WILEY SERIES IN PROBABILITY AND STATISTICS

A complete list of the titles in this series appears at the end of this volume.

APPLIED ECONOMETRIC
TIME SERIES

SECOND EDITION

APPLIED ECONOMETRIC TIME SERIES

Walter Enders
University of Alabama

www.wiley.com/college/enders

Executive Editor   *Leslie Kraham*
Editorial Assistant   *Jessica Bartelt*
Marketing Manager   *Charity Robey*
Managing Editor   *Lari Bishop*
Associate Production Manager   *Kelly Tavares*
Production Editor   *Sarah Wolfman–Robichaud*
Illustration Editor   *Jennifer Fisher*

This book was set in Times by Leyh Publishing LLC and printed and bound by Hamilton Printing. The cover was printed by Phoenix Color Corp.

This book is printed on acid free paper. ∞

To order books or for customer service please, call 1(800)-CALL-WILEY (225-5945).

Library of Congress Cataloging in Publication Data:
Enders, Walter, 1948–
  Applied econometric time series / Walter Enders.-- 2nd ed.
    p. cm.

Includes bibliographical references and index.
ISBN 978-0-471-23065-6 (cloth)
1. Econometrics. 2. Time-series analysis. I. Title

HB139.E55 2003
330'01'519232--dc21

USA ISBN: 978-0-471-23065-6
WIE ISBN: 0-471-45173-8

Printed in the United States of America

11 12 13 14 15

To Linda and to Lola's independence

PREFACE

In revising the text, I have tried to be careful about the trade-off between being complete and being concise. Textbook bloat has ruined the second editions of formerly fine manuscripts. No one wants to read an encyclopedic treatment of a topic or technique that has fallen out of style. The Internet now provides virtually unlimited access to papers on any number of specialized topics. As such, I tried to let readers of the first edition be my guide.

Most of the e-mail messages I received addressed a few key issues. People wanted to know how to compare the out-of-sample forecasts of alternative time-series models. Toward this end, the latter part of Chapter 2 has been restructured and the Granger–Newbold (1976) and Diebold–Mariano (1995) tests for comparing out-of-sample forecasts are discussed in a fair amount of detail. Chapter 3 contains a number of new developments in ARCH modeling including a discussion of IGARCH, EGARCH, and threshold–GARCH (TGARCH) models. Forecasting the conditional variance is also emphasized. Many readers of the first edition were concerned about multiple cointegrating vectors and inference in regressions with mixtures of stationary and nonstationary variables. Multiple cointegrating vectors and tests for cointegration with mixtures of $I(1)$ and $I(2)$ variables are examined in Chapter 6. I use the results of Sims, Stock, and Watson (1990) to discuss issues such as selecting the appropriate lag length in unit root tests, vector autoregressions, and cointegration tests. The issue also arises quite naturally in developing the general-to-specific modeling strategy (see Chapter 6) for nonstationary variables. The largest change is the addition of an entire chapter on nonlinear time-series models. Not only have many articles on nonlinear time-series models appeared in the top general journals, there are entire journals focusing on nonlinear economic and econometric models.

My original intent was to write a text in time-series macroeconometrics. Fortunately, a number of my colleagues convinced me to broaden the focus. Applied microeconomists have embraced time-series methods, and the political science journals have become more quantitative. As in the first edition, examples are drawn from macroeconomics, agricultural economics, international finance, and my work with Todd Sandler on the study of transnational terrorism. You should find the examples in the text to provide a reasonable balance between macroeconomic and microeconomic applications.

The text is intended for those with some background in multiple regression analysis. I presume the reader understands the assumptions underlying the use of ordinary least squares. All of my students are familiar with the concepts correlation and covariation; they also know how to use t-tests and F-tests in a regression framework. I use terms such as *mean square error, significance level,* and *unbiased estimate* without explaining their meaning. Two chapters of the text examine multiple time-series techniques. To work through these chapters, it is necessary to know how to solve a system of equations using matrix algebra. Chapter 1, entitled *Difference Equations,* is the cornerstone of the text. In my experience, this material and a knowledge of regression analysis is sufficient to bring students to the point where they are able to read the professional journals and to embark on a serious applied study.

I take the term *applied* that appears in the title very seriously. Towards this end, I believe in teaching by induction. The method is to take a simple example and build towards more general and more complicated models. Detailed examples of each procedure are provided. Each concludes with a step-by-step summary of the stages typically employed in using that procedure. The approach is one of learning by doing. A large number of solved problems are included in the body of each chapter. The *Questions and Exercises* section at the end of each chapter are especially important. You are encouraged to work through as many of the examples and exercises as possible. An *Instructors' Manual* is available to those adopting the text for their class.

Some of the techniques illustrated in the text need to be explicitly programmed. Structural VARs need to be estimated using a package that has the capacity to manipulate matrices. Nonlinear models need to be estimated using a package that can perform nonlinear least squares and maximum likelihood estimation. Completely menu-driven software packages are not able to estimate every form of time-series model. As I tell my students, by the time a procedure appears on the menu of an econometric software package, it's not new. As such, to work through all of the examples and exercises, it is necessary to have access to a software package such as EVIEWS, MICROFIT, PC-GIVE, RATS, SAS, SHAZAM, or STATA.

Matrix packages such as MATLAB and GAUSS are not as convenient for univariate models. All of these packages have their own programming language. To assist you in your programming, I have written a *Programming Guide* to accompany this text. You can download the guide (at no charge) from the Wiley Web site or from my personal Web page: www.cba.ua.edu/~wenders. ESTIMA has an extended version of the guide for RATS users available at www.estima.com. Of course, it is impossible for me to have versions of the guide for every possible platform. Most programmers should be able to transcribe a program written in one language into the language used by their personal software package.

In spite of all my efforts, some errors have undoubtedly crept into the text. If the first edition is any guide, the number is embarrassingly large. I will keep a list of typos and corrections on my Web page: www.cba.ua.edu/~wenders. Moreover, time-series methods and techniques keep evolving very rapidly. I will try to keep you updated by posting research notes and clarifications on my Web page. I would be happy to post any useful programs or communications you might have; my e-mail address is wenders@cba.ua.edu.

Many people made valuable suggestions for improving the organization, style, and clarity of the manuscript. I am grateful to my students, who kept me challenged and were quick to point out errors. Pierre Siklos and Mark Wohar made a number of important suggestions concerning the revised chapters. They also tested many of the programs used to obtain the estimations reported in the text. Pin Chung, Maria Crawford, and Jingan Yuan were especially helpful in carefully reading the many drafts of the manuscript and ferreting out numerous mistakes. Harvey Cutler, Selahattin Dibooglu, and Barry Falk made many helpful suggestions for the first edition that carry over to this edition. People I never met (including Denise Young, Jung Hoon Keem, and Celal Kuguker) wrote very nice letters pointing out a number of mistakes and errors in the first edition. Most of all, I would like to thank my loving wife, Linda, for putting up with me while I was working on the manuscript.

ABOUT THE AUTHOR

Walter Enders is the Lee Bidgood Professor of Economics at the University of Alabama. He received his doctorate in Economics in 1975 from Columbia University in New York. Dr. Enders' current research focuses on the development and application of time-series models to areas in economics and finance. Dr. Enders has published numerous research articles in such journals as the *Review of Economics and Statistics*, *Quarterly Journal of Economics*, and the *Journal of International Economics*. He has also published articles in the *American Economic Review* (a journal of the American Economic Association), the *Journal of Business and Economic Statistics* (a journal of the American Statistical Association), and *the American Political Science Review* (a journal of the American Political Science Association). He has formal editorial responsibilities for three different journals in the area of international economics and has served as a policy advisor to Ukraine. He is the current holder (along with Todd Sandler) of the National Academy of Sciences' Estes Award for Behavioral Research Relevant to the Prevention of Nuclear War. The award recognizes " … basic research in any field of cognitive or behavioral science that has employed rigorous formal or empirical methods, optimally a combination of these, to advance our understanding of problems or issues relating to the risk of nuclear war." The National Academy presented the award for their "… joint work on transnational terrorism using game theory and time series analysis to document the cyclic and shifting nature of terrorist attacks in response to defensive counteractions."

CONTENTS

CHAPTER *1*

DIFFERENCE EQUATIONS

INTRODUCTION

The theory of difference equations underlies all of the time-series methods employed in later chapters of this text. It is fair to say that time-series econometrics is concerned with the estimation of difference equations containing stochastic components. The traditional use of time-series analysis was to forecast the time path of a variable. Uncovering the dynamic path of a series improves forecasts since the predictable components of the series can be extrapolated into the future. The growing interest in economic dynamics has given a new emphasis to time-series econometrics. Stochastic difference equations arise quite naturally from dynamic economic models. Appropriately estimated equations can be used for the interpretation of economic data and for hypothesis testing.

This introductory chapter has three aims:

1. Explain how stochastic difference equations can be used for forecasting and illustrate how such equations can arise from familiar economic models. The chapter is not meant to be a treatise on the theory of difference equations. Only those techniques that are essential to the appropriate estimation of *linear* time-series models are presented. This chapter focuses on single equation models; multivariate models are considered in Chapters 5 and 6.

2. Explain what it means to *solve* a difference equation. The solution will determine whether a variable has a stable or an explosive time path. Knowledge of the stability conditions is essential to understanding the recent innovations in time-series econometrics. The contemporary time-series literature pays special attention to the issue of stationary versus nonstationary variables. The stability conditions underlie the conditions for stationarity.

3. Demonstrate how to find the solution to a stochastic difference equation. There are several different techniques that can be used; each has its own relative merits. A number of examples are presented to help you understand the different methods. Try to work through each example carefully. For extra practice, you should answer the exercises at the end of the chapter.

1. TIME-SERIES MODELS

The task facing the modern time-series econometrician is to develop reasonably simple models capable of forecasting, interpreting, and testing hypotheses concerning economic data. The challenge has grown over time; the original use of time-series analysis was primarily as an aid to forecasting. As such, a methodology was developed to decompose a series into a trend, a seasonal, a cyclical, and an irregular component. Uncovering the dynamic path of a series improves forecast accuracy because each of the predictable components can be extrapolated into the future.

Suppose you observe the fifty data points shown in Figure 1.1 and are interested in forecasting the subsequent values. Using the time-series methods discussed in the next several chapters, it is possible to decompose this series into the trend, seasonal, and irregular components shown in the lower panel of the figure. As you can see, the trend changes the mean of the series, and the seasonal component imparts a regular cyclical pattern with peaks occurring every twelve units of time. In practice, the trend and seasonal components will not be the simplistic deterministic functions shown in this figure. With economic data, it is typical to find that a series contains stochastic elements in the trend, seasonal, and irregular components. For the time being, it is wise to sidestep these complications so that the projection of the trend and seasonal components into periods 51 and beyond is straightforward.

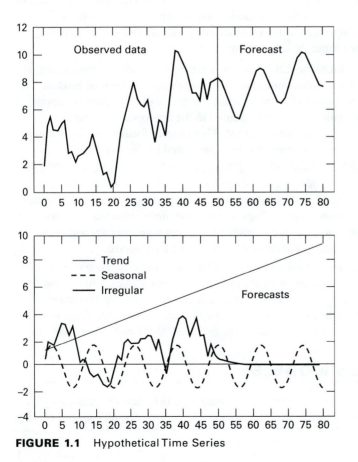

FIGURE 1.1 Hypothetical Time Series

Notice that the irregular component, while lacking a well-defined pattern, is somewhat predictable. If you examine the figure closely, you will see that the positive and negative values occur in runs; the occurrence of a large value in any period tends to be followed by another large value. Short-run forecasts will make use of this positive correlation in the irregular component. Over the entire span, however, the irregular component exhibits a tendency to revert to zero. As shown in the lower part, the projection of the irregular component past period 50 rapidly decays toward zero. The overall forecast, shown in the top part of the figure, is the sum of each forecasted component.

The general methodology used to make such forecasts entails finding the *equation of motion* driving a stochastic process and using that equation to predict subsequent outcomes. Let y_t denote the value of a data point at period t; if we use this notation, the example in Figure 1.1 assumes we observed y_1 through y_{50}. For $t = 1$ to 50, the equations of motion used to construct components of the y_t series are

$$\text{Trend: } T_t = 1 + 0.1t$$
$$\text{Seasonal: } S_t = 1.6 \sin(t\pi/6)$$
$$\text{Irregular: } I_t = 0.7 I_{t-1} + \varepsilon_t$$

where: T_t = value of the trend component in period t
S_t = value of the seasonal component in t
I_t = the value of the irregular component in t
ε_t = a pure random disturbance in t

Thus, the irregular disturbance in t is 70 percent of the previous period's irregular disturbance plus a random disturbance term.

Each of these three equations is a type of **difference equation.** In its most general form, a difference equation expresses the value of a variable as a function of its own lagged values, time, and other variables. The trend and seasonal terms are both functions of time and the irregular term is a function of its own lagged value and of the stochastic variable ε_t. The reason for introducing this set of equations is to make the point that *time-series econometrics is concerned with the estimation of difference equations containing stochastic components.* The time-series econometrician may estimate the properties of a single series or a vector containing many interdependent series. Both univariate and multivariate forecasting methods are presented in the text. Chapter 2 shows how to estimate the irregular part of a series. Chapter 3 considers estimating the variance when the data exhibit periods of volatility and tranquility. Estimation of the trend is considered in Chapter 4, which focuses on the issue of whether the trend is deterministic or stochastic. Chapter 5 discusses the properties of a vector of stochastic difference equations, and Chapter 6 is concerned with the estimation of trends in a multivariate model.

Although forecasting has always been the mainstay of time-series analysis, the growing importance of economic dynamics has generated new uses for time-series analysis. Many economic theories have natural representations as stochastic difference equations. Moreover, many of these models have testable implications concerning the time path of a key economic variable. Consider the following three examples:

1. **The Random Walk Hypothesis:** In its simplest form, the random walk model suggests that day-to-day changes in the price of a stock should have

a mean value of zero. After all, if it is known that a capital gain can be made by buying a share on day t and selling it for an expected profit the very next day, efficient speculation will drive up the current price. Similarly, no one will want to hold a stock if it is expected to depreciate. Formally, the model asserts that the price of a stock should evolve according to the stochastic difference equation

$$y_{t+1} = y_t + \varepsilon_{t+1}$$

or

$$\Delta y_{t+1} = \varepsilon_{t+1}$$

where: y_t = the price of a share of stock on day t
ε_{t+1} = a random disturbance term that has an expected value of zero

Now consider the more general stochastic difference equation:

$$\Delta y_{t+1} = \alpha_0 + \alpha_1 y_t + \varepsilon_{t+1}$$

The random walk hypothesis requires the testable restriction: $\alpha_0 = \alpha_1 = 0$. Rejecting this restriction is equivalent to rejecting the theory. Given the information available in period t, the theory also requires that the mean of ε_{t+1} be equal to zero; evidence that ε_{t+1} is predictable invalidates the random walk hypothesis. Again, the appropriate estimation of a single equation model is considered in Chapters 2 through 4.

2. **Reduced-Form and Structural Equations:** Often it is useful to collapse a system of difference equations into separate single-equation models. To illustrate the key issues involved, consider a stochastic version of Samuelson's (1939) classic model:

$$y_t = c_t + i_t \tag{1.1}$$

$$c_t = \alpha y_{t-1} + \varepsilon_{ct} \qquad\qquad 0 < \alpha < 1 \tag{1.2}$$

$$i_t = \beta(c_t - c_{t-1}) + \varepsilon_{it} \qquad\qquad \beta > 0 \tag{1.3}$$

where y_t, c_t, and i_t denote real GDP, consumption, and investment in time period t, respectively. In this Keynesian model, y_t, c_t, and i_t are endogenous variables. The previous period's GDP and consumption, y_{t-1} and c_{t-1}, are called predetermined or lagged endogenous variables. The terms ε_{ct} and ε_{it} are zero mean random disturbances for consumption and investment, and the coefficients α and β are parameters to be estimated.

The first equation equates aggregate output (GDP) with the sum of consumption and investment spending. The second equation asserts that consumption spending is proportional to the previous period's GDP plus a random disturbance term. The third equation illustrates the accelerator principle. Investment spending is proportional to the change in consumption; the idea is that growth in consumption necessitates new investment spending. The error terms ε_{ct} and ε_{it} represent the portions of consumption and investment not explained by the behavioral equations of the model.

Equation (1.3) is a **structural equation** since it expresses the endogenous variable i_t as being dependent on the current realization of another endogenous variable, c_t. A **reduced-form equation** is one expressing the value of a variable in terms of its own lags, lags of other endogenous variables, current and past values of exogenous variables, and disturbance terms. As formulated, the consumption function is already in reduced form; current consumption depends only on lagged income and the current value of the stochastic disturbance term ε_{ct}. Investment is not in reduced form because it depends on current period consumption.

To derive a reduced-form equation for investment, substitute (1.2) into the investment equation to obtain

$$i_t = \beta[\alpha y_{t-1} + \varepsilon_{ct} - c_{t-1}] + \varepsilon_{it}$$
$$= \alpha\beta y_{t-1} - \beta c_{t-1} + \beta\varepsilon_{ct} + \varepsilon_{it}$$

Notice that the reduced-form equation for investment is not unique. You can lag (1.2) one period to obtain: $c_{t-1} = \alpha y_{t-2} + \varepsilon_{ct-1}$. Using this expression, the reduced-form investment equation can also be written as

$$i_t = \alpha\beta y_{t-1} - \beta(\alpha y_{t-2} + \varepsilon_{ct-1}) + \beta\varepsilon_{ct} + \varepsilon_{it}$$
$$= \alpha\beta(y_{t-1} - y_{t-2}) + \beta(\varepsilon_{ct} - \varepsilon_{ct-1}) + \varepsilon_{it} \qquad (1.4)$$

Similarly, a reduced-form equation for GDP can be obtained by substituting (1.2) and (1.4) into (1.1):

$$y_t = \alpha y_{t-1} + \varepsilon_{ct} + \alpha\beta(y_{t-1} - y_{t-2}) + \beta(\varepsilon_{ct} - \varepsilon_{ct-1}) + \varepsilon_{it}$$
$$= \alpha(1+\beta)y_{t-1} - \alpha\beta y_{t-2} + (1+\beta)\varepsilon_{ct} + \varepsilon_{it} - \beta\varepsilon_{ct-1} \qquad (1.5)$$

Equation (1.5) is a **univariate** reduced-form equation; y_t is expressed solely as a function of its own lags and disturbance terms. A univariate model is particularly useful for forecasting since it enables you to predict a series based solely on its own current and past realizations. It is possible to estimate (1.5) using the univariate time-series techniques explained in Chapters 2 through 4. Once you have obtained estimates of α and β, it is straightforward to use the observed values of y_1 through y_t to predict all future values in the series (i.e., $y_{t+1}, y_{t+2}, \ldots$).

Chapter 5 considers the estimation of multivariate models when all variables are treated as jointly endogenous. The chapter also discusses the restrictions needed to recover (i.e., identify) the structural model from the estimated reduced-form model.

3. **Error-Correction: Forward and Spot Prices:** Certain commodities and financial instruments can be bought and sold on the spot market (for immediate delivery) or for delivery at some specified future date. For example, suppose that the price of a particular foreign currency on the spot market is s_t dollars and that the price of the currency for delivery one period into the future is f_t dollars. Now, consider a speculator who purchased forward currency at the price f_t dollars per unit. At the beginning of period $t + 1$, the speculator receives the currency and pays f_t dollars per unit

received. Since spot foreign exchange can be sold at s_{t+1}, the speculator can earn a profit (or loss) of $s_{t+1} - f_t$ per unit transacted.

The Unbiased Forward Rate (UFR) hypothesis asserts that expected profits from such speculative behavior should be zero. Formally, the hypothesis posits the following relationship between forward and spot exchange rates:

$$s_{t+1} = f_t + \varepsilon_{t+1} \tag{1.6}$$

where ε_{t+1} has a mean value of zero from the perspective of time period t.

In (1.6), the forward rate in t is an unbiased estimate of the spot rate in $t+1$. Thus, suppose you collected data on the two rates and estimated the regression

$$s_{t+1} = \alpha_0 + \alpha_1 f_t + \varepsilon_{t+1}$$

If you were able to conclude that $\alpha_0 = 0$, $\alpha_1 = 1$, and that the regression residuals ε_{t+1} have a mean value of zero from the perspective of time period t, the UFR hypothesis could be maintained.

The spot and forward markets are said to be in *long-run equilibrium* when $\varepsilon_{t+1} = 0$. Whenever s_{t+1} turns out to differ from f_t, some sort of adjustment must occur to restore the equilibrium in the subsequent period. Consider the adjustment process

$$s_{t+2} = s_{t+1} - \alpha[s_{t+1} - f_t] + \varepsilon_{st+2} \qquad \alpha > 0 \tag{1.7}$$

$$f_{t+1} = f_t + \beta[s_{t+1} - f_t] + \varepsilon_{ft+1} \qquad \beta > 0 \tag{1.8}$$

where ε_{st+2} and ε_{ft+1} both have a mean value of zero.

Equations (1.7) and (1.8) illustrate the type of simultaneous adjustment mechanism considered in Chapter 6. This dynamic model is called an **error-correction** model because the movement of the variables in any period is related to the previous period's gap from long-run equilibrium. If the spot rate s_{t+1} turns out to equal the forward rate f_t, (1.7) and (1.8) state that the spot rate and forward rates are expected to remain unchanged. If there is a positive gap between the spot and forward rates so that $s_{t+1} - f_t > 0$, (1.7) and (1.8) lead to the prediction that the spot rate will fall and the forward rate will rise.

2. DIFFERENCE EQUATIONS AND THEIR SOLUTIONS

Although many of the ideas in the previous section were probably familiar to you, it is necessary to formalize some of the concepts used. In this section, we will examine the type of difference equation used in econometric analysis and make explicit what it means to "solve" such equations. To begin our examination of difference equations, consider the function $y = f(t)$. If we evaluate the function when the independent variable t takes on the specific value t^*, we get a specific value for the dependent variable called y_{t^*}. Formally, $y_{t^*} = f(t^*)$. Using this same notation, y_{t^*+h} represents the value of y when t takes on the specific value $t^* + h$. The first difference of y is defined as the value of the function when evaluated at $t = t* + h$ minus the value of the function evaluated at $t*$:

$$\Delta y_{t*+h} \equiv f(t*+h) - f(t*)$$

$$\equiv y_{t*+h} - y_{t*} \qquad (1.9)$$

Differential calculus allows the change in the independent variable (i.e., the term h) to approach zero. Since most economic data is collected over discrete periods, however, it is more useful to allow the length of the time period to be greater than zero. Using difference equations, we normalize units so that h represents a unit change in t (i.e., $h = 1$) and consider the sequence of equally spaced values of the independent variable. Without any loss of generality, we can always drop the asterisk on $t*$. We can then form the **first differences:**

$$\Delta y_t = f(t) - f(t-1) \equiv y_t - y_{t-1}$$
$$\Delta y_{t+1} = f(t+1) - f(t) \equiv y_{t+1} - y_t$$
$$\Delta y_{t+2} = f(t+2) - f(t+1) \equiv y_{t+2} - y_{t+1}$$

Often it will be convenient to express the entire sequence of values $\{\ldots y_{t-2}, y_{t-1}, y_t, y_{t+1}, y_{t+2}, \ldots\}$ as $\{y_t\}$. We can then refer to any particular value in the sequence as y_t. Unless specified, the index t runs from $-\infty$ to $+\infty$. In time-series econometric models, we use t to represent "time" and h to represent the length of a time period. Thus, y_t and y_{t+1} might represent the realizations of the $\{y_t\}$ sequence in the first and second quarters of 2004, respectively.

In the same way we can form the **second difference** as the change in the first difference. Consider

$$\Delta^2 y_t \equiv \Delta(\Delta y_t) = \Delta(y_t - y_{t-1}) = (y_t - y_{t-1}) - (y_{t-1} - y_{t-2}) = y_t - 2y_{t-1} + y_{t-2}$$
$$\Delta^2 y_{t+1} \equiv \Delta(\Delta y_{t+1}) = \Delta(y_{t+1} - y_t) = (y_{t+1} - y_t) - (y_t - y_{t-1}) = y_{t+1} - 2y_t + y_{t-1}$$

The nth difference (Δ^n) is defined analogously. At this point, we risk taking the theory of difference equations too far. As you will see, the need to use second differences rarely arises in time-series analysis. It is safe to say that third and higher-order differences are never used in applied work.

Since this text considers linear time-series methods, it is possible to examine only the special case of an nth-order linear difference equation with constant coefficients. The form for this special type of difference equation is given by

$$y_t = a_0 + \sum_{i=1}^{n} a_i y_{t-i} + x_t \qquad (1.10)$$

The order of the difference equation is given by the value of n. The equation is linear because all values of the dependent variable are raised to the first power. Economic theory may dictate instances in which the various a_i are functions of variables within the economy. However, as long as they do not depend on any of the values of y_t or x_t, we can regard them as parameters. The term x_t is called the **forcing process.** The form of the forcing process can be very general; x_t can be any function of time, current and lagged values of other variables, and/or stochastic disturbances. From an appropriate choice of the forcing process, we can obtain a wide variety of important macroeconomic models. Re-examine equation (1.5), the reduced-form equation for GDP. This equation is a second-order difference equation since y_t depends on y_{t-2}. The forcing process is the expression $(1+\beta)\varepsilon_{ct} + \varepsilon_{it} - \beta\varepsilon_{ct-1}$. You will note that (1.5) has no intercept term corresponding to the expression a_0 in (1.10).

An important special case for the $\{x_t\}$ sequence is

$$x_t = \sum_{i=0}^{\infty} \beta_i \, \varepsilon_{t-i}$$

where the β_i are constants (some of which can equal zero) and the individual elements of the sequence $\{\varepsilon_t\}$ are not functions of the y_t. At this point it is useful to allow the $\{\varepsilon_t\}$ sequence to be nothing more than a sequence of unspecified exogenous variables. For example, let $\{\varepsilon_t\}$ be a random error term and set $\beta_0 = 1$ and $\beta_1 = \beta_2 = \ldots = 0$; in this case, (1.10) becomes the autoregression equation:

$$y_t = a_0 + a_1 y_{t-1} + a_2 y_{t-2} + \ldots + a_n y_{t-n} + \varepsilon_t$$

Let $n = 1$, $a_0 = 0$ and $a_1 = 1$ to obtain the random walk model. Notice that equation (1.10) can be written in terms of the **difference operator** (Δ). Subtracting y_{t-1} from (1.10), we obtain

$$y_t - y_{t-1} = a_0 + \left(a_1 - 1\right)y_{t-1} + \sum_{i=2}^{n} a_i y_{t-i} + x_t$$

or defining $\gamma = (a_1 - 1)$, we get

$$\Delta y_t = a_0 + \gamma y_{t-1} + \sum_{i=2}^{n} a_i y_{t-i} + x_t \tag{1.11}$$

Clearly, equation (1.11) is simply a modified version of (1.10).

A **solution** to a difference equation expresses the value of y_t as a function of the elements of the $\{x_t\}$ sequence and t (and possibly some given values of the $\{y_t\}$ sequence called **initial conditions**). Examining (1.11) makes it clear that there is a strong analogy to integral calculus, where the problem is to find a primitive function from a given derivative. We seek to find the primitive function $f(t)$, given an equation expressed in the form of (1.10) or (1.11). Notice that a solution is a function rather than a number. The key property of a solution is that it satisfies the difference equation for all permissible values of t and $\{x_t\}$. Thus, the substitution of a solution into the difference equation must result in an identity. For example, consider the simple difference equation $\Delta y_t = 2$ (or $y_t = y_{t-1} + 2$). You can easily verify that a solution to this difference equation is $y_t = 2t + c$, where c is any arbitrary constant. By definition, if $2t + c$ is a solution, it must hold for all permissible values of t. Thus for period $t-1$, $y_{t-1} = 2(t-1) + c$. Now substitute the solution into the difference equation to form

$$2t + c \equiv 2(t-1) + c + 2 \tag{1.12}$$

It is straightforward to carry out the algebra and verify that (1.12) is an identity. This simple example also illustrates that the solution to a difference equation need not be unique; there is a solution for any arbitrary value of c.

Another useful example is provided by the irregular term shown in Figure 1.1; recall that the equation for this expression is: $I_t = 0.7I_{t-1} + \varepsilon_t$. You can verify that the solution to this first-order equation is

$$I_t = \sum_{i=0}^{\infty} (0.7)^i \, \varepsilon_{t-i} \tag{1.13}$$

Since (1.13) holds for all time periods, the value of the irregular component in $t - 1$ is given by

$$I_{t-1} = \sum_{i=0}^{\infty} (0.7)^i \, \varepsilon_{t-1-i} \tag{1.14}$$

Now substitute (1.13) and (1.14) into $I_t = 0.7I_{t-1} + \varepsilon_t$ to obtain

$$\varepsilon_t + 0.7\varepsilon_{t-1} + (0.7)^2\varepsilon_{t-2} + (0.7)^3\varepsilon_{t-3} + \dots$$
$$= 0.7[\varepsilon_{t-1} + 0.7\varepsilon_{t-2} + (0.7)^2\varepsilon_{t-3} + (0.7)^3\varepsilon_{t-4} + \dots] + \varepsilon_t \tag{1.15}$$

The two sides of (1.15) are identical; this proves that (1.13) is a solution to the first-order stochastic difference equation $I_t = 0.7I_{t-1} + \varepsilon_t$. Be aware of the distinction between reduced-form equations and solutions. Since $I_t = 0.7I_{t-1} + \varepsilon_t$ holds for all values of t, it follows that $I_{t-1} = 0.7I_{t-2} + \varepsilon_{t-1}$. Combining these two equations yields

$$I_t = 0.7[0.7I_{t-2} + \varepsilon_{t-1}] + \varepsilon_t = 0.49I_{t-2} + 0.7\varepsilon_{t-1} + \varepsilon_t \tag{1.16}$$

Equation (1.16) is a reduced-form equation since it expresses I_t in terms of its own lags and disturbance terms. However, (1.16) does not qualify as a solution because it contains the "unknown" value of I_{t-2}. To qualify as a solution, (1.16) must express I_t in terms of the elements x_t, t, and any given initial conditions.

3. SOLUTION BY ITERATION

The solution given by (1.13) was simply postulated. The remaining portions of this chapter develop the methods you can use to obtain such solutions. Each method has its own merits; knowing the most appropriate to use in a particular circumstance is a skill that comes only with practice. This section develops the method of iteration. Although iteration is the most cumbersome and time-intensive method, most people find it to be very intuitive.

If the value of y in some specific period is known, a direct method of solution is to iterate forward from that period to obtain the subsequent time path of the entire y sequence. Refer to this known value of y as the initial condition or the value of y in time period 0 (denoted by y_0). It is easiest to illustrate the iterative technique using the first-order difference equation:

$$y_t = a_0 + a_1 y_{t-1} + \varepsilon_t \tag{1.17}$$

Given the value of y_0, it follows that y_1 will be given by

$$y_1 = a_0 + a_1 y_0 + \varepsilon_1$$

In the same way, y_2 must be

$$y_2 = a_0 + a_1 y_1 + \varepsilon_2$$
$$= a_0 + a_1[a_0 + a_1 y_0 + \varepsilon_1] + \varepsilon_2$$
$$= a_0 + a_0 a_1 + (a_1)^2 y_0 + a_1\varepsilon_1 + \varepsilon_2$$

Continuing the process in order to find y_3, we obtain

$$y_3 = a_0 + a_1 y_2 + \varepsilon_3 = a_0[1 + a_1 + (a_1)^2] + (a_1)^3 y_0 + a_1^2 \varepsilon_1 + a_1 \varepsilon_2 + \varepsilon_3$$

You can easily verify that for all $t > 0$, repeated iteration yields

$$y_t = a_0 \sum_{i=0}^{t-1} a_1^i + a_1^t y_0 + \sum_{i=0}^{t-1} a_1^i \varepsilon_{t-i} \tag{1.18}$$

Equation (1.18) is a solution to (1.17) since it expresses y_t as a function of t, the forcing process $x_t = \Sigma(a_1)^i \varepsilon_{t-i}$, and the known value of y_0. As an exercise, it is useful to show that iteration from y_t back to y_0 yields exactly the formula given by (1.18). Since $y_t = a_0 + a_1 y_{t-1} + \varepsilon_t$, it follows that

$$y_t = a_0 + a_1 [a_0 + a_1 y_{t-2} + \varepsilon_{t-1}] + \varepsilon_t$$
$$= a_0(1+a_1) + a_1 \varepsilon_{t-1} + \varepsilon_t + a_1^2[a_0 + a_1 y_{t-3} + \varepsilon_{t-2}]$$

Continuing the iteration back to period 0 yields equation (1.18).

Iteration without an Initial Condition

Suppose you were not given the initial condition for y_0. The solution given by (1.18) would no longer be appropriate because the value of y_0 is an unknown. You could not select this initial value of y and iterate forward, nor could you iterate backward from y_t and simply choose to stop at $t = t_0$. Thus, suppose we continued to iterate backward by substituting $a_0 + a_1 y_{-1} + \varepsilon_0$ for y_0 in (1.18):

$$y_t = a_0 \sum_{i=0}^{t-1} a_1^i + a_1^t [a_0 + a_1 y_{-1} + \varepsilon_0] + \sum_{i=0}^{t-1} a_1^i \varepsilon_{t-i}$$

$$= a_0 \sum_{i=0}^{t} a_1^i + \sum_{i=0}^{t} a_1^i \varepsilon_{t-i} + a_1^{t+1} y_{-1} \tag{1.19}$$

Continuing to iterate backward another m periods, we obtain

$$y_t = a_0 \sum_{i=0}^{t+m} a_1^i + \sum_{i=0}^{t+m} a_1^i \varepsilon_{t-i} + a_1^{t+m+1} y_{-m-1} \tag{1.20}$$

Now examine the pattern emerging from (1.19) and (1.20). If $|a_1| < 1$, the term a_1^{t+m+1} approaches zero as m approaches infinity. Also, the infinite sum $[1 + a_1 + (a_1)^2 + ...]$ converges to $1/(1 - a_1)$. Thus, if we temporarily assume that $|a_1| < 1$, after continual substitution, (1.20) can be written as

$$y_t = a_0 /(1 - a_1) + \sum_{i=0}^{\infty} a_1^i \varepsilon_{t-i} \tag{1.21}$$

You should take a few minutes to convince yourself that (1.21) is a solution to the original difference equation (1.17); substitution of (1.21) into (1.17) yields an identity. However, (1.21) is not a unique solution. For any arbitrary value of A, a solution to (1.17) is given by

$$y_t = A\, a_1^t + a_0\, /(1 - a_1) + \sum_{i=0}^{\infty} a_1^i\, \varepsilon_{t-i} \tag{1.22}$$

To verify that *for any arbitrary value of A* (1.22) is a solution, substitute (1.22) into (1.17) to obtain

$$a_0\, /(1 - a_1) + Aa_1^t + \sum_{i=0}^{\infty} a_1^i \varepsilon_{t-i} = a_0 + a_1[a_0\, /(1 - a_1) + Aa_1^{t-1} + \sum_{i=0}^{\infty} a_1^i\, \varepsilon_{t-1-i}] + \varepsilon_t$$

Since the two sides are identical, (1.22) is necessarily a solution to (1.17).

Reconciling the Two Iterative Methods

Given the iterative solution (1.22), suppose that you are now given an initial condition concerning the value of y in the arbitrary period t_0. It is straightforward to show that we can impose the initial condition on (1.22) to yield the same solution as (1.18). Since (1.22) must be valid for all periods (including t_0), when $t = 0$, it must be true that

$$y_0 = A + a_0\, /(1 - a_1) + \sum_{i=0}^{\infty} a_1^i \varepsilon_{-i} \quad \text{so that}$$

$$A = y_0 - a_0\, /(1 - a_1) - \sum_{i=0}^{\infty} a_1^i \varepsilon_{-i} \tag{1.23}$$

Since y_0 is given, we can view (1.23) as the value of A that renders (1.22) a solution to (1.17) given the initial condition. Hence, the presence of the initial condition eliminates the arbitrariness of A. Substituting this value of A into (1.22) yields

$$y_t = [y_0 - a_0\, /(1 - a_1) - \sum_{i=0}^{\infty} a_1^i \varepsilon_{-i}]\, a_1^t + a_0\, /(1 - a_1) + \sum_{i=0}^{\infty} a_1^i \varepsilon_{t-i} \tag{1.24}$$

Simplification of (1.24) results in

$$y_t = [y_0 - a_0\, /(1 - a_1)]\, a_1^t + a_0\, /(1 - a_1) + \sum_{i=0}^{t-1} a_1^i \varepsilon_{t-i} \tag{1.25}$$

You should take a moment to verify that (1.25) is identical to (1.18).

Nonconvergent Sequences

Given that $|a_1| < 1$, (1.21) is the limiting value of (1.20) as m grows infinitely large. What happens to the solution in other circumstances? If $|a_1| > 1$, it is not possible to move from (1.20) to (1.21) because the expression $|a_1|^{t+m}$ grows infinitely large as $t+m$ approaches infinity.[1] However, if there is an initial condition, there is no need to obtain the infinite summation. Simply select the initial condition y_0 and iterate forward; the result will be (1.18):

$$y_t = a_0 \sum_{i=0}^{t-1} a_1^i + a_1^t y_0 + \sum_{i=0}^{t-1} a_1^i \varepsilon_{t-i}$$

Although the successive values of the $\{y_t\}$ sequence will become progressively larger in absolute value, all values in the series will be finite.

A very interesting case arises if $a_1 = 1$. Rewrite (1.17) as:

$$y_t = a_0 + y_{t-1} + \varepsilon_t$$

or

$$\Delta y_t = a_0 + \varepsilon_t$$

As you should verify by iterating from y_t back to y_0, a solution to this equation is[2]

$$y_t = a_0 t + \sum_{i=1}^{t} \varepsilon_i + y_0 \tag{1.26}$$

After a moment's reflection, the form of the solution is quite intuitive. In every period t, the value of y_t changes by $a_0 + \varepsilon_t$ units. After t periods, there are t such changes; hence, the total change is ta_0 plus the t values of the $\{\varepsilon_t\}$ sequence. Notice that the solution contains summation of all disturbances from ε_1 through ε_t. Thus, when $a_1 = 1$, each disturbance has a permanent non-decaying effect on the value of y_t. You should compare this result to the solution found in (1.21). For the case in which $|a_1| < 1$, $|a_1|^t$ is a decreasing function of t so that the effects of past disturbances become successively smaller over time.

The importance of the magnitude of a_1 is illustrated in Figure 1.2. Twenty-five random numbers with a theoretical mean equal to zero were computer-generated and denoted by ε_1 through ε_{25}. Then the value of y_0 was set equal to unity and the next twenty-five values of the $\{y_t\}$ sequence were constructed using the formula $y_t = 0.9y_{t-1} + \varepsilon_t$. The result is shown by the thin line in Panel (a) of Figure 1.2. If you substitute $a_0 = 0$ and $a_1 = 0.9$ into (1.18), you will see that the time path of $\{y_t\}$ consists of two parts. The first part, 0.9^t, is shown by the slowly decaying thick line in the panel. This term dominates the solution for relatively small values of t. The influence of the random part is shown by the difference between the thin and the thick line; you can see that the first several values of $\{\varepsilon_t\}$ are negative. As t increases, the influence of the random component becomes more pronounced.

Using the previously drawn random numbers, we again set y_0 equal to unity and a second sequence was constructed using the formula $y_t = 0.5y_{t-1} + \varepsilon_t$. This second sequence is shown by the thin line in Panel (b) of Figure 1.2. The influence of the expression 0.5^t is shown by the rapidly decaying thick line. Again, as t increases, the random portion of the solution becomes more dominant in the time path of $\{y_t\}$. When we compare the first two panels, it is clear that reducing the magnitude of $|a_1|$ increases the rate of convergence. Moreover, the discrepancies between the simulated values of y_t and the thick line are less pronounced in the second panel. As you can see in (1.18), each value of ε_{t-i} enters the solution for y_t with a coefficient of $(a_1)^i$. The

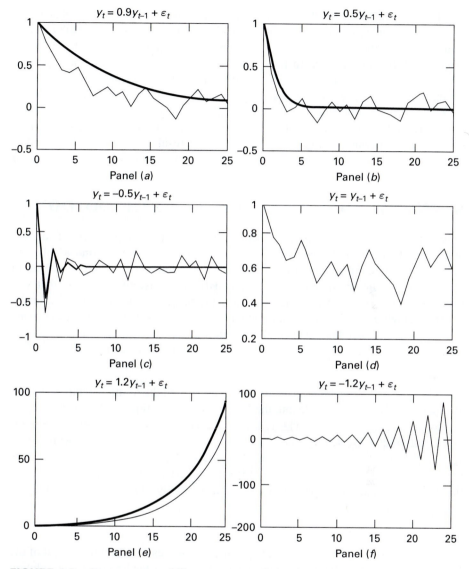

FIGURE 1.2   Convergent and Nonconvergent Sequences

smaller value of a_1 means that the past realizations of ε_{t-i} have a smaller influence on the current value of y_t.

Simulating a third sequence with $a_1 = -0.5$ yields the thin line shown in Panel (c). The oscillations are due to the negative value of a_1. The expression $(-0.5)^t$, shown by the thick line, is positive when t is even and negative when t is odd. Since $|a_1| < 1$, the oscillations are dampened.

The next three panels in Figure 1.2 all show nonconvergent sequences. Each uses the initial condition $y_0 = 1$ and the same twenty-five values of $\{\varepsilon_t\}$ used in the other simulations. The thin line in Panel (d) shows the time path of $y_t = y_{t-1} + \varepsilon_t$. Since each value of ε_t has an expected value of zero, Panel (d) illustrates a random-walk process. Here $\Delta y_t = \varepsilon_t$ so that the change in y_t is random. The nonconvergence is shown by the tendency of $\{y_t\}$ to meander. In Panel (e), the thick line representing the explosive expression $(1.2)^t$ dominates the random portion of the $\{y_t\}$ sequence. Also notice that the discrepancy between the simulated $\{y_t\}$ sequence and the thick line widens as t increases. The reason is that past values of ε_{t-i} enter the solution for y_t with the coefficient $(1.2)^i$. As i increases, the importance of these previous discrepancies becomes increasingly important. Similarly, setting $a_1 = -1.2$ results in the exploding oscillations shown in the lower-right panel of the figure. The value $(-1.2)^t$ is positive for even values of t and negative for odd values of t.

4. AN ALTERNATIVE SOLUTION METHODOLOGY

Solution by the iterative method breaks down in higher-order equations. The algebraic complexity quickly overwhelms any reasonable attempt to find a solution. Fortunately, there are several alternative solution techniques that can be helpful in solving the nth-order equation given by (1.10). If we use the principle that you should learn to walk before you learn to run, it is best to step through the first-order equation given by (1.17). Although you will be covering some familiar ground, the first-order case illustrates the general methodology extremely well. To split the procedure into its component parts, consider only the homogeneous portion of (1.17):[3]

$$y_t = a_1 y_{t-1} \tag{1.27}$$

The solution to this homogeneous equation is called the **homogeneous solution;** at times it will be useful to denote the homogeneous solution by the expression y_t^h. Obviously, the trivial solution $y_t = y_{t-1} = \ldots = 0$ satisfies (1.27). However, this solution is not unique. By setting a_0 and all values of $\{\varepsilon_t\}$ equal to zero, (1.18) becomes $y_t = a_1^t y_0$. Hence, $y_t = a_1^t y_0$ must be a solution to (1.27). Yet, even this solution does not constitute the full set of solutions. It is easy to verify that the expression a_1^t multiplied by any arbitrary constant A satisfies (1.27). Simply substitute $y_t = Aa_1^t$ and $y_{t-1} = Aa_1^{t-1}$ into (1.27) to obtain

$$Aa_1^t = a_1 Aa_1^{t-1}$$

Since $a_1^t = a_1 a_1^{t-1}$, it follows that $y_t = Aa_1^t$ also solves (1.27). With the aid of the thick lines in Figure 1.2, we can classify the properties of the homogeneous solution as follows:

1. If $|a_1| < 1$, the expression a_1^t converges to zero as t approaches infinity. Convergence is direct if $0 < a_1 < 1$ and oscillatory if $-1 < a_1 < 0$.

2. If $|a_1| > 1$, the homogeneous solution is not stable. If $a_1 > 1$, the homogeneous solution approaches infinity as t increases. If $a_1 < -1$, the homogeneous solution oscillates explosively.

3. If $a_1 = 1$, any arbitrary constant A satisfies the homogeneous equation $y_t = y_{t-1}$. If $a_1 = -1$, the system is *meta-stable*: $a_1^t = 1$ for even values of t and -1 for odd values of t.

Now consider (1.17) in its entirety. In the last section, you confirmed that (1.21) is a valid solution to (1.17). Equation (1.21) is called a **particular solution** to the difference equation; all such particular solutions will be denoted by the term y_t^p. The term "particular" stems from the fact that a solution to a difference equation may not be unique; hence, (1.21) is just one particular solution out of the many possibilities.

In moving to (1.22) you verified that the particular solution was not unique. The homogeneous solution Aa_1^t plus the particular solution given by (1.21) constituted the complete solution to (1.17). The **general solution** to a difference equation is defined to be a particular solution plus all homogeneous solutions. Once the general solution is obtained, the arbitrary constant A can be eliminated by imposing an initial condition for y_0.

The Solution Methodology

The results of the first-order case are directly applicable to the nth-order equation given by (1.10). In this general case, it will be more difficult to find the particular solution and there will be n distinct homogeneous solutions. Nevertheless, the solution methodology will always entail the following four steps:

STEP 1: Form the homogeneous equation and find all n homogeneous solutions;
STEP 2: Find a particular solution;
STEP 3: Obtain the general solution as the sum of the particular solution and a linear combination of all homogeneous solutions;
STEP 4: Eliminate the arbitrary constant(s) by imposing the initial condition(s) on the general solution.

Before we address the various techniques that can be used to obtain homogeneous and particular solutions, it is worthwhile to illustrate the methodology using the equation:

$$y_t = 0.9y_{t-1} - 0.2y_{t-2} + 3 \qquad (1.28)$$

Clearly, this second-order equation is in the form of (1.10) with $a_0 = 3$, $a_1 = 0.9$, $a_2 = -0.2$, and $x_t = 0$. Beginning with the first of the four steps, form the homogeneous equation:

$$y_t - 0.9y_{t-1} + 0.2y_{t-2} = 0 \qquad (1.29)$$

In the first-order case of (1.17), the homogeneous solution was Aa_1^t. Section 6 will show you how to find the complete set of homogeneous solutions. For now, it is sufficient to assert that the two homogeneous solutions are: $y_{1t}^h = (0.5)^t$ and $y_{2t}^h = (0.4)^t$. To verify the first solution, note that $y_{1t-1}^h = (0.5)^{t-1}$ and $y_{1t-2}^h = (0.5)^{t-2}$. Thus, y_{1t}^h is a solution if it satisfies

$$(0.5)^t - 0.9(0.5)^{t-1} + 0.2(0.5)^{t-2} = 0$$

If we divide by $(0.5)^{t-2}$, the issue is whether

$$(0.5)^2 - 0.9(0.5) + 0.2 = 0$$

Carrying out the algebra, $0.25 - 0.45 + 0.2$ does equal zero so that $(0.5)^t$ is a solution to (1.29). In the same way, it is easy to verify that $y_{2t}^h = (0.4)^t$ is a solution since

$$(0.4)^t - 0.9(0.4)^{t-1} + 0.2(0.4)^{t-2} = 0$$

Divide by $(0.4)^{t-2}$ to obtain $(0.4)^2 - 0.9(0.4) + 0.2 = 0.16 - 0.36 + 0.2 = 0$.

The second step is to obtain a particular solution; you can easily confirm that the particular solution $y_t^p = 10$ solves (1.28) as: $10 = 0.9(10) - 0.2(10) + 3$.

The third step is to combine the particular solution and a linear combination of both homogeneous solutions to obtain

$$y_t = A_1(0.5)^t + A_2(0.4)^t + 10$$

where A_1 and A_2 are arbitrary constants.

For the fourth step, assume you have two initial conditions for the $\{y_t\}$ sequence. So that we can keep our numbers reasonably round, suppose that $y_0 = 13$ and $y_1 = 11.3$. Thus, for periods zero and one, our solution must satisfy

$$13 = A_1 + A_2 + 10$$
$$11.3 = A_1(0.5) + A_2(0.4) + 10.$$

Solving simultaneously for A_1 and A_2, you should find $A_1 = 1$ and $A_2 = 2$. Hence, the solution is

$$y_t = (0.5)^t + 2(0.4)^t + 10$$

Generalizing the Method

To show that this method is applicable to higher-order equations, consider the homogeneous part of (1.10):

$$y_t = \sum_{i=1}^{n} a_i y_{t-i} \tag{1.30}$$

As shown in Section 6, there are n homogeneous solutions that satisfy (1.30). For now, it is sufficient to demonstrate the following proposition: *If y_t^h is a homogeneous solution to (1.30), Ay_t^h is also a solution for any arbitrary constant A.* By assumption, y_t^h solves the homogeneous equation so that

$$y_t^h = \sum_{i=1}^{n} a_i y_{t-i}^h \tag{1.31}$$

The expression Ay_t^h is also a solution if:

$$Ay_t^h = \sum_{i=1}^{n} a_i Ay_{t-i}^h \tag{1.32}$$

We know (1.32) is satisfied because dividing each term by A yields (1.31). Now suppose that there are two separate solutions to the homogeneous equation denoted by y_{1t}^h and y_{2t}^h. It is straightforward to show that for any two constants A_1 and A_2, the linear combination $A_1 y_{1t}^h + A_2 y_{2t}^h$ is also a solution to the homogeneous equation. If $A_1 y_{1t}^h + A_2 y_{2t}^h$ is a solution to (1.30), it must satisfy

$$A_1 y_{1t}^h + A_2 y_{2t}^h = a_1(A_1 y_{1t-1}^h + A_2 y_{2t-1}^h)$$
$$+ a_2(A_1 y_{1t-2}^h + A_2 y_{2t-2}^h) + \ldots + a_n(A_1 y_{1t-n}^h + A_2 y_{2t-n}^h)$$

Regrouping terms, we want to know if

$$(A_1 y_{1t}^h - \sum_{i=1}^{n} A_1 a_i y_{1t-i}^h) + (A_2 y_{2t}^h - \sum_{i=1}^{n} A_2 a_i y_{2t-i}^h) = 0$$

Since $A_1 y_{1t}^h$ and $A_2 y_{2t}^h$ are separate solutions to (1.30), each of the expressions in brackets is zero. Hence, the linear combination is necessarily a solution to the homogeneous equation. This result easily generalizes to all n homogeneous solutions to an nth-order equation.

Finally, the use of Step 3 is appropriate since *the sum of any particular solution and any linear combination of all homogeneous solutions is also a solution.* To prove this proposition, substitute the sum of the particular and homogeneous solutions into (1.10) to obtain

$$y_t^p + y_t^h = a_0 + \sum_{i=1}^{n} a_i (y_{t-i}^p + y_{t-i}^h) + x_t \tag{1.33}$$

Recombining the terms in (1.33), we want to know if

$$[y_t^p - a_0 - \sum_{i=1}^{n} a_i y_{t-i}^p - x_t] + [y_t^h - \sum_{i=1}^{n} a_i y_{t-i}^h] = 0 \tag{1.34}$$

Since y_t^p solves (1.10), the expression in the first bracket of (1.34) is zero. Since y_t^h solves the homogeneous equation, the expression in the second bracket is zero. Thus, (1.34) is an identity; the sum of the homogeneous and particular solutions solves (1.10).

5. THE COBWEB MODEL

An interesting way to illustrate the methodology outlined in the previous section is to consider a stochastic version of the traditional **cobweb model.** Since the model was originally developed to explain the volatility in agricultural prices, let the market for a product—say wheat—be represented by

$$d_t = a - \gamma p_t \qquad\qquad \gamma > 0 \tag{1.35}$$

$$s_t = b + \beta p_t^* + \varepsilon_t \qquad\qquad \beta > 0 \tag{1.36}$$

$$s_t = d_t \tag{1.37}$$

where: d_t = demand for wheat in period t
s_t = supply of wheat in t
p_t = market price of wheat in t
p_t^* = price that farmers expect to prevail at t
ε_t = a zero mean stochastic supply shock
and parameters a, b, γ, and β are all positive such that $a > b$.[4]

The nature of the model is such that consumers buy as much wheat as is desired at the market clearing price p_t. At planting time, farmers do not know the price prevailing at harvest time; they base their supply decision on the expected price (p_t^*). The actual quantity produced depends on the planned quantity $b + \beta p_t^*$ plus a random supply shock ε_t. Once the product is harvested, market equilibrium requires that the quantity supplied equal the quantity demanded. Unlike the actual market for wheat, the model does not allow for the possibility of storage. The essence of the cobweb model is that farmers form their expectations in a naive fashion; let farmers use last year's price as the expected market price

$$p_t^* = p_{t-1} \tag{1.38}$$

Point E in Figure 1.3 represents the long-run equilibrium price and quantity combination. Note that the equilibrium concept in this stochastic model differs from that of the traditional cobweb model. If the system is stable, successive prices will *tend* to converge to point E. However, the nature of the stochastic equilibrium is such that the ever-present supply shocks prevent the system from remaining at E. Nevertheless, it is useful to solve for the long-run price. If we set all values of the $\{\varepsilon_t\}$ sequence equal to zero, set $p_t = p_{t-1} = \ldots = p$, and equate supply and demand, the long-run equilibrium price is given by $p = (a - b)/(\gamma + \beta)$. Similarly, the equilibrium quantity (s) is given by $s = (a\beta + \gamma b)/(\gamma + \beta)$.

To understand the dynamics of the system, suppose that farmers in t plan to produce the equilibrium quantity s. However, let there be a negative supply shock such that the actual quantity produced turns out to be s_t. As shown by point 1 in Figure 1.3, consumers are willing to pay p_t for the quantity s_t; hence, market equilibrium in t occurs at point 1. Updating one period allows us to see the main result of the cobweb model. For simplicity, assume that all subsequent values of the supply shock are zero (i.e., $\varepsilon_{t+1} = \varepsilon_{t+2} = \ldots = 0$). At the beginning of period $t + 1$, farmers expect the price at harvest time to be the price of the previous period; thus $p_{t+1}^* = p_t$. Accordingly, they produce and market quantity s_{t+1} (see point 2 in the figure); consumers, however, are

FIGURE 1.3   The Cobweb Model

willing to buy quantity s_{t+1} only if the price falls to that indicated by p_{t+1} (see point 3 in the figure). The next period begins with farmers expecting to be at point 4. The process continually repeats until the equilibrium point E is attained.

As drawn, Figure 1.3 suggests that the market will always converge to the long-run equilibrium point. This result does not hold for all demand and supply curves. To formally derive the stability condition, combine (1.35) through (1.38) to obtain

$$b + \beta p_{t-1} + \varepsilon_t = a - \gamma p_t$$

or

$$p_t = (-\beta/\gamma)p_{t-1} + (a - b)/\gamma - \varepsilon_t/\gamma \qquad (1.39)$$

Clearly, (1.39) is a stochastic first-order linear difference equation with constant coefficients. To obtain the general solution, proceed using the four steps listed at the end of the last section:

1. Form the homogeneous equation: $p_t = (-\beta/\gamma)p_{t-1}$. In the next section you will learn how to find the solution(s) to a homogeneous equation. For now, it is sufficient to verify that the homogeneous solution is

$$p_t^h = A(-\beta/\gamma)^t$$

where A is an arbitrary constant.

2. If the ratio β/γ is less than unity, you can iterate (1.39) backward from p_t to verify that the particular solution for the price is

$$p_t^p = \frac{a-b}{\gamma+\beta} - \frac{1}{\gamma}\sum_{i=0}^{\infty}(-\beta/\gamma)^i \varepsilon_{t-i} \qquad (1.40)$$

If $\beta/\gamma \geq 1$, the infinite summation in (1.40) is not convergent. As discussed in the last section, it is necessary to impose an initial condition on (1.40) if $\beta/\gamma \geq 1$.

3. The general solution is the sum of the homogeneous and particular solutions; combining these two solutions, the general solution is

$$p_t = \frac{a-b}{\gamma+\beta} - \frac{1}{\gamma}\sum_{i=0}^{\infty}(-\beta/\gamma)^i \varepsilon_{t-i} + A(-\beta/\gamma)^t \qquad (1.41)$$

4. In (1.41), A is an arbitrary constant that can be eliminated if we know the price in some initial period. For convenience, let this initial period have a time subscript of zero. Since the solution must hold for every period, *including period zero,* it must be that case that

$$p_0 = \frac{a-b}{\gamma+\beta} - \frac{1}{\gamma}\sum_{i=0}^{\infty}(-\beta/\gamma)^i \varepsilon_{-i} + A(-\beta/\gamma)^0$$

Since $(-\beta/\gamma)^0 = 1$, the value of A is given by

$$A = p_0 - \frac{a-b}{\gamma+\beta} + \frac{1}{\gamma}\sum_{i=0}^{\infty}(-\beta/\gamma)^i \varepsilon_{-i}$$

Substituting this solution for A back into (1.41) yields

$$p_t = \frac{a-b}{\gamma+\beta} - \frac{1}{\gamma}\sum_{i=0}^{\infty}(-\beta/\gamma)^i \varepsilon_{t-i} + (-\frac{\beta}{\gamma})^t \left[p_0 - \frac{a-b}{\gamma+\beta} + \frac{1}{\gamma}\sum_{i=0}^{\infty}(-\beta/\gamma)^i \varepsilon_{-i} \right]$$

and after simplification of the two summations

$$p_t = \frac{a-b}{\gamma+\beta} - \frac{1}{\gamma}\sum_{i=0}^{t-1}(-\beta/\gamma)^i \varepsilon_{t-i} + (-\frac{\beta}{\gamma})^t \left[p_0 - \frac{a-b}{\gamma+\beta} \right] \tag{1.42}$$

We can interpret (1.42) in terms of Figure 1.3. In order to focus on the stability of the system, temporarily assume that all values of the $\{\varepsilon_t\}$ sequence are zero. Subsequently, we will return to a consideration of the effects of supply shocks. If the system begins in long-run equilibrium, the initial condition is such that $p_0 = (a-b)/(\gamma+\beta)$. In this case, inspection of equation (1.42) indicates that $p_t = (a-b)/(\gamma+\beta)$. Thus, if we begin the process at point E, the system remains in long-run equilibrium. Instead, suppose that the process begins at a price below long-run equilibrium: $p_0 < (a-b)/(\gamma+\beta)$. Equation (1.42) tells us that p_1 is

$$p_1 = (a-b)/(\gamma+\beta) + [p_0 - (a-b)/(\gamma+\beta)] (-\beta/\gamma)^1 \tag{1.43}$$

Since $p_0 < (a-b)/(\gamma+\beta)$ and $-\beta/\gamma < 0$, it follows that p_1 will be above the long-run equilibrium price $(a-b)/(\gamma+\beta)$. In period 2

$$p_2 = (a-b)/(\gamma+\beta) + [p_0 - (a-b)/(\gamma+\beta)] (-\beta/\gamma)^2$$

although $p_0 < (a-b)/(\gamma+\beta)$, $(-\beta/\gamma)^2$ is positive; hence, p_2 is below the long-run equilibrium. For the subsequent periods, note that $(-\beta/\gamma)^t$ will be positive for even values of t and negative for odd values of t. Just as we found graphically, the successive values of the $\{p_t\}$ sequence will oscillate above and below the long-run equilibrium price. Since $(\beta/\gamma)^t$ goes to zero if $\beta < \gamma$ and explodes if $\beta > \gamma$, the magnitude of β/γ determines whether the price actually converges toward the long-run equilibrium. If $\beta/\gamma < 1$, the oscillations will diminish in magnitude, and if $\beta/\gamma > 1$, the oscillations will be explosive.

The economic interpretation of this stability condition is straightforward. The slope of the supply curve (i.e., dp_t/ds_t) is $1/\beta$ and the absolute value of the slope of the demand curve [i.e., $-dp_t/d(d_t)$] is $1/\gamma$. If the supply curve is steeper than the demand curve, $1/\beta > 1/\gamma$ or $\beta/\gamma < 1$ so that the system is stable. This is precisely the case illustrated in Figure 1.3. As an exercise, you should draw a diagram with the demand curve steeper than the supply curve and show that the price oscillates and diverges from the long-run equilibrium.

Now consider the effects of the supply shocks. The contemporaneous effect of a supply shock on the price of wheat is the partial derivative of p_t with respect to ε_t; from (1.42):

$$\frac{\partial p_t}{\partial \varepsilon_t} = -\frac{1}{\gamma} \tag{1.44}$$

Equation (1.44) is called the **impact multiplier** since it shows the impact effect of a change in ε_t on the price in t. In terms of Figure 1.3, a negative value of ε_t implies a price above the long-run price p; the price in t rises by $1/\gamma$ units for each unit decline in current period supply. Of course, this terminology is not specific to the cobweb model; in terms of the nth-order model given by (1.10), the impact multiplier is the partial derivative of y_t with respect to the partial change in the forcing process.[5]

The effects of the supply shock in t persist into future periods. Updating (1.42) by one period yields the **one-period multiplier:**

$$\frac{\partial \, p_{t+1}}{\partial \, \varepsilon_t} = -\frac{1}{\gamma}(-\beta/\gamma)$$

$$= \beta/\gamma^2$$

Point 3 in Figure 1.3 illustrates how the price in $t+1$ is affected by the negative supply shock in t. It is straightforward to derive the result that the effects of the supply shock decay over time. Since $\beta/\gamma < 1$, the absolute value of $\partial p_t/\partial \varepsilon_t$ exceeds $\partial p_{t+1}/\partial \varepsilon_t$. All of the multipliers can be derived analogously; updating (1.42) by two periods:

$$\partial p_{t+2}/\partial \varepsilon_t = -(1/\gamma)(-\beta/\gamma)^2$$

and after n periods:

$$\partial p_{t+n}/\partial \varepsilon_t = -(1/\gamma)(-\beta/\gamma)^n$$

The time path of all such multipliers is called the **impulse response function.** This function has many important applications in time-series analysis because it shows how the entire time path of a variable is affected by a stochastic shock. Here, the impulse function traces the effects of a supply shock in the wheat market. In other economic applications, you may be interested in the time path of a money supply shock or a productivity shock on real GDP.

In actuality, the function can be derived without updating (1.42) because it is always the case that

$$\frac{\partial \, p_{t+j}}{\partial \, \varepsilon_t} = \frac{\partial \, p_t}{\partial \, \varepsilon_{t-j}}$$

To find the impulse response function, simply find the partial derivative of (1.42) with respect to the various ε_{t-j}. These partial derivatives are nothing more than the coefficients of the $\{\varepsilon_{t-j}\}$ sequence in (1.42).

Each of the three components in (1.42) has a direct economic interpretation. The deterministic portion of the particular solution $(a-b)/(\gamma+\beta)$ is the long-run equilibrium price; if the stability condition is met, the $\{p_t\}$ sequence tends to converge to this long-run value. The stochastic component of the particular solution captures the short-run price adjustments due to the supply shocks. The ultimate decay of the coefficients of the impulse response function guarantees that the effects of changes in the various ε_t are of a short-run duration. The third component is the expression $(-\beta/\gamma)^t A = (-\beta/\gamma)^t[p_0 - (a-b)/(\gamma+\beta)]$. The value of A is the initial period's deviation of the price from its long-run equilibrium level. Given that $\beta/\gamma < 1$, the importance of this initial deviation diminishes over time.

6. SOLVING HOMOGENEOUS DIFFERENCE EQUATIONS

Higher-order difference equations arise quite naturally in economic analysis. Equation (1.5)—the reduced-form GDP equation resulting from Samuelson's (1939) model—is an example of a second-order difference equation. Moreover, in time-series econometrics it is quite typical to estimate second and higher-order equations. To begin our examination of homogeneous solutions, consider the second-order equation

$$y_t - a_1 y_{t-1} - a_2 y_{t-2} = 0 \tag{1.45}$$

Given the findings in the first-order case, you should suspect that the homogeneous solution has the form $y_t^h = A\alpha^t$. Substitution of this trial solution into (1.45) yields

$$A\alpha^t - a_1 A\alpha^{t-1} - a_2 A\alpha^{t-2} = 0 \tag{1.46}$$

Clearly, any arbitrary value of A is satisfactory. If you divide (1.46) by $A\alpha^{t-2}$, the problem is to find the values of α that satisfy

$$\alpha^2 - a_1 \alpha - a_2 = 0 \tag{1.47}$$

Solving this quadratic equation—called the **characteristic equation**—yields two values of α, called the **characteristic roots.** Using the quadratic formula, we find that the two characteristic roots are

$$\alpha_1, \alpha_2 = \frac{a_1 \pm \sqrt{a_1^2 + 4a_2}}{2}$$

$$= (a_1 \pm \sqrt{d})/2 \tag{1.48}$$

where d is the discriminant $[(a_1)^2 + 4a_2]$.

Each of these two characteristic roots yields a valid solution for (1.45). Again, these solutions are not unique. In fact, for any two arbitrary constants A_1 and A_2, the linear combination $A_1(\alpha_1)^t + A_2(\alpha_2)^t$ also solves (1.45). As proof, simply substitute $y_t = A_1(\alpha_1)^t + A_2(\alpha_2)^t$ into (1.45) to obtain

$$A_1(\alpha_1)^t + A_2(\alpha_2)^t = a_1[A_1(\alpha_1)^{t-1} + A_2(\alpha_2)^{t-1}] + a_2[A_1(\alpha_1)^{t-2} + A_2(\alpha_2)^{t-2}]$$

Now, regroup terms as follows:

$$A_1[(\alpha_1)^t - a_1(\alpha_1)^{t-1} - a_2(\alpha_1)^{t-2}] + A_2[(\alpha_2)^t - a_1(\alpha_2)^{t-1} - a_2(\alpha_2)^{t-2}] = 0$$

Since α_1 and α_2 each solve (1.45), both terms in brackets must equal zero. As such, the complete homogeneous solution in the second-order case is

$$y_t^h = A_1(\alpha_1)^t + A_2(\alpha_2)^t$$

Without knowing the specific values of a_1 and a_2, we cannot find the two characteristic roots α_1 and α_2. Nevertheless, it is possible to characterize the nature of the solution; three possible cases are dependent on the value of the discriminant d.

CASE 1

If $a_1^2 + 4a_2 > 0$, d is a real number and there will be two distinct real characteristic roots. Hence, there are two separate solutions to the homogeneous equation denoted by $(\alpha_1)^t$ and $(\alpha_2)^t$. We already know that any linear combination of the two is also a solution. Hence,

$$y_t^h = A_1(\alpha_1)^t + A_2(\alpha_2)^t$$

It should be clear that if the absolute value of *either* α_1 or α_2 exceeds unity, the homogeneous solution will explode. Worksheet 1.1 examines two second-order equations showing real and distinct characteristic roots. In the first example, $y_t = 0.2y_{t-1} + 0.35y_{t-2}$, the characteristic roots are shown to be: $\alpha_1 = 0.7$ and $\alpha_2 = -0.5$. Hence, the full homogeneous solution is $y_t^h = A_1(0.7)^t + A_2(-0.5)^t$. Since both roots are less than unity in absolute value, the homogeneous solution is convergent. As you can see in the graph on the bottom left-hand side of Worksheet 1.1, convergence is not monotonic because of the influence of the expression $(-0.5)^t$.

In the second example, $y_t = 0.7y_{t-1} + 0.35y_{t-2}$. The worksheet indicates how to obtain the solution for the two characteristic roots. Given that one characteristic root is $(1.037)^t$, the $\{y_t\}$ sequence explodes. The influence of the negative root ($\alpha_2 = -0.337$) is responsible for the non-monotonicity of the time path. Since $(-0.337)^t$ quickly approaches zero, the dominant root is the explosive value 1.037.

CASE 2

If $a_1^2 + 4a_2 = 0$, it follows that $d = 0$ and $\alpha_1 = \alpha_2 = a_1/2$. Hence, a homogeneous solution is $a_1/2$. However, when $d = 0$, there is a second homogeneous solution given by $t(a_1/2)^t$. To demonstrate that $y_t^h = t(a_1/2)^t$ is a homogeneous solution, substitute it into (1.45) to determine whether

$$t(a_1/2)^t - a_1[(t-1)(a_1/2)^{t-1}] - a_2[(t-2)(a_1/2)^{t-2}] = 0$$

Divide by $(a_1/2)^{t-2}$ and form

$$-[(a_1^2/4) + a_2]t + [(a_1^2/2) + 2a_2] = 0$$

Since we are operating in the circumstance where $a_1^2 + 4a_2 = 0$, each bracketed expression is zero; hence, $t(a_1/2)^t$ solves (1.45). Again, for arbitrary constants A_1 and A_2, the complete homogeneous solution is

$$y_t^h = A_1(a_1/2)^t + A_2t(a_1/2)^t$$

Clearly, the system is explosive if $|a_1| > 2$. If $|a_1| < 2$, the term $A_1(a_1/2)^t$ converges, but you might think that the effect of the term $t(a_1/2)^t$ is ambiguous [since the diminishing $(a_1/2)^t$ is multiplied by t]. This ambiguity is correct in the limited sense that the behavior of the homogeneous solution is not monotonic. As illustrated in Figure 1.4 for $a_1/2 = 0.95$, 0.9, and -0.9, as long as $|a_1| < 2$, $\lim[\, t(a_1/2)^t\,]$ is necessarily zero as $t \to \infty$; thus, there is always convergence. For $0 < a_1 < 2$, the homogeneous solution appears to explode before ultimately converging to zero. For $-2 < a_1 < 0$, the behavior is wildly erratic; the homogeneous solution appears to oscillate explosively before the oscillations dampen and finally converge to zero.

WORKSHEET *1.1*

SECOND-ORDER EQUATIONS

Example 1: $y_t = 0.2y_{t-1} + 0.35y_{t-2}$. Hence: $a_1 = 0.2$ and $a_2 = 0.35$

Form the homogeneous equation: $y_t - 0.2y_{t-1} - 0.35y_{t-2} = 0$

A check of the discriminant reveals: $d = a_1^2 + 4a_2$ so that $d = 1.44$. Given that $d > 0$, the roots will be real and distinct.

Let the trial solution have the form: $y_t = \alpha^t$. Substitute the trial solution into the homogenous equation to obtain: $\alpha^t - 0.2\alpha^{t-1} - 0.35\alpha^{t-2} = 0$

Divide by α^{t-2} to obtain the characteristic equation: $\alpha^2 - 0.2\alpha^t - 0.35\alpha = 0$

Compute the two characteristic roots:

$$\alpha_1 = 0.5(a_1 + d^{1/2}) \qquad \alpha_2 = 0.5(a_1 - d^{1/2})$$
$$\alpha_1 = 0.7 \qquad\qquad\qquad \alpha_2 = -0.5$$

The homogeneous solution is: $A_1(0.7)^t + A_2(-0.5)^t$. The first graph shows the time path of this solution for the case in which the arbitrary constants equal unity and t runs from 1 to 20.

Example 2: $y_t = 0.7y_{t-1} + 0.35y_{t-2}$. Hence: $a_1 = 0.7$ and $a_2 = 0.35$

Form the homogeneous equation: $y_t - 0.7y_{t-1} - 0.35y_{t-2} = 0$

A check of the discriminant reveals: $d = a_1^2 + 4a_2$ so that $d = 1.89$. Given that $d > 0$, the roots will be real and distinct.

Form the characteristic equation $\alpha^t - 0.7\alpha^{t-1} - 0.35\alpha^{t-2} = 0$

Divide by α^{t-2} to obtain the characteristic equation: $\alpha^2 - 0.7\alpha - 0.35\alpha = 0$

Compute the two characteristic roots:

$$\alpha_1 = 0.5(a_1 + d^{1/2}) \qquad \alpha_2 = 0.5(a_1 - d^{1/2})$$
$$\alpha_1 = 1.037 \qquad\qquad\qquad \alpha_2 = -0.337$$

The homogeneous solution is: $A_1(1.037)^t + A_2(-0.337)^t$. The second graph shows the time path of this solution for the case in which the arbitrary constants equal unity and t runs from 1 to 20.

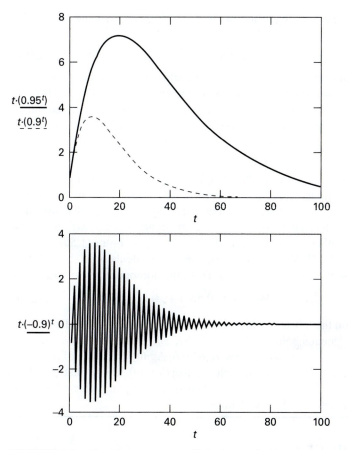

FIGURE 1-4 The Homogeneous Solution $t \cdot (a_1)^t$

CASE 3

If $a_1^2 + 4a_2 < 0$, it follows that d is negative so that the characteristic roots are imaginary. Since $a_1^2 \geq 0$, imaginary roots can occur only if $a_2 < 0$. Although this might be hard to interpret directly, if we switch to polar coordinates it is possible to transform the roots into more easily understood trigonometric functions. The technical details are presented in Appendix 1.1. For now, write the two characteristic roots as

$$\alpha_1 = (a_1 + i\sqrt{-d})/2 \qquad\qquad \alpha_2 = (a_1 - i\sqrt{-d})/2$$

where $i = \sqrt{-1}$.

As shown in Appendix 1.1, you can use de Moivre's theorem to write the homogeneous solution as

$$y_t^h = \beta_1 r^t \cos(\theta t + \beta_2) \tag{1.49}$$

where β_1 and β_2 are arbitrary constants, $r = (-a_2)^{1/2}$, and the value of θ is chosen so as to satisfy

$$\cos(\theta) = a_1/[2(-a_2)^{1/2}] \tag{1.50}$$

The trigonometric functions impart a wavelike pattern to the time path of the homogeneous solution; note that the frequency of the oscillations is determined by θ. Since $\cos(\theta t) = \cos(2\pi + \theta t)$, the stability condition is determined solely by the magnitude of $r = (-a_2)^{1/2}$. If $|a_2| = 1$, the oscillations are of unchanging amplitude; the homogeneous solution is periodic. The oscillations will dampen if $|a_2| < 1$ and explode if $|a_2| > 1$.

Example: It is worthwhile to work through an exercise using an equation with imaginary roots. The left-hand side of Worksheet 1.2 examines the behavior of the equation $y_t = 1.6y_{t-1} - 0.9y_{t-2}$. A quick check shows that the discriminant d is negative so that the characteristic roots are imaginary. If we transform to polar coordinates, the value of r is given by $(0.9)^{1/2} = 0.949$. From (1.50), $\cos(\theta) = 1.6/(2*0.949) = 0.843$. You can use a trig table or a calculator to show that $\theta = 0.567$ (i.e., if $\cos(\theta) = 0.843$, $\theta = 0.567$). Thus, the homogeneous solution is

$$y_t^h = \beta_1(0.949)^t \cos(0.567t + \beta_2) \tag{1.51}$$

The graph on the left-hand side of Worksheet 1.2 sets $\beta_1 = 1$ and $\beta_2 = 0$ and plots the homogeneous solution for $t = 1, \ldots, 30$. Example 2 uses the same value of a_2 (hence, $r = 0.949$) but sets $a_1 = -0.6$. Again, the value of d is negative; however, for this set of calculations, $\cos(\theta) = -0.316$ so that θ is 1.89. Comparing the two graphs, you can see that increasing the value of θ acts to increase the frequency of the oscillations.

Stability Conditions

The general stability conditions can be summarized using triangle ABC in Figure 1.5. Arc $A0B$ is the boundary between Cases 1 and 3; it is the locus of points where $d = a_1{}^2 + 4a_2 = 0$. The region above $A0B$ corresponds to Case 1 (since $d > 0$), and the region below $A0B$ corresponds to Case 3 (since $d < 0$).

In Case 1 (in which the roots are real and distinct), stability requires that the largest root be less than unity and the smallest root be greater than -1. The largest characteristic root, $\alpha_1 = (a_1 + \sqrt{d})/2$, will be less than unity if

$$a_1 + (a_1{}^2 + 4a_2)^{1/2} < 2 \quad \text{or} \quad (a_1{}^2 + 4a_2)^{1/2} < 2 - a_1$$

Hence, $a_1{}^2 + 4a_2 < 4 - 4a_1 + a_1{}^2$

or

$$a_1 + a_2 < 1 \tag{1.52}$$

The smallest root, $\alpha_2 = (a_1 - \sqrt{d})/2$, will be greater than minus one if

$$a_1 - (a_1{}^2 + 4a_2)^{1/2} > -2 \quad \text{or} \quad 2 + a_1 > (a_1{}^2 + 4a_2)^{1/2}$$

WORKSHEET *1.2*

IMAGINARY ROOTS

Example 1	**Example 2**
$y_t - 1.6y_{t-1} + 0.9y_{t-2}$	$y_t + 0.6y_{t-1} + 0.9y_{t-2}$

a) Check the discriminant $d = (a_1)^2 + 4a_2$

$$d = (1.6)^2 + 4(-0.9) \qquad\qquad d = (-0.6)^2 + 4(-0.9)$$
$$= -1.04 \qquad\qquad\qquad\qquad = -3.24$$

Hence, the roots are imaginary. The homogeneous solution has the form

$$y_t^h = \beta_1 r^t \cos(\theta t + \beta_2)$$

where β_1 and β_2 are arbitrary constants.

b) Obtain the value of $r = (-a_2)^{1/2}$

$$r = (0.9)^{1/2} \qquad\qquad\qquad r = (0.9)^{1/2}$$
$$= 0.949 \qquad\qquad\qquad\qquad = 0.949$$

c) Obtain θ from $\cos(\theta) = a_1/[2(-a_1)^{1/2}]$

$$\cos(\theta) = 1.6/[2(0.9)^{1/2}] \qquad \cos(\theta) = -0.6/[2(0.9)^{1/2}]$$
$$= 0.843 \qquad\qquad\qquad\qquad = -0.316$$

Given $\cos(\theta)$, use a trig-table to find θ

$$\theta = 0.567 \qquad\qquad\qquad \theta = 1.89$$

d) Form the homogeneous solution: $y_t^h = \beta_1 r^t \cos(\theta t + \beta_2)$

$$y_t^h = \beta_1(0.949)^t \cos(0.567t + \beta_2) \qquad y_t^h = \beta_1(0.949)^t \cos(1.89t + \beta_2)$$

For $\beta_1 = 1$ and $\beta_2 = 0$, the time paths of the homogeneous solutions are

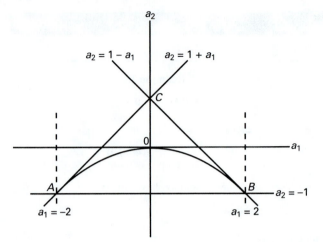

FIGURE 1.5   Characterizing the Stability Conditions

Hence: $4 + 4a_1 + a_1{}^2 > a_1{}^2 + 4a_2$

or

$$a_2 < 1 + a_1 \tag{1.53}$$

Thus, the region of stability in Case 1 consists of all points in the region bounded by $A0BC$. For any point in $A0BC$, conditions (1.52) and (1.53) hold and $d > 0$.

In Case 2 (repeated roots), $a_1{}^2 + 4a_2 = 0$. The stability condition is $|a_1| < 2$. Thus, the region of stability in Case 2 consists of all points on arc $A0B$. In Case 3 ($d < 0$), the stability condition is $r = (-a_2)^{1/2} < 1$. Hence

$$-a_2 < 1 \quad \text{(where } a_2 < 0) \tag{1.54}$$

Thus, the region of stability in Case 3 consists of all points in region $A0B$. For any point in $A0B$, (1.54) is satisfied and $d < 0$.

A succinct way to characterize the stability conditions is to state that the characteristic roots must lie within the unit circle. Consider the semicircle drawn in Figure 1.6. Real numbers are measured on the horizontal axis and imaginary numbers are measured on the vertical axis. If the characteristic roots α_1 and α_2 are both real, they can be plotted on the horizontal axis. Stability requires that they lie within a circle of radius one. Complex roots will lie somewhere in the complex plane. If $a_1 > 0$, the roots $\alpha_1 = (a_1 + i\sqrt{d})/2$ and $\alpha_2 = (a_1 - i\sqrt{d})/2$ can be represented by the two points shown in Figure 1.6. For example, α_1 is drawn by moving $a_1/2$ units along the real axis and $\sqrt{d}/2$ units along the imaginary axis. Using the distance formula, the length of the radius r is given by

$$r = \sqrt{(a_1/2)^2 + (d^{1/2}i/2)^2}$$

and, using the fact that $i^2 = -1$, we obtain

$$r = (-a_2)^{-1/2}$$

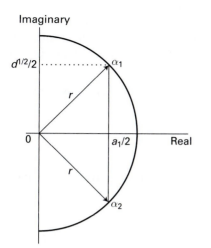

FIGURE 1.6   Characteristic Roots and the Unit Circle

The stability condition requires that $r < 1$. Therefore, when plotted on the complex plane, the two roots α_1 and α_2 must lie within a circle of radius equal to unity. In the time-series literature it is simply stated that *stability requires that all characteristic roots lie within the unit circle.*

Higher-Order Systems

The same method can be used to find the homogeneous solution to higher-order difference equations. The homogeneous equation for (1.10) is

$$y_t - \sum_{i=1}^{n} a_i y_{t-i} = 0 \qquad (1.55)$$

Given the results in Section 4, you should suspect each homogeneous solution to have the form $y_t^h = A\alpha^t$ where A is an arbitrary constant. Thus, to find the value(s) of α, we seek the solution for

$$A\alpha^t - \sum_{i=1}^{n} a_i A\alpha^{t-i} = 0 \qquad (1.56)$$

or, dividing through by α^{t-n}, we seek the values of α that solve

$$\alpha^n - a_1\alpha^{n-1} - a_2\alpha^{n-2} \ldots - a_n = 0 \qquad (1.57)$$

This nth-order polynomial will yield n solutions for α. Denote these n characteristic roots by $\alpha_1, \alpha_2, \ldots, \alpha_n$. Given the results in Section 4, the linear combination $A_1\alpha_1^t + A_2\alpha_2^t + \ldots + A_n\alpha_n^t$ is also a solution. The arbitrary constants A_1 through A_n can be eliminated by imposing n initial conditions on the general solution. The α_i may be real or complex numbers. Stability requires that all real valued α_i be less than unity in absolute value. Complex roots will necessarily come in pairs. Stability requires that all roots lie within the unit circle shown in Figure 1.6.

In most circumstances there is little need to directly calculate the characteristic roots of higher-order systems. Many of the technical details are included in Appendix 1.2 to this chapter. However, there are some useful rules for checking the stability conditions in higher-order systems.

1. In an nth-order equation, a necessary condition for all characteristic roots to lie inside the unit circle is

$$\sum_{i=1}^{n} a_i < 1$$

2. Since the values of the a_i can be positive or negative, a sufficient condition for all characteristic roots to lie inside the unit circle is

$$\sum_{i=1}^{n} |a_i| < 1$$

3. At least one characteristic root equals unity if

$$\sum_{i=1}^{n} a_i = 1$$

   Any sequence that contains one or more characteristic roots that equal unity is called a **unit root** process.

4. For a third-order equation, the stability conditions can be written as

$$1 - a_1 - a_2 - a_3 > 0$$
$$1 + a_1 - a_2 + a_3 > 0$$
$$1 - a_1 a_3 + a_2 - a_3^2 > 0$$
$$3 + a_1 + a_2 - 3a_3 > 0 \text{ or } 3 - a_1 + a_2 + 3a_3 > 0$$

   Given that the first three inequalities are satisfied, either of the last two can be checked. One of the last conditions is redundant, given that the other three hold.

7. PARTICULAR SOLUTIONS FOR DETERMINISTIC PROCESSES

Finding the particular solution to a difference equation is often a matter of ingenuity and perseverance. The appropriate technique depends heavily on the form of the $\{x_t\}$ process. We begin by considering those processes that contain only deterministic components. Of course, in econometric analysis, the forcing process will contain both deterministic and stochastic components.

CASE 1

$x_t = 0$. When all elements of the $\{x_t\}$ process are zero, the difference equation becomes

$$y_t = a_0 + a_1 y_{t-1} + a_2 y_{t-2} + \ldots + a_n y_{t-n} \tag{1.58}$$

Intuition suggests that an unchanging value of y (i.e., $y_t = y_{t-1} = \ldots = c$) should solve the equation. Substitute the trial solution $y_t = c$ into (1.58) to obtain

$$c = a_0 + a_1 c + a_2 c + \ldots + a_n c$$

so that

$$c = a_0/(1 - a_1 - a_2 - \ldots - a_n) \tag{1.59}$$

As long as $(1 - a_1 - a_2 - \ldots - a_n)$ does not equal zero, the value of c given by (1.59) is a solution to (1.58). Hence, the particular solution to (1.58) is given by $y_t^p = a_0/(1 - a_1 - a_2 - \ldots - a_n)$.

If $1 - a_1 - a_2 - \ldots - a_n = 0$, the value of c in (1.59) is undefined; it is necessary to try some other form for the solution. The key insight is that $\{y_t\}$ is a unit root process if $\Sigma a_i = 1$. Since $\{y_t\}$ is not convergent, it stands to reason that the constant solution does not work. Instead, recall equations (1.12) and (1.26); these solutions suggest that a linear time trend can appear in the solution of a unit root process. As such, try the solution: $y_t^p = ct$. For ct to be a solution it must be the case that

$$ct = a_0 + a_1 c(t-1) + a_2 c(t-2) + \ldots + a_n c(t-n)$$

or, combining like terms,

$$(1 - a_1 - a_2 - \ldots - a_n)ct = a_0 - c(a_1 + 2a_2 + 3a_3 + \ldots + na_n)$$

Since $1 - a_1 - a_2 - \ldots - a_n = 0$, select the value of c such that

$$c = a_0/(a_1 + 2a_2 + 3a_3 + \ldots + na_n)$$

For example, let

$$y_t = 2 + 0.75 y_{t-1} + 0.25 y_{t-2}$$

Here, $a_1 = 0.75$ and $a_2 = 0.25$; $\{y_t\}$ is a unit root process because $a_1 + a_2 = 1$. The particular solution has the form ct, where $c = 2/[0.75 + 2(0.25)] = 1.6$. In the event that the solution ct fails, sequentially try the solutions: $y_t^p = ct^2$, $ct^3, \ldots, ct^n$. For an nth-order equation, one of these solutions will always be the particular solution.

CASE 2

The Exponential Case. Let x_t have the exponential form $b(d)^{rt}$, where b, d, and r are constants. Since r has the natural interpretation as a growth rate, we would expect to encounter this type of forcing process case in a growth context. We illustrate the solution procedure using the first-order equation

$$y_t = a_0 + a_1 y_{t-1} + bd^{rt} \tag{1.60}$$

To try to gain an intuitive feel for the form of the solution, notice that if $b = 0$, (1.60) is a special case of (1.58). Hence, you should expect a constant to appear in the particular solution. Moreover, the expression d^{rt} grows at the constant rate r. Thus, you might expect the particular solution to have the form $y_t^p = c_0 + c_1 d^{rt}$, where c_0 and c_1 are constants. If this equation is actually a solution, you should be able to substitute it back into (1.60) and obtain an identity. Making the appropriate substitutions, we get

$$c_0 + c_1 d^{rt} = a_0 + a_1[c_0 + c_1 d^{r(t-1)}] + b d^{rt} \tag{1.61}$$

For this solution to work, it is necessary to select c_0 and c_1 such that

$$c_0 = a_0/(1 - a_1) \text{ and } c_1 = [bd^r]/(d^r - a_1)$$

Thus, a particular solution is

$$y_t^p = \frac{a_0}{1 - a_1} + \frac{b d^r}{d^r - a_1} d^{rt}$$

The nature of the solution is that y_t^p equals the constant $a_0/(1 - a_1)$ plus an expression that grows at the rate r. Note that for $|d^r| < 1$, the particular solution converges to $a_0/(1 - a_1)$.

If either $a_1 = 1$ or $a_1 = d^r$, use the trick suggested in Case 1. If $a_1 = 1$, try the solution $c_0 = ct$, and if $a_1 = d^r$, try the solution $c_1 = tb$. Use precisely the same methodology in higher-order systems.

CASE 3

Deterministic Time Trend. In this case, let the $\{x_t\}$ sequence be represented by the relationship $x_t = bt^d$ where b is a constant and d is a positive integer. Hence

$$y_t = a_0 + \sum_{i=1}^{n} a_i y_{t-i} + bt^d \tag{1.62}$$

Since y_t depends on t^d, it follows that y_{t-1} depends on $(t-1)^d$, y_{t-2} depends on $(t-2)^d$, and so on. As such, the particular solution has the form $y_t^p = c_0 + c_1 t + c_2 t^2 + \ldots + c_d t^d$. To find the values of the c_i, substitute the particular solution into (1.62). Then select the value of each c_i that results in an identity. Although various values of d are possible, in economic applications it is common to see models incorporating a linear time trend $(d = 1)$. For illustrative purposes, consider the second-order equation $y_t = a_0 + a_1 y_{t-1} + a_2 y_{t-2} + bt$. Posit the solution $y_t^p = c_0 + c_1 t$ where c_0 and c_1 are undetermined coefficients. Substituting this "challenge solution" into the second-order difference equation yields

$$c_0 + c_1 t = a_0 + a_1[c_0 + c_1(t-1)] + a_2[c_0 + c_1(t-2)] + bt \tag{1.63}$$

Now select values of c_0 and c_1 so as to force equation (1.63) to be an identity for all possible values of t. If we combine all constant terms and all terms involving t, the required values of c_0 and c_1 are

$$c_1 = b/(1 - a_1 - a_2)$$
$$c_0 = [a_0 - (2a_2 + a_1)c_1] / (1 - a_1 - a_2)$$

so that

$$c_0 = [a_0/(1 - a_1 - a_2)] - [b/(1 - a_1 - a_2)^2](2a_2 + a_1)$$

Thus, the particular solution will also contain a linear time trend. You should have no difficulty foreseeing the solution technique if $a_1 + a_2 = 1$. In this circumstance—which is applicable to higher order cases, as well—try multiplying the original challenge solution by t.

8. THE METHOD OF UNDETERMINED COEFFICIENTS

At this point, it is appropriate to introduce the first of two useful methods for finding particular solutions when there are stochastic components in the $\{y_t\}$ process. The key insight of the **method of undetermined coefficients** is that the particular solution to a linear difference equation is necessarily linear. Moreover, the solution can depend only on time, a constant, and the elements of the forcing process $\{x_t\}$. Thus, it is often possible to know the exact form of the solution even though the coefficients of the solution are unknown. The technique involves positing a solution—called a **challenge solution**—that is a linear function of all terms thought to appear in the actual solution. The problem becomes one of finding the set of values for those undetermined coefficients that solve the difference equation.

The actual technique for finding the coefficients is straightforward. Substitute the challenge solution into the original difference equation and solve for the values of the undetermined coefficients that yield an identity for all possible values of the included variables. If it is not possible to obtain an identity, the form of the challenge solution is incorrect. Try a new trial solution and repeat the process. In fact, we used the method of undetermined coefficients when positing the challenge solutions $y_t^p = c_0 + c_1 d^{rt}$ and $y_t^p = c_0 + c_1 t$ for Cases 2 and 3 in Section 7.

To begin, reconsider the simple first-order equation $y_t = a_0 + a_1 y_{t-1} + \varepsilon_t$. Since you have solved this equation using the iterative method, the equation is useful for illustrating the method of undetermined coefficients. The nature of the $\{y_t\}$ process is such that the particular solution can depend only on a constant term, time, and the individual elements of the $\{\varepsilon_t\}$ sequence. Since t does not explicitly appear in the forcing process, t can be in the particular solution only if the characteristic root is unity. Since the goal is to illustrate the method, posit the challenge solution:

$$y_t = b_0 + b_1 t + \sum_{i=0}^{\infty} \alpha_i \varepsilon_{t-i} \qquad (1.64)$$

where b_0, b_1, and all the α_i are the coefficients to be determined.

Substitute (1.64) into the original difference equation to form

$$b_0 + b_1 t + \alpha_0 \varepsilon_t + \alpha_1 \varepsilon_{t-1} + \alpha_2 \varepsilon_{t-2} + \dots$$
$$= a_0 + a_1 [b_0 + b_1 (t-1) + \alpha_0 \varepsilon_{t-1} + \alpha_1 \varepsilon_{t-2} + \dots] + \varepsilon_t$$

Collecting like terms, we obtain

$$(b_0 - a_0 - a_1 b_0 + a_1 b_1) + b_1 (1 - a_1) t + (\alpha_0 - 1) \varepsilon_t$$
$$+ (\alpha_1 - a_1 \alpha_0) \varepsilon_{t-1} + (\alpha_2 - a_1 \alpha_1) \varepsilon_{t-2} + (\alpha_3 - a_1 \alpha_2) \varepsilon_{t-3} + \dots = 0 \qquad (1.65)$$

Equation (1.65) must hold for all values of t and all possible values of the $\{\varepsilon_t\}$ sequence. Thus, each of the following conditions must hold:

$$\alpha_0 - 1 = 0$$
$$\alpha_1 - a_1\alpha_0 = 0$$
$$\alpha_2 - a_1\alpha_1 = 0$$
$$.$$
$$.$$
$$.$$
$$b_0 - a_0 - a_1b_0 + a_1b_1 = 0$$
$$b_1 - a_1b_1 = 0$$

Notice that the first set of conditions can be solved for the α_i recursively. The solution of the first condition entails setting $\alpha_0 = 1$. Given this solution for α_0, the next equation requires $\alpha_1 = a_1$. Moving down the list, $\alpha_2 = a_1\alpha_1$ or $\alpha_2 = a_1^2$. Continuing the recursive process, we find $\alpha_i = a_1^i$. Now consider the last two equations. There are two possible cases depending on the value of a_1. If $a_1 \neq 1$, it immediately follows that $b_1 = 0$ and $b_0 = a_0/(1 - a_1)$. For this case, the particular solution is

$$y_t = \frac{a_0}{1 - a_1} + \sum_{i=0}^{\infty} a_1^i \varepsilon_{t-i}$$

Compare this result to (1.21); you will see that it is precisely the same solution found using the iterative method. The general solution is the sum of this particular solution plus the homogeneous solution Aa_1^t. Hence, the general solution is

$$y_t = \frac{a_0}{1 - a_1} + \sum_{i=0}^{\infty} a_1^i \varepsilon_{t-i} + Aa_1^t$$

Now, if there is an initial condition for y_0, it follows that

$$y_0 = \frac{a_0}{1 - a_1} + \sum_{i=0}^{\infty} a_1^i \varepsilon_{-i} + A$$

Combining these two equations so as to eliminate the arbitrary constant A, we obtain

$$y_t = \frac{a_0}{1 - a_1} + \sum_{i=0}^{\infty} a_1^i \varepsilon_{t-i} + a_1^t \left[y_0 - a_0 /(1-a_1) - \sum_{i=0}^{\infty} a_1^i \varepsilon_{-i} \right]$$

so that

$$y_t = \frac{a_0}{1 - a_1} + \sum_{i=0}^{t-1} a_1^i \varepsilon_{t-i} + a_1^t \left[y_0 - a_0/(1-a_1) \right] \tag{1.66}$$

It can be easily verified that (1.66) is identical to (1.25). Instead, if $a_1 = 1$, b_0 can be any arbitrary constant and $b_1 = a_0$. The improper form of the solution is

$$y_t = b_0 + a_0 t + \sum_{i=0}^{\infty} \varepsilon_{t-i}$$

The form of the solution is "improper" because the sum of the $\{\varepsilon_t\}$ sequence may not be finite. Therefore, it is necessary to impose an initial condition. If the value y_0 is given, it follows that

$$y_0 = b_0 + \sum_{i=0}^{\infty} \varepsilon_{-i}$$

Imposing the initial condition on the improper form of the solution yields (1.26)

$$y_t = y_0 + a_0 t + \sum_{i=1}^{t} \varepsilon_i$$

To take a second example, consider the equation

$$y_t = a_0 + a_1 y_{t-1} + \varepsilon_t + \beta_1 \varepsilon_{t-1} \tag{1.67}$$

Again, the solution can depend only on a constant, the elements of the $\{\varepsilon_t\}$ sequence, and t raised to the first power. As in the previous example, t does not need to be included in the challenge solution if the characteristic root differs from unity. To reinforce this point, use the challenge solution given by (1.64). Substitute this tentative solution into (1.67) to obtain

$$b_0 + b_1 t + \sum_{i=0}^{\infty} \alpha_i\, \varepsilon_{t-i} = a_0 + a_1 [b_0 + b_1\,(t-1) + \sum_{i=0}^{\infty} a_i\, \varepsilon_{t-1-i}] + \varepsilon_t + \beta_1\, \varepsilon_{t-1}$$

Matching coefficients on all terms containing $\varepsilon_t, \varepsilon_{t-1}, \varepsilon_{t-2}, \ldots$, yields

$$\alpha_0 = 1$$
$$\alpha_1 = a_1 \alpha_0 + \beta_1 \qquad\qquad [\text{so that } \alpha_1 = a_1 + \beta_1]$$
$$\alpha_2 = a_1 \alpha_1 \qquad\qquad\quad\; [\text{so that } \alpha_2 = a_1(a_1 + \beta_1)]$$
$$\alpha_3 = a_1 \alpha_2 \qquad\qquad\quad\; [\text{so that } \alpha_3 = (a_1)^2(a_1 + \beta_1)]$$
$$\cdots$$
$$\alpha_i = a_1 \alpha_{i-1} \qquad\qquad\;\; [\text{so that } \alpha_i = (a_1)^{i-1}(a_1 + \beta_1)]$$

Matching coefficients of intercept terms and coefficients of terms containing t, we get

$$b_0 = a_0 + a_1 b_0 - a_1 b_1$$
$$b_1 = a_1 b_1$$

Again, there are two cases. If $a_1 \neq 1$, then $b_1 = 0$ and $b_0 = a_0/(1 - a_1)$. The particular solution is

$$y_t = \frac{a_0}{1 - a_1} + \varepsilon_t + (a_1 + \beta_1) \sum_{i=1}^{\infty} a_1^{i-1}\, \varepsilon_{t-i}$$

The general solution augments the particular solution with the term $A a_1^t$. You are left with the exercise of imposing the initial condition for y_0 on the general solution. Now consider the case in which $a_1 = 1$. The undetermined coefficients are such that $b_1 = a_0$ and b_0 is an arbitrary constant. The improper form of the solution is

$$y_t = b_0 + a_0 t + \varepsilon_t + (1 + \beta_1) \sum_{i=1}^{\infty} \varepsilon_{t-i}$$

If y_0 is given, it follows that

$$y_0 = b_0 + \varepsilon_0 + (1 + \beta_1) \sum_{i=1}^{\infty} \varepsilon_{-i}$$

Hence, imposing the initial condition, we obtain

$$y_t = y_0 + a_0 t + \varepsilon_t + (1 + \beta_1) \sum_{i=1}^{t-1} \varepsilon_{t-i}$$

Higher-Order Systems

The identical procedure is used for higher-order systems. As an example, let us find the particular solution to the second-order equation

$$y_t = a_0 + a_1 y_{t-1} + a_2 y_{t-2} + \varepsilon_t \tag{1.68}$$

Since we have a second-order equation, we use the challenge solution

$$y_t = b_0 + b_1 t + b_2 t^2 + \alpha_0 \varepsilon_t + \alpha_1 \varepsilon_{t-1} + \alpha_2 \varepsilon_{t-2} + \dots$$

where b_0, b_1, b_2, and the α_i are the undetermined coefficients.

Substituting the challenge solution into (1.68) yields

$$[b_0 + b_1 t + b_2 t^2] + \alpha_0 \varepsilon_t + \alpha_1 \varepsilon_{t-1} + \alpha_2 \varepsilon_{t-2} + \dots = a_0 + a_1 [b_0 + b_1(t-1) + b_2(t-1)^2$$
$$+ \alpha_0 \varepsilon_{t-1} + \alpha_1 \varepsilon_{t-2} + \alpha_2 \varepsilon_{t-3} + \dots] + a_2 [b_0 + b_1(t-2) + b_2(t-2)^2$$
$$+ \alpha_0 \varepsilon_{t-2} + \alpha_1 \varepsilon_{t-3} + \alpha_2 \varepsilon_{t-4} + \dots] + \varepsilon_t$$

There are several necessary and sufficient conditions for the values of the α_i's to render the equation above an identity for all possible realizations of the $\{\varepsilon_t\}$ sequence:

$$\alpha_0 = 1$$
$$\alpha_1 = a_1 \alpha_0 \qquad\qquad\qquad \text{[so that } \alpha_1 = a_1]$$
$$\alpha_2 = a_1 \alpha_1 + a_2 \alpha_0 \qquad\quad\;\, \text{[so that } \alpha_2 = (a_1)^2 + a_2]$$
$$\alpha_3 = a_1 \alpha_2 + a_2 \alpha_1 \qquad\quad\;\, \text{[so that } \alpha_3 = (a_1)^3 + 2a_1 a_2]$$
$$\cdot$$
$$\cdot$$

Notice that for any value of $j \geq 2$, the coefficients solve the second-order difference equation $\alpha_j = a_1 \alpha_{j-1} + a_2 \alpha_{j-2}$. Since we know α_0 and α_1, we can solve for all the α_j iteratively. The properties of the coefficients will be precisely those discussed when considering homogeneous solutions:

1. Convergence necessitates that $|a_2| < 1$, $a_1 + a_2 < 1$, and that $a_2 - a_1 < 1$. Notice that convergence implies that past values of the $\{\varepsilon_t\}$ sequence ultimately have a successively smaller influence on the current value of y_t.

2. If the coefficients converge, convergence will be direct or oscillatory if $(a_1^2 + 4a_2) > 0$, will follow a sine/cosine pattern if $(a_1^2 + 4a_2) < 0$, and will "explode" and then converge if $(a_1^2 + 4a_2) = 0$. Appropriately setting the α_i, we are left with the remaining expression:

$$b_2(1 - a_1 - a_2)t^2 + [b_1(1 - a_1 - a_2) + 2b_2(a_1 + 2a_2)]t +$$
$$[b_0(1 - a_1 - a_2) - a_0 + a_1(b_1 - b_2) + 2a_2(b_1 - 2b_2)] = 0 \tag{1.69}$$

Equation (1.69) must equal zero for all values of t. First, consider the case in which $a_1 + a_2 \neq 1$. Since $(1 - a_1 - a_2)$ does not vanish, it is necessary to set the value of b_2 equal to zero. Given that $b_2 = 0$ and that the coefficient of t must equal zero, it follows that b_1 must also be set equal to zero. Finally, given that $b_1 = b_2 = 0$, we must set $b_0 = a_0/(1 - a_1 - a_2)$. Instead, if $a_1 + a_2 = 1$, the solutions for the b_i depend on the specific values of a_0, a_1, and a_2. The key point is that *the stability condition for the homogeneous equation is precisely the condition for convergence of the particular solution. If any characteristic root of the homogeneous equation is equal to unity, a polynomial time trend will appear in the particular solution. The order of the polynomial is the number of unitary characteristic roots.* This result generalizes to higher-order equations.

If you are really clever, you can combine the discussion of the last section with the method of undetermined coefficients. Find the deterministic portion of the particular solution using the techniques discussed in the last section. Then use the method of undetermined coefficients to find the stochastic portion of the particular solution. In (1.67), for example, set $\varepsilon_t = \varepsilon_{t-1} = 0$ and obtain the solution $a_0/(1 - a_1)$. Now use the method of undetermined coefficients to find the particular solution of $y_t = a_1 y_{t-1} + \varepsilon_t + \beta_1 \varepsilon_{t-1}$. Add the deterministic and stochastic components to obtain all components of the particular solution.

A Solved Problem

To illustrate the methodology using a second-order equation, augment (1.28) with the stochastic term ε_t so that

$$y_t = 3 + 0.9 y_{t-1} - 0.2 y_{t-2} + \varepsilon_t \qquad (1.70)$$

You have already verified that the two homogeneous solutions are $A_1(0.5)^t$ and $A_2(0.4)^t$ and that the deterministic portion of the particular solution is $y_t^p = 10$. To find the stochastic portion of the particular solution, form the challenge solution

$$y_t = \sum_{i=0}^{\infty} \alpha_i \varepsilon_{t-i}$$

In contrast to (1.64), the intercept term b_0 is excluded (since we have already found the deterministic portion of the particular solution) and the time trend $b_1 t$ is excluded (since both characteristic roots are less than unity). For this challenge to work, it must satisfy

$$\alpha_0 \varepsilon_t + \alpha_1 \varepsilon_{t-1} + \alpha_2 \varepsilon_{t-2} + \alpha_3 \varepsilon_{t-3} + \ldots = 0.9[\alpha_0 \varepsilon_{t-1} + \alpha_1 \varepsilon_{t-2} + \alpha_2 \varepsilon_{t-3} + \alpha_3 \varepsilon_{t-4} + \ldots]$$
$$- 0.2 [\alpha_0 \varepsilon_{t-2} + \alpha_1 \varepsilon_{t-3} + \alpha_2 \varepsilon_{t-4} + \alpha_3 \varepsilon_{t-5} + \ldots] + \varepsilon_t \qquad (1.71)$$

Since (1.71) must hold for all possible realizations of $\varepsilon_t, \varepsilon_{t-1}, \varepsilon_{t-2}, \ldots$, each of the following conditions must hold:

$$\alpha_0 = 1$$
$$\alpha_1 = 0.9 \alpha_0$$

so that $\alpha_1 = 0.9$, and for all $i \geq 2$,

$$\alpha_i = 0.9 \alpha_{i-1} - 0.2 \alpha_{i-2} \qquad (1.72)$$

Now, it is possible to solve (1.72) iteratively so that $\alpha_2 = 0.9\alpha_1 - 0.2\alpha_0 = 0.61$, $\alpha_3 = 0.9(0.61) - 0.2(0.9) = 0.369$, and so forth. A more elegant solution method is to view (1.72) as a second-order difference equation in the $\{\alpha_i\}$ sequence with initial conditions $\alpha_0 = 1$ and $\alpha_1 = 0.9$. The solution to (1.72) is

$$\alpha_i = 5(0.5)^i - 4(0.4)^i \tag{1.73}$$

To obtain (1.73), note that the solution to (1.72) is: $\alpha_i = A_3(0.5)^i + A_4(0.4)^i$ where A_3 and A_4 are arbitrary constants. Imposing the conditions $\alpha_0 = 1$ and $\alpha_1 = 0.9$ yields (1.73). If we use (1.73), it follows that: $\alpha_0 = 5(0.5)^0 - 4(0.4)^0 = 1$; $\alpha_1 = 5(0.5)^1 - 4(0.4)^1 = 0.9$; $\alpha_2 = 5(0.5)^2 - 4(0.4)^2 = 0.61$; and so on.

The general solution to (1.70) is the sum of the two homogeneous solutions and the deterministic and stochastic portions of the particular solution:

$$y_t = 10 + A_1(0.5)^t + A_2(0.4)^t + \sum_{i=0}^{\infty} \alpha_i \varepsilon_{t-i} \tag{1.74}$$

where the α_i are given by (1.73).

Given initial conditions for y_0 and y_1, it follows that A_1 and A_2 must satisfy

$$y_0 = 10 + A_1 + A_2 + \sum_{i=0}^{\infty} \alpha_i \varepsilon_{-i} \tag{1.75}$$

$$y_1 = 10 + A_1(0.5) + A_2(0.4) + \sum_{i=0}^{\infty} \alpha_i \varepsilon_{1-i} \tag{1.76}$$

Although the algebra gets messy, (1.75) and (1.76) can be substituted into (1.74) to eliminate the arbitrary constants:

$$y_t = 10 + (0.4)^t [5(y_0 - 10) - 10(y_1 - 10)]$$
$$+ (0.5)^t [10(y_1 - 10) - 4(y_0 - 10)] + \sum_{i=0}^{t-2} \alpha_i \varepsilon_{t-i}$$

9. LAG OPERATORS

If it is not important to know the actual values of the coefficients appearing in the particular solution, it is often more convenient to use lag operators rather than the method of undetermined coefficients. The **lag operator** L is defined to be a *linear* operator such that for any value y_t

$$L^i y_t \equiv y_{t-i} \tag{1.77}$$

Thus, L^i preceding y_t simply means to lag y_t by i periods. It is useful to remember the following properties of lag operators:

1. The lag of a constant is a constant: $Lc = c$.
2. The distributive law holds for lag operators. We can set
   $(L^i + L^j)y_t = L^i y_t + L^j y_t = y_{t-i} + y_{t-j}$.

3. The associative law of multiplication holds for lag operators. We can set $L^i L^j y_t = L^i(L^j y_t) = L^i y_{t-j} = y_{t-i-j}$. Similarly, we can set $L^i L^j y_t = L^{i+j} y_t = y_{t-i-j}$. Note that $L^0 y_t = y_t$.

4. L raised to a negative power is actually a *lead* operator: $L^{-i} y_t = y_{t+i}$. To explain, define $j = -i$ and form $L^j y_t = y_{t-j} = y_{t+i}$.

5. For $|a| < 1$, the infinite sum $(1 + aL + a^2 L^2 + a^3 L^3 + ...) y_t = y_t/(1 - aL)$. This property of lag operators may not seem intuitive, but it follows directly from properties 2 and 3 above.

    Proof: Multiply each side by $(1 - aL)$ to form $(1 - aL)(1 + aL + a^2 L^3 + ...) y_t = y_t$. Multiply the two expressions to obtain $(1 - aL + aL - a^2 L^2 + a^2 L^2 - a^3 L^3 + ...) y_t = y_t$. Given that $|a| < 1$, the expression $a^n L^n y_t$ converges to zero as $n \to \infty$. Thus, the two sides of the equation are equal.

6. For $|a| > 1$, the infinite sum $[1 + (aL)^{-1} + (aL)^{-2} + (aL)^{-3} + ...] y_t = -aLy_t/(1 - aL)$. Thus,

$$y_t /(1 - aL) = -(aL)^{-1} \sum_{i=0}^{\infty} (aL)^{-i} y_t$$

    Proof: Multiply by $(1 - aL)$ to form $(1 - aL)[1 + (aL)^{-1} + (aL)^{-2} + (aL)^{-3} + ...] y_t = -aLy_t$. Perform the indicated multiplication to obtain $[1 - aL + (aL)^{-1} - 1 + (aL)^{-2} - (aL)^{-1} + (aL)^{-3} - (aL)^{-2} ...] y_t = -aLy_t$. Given that $|a| > 1$, the expression $a^{-n} L^{-n} y_t$ converges to zero as $n \to \infty$. Thus, the two sides of the equation are equal.

Lag operators provide a concise notation for writing difference equations. Using lag operators, we can write the *p*th-order equation $y_t = a_0 + a_1 y_{t-1} + ... + a_p y_{t-p} + \varepsilon_t$ as

$$(1 - a_1 L - a_2 L^2 - ... - a_p L^p) y_t = a_0 + \varepsilon_t$$

or, more compactly, as

$$A(L) y_t = a_0 + \varepsilon_t$$

where $A(L)$ is the polynomial $(1 - a_1 L - a_2 L^2 - ... - a_p L^p)$

Since $A(L)$ can be viewed as a polynomial in the lag operator, the notation $A(1)$ is used to denote the sum of the coefficients

$$A(1) = 1 - a_1 - a_2 ... - a_p$$

As a second example, lag operators can be used to express the equation $y_t = a_0 + a_1 y_{t-1} + ... + a_p y_{t-p} + \varepsilon_t + \beta_1 \varepsilon_{t-1} + ... + \beta_q \varepsilon_{t-q}$ as

$$A(L) y_t = a_0 + B(L) \varepsilon_t$$

where $A(L)$ and $B(L)$ are polynomials of orders p and q, respectively.

It is straightforward to use lag operators to solve linear difference equations. Again consider the first-order equation $y_t = a_0 + a_1 y_{t-1} + \varepsilon_t$ where $|a_1| < 1$. Use the definition of L to form

$$y_t = a_0 + a_1 L y_t + \varepsilon_t \qquad (1.78)$$

Solving for y_t, we obtain

$$y_t = \frac{a_0 + \varepsilon_t}{1 - a_1 L} \tag{1.79}$$

From property 1, we know that $La_0 = a_0$, so that $a_0/(1 - a_1 L) = a_0 + a_1 a_0 + a_1^2 a_0 + \ldots = a_0/(1 - a_1)$. From property 5, we know that $\varepsilon_t/(1 - a_1 L) = \varepsilon_t + a_1 \varepsilon_{t-1} + a_1^2 \varepsilon_{t-2} + \ldots$. Combining these two parts of the solution, we obtain the particular solution given by (1.21).

For practice, we can use lag operators to solve (1.67): $y_t = a_0 + a_1 y_{t-1} + \varepsilon_t + \beta_1 \varepsilon_{t-1}$, where $|a_1| < 1$. Use property 2 to form $(1 - a_1 L) y_t = a_0 + (1 + \beta_1 L) \varepsilon_t$. Solving for y_t yields

$$y_t = [a_0 + (1 + \beta_1 L) \varepsilon_t]/(1 - a_1 L)$$

so that

$$y_t = [a_0 / (1 - a_1)] + [\varepsilon_t / (1 - a_1 L)] + [\beta_1 \varepsilon_{t-1} / (1 - a_1 L)] \tag{1.80}$$

Expanding the last two terms of (1.80) yields the same solution found using the method of undetermined coefficients.

Now suppose $y_t = a_0 + a_1 y_{t-1} + \varepsilon_t$ but $|a_1| > 1$. The application of property 5 to (1.79) is inappropriate because it implies that y_t is infinite. Instead, expand (1.79) using property 6:

$$y_t = \frac{a_0}{1 - a_1} - \left(a_1 L \right)^{-1} \sum_{i=0}^{\infty} (a_1 L)^{-i} \varepsilon_t$$

$$= \frac{a_0}{1 - a_1} - \frac{1}{a_1} \sum_{i=0}^{\infty} (a_1 L)^{-i} \varepsilon_{t+1} \tag{1.81}$$

$$= \frac{a_0}{1 - a_1} - \left(\frac{1}{a_1} \right) \sum_{i=0}^{\infty} a_1^{-i} \varepsilon_{t+1+i} \tag{1.82}$$

Lag Operators in Higher-Order Systems

We can also use lag operators to transform the nth-order equation $y_t = a_0 + a_1 y_{t-1} + a_2 y_{t-2} + \ldots + a_n y_{t-n} + \varepsilon_t$ into

$$(1 - a_1 L - a_2 L^2 - \ldots - a_n L^n) y_t = a_0 + \varepsilon_t$$

or

$$y_t = (a_0 + \varepsilon_t)/(1 - a_1 L - a_2 L^2 - \ldots a_n L^n)$$

From our previous analysis (also see Appendix 1.2), we know that the stability condition is such that the characteristic roots of the equation $\alpha^n - a_1 \alpha^{n-1} - \ldots - a_n = 0$ all lie *within* the unit circle. Notice that the values of α solving the characteristic equation are the reciprocals of the values of L that solve the equation $1 - a_1 L \ldots - a_n L^n = 0$. In fact, the expression $1 - a_1 L \ldots - a_n L^n$ is often called the *inverse characteristic equation*. Thus, in the literature, it is often stated that the stability condition is for the characteristic roots of $(1 - a_1 L \ldots - a_n L^n)$ to lie *outside* of the unit circle.

In principle, one could use lag operators to actually obtain the coefficients of the particular solution. To illustrate using the second-order case, consider $y_t = (a_0 + \varepsilon_t)/(1 - a_1 L - a_2 L^2)$. If we knew the factors of the quadratic equation were such that $(1 - a_1 L - a_2 L^2) = (1 - b_1 L)(1 - b_2 L)$, we could write

$$y_t = (a_0 + \varepsilon_t)/[(1 - b_1 L)(1 - b_2 L)]$$

If both b_1 and b_2 are less than unity in absolute value, we can apply property 5 to obtain

$$y_t = \frac{[a_0/(1 - b_1)] + \displaystyle\sum_{i=0}^{\infty} b_1^i \, \varepsilon_{t-i}}{1 - b_2 \, L}$$

Reapply the rule to $a_0/(1 - b_1)$ and to each of the elements in the summation $\Sigma b_1^i \varepsilon_{t-i}$ to obtain the particular solution. If you want to know the actual coefficients of the process, it is preferable to use the method of undetermined coefficients. The beauty of lag operators is that they can be used to denote such particular solutions succinctly. The general model

$$A(L)y_t = a_0 + B(L)\varepsilon_t$$

has the particular solution

$$y_t = a_0/A(L) + B(L)\varepsilon_t/A(L)$$

As suggested by (1.82), there is a **forward-looking** solution to any linear difference equation. This text will not make much use of the forward-looking solution since future realizations of stochastic variables are not directly observable. Some of the details of forward-looking solutions can be found at www.cba.ua.edu/~enders.

10. SUMMARY

Time-series econometrics is concerned with the estimation of difference equations containing stochastic components. Originally, time-series models were used for forecasting. Uncovering the dynamic path of a series improves forecasts because the predictable components of the series can be extrapolated into the future. The growing interest in economic dynamics has given a new emphasis to time-series econometrics. Stochastic difference equations arise quite naturally from dynamic economic models. Appropriately estimated equations can be used for the interpretation of economic data and for hypothesis testing.

This introductory chapter focused on methods of "solving" stochastic difference equations. Although iteration can be useful, it is impractical in many circumstances. The solution to a linear difference equation can be divided into two parts: a *particular* solution and a *homogeneous* solution. One complicating factor is that the homogeneous solution is not unique. The *general* solution is a linear combination of the particular solution and all homogeneous solutions. Imposing n initial conditions on the general solution of an nth-order equation yields a unique solution.

The homogeneous portion of a difference equation is a measure of the *disequilibrium* in the initial period(s). The homogeneous equation is especially important in that it yields the characteristic roots; an nth-order equation has n such characteristic roots. If all of the characteristic roots lie within the unit circle, the series will be convergent. As you will see in Chapter 2, there is a direct relationship between the stability conditions and the issue of whether an economic variable is stationary or nonstationary.

The method of undetermined coefficients and the use of lag operators are powerful tools for obtaining the particular solution. The particular solution will be a linear function of the current and past values of the forcing process. In addition, this solution may contain an intercept term and a polynomial function of time. Unit roots and characteristic roots outside of the unit circle require the imposition of an initial condition for the particular solution to be meaningful. Some economic models allow for forward-looking solutions; in such circumstances, anticipated future events have consequences for the present period.

The tools developed in this chapter are aimed at paving the way for the study of time-series econometrics. It is a good idea to work all of the exercises presented below. Characteristic roots, the method of undetermined coefficients, and lag operators will be encountered throughout the remainder of the text.

QUESTIONS AND EXERCISES

1. Consider the difference equation $y_t = a_0 + a_1 y_{t-1}$ with the initial condition y_0. Jill solved the difference equation by iterating backward

$$
\begin{aligned}
y_t &= a_0 + a_1 y_{t-1} \\
&= a_0 + a_1(a_0 + a_1 y_{t-2}) \\
&= a_0 + a_0 a_1 + a_0 a_1^2 + \ldots + a_0 a_1^{t-1} + a_1^t y_0
\end{aligned}
$$

Bill added the homogeneous and particular solutions to obtain $y_t = a_0/(1 - a_1) + a_1^t[y_0 - a_0/(1 - a_1)]$.

   a. Show that the two solutions are identical for $|a_1| < 1$.

   b. Show that for $a_1 = 1$, Jill's solution is equivalent to $y_t = a_0 t + y_0$. How would you use Bill's method to arrive at this same conclusion in the case that $a_1 = 1$?

2. The cobweb model in Section 5 assumed *static* price expectations. Consider an alternative formulation called *adaptive expectations*. Let the expected price in t (denoted by p_t^*) be a weighted average of the price in $t-1$ and the price expectation of the previous period. Formally,

$$
p_t^* = \alpha p_{t-1} + (1 - \alpha) p_{t-1}^* \qquad\qquad 0 < \alpha \le 1
$$

   Clearly, when $\alpha = 1$, the static and adaptive expectations schemes are equivalent. An interesting feature of this model is that it can be viewed as a difference equation expressing the expected price as a function of its own lagged value and the forcing variable p_{t-1}.

   a. Find the homogeneous solution for p_t^*.

   b. Use lag operators to find the particular solution. Check your answer by substituting your answer into the original difference equation.

3. Suppose that the money supply process has the form $m_t = m + \rho m_{t-1} + \varepsilon_t$, where m is a constant and $0 < \rho < 1$.

   a. Show that it is possible to express m_{t+n} in terms of the known value m_t and the sequence $\{\varepsilon_{t+1}, \varepsilon_{t+2}, \ldots, \varepsilon_{t+n}\}$.

   b. Suppose that all values of ε_{t+i} for $i > 0$ have a mean value of zero. Explain how you could use your result in part a to forecast the money supply n periods into the future.

4. Find the particular solutions for each of the following:

   a. $y_t = a_1 y_{t-1} + \varepsilon_t + \beta_1 \varepsilon_{t-1}$

b. $y_t = a_1 y_{t-1} + \varepsilon_{1t} + \beta \varepsilon_{2t}$ (Hint: The form of the solution is
$y_t = \Sigma c_i \varepsilon_{1t-i} + \Sigma d_i \varepsilon_{2t-i}$)

5. The *unit root problem* in time-series econometrics is concerned with characteristic roots that are equal to unity. In order to preview the issue:

a. Find the homogeneous solution to each of the following (*Hint*: Each has at least one unit root):

    i. $y_t = 1.5 y_{t-1} - 0.5 y_{t-2} + \varepsilon_t$ **ii.** $y_t = y_{t-2} + \varepsilon_t$

    iii. $y_t = 2 y_{t-1} - y_{t-2} + \varepsilon_t$ **iv.** $y_t = y_{t-1} + 0.25 y_{t-2} - 0.25 y_{t-3} + \varepsilon_t$

b. Show that each of the backward-looking solutions is not convergent.

c. Show that Equation *i* can be written entirely in first differences; that is, $\Delta y_t = 0.5\Delta y_{t-1} + \varepsilon_t$. Find the particular solution for Δy_t. (*Hint*: Find the particular solution for the $\{\Delta y_t\}$ sequence in terms of the $\{\varepsilon_t\}$ sequence.)

d. Similarly transform the other equations into their first-difference form. Find the backward-looking particular solution, if it exists, for the transformed equations.

e. Given an initial condition y_0, find the solution for: $y_t = a_0 - y_{t-1} + \varepsilon_t$.

6. A researcher estimated the following relationship for the inflation rate (π_t):

$$\pi_t = -0.05 + 0.7\pi_{t-1} + 0.6\pi_{t-2} + \varepsilon_t$$

    a. Suppose that in periods 0 and 1, the inflation rate was 10 percent and 11 percent, respectively. Find the homogeneous, particular, and general solutions for the inflation rate.

    b. Discuss the shape of the impulse response function. Given that the United States is not headed for runaway inflation, why do you believe that the researcher's equation is poorly estimated?

7. Consider the stochastic process $y_t = a_0 + a_2 y_{t-2} + \varepsilon_t$.

    a. Find the homogeneous solution and determine the stability condition.

    b. Find the particular solution using the method of undetermined coefficients.

8. Consider the Cagan (1956) demand for money function in which $m_t - p_t = \alpha - \beta(p_{t+1} - p_t)$.

    a. Show that the backward-looking particular solution for p_t is divergent.

    b. Obtain the forward-looking particular solution for p_t in terms of the $\{m_t\}$ sequence. In forming the general solution, why is it necessary to assume that the money market is in long-run equilibrium?

    c. Find the impact multiplier. How does an increase in m_{t+2} affect p_t? Provide an intuitive explanation of the shape of the entire impulse response function.

9. For each of the following, verify that the posited solution satisfies the difference equation. The symbols c, c_0, and a_0 denote constants.

Equation	Solution
(a) $y_t - y_{t-1} = 0$	$y_t = c$
(b) $y_t - y_{t-1} = a_0$	$y_t = c + a_0 t$
(c) $y_t - y_{t-2} = 0$	$y_t = c + c_0(-1)^t$
(d) $y_t - y_{t-2} = \varepsilon_t$	$y_t = c + c_0(-1)^t + \varepsilon_t + \varepsilon_{t-2} + \varepsilon_{t-4} + \dots$

10. Part 1: For each of the following, determine whether $\{y_t\}$ represents a stable process. Determine whether the characteristic roots are real or imaginary and whether the real parts are positive or negative.

a. $y_t - 1.2y_{t-1} + 0.2y_{t-2}$ **b.** $y_t - 1.2y_{t-1} + 0.4y_{t-2}$

c. $y_t - 1.2y_{t-1} - 1.2y_{t-2}$ **d.** $y_t + 1.2y_{t-1}$

e. $y_t - 0.7y_{t-1} - 0.25y_{t-2} + 0.175y_{t-3} = 0$

[Hint: $(x - 0.5)(x + 0.5)(x - 0.7) = x^3 - 0.7x^2 - 0.25x + 0.175$.]

Part 2: Write each of the above equations using lag operators. Determine the characteristic roots of the inverse characteristic equation.

11. Consider the stochastic difference equation

$$y_t = 0.8y_{t-1} + \varepsilon_t - 0.5\varepsilon_{t-1}$$

     a. Suppose that the initial conditions are such that $y_0 = 0$ and $\varepsilon_0 = \varepsilon_{-1} = 0$. Now suppose that $\varepsilon_1 = 1$. Determine the values y_1 through y_5 by forward iteration.

     b. Find the homogeneous and particular solutions.

     c. Impose the initial conditions in order to obtain the general solution.

     d. Trace out the time path of an ε_t shock on the entire time path of the $\{y_t\}$ sequence.

12. Use equation (1.5) to determine the restrictions on α and β necessary to ensure that the $\{y_t\}$ process is stable.

ENDNOTES

1. Another possibility is to obtain the forward-looking solution; such solutions are discussed in Section 10.
2. Alternatively, you can substitute (1.26) into (1.17). Note that when ε_t is a pure random disturbance, $y_t = a_0 + y_{t-1} + \varepsilon_t$ is called a random walk plus drift model.
3. Any linear equation in the variables x_1 through x_n is homogeneous if it has the form $a_1x_1 + a_2x_2 + \ldots + a_nx_n = 0$. To obtain the homogeneous portion of (1.10), simply set the intercept term a_0 and the forcing process x_t equal to zero. Hence, the homogeneous equation for (1.10) is $y_t = a_1 y_{t-1} + a_2 y_{t-2} + \ldots + a_n y_{t-n}$.
4. If $b > a$, the demand and supply curves do not intersect in the positive quadrant. The assumption $a > b$ guarantees that the equilibrium price is positive.
5. For example, if the forcing process is $x_t = \varepsilon_t + \beta_1\varepsilon_{t-1} + \beta_2\varepsilon_{t-2} + \ldots$, the impact multiplier is the partial derivative of y_t with respect to ε_t.

APPENDIX 1.1: Imaginary Roots and de Moivre's Theorem

Consider a second-order difference equation $y_t = a_1 y_{t-1} + a_2 y_{t-2}$ such that the discriminant d is negative [i.e., $d = a_1^2 + 4a_2 < 0$]. From Section 6, we know that the full homogeneous solution can be written in the form

$$y_t^h = A_1\alpha_1^t + A_2\alpha_2^t \qquad (A1.1)$$

where the two imaginary characteristic roots are

$$\alpha_1 = (a_1 + i\sqrt{-d})/2 \text{ and } \alpha_2 = (a_1 - i\sqrt{-d})/2 \qquad (A1.2)$$

The purpose of this appendix is to explain how to rewrite and interpret (A1.1) in terms of standard trigonometric functions. You might first want to refresh your memory concerning two useful trig identities. For any two angles θ_1 and θ_2,

$$\sin(\theta_1 + \theta_2) = \sin(\theta_1)\cos(\theta_2) + \cos(\theta_1)\sin(\theta_2)$$
$$\cos(\theta_1 + \theta_2) = \cos(\theta_1)\cos(\theta_2) - \sin(\theta_1)\sin(\theta_2) \qquad (A1.3)$$

If $\theta_1 = \theta_2$, we can drop subscripts and form

$$\sin(2\theta) = 2\sin(\theta)\cos(\theta)$$
$$\cos(2\theta) = \cos(\theta)\cos(\theta) - \sin(\theta)\sin(\theta) \qquad (A1.4)$$

The first task is to demonstrate how to express imaginary numbers in the complex plane. Consider Figure A1.1 in which the horizontal axis measures real numbers and the vertical axis measures imaginary numbers. The complex number $a + bi$ can be represented by the point a units from the origin along the horizontal axis and b units from the origin along the vertical axis. It is convenient to represent the distance from the origin by the length of the vector denoted by r. Consider angle θ in triangle $0ab$ and note that $\cos(\theta) = a/r$ and $\sin(\theta) = b/r$. Hence, the lengths a and b can be measured by

$$a = r\cos(\theta) \quad \text{and} \quad b = r\sin(\theta)$$

In terms of (A1.2), we can define $a = a_1/2$ and $b = \sqrt{d}/2$. Thus, the characteristic roots α_1 and α_2 can be written as:

$$\alpha_1 = a + bi = r[\cos(\theta) + i\sin(\theta)]$$
$$\alpha_2 = a - bi = r[\cos(\theta) - i\sin(\theta)] \qquad (A1.5)$$

The next step is to consider the expressions $\alpha_1{}^t$ and $\alpha_2{}^t$. Begin with the expression $\alpha_1{}^2$ and recall that $i^2 = -1$:

$$\alpha_1{}^2 = \{r[\cos(\theta) + i\sin(\theta)]\}\{r[\cos(\theta) + i\sin(\theta)]\}$$
$$= r^2[\cos(\theta)\cos(\theta) - \sin(\theta)\sin(\theta) + 2i\sin(\theta)\cos(\theta)]$$

From (A1.4),

$$\alpha_1{}^2 = r^2[\cos(2\theta) + i\sin(2\theta)]$$

If we continue in this fashion, it is straightforward to demonstrate that

$$\alpha_1{}^t = r^t[\cos(t\theta) + i\sin(t\theta)] \text{ and } \alpha_2{}^t = r^t[\cos(t\theta) - i\sin(t\theta)]$$

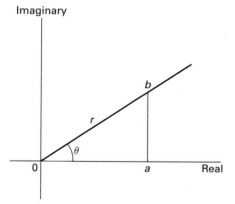

FIGURE A1.1 A Graphical Representation of Complex Numbers

Since y_t^h is a real number and α_1 and α_2 are complex, it follows that A_1 and A_2 must be complex. Although A_1 and A_2 are arbitrary complex numbers, they must have the form

$$A_1 = B_1[\cos(B_2) + i \sin(B_2)] \text{ and } A_2 = B_1[\cos(B_2) - i \sin(B_2)] \qquad (A1.7)$$

where B_1 and B_2 are arbitrary real numbers measured in radians.

In order to calculate $A_1(\alpha_1^t)$, use (A1.6) and (A1.7) to form

$$A_1\alpha_1^t = B_1[\cos(B_2) + i \sin(B_2)]r^t[\cos(t\theta) + i \sin(t\theta)]$$
$$= B_1r^t[\cos(B_2)\cos(t\theta) - \sin(B_2)\sin(t\theta) + i \cos(t\theta)\sin(B_2) + i \sin(t\theta)\cos(B_2)]$$

Using (A1.3), we obtain

$$A_1\alpha_1^t = B_1r^t[\cos(t\theta + B_2) + i \sin(t\theta + B_2)] \qquad (A1.8)$$

You should use the same technique to convince yourself that

$$A_2\alpha_2^t = B_1r^t[\cos(t\theta + B_2) - i \sin(t\theta + B_2)] \qquad (A1.9)$$

Since the homogeneous solution y_t^h is the sum of (A1.8) and (A1.9),

$$y_t^h = B_1r^t[\cos(t\theta + B_2) + i \sin(t\theta + B_2)] + B_1r^t[\cos(t\theta + B_2) - i \sin(t\theta + B_2)]$$
$$= 2B_1r^t\cos(t\theta + B_2) \qquad (A1.10)$$

Since B_1 is arbitrary, the homogeneous solution can be written in terms of the arbitrary constants B_2 and B_3

$$y_t^h = B_3r^t\cos(t\theta + B_2) \qquad (A1.11)$$

Now imagine a circle with a radius of unity superimposed on Figure A1.1. The stability condition is for the distance $r = 0b$ to be less than unity. Hence, in the literature it is said that the stability condition is for the characteristic root(s) to lie within this unit circle.

APPENDIX 1.2: Characteristic Roots in Higher-Order Equations

The characteristic equation to an nth-order difference equation is

$$\alpha^n - a_1\alpha^{n-1} - a_2\alpha^{n-2} \dots - a_n = 0 \qquad (A1.12)$$

As stated in Section 6, the n values of α which solve this characteristic equation are called the **characteristic roots**. Denote the n solutions by $\alpha_1, \alpha_2, \dots, \alpha_n$. Given the results in Section 4, the linear combination $A_1\alpha_1^t + A_2\alpha_2^t + \dots + A_n\alpha_n^t$ is also a solution to (A1.12)

A priori, the characteristic roots can take on any values. There is no restriction that they be real versus complex nor any restriction concerning their sign or magnitude. Consider the possibilities:

1. **All the α_i are real and distinct.** There are several important subcases. First suppose that each value of α_i is less than unity in absolute value. In this case, the homogeneous solution (A1.12) converges since the limit of each α_i^t equals zero as t approaches infinity. For a negative value of α_i,

the expression α_i^t is positive for even values of t and negative for odd values of t. Thus, if any of the α_i are negative (but less than one in absolute value), the solution will tend to exhibit some oscillation. If any of the α_i are greater than unity in absolute value, the solution will diverge.

2. **All of the α_i are real but $m \leq n$ of the roots are repeated.** Let the solution be such that $\alpha_1 = \alpha_2 = \ldots = \alpha_m$. Call the single distinct value of this root $\bar{\alpha}$ and let the other n-m roots be denoted by α_{m+1} through α_n. In the case of a second-order equation with a repeated root, you saw that one solution was $A_1 \bar{\alpha}^t$ and the other was $A_2 t \bar{\alpha}^t$. With m repeated roots, it is easily verified that $t \bar{\alpha}^t, t^2 \bar{\alpha}^t, \ldots, t^{m-1} \bar{\alpha}^t$ are also solutions to the homogeneous equation. With m repeated roots, the linear combination of all these solutions is

$$A_1 \bar{\alpha}^t + A_2 t \bar{\alpha}^t + A_3 t^2 \bar{\alpha}^t + \ldots + A_m t^{m-1} \bar{\alpha}^t + A_{m+1} \alpha_{m+1}^t + \ldots + A_n \alpha_n^t$$

3. **Some of the roots are complex.** Complex roots (which necessarily come in conjugate pairs) have the form $\alpha_i \pm i\theta$, where α_i and θ are real numbers and i is defined to be $\sqrt{-1}$. For any such pair, a solution to the homogeneous equation is: $A_1(\alpha_1 + i\theta)^t + A_2(\alpha_1 - i\theta)^t$ where A_1 and A_2 are arbitrary constants. Transforming to polar coordinates, the associated two solutions can be written in the form: $\beta_1 r^t \cos(\theta t + \beta_2)$ with arbitrary constants β_1 and β_2. Here stability hinges on the magnitude of r^t; if $|r| < 1$, the system converges. However, even if there is convergence, convergence is not direct because the sine and cosine functions impart oscillatory behavior to the time path of y_t. For example, if there are three roots, two of which are complex, the homogeneous solution has the form

$$\beta_1 r^t \cos(\theta t + \beta_2) + A_3(\alpha_3)^t$$

Stability of Higher-Order Systems: In practice, it is difficult to find the actual values of the characteristic roots. Unless the characteristic equation is easily factored, it is necessary to use numerical methods to obtain the characteristic roots. Fortunately software packages such as Mathematica, Maple, or Mathcad can easily obtain the characteristic roots of any specific difference equation. At one time it was popular to use the **Schur Theorem** to determine whether all of the roots lie within the unit circle. Rather than calculate all of these determinants, it is often possible to use the simple rules discussed in Section 6. Those of you familiar with matrix algebra may wish to consult the first edition of this text or Samuelson (1941) for the appropriate conditions.

CHAPTER 2

STATIONARY TIME-SERIES MODELS

The theory of linear difference equations can be extended to allow the forcing process $\{x_t\}$ to be stochastic. This class of linear stochastic difference equations underlies much of theory of time-series econometrics. Especially important is the Box–Jenkins (1976) methodology for estimating time-series models of the form

$$y_t = a_0 + a_1 y_{t-1} + \ldots + a_p y_{t-p} + \varepsilon_t + \beta_1 \varepsilon_{t-1} + \ldots + \beta_q \varepsilon_{t-q}$$

Such models are called autoregressive integrated moving-average (ARIMA) time-series models. This chapter has three aims:

1. Present the theory of stochastic linear difference equations and consider the time-series properties of stationary ARIMA models; a stationary ARIMA model is called an autoregressive moving-average (ARMA) model. It is shown that the stability conditions of the previous chapter are necessary conditions for stationarity.

2. Develop the tools used in estimating ARMA models. Especially useful are the autocorrelation and partial autocorrelation functions. It is shown how the Box–Jenkins methodology relies on these tools to estimate an ARMA model from sample data.

3. Consider various test statistics to check for model adequacy. Several examples of estimated ARMA models are analyzed in detail. It is shown how a properly estimated model can be used for forecasting.

1. STOCHASTIC DIFFERENCE EQUATION MODELS

In this chapter, we continue to work with **discrete,** rather than continuous, time-series models. Recall from the discussion in Chapter 1 that we can evaluate the function $y = f(t)$ at t_0 and $t_0 + h$ to form

$$\Delta y = f(t_0 + h) - f(t_0)$$

As a practical matter, most economic time-series data are collected for discrete time periods. Thus, we consider only the equidistant intervals t_0, $t_0 + h$, $t_0 + 2h$, $t_0 + 3h$, ..., and conveniently set $h = 1$. Be careful to recognize, however, that a discrete time-series implies that t, but not necessarily y_t, is discrete. For example, although Scotland's annual rainfall is a continuous variable, the sequence of such annual rainfall totals for years 1 through t is a discrete time series. In many economic applications, t refers to "time" so that h represents the change in time. However, t need not refer to the type of time interval as measured by a clock or calendar. Instead of allowing our measurement units to be minutes, days, quarters, or years, t can refer to an ordered event number. We could let y_t denote the outcome of spin t on a roulette wheel; y_t can then take on any of the 38 values 00, 0, 1, ..., 36.

A discrete variable y is said to be a **random** variable (i.e., stochastic) if for any real number r there exists a probability $p(y \leq r)$ that y will take on a value less than or equal to r. This definition is fairly general; in common usage, it is typically implied that there is at least one value of r for which $0 < p(y = r) < 1$. If there is some r for which $p(y = r) = 1$, y is deterministic rather than random.

It is useful to consider the elements of an observed time series $\{y_0, y_1, y_2, ..., y_t\}$ as being realizations (i.e., outcomes) of a stochastic process. As in Chapter 1, we continue to let the notation y_t to refer to an element of the entire sequence $\{y_t\}$. In our roulette example, y_t denotes the outcome of spin t on a roulette wheel. If we observe spins 1 through T, we can form the sequence $y_1, y_2, ..., y_T$ or, more compactly, $\{y_t\}$. In the same way, the term y_t could be used to denote gross domestic product (GDP) in time period t. Since we cannot forecast GDP perfectly, y_t is a random variable. Once we learn the value of GDP in period t, y_t becomes one of the realized values from a stochastic process. (Of course, measurement error may prevent us from ever knowing the "true" value of GDP.)

For discrete variables, the probability distribution of y_t is given by a formula (or table) that specifies each possible realized value of y_t and the probability associated with that realization. If the realizations are linked across time, there exists the joint probability distribution $p(y_1 = r_1, y_2 = r_2, ..., y_T = r_T)$ where r_i is the realized value of y in period i. Having observed the first t realizations, we can form the expected value of $y_{t+1}, y_{t+2}, ...$, conditioned on the observed values of y_1 through y_t. This conditional mean, or expected value, of y_{t+i} is denoted by $E_t[y_{t+i} \mid y_t, y_{t-1}, ..., y_1]$ or $E_t y_{t+i}$.

Of course, if y_t refers to the outcome of spinning a fair roulette wheel, the probability distribution is easily characterized. In contrast, we may never be able to completely describe the probability distribution for GDP. Nevertheless, the task of economic theorists is to develop models that capture the essence of the true datagenerating process. Stochastic difference equations are one convenient way of modeling dynamic economic processes. To take a simple example, suppose that the Federal Reserve's money supply target grows 3 percent each year. Hence,

$$m_t^* = 1.03 m_{t-1}^* \qquad (2.1)$$

so that, given the initial condition m_0^*, the particular solution is

$$m_t^* = (1.03)^t m_0^*$$

where: m_t^* = the logarithm of the money supply target in year t

$\qquad m_0^*$ = the initial condition for the target money supply in period zero

Of course, the actual money supply (m_t) and the target need not be equal. Suppose that at the end of period $t - 1$, there exists m_{t-1} outstanding dollars that are carried forward into period t. Hence, at the beginning of t there are m_{t-1} dollars so that the gap between the target and the actual money supply is $m_t^* - m_{t-1}$. Suppose that the Fed cannot perfectly control the money supply but attempts to change the money supply by ρ percent ($\rho < 100\%$) of any gap between the desired and actual money supply. We can model this behavior as

$$\Delta m_t = \rho[m_t^* - m_{t-1}] + \varepsilon_t$$

or using (2.1), we obtain

$$m_t = \rho(1.03)^t m_0^* + (1-\rho)m_{t-1} + \varepsilon_t \tag{2.2}$$

where ε_t is the uncontrollable portion of the money supply.

We assume the mean of ε_t is zero in all time periods.

Although the economic theory is overly simple, the model does illustrate the key points discussed above. Note the following:

1. Although the money supply is a continuous variable, (2.2) is a discrete difference equation. Since the forcing process $\{\varepsilon_t\}$ is stochastic, the money supply is stochastic; we can call (2.2) a linear stochastic difference equation.

2. If we knew the distribution of $\{\varepsilon_t\}$, we could calculate the distribution for each element in the $\{m_t\}$ sequence. Since (2.2) shows how the realizations of the $\{m_t\}$ sequence are linked across time, we would be able to calculate the various joint probabilities. Notice that the distribution of the money supply sequence is completely determined by the parameters of the difference equation (2.2) and the distribution of the $\{\varepsilon_t\}$ sequence.

3. Having observed the first t observations in the $\{m_t\}$ sequence, we can make forecasts of $m_{t+1}, m_{t+2}, \ldots$. For example, updating (2.2) by one period and taking the conditional expectation, the forecast of m_{t+1} is: $E_t m_{t+1} = \rho(1.03)^{t+1} m_0^* + (1 - \rho)m_t$.

Before we proceed too far along these lines, let's go back to the basic building block of discrete stochastic time-series models: the **white-noise** process. A sequence $\{\varepsilon_t\}$ is a white-noise process if each value in the sequence has a mean of zero, a constant variance, and is uncorrelated with all other realizations. Formally, if the notation $E(x)$ denotes the theoretical mean value of x, the sequence $\{\varepsilon_t\}$ is a white-noise process if for each time period t

$$E(\varepsilon_t) = E(\varepsilon_{t-1}) = \ldots = 0$$
$$E(\varepsilon_t^2) = E(\varepsilon_{t-1}^2) = \ldots = \sigma^2 \qquad [\text{or } var(\varepsilon_t) = var(\varepsilon_{t-1}) = \ldots = \sigma^2]$$
$$E(\varepsilon_t \, \varepsilon_{t-s}) = E(\varepsilon_{t-j} \, \varepsilon_{t-j-s}) = 0 \text{ for all } j \text{ and } s \qquad [\text{or } cov(\varepsilon_t, \varepsilon_{t-s}) = cov(\varepsilon_{t-j}, \varepsilon_{t-j-s}) = 0]$$

In the remainder of this text, $\{\varepsilon_t\}$ will always refer to a white-noise process and σ^2 will refer to the variance of that process. When it is necessary to refer to two or more white-noise processes, symbols such as $\{\varepsilon_{1t}\}$ and $\{\varepsilon_{2t}\}$ will be used. Now, use a white-noise process to construct the more interesting time-series

$$x_t = \sum_{i=0}^{q} \beta_i \, \varepsilon_{t-i} \tag{2.3}$$

For each period t, x_t is constructed by taking the values $\varepsilon_t, \varepsilon_{t-1}, \ldots, \varepsilon_{t-q}$ and multiplying each by the associated value of β_i. A sequence formed in this manner is called a **moving average** of order q and is denoted by MA(q). To illustrate a typical moving average process, suppose you win \$1 if a fair coin shows a head and lose \$1 if it shows a tail. Denote the outcome on toss t by ε_t (i.e., for toss t, ε_t is either +\$1 or –\$1). If you want to keep track of your hot streaks, you might want to calculate your average winnings on the last four tosses. For each coin toss t, your average payoff on the last four tosses is $1/4\varepsilon_t + 1/4\varepsilon_{t-1} + 1/4\varepsilon_{t-2} + 1/4\varepsilon_{t-3}$. In terms of (2.3), this sequence is a moving average process such that $\beta_i = 0.25$ for $i \leq 3$ and zero otherwise.

Although the $\{\varepsilon_t\}$ sequence is a white-noise process, the constructed $\{x_t\}$ sequence will *not* be a white-noise process if two or more of the β_i differ from zero. To illustrate using an MA(1) process, set $\beta_0 = 1$, $\beta_1 = 0.5$, and all other $\beta_i = 0$. In this circumstance, $E(x_t) = E(\varepsilon_t + 0.5\varepsilon_{t-1}) = 0$ and $\mathrm{var}(x_t) = \mathrm{var}(\varepsilon_t + 0.5\varepsilon_{t-1}) = 1.25\sigma^2$. You can easily convince yourself that $E(x_t) = E(x_{t-s})$ and that $\mathrm{var}(x_t) = \mathrm{var}(x_{t-s})$ for all s. Hence, the first two conditions for $\{x_t\}$ to be a white-noise process are satisfied. However $E(x_t x_{t-1}) = E[(\varepsilon_t + 0.5\varepsilon_{t-1})(\varepsilon_{t-1} + 0.5\varepsilon_{t-2})] = E(\varepsilon_t\varepsilon_{t-1} + 0.5(\varepsilon_{t-1})^2 + 0.5\varepsilon_t\varepsilon_{t-2} + 0.25\varepsilon_{t-1}\varepsilon_{t-2}) = 0.5\sigma^2$. Given that there exists a value of $s \neq 0$ such that $E(x_t x_{t-s}) \neq 0$, the $\{x_t\}$ sequence is not a white-noise process.

Exercise 1 at the end of this chapter asks you to find the mean, variance, and covariance of your hot streaks in coin tossing. For practice, you should work that exercise before continuing.

2. ARMA MODELS

It is possible to combine a moving average process with a linear difference equation to obtain an autoregressive moving average model. Consider the p-th order difference equation:

$$y_t = a_0 + \sum_{i=1}^{p} a_i\, y_{t-i} + x_t \tag{2.4}$$

Now let $\{x_t\}$ be the MA(q) process given by (2.3) so that we can write

$$y_t = a_0 + \sum_{i=1}^{p} a_i y_{t-i} + \sum_{i=0}^{q} \beta_i \varepsilon_{t-i} \tag{2.5}$$

We follow the convention of normalizing units so that β_0 is always equal to unity. If the characteristic roots of (2.5) are all in the unit circle, $\{y_t\}$ is called an **autoregressive moving-average** (ARMA) model for y_t. The autoregressive part of the model is the *difference equation* given by the homogeneous portion of (2.4) and the moving average part is the $\{x_t\}$ sequence. If the homogeneous part of the difference equation contains p lags and the model for x_t contains q lags, the model is called an ARMA(p, q) model. If $q = 0$, the process is called a pure autoregressive process denoted by AR(p) and if $p = 0$, the process is a pure moving-average process denoted by MA(q). In an ARMA model, it is perfectly permissible to allow p and/or q to be infinite. In this chapter we consider only models in which all of the characteristic roots of (2.5) are within the unit circle. However, if one or more characteristic roots of (2.5) is greater than or equal to unity, the $\{y_t\}$ sequence is said to be an **integrated** process and (2.5) is called an autoregressive integrated moving average (ARIMA) model.

Treating (2.5) as a difference equation suggests that we can "solve" for y_t in terms of the $\{\varepsilon_t\}$ sequence. The solution of an ARMA(p, q) model expressing y_t in terms of the $\{\varepsilon_t\}$ sequence is the **moving-average representation** of y_t. The procedure is no different from that discussed in Chapter 1. For the AR(1) model $y_t = a_0 + a_1 y_{t-1} + \varepsilon_t$, the moving-average representation was shown to be

$$y_t = a_0 / (1 - a_1) + \sum_{i=0}^{\infty} a_1^i \varepsilon_{t-i}$$

For the general ARMA(p, q) model, rewrite (2.5) using lag operators so that

$$(1 - \sum_{i=1}^{p} a_i L^i) y_t = a_0 + \sum_{i=0}^{q} \beta_i \varepsilon_{t-i}$$

so that the *particular* solution for y_t is

$$y_t = \left(a_0 + \sum_{i=0}^{q} \beta_i \varepsilon_{t-i} \right) / \left(1 - \sum_{i=1}^{p} a_i L^i \right) \tag{2.6}$$

Fortunately, it will not be necessary for us to expand (2.6) to obtain the specific coefficient for each element in $\{\varepsilon_t\}$. The important point to recognize is that the expansion will yield an MA(∞) process. The issue is whether such an expansion is convergent so that the stochastic difference equation given by (2.6) is stable. As you will see in the next section, the stability condition is that the roots of the polynomial $(1 - \Sigma a_i L^i)$ must lie outside of the unit circle. It is also shown *if y_t is a linear stochastic difference equation, the stability condition is a necessary condition for the time-series $\{y_t\}$ to be stationary.*

3. STATIONARITY

Suppose that the quality control division of a manufacturing firm samples four machines each hour. Every hour, quality control finds the mean of the machines' output levels. The plot of each machine's hourly output is shown in Figure 2.1. If y_{it} represents machine y_i's output at hour t, the means ($\bar{y}_t$) are readily calculated as

$$\bar{y}_t = \sum_{i=1}^{4} y_{it} / 4$$

For hours 5, 10, and 15, these mean values are 4.61, 5.14, and 5.03, respectively.

The sample variance for each hour can similarly be constructed. Unfortunately, applied econometricians do not usually have the luxury of being able to obtain an **ensemble** (i.e., multiple time-series data of the same process over the same time period). Typically, we observe only one set of realizations for any particular series. Fortunately, if $\{y_t\}$ is a **stationary** series, the mean, variance, and autocorrelations can usually be well approximated by sufficiently long **time averages** based on the single set of realizations. Suppose you observed only the output of machine 1 for 20

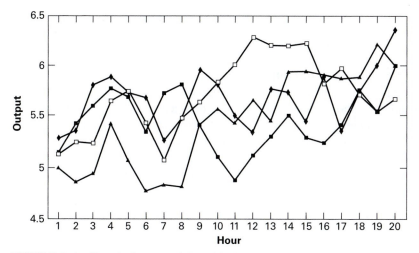

FIGURE 2.1   Hourly Output of Four Machines

periods. If you knew that the output was stationary, you could approximate the mean level of output by

$$\bar{y}_t \cong \sum_{t=1}^{20} y_{1t} / 20$$

In using this approximation, you would be assuming that the mean was the same for each period. Formally, a stochastic process having a finite mean and variance is **covariance stationary** if for all t and $t - s$,

$$E(y_t) = E(y_{t-s}) = \mu \tag{2.7}$$

$$E[(y_t - \mu)^2] = E[(y_{t-s} - \mu)^2] = \sigma_y^2 \quad [\text{var}(y_t) = \text{var}(y_{t-s}) = \sigma_y^2] \tag{2.8}$$

$$E[(y_t - \mu)(y_{t-s} - \mu)] = E[(y_{t-j} - \mu)(y_{t-j-s} - \mu)] = \gamma_s$$
$$[\text{cov}(y_t, y_{t-s}) = \text{cov}(y_{t-j}, y_{t-j-s}) = \gamma_s] \tag{2.9}$$

where μ, σ_y^2, and γ_s are all constants.

In (2.9), allowing $s = 0$ means that γ_0 is equivalent to the variance of y_t. Simply put, a time-series is covariance stationary if its mean and all autocovariances are unaffected by a change of time origin. In the literature, a covariance stationary process is also referred to as a weakly stationary, second-order stationary, or wide-sense stationary process. (Note that a **strongly** stationary process need not have a finite mean and/or variance). The text considers only covariance stationary series so that there is no ambiguity in using the terms stationary and covariance stationary interchangeably. One further word about terminology: In multivariate models, the term autocovariance is reserved for the covariance between y_t and its own lags. Cross-covariance refers to the covariance between one series and another. In univariate time-series models, there is no ambiguity and the terms autocovariance and covariance are used interchangeably.

For a covariance stationary series, we can define the **autocorrelation** between y_t and y_{t-s} as

$$\rho_s \equiv \gamma_s / \gamma_0$$

where γ_0 and γ_s are defined by (2.9).

Since γ_s and γ_0 are time-independent, the autocorrelation coefficients ρ_s are also time-independent. Although the autocorrelation between y_t and y_{t-1} can differ from the autocorrelation between y_t and y_{t-2}, the autocorrelation between y_t and y_{t-1} must be identical to that between y_{t-s} and y_{t-s-1}. Obviously, $\rho_0 = 1$.

Stationarity Restrictions for an AR(1) Process

For expositional convenience, first consider the necessary and sufficient conditions for an AR(1) process to be stationary. Let

$$y_t = a_0 + a_1 y_{t-1} + \varepsilon_t$$

where ε_t = white-noise.

Suppose that the process started in period zero, so that y_0 is a deterministic initial condition. In Section 3 of the last chapter, it was shown that the solution to this equation is (see also Question 2 at the end of this chapter)

$$y_t = a_0 \sum_{i=0}^{t-1} a_1^i + a_1^t y_0 + \sum_{i=0}^{t-1} a_1^i \, \varepsilon_{t-i} \tag{2.10}$$

Taking the expected value of (2.10), we obtain

$$E y_t = a_0 \sum_{i=0}^{t-1} a_1^i + a_1^t y_0 \tag{2.11}$$

Updating by s periods yields

$$E y_{t+s} = a_0 \sum_{i=0}^{t+s-1} a_1^i + a_1^{t+s} y_0 \tag{2.12}$$

Comparing (2.11) and (2.12), it is clear that both means are time dependent. Since $E y_t$ is not equal to $E y_{t+s}$, the sequence cannot be stationary. However, if t is large, we can consider the limiting value of y_t in (2.10). If $| a_1 | < 1$, the expression $(a_1)^t y_0$ converges to zero as t becomes infinitely large and the sum $a_0[1 + a_1 + (a_1)^2 + (a_1)^3 + ...]$ converges to $a_0/(1 - a_1)$. Thus, as $t \to \infty$ and if $| a_1 | < 1$

$$\lim y_t = \frac{a_0}{1 - a_1} + \sum_{i=0}^{\infty} a_1^i \, \varepsilon_{t-i} \tag{2.13}$$

Now take expectations of (2.13) so that for sufficiently large values of t, $E y_t = a_0/(1 - a_1)$. Thus, the mean value of y_t is finite and time independent so that $E y_t = E y_{t-s} = a_0/(1 - a_1) \equiv \mu$ for all t. Turning to the variance, we find

$$E(y_t - \mu)^2 = E[(\varepsilon_t + a_1\varepsilon_{t-1} + (a_1)^2\varepsilon_{t-2} + ...)^2]$$
$$= \sigma^2[1 + (a_1)^2 + (a_1)^4 + ...] = \sigma^2/(1 - (a_1)^2)$$

which is also finite and time-independent. Finally, it is easily demonstrated that the limiting values of all autocovariances are finite and time-independent:

$$E[(y_t - \mu)(y_{t-s} - \mu)] = E\{[\varepsilon_t + a_1\varepsilon_{t-1} + (a_1)^2\varepsilon_{t-2} + \ldots] \cdot$$
$$[\varepsilon_{t-s} + a_1\varepsilon_{t-s-1} + (a_1)^2\varepsilon_{t-s-2} + \ldots]\}$$
$$= \sigma^2(a_1)^s[1 + (a_1)^2 + (a_1)^4 + \ldots] = \sigma^2(a_1)^s/[1 - (a_1)^2] \qquad (2.14)$$

In summary, if we can use the limiting value of (2.10), the $\{y_t\}$ sequence will be stationary. For any given y_0 and $|a_1| < 1$, it follows that t must be sufficiently large. Thus, if a sample is generated by a process that has recently begun, the realizations may not be stationary. It is for this very reason that many econometricians assume that the data-generating process has been occurring for an infinitely long time. In practice, the researcher must be wary of any data generated from a "new" process. For example, $\{y_t\}$ could represent the daily change in the dollar/mark exchange rate beginning immediately after the demise of the Bretton Woods fixed exchange rate system. Such a series may not be stationary due to the fact there were deterministic initial conditions (exchange rate changes were essentially zero in the Bretton Woods era). The careful researcher wishing to use stationary series might consider excluding some of these earlier observations from the period of analysis.

Little would change were we not given the initial condition. Without the initial value y_0, the sum of the homogeneous and particular solutions for y_t is

$$y_t = a_0/(1 - a_1) + \sum_{i=0}^{\infty} a_1^i \varepsilon_{t-i} + A(a_1)^t \qquad (2.15)$$

where A = an arbitrary constant.

If you take the expectation of (2.15), it is clear that the $\{y_t\}$ sequence cannot be stationary unless the expression $A(a_1)^t$ is equal to zero. Either the sequence must have started infinitely long ago (so that $a_1^t = 0$) or the arbitrary constant A must be zero. Recall that the arbitrary constant is interpreted as a deviation from long-run equilibrium. The stability conditions can be stated succinctly:

1.   The homogeneous solution must be zero. Either the sequence must have started infinitely far in the past or the process must always be in equilibrium (so that the arbitrary constant is zero).

2.   The characteristic root a_1 must be less than unity in absolute value.

These two conditions readily generalize to all ARMA(p, q) processes. We know that the homogeneous solution to (2.5) has the form

$$\sum_{i=1}^{p} A_i \alpha_i^t$$

or if there are m repeated roots,

$$\alpha \sum_{i=1}^{m} A_i t^i + \sum_{i=m+1}^{p} A_i \alpha_i^t$$

where the A_i are all arbitrary constants, α is the repeated root, and the α_i are the distinct roots.

If any portion of the homogeneous equation is present, the mean, variance, and all covariances will be time-dependent. Hence, for any ARMA(p, q) model, stationarity necessitates that the homogeneous solution be zero. The next section addresses the stationarity restrictions for the particular solution.

4. STATIONARY RESTRICTIONS FOR AN ARMA(p, q) MODEL

As a prelude to the stationarity conditions for the general ARMA(p, q) model, first consider the restrictions necessary to ensure that an ARMA(2, 1) model is stationary. Since the magnitude of the intercept term does not affect the stability (or stationarity) conditions, set $a_0 = 0$ and write

$$y_t = a_1 y_{t-1} + a_2 y_{t-2} + \varepsilon_t + \beta_1 \varepsilon_{t-1} \tag{2.16}$$

From the previous section, we know that the homogeneous solution must be zero. As such, it is only necessary to find the particular solution. Using the method of undetermined coefficients, we can write the challenge solution as

$$y_t = \sum_{i=0}^{\infty} \alpha_i \varepsilon_{t-i} \tag{2.17}$$

For (2.17) to be a solution of (2.16), the various α_i must satisfy

$$\alpha_0 \varepsilon_t + \alpha_1 \varepsilon_{t-1} + \alpha_2 \varepsilon_{t-2} + \alpha_3 \varepsilon_{t-3} + \ldots = a_1(\alpha_0 \varepsilon_{t-1} + \alpha_1 \varepsilon_{t-2} + \alpha_2 \varepsilon_{t-3} + \alpha_3 \varepsilon_{t-4} + \ldots)$$
$$+ a_2(\alpha_0 \varepsilon_{t-2} + \alpha_1 \varepsilon_{t-3} + \alpha_2 \varepsilon_{t-4} + \alpha_3 \varepsilon_{t-5} + \ldots) + \varepsilon_t + \beta_1 \varepsilon_{t-1}$$

To match coefficients on the terms containing ε_t, ε_{t-1}, ε_{t-2}, ..., it is necessary to set

1. $\alpha_0 = 1$
2. $\alpha_1 = a_1 \alpha_0 + \beta_1$ $\Rightarrow \alpha_1 = a_1 + \beta_1$
3. $\alpha_i = a_1 \alpha_{i-1} + a_2 \alpha_{i-2}$ for all $i \geq 2$

The key point is that for $i \geq 2$, the coefficients satisfy the difference equation $\alpha_i = a_1 \alpha_{i-1} + a_2 \alpha_{i-2}$. If the characteristic roots of (2.16) are within the unit circle, the $\{\alpha_i\}$ must constitute a convergent sequence. For example, reconsider the case in which $a_1 = 1.6$, $a_2 = -0.9$, and let $\beta_1 = 0.5$. Worksheet 2.1 shows that the coefficients satisfying (2.17) are 1, 2.1, 2.46, 2.046, 1.06, –0.146, ... (also see Worksheet 1.2 of the previous chapter).

To verify that the $\{y_t\}$ sequence generated by (2.17) is stationary, take the expectation of (2.17) to form $Ey_t = Ey_{t-i} = 0$ for all t and i. Hence, the mean is finite and time-invariant. Since the $\{\varepsilon_t\}$ sequence is assumed to be a white-noise process, the variance of y_t is constant and time-independent; that is,

$$\text{Var}(y_t) = E[(\alpha_0 \varepsilon_t + \alpha_1 \varepsilon_{t-1} + \alpha_2 \varepsilon_{t-2} + \alpha_3 \varepsilon_{t-3} + \ldots)^2]$$
$$= \sigma^2 \sum_{i=0}^{\infty} \alpha_i^2$$

WORKSHEET *2.1*

COEFFICIENTS OF THE ARMA(2,1) PROCESS:
$$y_t = 1.6y_{t-1} - 0.9y_{t-2} + \varepsilon_t + 0.5\varepsilon_{t-1}$$

If we use the method of undetermined coefficients, the α_i must satisfy:

$$\alpha_0 = 1$$
$$\alpha_1 = 1.6 + 0.5 \qquad\qquad \text{hence, } \alpha_1 = 2.1$$
$$\alpha_i = 1.6\alpha_{i-1} - 0.9\alpha_{i-2} \qquad\qquad \text{for all } i = 2, 3, 4, \ldots$$

Notice that the coefficients follow a second-order difference equation with imaginary roots. If we use de Moivre's Theorem, the coefficients will satisfy
$$\alpha_i = 0.949^i\, \beta_1 \cos(0.567i + \beta_2)$$

Imposing the initial conditions for α_0 and α_1 yields
$$1 = \beta_1 \cos(\beta_2) \quad \text{and} \quad 2.1 = 0.949\beta_1\cos(0.567 + \beta_2)$$

Since $\beta_1 = 1/\cos(\beta_2)$, we seek the solution to
$$\cos(\beta_2) - (0.949/2.1) \cdot \cos(0.567 + \beta_2) = 0$$

From a trig table, the solution for β_2 is -1.197. Hence, the α_i satisfy
$$(-1/1.197) \cdot 0.949^i \cdot \cos(0.567i - 1.197)$$

Alternatively, we can use the initial values of α_0 and α_1 to find the other α_i by iteration. The sequence of the α_i is shown in the graph below.

The first 10 values of the sequence are

i	0	1	2	3	4	5	6	7	8	9	10
α_i	1.00	2.10	2.46	2.046	1.06	−0.146	1.187	−1.786	−1.761	−1.226	−0.378

Hence, $\text{var}(y_t) = \text{var}(y_{t-s})$ for all t and s. Finally, the covariance between y_t and y_{t-s} is

$$\text{Cov}(y_t, y_{t-1}) = E[(\varepsilon_t + \alpha_1\varepsilon_{t-1} + \alpha_2\varepsilon_{t-2} + \ldots)(\varepsilon_{t-1} + \alpha_1\varepsilon_{t-2} + \alpha_2\varepsilon_{t-3} + \alpha_3\varepsilon_{t-4} + \ldots)]$$
$$= \sigma^2(\alpha_1 + \alpha_2\alpha_1 + \alpha_3\alpha_2 + \ldots)$$

$$\text{Cov}(y_t, y_{t-2}) = E[(\varepsilon_t + \alpha_1\varepsilon_{t-1} + \alpha_2\varepsilon_{t-2} + \ldots)(\varepsilon_{t-2} + \alpha_1\varepsilon_{t-3} + \alpha_2\varepsilon_{t-4} + \alpha_3\varepsilon_{t-5} + \ldots)]$$
$$= \sigma^2(\alpha_2 + \alpha_3\alpha_1 + \alpha_4\alpha_2 + \ldots)$$

so that

$$\text{Cov}(y_t, y_{t-s}) = \sigma^2(\alpha_s + \alpha_{s+1}\alpha_1 + \alpha_{s+2}\alpha_2 + \ldots) \qquad (2.18)$$

Thus, $\text{cov}(y_t, y_{t-s})$ is constant and independent of t. Conversely, if the characteristic roots of (2.16) do not lie within the unit circle, the $\{\alpha_i\}$ sequence will *not* be convergent. As such, the $\{y_t\}$ sequence cannot be convergent.

It is not too difficult to generalize these results to the entire class of ARMA(p, q) models. Begin by considering the conditions ensuring the stationarity of a pure MA(∞) process. By appropriately restricting the β_i, all of the finite-order MA(q) processes can be obtained as special cases. Consider

$$x_t = \sum_{i=0}^{\infty} \beta_i \, \varepsilon_{t-i}$$

where $\{\varepsilon_t\}$ = a white-noise process with variance σ^2.

We have already determined that $\{x_t\}$ is not a white-noise process; now the issue is whether $\{x_t\}$ is covariance stationary. Given conditions (2.7), (2.8), and (2.9), we ask the following:

1. Is the mean finite and time-independent? Take the expected value of x_t and remember that the expectation of a sum is the sum of the individual expectations. Therefore,

$$E(x_t) = E(\varepsilon_t + \beta_1\varepsilon_{t-1} + \beta_2\varepsilon_{t-2} + \ldots)$$
$$= E\varepsilon_t + \beta_1 E\varepsilon_{t-1} + \beta_2 E\varepsilon_{t-2} + \ldots = 0$$

Repeat the procedure with x_{t-s}

$$E(x_{t-s}) = E(\varepsilon_{t-s} + \beta_1\varepsilon_{t-s-1} + \beta_2\varepsilon_{t-s-2} + \ldots) = 0$$

Hence, all elements in the $\{x_t\}$ sequence have the same finite mean ($\mu = 0$).

2. Is the variance finite and time-independent? Form $\text{var}(x_t)$ as

$$\text{Var}(x_t) = E[(\varepsilon_t + \beta_1\varepsilon_{t-1} + \beta_2\varepsilon_{t-2} + \ldots)^2]$$

Square the term in parentheses and take expectations. Since $\{\varepsilon_t\}$ is a white-noise process, all terms $E\varepsilon_t \varepsilon_{t-s} = 0$ for $s \neq 0$. Hence

$$\text{Var}(x_t) = E(\varepsilon_t)^2 + (\beta_1)^2 E(\varepsilon_{t-1})^2 + (\beta_2)^2 E(\varepsilon_{t-2})^2 + \ldots$$
$$= \sigma^2[1 + (\beta_1)^2 + (\beta_2)^2 + \ldots]$$

As long as $\Sigma(\beta_i)^2$ is finite, it follows that $\text{var}(x_t)$ is finite. Thus, $\Sigma(\beta_i)^2$ being finite is a necessary condition for $\{x_t\}$ to be stationary. To determine whether $\text{var}(x_t) = \text{var}(x_{t-s})$, form

$$\text{Var}(x_{t-s}) = E[(\varepsilon_{t-s} + \beta_1\varepsilon_{t-s-1} + \beta_2\varepsilon_{t-s-2} + \ldots)^2] = \sigma^2[1 + (\beta_1)^2 + (\beta_2)^2 + \ldots]$$

Thus, $\text{var}(x_t) = \text{var}(x_{t-s})$ for all t and t-s.

3. Are all autocovariances finite and time-independent? First form $E(x_t x_{t-s})$ as

$$E[x_t x_{t-s}] = E[(\varepsilon_t + \beta_1\varepsilon_{t-1} + \beta_2\varepsilon_{t-2} + \ldots)(\varepsilon_{t-s} + \beta_1\varepsilon_{t-s-1} + \beta_2\varepsilon_{t-s-2} + \ldots)]$$

Carrying out the multiplication and noting that $E(\varepsilon_t \varepsilon_{t-s}) = 0$ for $s \neq 0$, we get

$$E(x_t x_{t-s}) = \sigma^2(\beta_s + \beta_1\beta_{s+1} + \beta_2\beta_{s+2} + \ldots)$$

Restricting the sum $\beta_s + \beta_1\beta_{s+1} + \beta_2\beta_{s+2} + \ldots$ to be finite means that $E(x_t x_{t-s})$ is finite. Given this second restriction, it is clear that the covariance between x_t and x_{t-s}

only depends on the number of periods separating the variables (i.e., the value of s) but *not* on the time subscript t.

In summary, the necessary and sufficient conditions for any MA process to be stationary are for the sums (1), $\Sigma(\beta_i)^2$ and of (2), $(\beta_s + \beta_1\beta_{s+1} + \beta_2\beta_{s+2} + \ldots)$ to be finite. Since (2) must hold for all values of s and $\beta_0 = 1$, condition (1) is redundant. The direct implication is that a finite-order MA process will always be stationary. For an infinite-order process, (2) must hold for all $s \geq 0$. Some of the details involved with maximum likelihood estimation of MA processes are discussed in Appendix 2.1 of this chapter.

Stationarity Restrictions for the Autoregressive Coefficients

Now consider the pure autoregressive model

$$y_t = a_0 + \sum_{i=1}^{p} a_i \, y_{t-i} + \varepsilon_t \tag{2.19}$$

If the characteristic roots of the homogeneous equation of (2.19) all lie inside the unit circle, it is possible to write the particular solution as

$$y_t = \frac{a_0}{1 - \sum_{i=1}^{p} a_i} + \sum_{i=0}^{\infty} \alpha_i \, \varepsilon_{t-i} \tag{2.20}$$

where the α_i = undetermined coefficients.

Although it is possible to find the undetermined coefficients $\{\alpha_i\}$, we know that (2.20) is a convergent sequence so long as the characteristic roots of (2.19) are inside the unit circle. To sketch the proof, the method of undetermined coefficients allows us to write the particular solution in the form of (2.20). We also know that the sequence $\{\alpha_i\}$ will eventually solve the difference equation

$$\alpha_i - a_1\alpha_{i-1} - a_2\alpha_{i-2} - \ldots - a_p\alpha_{i-p} = 0 \tag{2.21}$$

If the characteristic roots of (2.21) are all inside the unit circle, the $\{\alpha_i\}$ sequence will be convergent. Although (2.20) is an infinite-order moving average process, the convergence of the MA coefficients implies that $\Sigma\alpha_i^2$ is finite. Thus, we can use (2.20) to check the three conditions for stationarity. Since $\alpha_0 = 1$,

$$Ey_t = Ey_{t-s} = a_0/(1 - \Sigma a_i)$$

You should recall from Chapter 1 that a necessary condition of all characteristic roots to lie inside the unit circle is $1 - \Sigma a_i > 0$. Hence, the mean of the sequence is finite and time-invariant.

$$\text{Var}(y_t) = E[(\varepsilon_t + \alpha_1\varepsilon_{t-1} + \alpha_2\varepsilon_{t-2} + \alpha_3\varepsilon_{t-3} + \ldots)^2] = \sigma^2\Sigma\alpha_i^2$$

and

$$\text{Var}(y_{t-s}) = E[(\varepsilon_{t-s} + \alpha_1\varepsilon_{t-s-1} + \alpha_2\varepsilon_{t-s-1} + \alpha_2\varepsilon_{t-s-2} + \alpha_3\varepsilon_{t-s-3} + \ldots)^2] = \sigma^2\Sigma\alpha_i^2$$

Given that $\Sigma\alpha_i^2$ is finite, the variance is finite and time-independent.

$$\text{Cov}(y_t, y_{t-s}) = E[(\varepsilon_t + \alpha_1\varepsilon_{t-1} + \alpha_2\varepsilon_{t-2} + \ldots)(\varepsilon_{t-s} + \alpha_1\varepsilon_{t-s-1} + \alpha_2\varepsilon_{t-s-2} + \ldots)]$$
$$= \sigma^2(\alpha_s + \alpha_1\alpha_{s+1} + \alpha_2\alpha_{s+2} + \ldots)$$

Thus, the covariance between y_t and y_{t-s} is constant and time-invariant for all t and $t-s$. Nothing of substance is changed by combining the AR(p) and MA(q) models into the general ARMA(p, q) model:

$$y_t = a_0 + \sum_{i=1}^{p} a_i\, y_{t-i} + x_t$$

$$x_t = \sum_{i=0}^{q} \beta_i \varepsilon_{t-i} \tag{2.22}$$

If the roots of the inverse characteristic equation lie outside of the unit circle [i.e., if the roots of the homogeneous form of (2.22) lie inside the unit circle] and if the $\{x_t\}$ sequence is stationary, the $\{y_t\}$ sequence will be stationary. Consider

$$y_t = \frac{a_0}{1-\sum_{i=1}^{p}a_i} + \frac{\varepsilon_t}{1-\sum_{i=1}^{p}a_i\,L^i} + \frac{\beta_1\,\varepsilon_{t-1}}{1-\sum_{i=1}^{p}a_i\,L^i} + \frac{\beta_2\,\varepsilon_{t-2}}{1-\sum_{i=1}^{p}a_i\,L^i} + \dots \tag{2.23}$$

With very little effort, you can convince yourself that the $\{y_t\}$ sequence satisfies the three conditions for stationarity. Each of the expressions on the right-hand side of (2.23) is stationary as long as the roots of $1 - \Sigma a_i L^i$ are outside the unit circle. Given that $\{x_t\}$ is stationary, only the roots of the autoregressive portion of (2.22) determine whether the $\{y_t\}$ sequence is stationary.

5. THE AUTOCORRELATION FUNCTION

The autocovariances and autocorrelations of the type found in (2.18) serve as useful tools in the Box–Jenkins (1976) approach to identifying and estimating time-series models. We illustrate by considering four important examples: the AR(1), AR(2), MA(1), and ARMA(1, 1) models. For the AR(1) model, $y_t = a_0 + a_1 y_{t-1} + \varepsilon_t$, (2.14) shows

$$\gamma_0 = \sigma^2/[1-(a_1)^2]$$
$$\gamma_s = \sigma^2(a_1)^s/[1-(a_1)^2]$$

Forming the autocorrelations by dividing each γ_s by γ_0, we find that $\rho_0 = 1$, $\rho_1 = a_1$, $\rho_2 = (a_1)^2$, ..., $\rho_s = (a_1)^s$. For an AR(1) process, a necessary condition for stationarity is for $|a_1| < 1$. Thus, the plot of ρ_s against s—called the autocorrelation function (ACF) or **correlogram**—should converge to zero geometrically if the series is stationary. If a_1 is positive, convergence will be direct, and if a_1 is negative, the autocorrelations will follow a dampened oscillatory path around zero. The first two graphs on the left-hand side of Figure 2.2 show the theoretical autocorrelation functions for $a_1 = 0.7$ and $a_1 = -0.7$ respectively. Here, ρ_0 is not shown since its value is necessarily unity.

The Autocorrelation Function of an AR(2) Process

Now consider the more complicated AR(2) process $y_t = a_1 y_{t-1} + a_2 y_{t-2} + \varepsilon_t$. We omit an intercept term (a_0) since it has no effect on the ACF. For the second-order process to be stationary, we know that it is necessary to restrict the roots of $(1 - a_1 L - a_2 L^2)$ to be outside the unit circle. In Section 4, we derived the autocovariances of an ARMA(2, 1)

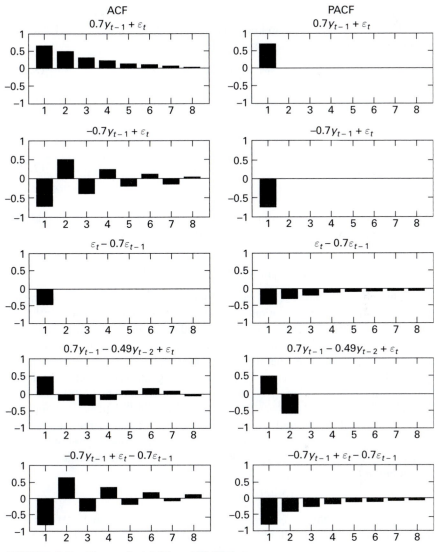

FIGURE 2.2 Theoretical ACF and PACF Patterns

process by use of the method of undetermined coefficients. Now we want to illustrate an alternative technique using the **Yule–Walker** equations. Multiply the second-order difference equation by y_{t-s} for $s = 0$, $s = 1$, $s = 2$, ... and take expectations to form

$$Ey_t y_t = a_1 Ey_{t-1} y_t + a_2 Ey_{t-2} y_t + E\varepsilon_t y_t$$
$$Ey_t y_{t-1} = a_1 Ey_{t-1} y_{t-1} + a_2 Ey_{t-2} y_{t-1} + E\varepsilon_t y_{t-1}$$
$$Ey_t y_{t-2} = a_1 Ey_{t-1} y_{t-2} + a_2 Ey_{t-2} y_{t-2} + E\varepsilon_t y_{t-2}$$

$$\cdot$$

$$Ey_t y_{t-s} = a_1 Ey_{t-1} y_{t-s} + a_2 Ey_{t-2} y_{t-s} + E\varepsilon_t y_{t-s} \tag{2.24}$$

By definition, the autocovariances of a stationary series are such that $Ey_t y_{t-s} = Ey_{t-s} y_t = Ey_{t-k} y_{t-k-s} = \gamma_s$. We also know that $E\varepsilon_t y_t = \sigma^2$ and $E\varepsilon_t y_{t-s} = 0$. Hence, we can use the equations in (2.24) to form

$$\gamma_0 = a_1 \gamma_1 + a_2 \gamma_2 + \sigma^2 \tag{2.25}$$

$$\gamma_1 = a_1 \gamma_0 + a_2 \gamma_1 \tag{2.26}$$

$$\gamma_s = a_1 \gamma_{s-1} + a_2 \gamma_{s-2} \tag{2.27}$$

Dividing (2.26) and (2.27) by γ_0 yields

$$\rho_1 = a_1 \rho_0 + a_2 \rho_1 \tag{2.28}$$

$$\rho_s = a_1 \rho_{s-1} + a_2 \rho_{s-2} \tag{2.29}$$

We know that $\rho_0 = 1$, so that from (2.28), $\rho_1 = a_1/(1 - a_2)$. Hence, we can find all ρ_s for $s \geq 2$ by solving the difference equation (2.29). For example, for $s = 2$, and $s = 3$,

$$\rho_2 = (a_1)^2/(1 - a_2) + a_2$$
$$\rho_3 = a_1[(a_1)^2/(1 - a_2) + a_2] + a_2 a_1/(1 - a_2)$$

Although the values of the ρ_s are cumbersome to derive, we can easily characterize their properties. Given the solutions for ρ_0 and ρ_1, the key point to note is that the ρ_s all satisfy the difference equation (2.29). As in the general case of a second-order difference equation, the solution may be oscillatory or direct. Note that the stationarity condition for y_t necessitates that the characteristic roots of (2.29) lie inside of the unit circle. Hence, the $\{\rho_s\}$ sequence must be convergent. The correlogram for an AR(2) process must be such that $\rho_0 = 1$ and that ρ_1 be determined by (2.28). These two values can be viewed as *initial values* for the second-order difference equation (2.29).

The fourth panel on the left-hand side of Figure 2.2 shows the ACF for the process $y_t = 0.7y_{t-1} - 0.49y_{t-2} + \varepsilon_t$. The properties of the various ρ_s follow directly from the homogeneous equation $y_t - 0.7y_{t-1} + 0.49y_{t-2} = 0$. The roots are obtained from the solution to

$$\alpha = \{0.7 \pm [(-0.7)^2 - 4(0.49)]^{1/2}\}/2$$

Since the discriminant $d = (-0.7)^2 - 4(0.49)$ is negative, the characteristic roots are imaginary so that the solution oscillates. However, since $a_2 = -0.49$, the solution is convergent and the $\{y_t\}$ sequence is stationary.

Finally, we may wish to find the autocovariances rather than the autocorrelations. Since we know all of the autocorrelations, if we can find the variance of y_t (i.e., γ_0), we can find all of the other γ_s. To find γ_0, use (2.25) and note that $\rho_i = \gamma_i / \gamma_0$ so that

$$\gamma_0(1 - a_1\rho_1 - a_2\rho_2) = \sigma^2$$

Substitution for ρ_1 and ρ_2 yields

$$\gamma_0 = \text{var}(y_t) = [(1 - a_2)/(1 + a_2)]\left| \frac{\sigma^2}{(a_1 + a_2 - 1)(a_2 - a_1 - 1)} \right|$$

The Autocorrelation Function of an MA(1) Process

Next consider the MA(1) process $y_t = \varepsilon_t + \beta\varepsilon_{t-1}$. Again, we can obtain the Yule–Walker equations by multiplying y_t by each y_{t-s} and take expectations

$$\gamma_0 = \text{var}(y_t) = Ey_t y_t = E[(\varepsilon_t + \beta\varepsilon_{t-1})(\varepsilon_t + \beta\varepsilon_{t-1})] = (1 + \beta^2)\sigma^2$$
$$\gamma_1 = Ey_t y_{t-1} = E[(\varepsilon_t + \beta\varepsilon_{t-1})(\varepsilon_{t-1} + \beta\varepsilon_{t-2})] = \beta\sigma^2$$

and

$$\gamma_s = Ey_t y_{t-s} = E[(\varepsilon_t + \beta\varepsilon_{t-1})(\varepsilon_{t-s} + \beta\varepsilon_{t-s-1})] = 0 \qquad \text{for all } s > 1$$

Hence, dividing each γ_s by γ_0, it can be immediately seen that the ACF is simply $\rho_0 = 1$, $\rho_1 = \beta/(1 + \beta^2)$, and $\rho_s = 0$ for all $s > 1$. The third graph on the left-hand side of Figure 2.2 shows the ACF for the MA(1) process $y_t = \varepsilon_t - 0.7\varepsilon_{t-1}$. As an exercise, you should demonstrate that the ACF for an MA(2) process has two spikes and then cuts to zero.

The Autocorrelation Function of an ARMA(1, 1) Process

Finally, let $y_t = a_1 y_{t-1} + \varepsilon_t + \beta_1\varepsilon_{t-1}$. Using the now-familiar procedure, we find the Yule–Walker equations

$$Ey_t y_t = a_1 Ey_{t-1} y_t + E\varepsilon_t y_t + \beta_1 E\varepsilon_{t-1} y_t \;\Rightarrow\; \gamma_0 = a_1\gamma_1 + \sigma^2 + \beta_1(a_1+\beta_1)\sigma^2 \quad (2.30)$$

$$Ey_t y_{t-1} = a_1 Ey_{t-1} y_{t-1} + E\varepsilon_t y_{t-1} + \beta_1 E\varepsilon_{t-1} y_{t-1} \;\Rightarrow\; \gamma_1 = a_1\gamma_0 + \beta_1\sigma^2 \quad (2.31)$$

$$Ey_t y_{t-2} = a_1 Ey_{t-1} y_{t-2} + E\varepsilon_t y_{t-2} + \beta_1 E\varepsilon_{t-1} y_{t-2} \;\Rightarrow\; \gamma_2 = a_1\gamma_1 \quad (2.32)$$

$$\cdot$$
$$\cdot$$

$$Ey_t y_{t-s} = a_1 Ey_{t-1} y_{t-s} + E\varepsilon_t y_{t-s} + \beta_1 E\varepsilon_{t-1} y_{t-s} \;\Rightarrow\; \gamma_s = a_1\gamma_{s-1} \quad (2.33)$$

Solving (2.30) and (2.31) simultaneously for γ_0 and γ_1 yields

$$\gamma_0 = \frac{1 + \beta_1^2 + 2a_1\beta_1}{(1 - a_1^2)}\sigma^2$$

$$\gamma_1 = \frac{(1 + a_1\beta_1)(a_1 + \beta_1)}{(1 - a_1^2)}\sigma^2$$

Hence,

$$\rho_1 = \frac{(1 + a_1\beta_1)(a_1 + \beta_1)}{(1 + \beta_1^2 + 2a_1\beta_1)} \qquad (2.34)$$

and $\rho_s = a_1\rho_{s-1}$ for all $s \geq 2$.

Thus, the ACF for an ARMA(1, 1) process is such that the magnitude of ρ_1 depends on both a_1 and β_1. Beginning with this value of ρ_1, the ACF of an ARMA(1, 1) process looks like that of the AR(1) process. If $0 < a_1 < 1$, convergence will be direct, and if $-1 < a_1 < 0$, the autocorrelations will oscillate. The ACF for the function $y_t = -0.7y_{t-1} + \varepsilon_t - 0.7\varepsilon_{t-1}$ is shown as the last graph on the left-hand side of Figure 2.2. The top portion of Worksheet 2.2 derives these autocorrelations.

We leave you with the exercise of deriving the correlogram of the ARMA(2, 1) process used in Worksheet 2.1. You should be able to recognize the point that the correlogram can reveal the pattern of the autoregressive coefficients. For an ARMA (p, q) model beginning after lag q, the values of the ρ_i will satisfy

$$\rho_i = a_1\rho_{i-1} + a_2\rho_{i-2} + \ldots + a_p\rho_{i-p}$$

WORKSHEET 2.2

CALCULATION OF THE PARTIAL AUTOCORRELATIONS OF $y_t = -0.7y_{t-1} + \varepsilon_t - 0.7\varepsilon_{t-1}$

Step 1: Calculate the autocorrelations. Use (2.34) to calculate ρ_1 as

$$\rho_1 = \frac{(1+0.49)(-0.7-0.7)}{1+0.49+2(0.49)} = -0.8445$$

The remaining autocorrelations decay at the rate $\rho_i = -0.7\rho_{i-1}$ so that

$$\rho_2 = 0.591, \rho_3 = -0.414, \rho_4 = 0.290, \rho_5 = -0.203, \rho_6 = 0.142, \rho_7 = -0.099, \rho_8 = 0.07$$

Step 2: Calculate the first two partial autocorrelations using (2.35) and (2.36). Hence
$$\phi_{11} = \rho_1 = -0.8445$$
$$\phi_{22} = [0.591 - (-0.8445)^2]/[1 - (-0.8445)^2] = -0.426$$

Step 3: Construct all remaining ϕ_{ss} iteratively using (2.37). To find ϕ_{33}, note that $\phi_{21} = \phi_{11} - \phi_{22}\phi_{11} = -1.204$ and form

$$\phi_{33} = \left(\rho_3 - \sum_{j=1}^{2}\phi_{2j}\rho_{3-j}\right)\left(1 - \sum_{j=1}^{2}\phi_{2j}\rho_j\right)^{-1}$$

$$= [-0.414 - (-1.204)(0.591) - (-0.426)(-0.8445)]/[1 - (-1.204)(-0.8445) - (-0.426)(0.591)]$$

$$= -0.262$$

Similarly, to find ϕ_{44} use

$$\phi_{44} = \left(\rho_4 - \sum_{j=1}^{3}\phi_{3j}\rho_{4-j}\right)\left(1 - \sum_{j=1}^{3}\phi_{3j}\rho_j\right)^{-1}$$

Since $\phi_{3j} = \phi_{2j} - \phi_{33}\phi_{2,2-j}$, it follows that $\phi_{31} = -1.315$, and $\phi_{32} = -0.74$. Hence

$$\phi_{44} = -0.173$$

If we continue in this fashion, it is possible to demonstrate that $\phi_{55} = -0.117$, $\phi_{66} = -0.081$, $\phi_{77} = -0.056$ and $\phi_{88} = -0.039$

The previous p values can be treated as initial conditions that satisfy the Yule–Walker equations. For these lags, the shape of the ACF is determined by the characteristic equation.

6. THE PARTIAL AUTOCORRELATION FUNCTION

In an AR(1) process, y_t and y_{t-2} are correlated even though y_{t-2} does not directly appear in the model. The correlation between y_t and y_{t-2} (i.e., ρ_2) is equal to the correlation between y_t and y_{t-1} (i.e., ρ_1) multiplied by the correlation between y_{t-1} and y_{t-2} (i.e., ρ_1 again) so that $\rho_2 = (\rho_1)^2$. It is important to note that all such *indirect* correlations are present in the ACF of any autoregressive process. In contrast, the **partial autocorrelation** between y_t and y_{t-s} eliminates the effects of the intervening values y_{t-1} through y_{t-s+1}. As such, in an AR(1) process the partial autocorrelation between y_t and y_{t-2} is equal to zero. The most direct way to find the partial autocorrelation function is to first form the series $\{y_t^*\}$ by subtracting the mean of the series (i.e., μ) from each observation to obtain $y_t^* \equiv y_t - \mu$. Next, form the first-order autoregression

$$y_t^* = \phi_{11} y_{t-1}^* + e_t$$

where e_t is an error term.

Here the symbol $\{e_t\}$ is used since this error process may not be white noise.

Since there are no intervening values, ϕ_{11} is both the autocorrelation and the partial autocorrelation between y_t and y_{t-1}. Now form the second-order autoregression equation

$$y_t^* = \phi_{21} y_{t-1}^* + \phi_{22} y_{t-2}^* + e_t$$

Here ϕ_{22} is the partial autocorrelation coefficient between y_t and y_{t-2}. In other words, ϕ_{22} is the correlation between y_t and y_{t-2} controlling for (i.e., "netting out") the effect of y_{t-1}. Repeating this process for all additional lags s yields the partial autocorrelation function (PACF). In practice, with sample size T, only $T/4$ lags are used in obtaining the sample PACF.

Since most statistical computer packages perform these transformations, there is little need to elaborate on the computational procedure. However, it should be pointed out that a simple computational method relying on the so-called Yule–Walker equations is available. One can form the partial autocorrelations from the autocorrelations as

$$\phi_{11} = \rho_1 \tag{2.35}$$

$$\phi_{22} = (\rho_2 - \rho_1^2)/(1 - \rho_1^2) \tag{2.36}$$

and for additional lags,

$$\phi_{ss} = \frac{\rho_s - \sum_{j=1}^{s-1} \phi_{s-1,j}\, \rho_{s-j}}{1 - \sum_{j=1}^{s-1} \phi_{s-1,j}\, \rho_j}, \qquad s = 3,\ 4,\ 5, \dots \tag{2.37}$$

where $\phi_{sj} = \phi_{s-1,j} - \phi_{ss}\phi_{s-1,s-j}, j = 1, 2, 3, \dots, s-1$.

For an AR(p) process, there is no direct correlation between y_t and y_{t-s} for $s > p$. Hence, for $s > p$, all values of ϕ_{ss} will be zero and the PACF for a pure AR(p) process should cut to zero for all lags greater than p. This is a useful feature of the PACF that can aid in the identification of an AR(p) model. In contrast, consider the PACF for the MA(1) process: $y_t = \varepsilon_t + \beta\varepsilon_{t-1}$. As long as $\beta \neq -1$, we can write $y_t / (1 + \beta L) = \varepsilon_t$, which we know has the infinite-order autoregressive representation

$$y_t - \beta y_{t-1} + \beta^2 y_{t-2} - \beta^3 y_{t-3} + \ldots = \varepsilon_t$$

As such, the PACF will *not* jump to zero since y_t will be correlated with all of its own lags. Instead, the PACF coefficients exhibit a geometrically decaying pattern. If $\beta < 0$, decay is direct and if $\beta > 0$, the PACF coefficients oscillate.

Worksheet 2.2 illustrates the procedure used in constructing the PACF for the ARMA(1, 1) model shown in the fifth panel on the right-hand side of Figure 2.2:

$$y_t = -0.7y_{t-1} + \varepsilon_t - 0.7\varepsilon_{t-1}$$

First, calculate the autocorrelations. Clearly, $\rho_0 = 1$; use equation (2.34) to calculate as $\rho_1 = -0.8445$. Thereafter, the ACF coefficients decay at the rate $\rho_i = (-0.7)\rho_{i-1}$ for $i \geq 2$. Using (2.35) and (2.36), we obtain $\phi_{11} = -0.8445$ and $\phi_{22} = -0.4250$. All subsequent ϕ_{ss} and ϕ_{sj} can be calculated from (2.37) as in Worksheet 2.2.

More generally, the PACF of a stationary ARMA(p, q) process must ultimately decay toward zero beginning at lag p. The decay pattern depends on the coefficients of the polynomial $(1 + \beta_1 L + \beta_2 L^2 + \ldots + \beta_q L^q)$. Table 2.1 summarizes some of the properties of the ACF and PACF for various ARMA processes. Also, the right-hand side graphs of Figure 2.2 show the partial autocorrelation functions of the five indicated processes.

For stationary processes, the key points to note are the following:

1. The ACF of an ARMA(p, q) process will begin to decay after lag q. After lag q, the coefficients of the ACF (i.e., the ρ_i) will satisfy the difference

Table 2.1 Properties of the ACF and PACF

Process	ACF	PACF
White noise	All $\rho_s = 0$ ($s \neq 0$)	All $\phi_{ss} = 0$
AR(1): $a_1 > 0$	Direct exponential decay: $\rho_s = a_1^s$	$\phi_{11} = \rho_1$; $\phi_{ss} = 0$ for $s \geq 2$
AR(1): $a_1 < 0$	Oscillating decay: $\rho_s = a_1^s$	$\phi_{11} = \rho_1$; $\phi_{ss} = 0$ for $s \geq 2$
AR(p)	Decays toward zero. Coefficients may oscillate.	Spikes through lag p. All $\phi_{ss} = 0$ for $s > p$.
MA(1): $\beta > 0$	Positive spike at lag 1. $\rho_s = 0$ for $s \geq 2$	Oscillating decay: $\phi_{11} > 0$.
MA(1): $\beta < 0$	Negative spike at lag 1. $\rho_s = 0$ for $s \geq 2$	Geometric decay: $\phi_{11} < 0$.
ARMA(1, 1): $a_1 > 0$	Exponential decay beginning at lag 1. Sign $\rho_1 = \text{sign}(a_1 + \beta)$	Oscillating decay beginning at lag 1. $\phi_{11} = \rho_1$
ARMA(1, 1): $a_1 < 0$	Oscillating decay beginning at lag 1. Sign $\rho_1 = \text{sign}(a_1 + \beta)$	Exponential decay beginning at lag 1. $\phi_{11} = \rho_1$ and $\text{sign}(\phi_{ss}) = \text{sign}(\phi_{11})$.
ARMA (p, q)	Decay (either direct or oscillatory) beginning at lag q.	Decay (either direct or oscillatory) after lag p.

equation ($\rho_i = a_1\rho_{i-1} + a_2\rho_{i-2} + \ldots + a_p\rho_{i-p}$). Since the characteristic roots are inside the unit circle, the autocorrelations will decay after lag q. Moreover, the pattern of the autocorrelation coefficients will mimic that suggested by the characteristic roots.

2. The PACF of an ARMA(p, q) process will begin to decay after lag p. After lag p, the coefficients of the PACF (i.e., the ϕ_{ss}) will mimic the ACF coefficients from the model $y_t /(1 + \beta_1 L + \beta_2 L^2 + \ldots + \beta_q L^q)$.

We can illustrate the usefulness of the ACF and PACF functions using the model $y_t = a_0 + 0.7y_{t-1} + \varepsilon_t$. If we compare the top two graphs in Figure 2.2, the ACF shows the monotonic decay of the autocorrelations while the PACF exhibits the single spike at lag 1. Suppose that a researcher collected sample data and plotted the ACF and PACF functions. If the actual patterns compared favorably to the theoretical patterns, the researcher might try to estimate data using an AR(1) model. Correspondingly, if the ACF exhibited a single spike and the PACF exhibited monotonic decay (see the third graph for the model $y_t = \varepsilon_t - 0.7\varepsilon_{t-1}$) the researcher might try an MA(1) model.

7. SAMPLE AUTOCORRELATIONS OF STATIONARY SERIES

In practice, the theoretical mean, variance, and autocorrelations of a series are unknown to the researcher. Given that a series is stationary, we can use the sample mean, variance and autocorrelations to estimate the parameters of the actual data generating process. Let there be T observations labeled y_1 through y_T. We can let $\bar{y}$, $\hat{\sigma}^2$, and r_s be estimates of μ, σ^2, and ρ_s respectively where[1]

$$\bar{y} = (1/T)\sum_{t=1}^{T} y_t \tag{2.38}$$

$$\hat{\sigma}^2 = (1/T)\sum_{t=1}^{T}(y_t - \bar{y})^2 \tag{2.39}$$

and for each value of $s = 1, 2, \ldots$.

$$r_s = \frac{\sum\limits_{t=s+1}^{T} (y_t - \bar{y})(y_{t-s} - \bar{y})}{\sum\limits_{t=1}^{T}(y_t - \bar{y})^2} \tag{2.40}$$

The sample autocorrelation function [i.e., the ACF derived from (2.40)] and the sample PACF can be compared to various theoretical functions to help identify the actual nature of the data generating process. Box and Jenkins (1976) discuss the distribution of the sample values of r_s under the null that y_t is stationary with normally distributed errors. Allowing var(r_s) to denote the sampling variance of r_s, they obtain

$$\text{Var}(r_s) = T^{-1} \qquad \text{for } s = 1$$

$$= T^{-1}\left(1 + 2\sum_{j=1}^{s-1}r_j^2\right) \quad \text{for } s > 1 \tag{2.41}$$

if the true value of $r_s = 0$ [i.e., if the true data-generating process is an MA(s–1) process]. Moreover, in large samples (i.e., for large values of T), r_s will be normally distributed with a mean equal to zero. For the PACF coefficients, under the null hypothesis of an AR(p) model (i.e., under the null that all $\phi_{p+i,p+i}$ are zero), the variance of the $\hat{\phi}_{p+i,p+i}$ is approximately $1/T$.

In practice, we can use these sample values to form the sample autocorrelation and partial autocorrelation functions and test for significance using (2.41). For example, if we use a 95 percent confidence interval (i.e., two standard deviations), and the calculated value of r_1 exceeds $2T^{-1/2}$, it is possible to reject the null hypothesis that the first-order autocorrelation is not statistically different from zero. Rejecting this hypothesis means rejecting an MA(s – 1) = MA(0) process and accepting the alternative $q > 0$. Next, try $s = 2$; var(r_2) is: $(1+2r_1^2)/T$. If r_1 is 0.5 and T is 100, the variance of r_2 is 0.015 and the standard deviation is about 0.123. Thus, if the calculated value of r_2 exceeds 2(0.123), it is possible to reject the hypothesis $r_2 = 0$. Here, rejecting the null means accepting the alternative that $q > 1$. Repeating for the various values of s is helpful in identifying the order to the process. The maximum number of sample autocorrelations and partial autocorrelations to use is typically set equal to $T/4$.

Within any large group of autocorrelations, some will exceed two standard deviations as a result of pure chance even though the true values in the data-generating process are zero. The Q-statistic can be used to test whether a group of autocorrelations is significantly different from zero. Box and Pierce (1970) used the sample autocorrelations to form the statistic

$$Q = T \sum_{k=1}^{s} r_k^2$$

Under the null hypothesis that all values of $r_k = 0$, Q is asymptotically χ^2 distributed with s degrees of freedom. The intuition behind the use of the statistic is that high sample autocorrelations lead to large values of Q. Certainly, a white-noise process (in which all autocorrelations should be zero) would have a Q value of zero. If the calculated value of Q exceeds the appropriate value in a χ^2 table, we can reject the null of no significant autocorrelations. Note that rejecting the null means accepting an alternative that at least one autocorrelation is not zero.

A problem with the Box–Pierce Q-statistic is that it works poorly even in moderately large samples. Ljung and Box (1978) report superior small sample performance for the modified Q-statistic calculated as

$$Q = T(T+2) \sum_{k=1}^{s} r_k^2 / (T-k) \tag{2.42}$$

If the sample value of Q calculated from (2.42) exceeds the critical value of χ^2 with s degrees of freedom, then *at least* one value of r_k is statistically different from zero at the specified significance level. The Box–Pierce and Ljung–Box Q-statistics also serve as a check to see if the *residuals* from an estimated ARMA(p, q) model behave as a white-noise process. However, when the s correlations from an estimated ARMA(p, q) model are formed, the degrees of freedom are reduced by the number of estimated coefficients.

Hence, using the residuals of an ARMA(p, q) model, Q has a χ^2 with $s - p - q$ degrees of freedom (if a constant is included, the degrees of freedom are $s - p - q - 1$).

Model Selection Criteria

One natural question to ask of any estimated model is: How well does it fit the data? Adding additional lags for p and/or q will necessarily reduce the sum of squares of the estimated residuals. However, adding such lags entails the estimation of additional coefficients and an associated loss of degrees of freedom. Moreover, the inclusion of extraneous coefficients will reduce the forecasting performance of the fitted model. As discussed in some detail in Appendix 2.2 of this chapter, there exist various model selection criteria that trade off a reduction in the sum of squares of the residuals for a more **parsimonious** model. The two most commonly used model selection criteria are the Akaike Information Criterion (AIC) and the Schwartz Bayesian Criterion (SBC). Although there are several different ways to report the criteria (as illustrated by question 10 at the end of this chapter), all will select the same model. In the text, we will use the following formulas

$$AIC = T \ln \text{(sum of squared residuals)} + 2n$$
$$SBC = T \ln \text{(sum of squared residuals)} + n \ln(T)$$

where: n = number of parameters estimated ($p + q +$ possible constant term)
T = number of usable observations
When you estimate a model using lagged variables, some observations are lost. To adequately compare the alternative models, T should be kept fixed. Otherwise, you will be comparing the performance of the models over different sample periods. Moreover, decreasing T has direct effect of reducing the AIC and the SBC; the goal is not to select a model because it has the smallest number of usable observations. For example, with 100 data points, estimate an AR(1) and an AR(2) using only the last 98 observations in each estimation. Compare the two models using $T = 98$.

Ideally, the AIC and SBC will be as small as possible (note that both can be negative). As the fit of the model improves, the AIC and SBC will approach $-\infty$. We can use these criteria to aid in selecting the most appropriate model; model A is said to fit better than model B if the AIC (or SBC) for A is smaller than for model B. In using the criteria to compare alternative models, we must estimate them over the same sample period so that they will be comparable. For each, increasing the number of regressors increases n but should have the effect of reducing the sum of squared residuals. Thus, if a regressor has no explanatory power, adding it to the model will cause both the AIC and SBC to increase. Since $\ln(T)$ will be greater than 2, the SBC will always select a more parsimonious model than will the AIC; the marginal cost of adding regressors is greater with the SBC than with the AIC.

Of the two criteria, the SBC has superior large sample properties. Let the true order of the data generating process be (p^*, q^*) and suppose that we use the AIC and SBC to estimate all ARMA models of order (p, q) where $p \geq p^*$ and $q \geq q^*$. Both the AIC and the SBC will select models of orders greater than or equal to (p^*, q^*) as the sample size approaches infinity. However, the SBC is asymptotically consistent while the AIC is biased toward selecting an overparameterized model. However, in small samples, the AIC can work better than the SBC. You can be quite confident in your results if both the AIC and the SBC select the same model. If they select different models, you need to proceed cautiously. Since SBC selects the more parsimonious model, you should check to determine if the residuals appear to be white noise. Since the AIC can select an overparameterized model, the t-statistics of all coefficients should be significant at conventional levels. A number of other diagnostic checks that can be used to compare alternative models are presented in Sections 8 and 9. Nevertheless, it is wise to retain a healthy skepticism of your estimated models. With many data sets, it is just not possible to find the one model that clearly dominates all others. There is nothing wrong with reporting the results and the forecasts using alternative estimations.

Estimation of an AR(1) Model

Let us use a specific example to see how the sample autocorrelation function and partial autocorrelation function can be used as an aid in identifying an ARMA model. A computer program was used to draw 100 normally distributed random numbers with a theoretical variance equal to unity. Call these random variates ε_t, where t runs from 1 to 100. Beginning with $t = 1$, values of y_t were generated using the formula $y_t = 0.7y_{t-1} + \varepsilon_t$ and the initial condition $y_0 = 0$. Note that the problem of nonstationarity is avoided since the initial condition is consistent with long-run equilibrium. The upper-left-hand graph of Figure 2.3 shows the sample correlogram and the upper-right-hand graph shows the sample PACF. You should take a minute to compare the ACF and PACF to those of the theoretical processes shown in Figure 2.2.

   In practice, we never know the true data-generating process. However, suppose we were presented with these 100 sample values and were asked to uncover the true process. The first step might be to compare the sample ACF and PACF to those of the various theoretical models. The decaying pattern of the ACF and the single large spike at lag 1 in the sample PACF suggests an AR(1) model. The first three autocorrelations are $r_1 = 0.74$, $r_2 = 0.58$, and $r_3 = 0.47$ (which are somewhat greater than the theoretical values of 0.7, 0.49 ($0.7^2 = 0.49$), and 0.343. In the PACF, there is a sizable spike of 0.74 at lag 1, and all other partial autocorrelations (except for lag 12) are very small.

   Under the null hypothesis of an MA(0) process, the standard deviation of r_1 is $T^{-1/2} = 0.1$. Since the sample value of $r_1 = 0.74$ is more than seven standard deviations from zero, we can reject the null hypothesis that r_1 equals 0. The standard deviation of r_2 is obtained by applying (2.41) to the sampling data, where $s = 2$:

$$\text{Var}(r_2) = (1 + 2(0.74)^2)/100 = 0.021$$

   Since $(0.021)^{1/2} = 0.1449$, the sample value of r_2 is more than three standard deviations from zero; at conventional significance levels, we can reject the null hypothesis that r_2 equals zero. We can similarly test the significance of the other values of the autocorrelations.

   As you can see in the second panel of the figure, other than ϕ_{11}, all partial autocorrelations (except for lag 12) are less than $2T^{-1/2} = 0.2$. The decay of the ACF and the single spike of the PACF give the strong impression of a first-order

FIGURE 2.3   ACF and PACF for Two Simulated Processes

autoregressive model. Nevertheless, if we did not know the true underlying process, and happened to be using monthly data, we might be concerned with the significant partial autocorrelation at lag 12. After all, with monthly data we might expect some direct relationship between y_t and y_{t-12}.

Although we know that the data was actually generated from an AR(1) process, it is illuminating to compare the estimates of two different models. Suppose we estimate an AR(1) model and also try to capture the spike at lag 12 with an MA coefficient. Thus, we can consider the two tentative models

$$\text{Model 1: } y_t = a_1 y_{t-1} + \varepsilon_t$$
$$\text{Model 2: } y_t = a_1 y_{t-1} + \varepsilon_t + \beta_{12} \varepsilon_{t-12}.$$

Table 2.2 reports the results of the two estimations. The coefficient of model 1 satisfies the stability condition $| a_1 | < 1$ and has a low standard error (the associated t-statistic for a null of zero is more than 12). As a useful diagnostic check, we plot the correlogram of the **residuals** of the fitted model in Figure 2.4. The Q-statistics for these residuals indicate that each one of the autocorrelations is less than 2 standard deviations from zero. The Ljung–Box Q-statistics of these residuals indicate that *as a group,* lags 1 through 8, 1 through 16, and 1 through 24 are not significantly different from zero. This is strong evidence that the AR(1) model "fits" the data well. After all, if residual autocorrelations were significant, the AR(1) model would not utilize

Table 2.2 Estimates of an AR(1) Model

	Model 1 $y_t = a_1 y_{t-1} + \varepsilon_t$	Model 2 $y_t = a_1 y_{t-1} + \varepsilon_t + \beta_{12} \varepsilon_{t-12}$
Degrees of freedom	99	98
Sum of squared residuals	85.21	85.17
Estimated a_1	0.7910	0.7953
(standard error)	(0.0622)	(0.0638)
Estimated β		−0.033
(standard error)		(0.1134)
AIC; SBC	AIC = 441.9; SBC = 444.5	AIC = 443.9; SBC = 449.1
Ljung–Box Q-statistics for the residuals (significance level in parentheses)	Q(8) = 6.43 (0.490) Q(16) = 15.86 (0.391) Q(24) = 21.74 (0.536)	Q(8) = 6.48 (0.485) Q(16) = 15.75 (0.400) Q(24) = 21.56 (0.547)

FIGURE 2.4 ACF of Residuals from Model 1

all available information concerning movements in the $\{y_t\}$ sequence. For example, suppose we wanted to forecast y_{t+1} conditioned on all available information up to and including period t. With model 1, the value of y_{t+1} is $y_{t+1} = a_1 y_t + \varepsilon_{t+1}$. Hence, the forecast from model 1 is $a_1 y_t$. If the residual autocorrelations had been significant, this forecast would not capture all of the available information set.

Examining the results for model 2, note that both models yield similar estimates for the first-order autoregressive coefficient and the associated standard error. However, the estimate for β_{12} is of poor quality; the insignificant t value suggests that it should be dropped from the model. Moreover, comparing the AIC and the SBC values of the two models suggests that any benefits of a reduced sum of squared residuals is overwhelmed by the detrimental effects of estimating an additional parameter. All of these indicators point to the choice of model 1.

Exercise 7 at the end of this chapter entails various estimations using this data set. In this exercise you are asked to show that the AR(1) model performs better than some alternative specifications. It is important that you complete this exercise.

Estimation of an ARMA(1, 1) Model

A second $\{y_t\}$ sequence was constructed to illustrate the estimation of an ARMA(1, 1). Given 100 normally distributed values of $\{\varepsilon_t\}$, 100 values of $\{y_t\}$ were generated using

$$y_t = -0.7y_{t-1} + \varepsilon_t - 0.7\varepsilon_{t-1}$$

where y_0 and ε_0 were both set equal to zero.

Both the sample ACF and the PACF from the simulated data (see the second set of graphs in Figure 2.3) are roughly equivalent to those of the theoretical model shown in Figure 2.2. However, if the true data-generating process were unknown, the researcher might be concerned about certain discrepancies. An AR(2) model could yield a sample ACF and PACF similar to those in the figure. Table 2.3 reports the results of estimating the data using the following three models:

Model 1: $y_t = a_1 y_{t-1} + \varepsilon_t$
Model 2: $y_t = a_1 y_{t-1} + \varepsilon_t + \beta_1 \varepsilon_{t-1}$
Model 3: $y_t = a_1 y_{t-1} + a_2 y_{t-2} + \varepsilon_t$

In examining Table 2.3, notice that all of the estimated values of a_1 are highly significant; each of the estimated values is *at least* eight standard deviations from zero. It is clear that the AR(1) model is inappropriate. The Q-statistics for model 1 indicate that there is significant autocorrelation in the residuals. The estimated ARMA(1, 1) model does not suffer from this problem. Moreover, both the AIC and the SBC select model 2 over model 1.

The same type of reasoning indicates that model 2 is preferred to model 3. Note that for each model, the estimated coefficients are highly significant and the point estimates imply convergence. Although the Q-statistic at 24 lags indicates that these

Table 2.3 Estimates of an ARMA (1, 1) Model

		Estimates[1]	Q-Statistics[2]	AIC/SBC[3]
Model 1	a_1: −0.835 (.053)	$Q(8) = 26.19$ (.000)	AIC = 496.5
		$Q(24) = 41.10$ (.001)	SBC = 499.0
Model 2	a_1: −0.679 (.076)	$Q(8) = 3.86$ (.695)	AIC = 471.0
	β_1: −0.676 (.081)	$Q(24) = 14.23$ (.892)	SBC = 476.2
Model 3	a_1: −1.16 (.093)	$Q(8) = 11.44$ (.057)	AIC = 482.8
	a_2: −0.378 (.092)	$Q(24) = 22.59$ (.424)	SBC = 487.9

Notes:
[1] Standard errors in parentheses.
[2] Ljung–Box Q-statistics of the residuals from the fitted model. The significance levels are in parentheses.
[3] For comparability, the AIC and SBC values are reported for estimations that used only observations 3 through 100. If the AR(1) is estimated using 99 observations, the AIC and SBC are 502.3 and 504.9, respectively. If the ARMA(1, 1) is estimated using 99 observations, the AIC and SBC are 476.6 and 481.1, respectively.

two models do not suffer from correlated residuals, the Q-statistic at 8 lags indicates serial correlation in the residuals of model 3. Thus, the AR(2) model does not capture short-term dynamics as well as the ARMA(1, 1) model. Also note that the AIC and SBC both select model 2.

Estimation of an AR(2) Model

A third data series was simulated as

$$y_t = 0.7y_{t-1} - 0.49y_{t-2} + \varepsilon_t$$

The estimated ACF and the PACF of the series follow:

ACF

Lags:

1–12: 0.466 −0.161 −0.322 −0.108 −0.052 −0.165
      −0.010 0.128 0.180 0.034 −0.087 −0.113

13–24: −0.164 −0.058 0.115 0.254 0.046 −0.175
       0.150 0.010 0.032 −0.089 −0.046 0.052

PACF

1–12: 0.466 −0.482 0.023 0.045 −0.253 −0.121
      0.101 0.037 −0.076 0.023 −0.020 −0.139

13–24: −0.167 0.207 0.007 0.085 −0.216 0.013
       −0.022 −0.032 0.015 −0.061 0.038 −0.184

Note the large autocorrelation at lag 16 and the large partial autocorrelations at lags 14 and 17. Given the way the process was simulated, the presence of these autocorrelations is due to nothing more than chance. However, an econometrician unaware of the actual data-generating process might be concerned about these autocorrelations. The coefficients of the AR(2) model are estimated as

Coefficient	Estimate	Standard Error	t-Statistic	Significance Level
a_1	0.692389807	0.089515769	7.73484	0.00000000
a_2	−0.480874620	0.089576524	−5.36831	0.00000055
	AIC = 219.87333		SBC = 225.04327	

Overall, the model appears to be adequate. However, the two AR(2) coefficients are unable to capture the correlations at very long lags. For example, the partial autocorrelations of the *residuals* for lags 14 and 17 are both greater than 0.2 in absolute value. The calculated Ljung–Box statistic for 16 lags is 24.6248 (which is significant at the 0.038 level). At this point, it might be tempting to try to model the correlation at lag 16 by including the moving average term $\beta_{16}\varepsilon_{t-16}$. Such an estimation results in[2]

Coefficient	Estimate	Standard Error	t-Statistic	Significance Level
a_1	0.716681247	0.091069451	7.86961	0.00000000
a_2	−0.464999924	0.090958095	−5.11224	0.00000165
β_{16}	0.305813568	0.109936945	2.78172	0.00652182
	AIC = 213.40055		SBC = 221.15545	

All estimated coefficients are significant and the Ljung–Box Q-statistics for the residuals are all insignificant at conventional levels. In conjunction with the fact that the AIC and SBC both select this second model, the researcher unaware of the true process might be tempted to conclude that the data-generating process includes a moving average term at lag 16.

A useful model check is to split the sample into two parts. If a coefficient is present in the data-generating process, its influence should be seen in both subsamples. If the simulated series is split into two parts, the ACF and PACF using observations 50 through 100 follow:

ACF

Lags

1–12:	0.460	−0.207	−0.280	0.035	0.095	−0.153
	−0.133	0.102	0.181	0.027	−0.009	0.009
13–24:	−0.058	−0.088	0.042	0.205	0.064	−0.162
	−0.184	−0.050	−0.033	−0.145	−0.107	−0.036

PACF

1–12:	0.460	−0.531	0.193	0.063	−0.197	−0.130
	0.234	−0.078	0.004	0.065	0.154	−0.257
13–24:	0.026	0.146	0.038	0.004	−0.054	−0.009
	−0.137	−0.076	−0.034	−0.083	−0.029	−0.220

As you can see, the size of the partial autocorrelations at lags 14 and 17 is diminished. Now, estimating a pure AR(2) model over this second part of the sample yields

Coefficient	Estimate	Standard Error	t-Statistic	Significance Level
a_1	0.713855785	0.120541523	5.92207	0.00000031
a_2	−0.537843744	0.120420318	−4.46639	0.00004687

$Q(8) = 7.83$, significance level 0.251
$Q(16) = 15.93$, significance level 0.317
$Q(24) = 26.06$, significance level 0.249

All estimated coefficients are significant, and the Ljung–Box Q-statistics do not indicate any significant autocorrelations in the residuals. In fact, this model does capture the actual data-generating process quite well. In this example, the large spurious autocorrelations of the long lags can be eliminated by changing the sample period. Thus, it is hard to maintain that the correlation at lag 16 is meaningful. Most sophisticated practitioners warn against trying to fit any model to the very long lags. As you can infer from (2.41), the variance of r_s can be sizable when s is large. Moreover, in small samples, a few "unusual" observations can create the appearance of significant autocorrelations at long lags. Since econometric estimation involves unknown data-generating processes, the more general point is that we always need to be wary of our estimated model. Fortunately, Box and Jenkins (1976) established a set of procedures that can be used to check a model's adequacy.

8. BOX–JENKINS MODEL SELECTION

The estimates of the AR(1), ARMA(1, 1) and AR(2) models in the previous section illustrate the Box–Jenkins (1976) strategy for appropriate model selection. Box and Jenkins popularized a three-stage method aimed at selecting an appropriate model for the purpose of estimating and forecasting a univariate time series. In the **identification stage,** the researcher visually examines the time plot of the series, the autocorrelation function, and the partial correlation function. Plotting the time path of the $\{y_t\}$ sequence provides useful information concerning outliers, missing values, and structural breaks in the data. Nonstationary variables may have a pronounced trend or appear to meander without a constant long-run mean or variance. Missing values and outliers can be corrected at this point. At one time, the standard practice was to first-difference any series deemed to be nonstationary. Currently, a large literature is evolving that develops formal procedures to check for nonstationarity. We defer this discussion until Chapter 4 and assume that we are working with stationary data. A comparison of the sample ACF and PACF to those of various theoretical ARMA processes may suggest several plausible models. In the **estimation stage,** each of the tentative models is fit and the various a_i and β_i coefficients are examined. In this second stage, the estimated models are compared using the following criteria.

Parsimony

A fundamental idea in the Box–Jenkins approach is the principle of **parsimony.** Parsimony (meaning sparseness or stinginess) should come as second nature to economists. Incorporating additional coefficients will necessarily increase fit (e.g., the value of R^2 will increase) at a cost of reducing degrees of freedom. Box and Jenkins argue that parsimonious models produce better forecasts than overparameterized models. A parsimonious model fits the data well without incorporating any needless coefficients. The aim is to approximate the true data-generating process but not to pin down the exact process. The goal of parsimony suggested eliminating the MA(12) coefficient in the simulated AR(1) model shown earlier.

In selecting an appropriate model, the econometrician needs to be aware that several different models may have similar properties. As an extreme example, note that the AR(1) model $y_t = 0.5y_{t-1} + \varepsilon_t$ has the equivalent infinite-order moving-average representation of $y_t = \varepsilon_t + 0.5\varepsilon_{t-1} + 0.25\varepsilon_{t-2} + 0.125\varepsilon_{t-3} + 0.0625\varepsilon_{t-4} + \ldots$. In most samples, approximating this MA(∞) process with an MA(2) or MA(3) model will give a very good fit. However, the AR(1) model is the more parsimonious model and is preferred. As a test, you should show that this AR(1) model has the equivalent representation of $y_t = 0.25y_{t-2} + 0.5\varepsilon_{t-1} + \varepsilon_t$.

Also, be aware of the **common factor problem.** Suppose we wanted to fit the ARMA(2, 3) model

$$(1 - a_1L - a_2L^2)y_t = (1 + \beta_1L + \beta_2L^2 + \beta_3L^3)\varepsilon_t \qquad (2.43)$$

Suppose that $(1 - a_1L - a_2L^2)$ and $(1 + \beta_1L + \beta_2L^2 + \beta_3L^3)$ can each be factored as $(1 + cL)(1 + aL)$ and $(1 + cL)(1 + b_1L + b_2L^2)$, respectively. Since $(1 + cL)$ is a common factor to each, (2.43) has the equivalent, but more parsimonious, form[3]

$$(1 + aL)y_t = (1 + b_1L + b_2L^2)\varepsilon_t \qquad (2.44)$$

If you passed the last quiz, you know that $(1 - 0.25L^2)y_t = (1 + 0.5L)\varepsilon_t$ is equivalent to $(1 + 0.5L)(1 - 0.5L)y_t = (1 + 0.5L)\varepsilon_t$ so that $y_t = 0.5y_{t-1} + \varepsilon_t$. In practice, the polynomials will not factor exactly. However, if the factors are similar, you should try a more parsimonious form.

In order to ensure that the model is parsimonious, the various a_i and β_i should all have t-statistics of 2.0 or greater (so that each coefficient is significantly different from zero at the 5% level). Moreover, the coefficients should not be strongly correlated with each other. Highly collinear coefficients are unstable; usually one or more can be eliminated from the model without reducing forecast performance.

Stationarity and Invertibility

The distribution theory underlying the use of the sample ACF and PACF as approximations to those of the true data-generating process assumes that the $\{y_t\}$ sequence is stationary. Moreover, t-statistics and Q-statistics also presume that the data are stationary. The estimated autoregressive coefficients should be consistent with this underlying assumption. Hence, we should be suspicious of an AR(1) model if the estimated value of a_1 is close to unity. For an ARMA(2, q) model, the characteristic roots of the estimated polynomial $(1 - a_1L - a_2L^2)$ should lie outside of the unit circle.

As discussed in greater detail in Appendix 2.1, the Box–Jenkins approach also necessitates that the model be **invertible.** Formally, $\{y_t\}$ is invertible if it can be represented by a finite-order or convergent autoregressive process. Invertibility is important because the use of the ACF and PACF implicitly assume that the $\{y_t\}$ sequence can be represented by an autoregressive model. As a demonstration, consider the simple MA(1) model:

$$y_t = \varepsilon_t - \beta_1\varepsilon_{t-1} \tag{2.45}$$

so that if $|\beta_1| < 1$,

$$y_t /(1 - \beta_1 L) = \varepsilon_t$$

or

$$y_t + \beta_1 y_{t-1} + \beta_1^2 y_{t-2} + \beta_1^3 y_{t-3} + \ldots = \varepsilon_t \tag{2.46}$$

If $|\beta_1| < 1$, (2.46) can be estimated using the Box–Jenkins method. However, if $|\beta_1| \geq 1$, the $\{y_t\}$ sequence cannot be represented by a finite-order AR process; as such, it is not invertible. More generally, for an ARMA model to have a convergent AR representation, the roots of the polynomial $(1 + \beta_1 L + \beta_2 L^2 + \ldots + \beta_q L^q)$ must lie outside of the unit circle. Note that there is nothing improper about a noninvertible model. The $\{y_t\}$ sequence implied by $y_t = \varepsilon_t - \varepsilon_{t-1}$ is stationary in that it has a constant time-invariant mean $[Ey_t = Ey_{t-s} = 0]$, a constant time-invariant variance $[\text{var}(y_t) = \text{var}(y_{t-s}) = \sigma^2(1 + \beta_1^2) + 2\sigma^2]$, and the autocovariances $\gamma_1 = -\beta_1\sigma^2$ and all other $\gamma_s = 0$. The problem is that the technique does not allow for the estimation of such models. If $\beta_1 = 1$, (2.46) becomes

$$y_t + y_{t-1} + y_{t-2} + y_{t-3} + y_{t-4} + \ldots = \varepsilon_t$$

Clearly, the autocorrelations and partial autocorrelations between y_t and y_{t-s} will never decay.

Goodness of Fit

A good model will fit the data well. Obviously, R^2 and the average of the residual sum of squares are common *goodness-of-fit* measures in ordinary least squares. The problem with these measures is that the fit necessarily improves as more parameters are included in the model. Parsimony suggests using the AIC and/or SBC as more appropriate measures of the overall fit of the model. Also be cautious of estimates that fail to converge rapidly. Most software packages estimate the parameters of an ARMA model using a nonlinear search procedure. If the search fails to converge rapidly, it is possible that the estimated parameters are unstable. In such circumstances, adding an additional observation or two can greatly alter the estimates.

The third stage of the Box–Jenkins methodology involves **diagnostic checking.** The standard practice is to plot the residuals to look for outliers and for evidence of periods in which the model does not fit the data well. If all plausible ARMA models show evidence of a poor fit during a reasonably long portion of the sample, it is wise to consider using intervention analysis, transfer function analysis, or any other of the multivariate estimation methods discussed in later chapters. If the variance of the residuals is increasing, a logarithmic transformation may be appropriate. Alternatively, you may wish to actually model any tendency of the variance to change using the ARCH techniques discussed in Chapter 3.

It is particularly important that the residuals from an estimated model be serially uncorrelated. Any evidence of serial correlation implies a systematic movement in the $\{y_t\}$ sequence that is not accounted for by the ARMA coefficients included in the model. Hence, any of the tentative models yielding nonrandom residuals should be eliminated from consideration. To check for correlation in the residuals, construct the ACF and the PACF of the *residuals* of the estimated model. You can then use (2.41) and (2.42) to determine whether any or all of the residual autocorrelations or partial autocorrelations are statistically significant.[4] Although there is no significance level that is deemed "most appropriate," be wary of any model yielding (1) several residual correlations that are marginally significant and (2) a Q-statistic that is barely significant at the 10 percent level. In such circumstances, it is usually possible to formulate a better performing model. If there are sufficient observations, fitting the same ARMA model to each of two subsamples can provide useful information concerning the assumption that the data-generating process is unchanging. In the AR(2) model that was estimated in the last section, the sample was split in half. In general, suppose you estimated an ARMA(p, q) model using a sample size of T observations. Denote the sum of the squared residuals as SSR. Divide the T observations into two subsamples with t_m observations in the first and $t_n = T - t_m$ observations in the second. Use each subsample to estimate the two models

$$y_t = a_0(1) + a_1(1)y_{t-1} + \ldots + a_p(1)y_{t-p} + \varepsilon_t + \beta_1(1)\varepsilon_{t-1} + \ldots + \beta_q(1)\varepsilon_{t-q}$$
$$\text{using } t_1, \ldots, t_m$$

$$y_t = a_0(2) + a_1(2)y_{t-1} + \ldots + a_p(2)y_{t-p} + \varepsilon_t + \beta_1(2)\varepsilon_{t-1} + \ldots + \beta_q(2)\varepsilon_{t-q}$$
$$\text{using } t_{m+1}, \ldots, t_T$$

Let the sum of the squared residuals from each model be SSR_1 and SSR_2 respectively. To test the restriction that all coefficients are equal [i.e., $a_0(1) = a_0(2)$ and $a_1(1) = a_1(2)$ and ... $a_p(1) = a_p(2)$ and $\beta_1(1) = \beta_1(2)$ and ... $\beta_q(1) = \beta_q(2)$], use an F-test and form[5]

$$F = \frac{(SSR - SSR_1 - SSR_2)/n}{(SSR_1 + SSR_2)/(T - 2n)} \qquad (2.47)$$

where n = number of parameters estimated ($n = p + q + 1$ if an intercept is included and $p + q$ otherwise) and the number of degrees of freedom are (n, $T - 2n$).

Intuitively, if the restriction is not binding (i.e., if the coefficients are equal), the sum $SSR_1 + SSR_2$ should equal the sum of the squared residuals from the entire sample estimation. Hence, F should equal zero. The larger the calculated value of F, the more restrictive is the assumption that the coefficients are equal.

Similarly, a model can be estimated over only a portion of the data set. The estimated model can then be used to forecast the known values of the series. The sum of the squared forecast errors is a useful way to compare the adequacy of alternative models. Those models with poor *out-of-sample* forecasts should be eliminated. Some of the details in constructing out-of-sample forecasts are discussed in the next section.

9. PROPERTIES OF FORECASTS

Perhaps the most important use of an ARMA model is to forecast future values of the $\{y_t\}$ sequence. To simplify the following discussion, it is assumed that the actual data-generating process and the current and past realizations of the $\{\varepsilon_t\}$ and $\{y_t\}$ sequences are known to the researcher. First consider the forecasts from the AR(1) model $y_t = a_0 + a_1 y_{t-1} + \varepsilon_t$. Updating one period, we obtain

$$y_{t+1} = a_0 + a_1 y_t + \varepsilon_{t+1}$$

If you know the coefficients a_0 and a_1, you can forecast y_{t+1} conditioned on the information available at period t as

$$E_t y_{t+1} = a_0 + a_1 y_t \qquad (2.48)$$

where $E_t y_{t+j}$ is a short-hand way to write the conditional expectation of y_{t+j} given the information available at t.

Formally, $E_t y_{t+j} = E(y_{t+j} \mid y_t, y_{t-1}, y_{t-2}, \ldots, \varepsilon_t, \varepsilon_{t-1}, \ldots)$.

In the same way, since $y_{t+2} = a_0 + a_1 y_{t+1} + \varepsilon_{t+2}$, the forecast of y_{t+2} conditioned on the information available at period t is

$$E_t y_{t+2} = a_0 + a_1 E_t y_{t+1}$$

and using (2.48)

$$E_t y_{t+2} = a_0 + a_1(a_0 + a_1 y_t)$$

Thus, the forecast of y_{t+1} can be used to forecast y_{t+2}. The point is that forecasts can be constructed using forward iteration; the forecast of y_{t+j} can be used to forecast y_{t+j+1}. Since $y_{t+j+1} = a_0 + a_1 y_{t+j} + \varepsilon_{t+j+1}$, it immediately follows that

$$E_t y_{t+j+1} = a_0 + a_1 E_t y_{t+j} \qquad (2.49)$$

From (2.48) and (2.49) it should be clear that it is possible to obtain the entire sequence of j-step-ahead forecasts by forward iteration. Consider

$$E_t y_{t+j} = a_0(1 + a_1 + a_1^2 + \ldots + a_1^{j-1}) + a_1^j y_t$$

This equation, called the **forecast function**, expresses all of the j-step-ahead forecasts as a function of the information set in period t. Unfortunately, the quality of the forecasts declines as we forecast further out into the future. Think of (2.49) as a first-order difference equation in the $\{E_t y_{t+j}\}$ sequence. Since $|a_1| < 1$, the difference equation is stable, and it is straightforward to find the particular solution to the difference equation. If we take the limit of $E_t y_{t+j}$ as $j \rightarrow \infty$, we find that $E_t y_{t+j} \rightarrow a_0/(1 - a_1)$. This result is really quite general: *For any stationary ARMA model, the conditional forecast of y_{t+j} converges to the unconditional mean as $j \rightarrow \infty$.*

Because the forecasts from an ARMA model will not be perfectly accurate, it is important to consider the properties of the forecast errors. Forecasting from time period t, we can define the j-step-ahead forecast error—$e_t(j)$—as the difference between the realized value of y_{t+j} and the forecasted value

$$e_t(j) \equiv y_{t+j} - E_t y_{t+j}$$

Hence, the one-step-ahead forecast error is $e_t(1) = y_{t+1} - E_t y_{t+1} = \varepsilon_{t+1}$ (i.e., the "unforecastable" portion of y_{t+1} given the information available in t).

To find the two-step-ahead forecast error, we need to form $e_t(2) = y_{t+2} - E_t y_{t+2}$. Since $y_{t+2} = a_0 + a_1 y_{t+1} + \varepsilon_{t+2}$ and $E_t y_{t+2} = a_0 + a_1 E_t y_{t+1}$, it follows that

$$e_t(2) = a_1(y_{t+1} - E_t y_{t+1}) + \varepsilon_{t+2} = \varepsilon_{t+2} + a_1 \varepsilon_{t+1}$$

You should take a few moments to demonstrate that for the AR(1) model, the j-step-ahead forecast error is given by

$$e_t(j) = \varepsilon_{t+j} + a_1 \varepsilon_{t+j-1} + a_1^2 \varepsilon_{t+j-2} + a_1^3 \varepsilon_{t+j-3} + \ldots + a_1^{j-1} \varepsilon_{t+1} \qquad (2.50)$$

Since the mean of (2.50) is zero, the forecasts are unbiased estimates of each value y_{t+j}. The proof is trivial. Since $E_t \varepsilon_{t+j} = E_t \varepsilon_{t+j-1} = \ldots = E_t \varepsilon_{t+1} = 0$, the conditional expectation of (2.50) is $E_t e_t(j) = 0$. Since the expected value of the forecast error is zero, the forecasts are unbiased.

Although unbiased, the forecasts from an ARMA model are necessarily inaccurate. To find the variance of the forecast error, continue to assume that the elements of the $\{\varepsilon_t\}$ sequence are independent with a variance equal to σ^2. Hence, from (2.50) the variance of the forecast error is

$$\text{Var}[e_t(j)] = \sigma^2[1 + a_1^2 + a_1^4 + a_1^6 + \ldots + a_1^{2(j-1)}] \qquad (2.51)$$

Thus, the one-step-ahead forecast error variance is σ^2, the two-step-ahead forecast error variance is $\sigma^2(1 + a_1^2)$, and so forth. The essential point to note is that the variance of the forecast error is an increasing function of j. As such, you can have more confidence in short-term forecasts than in long-term forecasts. In the limit as $j \rightarrow \infty$, the forecast error variance converges to $\sigma^2/(1 - a_1^2)$; hence, the forecast error variance converges to the unconditional variance of the $\{y_t\}$ sequence.

Moreover, assuming the $\{\varepsilon_t\}$ sequence is normally distributed, you can place confidence intervals around the forecasts. The one-step-ahead forecast of y_{t+1} is $a_0 + a_1 y_t$

and the forecast error is σ^2. As such, the 95 percent confidence interval for the one-step-ahead forecast can be constructed as

$$a_0 + a_1y_t \pm 1.96\sigma$$

We can construct a confidence interval for the two-step-ahead forecast error in the same way. From (2.49), the two-step-ahead forecast is $a_0(1 + a_1) + a_1^2 y_t$ and (2.51) indicates that var$[e_t(2)]$ is $\sigma^2(1 + a_1^2)$. Thus, the 95 percent confidence interval for the two-step-ahead forecast is

$$a_0(1 + a_1) + a_1^2 y_t \pm 1.96\sigma(1 + a_1^2)^{1/2}$$

Higher-Order Models

To generalize the discussion, it is possible to use the iterative technique to derive the forecasts for any ARMA(p, q) model. To keep the algebra simple, consider the ARMA(2, 1) model

$$y_t = a_0 + a_1y_{t-1} + a_2y_{t-2} + \varepsilon_t + \beta_1\varepsilon_{t-1} \tag{2.52}$$

Updating one period yields

$$y_{t+1} = a_0 + a_1y_t + a_2y_{t-1} + \varepsilon_{t+1} + \beta_1\varepsilon_t$$

If we continue to assume that (1) all coefficients are known; (2) all variables subscripted t, $t-1$, $t-2$, ... are known at period t; and (3) $E_t\,\varepsilon_{t+j} = 0$ for $j > 0$, the conditional expectation of y_{t+1} is

$$E_ty_{t+1} = a_0 + a_1y_t + a_2y_{t-1} + \beta_1\varepsilon_t \tag{2.53}$$

Equation (2.53) is the one-step-ahead forecast of y_{t+1}. The one-step-ahead forecast error is the difference between y_{t+1} and E_ty_{t+1} so that $e_t(1) = \varepsilon_{t+1}$. To find the two-step-ahead forecast, update (2.52) by two periods

$$y_{t+2} = a_0 + a_1y_{t+1} + a_2y_t + \varepsilon_{t+2} + \beta_1\varepsilon_{t+1}$$

The conditional expectation of y_{t+2} is

$$E_ty_{t+2} = a_0 + a_1E_ty_{t+1} + a_2y_t \tag{2.54}$$

Equation (2.54) expresses the two-step-ahead forecast in terms of the one-step-ahead forecast and current value of y_t. Combining (2.53) and (2.54) yields

$$E_ty_{t+2} = a_0 + a_1[a_0 + a_1y_t + a_2y_{t-1} + \beta_1\varepsilon_t] + a_2y_t$$
$$= a_0(1 + a_1) + [a_1^2 + a_2]y_t + a_1a_2y_{t-1} + a_1\beta_1\varepsilon_t$$

To find the two-step-ahead forecast error, subtract (2.54) from y_{t+2}. Thus,

$$e_t(2) = a_1(y_{t+1} - E_ty_{t+1}) + \varepsilon_{t+2} + \beta_1\varepsilon_{t+1} \tag{2.55}$$

Since $y_{t+1} - E_ty_{t+1}$ is the one-step-ahead forecast error, we can write the forecast error as

$$e_t(2) = (a_1 + \beta_1)\varepsilon_{t+1} + \varepsilon_{t+2} \tag{2.56}$$

Finally, all j-step-ahead forecasts can be obtained from

$$E_ty_{t+j} = a_0 + a_1E_ty_{t+j-1} + a_2E_ty_{t+j-2}, j \geq 2 \tag{2.57}$$

Equation (2.57) suggests that the forecasts will satisfy a second-order difference equation. As long as the characteristic roots of (2.57) lie inside the unit circle, the forecasts will converge to the unconditional mean: $a_0/(1 - a_1 - a_2)$. We can use (2.57) to find the j-step-ahead forecast errors. Since $y_{t+j} = a_0 + a_1 y_{t+j-1} + a_2 y_{t+j-2} + \varepsilon_{t+j} + \beta_1 \varepsilon_{t+j-1}$, the j-step-ahead forecast error is

$$
\begin{aligned}
e_t(j) &= a_1(y_{t+j-1} - E_t y_{t+j-1}) + a_2(y_{t+j-2} - E_t y_{t+j-2}) + \varepsilon_{t+j} + \beta_1 \varepsilon_{t+j-1} \\
&= a_1 e_t(j-1) + a_2 e_t(j-2) + \varepsilon_{t+j} + \beta_1 \varepsilon_{t+j-1}
\end{aligned}
\tag{2.58}
$$

In practice, you will not know the actual order of the ARMA process or the actual values of the coefficients of that process. Instead, to create out-of-sample forecasts, it is necessary to use the estimated coefficients from what you believe to be the most appropriate form of an ARMA model. The rule of thumb is that forecasts from an ARMA model should never be trusted if the model is estimated with fewer than 50 observations. Suppose you have T observations of the $\{y_t\}$ sequence and choose to fit an ARMA(2, 1) model to the data. Let a hat or caret (i.e.: ^) over a parameter denote the estimated value of a parameter, and let $\{\hat{\varepsilon}_t\}$ denote the residuals of the estimated model. Hence, the estimated ARMA(2, 1) model can be written as

$$
y_t = \hat{a}_0 + \hat{a}_1 y_{t-1} + \hat{a}_2 y_{t-2} + \hat{\varepsilon}_t + \hat{\beta}_1 \hat{\varepsilon}_{t-1}
$$

Given that the sample contains T observations, the out-of-sample forecasts are easily constructed. For example, you can use (2.53) to forecast the value of y_{T+1} conditional on the T observations as

$$
E_T y_{T+1} = \hat{a}_0 + \hat{a}_1 y_T + \hat{a}_2 y_{T-1} + \hat{\beta}_1 \hat{\varepsilon}_T
\tag{2.59}
$$

Once you know the values of $\hat{a}_0, \hat{a}_1, \hat{a}_2$, and $\hat{\beta}_1$, (2.59) can easily be constructed using the actual values y_T, y_{T-1}, and $\hat{\varepsilon}_T$ (i.e., the last residual of your estimated model). Similarly, the forecast of y_{T+2} can be constructed as

$$
E_T y_{T+2} = \hat{a}_0 + \hat{a}_1 E_T y_{T+1} + \hat{a}_2 y_T
$$

where $E_T y_{T+1}$ is the forecast from (2.59).

Given these two forecasts, all subsequent forecasts can be obtained from the difference equation

$$
E_T y_{T+j} = \hat{a}_0 + \hat{a}_1 E_T y_{T+j-1} + \hat{a}_2 E_T y_{T+j-2} \quad \text{for } j \geq 2
$$

Unfortunately, it is much more difficult to construct confidence intervals for the forecast errors. Not only is it necessary to include the effects of the stochastic variation in the future values of $\{y_{T+i}\}$, it is also necessary to incorporate the fact that the coefficients are estimated with error.

Forecast Evaluation

Now that you have estimated a series and have forecasted its future values, the obvious question is, "How good are my forecasts?" Typically, there will be several plausible models that you can select to use for your forecasts. Do not be fooled into thinking that the one with the best fit is the one that will forecast the best. To make a simple point, suppose you wanted to forecast the future values of the ARMA(2, 1) process given by (2.52). If you could forecast the value of y_{T+1} using (2.53), you would obtain the one-step-ahead forecast error

$$e_T(1) = y_{T+1} - a_0 - a_1 y_T - a_2 y_{T-1} - \beta_1 \varepsilon_T = \varepsilon_{T+1}$$

Since the forecast error is the pure *unforecastable* portion of y_{T+1}, no other ARMA model can provide you with superior forecasting performance. However, we need to estimate the parameters of the process, so our forecasts must be made using (2.59). As such, our forecast error will be

$$e_T = y_{T+1} - (\hat{a}_0 + \hat{a}_1 y_T + \hat{a}_2 y_{T-1} + \hat{\beta}_1 \hat{\varepsilon}_T)$$

Clearly, the two forecast errors are not identical. When we forecast using (2.59), the coefficients (and the residuals) are estimated imprecisely. The forecasts made using the estimated model extrapolate this coefficient uncertainty into the future. Since coefficient uncertainty increases as the model becomes more complex, it could be that an estimated AR(1) model forecasts the process given by (2.52) better than an estimated ARMA(2, 1) model.

How do you know which one of several reasonable models has the best forecasting performance? One way to answer these questions is to put the alternative models to a head-to-head test. Since the future values of the series are unknown, you can hold back a portion of the observations from the estimation process. As such, you can estimate the alternative models over the shortened span of data and use these estimates to forecast the observations of the holdback period. You can then compare the properties of the forecast errors from the two models. To take a simple example, suppose that $\{y_t\}$ contains a total of 150 observations and that you are unsure as to whether an AR(1) or an MA(1) model best captures the behavior of the series.

One way to proceed is to use the first 100 observations to estimate both models and use each to forecast the value of y_{101}. Since you know the actual value of y_{101}, you can construct the forecast error obtained from the AR(1) and from the MA(1). These two forecast errors are precisely those that someone would have made if they had been making a one-step-ahead forecast in period 100. Now, re-estimate an AR(1) and an MA(1) model using the first 101 observations. Although the estimated coefficients will change somewhat, they are those that someone would have obtained in period 101. Use the two models to forecast the value of y_{102}. Given that you know the actual value of y_{102}, you can construct two more forecast errors. Since you know all values of the $\{y_t\}$ sequence through period 150, you can continue this process so as to obtain two series of one-step-ahead forecast errors, each containing 50 observations. To keep the notation simple, let $\{f_{1i}\}$ and $\{f_{2i}\}$ denote the sequence of forecasts from the AR(1) and the MA(1), respectively. Similarly, $\{e_{1i}\}$ and $\{e_{2i}\}$ denote the sequences of forecast errors from the AR(1) and the MA(1), respectively. If you understand the notation, it should be clear that $f_{11} = E_{100} y_{101}$ is the first forecast using the AR(1), $e_{11} = y_{101} - f_{11}$ is the first forecast error (where the first hold back observation is y_{101}), and $e_{2,50}$ is the last forecast error from the MA(1).

Obviously, it is desirable that the forecast errors have a mean near zero and a small variance. A regression-based method to assess the forecasts is to use the 50 forecasts from the AR(1) to estimate an equation of the form

$$y_{100+t} = a_0 + a_1 f_{1t} + v_{1t}$$

If the forecasts are unbiased, an F-test should allow you to impose the restriction $a_0 = 0$ and $a_1 = 1$. Similarly, the residual series $\{v_{1t}\}$ should act as a white-noise process. It is a good idea to plot $\{v_{1t}\}$ against $\{y_{100+t}\}$ to determine if there are periods in which your forecasts are especially poor. Now repeat the process with the forecasts from the MA(1). In particular, use the 50 forecasts from the MA(1) to estimate

$$y_{100+t} = b_0 + b_1 f_{2t} + v_{2t} \qquad\qquad t = 1, \ldots, 50$$

Again, if you use an F-test, you should not be able to reject the joint hypothesis $b_0 = 0$ and $b_1 = 1$. If the significance levels from the two F-tests are similar, you might select the model with the smallest residual variance; that is, select the AR(1) if $\mathrm{var}(v_{1t}) < \mathrm{var}(v_{2t})$.

More generally, you might want to have a holdback period that differs from 50 observations. With a very small sample, it may not be possible to hold back 50 observations. Small samples are a problem since Ashley (1997) shows that very large samples are often necessary to reveal a significant difference between the out-of-sample forecasting performances of similar models. Hence, you need to have enough observations to have well-estimated coefficients for the in-sample period and enough out-of-sample forecasts so that the test has good power. If you have a large sample, it is typical to hold back as much as 50 percent of the data set. Also, you might want to use j-step-ahead forecasts instead of one-step-ahead forecasts. For example, if you have quarterly data and want to forecast one year into the future, you can perform the analysis using four-step-ahead forecasts. Nevertheless, once you have the two sequences of forecast errors, you can compare their properties.

Instead of using a regression-based approach, many researchers would select the model with the smallest mean square prediction error (MSPE). If there are H observations in the holdback periods, the MSPE for the AR(1) can be calculated as

$$MSPE = \frac{1}{H}\sum_{i=1}^{H} e_{1i}^{2}$$

Several methods have been proposed to determine whether one MSPE is statistically different from the other. If you put the larger of the two MSPEs in the numerator, a standard recommendation is to use the F-statistic

$$F = \sum_{i=1}^{H} e_{1i}^{2} \Big/ \sum_{i=1}^{H} e_{2i}^{2} \qquad\qquad (2.60)$$

The intuition is that the value of F will equal unity if the forecast errors from the two models are identical. A very large value of F implies that the forecast errors from the first model are substantially larger than those from the second. Under the null hypothesis of equal forecasting performance, (2.60) has a standard F-distribution with (H, H) degrees of freedom if the following three assumptions hold:

1. The forecast errors have zero mean and are normally distributed
2. The forecast errors are serially uncorrelated
3. The forecast errors are contemporaneously uncorrelated with each other

Although it is common practice to assume that the $\{\varepsilon_t\}$ sequence is normally distributed, it is not necessarily the case that the forecast errors are normally distributed with a mean value of zero. Similarly, the forecasts may be serially correlated; this is particularly true if you use multi-step-ahead forecasts. For example, equation (2.56) indicated that the two-step-ahead forecast error for y_{t+2} is

$$e_t(2) = (a_1 + \beta_1)\varepsilon_{t+1} + \varepsilon_{t+2}$$

and updating by one period yields the two-step-ahead forecast error for y_{t+3}

$$e_{t+1}(2) = (a_1 + \beta_1)\varepsilon_{t+2} + \varepsilon_{t+3}$$

It should be clear that the two forecast errors are correlated. In particular,

$$E[e_t(2)e_{t+1}(2)] = (a_1 + \beta_1)\sigma^2$$

The point is that predicting y_{t+2} from the perspective of period t and predicting y_{t+3} from the perspective of period $t+1$ both contain an error due to the presence of ε_{t+2}. However, for $i > 1$, $E[e_t(2)e_{t+i}(2)] = 0$ since there are no overlapping forecasts. Hence, the autocorrelations of the two-step-ahead forecast errors cut to zero after lag 1. You should be able to demonstrate the general result that j-step-ahead forecast errors act as an MA($j-1$) process.

Finally, the forecast errors from the two alternative models will usually be highly correlated with each other. For example, a negative realization of ε_{t+1} will tend to cause the forecasts from both models to be too high. Unfortunately, the violation of any one of these assumptions means that the ratio of the MSPEs in (2.60) does not have an F-distribution.

THE GRANGER–NEWBOLD TEST   Granger and Newbold (1976) show how to overcome the problem of contemporaneously correlated forecast errors. Use the two sequences of forecast errors to form

$$x_t = e_{1t} + e_{2t} \text{ and } z_t = e_{1t} - e_{2t}$$

Given that the first two assumptions above are valid, under the null hypothesis of equal forecast accuracy, x_t and z_t should be uncorrelated

$$\rho_{xz} = Ex_t z_t = E(e_{1t}^2 - e_{2t}^2)$$

Model 1 has a larger MSPE if ρ_{xz} is positive and model 2 has a larger MSPE if ρ_{xz} is negative. Let r_{xz} denote the sample correlation coefficient between $\{x_t\}$ and $\{z_t\}$. Granger and Newbold (1976) show that

$$r_{xz} / \sqrt{(1 - r_{xz}^2)/(H-1)} \tag{2.61}$$

has a t-distribution with $H - 1$ degrees of freedom. Thus, if r_{xz} is statistically different from zero, model 1 has a larger MSPE if r_{xz} is positive and model 2 has a larger MSPE if r_{xz} is negative.

THE DIEBOLD–MARIANO TEST   There is a very large literature trying to extend the Granger–Newbold test so as to relax assumptions 1 and 2. Moreover, applied econometricians might be interested in measures of forecasting performance other than the sum of squared errors. Indeed, it should be clear that using the sum of squared errors as a criterion makes sense only if the loss from making an incorrect forecast is quadratic. However, there are many other possibilities. For example, if your loss depends on the size of the forecast error, you should be concerned with the absolute values of the forecast errors. Alternatively, an options trader receives a pay-off of zero if the value of the underlying asset lies below the strike price but receives a one-dollar payoff for each dollar the asset price rises above the strike price. Diebold and Mariano (1995) have developed a test that relaxes assumptions 1 to 3 and allows for an objective function that is not quadratic.

If we consider only one-step-ahead forecasts, we can eliminate the subscript j. As such, we can let the loss from a forecast error in period i be denoted by $g(e_i)$. In the typical case of mean squared errors, the loss is e_i^2. Nevertheless, to allow the loss function to be general, we can write the differential loss in period i from using model 1 versus model 2 as $d_i = g(e_{1i}) - g(e_{2i})$. The mean loss can be obtained as

$$\bar{d} = \frac{1}{H} \sum_{i=1}^{H} [g(e_{1i}) - g(e_{2i})] \tag{2.62}$$

Under the null hypothesis of equal forecast accuracy, the value of $\bar{d}$ is zero. Since $\bar{d}$ is the mean of the individual losses, under fairly weak conditions, the central limit theorem implies that $\bar{d}$ should have a normal distribution. Hence, it is not necessary to assume that the individual forecast errors are normally distributed. Thus, if we knew $\text{var}(\bar{d})$, we could construct the ratio $\bar{d}/\sqrt{\text{var}(\bar{d})}$ and test the null hypothesis of equal forecast accuracy using a standard normal distribution. In practice, the implementation of the test is complicated by the fact that we need to estimate $\text{var}(\bar{d})$.

If the $\{d_i\}$ series is serially uncorrelated with a sample variance of γ_0, the estimate of $\text{var}(\bar{d})$ is simply $\gamma_0/(H-1)$. Since we use the estimated value of the variance, the expression $\bar{d}/\sqrt{\gamma_0/(H-1)}$ has a t-distribution with $H-1$ degrees of freedom.

There is a very large literature on the best way to estimate the standard deviation of $\bar{d}$ in the presence of serial correlation. Many of the technical details are not appropriate here. Diebold and Mariano let γ_i denote the i-th autocovariance of the d_t sequence. Suppose that the first q values of γ_i are different from zero. The variance of $\bar{d}$ can be approximated by $\text{var}(\bar{d}) = [\gamma_0 + 2\gamma_1 + \dots + 2\gamma_q](H-1)^{-1}$; the standard deviation is the square root. As such, Harvey, Leybourne, and Newbold (1998) recommend constructing the Diebold–Mariano (DM) statistic as

$$\text{DM} = \bar{d}/\sqrt{(\gamma_0 + 2\gamma_1 + \dots + 2\gamma_q)/(H-1)} \tag{2.63}$$

Compare the sample value of (2.63) to a t-statistic with $H-1$ degrees of freedom.[6] It is also possible to use the method for j-step-ahead forecasts. If $\{e_{1t}\}$ and $\{e_{2t}\}$ denote two sequences of j-step-ahead forecasts, the DM statistic is

$$\text{DM} = \bar{d}/\sqrt{(\gamma_0 + 2\gamma_1 + \dots + 2\gamma_q)/[H+1-2j+H^{-1}j(j-1)]}$$

An example showing the appropriate use of the Granger–Newbold and Diebold–Mariano tests is provided in the next section.

10. A MODEL OF THE PRODUCER PRICE INDEX

The ARMA estimations performed in Section 7 were almost too straightforward. In practice, we rarely find a data series precisely conforming to a theoretical ACF or PACF. This section is intended to illustrate some of the ambiguities frequently encountered in the Box–Jenkins technique. These ambiguities may lead two equally skilled econometricians to estimate and forecast the same series using very different ARMA processes. Many view the necessity of relying on the researcher's judgment and experience as a serious weakness of a procedure that is designed to be scientific. Yet, if you make reasonable choices, you will select models that come very close to mimicking the actual data-generating process.

It is useful to illustrate the Box–Jenkins modeling procedure by estimating a quarterly model of the U.S. Producer Price Index (PPI). The data used in this section are the series labeled PPI on the file QUARTERLY.XLS. Exercise 11 at the end of this chapter asks you to reproduce the results reported below.

Panel (*a*) of Figure 2.5 clearly reveals that there is little point in modeling the series as being stationary; there is a decidedly positive trend or drift throughout the period 1960Q1 to 2002Q1. The first difference of the series seems to have a constant mean, although inspection of Panel (*b*) suggests that the variance is an increasing function of time. As shown in Panel (*c*), the first difference of the logarithm (denoted by $\Delta lppi$) is the most likely candidate to be covariance stationary. Moreover, there is a strong economic reason to be interested in the logarithmic change since $\Delta lppi_t$ is a measure of inflation. However, the large volatility of the PPI accompanying the oil price shocks in the 1970s should make us somewhat wary of the assumption that the process is covariance stationary. At this point, some researchers would make additional transformations intended to reduce the volatility exhibited in the 1970s. However, it seems reasonable to estimate a model of the $\{\Delta lppi_t\}$ sequence without any further transformations. As always, you should maintain a healthy skepticism of the accuracy of your model.

Before reading on, you should examine the autocorrelation and partial autocorrelation functions of the $\{\Delta lppi_t\}$ sequence shown in Figure 2.6. Try to identify the tentative models that you would want to estimate. In making your decision, note the following:

1. The ACF and PACF converge to zero reasonably quickly. We do not want to *overdifference* the data and try to model the $\{\Delta^2 lppi_t\}$ sequence.

2. The theoretical ACF of a pure MA(q) process cuts off to zero at lag q and the theoretical ACF of an AR(1) model decays geometrically. Examination of Figure 2.6 suggests that neither of these specifications seems appropriate for the sample data.

3. The ACF does not decay geometrically. The value of ρ_1 is 0.603 and the values of ρ_2, ρ_3, and ρ_4 are 0.494, 0.451, and 0.446, respectively. Thus, the ACF is suggestive of an AR(2) process or a process with both autoregressive and moving average components. The PACF is such that $\phi_{11} = 0.604$ and cuts off to 0.203 abruptly (i.e., $\phi_{22} = 0.203$). Overall, the PACF suggests that we should consider models such that $p = 1$ and $p = 2$.

Panel (*a*): The Producer Price Index: (1995 = 100)

Panel (*b*): First Difference of the PPI

Panel (*c*): Logarithmic Difference of the PPI

FIGURE 2.5 U.S. Producer Price Index (1995 = 100)

4. Note the jump in ACF after lag 4 and the small jump in the PACF at lag 4 ($\phi_{44} = 0.148$ while $\phi_{55} = -0.114$). Since we are using quarterly data, we might want to incorporate a seasonal factor at lag 4.

Points 1 to 4 suggest an ARMA(1,1) or an AR(2) model. In addition, we might want to consider models with a seasonal term at lag 4. Since computing time is

FIGURE 2.6   ACF and PACF for the Logarithmic Change in the PPI

inexpensive, we can estimate a variety of models and compare their results. Table 2.4 reports estimates of six tentative models. To ensure comparability, all were estimated over the same sample period.[7] Note the following points:

1. The estimated AR(1) model confirms our analysis conducted in the identification stage. Even though the estimated value of a_1 (0.603) is less than unity in absolute value and almost four standard deviations from zero, the AR(1) specification is inadequate. Forming the Ljung–Box Q-statistic for 4 lags of the residuals yields a value of 13.9; we can reject the null that $Q(4) = 0$ at the 1 percent significance level. Hence, the lagged residuals of this model exhibit substantial serial autocorrelation. As such, we must eliminate this model from consideration.

2. The AR(2) model is an improvement over the AR(1) specification. The estimated coefficients ($a_1 = 0.480$ and $a_2 = 0.209$) are each significantly different from zero at conventional levels and imply characteristic roots in the unit circle. However, there is some ambiguity about the information content of the residuals. The Q-statistics indicate that the autocorrelations of the residuals are not statistically significant at the 5 percent level but are significant at the 10 percent level. As measured by the AIC and SBC, the fit of the AR(2) model is superior to that of the AR(1). Overall, the AR(2) model dominates the AR(1) specification.

3. The ARMA(1, 1) specification is superior to the AR(2) model. The estimated coefficients are of high quality (with t-values of 14.9 and –4.41). The estimated value of a_1 is positive and less than unity and the Q-statistics indicate that the autocorrelations of the residuals are not significant at conventional levels of statistical significance. Moreover, all goodness-of-fit measures select the ARMA(1, 1) specification over the AR(2) model. Thus, there is little reason to maintain the AR(2) specification.

Table 2.4 Estimates of the PPI

	$p = 1$ $q = 0$	$p = 2$ $q = 0$	$p = 1$ $q = 1$	$p = 1$ $q = 1, 4$	$p = 2$ $q = 1$	$p = 2$ $q = \|4\|$
a_0	0.003 (3.28)	0.003 (2.48)	0.003 (2.27)	0.003 (2.31)	0.003 (2.23)	0.003 (2.87)
a_1	0.603 (9.69)	0.480 (6.24)	0.871 (14.9)	0.768 (9.46)	0.949 (3.97)	0.460 (5.87)
a_2		0.209 (2.65)			−0.061 (−0.348)	0.163 (2.03)
β_1			−0.455 (−4.41)	−0.358 (−3.41)	−0.517 (−2.33)	
β_4				0.297 (3.63)		0.261 (3.23)
SSR	0.0210	0.0201	0.0196	0.0188	0.0196	0.0191
AIC	−637.2	−642.3	−646.5	−651.4	−644.7	−648.3
SBC	−631.0	−632.9	−637.2	−639.0	−632.3	−635.9
$Q(4)$	13.9 (0.008)	8.5 (0.074)	4.5 (0.339)	1.4 (0.846)	4.3 (0.367)	2.1 (0.720)
$Q(8)$	21.9 (0.005)	15.3 (0.053)	11.5 (0.176)	7.3 (0.505)	11.4 (0.181)	8.3 (0.401)
$Q(12)$	27.2 (0.007)	20.7 (0.054)	18.0 (0.104)	11.2 (0.513)	18.7 (0.096)	12.2 (0.426)

Notes:
Each coefficient is reported with the associated t-statistic for the null hypothesis that the estimated value is equal to zero.
SSR is the sum of squared residuals.
$Q(n)$ reports the Ljung–Box Q-statistic for the autocorrelations of the n residuals of the estimated model. Significance levels are in parentheses.
$\|4\|$ denotes that only the fourth MA term was included in the estimated model.

4. In order to account for the possibility of seasonality, we estimated the ARMA(1, 1) model with an additional moving average coefficient at lag 4—that is, we estimated a model of the form $y_t = a_0 + a_1 y_{t-1} + \varepsilon_t + \beta_1 \varepsilon_{t-1} + \beta_4 \varepsilon_{t-4}$. Other seasonal patterns are considered in the next section. For now, note that the additive expression $\beta_4 \varepsilon_{t-4}$ is often preferable to an additive autoregressive term of the form $a_4 y_{t-4}$. For truly seasonal shocks, the expression $\beta_4 \varepsilon_{t-4}$ best captures spikes—not decay—at the quarterly lags. The slope coefficients of the estimated ARMA(1, (1, 4)) model are all highly significant with t-statistics of 9.46, −3.41, and 3.63.[8] The Q-statistics of the residuals are all very low, implying that the autocorrelations are not statistically different from zero. Moreover, the AIC and SBC select this model over the ARMA(1, 1) model.

5. In contrast, the ARMA(2, 1) contains a superfluous coefficient. The t-statistic for a_2 is sufficiently low that we should eliminate this model.

6. Since a seasonal term seems to fit the data well, we estimated an equation of the form $y_t = a_0 + a_1 y_{t-1} + a_2 y_{t-2} + \varepsilon_t + \beta_4 \varepsilon_{t-4}$. Notice that all coefficients have t-values in excess of 2.0 and that the Q-statistics are not significant. However, as measured by the AIC and the SBC, this model does not fit the data as well as the ARMA(1, (1, 4)).

Having identified and estimated a plausible model, we want to perform additional diagnostic checks of model adequacy. Due to the high volatility in the 1970s, the sample was split into the two subperiods: $1960Q3 - 1971Q4$ and $1972Q1 - 2002Q1$. Model estimates for each subperiod are

$$\Delta lppi_t = 0.002 + 0.621\Delta lppi_{t-1} + \varepsilon_t - 0.329\varepsilon_{t-1} + 0.263\varepsilon_{t-4} \qquad (1960Q3 - 1971Q4)$$

and

$$\Delta lppi_t = 0.002 + 0.763\Delta lppi_{t-1} + \varepsilon_t - 0.350\varepsilon_{t-1} + 0.301\varepsilon_{t-4} \qquad (1972Q1 - 2002Q1)$$

The coefficients of the two models appear to be quite similar; we can formally test for the equality of coefficients using (2.47). Respectively, the sum of squared residuals for the two models are $SSR_1 = 0.001267$ and $SSR_2 = 0.017551$. Estimating the model over the full sample period yields $SSR = 0.018870$. Since $T = 167$ and $n = 4$ (including the intercept means that there are four estimated coefficients), (2.47) becomes

$$F = [(0.018870 - 0.001267 - 0.017551)/4] / [(0.001267 + 0.017551)/(167 - 8)]$$
$$= 0.10984$$

With 4 degrees of freedom in the numerator and 159 in the denominator, we cannot reject the null of no structural change in the coefficients (i.e., we accept the hypothesis that there is no change in the structural coefficients).

Out-of-Sample Forecasts

We can assess the forecasting performance of the ARMA(1, 1) and ARMA(1, (1, 4)) by using the Granger–Newbold and Diebold–Mariano tests discussed in the previous section. Given that the data set contains a total of 167 usable observations, it is possible to use a holdback period of 50 observations. This way, there are at least 117 observations in each of the estimated models and an adequate number of out-of-sample forecasts. First, the two models were estimated using all available observations through $1989Q3$ and two one-step-ahead forecasts were obtained. The actual value of $\Delta lppi_{1989:4} = 0.00385$; the ARMA(1, 1) predicted a value of 0.00715 and the ARMA(1, (1, 4)) model predicted a value of 0.00415. Thus, the forecast of the ARMA(1, (1, 4)) is superior to that of the ARMA(1, 1) for this first period. An additional 49 forecasts were obtained for periods $1990Q1$ to $2002Q1$. Let e_{1t} denote the forecast errors from the ARMA(1, 1) model and e_{2t} denote the forecast errors from the ARMA(1, (1, 4)) model. The mean of e_{1t} is -0.00210, the mean of e_{2t} is -0.002250, and the estimated variances are such that $\text{var}(e_{1t}) = 0.000127$ and $\text{var}(e_{2t}) = 0.000133$. As such, there is an advantage in the forecasting performance of the ARMA(1, 1). To ascertain whether this difference is statistically significant, we first use the Granger–Newbold test. Form the x_t and z_t series as $x_t = e_{1t} + e_{2t}$ and $z_t = e_{1t} - e_{2t}$. The correlation coefficient between x_t and z_y is $r_{xz} = -0.0767$. Given that there are 50 observations in the holdback period, form the Granger–Newbold statistic

$$r_{xz} / \sqrt{(1 - r_{xz}^2)/(H - 1)} = -0.0767 / \sqrt{(1 - (-0.0767)^2 / 49} = -0.5387$$

With 49 degrees of freedom, a value of $t = -0.5387$ is not statistically significant. We can conclude that the forecasting performance of the ARMA(1, 1) is not statistically different from that of the ARMA(1, (1, 4)).

We obtain virtually the same answer using the DM statistic. Oftentimes forecasters are concerned about the MSPE. However, there are many other possibilities. In Exercise 11 at the end of this chapter, you will be asked to use the mean absolute error. Now, to illustrate the use of the DM test, suppose that the cost of a forecast error rises extremely quickly in the size of the error. In such circumstances, the loss function might be best represented by the forecast error raised to the fourth power. Hence,

$$d_t = e_{1t}^4 - e_{2t}^4$$

The mean value of the $\{d_t\}$ sequence (i.e., $\bar{d}$) is $-2.995 \cdot 10^{-9}$ and the estimated variance is $4.6487 \cdot 10^{-16}$. Since $H = 50$, we can form the DM-statistic

$$DM = -2.995 \cdot 10^{-9} / (4.6487 \cdot 10^{-16} / 49)^{1/2} = -0.972$$

If there were serial correlation in the $\{d_t\}$ series, we would need to use the specification in (2.62). Toward this end, we would select the statistically significant values of γ_q. However, in this example, we do not need to worry about serial correlation in the $\{d_t\}$ sequence because the Ljung–Box statistics do not indicate that the autocorrelations are significant. The individual autocorrelations are

ρ_1	ρ_2	ρ_3	ρ_4	ρ_5	ρ_6	ρ_7	ρ_8	ρ_9	ρ_{10}	ρ_{11}	ρ_{12}
−0.18	0.06	−0.17	−0.10	0.07	0.12	0.13	−0.05	0.08	0.00	0.12	0.12

Instead, suppose we used the squared forecast errors as a measure of the loss so that $d_t = e_{1t}^2 - e_{2t}^2$. Now $\bar{d} = -5.863 \cdot 10^{-6}$ and the estimated variance is $1.8703 \cdot 10^{-9}$. If you check the autocorrelations, you will find the following:

ρ_1	ρ_2	ρ_3	ρ_4	ρ_5	ρ_6	ρ_7	ρ_8	ρ_9	ρ_{10}	ρ_{11}	ρ_{12}
0.08	−0.09	−0.23	−0.30	0.32	0.16	0.29	0.13	−0.27	−0.06	0.08	0.22

The Ljung–Box $Q(4)$ is not significant at the 5 percent level, but the $Q(8)$ has a *prob*-value of 0.004. If we construct the DM statistic using all 12 autocovariances (recall $\rho_i = \gamma_i / \gamma_0$), we find that $\gamma_0 + 2\gamma_1 + \ldots + 2\gamma_{12} = 5.957 \cdot 10^{-9}$. Thus, the desired value of the DM statistic is

$$DM = -5.863 \cdot 10^{-6} / (5.957 \cdot 10^{-9} / 49)^{1/2} = -0.532$$

If we now compare this value to a t-statistic with 49 degrees of freedom, we conclude that the difference between the forecasting abilities of the two models is not statistically significant. This is not too surprising since Ashley (1997) shows that very large samples are often necessary to reveal a significant difference between the out-of-sample forecasting performances of similar models.

Although the ARMA(1, 1) and ARMA(1, (1, 4)) appear to be adequate, other researchers might have selected a decidedly different model. Consider some of the alternatives:

1. **Trends:** Although the logarithmic change of the PPI appears to be stationary, the ACF converges to zero rather slowly. Moreover, both the

ARMA(1, 1) and ARMA(1, (1, 4)) models yield estimated values of a_1 (0.871 and 0.768, respectively), which are close to unity. Some researchers might have chosen to model the second-order difference of the series. Others might have detrended the data using a deterministic time trend.

2. **Seasonality:** The seasonality of the data was modeled using a moving average term at lag 4. However, there are many other plausible ways to model the seasonality in the data, as will be discussed in the next section. For example, many computer programs are capable of estimating multiplicative seasonal coefficients. Consider the multiplicative seasonal model

$$(1 - a_1L)y_t = (1 + \beta_1 L)(1 + \beta_4 L^4)\varepsilon_t$$

Here the seasonal expression $\beta_4 \varepsilon_{t-4}$ enters the model in a multiplicative, rather than a linear, fashion. Experimenting with various multiplicative seasonal coefficients might be a way to improve forecasting performance.

3. **Volatility:** Given the volatility of the $\{\Delta lppi_t\}$ sequence during the 1970s, the assumption of a constant variance might not be appropriate. Transforming the data using a square root, rather than the logarithm, might be more appropriate. A general class of transformations was proposed by Box and Cox (1964). Suppose that all values of $\{y_t\}$ are positive so that it is possible to construct the transformed $\{y_t^*\}$ sequence as

$$y_t^* = (y_t^\lambda - 1)/\lambda \qquad\qquad \lambda \neq 0$$
$$= \ln(y_t) \qquad\qquad \lambda = 0$$

The common practice is to transform the data using a preselected value of λ. Selecting a value of λ that is close to zero acts to smooth the sequence. As in the PPI example, an ARMA model can be fitted to the transformed data. Although some software programs have the capacity to simultaneously estimate λ along with the other parameters of the ARMA model, this approach has fallen out of fashion. Instead, it is possible to actually model the variance using the methods discussed in Chapter 3.

11. SEASONALITY

Many economic processes exhibit some form of seasonality. The agricultural, construction, and travel sectors have obvious seasonal patterns resulting from their dependence on the weather. Similarly, the Thanksgiving-to-Christmas holiday season has a pronounced influence on the retail trade. In fact, the seasonal variation of a series may account for the preponderance of its total variance. Forecasts that ignore important seasonal patterns will have a high variance. In the last section, we saw how the inclusion of a four-quarter seasonal factor could help improve the model of the PPI. This section expands that discussion by illustrating some of the techniques that can be used to identify seasonal patterns.

Too many people fall into the trap of ignoring seasonality if they are working with **deseasonalized** or **seasonally adjusted** data. Suppose you collect a data set that the U.S. Census Bureau has "seasonally adjusted" using its X-11 method.[9] In principle, the seasonally adjusted data should have the seasonal pattern removed. However, caution is necessary. Although a standardized procedure may be necessary for a government agency reporting hundreds of series, the procedure might not be best for an individual wanting to model a single series. Even if you use seasonally adjusted data, a seasonal pattern might remain. This is particularly true if you do not use the entire span of data; the portion of the data used in your study can display more (or less) seasonality than the overall span. In fact, the PPI sequence used in the previous section had been *deseasonalized* by the Bureau of Economic Analysis. There is another important reason to be concerned about seasonality when using deseasonalized data. Implicit in any method of seasonal adjustment is a two-step procedure. First, the seasonality is removed and second, the autoregressive and moving average coefficients are estimated using Box–Jenkins techniques. As surveyed in Bell and Hillmer (1984), oftentimes the seasonal and the ARMA coefficients are best identified and estimated jointly. In such circumstances, it is wise to avoid using seasonally adjusted data.

Models of Seasonal Data

The Box–Jenkins technique for modeling seasonal data is only a bit different from that of nonseasonal data. The twist introduced by seasonal data of period s is that the seasonal coefficients of the ACF and PACF appear at lags s, $2s$, $3s$, …, rather than at lags 1, 2, 3, …. For example, two purely seasonal models for quarterly data might be

$$y_t = a_4 y_{t-4} + \varepsilon_t \qquad (2.64)$$

and

$$y_t = \varepsilon_t + \beta_4 \varepsilon_{t-4} \qquad (2.65)$$

You can easily convince yourself that the theoretical correlogram for (2.64) is such that: $\rho_i = (a_4)^{i/4}$ if $i/4$ is an integer and $\rho_i = 0$ otherwise; thus, the ACF exhibits decay at lags 4, 8, 12, …. For model (2.65), the ACF exhibits a single spike at lag 4 and all other correlations are zero.

In practice, identification will be complicated by the fact that the seasonal pattern will interact with the nonseasonal pattern in the data. The ACF and PACF for a combined seasonal/nonseasonal process will reflect both elements. Note that the final model of the PPI estimated in the last section had the form

$$y_t = a_1 y_{t-1} + \varepsilon_t + \beta_1 \varepsilon_{t-1} + \beta_4 \varepsilon_{t-4} \qquad (2.66)$$

Alternatively, an autoregressive coefficient at lag 4 might have been used to capture the seasonality

$$y_t = a_1 y_{t-1} + a_4 y_{t-4} + \varepsilon_t + \beta_1 \varepsilon_{t-1}$$

Both of these methods treat the seasonal coefficients additively; an AR or an MA coefficient is added at the seasonal period. **Multiplicative seasonality** allows for the interaction of the ARMA and the seasonal effects. Consider the multiplicative specifications

$$(1 - a_1 L)y_t = (1 + \beta_1 L)(1 + \beta_4 L^4)\varepsilon_t \qquad (2.67)$$

$$(1 - a_1 L)(1 - a_4 L^4)y_t = (1 + \beta_1 L)\varepsilon_t \qquad (2.68)$$

Equation (2.67) differs from (2.66) in that it allows the moving average term at lag 1 to interact with the seasonal moving average effect at lag 4. In the same way, (2.68) allows the autoregressive term at lag 1 to interact with the seasonal autoregressive effect at lag 4. Many researchers prefer the multiplicative form since a rich interaction pattern can be captured with a small number of coefficients. Rewrite (2.67) as

$$y_t = a_1 y_{t-1} + \varepsilon_t + \beta_1 \varepsilon_{t-1} + \beta_4 \varepsilon_{t-4} + \beta_1 \beta_4 \varepsilon_{t-5}$$

Estimating only three coefficients (i.e., a_1, β_1, and β_4) allows us to capture the effects of an autoregressive term and the effects of moving average terms at lags 1, 4, and 5. Of course, you do not really get something for nothing. The estimates of the three moving average coefficients are interrelated. A researcher estimating the unconstrained model $y_t = a_1 y_{t-1} + \varepsilon_t + \beta_1 \varepsilon_{t-1} + \beta_4 \varepsilon_{t-4} + \beta_5 \varepsilon_{t-5}$ would necessarily obtain a smaller residual sum of squares. However, (2.67) is clearly the more parsimonious model. If the unconstrained value of β_5 approximates the product $\beta_1 \beta_4$, the multiplicative model will be preferable. For this reason, most software packages have routines capable of estimating multiplicative models. Otherwise, there are no theoretical grounds leading us to prefer one form of seasonality over another. As illustrated in the last section, experimentation and diagnostic checks are probably the best way to obtain the most appropriate model.

Seasonal Differencing

The Christmas shopping season is accompanied by an unusually large number of transactions, and the Federal Reserve expands the money supply to accommodate the increased demand for money. As shown by the dashed line in Figure 2.7, the U.S. money supply, as measured by M1, has a decidedly upward trend. The series, called M1NSA, is contained on the file QUARTERLY.XLS. You can use the data to follow along with

FIGURE 2.7 The Level and Growth Rate of M1

the discussion below. The logarithmic change, shown by the solid line, appears to be stationary. Nevertheless, there is a clear seasonal pattern in that the value of the fourth quarter for any year is substantially higher than that for the adjacent quarters.

This combination of strong seasonality and nonstationarity is often found in economic data. The ACF for a process with strong seasonality is similar to that for a non-seasonal process; the main difference is that the spikes at lags s, $2s$, $3s$, ... do not exhibit rapid decay. We know that it is necessary to difference (or take the logarithmic change of) a nonstationary process. Similarly, if the autocorrelations at the seasonal lags do not decay, it is necessary to take the seasonal difference so that the other autocorrelations are not dwarfed by the seasonal effects. The ACF and PACF for the growth rate of M1 are shown in Panel (a) of Figure 2.8. For now, just focus on the autocorrelations at the seasonal lags. All seasonal autocorrelations are large and show no tendency to decay. In particular, $\rho_4 = 0.66$, $\rho_8 = 0.52$, $\rho_{12} = 0.43$, $\rho_{16} = 0.42$, $\rho_{20} = 0.47$, and $\rho_{24} = 0.49$. These autocorrelations reflect the fact that the change in M1 from one Christmas season to the next is not as pronounced as the change between the fourth quarter and other quarters.

The first step in the Box–Jenkins method is to transform the data so as to make it stationary. As such, a logarithmic transformation is helpful because it can straighten the nonlinear trend in M1. Let y_t denote the log of M1. As mentioned above, the first difference of the $\{y_t\}$ sequence, illustrated by the solid line in Figure 2.7, appears to be stationary. However, to remove the strong seasonal persistence in the data, we need to take the seasonal difference. For quarterly data, the seasonal difference is $y_t - y_{t-4}$. Since the order of differencing is irrelevant, we can form the transformed sequence

$$m_t = (1 - L)(1 - L^4)y_t$$

FIGURE 2.8 ACF and PACF

Thus, we use the seasonal difference of the first difference. The ACF and PACF for the $\{m_t\}$ sequence are shown in Panel (b) of Figure 2.8; the properties of this series are much more amenable to the Box–Jenkins methodology. The autocorrelation and partial autocorrelations for the first few lags are strongly suggestive of an AR(1) process ($\rho_1 = \phi_{11} = 0.38$, $\rho_2 = 0.16$, and $\phi_{22} = 0.02$). Recall that the ACF for an AR(1) process will decay and the PACF will cut to zero after lag 1. Given that $\rho_4 = -0.28$, $\rho_5 = 0.01$, $\phi_{44} = -0.34$, and $\phi_{55} = 0.28$, there is evidence of remaining seasonality in the $\{m_t\}$ sequence. The seasonal term is most likely to be in the form of an MA coefficient since the autocorrelation cuts to zero whereas the PACF does not. Nevertheless, it is best to estimate several similar models and then select the best. Estimates of the following three models are reported in Table 2.5:

$m_t = a_0 + a_1 m_{t-1} + \varepsilon_t + \beta_4 \varepsilon_{t-4}$ Model 1: AR(1) with Seasonal MA
$m_t = a_0 + (1 + a_1 L)(1 + a_4 L^4) m_{t-1} + \varepsilon_t$ Model 2: Multiplicative Autoregressive
$m_t = a_0 + (1 + \beta_1 L)(1 + \beta_4 L^4) \varepsilon_t$ Model 3: Multiplicative Moving Average

The point estimates of the coefficients all imply stationarity and invertibility. Moreover, all are at least six standard deviations from zero. However, the diagnostic statistics all suggest that model 1 is preferred. Model 1 has the best fit in that it has the lowest sum of squared residuals (SSR). Moreover, the Q-statistics for lags 4, 8, and 12 indicate that the residual autocorrelations are insignificant. In contrast, the residual correlations for model 2 are significant at the long lags [i.e., $Q(8)$ and $Q(12)$ are significant at the 0.007 and 0.002 levels]. This is because the multiplicative seasonal autoregressive (SAR) term does not adequately capture the seasonal pattern. An SAR term implies autoregressive decay from period s into period $s + 1$. In Panel (b) of Figure 2.8, the value

Table 2.5 Three Models of Money Growth

	Model 1	Model 2	Model 3
a_1	0.543	0.492	
	(7.98)	(6.98)	
a_4		−0.437	
		(−5.81)	
β_1			0.460
			(6.30)
β_4	−0.763		−0.752
	(−14.27)		(−13.88)
SSR	0.0161	0.0196	0.0175
AIC	−650.7	−619.4	−637.0
SBC	−641.5	−610.2	−627.8
$Q(4)$	2.03 (0.680)	3.63 (0.458)	21.35 (0.000)
$Q(8)$	6.41 (0.601)	22.20 (0.007)	28.37 (0.000)
$Q(12)$	14.11 (0.294)	30.89 (0.002)	40.04 (0.000)

To ensure comparability, the three models are estimated over the 1963$Q$3–2002$Q$1 period. The estimated intercepts are not reported since all were insignificant from zero.

of ρ_4 is –0.28 but ρ_5 is almost zero. As such, a multiplicative seasonal moving average (SMA) term is more appropriate. Model 3 properly captures the seasonal pattern, but the MA(1) term does not capture the autoregressive decay present at the short lags. Other diagnostic methods, including splitting the sample, suggest that model 1 is appropriate.

The out-of-sample forecasts are shown in Figure 2.9. To create the one- through twelve-step-ahead forecasts, model 1 was estimated over the full sample period 1961Q3 – 2002Q1. The estimated model is

$$m_t = 0.529m_{t-1} + \varepsilon_t - 0.758\varepsilon_{t-4} \tag{2.69}$$

Given that $m_{2002:1} = 0.00795$ and the residual for 2001:02 was 0.0119 (i.e., $\hat{\varepsilon}_{2001Q2} = 0.0119$), the forecast of $m_{2002:2}$ is –0.00490. Now, use this forecast and the value of $\hat{\varepsilon}_{2001Q3}$ to forecast m_{2002Q3}. You can continue in this fashion so as to obtain the out-of-sample forecasts for the $\{m_t\}$ sequence. Although you do not have the residuals for periods beyond 2002Q1, you can simply use their forecasted values of zero. The trick to forecasting future values of M1 from the $\{m_t\}$ sequence is to sum the changes and the seasonal changes so as to obtain the logarithm of the forecasted values of M1. Since $m_t = (1 – L)(1 – L^4)\ln(M1_t)$, it follows that the value of $\ln(M1_t)$ can be obtained from $m_t + \ln(M1_{t-1}) + \ln(M1_{t-4}) – \ln(M1_{t-5})$. The first 12 of the forecasted values are plotted in Figure 2.9.

The procedures illustrated in this example of fitting a model to highly seasonal data are typical of many other series. With highly seasonal data it is necessary to supplement the Box–Jenkins method:

1.   In the identification stage, it is usually necessary to seasonally difference the data and to check the ACF of the resultant series. Oftentimes, the seasonally differenced data will not be stationary. In such instances, the data may also need to be first differenced.

2.   Use the ACF and PACF to identify potential models. Try to estimate models with low-order nonseasonal ARMA coefficients. Consider both additive and multiplicative seasonality. Allow the appropriate form of seasonality to be determined by the various diagnostic statistics.

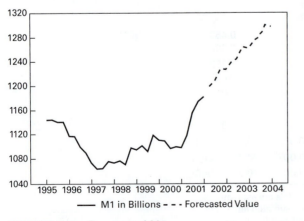

FIGURE 2.9   Forecast of M1

A compact notation has been developed that allows for the efficient representation of intricate models. As in previous sections, the dth difference of a series is denoted by Δ^d. Hence,

$$\Delta^2 y_t = \Delta(y_t - y_{t-1})$$
$$= y_t - 2y_{t-1} + y_{t-2}$$

A seasonal difference is denoted by Δ_s where s is the period of the data. The D-th such seasonal difference is Δ_s^D. For example, if we want the second seasonal difference of a monthly series, we can form

$$\Delta_{12}^2 y_t = \Delta_{12}(y_t - y_{t-12})$$
$$= \Delta_{12} y_t - \Delta_{12} y_{t-12}$$
$$= y_t - y_{t-12} - (y_{t-12} - y_{t-24})$$
$$= y_t - 2y_{t-12} + y_{t-24}$$

Combining the two types of differencing yields $\Delta^d \Delta_s^D$. Multiplicative models are written in the form ARIMA$(p, d, q)(P, D, Q)_s$

where: p and q = the nonseasonal ARMA coefficients

d = number of nonseasonal differences

P = number of multiplicative autoregressive coefficients

D = number of seasonal differences

Q = number of multiplicative moving average coefficients

s = seasonal period

Using this notation, we can say that the fitted model of PPI is an ARIMA(1, 1, 0)(0, 1, 1)$_4$ model. Moreover, the value of m_t can be written as $m_t = \Delta \Delta^4 \ln(\text{M1}_t)$. In applied work, the ARIMA(1, 1, 0)(0, 1, 1)$_s$ and the ARIMA(0, 1, 1)(0, 1, 1)$_s$ models occurs routinely; the latter is called the *airline model* ever since Box and Jenkins (1976) used this model to analyze airline travel data.

12. SUMMARY AND CONCLUSIONS

The chapter focuses on the Box–Jenkins (1976) approach to identification, estimation, diagnostic checking, and forecasting a univariate time-series. ARMA models can be viewed as a special class of linear stochastic difference equations. By definition, an ARMA model is covariance stationary in that it has a finite and time-invariant mean and covariances. For an ARMA model to be stationary, the characteristic roots of the difference equation must lie inside the unit circle. Moreover, the process must have started infinitely far in the past or the process must always be in equilibrium.

In the identification stage, the series is plotted and the sample autocorrelations and partial correlations are examined. As illustrated using the U.S. PPI, a slowly decaying autocorrelation function suggests nonstationarity behavior. In such circumstances, Box and Jenkins recommend differencing the data. Formal tests for nonstationarity are presented in Chapter 4. A common practice is to use a logarithmic or Box–Cox transformation if the variance does not appear to be constant. Chapter 3 presents some modern techniques that can be used to model the variance.

The sample autocorrelations and partial correlations of the suitably transformed data are compared to those of various theoretical ARMA processes. All plausible models are estimated and compared using a battery of diagnostic criteria. A well-estimated model: (i) is parsimonious; (ii) has coefficients that imply stationarity and invertibility; (iii) fits the data well; (iv) has residuals that approximate a white-noise process; (v) has coefficients that do not change over the sample period; and (vi) has good out-of-sample forecasts.

In utilizing the Box–Jenkins methodology, you will find yourself making many seemingly *ad hoc* choices. The most parsimonious model may not have the best fit, but may have the best out-of-sample forecasts. You will find yourself addressing the following types of questions: What is the most appropriate data transformation? Is an ARMA(2, 1) model more appropriate than an ARMA(1, 2) specification? How can seasonality best be modeled? Given this latitude, many view the Box–Jenkins methodology as an art rather than a science. Nevertheless, the technique is best learned through experience. The exercises at the end of this chapter are designed to guide you through the types of choices you will encounter in your own research.

QUESTIONS AND EXERCISES

1. In the coin-tossing example of Section 1, your average winnings on the last four tosses (w_t) can be denoted by

    $$w_t = 1/4\varepsilon_t + 1/4\varepsilon_{t-1} + 1/4\varepsilon_{t-2} + 1/4\varepsilon_{t-3}$$

    a. Find the expected value of your winnings. Find the expected value given that $\varepsilon_{t-3} = \varepsilon_{t-2} = 1$.
    b. Find var(w_t). Find var(w_t) conditional on $\varepsilon_{t-3} = \varepsilon_{t-2} = 1$.
    c. Find cov(w_t, w_{t-1}), cov(w_t, w_{t-2}) and cov(w_t, w_{t-5}).

2. Substitute (2.10) into $y_t = a_0 + a_1 y_{t-1} + \varepsilon_t$. Show that the resulting equation is an identity.
    a. Find the homogeneous solution to $y_t = a_0 + a_1 y_{t-1} + \varepsilon_t$.
    b. Find the particular solution given that $|a_1| < 1$.
    c. Show how to obtain (2.10) by combining the homogeneous and particular solutions.

3. Consider the second-order autoregressive process $y_t = a_0 + a_2 y_{t-2} + \varepsilon_t$ where $|a_2| < 1$.
    a. Find: i. $E_{t-2}y_t$ ii. $E_{t-1}y_t$ iii. $E_t y_{t+2}$ iv. Cov(y_t, y_{t-1})
         v. Cov(y_t, y_{t-2})   vi. the partial autocorrelations ϕ_{11} and ϕ_{22}
    b. Find the impulse response function. Given y_{t-2}, trace out the effects on an ε_t shock on the $\{y_t\}$ sequence.
    c. Determine the forecast function: $E_t y_{t+s}$. The forecast error $e_t(s)$ is the difference between y_{t+s} and $E_t y_{t+s}$. Derive the correlogram of the $\{e_t(s)\}$ sequence. {*Hint*: Find $E_t e_t(s)$, var[$e_t(s)$], and $E_t[e_t(s)e_t(s-j)]$ for $j = 0$ to s}.

4. Two different balls are drawn from a jar containing three balls numbered 1, 2, and 4. Let x denote number on the first ball drawn and y denote sum of the two balls drawn.
    a. Find the joint probability distribution for x and y; that is, find prob($x = 1$, $y = 3$), prob($x = 1$, $y = 5$), ..., prob ($x = 4$, $y = 6$).
    b. Find each of the following: $E(x)$, $E(y)$, $E(y|x = 1)$, $E(x|y = 5)$, var($x|y = 5$), and $E(y^2)$.
    c. Consider the two functions $w_1 = 3x^2$ and $w_2 = x^{-1}$. Find $E(w_1 + w_2)$ and $E(w_1 + w_2|y = 3)$.
    d. How would your answers change if the balls were drawn with replacement?

5. The general solution to an *n*th-order difference equation requires *n* arbitrary constants. Consider the second-order equation $y_t = a_0 + 0.75 y_{t-1} - 0.125 y_{t-2} + \varepsilon_t$.
    a. Find the homogeneous and particular solutions. Discuss the shape of the impulse response function.
    b. Find the values of the initial conditions that ensure the $\{y_t\}$ sequence is stationary.
    c. Given your answer to part b, derive the correlogram for the $\{y_t\}$ sequence.

6. Consider the second-order stochastic difference equation: $y_t = 1.5y_{t-1} - 0.5y_{t-2} + \varepsilon_t$.

    a. Find the characteristic roots of the homogeneous equation.

    b. Demonstrate that the roots of $1 - 1.5L + 0.5L^2$ are the reciprocals of your answer in part a.

    c. Given initial conditions for y_0 and y_1, find the solution for y_t in terms of the current and past values of the $\{\varepsilon_t\}$ sequence. Explain why it is not possible to obtain the backward looking solution for y_t unless such initial conditions are given.

    d. Find the forecast function for y_{T+s} (i.e., find the solution for any value of y_{T+s} given the values of y_T and y_{T-1}).

    e. Find Ey_t, Ey_{t+1}, var(y_t), var(y_{t+1}), and cov(y_{t+1}, y_t).

7. The file entitled SIM_2.XLS contains the simulated data sets used in this chapter. The first series, denoted Y1, contains the 100 values of the simulated AR(1) process used in Section 7. Use this series to perform the following tasks (*Note:* Due to differences in data handling and rounding, your answers need only approximate those presented here):

    a. Plot the sequence against time. Does the series appear to be stationary?

    b. Verify that the first 12 coefficients of the ACF and the PACF are as follows:

    ACF

    1:   0.7394472   0.5842742   0.4711050   0.3885974   0.3443779   0.3350913

    7:   0.2972263   0.3251532   0.2689484   0.2007989   0.1886648   0.0824283

    PACF

    1: 0.7394472 0.0827240   0.0302925   0.0255945   0.0601115   0.0889358

    7: −0.0165339 0.1438633 −0.1002335 −0.0653566 0.0699036   −0.2040202

    Ljung–Box Q-Statistics: $Q(8) = 177.58$, $Q(16) = 197.84$, $Q(24) = 201.28$.

    c. Use the data to verify the results given in Table 2.2.

    d. Estimate the series as an AR(2) process without an intercept. You should obtain:

    Included observations: 98

Coefficient	Estimate	Standard Error	t-Statistic	Probability
a_1	0.701	0.102	6.878	0.0000
a_2	0.105	0.101	1.036	0.3030

    Ljung–Box Q-Statistics: $Q(8) = 5.1317$. $Q(16) = 15.8647$. $Q(24) = 21.0213$

    e. Estimate the series as an ARMA(1, 1) process without an intercept. You should obtain:

    Included observations: 99

Coefficient	Estimate	Standard Error	t-Statistic	Probability
a_1	0.846	0.069	12.248	0.0000
β_1	−0.147	0.126	−1.162	0.2481

    Verify that the ACF and PACF of the residuals do not indicate any serial correlation.

8. The second column in file SIM_2.XLS contains the 100 values of the simulated ARMA(1, 1) process used in Section 7. This series is entitled Y2. Use this series to perform the following tasks (*Note:* Due to differences in data handling and rounding, your answers need only approximate those presented here):

    a. Plot the sequence against time. Does the series appear to be stationary? Verify that the first 12 coefficients of the ACF and the PACF are as follows:

ACF

1: −0.8343833   0.5965289   −0.4399659   0.3497724   −0.3187446   0.3316348
7: −0.3371782   0.3166057   −0.2761498   0.1789268   −0.0839171   0.0375968

PACF

1: −0.8343833   −0.3280611   −0.1942907   −0.0145160   −0.1398293   0.0891764
7: 0.0004335   0.0143663   0.0166776   −0.1987829   −0.0462213   −0.0212410

b. Verify the results in Table 2.3.

c. Estimate the process using a pure MA(2) model. You should obtain:

Included observations: 100

Coefficient	Estimate	Standard Error	t-Statistic	Probability
β_1	−1.191	0.068	−17.41	0.0000
β_2	0.468	0.081	5.77	0.0000

Verify that the Ljung–Box Q-Statistics are:

$Q(8) = 28.4771$. Significance level 0.00007638
$Q(16) = 37.4666$. Significance level 0.00062675
$Q(24) = 38.8424$. Significance level 0.01470990

d. Compare the MA(2) to the ARMA(1, 1).

9. The third column in file SIM_2.XLS contains the 100 values of the simulated AR(2) process used in Section 7. This series is entitled Y3. Use this series to perform the following tasks (*Note*: Due to differences in data handling and rounding, your answers need only approximate those presented here):

a. Plot the sequence against time. Verify the ACF and the PACF coefficients reported in Section 7. Compare the sample ACF and PACF to the those of a theoretical AR(2) process.

b. Estimate the series as an AR(1) process. You should find that the estimated AR(1) coefficient and the *t*-statistic are

$$y_t = 0.467y_{t-1} + e_t$$
$$(5.24)$$

Why is an AR(1) model inadequate?

c. Could an ARMA(1, 1) process generate the type of sample ACF and PACF found in part a? Estimate the series as an ARMA(1,1) process. You should obtain:

Included observations: 99

Coefficient	Estimate	Standard Error	t-Statistic	Probability
a_1	0.183	0.159	1.15	0.2523
β_1	0.510	0.140	3.64	0.0004

Use the Ljung–Box Q-Statistics to show that the ARMA(1,1) model is inadequate.

d. Estimate the series as an AR(2) process to verify the results reported in the text.

10. As you read more of the time-series literature, you will find that different authors and different software packages report the AIC and the SBC in various ways. The examples in the text use AIC = $T \ln(SSR) + 2n$ and SBC = $T \ln(SSR) + n \ln(T)$ where SSR = sum of squared residuals. However, other common formulas include

$$AIC = -2 \ln(L)/T + 2n/T \text{ and } SBC = -2 \ln(L)/T + n \ln(T)/T$$

where L = maximized value of the likelihood function
and

$$AIC = \exp(2n/T) \cdot SSR/T \quad SBC = T^{n/T} \cdot SSR/T$$

a. Show that all three methods of calculating the AIC will necessarily select the same model. [*Hint:* The AIC will select model 1 over model 2 if the AIC from model 1 is smaller than that from model 2. Show that all three ways of calculating the AIC are monotonic transformations of each other.]

b. Show that all three methods of calculating the SBC will necessarily select the same model.

c. Select one of the three pairs above. Show that the AIC will never select a more parsimonious model than the SBC.

11. The file QUARTERLY.XLS contains U.S. PPI data from 1960:$Q1$ to 2002:$Q1$. Make the data transformations indicated in Section 10 of the text.

a. Use the full sample period to obtain the estimates of the ARMA(1, 1) and ARMA(1, (1, 4)) and AR(2) model reported in Section 10.

b. Estimate the ARMA(1, 1) and ARMA(1, (1, 4)) models over the period 1960:$Q1$ to 1989:$Q3$. Obtain the one-step-ahead forecast and the one-step-ahead forecast error from each. As in Section 10, continue to update the estimation period so as to obtain the fifty one-step-ahead forecast errors from each model. Let $\{e_{1t}\}$ denote the forecast errors from the ARMA(1, 1) and $\{e_{2t}\}$ denote the forecast errors from the ARMA(1, (1, 4)). You should find that the properties of the forecast errors are such that

Series	Obs	Mean	Standard Error	Minimum	Maximum
e_{1t}	50	−0.00210	0.011283	−0.03892	0.01861
e_{2t}	50	−0.00225	0.011516	−0.03894	0.02006

c. Construct the Diebold–Mariano test using the mean absolute error. How do the results compare to those reported in Section 10?

d. Use the Granger–Newbold test to compare the AR(2) model to the ARMA(1, 1).

12. The file QUARTERLY.XLS contains the U.S. money supply as measured by M1 (M1NSA) and demand deposits reported by commercial banks (DDNSA). Neither series is seasonally adjusted. The series are quarterly averages over the period 1960:$Q1$ to 2002:$Q1$.

a. Plot the M1NSA sequence against time. Create the growth rate series and replicate the results in Section 11.

b. Form the growth rate of the demand deposit series as $\log(DDNSA_t/DDNSA_{t-1})$. You should find the ACF and PACF are such that

ACF
1: 0.0349076 0.0428105 −0.0264426 0.6357616 −0.0792992 −0.0506527
7: −0.1681839 0.5227466 −0.1962156 −0.1354325 −0.1646850 0.4345867

PACF
1: 0.0349076 0.0416427 −0.0294152 0.6383146 −0.2252285 −0.1047281
7: −0.1629304 0.2796482 −0.2431228 −0.0673336 0.0813827 0.0557702

Explain the observed pattern at lags 4, 8, and 12. What tentative models seem plausible? Does the ACF seem to exhibit geometric decay?

c. Seasonally difference demand deposits using: $\Delta_4\log(DDNSA_t) = \log(DDNSA)_t - \log(DDNSA)_{t-4}$. You should find the following:

ACF
1: 0.9175642 0.7945739 0.6495668 0.4846487 0.3741205 0.2631638
7: 0.1548070 0.0803462 0.0129742 −0.0458305 −0.0836976 −0.1308542

d.   For convenience, let d_t denote the series $(1 - L)(1 - L^4)$DDNSA$_t$. Find the most appropriate model for the $\{d_t\}$ series. In particular, compare the following three models for the series

$$d_t = a_0 + a_1 d_{t-1} + \varepsilon_t + \beta_4 \varepsilon_{t-4} \qquad \text{Model 1: AR(1) with Seasonal MA}$$
$$d_t = a_0 + (1 + a_1 L)(1 + a_4 L^4)d_{t-1} + \varepsilon_t \qquad \text{Model 2: Multiplicative Autoregressive}$$
$$d_t = a_0 + (1 + \beta_1 L)(1 + \beta_4 L^4)\varepsilon_t \qquad \text{Model 3: Multiplicative Moving Average}$$

ENDNOTES

1.   Often, the variance is estimated as

$$\hat{\sigma}^2 = [1/(T-1)]\sum_{t=1}^{T}(y_t - \bar{y})^2$$

2.   As discussed in Appendix 2.1, the estimation of lagged MA coefficients does not entail a loss of any usable observations. Hence, the two models are estimated over the same sample period.

3.   Most software programs will not be able to estimate (2.43) since there is not a unique set of parameter values that minimizes the likelihood function.

4.   Some software programs report the Durbin–Watson test statistic as a check for first-order serial correlation. This well-known test statistic is biased toward finding no serial correlation in the presence of lagged dependent variables. Hence, it is usually not used in ARMA models.

5.   Estimation of an AR(p) model usually entails a loss of the number of usable observations. Hence, to estimate a sample using T observations it will be necessary to have $(T + p)$ observations. Also note that the procedure outlined necessitates that the second subsample period incorporate the lagged values $t_m, t_{m-1}, \dots, t_{m-p+1}$.

6.   Unfortunately, the construction of (2.63) can be sensitive to the choice of q and, if one or more of the $\gamma_i < 0$, the estimated variance can be negative. In such circumstances, it is preferable to use a Newey–West (1987) estimator. A number of software packages allow you to directly obtain the Newey–West estimator of the variance.

7.   To ensure comparability, each was estimated over the 1960:4 - 2002:1 sample period. Note that one usable observation is lost as a result of differencing. In a pure AR(p) model, one observation is also lost for each lag. Thus, estimation of the AR(2) model can begin no earlier than 1960:4. Note that no usable observations are lost in estimating MA(q) models. Some software programs initialize the values of $\varepsilon_1, \dots, \varepsilon_q$ to be zero so that no additional usable observations are lost. Others will backcast the initial values of $\varepsilon_1, \dots, \varepsilon_q$.

8.   In essence, the estimated equation is an ARMA(1, 4) model with the coefficients β_2 and β_3 constrained to be equal to zero. In order to distinguish between the two specifications, the notation ARMA(1,(1, 4)) or ARMA(1, $\|$ 1, 4$\|$) is used to indicate that only the moving-average terms at lags 1 and 4 are included in the model.

9.   The details of the X-11 procedure are not important for our purposes. A number of well-known statistical packages, such as EViews, SAS and RATS, can perform the X-11 procedure. The technical details of the procedure are explained by the Bureau of the Census (1969). Also note that X-12 is replacing X-11.

APPENDIX 2.1: ESTIMATION OF AN MA(1) PROCESS

How do you estimate an MA or an ARMA process? When you estimate a regression using ordinary least squares (OLS), you have a dependent variable and a set of independent variables. In an AR model, the list of regressors is simply the lagged values of the $\{y_t\}$ series. Estimating an MA process is different because you do not know the values of the $\{\varepsilon_t\}$ sequence. Since you cannot directly estimate a regression equation, maximum likelihood estimation is used. Suppose that $\{\varepsilon_t\}$ is a white-noise sequence drawn from a normal distribution. The likelihood of any realization ε_t is

$$\frac{1}{\sqrt{2\pi\sigma^2}}\exp\left(\frac{-\varepsilon_t^2}{2\sigma^2}\right)$$

Since the ε_t are independent, the likelihood of the joint realizations $\varepsilon_1, \varepsilon_2, \ldots, \varepsilon_T$ is

$$\prod_{t=1}^{T}\frac{1}{\sqrt{2\pi\sigma^2}}\exp\left(\frac{-\varepsilon_t^2}{2\sigma^2}\right)$$

If you take the log of the likelihood, you obtain

$$\ln L = \frac{-T}{2}\ln(2\pi) - \frac{T}{2}\ln\sigma^2 - \frac{1}{2\sigma^2}\sum_{t=1}^{T}\varepsilon_t^2$$

Now suppose that we observe T values of the MA(1) series $y_t = \beta\varepsilon_{t-1} + \varepsilon_t$. The problem is to construct the $\{\varepsilon_t\}$ sequence from the observed values of $\{y_t\}$. If we knew the true value of β and knew that $\varepsilon_0 = 0$, we could construct $\varepsilon_1, \ldots, \varepsilon_T$ recursively. Given that $\varepsilon_0 = 0$, it follows that

$$\varepsilon_1 = y_1$$
$$\varepsilon_2 = y_2 - \beta\varepsilon_1 = y_2 - \beta y_1$$
$$\varepsilon_3 = y_3 - \beta\varepsilon_2 = y_3 - \beta(y_2 - \beta y_1)$$
$$\varepsilon_4 = y_4 - \beta\varepsilon_3 = y_4 - \beta[y_3 - \beta(y_2 - \beta y_1)]$$

In general, $\varepsilon_t = y_t - \beta\varepsilon_{t-1}$ so that if L is the lag operator

$$\varepsilon_t = y_t/(1+\beta L) = \sum_{i=0}^{t-1}(-\beta)^i y_{t-i}$$

As long as $|\beta| < 1$, the values of ε_t will represent a convergent process. This is the justification for the assumption that the MA process be invertible. If $|\beta| > 1$, we cannot represent the $\{\varepsilon_t\}$ series in terms of the observed $\{y_t\}$ series. If we now substitute the solution for ε_t into the formula for the log likelihood, we obtain

$$\ln L = \frac{-T}{2}\ln(2\pi) - \frac{T}{2}\ln\sigma^2 - \frac{1}{2\sigma^2}\sum_{t=1}^{T}\left(\sum_{i=0}^{t-1}(-\beta)^i y_{t-i}\right)^2$$

Now that we have expressed $\ln L$ in terms of the observable $\{y_t\}$ series, it is possible to select the values of β and σ^2 that maximize the value of $\ln L$. Unlike OLS, if you actually take the partial derivatives of $\ln L$ with respect to β and σ^2 you will not obtain a simple set of first-order conditions. Moreover, the formula becomes much more complicated in higher-order MA(q) processes. Nevertheless, computers can use a number of available search algorithms to find the values of β and σ^2 that maximize $\ln L$.

APPENDIX 2.2: MODEL SELECTION CRITERIA

Hypothesis testing is not particularly well suited to testing non-nested models. For example, if you wanted to chose between an AR(1) and an MA(2) you could estimate an ARMA(1, 2) and then try to restrict the MA(2) coefficients to equal zero. Alternatively, you could try to restrict the AR(1) coefficient to equal zero. Nevertheless, the method is unsatisfactory because it necessitates estimating the over-parameterized ARMA(1, 2) model. Instead, model selection criteria, such as the AIC and the SBC, can be used to choose between alternative models. Such model selection criteria can be viewed as measures of *goodness-of-fit* that include a cost, or penalty, for each parameter estimated.

One reason it is not desirable to have an overparameterized model is that forecast error variance increases as a result of errors arising from parameter estimation. In other words, small models tend to have better out-of-sample performance than large models. Suppose that the actual data-generating process (DGP) is the AR(1) model

$$y_t = a y_{t-1} + \varepsilon_t$$

If a is known, the one-step-ahead forecast of y_{t+1} is $E_t y_{t+1} = a y_t$. Hence, the mean squared forecast error is $E_t(y_{t+1} - a y_t)^2 = E_t \varepsilon_{t+1}^2 = \sigma^2$. However, when a is estimated from the data, the one-step-ahead forecast of y_{t+1} is

$$E_t y_{t+1} = \hat{a} y_t$$

where $\hat{a}$ is the estimated value of a.

Hence, the mean squared forecast, or prediction, error is

$$\text{MSPE} = E_t(y_{t+1} - \hat{a} y_t)^2 = E_t[(a y_t - \hat{a} y_t) + \varepsilon_{t+1}]^2$$

Since ε_{t+1} is independent of $\hat{a}$ and y_t, it follows that

$$E_t(y_{t+1} - \hat{a} y_t)^2 = E_t[(a - \hat{a}) y_t]^2 + \sigma^2$$

$$\approx E_t[(a - \hat{a})]^2 (y_t)^2 + \sigma^2$$

Since $E_t[(a - \hat{a})]^2$ is strictly positive, parameter uncertainty contributes to forecast error variance in that the mean squared forecast error exceeds σ^2. The point is that errors in parameter estimation contribute to forecast error variance. Moreover, the more parameters estimated, the greater the parameter uncertainty. It is easy to show that the problem is particularly acute in small samples. Since $\text{var}(y_t) = \sigma^2 / (1 - a^2)$ and, in large samples, $\text{var}(\hat{a}) = E_t[(a - \hat{a})]^2 \approx (1 - a^2)/T$ it follows that

$$E_t[(a - \hat{a})]^2 (y_t)^2 + \sigma^2 \approx [(1 - a^2)/T](1 - a^2)^{-1} \sigma^2 + \sigma^2$$

$$= [1 + (1/T)]\sigma^2$$

Thus, as T increases, the MSPE approaches σ^2.

The Finite Prediction Error (FPE) Criterion

The FPE criterion seeks to minimize the one-step-ahead mean squared prediction error. Now consider the AR(p) process

$$y_t = a_1 y_{t-1} + \dots + a_p y_{t-p} + \varepsilon_t$$

If you use the argument in the previous section, the MSPE can be shown to be equal to

$$[1 + (p/T)]\sigma^2$$

We do not know the true variance σ^2. However, σ^2 can be replaced by its unbiased estimate $SSR/(T-p)$ to get

$$FPE = [1 + (p/T)][SSR/(T\text{-}p)]$$

Select p so as to minimize FPE. We can use logs and note that $\ln(1 + p/T)$ can be approximated by p/T. Hence, it is possible to select p to minimize

$$p/T + \ln(SSR) - \ln(T - p)$$

which is the same as minimizing

$$p + T\ln(SSR) - T\ln(T - p)$$

Since $\ln(T - p) \cong \ln T - p/T$, the problem can be written in terms of selecting p so as to minimize

$$p + T\ln(SSR) - \ln(T) + p$$

which has the same solution as minimizing

$$T\ln(SSR) + 2p$$

The AIC and the SBC

The more general AIC selects the $(1 + p + q)$ parameters of an ARMA model so as to maximize the log likelihood function including a penalty for each parameter estimated

$$AIC = -2 \ln \text{ maximized value of log likelihood} + (1 + p + q)/T$$

For a given value of T, selecting the values of p and q so as to minimize $\ln(AIC)$ is equivalent to selecting p and q so as to minimize the sum

$$T \ln (SSR) + 2(1 + p + q)$$

Notice that if $q = 0$ and there is no intercept, this is the result obtained using the FPE. Minimizing the value of the AIC implies that each estimated parameter entails a benefit and a cost. Clearly, a benefit of adding another parameter is that the value of SSR is reduced. The cost is that degrees of freedom are reduced and there is added parameter uncertainty. Thus, adding additional parameters will decrease ln (SSR) but will increase $(1 + p + q)$. The AIC allows you to add parameters until the marginal cost (i.e., the marginal cost is 2 for each parameter estimated) equals the marginal benefit. The SBC incorporates the larger penalty $(1 + p + q) \ln T$. To use the SBC, select the values of p and q so as to minimize

$$T \ln (SSR) + (1 + p + q) \ln(T)$$

For any reasonable sample size, $\ln(T) > 2$ so that the marginal cost of adding parameters using the SBC exceeds that of the AIC. Hence, the SBC will select a more parsimonious model than the AIC. As indicated in the text, the SBC has superior large sample properties. It is possible to prove that the SBC is asymptotically consistent while the AIC is biased toward selecting an overparameterized model. However, Monte Carlo studies have shown that in small samples, the AIC can work better than the SBC.

CHAPTER *3*

MODELING VOLATILITY

Many economic time series do not have a constant mean, and most exhibit phases of relative tranquility followed by periods of high volatility. Much of the current econometric research is concerned with extending the Box–Jenkins methodology to analyze these types of time-series variables. This chapter has three aims:

1. Examine the so-called *stylized facts* concerning the properties of economic time-series data. Casual inspection of GDP, financial aggregates, interest rates and exchange rates suggests they do not have a constant mean and variance. Many seem to have a decidedly upward trend while others seem to meander and show periods of high and low volatility. A stochastic variable with a constant variance is called **homoskedastic** as opposed to **heteroskedastic.**[1] For series exhibiting volatility, the unconditional variance may be constant even though the variance during some periods is unusually large.

2. Formalize simple models of variables with exhibiting heteroskedasticity. Asset holders are interested in the volatility returns over the holding period, not over some historical period. This forward-looking view of risk means that it is important to be able to estimate and forecast the risk associated with holding a particular asset. As such, this chapter will develop the tools necessary to model and forecast conditional heteroskedasticity.

3. Examine a number of variants of the basic model for conditional volatility. The simplest model posits that the conditional heteroskedasticity can be estimated as an autoregressive process (ARCH). This chapter examines a number of important generalizations of the basic ARCH model.

1. ECONOMIC TIME SERIES: THE STYLIZED FACTS

Figures 3.1 through 3.6 illustrate the behavior of some of the more important variables encountered in macroeconomic analysis. Casual inspection does have its perils, and formal testing is necessary to substantiate any first impressions. However, the strong visual pattern is that these series are *not* stationary; the sample means do not appear to be constant and/or there is the strong appearance of heteroskedasticity. We can characterize the key features of the various series with these *stylized facts:*

1. **Most of the series contain a clear trend.** Real GDP and consumption (see Figure 3.1) exhibit a decidedly upward trend. Although the other components of real GDP (see Figure 3.2) also have an upward trend, real investment and government spending are more volatile than real GDP and consumption.

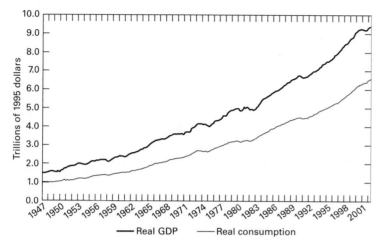

FIGURE 3.1 U.S. GDP and Consumption

FIGURE 3.2 Investment and Government Consumption

2. **Shocks to a series can display a high degree of persistence.** Neither of the interest rate series shown in Figure 3.3 have a clear upward or downward trend. Nevertheless, both show a high degree of persistence. Notice that the Federal Funds Rate experienced a violent upward surge in 1973 and remained at that high level for nearly two years. Similarly, after a number of sharp decreases in 1987, the rate never again displayed the levels attained in the early 1980s.

3. **The volatility of many series is not constant over time.** Real investment grew smoothly throughout most of the 1960s but also became highly variable

FIGURE 3.3 Short- and Long-Term Interest Rates

in the 1970s. Also during the 1970s, the U.S. producer price index shown in Figure 2.5 of the last chapter fluctuated wildly as compared with the 1960s and 1980s. Most dramatic are the daily changes in the NYSE composite index. In Figure 3.4 you can see the periods where the stock market seems tranquil alongside periods with large increases and decreases in the market. Such series are called *conditionally heteroskedastic* if the unconditional (or long-run) variance is constant, but there are periods in which the variance is relatively high.

4. **Some series seem to meander.** The real effective exchange rates (see Figure 3.5) show no particular tendency to increase or decrease. The real values of the U.S. and the Canadian dollar seem to go through sustained periods of appreciation and then depreciation with no tendency to revert to a long-run mean. This type of "random walk" behavior is typical of nonstationary series. On the other hand, without any formal testing, it is difficult to tell if the real German mark is mean-reverting.

5. **Some series share co-movements with other series.** Individually, the federal funds rate and the ten-year yield on U.S. government securities show no tendency to revert to a long-run mean. However, it is clear that the two series never drift too far apart. Moreover, large shocks to the federal funds rate appear to be timed similarly with those to the ten-year rate. The presence of such co-movements should not be too surprising since the forces driving short-term and long-term rates should be similar. On the other hand, it is not clear whether the various indices of real GDP levels (see Figure 3.6) share the same trend. The movements in the three GDP series

FIGURE 3.4   Daily Changes in the NYSE Composite Index,
January 3, 1995–August 30, 2002

FIGURE 3.5   Real Effective Exchange Rates

are such that all seem to experience recessions and expansions simultaneously. However, it is not clear whether the differences among the trend
rates of growth are statistically significant.

Please be aware that "eyeballing" the data is not a substitute for formally testing
for the presence of conditional heteroskedasticity or nonstationary behavior.[2]
Although most of the variables shown in the figures are neither stationary nor

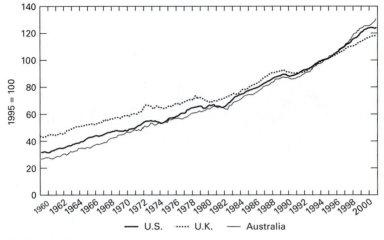

FIGURE 3.6 Real GDP Indices

homoskedastic ARMA processes, the issue will not always be so obvious. Fortunately, it is possible to modify the tools developed in the last chapter to help in the identification and estimation of such series. The remainder of this chapter considers the issue of conditional heteroskedasticity. Models and formal tests for the presence of trends (either deterministic and/or stochastic) are contained in the next chapter. The order in which you read Chapters 3 and 4 is immaterial; some instructors may wish to cover the material in Chapter 4 and then the material in Chapter 3. However, the issue of co-movements in multivariate time series must wait until Chapters 5 and 6.

2. ARCH PROCESSES

In conventional econometric models, the variance of the disturbance term is assumed to be constant. However, Figures 3.1 to 3.6 demonstrate that many economic time series exhibit periods of unusually large volatility, followed by periods of relative tranquility. In such circumstances, the assumption of a constant variance (**homoskedasticity**) is inappropriate. It is easy to imagine instances in which you might want to forecast the conditional variance of a series. As an asset holder, you would be interested in forecasts of the rate of return *and* its variance over the holding period. The unconditional variance (i.e., the long-run forecast of the variance) would be unimportant if you plan to buy the asset at t and sell at $t + 1$.

One approach to forecasting the variance is to explicitly introduce an independent variable that helps to predict the volatility. Consider the simplest case in which

$$y_{t+1} = \varepsilon_{t+1} x_t$$

where: y_{t+1} = the variable of interest
ε_{t+1} = a white-noise disturbance term with variance σ^2
x_t = an independent variable that can be observed at period t

If $x_t = x_{t-1} = x_{t-2} = \ldots =$ constant, the $\{y_t\}$ sequence is the familiar white-noise process with a constant variance. However, when the realizations of the $\{x_t\}$ sequence are not all equal, the variance of y_{t+1} conditional on the observable value of x_t is

$$\mathrm{Var}(y_{t+1} \mid x_t) = x_t^2 \sigma^2$$

Here the conditional variance of y_{t+1} is dependent on the realized value of x_t. Since you can observe x_t at time period t, you can form the variance of y_{t+1} conditionally on the realized value of x_t. If the magnitude $(x_t)^2$ is large (small), the variance of y_{t+1} will be large (small) as well. Furthermore, if the successive values of $\{x_t\}$ exhibit positive serial correlation (so that a large value of x_t tends to be followed by a large value of x_{t+1}), the conditional variance of the $\{y_t\}$ sequence will exhibit positive serial correlation as well. In this way, the introduction of the $\{x_t\}$ sequence can explain periods of volatility in the $\{y_t\}$ sequence. In practice, you might want to modify the basic model by introducing the coefficients a_0 and a_1 and estimating the regression equation in logarithmic form as

$$\ln(y_t) = a_0 + a_1 \ln(x_{t-1}) + e_t$$

where e_t is the error term [formally, $e_t = \ln(\varepsilon_t)$].

This procedure is simple to implement since the logarithmic transformation results in a linear regression equation; OLS can be used to estimate a_0 and a_1 directly. A major difficulty with this strategy is that it assumes a specific cause for the changing variance. Moreover, the methodology also forces $\{x_t\}$ to affect the mean of $\ln(y_t)$. Oftentimes, you might not have a firm theoretical reason for selecting one candidate for the $\{x_t\}$ sequence over other reasonable choices. Was it the oil price shocks, a change in the conduct of monetary policy, and/or the breakdown of the Bretton-Woods system that was responsible for the volatile PPI during the 1970s? Moreover, the technique necessitates a transformation of the data such that the resulting series has a constant variance. In the example at hand, the $\{e_t\}$ sequence is assumed to have a constant variance. If this assumption is violated, some other transformation of the data is necessary.

ARCH Processes

Instead of using ad hoc variable choices for x_t and/or data transformations, Engle (1982) shows that it is possible to simultaneously model the mean *and* the variance of a series. As a preliminary step to understanding Engle's methodology, note that conditional forecasts are vastly superior to unconditional forecasts. To elaborate, suppose you estimate the stationary ARMA model $y_t = a_0 + a_1 y_{t-1} + \varepsilon_t$ and want to forecast y_{t+1}. The conditional mean of y_{t+1} is

$$E_t y_{t+1} = a_0 + a_1 y_t$$

If we use this conditional mean to forecast y_{t+1}, the forecast error variance is $E_t[(y_{t+1} - a_0 - a_1 y_t)^2] = E_t \varepsilon_{t+1}^2 = \sigma^2$. However, if unconditional forecasts are used, the unconditional forecast is always the long-run mean of the $\{y_t\}$ sequence that is equal to $a_0/(1 - a_1)$. The unconditional forecast error variance is

$$E\{[y_{t+1} - a_0/(1 - a_1)]^2\} = E[(\varepsilon_{t+1} + a_1 \varepsilon_t + a_1^2 \varepsilon_{t-1} + a_1^3 \varepsilon_{t-2} + \ldots)^2]$$
$$= \sigma^2/(1 - a_1^2)$$

Since $1/(1 - a_1^2) > 1$, the unconditional forecast has a greater variance than the conditional forecast. Thus, conditional forecasts (since they take into account the known current and past realizations of series) are preferable.

Similarly, if the variance of $\{\varepsilon_t\}$ is not constant, you can estimate any tendency for sustained movements in the variance using an ARMA model. For example, let $\{\hat{\varepsilon}_t\}$ denote the estimated residuals from the model $y_t = a_0 + a_1 y_{t-1} + \varepsilon_t$ so that the conditional variance of y_{t+1} is

$$\text{Var}(y_{t+1} \mid y_t) = E_t[(y_{t+1} - a_0 - a_1 y_t)^2]$$
$$= E_t(\varepsilon_{t+1})^2$$

To this point, we have set $E_t(\varepsilon_{t+1})^2$ equal to the constant σ^2. Now suppose that the conditional variance is not constant. One simple strategy is to forecast the conditional variance as an AR(q) process using *squares* of the estimated residuals

$$\hat{\varepsilon}_t^2 = \alpha_0 + \alpha_1 \hat{\varepsilon}_{t-1}^2 + \alpha_2 \hat{\varepsilon}_{t-2}^2 + \ldots + \alpha_q \hat{\varepsilon}_{t-q}^2 + v_t \tag{3.1}$$

where v_t is a white-noise process.

If the values of $\alpha_1, \alpha_2, \ldots, \alpha_n$ all equal zero, the estimated variance is simply the constant α_0. Otherwise, the conditional variance of y_t evolves according to the autoregressive process given by (3.1). As such, you can use (3.1) to forecast the conditional variance at $t + 1$ as

$$E_t \hat{\varepsilon}_{t+1}^2 = \alpha_0 + \alpha_1 \hat{\varepsilon}_t^2 + \alpha_2 \hat{\varepsilon}_{t-1}^2 + \ldots + \alpha_q \hat{\varepsilon}_{t+1-q}^2$$

For this reason, an equation like (3.1) is called an **autoregressive conditional heteroskedastic** (ARCH) model. There are many possible applications for ARCH models since the residuals in (3.1) can come from an autoregression, an ARMA model, or a standard regression model.

In actuality, the linear specification of (3.1) is not the most convenient. The reason is that the model for $\{y_t\}$ and the conditional variance are best estimated simultaneously using maximum likelihood techniques. Instead of the specification given by (3.1), it is more tractable to specify v_t as a multiplicative disturbance.

The simplest example from the class of multiplicative conditionally heteroskedastic models proposed by Engle (1982) is

$$\varepsilon_t = v_t \sqrt{\alpha_0 + \alpha_1 \varepsilon_{t-1}^2} \tag{3.2}$$

where v_t = white-noise process such that $\sigma_v^2 = 1$, v_t and ε_{t-1} are independent of each other, and α_0 and α_1 are constants such that $\alpha_0 > 0$ and $0 < \alpha_1 < 1$.

Consider the properties of the $\{\varepsilon_t\}$ sequence. Since v_t is white noise and is independent of ε_{t-1}, it is easy to show that the elements of the $\{\varepsilon_t\}$ sequence have a mean of zero and are uncorrelated. The proof is straightforward. Take the unconditional expectation of ε_t. Since $Ev_t = 0$, it follows that

$$E\varepsilon_t = E[v_t(\alpha_0 + \alpha_1 \varepsilon_{t-1}^2)^{1/2}]$$
$$= Ev_t E(\alpha_0 + \alpha_1 \varepsilon_{t-1}^2)^{1/2} = 0 \tag{3.3}$$

Since $Ev_t v_{t-i} = 0$, it also follows that

$$E\varepsilon_t \varepsilon_{t-i} = 0, \quad i \neq 0 \tag{3.4}$$

The derivation of the unconditional variance of ε_t is also straightforward. Square ε_t and take the unconditional expectation to form

$$E\varepsilon_t^2 = E[v_t^2(\alpha_0 + \alpha_1 \varepsilon_{t-1}^2)]$$
$$= Ev_t^2 E(\alpha_0 + \alpha_1 \varepsilon_{t-1}^2)$$

Since $\sigma_v^2 = 1$ and the unconditional variance of ε_t is identical to that of ε_{t-1} (i.e., $E\varepsilon_t^2 = E\varepsilon_{t-1}^2$), the unconditional variance is

$$E\varepsilon_t^2 = \alpha_0 / (1 - \alpha_1) \tag{3.5}$$

Thus, the unconditional mean and variance are unaffected by the presence of the error process given by (3.2). Similarly, it is easy to show that the conditional mean of ε_t is equal to zero. Given that v_t and ε_{t-1} are independent and that $Ev_t = 0$, the conditional mean of ε_t is

$$E(\varepsilon_t | \varepsilon_{t-1}, \varepsilon_{t-2}, \ldots) = E_{t-1} v_t E_{t-1}(\alpha_0 + \alpha_1 \varepsilon_{t-1}^2)^{1/2} = 0$$

At this point you might be thinking that the properties of the $\{\varepsilon_t\}$ sequence are not affected by (3.2) since the mean is zero, the variance is constant, and all autocovariances are zero. However, the influence of (3.2) falls entirely on the conditional variance. Because $Ev_t^2 = 1$, the variance of ε_t conditioned on the past history of ε_{t-1}, ε_{t-2}, ... is

$$E[\varepsilon_t^2 | \varepsilon_{t-1}, \varepsilon_{t-2}, \ldots] = \alpha_0 + \alpha_1 \varepsilon_{t-1}^2 \tag{3.6}$$

In (3.6), the conditional variance of ε_t is dependent on the realized value of ε_{t-1}^2. If the realized value of ε_{t-1}^2 is large, the conditional variance in t will be large as well. In (3.6) the conditional variance follows a first-order autoregressive process denoted by ARCH(1). As opposed to a usual autoregression, the coefficients α_0 and α_1 have to be restricted. In order to ensure that the conditional variance is never negative, it is necessary to assume that both α_0 and α_1 are positive. After all, if α_0 is negative, a sufficiently small realization of ε_{t-1} will mean that (3.6) is negative. Similarly, if α_1 is negative, a sufficiently large realization of ε_{t-1} can render a negative value for the conditional variance. Moreover, to ensure the stability of the process, it is necessary to restrict α_1 such that $0 < \alpha_1 < 1$.

Equations (3.3), (3.4), (3.5), and (3.6) illustrate the essential features of any ARCH process. In an ARCH model, the error structure is such that the conditional and unconditional means are equal to zero. Moreover, the $\{\varepsilon_t\}$ sequence is serially uncorrelated because for all $s \neq 0$, $E\varepsilon_t \varepsilon_{t-s} = 0$. The key point is that the errors are *not* independent since they are related through their second moment (recall that correlation is a linear relationship). The conditional variance itself is an autoregressive process resulting in conditionally heteroskedastic errors. When the realized value of

ε_{t-1} is far from zero—so that $\alpha_1(\varepsilon_{t-1})^2$ is relatively large—the variance of ε_t will tend to be large. As you will see momentarily, the conditional heteroskedasticity in $\{\varepsilon_t\}$ will result in $\{y_t\}$ being heteroskedastic itself. Thus, the ARCH model is able to capture periods of tranquility and volatility in the $\{y_t\}$ series.

The four graphs of Figure 3.7 depict two different ARCH models. The upper-left-hand graph (a), representing the $\{v_t\}$ sequence, shows 100 serially uncorrelated and normally distributed random deviates. From casual inspection, the $\{v_t\}$ sequence appears to fluctuate around a mean of zero and have a constant variance. Note the moderate increase in volatility between periods 50 and 60. Given the initial condition $\varepsilon_0 = 0$, these realizations of the $\{v_t\}$ sequence were used to construct the next 100 values of the $\{\varepsilon_t\}$ sequence using equation (3.2) and setting $\alpha_0 = 1$ and $\alpha_1 = 0.8$. As illustrated in Panel (b), the $\{\varepsilon_t\}$ sequence also has a mean of zero, but the variance appears to experience an increase in volatility around $t = 50$.

How does the error structure affect the $\{y_t\}$ sequence? Clearly if the autoregressive parameter a_1 is zero, y_t is nothing more than ε_t. Thus, the upper-right-hand

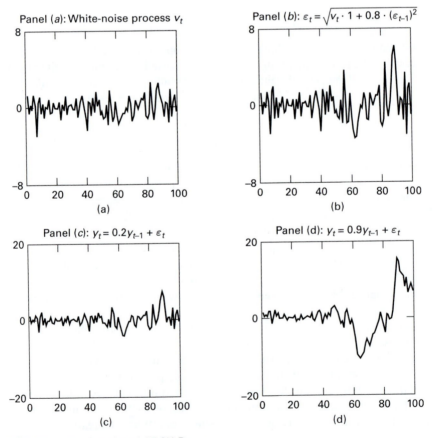

FIGURE 3.7　Simulated ARCH Processes

graph can be used to depict the time path of the $\{y_t\}$ sequence for the case of $a_1 = 0$. Panels (c) and (d) show the behavior of the $\{y_t\}$ sequence for the cases of $a_1 = 0.2$ and 0.9, respectively. The essential point to note is that the ARCH error structure and the autocorrelation parameters of the $\{y_t\}$ process interact with each other. Comparing Panels (c) and (d) illustrates that the volatility of $\{y_t\}$ is increasing in a_1 and α_1. The explanation is intuitive. Any unusually large (in absolute value) shock in v_t will be associated with a persistently large variance in the $\{\varepsilon_t\}$ sequence; the larger is α_1, the longer the persistence. Moreover, the greater the autoregressive parameter a_1, the more persistent is any given change in y_t. The stronger the tendency for $\{y_t\}$ to remain away from its mean, the greater the variance.

To formally examine the properties of the $\{y_t\}$ sequence, the conditional mean and variance are given by

$$E_{t-1}y_t = a_0 + a_1 y_{t-1}$$

and

$$\begin{aligned}\text{Var}(y_t \mid y_{t-1}, y_{t-2}, \ldots) &= E_{t-1}(y_t - a_0 - a_1 y_{t-1})^2 \\ &= E_{t-1}(\varepsilon_t)^2 \\ &= \alpha_0 + \alpha_1(\varepsilon_{t-1})^2\end{aligned}$$

Since α_1 and ε_{t-1}^2 cannot be negative, the minimum value for the conditional variance is α_0. For any nonzero realization of ε_{t-1}, the conditional variance of y_t is positively related to α_1. The unconditional mean and variance of y_t can be obtained by solving the difference equation for y_t and then taking expectations. If the process began sufficiently far in the past (so that the arbitrary constant A can safely be ignored), the solution for y_t is

$$y_t = \frac{a_0}{1 - a_1} + \sum_{i=0}^{\infty} a_1^i \varepsilon_{t-i} \tag{3.7}$$

Since $E\varepsilon_t = 0$ for all t, the unconditional expectation of (3.7) is $Ey_t = a_0/(1 - a_1)$. The unconditional variance can be obtained in a similar fashion using (3.7). Given that $E\varepsilon_t \varepsilon_{t-i}$ is zero for all $i \neq 0$, the unconditional variance of y_t follows directly from (3.7) as

$$\text{Var}(y_t) = \sum_{i=0}^{\infty} a_1^{2i} \text{var}(\varepsilon_{t-i})$$

From the result that the unconditional variance of ε_t is constant [i.e., $\text{var}(\varepsilon_t) = \text{var}(\varepsilon_{t-1}) = \text{var}(\varepsilon_{t-2}) = \ldots = \alpha_0/(1 - \alpha_1)$], it follows that

$$\text{Var}(y_t) = \left(\frac{\alpha_0}{1 - \alpha_1}\right)\left(\frac{1}{1 - a_1^2}\right)$$

Clearly, the variance of the $\{y_t\}$ sequence is increasing in α_1 and in the absolute value of a_1. Although the algebra can be a bit tedious, the essential point is that an ARCH error process can be used to model periods of volatility within the univariate framework.

The ARCH process given by (3.2) has been extended in several interesting ways. Engle's (1982) original contribution considered the entire class of higher-order ARCH(q) processes:

$$\varepsilon_t = v_t \sqrt{\alpha_0 + \sum_{i=1}^{q} \alpha_i \varepsilon_{t-i}^2} \qquad (3.8)$$

In (3.8), all shocks from ε_{t-1} to ε_{t-q} have a direct effect on ε_t, so that the conditional variance acts like an autoregressive process of order q. It is a good exercise to demonstrate that the forecast for $E_t \varepsilon_{t+1}^2$ arising from (3.1) and (3.8) have precisely the same form.

The GARCH Model

Bollerslev (1986) extended Engle's original work by developing a technique that allows the conditional variance to be an ARMA process. Now let the error process be such that

$$\varepsilon_t = v_t \sqrt{h_t}$$

where $\sigma_v^2 = 1$ and

$$h_t = \alpha_0 + \sum_{i=1}^{q} \alpha_i \varepsilon_{t-i}^2 + \sum_{i=1}^{p} \beta_i h_{t-i} \qquad (3.9)$$

Since $\{v_t\}$ is a white-noise process, the conditional and unconditional means of ε_t are equal to zero. Taking the expected value of ε_t, it is easy to verify that

$$E\varepsilon_t = Ev_t(h_t)^{1/2} = 0$$

The important point is that the conditional variance of ε_t is given by $E_{t-1}\varepsilon_t^2 = h_t$. Thus, *the conditional variance of ε_t is the ARMA process given by the expression h_t in (3.9)*.

This **generalized** ARCH(p, q) model—called GARCH(p, q)—allows for both autoregressive and moving average components in the heteroskedastic variance. If we set $p = 0$ and $q = 1$, it is clear that the first-order ARCH model given by (3.2) is simply a GARCH(0, 1) model. Hence, if all values of β_i equal zero, the GARCH (p, q) model is equivalent to an ARCH(q) model. The benefits of the GARCH model should be clear; a high-order ARCH model may have a more parsimonious GARCH representation that is much easier to identify and estimate. This is particularly true since all coefficients in (3.9) must be positive. Moreover, to ensure that the variance is finite, all characteristic roots of (3.9) must lie inside the unit circle. Clearly, the more parsimonious model will entail fewer coefficient restrictions.[3]

The key feature of GARCH models is that the conditional variance of the *disturbances* of the $\{y_t\}$ sequence constitutes an ARMA process. Hence, it is to be expected that the residuals from a fitted ARMA model should display this characteristic pattern. To explain, suppose you estimate $\{y_t\}$ as an ARMA process. If your model of $\{y_t\}$ is adequate, the ACF and PACF of the residuals should be indicative of a white-noise process. However, the ACF of the *squared* residuals can help identify the order of the GARCH process. Equation (3.9) looks very much like a standard ARMA(p, q) process. As such, if there is conditional heteroskedasticity, the correlogram should be suggestive of such a process. The technique to construct the correlogram of the squared residuals is as follows:

STEP 1: Estimate the $\{y_t\}$ sequence using the "best fitting" ARMA model (or regression model) and obtain the squares of the fitted errors $\{\hat{\varepsilon}_t^2\}$. Also calculate the sample variance of the residuals ($\hat{\sigma}^2$) defined as

$$\hat{\sigma}^2 = \sum_{t=1}^{T} \hat{\varepsilon}_t^2 / T$$

where T = number of residuals.

STEP 2: Calculate and plot the sample autocorrelations of the squared residuals as

$$\rho_i = \frac{\sum_{t=i+1}^{T} (\hat{\varepsilon}_t^2 - \hat{\sigma}^2)(\hat{\varepsilon}_{t-i}^2 - \hat{\sigma}^2)}{\sum_{t=1}^{T} (\hat{\varepsilon}_t^2 - \hat{\sigma}^2)^2}$$

STEP 3: In large samples, the standard deviation of ρ_i can be approximated by $T^{-0.5}$. Individual values of ρ_i that are significantly different from zero are indicative of GARCH errors. Ljung–Box Q-statistics can be used to test for groups of significant coefficients. As in Chapter 2, the statistic

$$Q = T (T+2) \sum_{i=1}^{n} \rho_i / (T - i)$$

has an asymptotic χ^2 distribution with n degrees of freedom if the $\{\hat{\varepsilon}_t^2\}$ sequence is serially uncorrelated. Rejecting the null hypothesis that the $\{\hat{\varepsilon}_t^2\}$ are serially uncorrelated is equivalent to rejecting the null hypothesis of no ARCH or GARCH errors. In practice, you should consider values of n up to $T/4$.

The more formal Lagrange multiplier test for ARCH disturbances has been proposed by Engle (1982). The methodology involves the following two steps:[4]

STEP 1: Use OLS to estimate the most appropriate regression equation or ARMA model and let $\{\hat{\varepsilon}_t^2\}$ denote the squares of the fitted errors.

STEP 2: Regress these squared residuals on a constant and on the q lagged values $\hat{\varepsilon}_{t-1}^2$, $\hat{\varepsilon}_{t-2}^2$, $\hat{\varepsilon}_{t-3}^2$, ..., $\hat{\varepsilon}_{t-q}^2$, that is, estimate a regression of the form

$$\hat{\varepsilon}_t^2 = \alpha_0 + \alpha_1 \hat{\varepsilon}_{t-1}^2 + \alpha_2 \hat{\varepsilon}_{t-2}^2 + ... + \alpha_q \hat{\varepsilon}_{t-q}^2$$

If there are no ARCH or GARCH effects, the estimated values of α_1 through α_q should be zero. Hence, this regression will have little explanatory power so that the coefficient of determination (i.e., the usual R^2) will be quite low. Using a sample of T residuals, under the null hypothesis of no ARCH errors, the test statistic

TR^2 converges to a χ^2 distribution with q degrees of freedom. If TR^2 is sufficiently large, rejection of the null hypothesis that α_1 through α_q are jointly equal to zero is equivalent to rejection of the null hypothesis of no ARCH errors. On the other hand, if TR^2 is sufficiently low, it is possible to conclude that there are no ARCH effects. In the small sample sizes typically used in applied work, an F-test for the null hypothesis $\alpha_1 = \ldots = \alpha_q = 0$ has been shown to be superior to a χ^2 test. Compare the sample value of F to the values in an F-table with q degrees of freedom in the numerator and $T - q$ degrees of freedom in the denominator.

3. ARCH AND GARCH ESTIMATES OF INFLATION

ARCH and GARCH models have become very popular in that they enable the econometrician to estimate the variance of a series at a particular point in time. Clearly, asset-pricing models indicate that the risk premium will depend on the expected return and the variance of that return. The relevant measure is the risk over the holding period, not the unconditional risk. Similarly, a portfolio manager who uses **value-at-risk** might be unwilling to hold a portfolio with a 5 percent chance of losing $1 million. The assessment of the risk should be determined using the conditional distribution of asset returns. To use Engle's example of the importance of using the conditional variance rather than the unconditional variance, consider the nature of the wage-bargaining process. Clearly, firms and unions need to forecast the inflation rate over the duration of the labor contract. Economic theory suggests that the terms of the wage contract will depend on the inflation forecasts and the uncertainty concerning the accuracy of these forecasts. Let $E_t \pi_{t+1}$ denote the conditional expected rate of inflation for $t + 1$ and let σ_m^2 denote the conditional variance. If parties to the contract have rational expectations, the terms of the contract will depend on $E_t \pi_{t+1}$ and σ_m^2 as opposed to the unconditional mean or the unconditional variance.

This example illustrates a very important point. The rational expectations hypothesis asserts that agents do not waste useful information. In forecasting any time series, rational agents use the conditional, rather than the unconditional, distribution of the series. Hence, any test of the wage bargaining model above that uses the historical variance of the inflation rate would be inconsistent with the notion that rational agents make use of all available information (i.e., conditional means and variances). A student of the *economics of uncertainty* can immediately see the importance of ARCH and GARCH models. Theoretical models using *variance as a measure of risk (such as mean-variance analysis), can be tested using the conditional variance.* As such, the growth in the use of ARCH/GARCH methods has been nothing short of impressive. In fact, there are so many types of models of conditional volatility that it is common practice to refer to the entire class of models as ARCH or GARCH models.

Engle's Model of U.K. Inflation

Although Section 2 focused on the residuals of a pure ARMA model, it is possible to estimate the residuals of a standard multiple regression model as ARCH or GARCH processes. In fact, Engle's (1982) seminal paper considered the residuals of a simple model of the wage/price spiral for the U.K over the 1958:II – 1977:II period. Let p_t denote the log of the U.K. consumer price index and w_t denote the log of the index of nominal wage rates. Thus, the rate of inflation is $\pi_t = p_t - p_{t-1}$ and the real wage is $r_t = w_t - p_t$. Engle reports that after some experimentation, he chose the following model of the U.K. inflation rate (standard errors are in parentheses):

$$\pi_t = 0.0257 + 0.334\,\pi_{t-1} + 0.408\,\pi_{t-4} - 0.404\,\pi_{t-5} + 0.0559 r_{t-1} + \varepsilon_t \quad (3.10)$$
$$\quad\;(0.0057)\;(0.103) \qquad (0.110) \qquad (0.114) \qquad (0.0136)$$
$$h_t = 0.000089$$

where h_t is the variance of $\{\varepsilon_t\}$.

The nature of the model is such that increases in the previous period's real wage increase the current inflation rate. Lagged inflation rates at $t-4$ and $t-5$ are intended to capture seasonal factors. All coefficients have a t-statistic greater than 3.0 and a battery of diagnostic tests did not indicate the presence of serial correlation. The estimated variance was the constant value $8.9E - 5$. In testing for ARCH errors, the Lagrange multiplier test for ARCH(1) errors was not significant but the test for an ARCH(4) error process yielded a value of TR^2 equal to 15.2. At the 0.01 significance level, the critical value of χ^2 with four degrees of freedom is 13.28; hence, Engle concludes that there are ARCH errors.

Engle specified an ARCH(4) process forcing the following declining set of weights on the errors:

$$h_t = \alpha_0 + \alpha_1(0.4\varepsilon_{t-1}^2 + 0.3\varepsilon_{t-2}^2 + 0.2\varepsilon_{t-3}^2 + 0.1\varepsilon_{t-4}^2) \quad (3.11)$$

The rationale for choosing a two-parameter variance function was to ensure the nonnegativity and stationarity constraints that might not be satisfied using an unrestricted estimating equation. Given this particular set of weights, the necessary and sufficient conditions for the two constraints to be satisfied are $\alpha_0 > 0$ and $0 < \alpha_1 < 1$.

Engle shows that the estimation of the parameters of (3.10) and (3.11) can be considered separately without loss of asymptotic efficiency. One procedure is to estimate (3.10) using OLS and to save the residuals. From these residuals, an estimate of the parameters of (3.11) can be constructed, and based on these estimates, new estimates of (3.10) can be obtained. To estimate both with full efficiency, continued iterations can be checked to determine whether the separate estimates are converging. Now that many statistical software packages contain nonlinear maximum likelihood estimation routines, the current procedure is to simultaneously estimate both equations using the methodology discussed in Section 8.

Engle's maximum likelihood estimates of the model are

$$\pi_t = 0.0328 + 0.162\,\pi_{t-1} + 0.264\,\pi_{t-4} - 0.325\,\pi_{t-5} + 0.0707 r_{t-1} + \varepsilon_t \quad (3.12)$$
$$\quad(0.0049)\;(0.108) \qquad (0.089) \qquad (0.099) \qquad (0.0115)$$

$$h_t = 1.4E - 5 + 0.955(0.4\varepsilon_{t-1}^2 + 0.3\varepsilon_{t-2}^2 + 0.2\varepsilon_{t-3}^2 + 0.1\varepsilon_{t-4}^2)$$
$$\quad(8.5) \qquad (0.298)$$

The estimated values of h_t are one-step-ahead forecast error variances. All coefficients (except the own lag of the inflation rate) are significant at conventional levels.

For a given real wage, the point estimates of (3.12) imply that the inflation rate is a convergent process. Using the calculated values of the $\{h_t\}$ sequence, Engle finds that the standard deviation of inflation forecasts more than doubled as the economy moved from the "predictable sixties into the chaotic seventies." The point estimate of 0.955 indicates an extreme amount of persistence.

Bollerslev's Estimates of U.S. Inflation

Bollerslev's (1986) estimate of U.S. inflation provides an interesting comparison of a standard autoregressive time-series model (which assumes a constant variance), a model with ARCH errors, and a model with GARCH errors. He notes that the ARCH procedure has been useful in modeling different economic phenomena but points out (see pp. 307–308):

> Common to most ... applications, however, is the introduction of a rather arbitrary linear declining lag structure in the conditional variance equation to take account of the long memory typically found in empirical work, since estimating a totally free lag distribution often will lead to violation of the nonnegativity constraints.

There is no doubt that the lag structure Engle used to model h_t in (3.12) is subject to this criticism. Using quarterly data over the 1948.II to 1983.IV period, Bollerslev (1986) calculates the inflation rate (π_t) as the logarithmic change in the U.S. GNP deflator. He then estimates the autoregression:

$$\pi_t = 0.240 + 0.552\,\pi_{t-1} + 0.177\,\pi_{t-2} + 0.232\,\pi_{t-3} - 0.209\,\pi_{t-4} + \varepsilon_t \qquad (3.13)$$
$$\quad\;\; (0.080)\;(0.083)\qquad (0.089)\qquad (0.090)\qquad (0.080)$$

$$h_t = 0.282$$

Equation (3.13) seems to have all the properties of a well-estimated time-series model. All coefficients are significant at conventional levels (the standard errors are in parentheses) and the estimated values of the autoregressive coefficients imply stationarity. Bollerslev reports that the ACF and PACF do not exhibit any significant coefficients at the 5 percent significance level. However, as is typical of ARCH errors, the ACF and PACF of the *squared* residuals [i.e., ε_t^2] show significant correlations. The Lagrange multiplier tests for ARCH(1), ARCH(4), and ARCH(8) errors are all highly significant.

Bollerslev next estimates the restricted ARCH(8) model originally proposed by Engle and Kraft (1983). By way of comparison to (3.13), he finds

$$\pi_t = 0.138 + 0.423\,\pi_{t-1} + 0.222\,\pi_{t-2} + 0.377\,\pi_{t-3} - 0.175\,\pi_{t-4} + \varepsilon_t \qquad (3.14)$$
$$\quad\;\; (0.059)\;(0.081)\qquad (0.108)\qquad (0.078)\qquad (0.104)$$

$$h_t = 0.058 + 0.802 \sum_{i=1}^{8} [(9-i)/36]\,\varepsilon_{t-i}^2$$

$$(0.003)\;(0.265)$$

Note that the autoregressive coefficients of (3.13) and (3.14) are similar. The models of the variance, however, are quite different. Equation (3.13) assumes a constant variance, whereas (3.14) assumes that the variance (h_t) is a geometrically declining weighted average of the variance in the previous eight quarters.[5] Hence, the inflation rate predictions of the two models should be similar, but the confidence intervals surrounding the forecasts will differ. Equation (3.13) yields a constant interval of unchanging width. Equation (3.14) yields a confidence interval that expands during periods of inflation volatility and contracts in relatively tranquil periods.

In order to test for the presence of a first-order GARCH term in the conditional variance, it is possible to estimate the equation

$$h_t = \alpha_0 + \alpha_1 \sum_{i=1}^{8} [(9-i)/36] \, \varepsilon_{t-i}^2 + \beta_1 h_{t-1} \tag{3.15}$$

The finding that $\beta_1 = 0$ would imply an absence of a first-order moving average term in the conditional variance. Given the difficulties of estimating (3.15), Bollerslev (1986) uses the simpler Lagrange multiplier (LM) test. Formally, the test involves constructing the residuals of the conditional variance of (3.14). The next step is to regress these residuals on a constant and h_{t-1}; the expression TR^2 has a χ^2 distribution with one degree of freedom. Bollerslev finds that $TR^2 = 4.57$; at the 5 percent significance level, he cannot reject the presence of a first-order GARCH process. He then estimates the following GARCH(1, 1) model:

$$\pi_t = 0.141 + 0.433\,\pi_{t-1} + 0.229\,\pi_{t-2} + 0.349\,\pi_{t-3} - 0.162\,\pi_{t-4} + \varepsilon_t$$
$$(0.060)\ (0.081)\quad\ (0.110)\quad\ \ (0.077)\quad\ \ (0.104)$$

$$h_t = 0.007 + 0.135\varepsilon_{t-1}^2 + 0.829 h_{t-1}$$
$$(0.006)\ (0.070)\quad\ (0.068)$$

Diagnostic checks indicate that the ACF and PACF of the squared residuals do not reveal any coefficients exceeding $2T^{-0.5}$. LM tests for the presence of additional lags of ε_t^2 and for the presence of h_{t-2} are not significant at the 5 percent level.

4. A GARCH MODEL OF THE PPI: AN EXAMPLE

To get a better idea of the actual process of fitting a GARCH model, reconsider the U.S. producer price index data used in the last chapter. Recall that the Box–Jenkins approach led us to select the following model of the logarithmic change in the producer price index

$$\pi_t = 0.003 + 0.768\,\pi_{t-1} + \varepsilon_t - 0.358\varepsilon_{t-1} + 0.297\varepsilon_{t-4} \tag{3.16}$$

where we now use the symbol π_t to denote $\Delta ln(ppi_t)$.

As shown in Chapter 2, the estimated model performed quite well. All estimated parameters were significant at conventional levels, and both the AIC and SBC selected the ARMA[(1, (1, 4)] specification. The ACF and PACF of the residuals do not indicate any serial correlation. Recall that the only suspect autocorrelation coefficient is for lag 6; the value $\rho_6 = 0.136$ is about 1.7 standard deviations from zero. All other autocorrelations and partial autocorrelations are less than 0.11. The Ljung–Box Q-statistics for lags of 4, 12, and 24 quarters are 1.43, 11.32, and 19.13; none of these values are significant at conventional levels. Moreover, there was no evidence of structural change in the estimated coefficients. Nevertheless, during the 1970s, there was a period of unusual volatility that is characteristic of a GARCH process. The aim of this section is to illustrate a step-by-step analysis of a GARCH estimation of the rate of inflation as measured by the producer price index. The data series is contained in the file labeled QUARTERLY.XLS. You should use this data to replicate the following results.

Although the model appears adequate, the volatility during the 1970s suggests an examination of the ACF and PACF of the squared residuals. The autocorrelations of the *squared* residuals are such that $\rho_1 = 0.128$, $\rho_2 = 0.319$, $\rho_3 = 0.098$, and $\rho_4 = 0.295$. Other values for ρ_i are generally 0.10 or less. The Ljung–Box Q-statistics for the squared residuals are all highly significant; for example, $Q(4) = 36.91$ and $Q(12) = 46.83$, which are both significant at the 0.00001 level.

Formal Tests for ARCH Errors

Next, let $\hat{\varepsilon}_t$ denote the residuals of (3.16) and consider the ARCH(q) model for lag lengths of one, four, and eight quarters:

$$\hat{\varepsilon}_t^2 = \alpha_0 + \sum_{i=1}^{q} \alpha_i \, \hat{\varepsilon}_{t-i}^2 \qquad (3.17)$$

Estimating (3.17) using OLS, the calculated values of TR^2 for $q = 1, 4$, and 8 are 29.73, 47.36, and 49.53, respectively. Hence, there appear to be ARCH errors at the 1 percent significance level; the critical values of χ^2 with one, four, and eight degrees of freedom are 5.41, 11.67, and 18.17, respectively. In small samples, it is common to use an F-test to determine whether it is possible to reject the restriction $\alpha_1 = \alpha_2 = \ldots = \alpha_q = 0$. For values of $q = 4$, the sample value of F is 6.97; with four degrees of freedom, the significance level is 0.00003. Hence, we can be confident that there are ARCH effects in the model of the inflation rate.

Since the autocorrelations of the squared residuals are all quite small after lag 4, it seems worthwhile to try to pin down the lag length to an ARCH(4) process. A straightforward method is to estimate (3.17) for $q = 8$. In this instance, the sample value of F for the null hypothesis $\alpha_5 = \alpha_6 = \alpha_7 = \alpha_8 = 0$ is 1.05. We can conclude that only four lags are necessary since, with four degrees of freedom, this value has a significance level of 0.38.

The same procedure can be used to test whether the model is an ARCH(1) or an ARCH(4) process. To perform the test, regress $\hat{\varepsilon}_t^2$ on a constant and on its own four lags. The sample F-value for the null hypothesis $\alpha_2 = \alpha_3 = \alpha_4 = 0$ is 8.29. With three degrees of freedom in the numerator (since there are three restrictions) and 158 degrees of freedom in the denominator, the 5 percent and 1 percent critical values of F are 2.66 and 3.90, respectively. Hence, it hardly seems plausible to conclude that an ARCH(1) characterizes the error process; lags 2 through 4 cannot be excluded from (3.17).

Alternative Estimates of the Model

At this point, one might be tempted to plot the ACF and PACF of the squared residuals and estimate the squared residuals using Box–Jenkins methods. In this way, a parsimonious model of the error process could be obtained. However, a word of caution is in order. The problem with this strategy is that (3.16) was estimated under the assumption that the conditional variance was constant. As such, it does not make sense to use the residuals of (3.16) to estimate a model in which the conditional variance is not constant. The point is that it is necessary to be cautious about pinning down the conditional variance to an ARCH(4) process. The simplest way to circumvent the problem is to estimate the model of the inflation rate and the model of the conditional variance simultaneously. As such, GARCH processes are typically estimated by maximum likelihood techniques so as to obtain estimates that are fully efficient. The ARCH(4) process is a good starting point for a model of the conditional variance.

Overall, these tests suggest estimating the inflation rate using an ARMA(1, (1, 4)) model assuming an ARCH(4) error process. The results from maximum likelihood estimation are (with t-statistics in parentheses)

$$\pi_t = 0.0033 + 0.5727\,\pi_{t-1} + \varepsilon_t - 0.0389\varepsilon_{t-1} + 0.2830\varepsilon_{t-4}$$
$$\quad (0.167)\quad (6.12)\qquad\qquad (-0.370)\qquad (3.47)$$

$$h_t = 4.53E-5 + 0.094\varepsilon_{t-1}^2 + 0.299\varepsilon_{t-2}^2 - 0.055\varepsilon_{t-3}^2 + 0.307\varepsilon_{t-4}^2$$
$$\quad (5.04)\qquad (1.08)\qquad (2.18)\qquad (-1.38)\qquad (2.90)$$

The first problem is that the estimated coefficient on ε_{t-3}^2 is negative. The implication is that a large enough realization of ε_{t-3}^2 can render h_t negative. Since the t-statistic is low, one possibility is to eliminate ε_{t-3}^2 from the model of the conditional variance. Some software packages allow you to estimate a GARCH model that constrains all coefficients of the conditional variance to be nonnegative. Although this is a possible solution, you should also be concerned that there are a number of insignificant coefficients. Also note that the estimated coefficient on ε_{t-1} in the equation for π_t is about one standard error from zero; we know, however, that eliminating this coefficient from the ARMA(1, (1, 4)) model of inflation leads to residuals which are serially correlated. Moreover, three values of the ARCH(4) error process are insignificantly different from zero at conventional significance levels. The likely solution to the problem concerns the modeling of the ARCH process; perhaps a more parsimonious model is in order.

One approach to reducing the number of estimated parameters is to constrain the conditional variance to have the same declining weights that Engle used in (3.11). The maximum likelihood estimates of this constrained ARCH(4) process are

$$\pi_t = 0.0026 + 0.5800\,\pi_{t-1} + \varepsilon_t - 0.1162\varepsilon_{t-1} + 0.2827\varepsilon_{t-4}$$
$$\quad (2.52)\quad (4.20)\qquad\qquad (-0.77)\qquad (3.74)$$

$$h_t = 4.92E-5 + 0.6005(0.4\varepsilon_{t-1}^2 + 0.3\varepsilon_{t-2}^2 + 0.2\varepsilon_{t-3}^2 + 0.1\varepsilon_{t-4}^2)$$
$$\quad (4.25)\qquad (3.38)$$

Here, the estimated parameters of the ARCH process are both positive and significantly different from zero. The estimated value of α_1 ($= 0.6005$) implies that h_t is convergent. One problem with this model is that the MA(1) coefficient in the equation for π_t are not significant at the 5 percent level. One way to proceed is to try alternative weighting patterns and to select the "best" pattern. Of course, this approach is subject to Bollerslev's criticism of being completely ad hoc.

A better alternative is to use a GARCH(1, 1) model. As such, the process is estimated as

$$\pi_t = 0.0050 + 0.7155\,\pi_{t-1} + \varepsilon_t - 0.2831\,\varepsilon_{t-1} + 0.2647\,\varepsilon_{t-4}$$
$$\qquad\;\;(1.82)\quad\;\;(7.42)\qquad\qquad\;(-2.26)\qquad\quad(2.67)$$
$$h_t = 1.74E-5 + 0.2100\,\varepsilon_{t-1}^2 + 0.6410\,h_{t-1}$$
$$\quad(1.54)\qquad\;\;(2.14)\qquad\quad\;\;(3.62)$$

It might be argued that the intercept term in the model for π_t should be excluded. All of the other coefficients imply stationarity and are significant at conventional levels. The intercept in the equation for h_t is not significant at conventional levels. Nevertheless, we would not want to exclude this term; a zero intercept would mean that the long-run value of the variance would be zero. The other coefficients in the equation for h_t are significant and imply substantial persistence in conditional volatility. The value of the maximized likelihood function is greater for the GARCH(1, 1) model than for the pure ARCH processes even though all models were estimated over the same time period.[6]

Diagnostic tests did not indicate the need to include other lags into the GARCH(1, 1) model. The Lagrange multiplier tests for the presence of additional values of α_i or β_i were insignificant at conventional levels. The solid line in Figure 3.8 shows the one-step-ahead forecast $E_t \pi_{t+1}$. Since h_t is an estimate of the conditional variance of π_t, $(h_{t+1})^{1/2}$ is the standard error of the one-step-ahead forecast. The dashed lines in the figure represent a band of $\pm 2\,(h_{t+1})^{1/2}$ surrounding the one-step-ahead forecast of π_{t+1}. In

— Forecasts
···· +2 Standard deviations
···· −2 Standard deviations

FIGURE 3.8 Inflation Forecasts

contrast to the assumption of a constant conditional variance, note that the band width increases in the mid-1970s and in the latter part of the 1980s through the early 1990s.

5. A GARCH MODEL OF RISK

An interesting application of GARCH modeling is provided by Holt and Aradhyula (1990). Their theoretical framework stands in contrast to the cobweb model (see Section 5 of Chapter 1) in that rational expectations are assumed to prevail in the agricultural sector. The aim of the study is to examine the extent to which producers in the U.S. broiler (i.e., chicken) industry exhibit risk-averse behavior. To this end, the supply function for the U.S. broiler industry takes the form[7]

$$q_t = a_0 + a_1 p_t^e - a_2 h_t - a_3 pfeed_{t-1} + a_4 hatch_{t-1} + a_5 q_{t-4} + \varepsilon_{1t} \quad (3.18)$$

where: q_t = quantity of broiler production (in millions of pounds) in t
p_t^e = expected real price of broilers at t conditioned on the information at
  $t - 1$ (so that $p_t^e = E_{t-1} p_t$)
h_t = expected variance of the price of broilers in t conditioned on the
  information at $t - 1$
$pfeed_{t-1}$ = real price of broiler feed (in cents per pound) at $t - 1$
$hatch_{t-1}$ = hatch of broiler-type chicks in commercial hatcheries (measured in
  thousands) in period $t - 1$
ε_{1t} = supply shock in t
and the length of the time period is one quarter.

The supply function is based on the biological fact that the production cycle of broilers is about two months. Since bimonthly data are unavailable, the model assumes that the supply decision is positively related to the price expectation formed by producers in the previous quarter. Given that feed accounts for the bulk of production costs, real feed prices lagged one quarter are negatively related to broiler production in t. Obviously, the *hatch* available in $t - 1$ increases the number of broilers that can be marketed in t. The fourth lag of broiler production is included to account for the possibility that production in any period may not fully adjust to the desired level of production.

For our purposes, the most interesting part of the study is the negative effect of the conditional variance of price on broiler supply. The timing of the production process is such that feed and other production costs must be incurred before output is sold in the market. In the planning stage, producers must forecast the price that will prevail two months hence. The greater p_t^e, the greater the number of chicks that will be fed and brought to market. If price variability is very low, these forecasts can be held with confidence. Increased price variability decreases the accuracy of the forecasts and decreases broiler supply. Risk-averse producers will opt to raise and market fewer broilers when the conditional volatility of price is high.

In the initial stage of the study, broiler prices are estimated as the AR(4) process

$$(1 - \beta_1 L - \beta_2 L^2 - \beta_3 L^3 - \beta_4 L^4) p_t = \beta_0 + \varepsilon_{2t} \quad (3.19)$$

Ljung–Box Q-statistics for various lag lengths indicate that the residual series appear to be white noise at the 5 percent level. However, the Ljung–Box Q-statistics for the squared residuals—that is, the $\{\varepsilon_{2t}^2\}$—of 32.4 is significant at the 5 percent level. Thus, Holt and Aradhyula conclude that the variance of the price is heteroskedastic.

In the second stage of the study, several low-order GARCH estimates of (3.19) are compared. Goodness-of-fit statistics and significance tests suggest a GARCH(1, 1) process. In the third stage, the supply equation (3.18) and a GARCH(1, 1) process are simultaneously estimated. The estimated price equation (with standard errors in parentheses) is

$$(1 - 0.511L - 0.129L^2 - 0.130L^3 - 0.138L^4)p_t = 1.632 + \varepsilon_{2t} \quad (3.20)$$
$$\quad (0.092) \quad (0.098) \quad (0.094) \quad (0.073) \qquad (1.347)$$

$$h_t = 1.353 + 0.162\varepsilon_{2t-1}^2 + 0.591h_{t-1} \qquad (3.21)$$
$$(0.747) \quad (0.80) \qquad (0.175)$$

Equations (3.20) and (3.21) are well-behaved in that (1) all estimated coefficients are significant at conventional significance levels; (2) all coefficients of the conditional variance equation are positive; and (3) the coefficients all imply convergent processes.

Holt and Aradhyula assume that producers use (3.20) and (3.21) to form their price expectations. Combining these estimates with (3.18) yields the supply equation

$$q_t = 2.767p_t^e - 0.521h_t - 4.325pfeed_{t-1} + 1.887hatch_{t-1} + 0.603q_{t-4} + \varepsilon_{1t}$$
$$(0.585) \quad (0.344) \quad (1.463) \qquad (0.205) \qquad (0.065)$$

All estimated coefficients are significant at conventional levels and have the appropriate sign. An increase in the expected price increases broiler output. Increased uncertainty, as measured by conditional variance, acts to decrease output. This forward-looking rational expectations formulation is at odds with the more traditional cobweb model discussed in Chapter 1. In order to compare the two formulations, Holt and Aradhyula (1990) also consider an adaptive expectations formulation (see Exercise 2 in Chapter 1). Under adaptive expectations, price expectations are formed according to a weighted average of the previous period's price and the previous period's price expectation:

$$p_t^e = \alpha p_{t-1} + (1 - \alpha)p_{t-1}^e$$

or solving for p_t^e in terms of the $\{p_t\}$ sequence, we obtain

$$p_t^e = \alpha \sum_{i=0}^{\infty} (1 - \alpha)^i p_{t-1-i}$$

Similarly, the adaptive expectations formulation for conditional risk is given by

$$h_t = \beta \sum_{i=0}^{\infty} (1 - \beta)^i (p_{t-1-i} - p_{t-1-i}^e)^2 \qquad (3.22)$$

where $0 < \beta < 1$ and $(p_{t-1-i} - p_{t-1-i}^e)^2$ is the forecast-error variance for period $t-i$.

Note that in (3.22) the expected measure of risk as viewed by producers is not necessarily the actual conditional variance. The estimates of the two models differ concerning the implied long-run elasticities of supply with respect to expected price and conditional variance.[8] Respectively, the estimated long-run elasticities of supply with respect to expected price are 0.587 and 0.399 in the rational expectations and adaptive expectations formulations. Similarly, rational and adaptive expectations formulations yield long-run supply elasticities of conditional variance of –0.030 and –0.013, respectively. Not surprisingly, the adaptive expectations model suggests a more sluggish supply response than does the forward-looking rational expectations model.

6. THE ARCH-M MODEL

Engle, Lilien, and Robins (1987) extend the basic ARCH framework to allow the mean of a sequence to depend on its own conditional variance. This class of model, called the ARCH in mean (ARCH-M) model, is particularly suited to the study of asset markets. The basic insight is that risk-averse agents will require compensation for holding a risky asset. Given that an asset's *riskiness* can be measured by the variance of returns, the risk premium will be an increasing function of the conditional variance of returns.[9] Engle, Lilien, and Robins express this idea by writing the excess return from holding a risky asset as

$$y_t = \mu_t + \varepsilon_t \tag{3.23}$$

where: y_t = excess return from holding a long-term asset relative to a one-period treasury bill

μ_t = risk premium necessary to induce the risk-averse agent to hold the long-term asset rather than the one-period bond

ε_t = unforecastable shock to the excess return on the long-term asset

To explain (3.23), note that the expected excess return from holding the long-term asset must be just equal to the risk premium:[10]

$$E_{t-1}y_t = \mu_t$$

Engle, Lilien, and Robins assume that the risk premium is an increasing function of the conditional variance of ε_t; in other words, the greater the conditional variance of returns, the greater the compensation necessary to induce the agent to hold the long-term asset. Mathematically, if h_t is the conditional variance of ε_t, the risk premium can be expressed as

$$\mu_t = \beta + \delta h_t \qquad \delta > 0 \tag{3.24}$$

where h_t is the ARCH(q) process:

$$h_t = \alpha_0 + \sum_{i=1}^{q} \alpha_i \varepsilon_{t-i}^2 \tag{3.25}$$

As a set, equations (3.23), (3.24), and (3.25) constitute the basic ARCH-M model. From (3.23) and (3.24), the conditional mean of y_t depends on the conditional variance h_t. From (3.25), the conditional variance is an ARCH(q) process. It should be pointed out that if the conditional variance is constant (i.e., if $\alpha_1 = \alpha_2 = \ldots = \alpha_q = 0$) the ARCH-M model degenerates into the more traditional case of a constant risk premium.

Figure 3.9 illustrates two different ARCH-M processes. The upper-left-hand graph (a) of the figure shows 60 realizations of a simulated white-noise process denoted by $\{\varepsilon_t\}$. Note the temporary increase in volatility during periods 20 to 30. By initializing $\varepsilon_0 = 0$, the conditional variance was constructed as the first-order ARCH process:

$$h_t = 1 + 0.65\varepsilon_{t-1}^2$$

As you can see in the upper-right-hand graph (b), the volatility in $\{\varepsilon_t\}$ translates into increases in conditional variance. Note that large positive *and* negative changes realizations of ε_{t-1} result in a large value of h_t; it is the square of each $\{\varepsilon_t\}$ realization that enters the conditional variance. In the lower-left graph (c), the values of β and δ are set equal to –4 and +4, respectively. As such, the y_t sequence is constructed as $y_t = -4 + 4h_t + \varepsilon_t$. You can clearly see that y_t is above its long-run value during the period of volatility. In the simulation, conditional volatility translates itself into increases in the values of $\{y_t\}$. In the latter portion of the sample, the volatility of $\{\varepsilon_t\}$ diminishes and the values y_{30} through y_{60} fluctuate around their long-run mean.

The lower-right-hand graph (d) reduces the influence of ARCH-M effects by reducing the magnitude of δ and β (see Exercise 4 at the end of this chapter). Obviously, if $\delta = 0$, there are no ARCH-M effects at all. As you can see by comparing the two lower graphs, y_t more closely mimics the ε_t sequence when the magnitude of δ is diminished from $\delta = 4$ to $\delta = 1$.[11]

As in any ARCH or GARCH model, a Lagrange multiplier test can be used to detect the presence of conditional volatility. The LM tests are relatively simple to conduct since they do not require estimation of the full model. The statistic TR^2 is

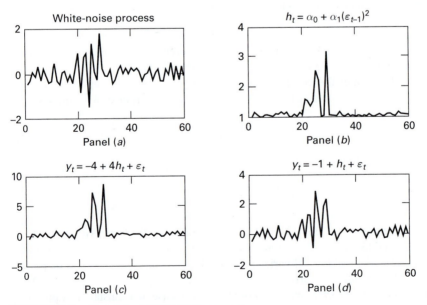

FIGURE 3.9 Simulated ARCH-M Processes

asymptotically distributed as χ^2 with degrees of freedom equal to the number of restrictions. Nevertheless, as in the model for the PPI, some trial and error is necessary to arrive at the most appropriate model of the conditional variance.

Implementation

Using quarterly data from 1960:I to 1984:II, Engle, Lilien, and Robins (1987) constructed the excess yield on six-month treasury bills as follows. Let r_t denote the quarterly yield on a three-month treasury bill held from t to $(t + 1)$. Rolling over all proceeds, at the end of two quarters an individual investing \$1 at the beginning of period t will have $(1 + r_t)(1 + r_{t+1})$ dollars. In the same fashion, if R_t denotes the quarterly yield on a six-month treasury bill, buying and holding the six-month bill for the full two quarters will result in $(1 + R_t)^2$ dollars. The excess yield, y_t, due to holding the six-month bill is

$$y_t = (1 + R_t)^2 - (1 + r_{t+1})(1 + r_t)$$

which is approximately equal to

$$y_t = 2R_t - r_{t+1} - r_t$$

The results from regressing the excess yield on a constant are as follows, with the t-statistic in parentheses:

$$y_t = 0.142 + \varepsilon_t \qquad (3.26)$$
$$(4.04)$$

The excess yield of 0.142 percent per quarter is more than four standard deviations from zero. The problem with this estimation method is that the post-1979 period showed markedly higher volatility than the earlier sample period. To test for the presence of ARCH errors, the squared residuals were regressed on a weighted average of past squared residuals, as in (3.11). The LM test for the restriction $\alpha_1 = 0$ yields a value of $TR^2 = 10.1$, which has a χ^2 distribution with one degree of freedom. At the 1 percent significance level, the critical value of χ^2 with one degree of freedom is 6.635; hence, there is strong evidence of heteroskedasticity. Thus, there appear to be ARCH errors; as a result, (3.26) is misspecified if individuals demand a risk premium.

The maximum likelihood estimates of the ARCH-M model and the associated t-statistics are

$$y_t = -0.0241 + 0.687h_t + \varepsilon_t$$
$$(-1.29) \quad (5.15)$$

$$h_t = 0.0023 + 1.64(0.4\varepsilon_{t-1}^2 + 0.3\varepsilon_{t-2}^2 + 0.2\varepsilon_{t-3}^2 + 0.1\varepsilon_{t-4}^2)$$
$$(1.08) \quad (6.30)$$

The estimated coefficients imply a time varying risk premium. The estimated parameter of the ARCH equation of 1.64 implies that the unconditional variance is infinite. Although this is troublesome, the conditional variance is finite. Shocks to ε_{t-i} act to increase the conditional variance so that there are periods of tranquility and volatility. During volatile periods, the risk premium rises as risk-averse agents seek assets that are conditionally less risky.

Exercise 7 at the end of this chapter asks you to estimate such an ARCH-M model using simulated data. The questions are designed to guide you through a typical estimation procedure.

7. ADDITIONAL PROPERTIES OF GARCH PROCESSES

Whenever you estimate a GARCH process, you will be estimating the two interrelated equations

$$y_t = a_0 + \beta x_t + \varepsilon_t$$

and

$$\varepsilon_t = v_t(\alpha_0 + \alpha_1 \varepsilon_{t-1}^2 + \dots + \alpha_q \varepsilon_{t-q}^2 + \beta_1 h_{t-1} + \dots + \beta_p h_{t-p})^{0.5} \quad (3.27)$$

where x_t can be an ARMA process of order (p^m, q^m). Moreover, x_t can contain exogenous variables.

The first equation is a model of the mean and the second yields the model of the variance. The symbols p^m and q^m are used to denote that the order of the ARMA process for the mean need not equal the order of the GARCH(p, q) equation. The two equations are related in that h_t is the conditional variance of ε_t; hence, the GARCH process of (3.27) is the conditional variance of the mean equation. Do not make the mistake of assuming that ε_t^2 is the conditional variance itself. Given that $\varepsilon_t = v_t(h_t)^{0.5}$, it follows that the relationship between h_t and ε_t^2 is

$$\varepsilon_t^2 = v_t^2 h_t$$

and, since $Ev_t^2 = E_{t-1}v_t^2 = 1$,

$$E_{t-1}\varepsilon_t^2 = h_t$$

Thus, h_t is the conditional variance of the $\{\varepsilon_t\}$ sequence.

A GARCH(1, 1) specification is the most popular form of conditional volatility. This is especially true for financial data where volatility shocks are very persistent. As such, it is worthwhile to pay special attention to this form of GARCH process.

Properties of GARCH(1, 1) Error Processes

In the absence of conditional heteroskedasticity, the $\{\varepsilon_t\}$ sequence has a mean of zero, a constant variance, and all autocorrelations between ε_t and ε_{t-j} are zero. The situation is clearly more complicated with GARCH processes. At this point, it is desirable to establish the properties of the GARCH(1, 1) error process. In doing so, we can generalize some of the discussion of ARCH(1) models presented in Section 2. If you take the conditional expectation of the GARCH(1, 1) process, you should have no trouble verifying that

$$E_{t-1}\varepsilon_t^2 = \alpha_0 + \alpha_1 \varepsilon_{t-1}^2 + \beta_1 h_{t-1}$$

or

$$h_t = \alpha_0 + \alpha_1 \varepsilon_{t-1}^2 + \beta_1 h_{t-1} \quad (3.28)$$

The mean of ε_t: The unconditional mean of ε_t is zero. If you take the expected value of (3.27), you obtain

$$E\varepsilon_t = E[v_t(h_t)^{1/2}]$$

Since h_t does not depend on v_t and $Ev_t = 0$, it immediately follows that $E\varepsilon_t = 0$.
The variance of ε_t: Since

$$\varepsilon_t^2 = v_t^2(\alpha_0 + \alpha_1 \varepsilon_{t-1}^2 + \beta_1 h_{t-1})$$

it follows that the unconditional variance of a GARCH(1, 1) process is

$$E\varepsilon_t^2 = Ev_t^2(\alpha_0 + \alpha_1 E\varepsilon_{t-1}^2 + \beta_1 Eh_{t-1}) \tag{3.29}$$

We can simplify this expression if we recognize that $Ev_t^2 = 1$ and $E\varepsilon_{t-i}^2 = Eh_{t-i}$. This second relationship follows from the **law of iterated expectations.** The form of the law we need guarantees that $E\varepsilon_t^2 = E(E_{t-1}\varepsilon_t^2)$. In essence, the unconditional expectation of the conditional variance is just the unconditional variance. As such, we can lag the relationship one period and write $E\varepsilon_{t-i}^2 = E(E_{t-2}\varepsilon_{t-i}^2)$, so that $E\varepsilon_{t-i}^2 = E(h_{t-1})$. If we substitute this condition into (3.29), it follows that

$$E\varepsilon_t^2 = \alpha_0 + (\alpha_1 + \beta_1)E\varepsilon_{t-1}^2 \tag{3.30}$$

Thus, (3.30) yields the solution for the unconditional variance. Given that $\alpha_1 + \beta_1 < 0$, the unconditional variance is

$$E\varepsilon_t^2 = \alpha_0 / (1 - \alpha_1 - \beta_1)$$

For the more general GARCH(p, q) model, it follows that the variance will be finite if

$$1 - \sum_{i=1}^{q}\alpha_i - \sum_{i=1}^{p}\beta_i > 0$$

The autocorrelation function: The autocorrelations $E\varepsilon_t \varepsilon_{t-j}$ are all equal to zero. Consider

$$E\varepsilon_t \varepsilon_{t-j} = E[v_t(h_t)^{1/2}v_{t-j}(h_{t-j})^{1/2}]$$

Since h_t, v_{t-j}, and h_{t-j} do not depend on the value of v_t and $Ev_t = 0$, it follows that all autocorrelations are zero for $j \neq 0$.
The conditional variance: The conditional variance of the error process is h_t. Consider

$$E_{t-1}\varepsilon_t^2 = E_{t-1}v_t^2 h_t = h_t$$

This simple result is the essential feature of GARCH modeling. The conditional variance of the error process is *not* constant. With the appropriate specification of the parameters of h_t, it is possible to model and forecast the conditional variance of the $\{y_t\}$ process.
Volatility persistence: In a GARCH process, the errors are uncorrelated in that $E\varepsilon_t \varepsilon_{t-j} = 0$. However, as shown in (3.28), the squared errors of a GARCH(1, 1) process are correlated. You should be able to show that the degree of autoregressive

decay of the squared residuals is $(\alpha_1 + \beta_1)$. In fact, the ACF of the squared residuals of GARCH(1, 1) process tend to behave like that of an ARMA(1, 1) process.

Large values of α_1 and β_1 both act to increase the conditional volatility, but they do so in different ways. The larger is α_1, the larger is the response of h_t to new information; clearly, if α_1 is large, a v_t shock has a sizable effect on ε_t^2 and h_{t+1}. To illustrate the point, two GARCH(1, 1) processes were simulated using the identical set of random numbers for the $\{v_t\}$ sequence. In both cases, h_0 and ε_0 were initialized and the remaining values of the series were constructed using the relationship $\varepsilon_t^2 = v_t^2 h_t$ and

$$\text{Model 1:} \qquad h_t = 1 + 0.7\varepsilon_{t-1}^2 + 0.2h_{t-1}$$

$$\text{Model 2:} \qquad h_t = 1 + 0.2\varepsilon_{t-1}^2 + 0.7h_{t-1}$$

In order to avoid the effect of selecting the specific values for the initial conditions, the first 100 realizations were eliminated; the remaining 250 realizations are shown in Figure 3.10. Given the value of h_t, a large v_t shock has its immediate effect on ε_t^2. Since model 1 has a larger value of α_1, the effect of this shock is more pronounced in the subsequent period. In contrast, the peaks in the series generated using model 2 are more persistent. Since model 2 has the larger value of β_1, its conditional variance displays more autoregressive persistence.

FIGURE 3.10   Persistence in the GARCH(1, 1) Model

Also note that the value of α_1 must be strictly positive. Hence, the analogy between the ACF of the squared residuals of a GARCH(1, 1) and the ACF of the residuals from an ARMA(1, 1) process is not perfect. If $\alpha_1 = 0$, it is possible to write (3.28) as

$$h_t = \alpha_0 + \beta_1 h_{t-1}$$

so that there is no interaction between $\{v_t\}$ and h_t. As such, the model for the conditional variance cannot be identified. The analogy is even less clear in the more general case of a GARCH(p, q) process. Bollerslev (1986) proves that the ACF of the squared residuals resulting from a GARCH(p, q) process acts like that of an ARMA(m, p) process where $m = \max(p, q)$. This makes identification of the most appropriate values of p and q somewhat difficult. Question 3 at the end of the chapter guides you through a proof that the ACF of a GARCH(2, 1) has the same properties as the ACF of a GARCH(2, 2) model.

Assessing the Fit

One way to assess the adequacy of a GARCH model is to see how well it fits the data. Some authors use the AIC and SBC discussed in Chapter 2. Moreover, some statistical software packages report these same goodness-of-fit measures for any type of GARCH estimation. However, you need to be careful in interpreting these results since, as stated by Bollerslev, Engle, and Nelson (1994), "... their statistical properties in the ARCH context are largely unknown." Consider the AIC

$$\text{AIC} = T \ln(\text{residual sum of squares}) + 2n$$

Note that *residual sum of squares* is identical to $\Sigma \varepsilon_t^2$; hence, the AIC and SBC measure squared deviations of the model of the mean. Instead, suppose you want to know how well the model of the variance fits the data. For example, you might want to see if an ARCH(2) provides a better fit of the variance than a GARCH(1, 1). As an analogy to the residual sum of squares, consider

$$\text{RSS}' = \sum_{t=1}^{T} (\varepsilon_t^2 - h_t)^2$$

Here, RSS' is the sum of the squared differences between ε_t^2 and the fitted value of the conditional variance. Since RSS' will be small if the fitted values of h_t are close to ε_t^2, you can select the model that yields the smallest value of RSS'. One way to compare alternative models is to estimate a regression of the fitted values of $(\varepsilon_t)^2$ on the values of h_t. The model yielding the largest R^2 (i.e., the one with the best fit) is deemed to be the most appropriate model. Note that RSS' does not provide a penalty for the estimation of additional parameters.

Although little is known about the various selection criteria for assessing models of the variance, a suggestion that seems promising is to use measures analogous to the AIC and SBC. As explained in more detail in Section 8, if you assume that the error process is normal, the maximized value of the likelihood function depends on

$$L = -\sum_{t=1}^{T} [\ln(h_t) + \varepsilon_t^2 / h_t]$$

where: $\hat{h}_t$ = estimated values of the conditional variance
$\hat{\varepsilon}_t^2$ = fitted values of the squared residuals
L = maximized value of the log-likelihood function

Notice that L does not include a penalty for the estimation of additional parameters. However, you can construct the AIC and SBC using

$$AIC' = -\ln L + 2n$$
$$SBC' = -\ln L + n \ln(T)$$

where L is defined above and n is the number of estimated parameters.

Diagnostic Checks for Model Adequacy

In addition to providing a good fit, an estimated GARCH model should capture all dynamic aspects of the model of the mean and the model of the variance. The estimated residuals should be serially uncorrelated and should not display any remaining conditional volatility. You can test to ensure that your model has captured these properties by standardizing the residuals; simply divide $\hat{\varepsilon}_t$ by $\hat{h}_t^{1/2}$. Thus, you standardize each residual using its conditional standard deviation. The resulting series, which we call $\hat{s}_t$, should have a mean of zero and a variance of unity.

If there is any serial correlation in the $\{\hat{s}_t\}$ sequence, the model of the mean is not properly specified. To test the model of the mean, form the Ljung–Box Q-statistics for the $\{\hat{s}_t\}$ sequence. You should not be able to reject the null hypothesis that the various Q-statistics are equal to zero.

To test for remaining GARCH effects, form the Ljung–Box Q-statistics of the squared standardized residuals (i.e., $\hat{s}_t^2$). If there are no remaining GARCH effects, you should not be able to reject the null hypothesis that the sample values of the Q-statistics are equal to zero. The basic idea is that $\hat{s}_t^2$ is an estimate of $\varepsilon_t^2 / h_t = v_t^2$. Hence, the properties of the $\hat{s}_t^2$ sequence should mimic those of a white-noise process.

Once you have obtained a satisfactory model, you can forecast future values of y_t and its conditional variance. Moreover, you can place confidence bands around the forecast using the estimates of conditional standard deviation. Since $E_t \varepsilon_{t+1}^2 = h_{t+1}$, a two-standard deviation confidence interval for your forecast can be constructed using

$$E_t y_{t+1} \pm 2(h_{t+1})^{0.5}$$

The result is quite general; since the mean of any GARCH process is zero, *the optimal j-step-ahead forecast of y_{t+j} does not depend on the presence of GARCH errors.* However, the size of any confidence interval surrounding the forecasts does depend on the conditional volatility.

Clearly, in times when there is substantial conditional volatility (i.e, when h_{t+1} is large), the variance of the forecast error will be large. Simply put, we cannot be as confident of our forecasts in periods when conditional volatility is high.

Forecasting the Conditional Variance

The one-step-ahead forecast of the conditional variance is easy to obtain. If we update h_t by one period, we find

$$h_{t+1} = \alpha_0 + \alpha_1 \varepsilon_t^2 + \beta_1 h_t$$

Since ε_t^2 and h_t are known in period t, the one-step-ahead forecast is simply $\alpha_0 + \alpha_1 \varepsilon_t^2 + \beta_1 h_t$. It is only somewhat more difficult to obtain the j-step-ahead forecasts. To begin, use the fact that $\varepsilon_t^2 = v_t^2 h_t$ so that $\varepsilon_{t+j}^2 = v_{t+j}^2 h_{t+j}$. If you update by j periods and take the conditional expectation of each side, it should be clear that

$$E_t \varepsilon_{t+j}^2 = E_t(v_{t+j}^2 h_{t+j})$$

Since v_{t+j} is independent of h_{t+j} and $E_t v_{t+j}^2 = 1$, it follows that

$$E_t \varepsilon_{t+j}^2 = E_t h_{t+j} \tag{3.31}$$

We can use (3.31) to obtain the forecasts of the conditional variance of the GARCH(1, 1) process. Update (3.28) by j periods to obtain,

$$h_{t+j} = \alpha_0 + \alpha_1 \varepsilon_{t+j-1}^2 + \beta_1 h_{t+j-1}$$

and take the conditional expectation

$$E_t h_{t+j} = \alpha_0 + \alpha_1 E_t \varepsilon_{t+j-1}^2 + \beta_1 E_t h_{t+j-1}$$

If you combine this relationship with (3.31), it is easy to verify that

$$E_t h_{t+j} = \alpha_0 + (\alpha_1 + \beta_1) E_t h_{t+j-1} \tag{3.32}$$

Given h_{t+1}, we can use (3.32) to forecast all subsequent values of the conditional variance as

$$E_t h_{t+j} = \alpha_0 [1 + (\alpha_1 + \beta_1) + (\alpha_1 + \beta_1)^2 + \ldots + (\alpha_1 + \beta_1)^{j-1}] + (\alpha_1 + \beta_1)^j h_t$$

If $\alpha_1 + \beta_1 < 1$, the conditional forecasts of h_{t+j} will converge to the long-run value

$$E h_t = \alpha_0 / (1 - \alpha_1 - \beta_1)$$

Similarly, we can forecast the conditional variance of the ARCH(q) process

$$h_t = \alpha_0 + \alpha_1 \varepsilon_{t-1}^2 + \ldots + \alpha_q \varepsilon_{t-q}^2 \tag{3.33}$$

If we update (3.33) by one period, we obtain

$$h_{t+1} = \alpha_0 + \alpha_1 \varepsilon_t^2 + \ldots + \alpha_q \varepsilon_{t-q+1}^2$$

As mentioned above, at period t, we have all of the information necessary to calculate the value of h_{t+1} for any GARCH process. Now, if we update (3.33) by two periods and take the conditional expectation, we obtain

$$E_t h_{t+2} = \alpha_0 + \alpha_1 E_t \varepsilon_{t+1}^2 + \ldots + \alpha_q \varepsilon_{t-q+2}^2$$

Since $E_t\varepsilon_{t+1}^2 = h_{t+1}$, it follows that

$$E_t h_{t+2} = \alpha_0 + \alpha_1 h_{t+1} + \ldots + \alpha_q \varepsilon_{t-q+2}^2$$

The point is that it is possible to obtain the j-step-ahead forecasts of the conditional variance recursively. As the value of $j \to \infty$, the forecasts of h_{t+j} should converge to the unconditional mean

$$E\varepsilon_t^2 = \alpha_0 / (1 - \alpha_1 - \alpha_2 - \ldots - \alpha_q)$$

It should be clear that a necessary condition for convergence is for the roots of the inverse characteristic equation $1 - \alpha_1 L - \ldots - \alpha_q L^q$ to lie outside the unit circle. This is a necessary condition for the long-run mean to have the representation $\alpha_0/(1 - \Sigma\alpha_i)$. To ensure that the variance is always positive, we also require that $\alpha_0 > 0$ and $\alpha_i \geq 0$ for $i \geq 1$.

You should have no trouble generalizing these results to the general GARCH(p, q) process. Fortunately, most statistical software packages can perform these calculations automatically.

8. MAXIMUM LIKELIHOOD ESTIMATION OF GARCH MODELS

Many software packages contain built-in routines that estimate GARCH and ARCH-M models such that the researcher simply specifies the order of the process and the computer does the rest. Even if you have access to an automated routine, it is important to understand the numerical procedures used by your software package. Other packages require user input in the form of a small optimization algorithm. This section explains the maximum likelihood methods required to understand and write a program for GARCH-type models.

Suppose that values of $\{\varepsilon_t\}$ are drawn from a normal distribution having a mean of zero and a **constant** variance σ^2. From standard distribution theory, the likelihood of any realization of ε_t is

$$L_t = \left(\frac{1}{\sqrt{2\pi\sigma^2}}\right)\exp\left(\frac{-\varepsilon_t^2}{2\sigma^2}\right)$$

where L_t is the likelihood of ε_t.

Since the realizations of $\{\varepsilon_t\}$ are independent, the likelihood of the joint realizations of ε_1, ε_2, ..., ε_T is the product in the individual likelihoods. Hence, if all have the same variance, the likelihood of the joint realizations is

$$L = \prod_{t=1}^{T}\left(\frac{1}{\sqrt{2\pi\sigma^2}}\right)\exp\left(\frac{-\varepsilon_t^2}{2\sigma^2}\right)$$

It is far easier to work with a sum than with a product. As such, it is convenient to take the natural log of each side so as to obtain

$$\ln L = -\frac{T}{2}\ln(2\pi) - \frac{T}{2}\ln\sigma^2 - \frac{1}{2\sigma^2}\sum_{t=1}^{T}(\varepsilon_t)^2 \qquad (3.34)$$

The procedure used in maximum likelihood estimation is to select the distributional parameters so as to maximize the likelihood of drawing the observed sample. In Appendix 1 of Chapter 2, we considered the case where the $\{\varepsilon_t\}$ sequence was an MA(1) process. In the example at hand, suppose that $\{\varepsilon_t\}$ is generated by the following model:

$$\varepsilon_t = y_t - \beta x_t \qquad (3.35)$$

In the classical regression model, the mean of ε_t is assumed to be zero, the variance is the constant σ^2, and the various realizations of $\{\varepsilon_t\}$ are independent. Using a sample with T observations, we can substitute (3.37) into the log likelihood function given by (3.34) to obtain

$$\ln L = -\frac{T}{2}\ln(2\pi) - \frac{T}{2}\ln\sigma^2 - \frac{1}{2\sigma^2}\sum_{t=1}^{T}(y_t - \beta x_t)^2 \qquad (3.36)$$

Maximizing the log likelihood function (3.36) with respect to σ^2 and β yields:

$$\frac{\partial \ln L}{\partial \sigma^2} = -\frac{T}{2\sigma^2} + \frac{1}{2\sigma^4}\sum_{t=1}^{T}(y_t - \beta x_t)^2$$

and

$$\frac{\partial \ln L}{\partial \beta} = \frac{1}{\sigma^2}\sum_{t=1}^{T}(y_t x_t - \beta x_t^2) \qquad (3.37)$$

Setting these partial derivatives equal to zero and solving for the values of σ^2 and β and that yield the maximum value of $\ln L$ results in the familiar OLS estimates of the variance and β (denoted by $\hat{\beta}$ and $\hat{\sigma}^2$). Hence,

$$\hat{\sigma}^2 = \sum \varepsilon_t^2 / T \qquad (3.38)$$

and

$$\hat{\beta} = \sum x_t y_t / \sum x_t^2 \qquad (3.39)$$

All of this should be familiar ground since most econometric texts concerned with regression analysis discuss maximum likelihood estimation. The point to emphasize here is that the first-order conditions are easily solved since they are all linear. Calculating the appropriate sums may be tedious, but the methodology is straightforward. Unfortunately, this is not the case in estimating an ARCH or GARCH model since the first-order equations are nonlinear. Instead, the solution requires some sort of search algorithm. The simplest way to illustrate the issue is to introduce an ARCH(1) error process into the regression model given by (3.35). Continue to assume that ε_t is the error term in linear equation $y_t - \beta x_t = \varepsilon_t$. Now let ε_t be given by

$$\varepsilon_t = v_t(h_t)^{0.5}$$

Although the conditional variance of ε_t is not constant, the necessary modification of (3.34) is clear. Since each realization of ε_t has the conditional variance h_t, the joint likelihood of realization ε_1 through ε_T is

$$L = \prod_{t=1}^{T}\left(\frac{1}{\sqrt{2\pi h_t}}\right)\exp\left(\frac{-\varepsilon_t^2}{2h_t}\right)$$

so that the log likelihood function is

$$\ln L = -\frac{T}{2}\ln(2\pi) - 0.5\sum_{t=1}^{T}\ln h_t - 0.5\sum_{t=1}^{T}(\varepsilon_t^2 / h_t)$$

Now suppose that $\varepsilon_t = y_t - \beta x_t$ and that the conditional variance is the ARCH(1) process $h_t = a_0 + a_1\varepsilon_{t-1}^2$. Substituting for h_t and y_t yields

$$\ln L = -\frac{T-1}{2}\ln(2\pi) - 0.5\sum_{t=2}^{T}\ln(a_0 + a_1\varepsilon_{t-1}^2) - \frac{1}{2}\sum_{t=2}^{T}[(y_t - \beta x_t)^2 / (a_0 + a_1\varepsilon_{t-1}^2)]$$

Note that the initial observation is lost since ε_0 is outside the sample. Once you substitute $(y_{t-1} - \beta x_{t-1})^2$ for ε_{t-1}^2, it is possible to maximize ln L with respect to a_0, a_1, and β. As you can surmise, there are no simple solutions to the first-order conditions for a maximum. Fortunately, computers are able to select the parameter values that maximize this log likelihood function. In most time-series software packages, the procedure necessary to write such programs is quite simple.

9. OTHER MODELS OF CONDITIONAL VARIANCE

Financial analysts are especially keen to obtain precise estimates of the conditional variance of an asset price. Since GARCH models can forecast conditional volatility, they are able to measure the risk of an asset over the holding period. As such, a number of extensions of the basic GARCH model have been developed that are especially suited to estimating the conditional volatility of financial instruments.

The IGARCH Model

In financial time series, the conditional volatility is persistent. In fact, if you estimate a GARCH(1, 1) model using a long time-series of stock returns, you will find that the sum of a_1 and β_1 is very close to unity. Nelson (1990) argued that constraining $a_1 + \beta_1$ to equal unity can yield a very parsimonious representation of the distribution of an asset's return. In some respects, this constraint forces the conditional variance to act like a process with a unit-root. This integrated-GARCH (IGARCH) has some very interesting properties. From (3.32), if $a_1 + \beta_1 = 1$, the one-step-ahead forecast of the conditional variance is

$$E_t h_{t+1} = a_0 + h_t$$

and the j-step-ahead forecast is

$$E_t h_{t+j} = ja_0 + h_t$$

Thus, except for the intercept term a_0, the forecast of the conditional variance for the next period is the current value of the conditional variance. Moreover, the unconditional variance is clearly infinite. Nevertheless, Nelson (1990) shows that the analogy between the IGARCH process and an ARIMA process with a unit root is not perfect. Given that $a_1 + \beta_1 = 1$, and that $h_{t-1} = Lh_t$, we can write the conditional variance as

$$h_t = a_0 + (1 - \beta_1)\varepsilon_{t-1}^2 + \beta_1 Lh_t$$

and, solving for h_t,

$$h_t = \alpha_0 / (1 - \beta_1) + (1 - \beta_1) \sum_{i=0}^{\infty} \beta_1^i \varepsilon_{t-1-i}^2$$

Thus, unlike a true nonstationary process, the conditional variance is a geometrically *decaying* function of the current and past realizations of the $\{\varepsilon_t^2\}$ sequence. As such, an IGARCH model can be estimated like any other GARCH model.

Models with Explanatory Variables

Just as the model of the mean can contain explanatory variables, the specification of h_t also allows for exogenous variables. For example, suppose that you want to determine whether the terrorist attacks of September 11, 2001, increased the volatility of asset returns. One way to accomplish the task would be to create a dummy variable D_t equal to 0 before September 11 and equal to 1 thereafter. Consider the following modification of the GARCH(1, 1) specification

$$h_t = \alpha_0 + \alpha_1 \varepsilon_{t-1}^2 + \beta_1 h_{t-1} + \gamma D_t$$

If it is found that $\gamma > 0$, it is possible to conclude that the terrorist attacks increased the mean of the conditional volatility.

Models with Asymmetry: TARCH and EGARCH

An interesting feature of asset prices is that "bad" news seems to have a more pronounced effect on volatility than does "good" news. For many stocks, there is a strong negative correlation between the current return and the future volatility. The tendency for volatility to decline when returns rise and to rise when returns fall is often called the **leverage effect.** The idea of the leverage effect is captured in Figure 3.11, where "new information" is measured by the size of ε_t. If $\varepsilon_t = 0$, expected volatility ($E_t h_{t+1}$) is $0a$. Any news increases volatility; however, if the news is "good" (i.e., if ε_t is positive), volatility increases along ab. If the news is "bad," volatility increases along ac. Since segment ac is steeper than ab, a positive ε_t shock will have a smaller effect on volatility than a negative shock of the same magnitude.

Glosten, Jaganathan, and Runkle (1994) showed how to allow the effects of good and bad news to have different effects on volatility. In a sense, $\varepsilon_{t-1} = 0$ is a threshold such that shocks greater than the threshold have different effects than shocks below the threshold. Consider the threshold-GARCH (TARCH) process

$$h_t = \alpha_0 + \alpha_1 \varepsilon_{t-1}^2 + \lambda_1 d_{t-1} \varepsilon_{t-1}^2 + \beta_1 h_{t-1}$$

where d_{t-1} is a dummy variable that is equal to one if $\varepsilon_{t-1} < 0$ and is equal to zero if $\varepsilon_{t-1} \geq 0$.

The intuition behind the TARCH model is that positive values of ε_{t-1} are associated with a zero value of d_{t-1}. Hence, if $\varepsilon_{t-1} \geq 0$, the effect of an ε_{t-1} shock on h_t is $\alpha_1 \varepsilon_{t-1}^2$. When $\varepsilon_{t-1} < 0$, $d_{t-1} = 1$, and the effect of an ε_{t-1} shock on h_t is $(\alpha_1 + \lambda_1)\varepsilon_{t-1}^2$. If $\lambda_1 > 0$, negative shocks will have larger effects on volatility than positive shocks. You can

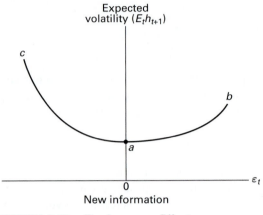

FIGURE 3.11 The Leverage Effect

easily create a dummy variable d_t and the product $d_{t-1}\varepsilon_{t-1}^2$. If the coefficient λ_1 is statistically different from zero, you can conclude that your data contain a threshold effect.

Another model that allows for the asymmetric effect of news is the exponential-GARCH (EGARCH) model. One problem with a standard GARCH model is that it is necessary to ensure that all of the estimated coefficients are positive. Nelson (1991) proposed a specification that does not require nonnegativity constraints. Consider

$$\ln(h_t) = \alpha_0 + \alpha_1(\varepsilon_{t-1}/h_{t-1}^{0.5}) + \lambda_1 \mid \varepsilon_{t-1}/h_{t-1}^{0.5} \mid + \beta_1 \ln(h_{t-1}) \qquad (3.40)$$

Equation (3.40) is called the exponential-GARCH or EGARCH model. There are three interesting features to notice about the EGARCH model:

1. The equation for the conditional variance is in log-linear form. Regardless of the magnitude of $\ln(h_t)$, the implied value of h_t can never be negative. Hence, it is permissible for the coefficients to be negative.

2. Instead of using the value of ε_{t-1}^2, the EGARCH model uses the level of standardized value of ε_{t-1} [i.e., ε_{t-1} divided by $(h_{t-1})^{0.5}$]. Nelson argues that this standardization allows for a more natural interpretation of the size and persistence of shocks. After all, the standardized value of ε_{t-1} is a unit-free measure.

3. The EGARCH model allows for leverage effects. If $\varepsilon_{t-1}/(h_{t-1})^{0.5}$ is positive, the effect of the shock on the log of the conditional variance is $\alpha_1 + \lambda_1$. If $\varepsilon_{t-1}/(h_{t-1})^{0.5}$ is negative, the effect of the shock on the log of the conditional variance is $-\alpha_1 + \lambda_1$.

Although the EGARCH model has some advantages over the TARCH model, it is difficult to forecast the conditional variance of an EGARCH model. For the TARCH model, it makes sense to assume that $E_t d_{t+j} = 0.5$. If asset returns are symmetric, there is a 50:50 chance that the realized value of ε_{t+j} will be positive.

Testing for Leverage Effects

One way to test for leverage is to estimate the TARCH or EGARCH model and perform a t-test for the null hypothesis $\hat{\lambda}_1 = 0$. However, there is a specific diagnostic test that allows you to determine whether there are any remaining leverage effects in your residuals. After you estimate an ARCH or GARCH model, form the standardized residuals

$$s_t = \hat{\varepsilon}_t / \hat{h}_t^{1/2}$$

Thus, the $\{s_t\}$ sequence consists of each residual divided by its standard deviation. To test for leverage effects, estimate a regression of the form

$$s_t^2 = a_0 + a_1 s_{t-1} + a_2 s_{t-2} + ...$$

If there are no leverage effects, the squared errors should be uncorrelated with the level of the error terms. Hence, you can conclude there are leverage effects if the sample value of F for the null hypothesis $a_1 = a_2 = ...$ exceeds the critical value obtained from an F table.

Engle and Ng (1993) developed a second way to determine whether positive and negative shocks have different effects on the conditional variance. Again, let d_{t-1} be a dummy variable that is equal to 1 if $\hat{\varepsilon}_{t-1} < 0$ and is equal to zero if $\hat{\varepsilon}_{t-1} \geq 0$. The test is to determine whether the estimated squared residuals can be predicted using the $\{d_{t-1}\}$ sequence. The Sign Bias test uses the regression equation of the form

$$s_t^2 = a_0 + a_1 d_{t-1} + \varepsilon_{1t}$$

where ε_{1t} is a regression residual.

If a t-test indicates that a_1 is statistically different from zero, the sign of the current period shock is helpful in predicting the conditional volatility. To generalize the test, you can estimate the regression

$$s_t^2 = a_0 + a_1 d_{t-1} + a_2 d_{t-1} s_{t-1} + a_3 (1 - d_{t-1}) s_{t-1} + \varepsilon_{1t}$$

The presence of $d_{t-1}s_{t-1}$ and $(1 - d_{t-1})s_{t-1}$ is designed to determine whether the effects of positive and negative shocks also depend on their size. You can use an F-statistic to test the null hypothesis $a_1 = a_2 = a_3 = 0$. If you conclude that there is a leverage effect, you can estimate a specific form of the TARCH of EGARCH model.[12]

Non-normal Errors

For most financial assets, the distribution function for the rate of return is **fat-tailed.** A fat-tailed distribution has more weight in the tails than a normal distribution. Suppose that the rate of return on a particular stock has a higher probability of a very large loss (or gain) than indicated by the normal distribution. As such, you might not want to perform a maximum likelihood estimation using a normal distribution. Figure 3.12 compares the standardized normal distribution to a t-distribution with one degree of freedom. You can see that the t-distribution places a greater likelihood on large realizations than does the normal distribution. As such, many computer packages allow you to estimate a GARCH model using a t-distribution.[13]

10. ESTIMATING THE NYSE COMPOSITE INDEX

We can illustrate the process of fitting a GARCH model to financial data by using the logarithmic change in the NYSE Composite Index shown in Figure 3.4. The series

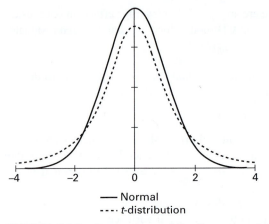

— Normal
---- *t*-distribution

FIGURE 3.12 Comparison of the Normal and *t*-Distributions

labeled COMPOSITE in the data set NYSE.XLS contains the daily closing values of the index over the period January 3, 1995, through August 30, 2002.[14] The series is a good candidate to be a GARCH process; you can clearly see periods in which there are only small changes in the series and others (especially near the end of the series) where there are clusters of large increases and decreases in the index.

The main focus of the PPI example was to estimate a model of the mean and to estimate the appropriate conditional confidence intervals. Here, the model of the mean is of little interest. Asset prices tend to behave as random walks or as random walks with a drift term. For this reason, there is little information content in the model of the mean. Instead, our goal is to accurately capture the behavior of the conditional volatility. Accurately modeling the conditional variance requires a large number of observations. Moreover, since financial data are readily available, GARCH models of asset prices typically use large data sets.

The Model of the Mean

The first step in modeling any GARCH process is to estimate the model of the mean. Since the level of the index is clearly nonstationary, we construct the daily rate of return on the index as

$$r_t = \ln(COMPOSITE_t / COMPOSITE_{t-1})$$

The 1,930 observations in the $\{r_t\}$ series have a mean value of 0.000353 and a sample variance of 0.000101. These 1,930 observations are plotted in Figure 3.4 while the distribution of the $\{r_t\}$ sequence is shown in Figure 3.13. Although the distribution of returns is more peaked than a normal distribution, you can see that it makes little sense to estimate the $\{r_t\}$ series using a *t*-distribution. As such, we will proceed as if the return series were normally distributed.

The autocorrelations of the $\{r_t\}$ sequence are all very small. Nevertheless, with such a large number of observations, the first several are statistically significant. For

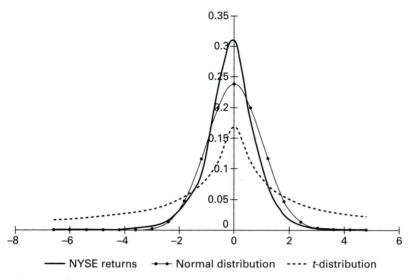

FIGURE 3.13 The Distribution of NYSE Returns

example, $\rho_1 = 0.068$ and $\rho_2 = -0.0458$. Since $2/(1930)^{0.5} = 0.0456$, these two correlations are significant at the 5 percent level. If you form the $\{r_t\}$ series, you can verify that the AIC and the SBC select the following two models of the mean, respectively:

$$r_t = 0.000353 + \varepsilon_t + 0.0705\varepsilon_{t-1} - 0.0413\varepsilon_{t-2} \qquad (3.41)$$
$$\quad\;(1.50) \qquad\qquad (3.31) \qquad\;\; (-1.82)$$

$$r_t = 0.000353 + 0.0705\varepsilon_{t-1} + \varepsilon_t$$
$$\quad\;(1.44) \qquad\;\; (3.31)$$

The AIC selects the MA(2) model and the SBC selects the more parsimonious MA(1) model. There is some ambiguity as to which is the most appropriate since the coefficient on ε_{t-2} has a *prob*-value of 0.069. For now, there is no need to select the "best" because each was estimated assuming that the variance is constant. If the variance is actually time-varying, the standard errors of the coefficients can change substantially once the models of the mean and the variance are simultaneously estimated. Notice that it is possible to eliminate the intercept terms from the regressions since the t-statistics are relatively low. Nevertheless, there are advantages to using regressions containing intercept terms. As the t-statistics can change as we posit different models for the conditional variance, intercepts will be included in the model of the mean. Once we have found the most appropriate GARCH representation for h_t, we can consider re-estimating a model without an intercept term.

Testing for GARCH Errors

The residuals from the two models are virtually identical. However, we do not want any possible serial correlation in the residuals to contaminate the test for conditional volatility. To ensure against this possibility, we test for the presence of GARCH errors using (3.41) To perform the Lagrange multiplier test, let $\hat{\varepsilon}_t^2$ denote the squared residuals from (3.41). Using four lags of the $\hat{\varepsilon}_t^2$ series, we obtain

$$\hat{\varepsilon}_t^2 = 5.877E-5+0.154\hat{\varepsilon}_{t-1}^2+0.102\hat{\varepsilon}_{t-2}^2+0.119\hat{\varepsilon}_{t-3}^2+0.041\hat{\varepsilon}_{t-4}^2$$
$$(8.93) \qquad (6.76) \qquad (4.46) \qquad (5.20) \qquad (1.81)$$

The sample F-statistic for the null hypothesis that all coefficients on the lagged values of $\{\hat{\varepsilon}_t^2\}$ are equal to zero is 37.77; with four degrees of freedom in the numerator and 1921 in the denominator (we estimate five coefficients and lose four usable observations), the *prob*-value is 0.000. Hence, we can conclude that there are GARCH errors.

Now take a little quiz. How accurately does the lag length need to be estimated to perform the test? The obvious answer ("As accurately as possible!") begs the question. Clearly, you do not want to include lags that have very small t-values; including lags that are insignificant will reduce the power of the test. If your lag length is too short, you could fail to detect the presence of conditional volatility. However, if your lag length is shorter than the true structure, and if you still detect GARCH effects, you can conclude that GARCH effects are present in the data. To take a simple example, if you find GARCH effects using only $\hat{\varepsilon}_{t-1}$, you can conclude there is some type of ARCH effect.

Alternative Estimates of the Model

As in the Box–Jenkins method, we want to estimate a parsimonious model. Not only can we alter the lag lengths for the GARCH(p, q) process, we can also allow for ARCH-M effects and for specifications with asymmetry. Given the tremendous number of possible specifications, it is very easy to over-fit the data. Consequently, it is best to start with a simple model and determine whether or not is it adequate. If it fails any of the diagnostic checks, it is possible to use a more complicated model. We begin by estimating (3.41) using a GARCH(1, 1) error process. The results from maximum likelihood estimation are

$$r_t = 7.24E-4 + \varepsilon_t - 0.1034\varepsilon_{t-1} - 0.0003\varepsilon_{t-2}$$
$$(3.42) \qquad\qquad (-4.17) \qquad (-0.13)$$

$$h_t = 1.33E-6+0.119\varepsilon_{t-1}^2+0.877h_{t-1}$$
$$(4.09) \qquad (11.58) \qquad (83.48)$$

Notice that some of the ambiguity concerning the model of the mean has been eliminated; the term ε_{t-2} can be eliminated from the model of the mean. We can now estimate the MA(1)–GARCH(1, 1) process:

$$r_t = 7.25E-4 + \varepsilon_t - 0.1030\varepsilon_{t-1}$$
$$(3.47) \qquad\qquad (-4.29)$$
$$h_t = 1.32E-6+0.119\varepsilon_{t-1}^2+0.878h_{t-1}$$
$$(4.09) \qquad (12.42) \qquad (85.00)$$

Since the sum of the coefficients on ε_{t-1}^2 and h_{t-1} is almost identically equal to unity, we can estimate the IGARCH(1, 1) model:

$$r_t = 7.26E-4 + \varepsilon_t - 0.1031\varepsilon_{t-1}$$
$$(3.50) \qquad\qquad (-4.27)$$

$$h_t = 1.18E-6+0.1219\varepsilon_{t-1}^2+(1-0.1219)h_{t-1}$$
$$(6.00) \qquad (12.65)$$

The fit of the IGARCH model will not be as good as that from the GARCH(1, 1) model since the IGARCH model imposes a constraint of the sum of the coefficients. However, the IGARCH model is more parsimonious than the GARCH(1, 1) model. If you experiment with alternative values of p and/or q in a GARCH(p, q) or an IGARCH(p, q) model, you will find that the longer lags are not statistically significant. Moreover, the ARCH-M specification is not favorable to the presumption that the return on the NYSE Composite Index contains a risk premium. For example, if we use the GARCH(1, 1) specification, we find that the model for the mean is

$$r_t = 1.20E - 4 + \varepsilon_t - 0.103\varepsilon_{t-1} + 0.081h_t$$
$$\quad (0.189) \qquad\qquad (-4.26) \qquad\quad (1.00)$$

Another possibility is that the conditional standard deviation (as opposed to the conditional variance) affects the return in the index. However, this specification also yields an insignificant coefficient for the ARCH-M effect. Consider the equation

$$r_t = 3.70E - 4 + \varepsilon_t - 0.103\varepsilon_{t-1} + 5.61h_t^{0.5}$$
$$\quad (0.116) \qquad\qquad (-4.25) \qquad\quad (1.41)$$

Diagnostic Checking

Now we need to know whether the IGARCH(1, 1) model passes the various diagnostic checks for model adequacy. As all diagnostic tests are performed on the standardized residuals, form the series $s_t = \hat{\varepsilon}_t / \hat{h}_t^{0.5}$.

Remaining Serial Correlation: The autocorrelations of the $\{s_t\}$ series are all very small; the Ljung–Box $Q(5)$, $Q(10)$, and $Q(25)$ statistics are 6.39, 10.36, and 29.63, respectively. None of these values is significant at conventional levels; hence, we conclude that the standardized residuals are serially uncorrelated.

Remaining GARCH Effects: Now form the standardized squared residuals s_t^2 and estimate a regression of the form

$$s_t^2 = a_0 + a_1 s_{t-1}^2 + \ldots + a_n s_{t-n}^2$$

If you use various values of n, you will find that none of the a_1 through a_n is statistically significant. More importantly, you cannot reject any test of the null hypothesis $a_1 = a_2 = \ldots = a_n = 0$. For example, if you estimate the regression

$$s_t^2 = 0.95 - 0.001 s_{t-1}^2 + 0.0351 s_{t-2}^2$$

you will find that the restriction $a_1 = a_2 = 0$ has an F-value of 1.18 and a *prob*-value of 0.38. Hence, you conclude that there are no remaining GARCH effects.

Similarly, the Ljung–Box $Q(5)$, $Q(10)$, and $Q(25)$ statistics for the $\{s_t^2\}$ series are 3.89, 4.57, and 11.15, respectively. None of these values is significant at conventional levels; hence, we conclude that the standardized squared residuals are not serially correlated.

Leverage Effects: If there are no leverage effects, s_t^2 should be uncorrelated with the lagged levels of $\{s_t\}$. However, consider the regression equation

$$s_t^2 = 0.964 - 0.157 s_{t-1} - 0.250 s_{t-2} - 0.084 s_{t-3}$$
$$\quad (21.29)\ (-3.49) \qquad (-5.49) \qquad\quad (-1.85)$$

The coefficients on s_{t-1} and s_{t-2} are highly significant. Moreover, the F-statistic for the null hypothesis that the coefficients on all three lagged values are jointly equal to zero is 15.23 with a *prob*-value of 0.000. Given that the signs are negative, we conclude that negative shocks are associated with large values of the conditional variance. This result is reinforced by the Engle–Ng sign test. Set $d_{t-1} = 1$ if $s_{t-1} < 0$; otherwise, set $d_{t-1} = 0$. Now if you perform the sign bias test, you will find

$$s_t^2 = 0.858 + 0.245d_{t-1}$$
$$(13.04) \quad (2.70)$$

Since the coefficient on d_{t-1} is significant, we again conclude that negative shocks tend to increase the conditional variance of r_t. The strong suggestion is that we should consider a TARCH or an EGARCH model.

The Asymmetric Models

The TARCH model is unsatisfactory since the estimated value of α_1 is negative. Consider the estimated equation for the conditional variance

$$h_t = 1.81E - 6 - 0.0064\varepsilon_{t-1}^2 + 0.1947d_{t-1}\varepsilon_{t-1} + 0.8937h_{t-1}$$
$$(6.48) \quad\quad (-0.662) \quad\quad (12.33) \quad\quad\quad (96.85)$$

It is not possible to re-estimate the model without the variable ε_{t-1}^2. Recall the argument demonstrating that α_1 must be positive for a GARCH(1, 1) model to be identified. You should be able to show that the identical reasoning applies to the TARCH model. One possibility is to constrain the coefficients to be positive. An alternative is to estimate an EGARCH model. Consider

$$r_t = 2.77E - 4 + 0.1186\varepsilon_{t-1} + \varepsilon_t$$
$$(1.45) \quad\quad (5.00)$$

$$\ln(h_t) = -0.4321 - 0.1553\varepsilon_{t-1}/h_{t-1}^{0.5} + 0.1263|\varepsilon_{t-1}/h_{t-1}^{0.5}| + 0.9646\ \ln(h_{t-1})$$
$$(-9.61)\ (-13.71) \quad\quad\quad (7.72) \quad\quad\quad (230.71)$$

Since there are not any restrictions on the signs of the coefficients, the model appears to be satisfactory. Moreover, all of the coefficients in the equation for $\ln(h_t)$ are highly significant. It is interesting that α_1 is negative, λ_1 positive and $\alpha_1 + \lambda_1$ is negative. Given the value of h_{t-1}, a one-unit decline in ε_{t-1} will induce a change in the log of the conditional variance by 0.2816 units $[-(-0.1553) + 0.1263 = 0.2816]$. However, the point estimates of the coefficients imply that if ε_{t-1} rises by one unit, the conditional volatility actually declines by 0.0290 units ($-0.1553 + 0.1263 = -0.0290$). The implication is that "good news" reduces the conditional volatility. Nevertheless, you might want to test the restriction $\alpha_1 + \lambda_1 = 0$. In this case, positive shocks would have no effect on $\ln(h_t)$ and negative shocks would increase $\ln(h_t)$.

The two plausible models seem to be the IGARCH and EGARCH models. Not only does the EGARCH model capture the leverage effect, but it also fits the data better than the IGARCH model. The maximized value of log likelihood function is 6356.146 for the IGARCH model and 6414.779 for the EGARCH model. As a final check on the adequacy of the EGARCH model, the following diagnostic checks were performed:

1. **Checks of the standardized residuals:** The standardized residuals were checked to determine whether they exhibited no serial correlation. Similarly, the squares of the standardized residuals were checked for serial correlation. Any correlation in the $\{s_t^2\}$ series implies that there are neglected GARCH effects in the residuals. These tests and the sign bias test on s_t^2 did not reveal any remaining information in the residuals.

2. **Alternative goodness-of-fit measures:** The values of RSS', AIC', and SBC' from the IGARCH model are 1902.59, 14577.37, and 14588.51, respectively. However, the same values for the EGARCH model are larger. In particular, the values of RSS', AIC', and SBC' from the EGARCH model are 1936.22, 14611.19, and 14622.33, respectively. Hence, the parsimonious IGARCH model seems to fit the conditional variance better than the EGARCH model. Nevertheless, it is not clear how to interpret these results because the sums of squares do not take differentiate between positive and negative errors. Moreover, the ability of AIC' and SBC' to select the best model are unproven.

3. **Normally distributed errors:** In order to determine whether the standardized errors are normally distributed, the fractiles of the $\{s_t\}$ sequence can be plotted against the fractiles of the normal distribution. After all, if $\{s_t\}$ has a standardized normal distribution, 0.5 percent should be below −2.54, 2.5 percent of the values should be below −1.64, 50 percent should be negative, 95 percent should be above 1.64 standard deviations, and 99.5 percent should be above 2.54. The point is that if $\{s_t\}$ is truly normally distributed, the fractiles should lie along a straight line when plotted against the fractiles of the normal distribution. As you can see in Figure 3.14, except for the extreme observations, the standardized residuals do appear to be normally distributed. Nevertheless, to ensure the appropriateness of the estimates, when the

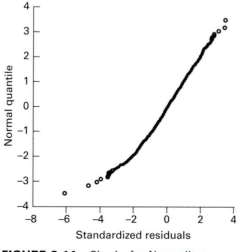

FIGURE 3.14 Checks for Normality

EGARCH model of the $\{r_t\}$ series is estimated using a t-distribution, the results are very similar to those shown earlier.

Figure 3.15 shows the fitted values of h_t for the EGARCH model from July 2000 through August 2002. Also shown in the figure are the forecasted values from September 1, 2002, through April 1, 2003. You can see that the $\{\ln(h_t)\}$ sequence decays very slowly; the degree of persistence is more than 96 percent.

11. SUMMARY AND CONCLUSIONS

Many economic time series exhibit periods of volatility. Conditionally heteroskedastic models (ARCH or GARCH) allow the conditional variance of a series to depend on the past realizations of the error process. A large realization of the current period's disturbance increases the conditional variance in subsequent periods. For a stable process, the conditional variance will eventually decay to the long-run (unconditional) variance. As such, ARCH and GARCH models can capture periods of turbulence and tranquility.

Conditional variance is a measure of risk. ARCH and GARCH effects have been included in a regression framework to test hypotheses of risk-averse agents. For example, if producers are risk averse, conditional price variability will affect product supply. Producers may reduce their exposure by withdrawing from the market in periods of substantial risk. Similarly, asset prices should be negatively related to their conditional volatility. Such ARCH effects in the mean of a series (ARCH-M) are a natural implication of asset pricing models.

The basic ARCH and GARCH models have been extended in a number of interesting ways. The IGARCH model allows volatility shocks to be permanent and the TARCH and EGARCH models allow negative shocks to behave differently than positive shocks. You can also include explanatory variables in the equation for the conditional volatility.

FIGURE 3.15 The Fitted and Forecasted Variance, Estimated through August 2002

One interesting development is the application of GARCH models in a multivariate setting. There is little conceptual difficulty in formulating a multivariate model such that the conditional volatilities are interdependent. For example, in a two-variable system, we can let ε_{it} and h_{it} denote the shocks and the conditional volatility of variable i, respectively. As such, a simple multivariate GARCH process is

$$h_{1t} = \alpha_{10} + \alpha_{11}\varepsilon_{1t-1}^2 + \alpha_{12}\varepsilon_{2t-1}^2 + \beta_{11}h_{1t-1} + \beta_{12}h_{2t-1}$$

$$h_{2t} = \alpha_{20} + \alpha_{21}\varepsilon_{1t-1}^2 + \alpha_{22}\varepsilon_{2t-1}^2 + \beta_{21}h_{1t-1} + \beta_{22}h_{2t-1}$$

Although simple to conceptualize, multivariate GARCH models can be very difficult to estimate. This is especially true in higher-order systems in several variables because all of the coefficients need to be positive to ensure that the conditional variance is never negative. As such, a number of estimation strategies have been designed to overcome this problem. Engle and Kroner (1995), Bollerslev, Engle, and Wooldridge (1988) and Bollerslev, Engle and Nelson (1994) discuss some of these strategies. Fortunately, a number of software packages have incorporated a number of these suggestions. For example, EVIEWS and RATS come with sample programs that illustrate the Engle and Kroner (1995) method.

QUESTIONS AND EXERCISES

1. Suppose that the $\{\varepsilon_t\}$ sequence is the ARCH(q) process

$$\varepsilon_t = v_t(\alpha_0 + \alpha_1\varepsilon_{t-1}^2 + \ldots + a_q\varepsilon_{t-q}^2)^{1/2}$$

    Show that the conditional expectation $E_{t-1}\varepsilon_t^2$ has the same form as the conditional expectation as (3.1).

2. Consider the ARCH-M model represented by equations (3.23) to (3.25). Recall that $\{\varepsilon_t\}$ is a white-noise disturbance; for simplicity, let $E\varepsilon_t^2 = E\varepsilon_{t-1}^2 = \ldots = 1$.

    a. Find the unconditional mean Ey_t. How does a change in δ affect the mean? Using the example of Section 6, show that changing β and δ from $(-4, 4)$ to $(-1, 1)$ preserves the mean of the $\{y_t\}$ sequence.

    b. Show that the unconditional variance of y_t when $h_t = \alpha_0 + \alpha_1\varepsilon_{t-1}^2$ does not depend on β, δ or α_0.

3. Bollerslev (1986) proves that the ACF of the squared residuals resulting from the GARCH(p, q) process represented by (3.9) act as an ARMA(m, p) process where $m = \max(p, q)$. You are to illustrate this result using the examples below.

    a. Consider the GARCH(1, 2) process: $h_t = \alpha_0 + \alpha_1\varepsilon_{t-1}^2 + \alpha_2\varepsilon_{t-2}^2 + \beta_1 h_{t-1}$. Add the expression $(\varepsilon_t^2 - h_t)$ to each side so that

$$\varepsilon_t^2 = \alpha_0 + \alpha_1\varepsilon_{t-1}^2 + \alpha_2\varepsilon_{t-2}^2 + \beta_1 h_{t-1} + (\varepsilon_t^2 - h_t)$$
$$= \alpha_0 + (\alpha_1 + \beta_1)\varepsilon_{t-1}^2 + \alpha_2\varepsilon_{t-2}^2 - \beta_1(\varepsilon_{t-1}^2 - h_{t-1}) + (\varepsilon_t^2 - h_t)$$

    Define $\eta_t = (\varepsilon_t^2 - h_t)$, so that:

$$\varepsilon_t^2 = \alpha_0 + (\alpha_1 + \beta_1)\varepsilon_{t-1}^2 + \alpha_2\varepsilon_{t-2}^2 - \beta_1\eta_{t-1} + \eta_t$$

    Show that:

    i. η_t is serially uncorrelated

    ii. The $\{\varepsilon_t^2\}$ sequence acts as an ARMA(2, 1) process.

b.   Consider the GARCH(2, 1) process $h_t = \alpha_0 + \alpha_1 \varepsilon_{t-1}^2 + \beta_1 h_{t-1} + \beta_2 h_{t-2}$. Show that it is possible to add η_t to each side so as to obtain:

$$\varepsilon_t^2 = \alpha_0 + \alpha_1 \varepsilon_{t-1}^2 + \beta_1 h_{t-1} + \eta_t + \beta_2 h_{t-2}$$

Show that adding and subtracting the terms $\beta_1 \eta_{t-1}$ and $\beta_2 \eta_{t-2}$ to the right-hand side of this equation yields an ARMA(2, 2) process.

c.   Provide an intuitive explanation of the statement: "The Lagrange multiplier for ARCH errors test cannot be used to test the null of white noise squared residuals against an alternative of a specific GARCH(p, q) process."

d.   Sketch the proof of the general statement that the ACF of the squared residuals resulting from the GARCH(p, q) process represented by (3.9) act as an ARMA(m, p) process where $m = \max(p, q)$.

4.   Let $y_0 = 0$, and let the first five realizations of the $\{\varepsilon_t\}$ sequence be (1, –1, –2, 1, 1). Plot each of the following sequences:

$$\text{Model 1: } y_t = 0.5 y_{t-1} + \varepsilon_t$$

$$\text{Model 2: } y_t = \varepsilon_t - \varepsilon_{t-1}^2$$

$$\text{Model 3: } y_t = 0.5 y_{t-1} + \varepsilon_t - \varepsilon_{t-1}^2$$

a.   How does the ARCH-M specification affect the behavior of the $\{y_t\}$ sequence? What is the influence of the autoregressive term in model 3?

b.   For each of the three models, calculate the sample mean and variance of $\{y_t\}$.

5.   The file labeled ARCH.XLS contains the 100 realizations of the simulated $\{y_t\}$ sequence used to create the Panel (d) of Figure 3.7. Recall that this series was simulated as $y_t = 0.9 y_{t-1} + \varepsilon_t$ where ε_t is the ARCH(1) error process $\varepsilon_t = v_t (1 + 0.8 \varepsilon_{t-1})^{1/2}$. You should find the series has a mean of 0.263369480, a standard deviation of 4.89409139 with minimum and maximum values of –10.8 and 15.15, respectively.

a.   Estimate the series using OLS and save the residuals. You should obtain:

$$y_t = 0.9444053245 y_{t-1} + \varepsilon_t$$

The t-statistic for a_1 is 26.50647.

Note that the estimated value of a_1 differs from the theoretical value of 0.9. This is due to nothing more than sampling error; the simulated values of $\{v_t\}$ do not precisely conform to the theoretical distribution. However, can you provide an intuitive explanation of why positive serial correlation in the $\{v_t\}$ sequence might shift the estimate of a_1 upward in small samples?

b.   Obtain the ACF and the PACF of the residuals. Use Ljung–Box Q-statistics to determine whether the residuals approximate white noise. You should find:

ACF of the residuals:

1: 0.1489160	0.0044162	–0.0178424	–0.0124788	0.0682729	0.0028705
7: –0.0994202	–0.1508656	0.0643873	0.1012332	0.0898023	–0.0379116

PACF of the residuals:

1: 0.1489160	–0.0181625	–0.0161712	–0.0074713	0.0727149	–0.0192058
7: –0.0996379	–0.1234779	0.111544	0.0731477	0.0606913	–0.0565566

Ljung–Box Q-Statistics: $Q(4)$ = 2.3142, Significance level 0.50980859
$Q(8)$ = 6.3861, Significance level 0.49546069
$Q(24)$ = 18.4914, Significance level 0.73031863

c.   Obtain the ACF and the PACF of the squared residuals. You should find:

ACF of the squared residuals:

1: 0.473047   0.1268669   −0.0573466   −0.0777808   0.0570613   0.2424039
7: 0.2727332   0.2140628   0.1368675   −0.0053388   −0.0660162   −0.0942429

PACF of the squared residuals:

1: 0.4730473   −0.1248437   −0.0861060   0.0037908   0.1351502   0.1981716
7: 0.0702680   0.0620095   0.0682656   −0.0656655   −0.0381717   −0.1030398

Ljung–Box Q-Statistics: $Q(4)$ = 25.4702, Significance level 0.00001231
                            $Q(8)$ = 45.2535, Significance level 0.00000012
                            $Q(24)$ = 50.6029, Significance level 0.00076745

Based on the ACF and PACF of the residuals and the squared residuals, what can you conclude about the presence of ARCH errors?

d.   Estimate the squared residuals as: $\varepsilon_t^2 = \alpha_0 + \alpha_1 \varepsilon_{t-1}^2$. You should verify

Coefficient	Estimate	Std Error	T-Stat	Signif
α_0	1.5501077352	0.5484906416	2.82613	0.00573246
α_1	0.4745095418	0.0899397119	5.27586	0.00000082

Show that the Lagrange multiplier ARCH(1) errors is: $TR^2 = 22.027771$ with a significance level of 0.00000269.

e.   Simultaneously estimate the $\{y_t\}$ sequence and the ARCH(1) error process using maximum likelihood estimation. You should find:

Coefficient	Estimate	Std Error	T-Stat	Signif
a_1	0.8864631666	0.0270362312	32.78797	0.00000000
α_0	1.1735726519	0.2703953538	4.34021	0.00001423
α_1	0.6663896955	0.2221985284	2.99907	0.00270802

6.   The file QUARTERLY.XLS contains the quarterly values of the U.S. producer price index that were used in Section 4. Use the data to construct the logarithmic change as:

$$\pi_t = \log(ppi_t) - \log(ppi_{t-1})$$

a.   Use the entire sample period to estimate equation (3.16). Perform diagnostic checks to determine whether the residuals appear to be white noise.

b.   Plot the ACF and PACF of the squared residuals.

c.   Replicate the results for the various GARCH models reported in Section 4.

7.   The second series on the file ARCH.XLS contains 100 observations of a simulated ARCH-M process.

a.   Estimate the $\{y_t\}$ sequence using the Box–Jenkins methodology. Try to improve on the model

$$y_t = a_0 + \varepsilon_t + \beta_3 \varepsilon_{t-3} + \beta_6 \varepsilon_{t-6}$$

where

Coefficient	Estimate	Std Error	T-Stat	Significance
a_0	1.071771081	0.048009924	22.32395	0.00000000
β_3	0.254214138	0.098929960	2.56964	0.01170287
β_6	−0.262006589	0.099273537	−2.63924	0.00968214

b. Examine the ACF and the PACF of the residuals from the MA($\|3, 6\|$) model above. Why might someone conclude that the residuals appear to be white noise? Now examine the ACF and PACF of the squared residuals. You should find:

ACF of the squared residuals:
0.4981203 0.2509847 0.2895971 0.1625192 0.0430988 0.1141240

PACF of the squared residuals:
0.4981203 0.0038049 0.2170029 –0.0878890 –0.0413535 0.1013672

Perform the LM test for ARCH errors.

c. Estimate the $\{y_t\}$ sequence as the ARCH-M process:

$$y_t = a_0 + a_1 h_1 + \varepsilon_t$$
$$h_t = \alpha_0 + \alpha_1 \varepsilon_{t-1}^2$$

You should find:

Coefficient	Estimate	Std Error	T–Stat	Significance
a_0	0.9081809340	0.0646439764	14.04896	0.00000000
a_1	0.6252387171	0.3491817146	1.79058	0.07336030
α_0	0.1079170551	0.0193136878	5.58759	0.00000002
α_1	0.5973791022	0.2387112973	2.50252	0.01233137

d. Check the ACF and the PACF of the estimated $\{\varepsilon_t\}$ sequence. Do they appear to be satisfactory? Experiment with several other simple formulations of the ARCH-M process.

8. Consider the ARCH(2) process $E_{t-1}\varepsilon_t^2 = \alpha_0 + \alpha_1 \varepsilon_{t-1}^2 + \alpha_2 \varepsilon_{t-2}^2$

a. Suppose that the residuals come from the model $y_t = a_0 + a_1 y_{t-1} + \varepsilon_t$. Find the conditional and unconditional variance of $\{y_t\}$ in terms of the parameters a_1, α_0, α_1, and α_2.

b. Suppose that $\{y_t\}$ is an ARCH-M process such the level of y_t is positively related to its own conditional variance. For simplicity, let: $y_t = \alpha_0 + \alpha_1 \varepsilon_{t-1}^2 + \alpha_2 \varepsilon_{t-2}^2 + \varepsilon_t$. Trace out the impulse response function of $\{y_t\}$ to an $\{\varepsilon_t\}$ shock. You may assume that the system has been in long-run equilibrium ($\varepsilon_{t-2} = \varepsilon_{t-1} = 0$) but now $\varepsilon_t = 1$. Thus, the issue is to find the values of y_1, y_2, y_3, and y_4 given that $\varepsilon_2 = \varepsilon_3 = \ldots = 0$.

c. Use your answer to part b to explain the following result. A student estimated $\{y_t\}$ as an MA(2) process and found the residuals to be white noise. A second student estimated the same series as the ARCH-M process: $y_t = \alpha_0 + \alpha_1 \varepsilon_{t-1}^2 + \alpha_2 \varepsilon_{t-2}^2 + \varepsilon_t$. Why might both estimates appear reasonable? How would you decide which is the better model?

d. In general, explain why an ARCH-M model might appear to be a moving average process.

9. The file NYSE.XLS contain the daily values of the New York Stock Exchange Composite Index that was used in Section 10. Reproduce the results of Section 10.

10. Chapter 1.6 of the Programming Manual that accompanies this text contains a discussion of nonlinear least squares and maximum likelihood estimation. If you have not already done so, download the manual from the Wiley Web site. Also download the data set MONEYDEM.XLS and the programs.

Program 1.4 creates the interest rate spread (s_t) as tb1yr – tb3mo. As indicated in the programming manual, estimate the spread as an AR(3) process. You should find:

$$s_t = 0.0476 + 0.890s_{t-1} - 0.39s_{t-2} + 0.162s_{t-3} + \varepsilon_t$$

a. Show that the residuals pass the standard diagnostic tests for serial correlation.

b. Form the squared residuals and perform the test for ARCH errors. You should find

$$\hat{\varepsilon}_t^2 = 0.046 + 0.217\hat{\varepsilon}_{t-1}^2 - 0.026\hat{\varepsilon}_{t-2}^2 + 0.160\hat{\varepsilon}_{t-3}^2$$

Determine the value of TR^2 for this equation.

c. Estimate the spread as an AR(3) process with ARCH(3) errors.

d. As shown in Program 1.4, estimate the spread as an ARMA(1, 1) process with GARCH(1, 1) errors. Show that this model is preferable to that from part c.

ENDNOTES

1. Some authors prefer the spelling homoscedastic and heteroscedastic; both forms are correct.
2. If the unconditional variance of a series is not constant, the series is nonstationary. However, *conditional* heteroskedasticy is *not* a source of nonstationarity.
3. Letting $\alpha(L)$ and $\beta(L)$ be polynomials in the lag operator L, we can rewrite h_t in the form
   $$h_t = \alpha_0 + \alpha(L)\varepsilon_t^2 + \beta(L)h_{t-1}$$
   The notation $\alpha(1)$ denotes the polynomial $\alpha(L)$ evaluated at $L = 1$; i.e., $\alpha(1) = \alpha_1 + \alpha_2 + \dots + \alpha_q$. Bollerslev (1986) shows that the GARCH process is stationary with $E\varepsilon_t = 0$, $\text{var}(\varepsilon_t) = \alpha_0/(1 - \alpha(1) - \beta(1))$ and $\text{Cov}(\varepsilon_t, \varepsilon_{t-s}) = 0$ for $s \neq 0$ if $\alpha(1) + \beta(1) < 1$.
4. Unfortunately, there is no available method to test the null of white-noise errors versus the specific alternative of GARCH(p, q) errors. Bollerslev (1986) proves that the ACF of the squared residuals resulting from (3.9) are an ARMA(m, p) model where $m = \max(p,q)$.
5. Constraining the coefficients of h_t to follow a decaying pattern conserves degrees of freedom and considerably eases the estimation process. Moreover, the lagged coefficients given by $(9 - i)$ are necessarily positive.
6. Estimating a model with p lags usually entails a loss of the first p observations. To correct for this problem, the ARCH and GARCH models should be compared over the identical sample period.
7. In addition to the intercept term, three seasonal dummy variables were included in the supply equation.
8. If the underlying data-generating process is autoregressive, adaptive expectations and rational expectations can be perfectly consistent with each other.
9. If the utility function is quadratic and/or if the excess returns from holding the asset are normally distributed, an increase in the variance of returns is equivalent to an increase in "risk."
10. Of course, to the individual contemplating the purchase of a risky asset, the value of μ_t is not stochastic. Note that μ_t is the expected return that the individual would demand in order to hold the long-term asset.
11. The unconditional mean of y_t is altered by changing only δ. Changing β and δ commensurately maintains the mean value of the $\{y_t\}$ sequence.
12. A t-test on only the coefficient a_2 is called the Negative Size Bias test, and the test on only the coefficient a_3 is called the Positive Size Bias test.
13. In large samples, it is permissible to ignore the issue of a fat-tailed distribution. Quasi-maximum likelihood estimates use the normal distribution even though the actual distribution of the $\{\varepsilon_t\}$ sequence is fat-tailed. Under fairly weak assumptions, the parameter estimates for the model of the mean and the conditional variance are consistent and normally distributed.
14. No attempt was made to account for the fact that the market is closed on holidays and on important key dates such as September 11, 2001.

CHAPTER *4*

MODELS WITH TREND

Inspection of the autocorrelation function serves as a rough indicator of whether a trend is present in a series. A slowly decaying ACF is indicative of a large characteristic root, a true unit root process, or a trend stationary process. Formal tests can help determine whether a system contains a trend and whether the trend is deterministic or stochastic. However, the existing tests have little power to distinguish between near-unit root and unit root processes. This chapter has five aims:

1. Formalize simple models of variables with a time-dependent mean. A trend can be completely deterministic or may contain stochastic components. It is essential to properly model the trend if you intend to do any hypothesis testing or long-term forecasting.

2. Develop and illustrate the Dickey–Fuller and augmented Dickey–Fuller tests for the presence of a unit root. These tests can also be used to help detect the presence of a stochastic trend. Several variants of the test are presented, including a test for seasonal unit roots. In order to develop the test statistics it is necessary to understand the nature of Monte Carlo experiments.

3. Consider tests for unit roots in the presence of structural change. Structural change can complicate the tests for trends; a policy regime change can result in a structural break that makes an otherwise stationary series appear to be nonstationary.

4. Illustrate a general procedure to determine whether a series contains a unit root. Unit root tests are sensitive to the presence of deterministic regressors, such as an intercept term or a deterministic time trend. As such, there is a sophisticated set of procedures that can aid in the identification process. These procedures can be used if it is not known which deterministic elements are parts of the true data-generating process. It is important to be wary of the results from such tests since (i) they all have low power to discriminate between a unit root and a near-unit root process and (ii) they may have used an inappropriate set of deterministic regressors.

5. Decompose a series with a trend into its stationary and trend components. Several methodologies that can be used to decompose a series into its temporary and permanent components are presented.

1. DETERMINISTIC AND STOCHASTIC TRENDS

It is helpful to represent the general solution to a linear stochastic difference equation as consisting of these three distinct parts:[1]

$$y_t = \text{trend} + \text{stationary component} + \text{noise}$$

Chapter 2 explained how to model the stationary component using the Box–Jenkins methodology. Chapter 3 showed you how to model the variance of the error (i.e., noise) component. A critical task for applied econometricians is to develop simple stochastic difference equation models that mimic the behavior of trending variables. If you examine Figure 4.1, it is clear that the distinguishing feature of real GDP $\{rgdp_t\}$ is that it increases over time. For such a series, a naïve forecaster might estimate the sustained increase using the following cubic polynomial model for the trend:

$$rgdp_t = 2.224 + 0.385t - 0.0002t^2 + 1.85E - 6t^3 \qquad (4.1)$$
$$(61.27)\ (20.89)\ (-6.78)\quad (12.17)$$

The fitted values are shown as the dashed lines in the figure and the forecasted values are shown as the solid line extending past 2002:1. Regardless of the t-statistics, the use of such a model for the trend of real GDP is problematic. Since there are no stochastic components in the trend, (4.1) implies that there is a deterministic (and accelerating) long-run growth rate of the real economy. The "Real Business Cycle" school argues that technological advancements have permanent effects on the trend of the macroeconomy. Since technological innovations are stochastic, the trend should reflect this underlying randomness. Adherents to other schools of macroeconomics would also argue that the trend is not completely deterministic. For example, they might point out that an oil price shock or a targeted tax reduction could affect investment and the economy's long-term growth rate.

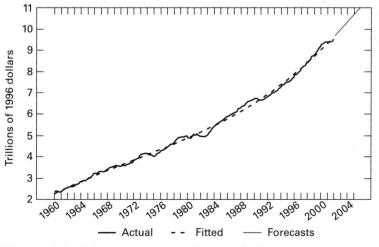

FIGURE 4.1   A Deterministic Trend in Real GDP?

The federal funds rate and the yield on 10-year U.S. federal government securities are shown in Figure 4.2. The two interest rates have no obvious tendency to increase or decrease. Moreover, there are no decided structural breaks that induce one-time shifts in the mean. Nevertheless, there is no pronounced tendency for either series to revert to a long-run mean. The key feature of a trend is that it has a permanent effect on a series. If the trend is defined as the "permanent" or nondecaying component of a time series, the two interest rates have a trend.

Suppose that a series always changes by the same fixed amount from one period to the next. To be more specific, suppose that

$$\Delta y_t = a_0$$

As you know from Chapter 1, the solution to this linear difference equation is

$$y_t = y_0 + a_0 t$$

where y_0 is the initial condition for period zero.

Hence, the solution for $\Delta y_t = a_0$ turns out to be nothing more than a deterministic linear time trend; the intercept is y_0 and the slope is a_0. Now, if we add the stationary component $A(L)\varepsilon_t$ to the trend, we obtain

$$y_t = y_0 + a_0 t + A(L)\varepsilon_t \tag{4.2}$$

In (4.2), y_t can differ from its trend value by the amount $A(L)\varepsilon_t$. Since this deviation is stationary, the $\{y_t\}$ sequence will exhibit only temporary departures from the trend. As such, the long-term forecast of y_{t+s} will converge to the trend line $y_0 + a_0(t + s)$. In the jargon of the profession, this type of model is called a **trend stationary (TS) model.**

FIGURE 4.2   Short- and Long-Term Interest Rates

Now suppose that the *expected* change in y_t is a_0 units. In particular, let Δy_t be equal to a_0 plus a white-noise term:

$$\Delta y_t = a_0 + \varepsilon_t \tag{4.3}$$

Sometimes Δy_t exceeds a_0 and sometimes it falls short of a_0. Since $E_{t-1}\varepsilon_t = 0$, (4.3) implies that y_t is expected to change by a_0 units from one period to the next. The seemingly innocuous modification of (4.2) has profound differences for the trend. If y_0 is the initial condition, it is readily verified that the general solution to the first-order difference equation represented by (4.3) is

$$y_t = y_0 + \sum_{i=1}^{t} \varepsilon_i + a_0 t$$

Here, y_t consists of the deterministic trend component $a_0 t$ and the component $y_0 + \Sigma \varepsilon_i$. We can think of this second component as a stochastic intercept term. In the absence of any shocks, the intercept is y_0. However, each ε_i shock represents a shift in the intercept. Since all values of $\{\varepsilon_i\}$ have a coefficient of unity, the effect of each shock on the intercept term is permanent. In the time-series literature, such a sequence is said to have a **stochastic trend** since each ε_i shock imparts a permanent, albeit random, change in the conditional mean of the series. If $a_0 = 0$ this type of model seems to capture some of the behavior of the interest rates shown in Figure 4.2. The two rates have no particular tendency to increase or decrease over time; neither do they exhibit any tendency to revert to a given mean value.

The Random Walk Model

Equation (4.3) is the basic building block for modeling series containing stochastic trends. Since these models are probably unfamiliar to you, the remainder of this section explores the nature of stochastic trends. We begin by considering the special case of (4.3) when $a_0 = 0$. This model, known as the **random walk model,** has a special place in the economics and finance literature. For example, some formulations of the efficient market hypothesis posit that the change in the price of a stock from one day to the next is completely random. As such, the current price (y_t) should be equal to last period's price plus a white-noise term, so that

$$y_t = y_{t-1} + \varepsilon_t \quad (\text{or } \Delta y_t = \varepsilon_t) \tag{4.4}$$

Similarly, suppose you were betting on the outcome of a coin toss, and a head added $1 to your wealth while a tail cost you $1. We could let $\varepsilon_t = +\$1$ if a head appears and $-\$1$ in the event of a tail. Thus, your current wealth (y_t) equals last period's wealth (y_{t-1}) plus the realized value of ε_t. If you play again, your wealth in $t + 1$ is $y_{t+1} = y_t + \varepsilon_{t+1}$.

If y_0 is a given initial condition, it can be readily verified that the general solution to the first-order difference equation represented by the random walk model is

$$y_t = y_0 + \sum_{i=1}^{t} \varepsilon_i$$

Taking expected values we obtain $Ey_t = Ey_{t-s} = y_0$; thus, the mean of a random walk is a constant. However, all stochastic shocks have nondecaying effects on the $\{y_t\}$ sequence. Given the first t realizations of the $\{\varepsilon_t\}$ process, the conditional mean of y_{t+1} is

$$E_t y_{t+1} = E_t(y_t + \varepsilon_{t+1}) = y_t$$

Similarly, the conditional mean of y_{t+s} (for any $s > 0$) can be obtained from

$$y_{t+s} = y_t + \sum_{i=1}^{s} \varepsilon_{t+i}$$

so that

$$E_t y_{t+s} = y_t + E_t \sum_{i=1}^{s} \varepsilon_{t+i} = y_t$$

For any positive value of s, the conditional means for all values of y_{t+s} are equivalent. Hence, the constant value of y_t is the unbiased estimator of all future values of y_{t+s}. To interpret, note that an ε_t shock has a permanent effect on y_t. This permanence is directly reflected in the forecasts for y_{t+s}.

It is easy to show that the variance is time-dependent. Given the value of y_0, the variance can be constructed as

$$\text{Var}(y_t) = \text{var}(\varepsilon_t + \varepsilon_{t-1} + \ldots + \varepsilon_1) = t\sigma^2$$

and

$$\text{Var}(y_{t-s}) = \text{var}(\varepsilon_{t-s} + \varepsilon_{t-s-1} + \ldots + \varepsilon_1) = (t - s)\sigma^2$$

Since the variance is not constant [i.e., $\text{var}(y_t) \neq \text{var}(y_{t-s})$], the random walk process is nonstationary. Moreover, as $t \to \infty$ the variance of y_t also approaches infinity. Thus, the random walk meanders without exhibiting any tendency to increase or decrease. It is also instructive to calculate the covariance of y_t and y_{t-s}. Since the mean is constant, we can form the covariance γ_{t-s} as

$$\begin{aligned}
E[(y_t - y_0)(y_{t-s} - y_0)] &= E[(\varepsilon_t + \varepsilon_{t-1} + \ldots + \varepsilon_1)(\varepsilon_{t-s} + \varepsilon_{t-s-1} + \ldots + \varepsilon_1)] \\
&= E[(\varepsilon_{t-s})^2 + (\varepsilon_{t-s-1})^2 + \ldots + (\varepsilon_1)^2] \\
&= (t - s)\sigma^2
\end{aligned}$$

To form the correlation coefficient ρ_s, we can divide γ_{t-s} by the product of the standard deviation of y_t multiplied by the standard deviation of y_{t-s}. Thus, the correlation coefficient ρ_s is

$$\rho_s = (t - s)/\sqrt{(t - s)t}$$
$$= [(t - s)/t]^{0.5}$$

This result plays an important role in the detection of nonstationary series. For the first few autocorrelations, the sample size t will be large relative to the number of autocorrelations formed; for small values of s, the ratio $(t - s)/t$ is approximately equal to unity. However, as s increases, the values of ρ_s will decline. Hence, in using sample data, *the autocorrelation function for a random walk process will show a slight tendency to decay.* Thus, it will not be possible to use the autocorrelation function to distinguish between a unit root process and a stationary process with an autoregressive coefficient that is close to unity.

Panel (*a*) in Figure 4.3 shows the time path of a simulated random walk process. First, 100 normally distributed random deviates were drawn from a theoretical distribution with a mean of zero and a variance equal to unity. By setting $y_0 = 0$, each value of y_t ($t = 1, ..., 100$) was constructed by adding the random variable to the value of y_{t-1}. As expected, the series meanders without any tendency to revert to a long-run value. However, there does appear to be a slight positive trend in the simulated data. The reason for the upward trend is that this particular simulation happened to contain more positive values than negative values. The impression of a steadily increasing trend in the true data-generating process is false and serves as a reminder against relying solely on causal inspection.

The Random Walk Plus Drift Model

Now let the change in y_t be partially deterministic and partially stochastic. The **random walk plus drift model** augments the random walk model by adding a constant term a_0, so that

$$y_t = y_{t-1} + a_0 + \varepsilon_t$$

Hence, you can see that (4.3) is a random walk plus drift. Given the initial condition y_0, the general solution for y_t is given by

$$y_t = y_0 + a_0 t + \sum_{i=1}^{t} \varepsilon_i \tag{4.5}$$

FIGURE 4.3   Four Series with Trends

Here, the behavior of y_t is governed by two nonstationary components: a linear deterministic trend and the stochastic trend $\Sigma \varepsilon_i$. As such, a random walk plus drift is a pure model of a trend; there is no separate stationary component in (4.5).

If we take expectations, the mean of y_t is $y_0 + a_0 t$ and the mean of y_{t+s} is $E y_{t+s} = y_0 + a_0(t + s)$. To explain, the deterministic change in each realization of $\{y_t\}$ is a_0; after t periods the cumulated change is $a_0 t$. In addition, there is the stochastic trend $\Sigma \varepsilon_i$; each ε_i shock has a permanent effect on the mean of y_t. Notice that the first difference of the series is stationary; taking the first difference yields the stationary sequence $\Delta y_t = a_0 + \varepsilon_t$.

Panel (*b*) of Figure 4.3 illustrates a simulated random walk plus drift model. The value of a_0 was set equal to 0.5 and (4.5) was simulated using the same 100 deviates used for the random walk model above. Clearly, the deterministic time trend dominates the time path of the series. In a very large sample, asymptotic theory suggests this will always be the case. However, you should not conclude that it is always easy to discern the difference between a random walk model and a model with drift. In a small sample, increasing the variance of $\{\varepsilon_t\}$ or decreasing the absolute value of a_0 could cloud the long-run properties of the sequence. Panel (*c*) uses the same random numbers to generate the trend stationary (TS) series $y_t = 0.5t + \varepsilon_t$. The patterns evident in the random walk plus drift model and in the TS series look strikingly similar to each other and to the real GDP series shown in Figure 4.1.

To obtain the *s*-step-ahead forecast for a random walk plus drift, update (4.5) by *s* periods to obtain

$$y_{t+s} = y_0 + a_0(t + s) + \sum_{i=1}^{t+s} \varepsilon_i$$

$$= y_t + a_0 s + \sum_{i=1}^{s} \varepsilon_{t+i}$$

Taking the conditional expectation of y_{t+s}, it follows that

$$E_t y_{t+s} = y_t + a_0 s$$

In contrast to the pure random walk model, the forecast function is not flat. The fact that the average change in y_t is always the constant a_0 is reflected in the forecast function. In addition to the given value of y_t, we project this deterministic change s times into the future.

Generalizations of the Stochastic Trend Model

It is not too difficult to generalize the random walk model to allow y_t to be the sum of a stochastic trend and a white-noise component. Formally, this third model—called a **random walk plus noise**—is represented by

$$y_t = y_0 + \sum_{i=1}^{t} \varepsilon_i + \eta_t \tag{4.6}$$

where $\{\eta_t\}$ is a white-noise process with variance σ_η^2; and ε_t and η_{t-s} are independently distributed for all t and s [i.e., $E(\varepsilon_t \eta_{t-s}) = 0$]

An alternative representation of the random walk plus noise model is

$$\Delta y_t = \varepsilon_t + \Delta \eta_t \qquad (4.7)$$

You can easily verify that (4.6) and (4.7) are equivalent by writing y_{t-1} as

$$y_{t-1} = y_0 + \sum_{i=1}^{t-1} \varepsilon_i + \eta_{t-1}$$

Subtract this expression from (4.6) to obtain (4.7). From (4.6), you can see that the key properties of the random walk plus noise model are:

1. Given the value y_0, the mean of the $\{y_t\}$ sequence is constant: $Ey_t = y_0$ and updating by s periods yields $Ey_{t+s} = y_0$. Notice that the successive ε_t shocks have permanent effects on the $\{y_t\}$ sequence in that there is no decay factor on past values of ε_{t-i}. Hence, y_t has the stochastic trend component $\Sigma \varepsilon_i$.

2. The $\{y_t\}$ sequence has a pure noise component in that the $\{\eta_t\}$ sequence has only a temporary effect on the $\{y_t\}$ sequence. The current realization of η_t affects only y_t but not the subsequent values y_{t+s}.

3. The variance of $\{y_t\}$ is not constant: $\text{var}(y_t) = t\sigma^2 + \sigma_\eta^2$ and $\text{var}(y_{t-s}) = (t-s)\sigma^2 + \sigma_\eta^2$. As in the other models with a stochastic trend, the variance of y_t approaches infinity as t increases. The presence of the noise component means that the correlation coefficient between y_t and y_{t-s} is smaller than that for the pure random walk model.

To prove that the sample correlogram will exhibit even faster decay than in the pure random walk model, note that the covariance between y_t and y_{t-s} is

$$\text{Cov}(y_t, y_{t-s}) = E[(y_t - y_0)(y_{t-s} - y_0)]$$
$$= E[(\varepsilon_1 + \varepsilon_2 + \varepsilon_3 + \ldots + \varepsilon_t + \eta_t)(\varepsilon_1 + \varepsilon_2 + \varepsilon_3 + \ldots + \varepsilon_{t-s} + \eta_{t-s})]$$

Since $\{\varepsilon_t\}$ and $\{\eta_t\}$ are independent white-noise sequences

$$\text{Cov}(y_t, y_{t-s}) = (t-s)\sigma^2$$

Thus, the correlation coefficient ρ_s is

$$\rho_s = \frac{(t-s)\sigma^2}{\sqrt{(t\sigma^2 + \sigma_\eta^2)[(t-s)\sigma^2 + \sigma_\eta^2]}}$$

Comparison of ρ_s with the correlation coefficient for the pure random walk model verifies that the autocorrelations for the random walk plus noise model are always smaller for $\sigma_\eta^2 > 0$. Panel (d) of Figure 4.3 shows a random walk plus noise model. The series was simulated by drawing a second 100 normally distributed random terms to represent the $\{\eta_t\}$ series. For each value of t, y_t was calculated using (4.6). If we compare Panels (a) and (d), it can be seen that the two series track each other quite well. The random walk plus noise model could mimic the same set of macroeconomic variables as the random walk model. The effect of the "noise" component $\{\eta_t\}$ is to increase the variance of $\{y_t\}$ without affecting its long-run behavior.

After all, the random walk plus noise series is nothing more than the random walk model with a purely temporary component added.

The random walk plus noise and the random walk plus drift models are the building blocks of more complex time-series models. For example, the noise and drift components can easily be incorporated into a single model by modifying (4.6) such that the trend in y_t contains a deterministic and a stochastic component. Specifically, replace (4.6) with

$$\Delta y_t = a_0 + \varepsilon_t + \Delta \eta_t$$

or

$$y_t = y_0 + a_0 t + \sum_{i=1}^{t} \varepsilon_i + \eta_t \tag{4.8}$$

Equation (4.8) is called the **trend plus noise model**; y_t is the sum of a deterministic trend, a stochastic trend and a pure white-noise term. Moreover, the noise sequence does not need to be a white-noise process. Let $A(L)$ be a polynomial in the lag operator L; it is possible to augment a random walk plus drift process with the stationary process $A(L)\eta_t$ so that the **general trend plus irregular model** is

$$y_t = y_0 + a_0 t + \sum_{i=1}^{t} \varepsilon_i + A(L)\ \eta_t \tag{4.9}$$

Thus, (4.9) has a deterministic trend, a stochastic trend and a stationary component.

2. REMOVING THE TREND

From the previous section, it should be clear that there are important differences between a series with a trend and a stationary series. Shocks to a stationary time series are necessarily temporary; over time, the effects of the shocks will dissipate and the series will revert to its long-run mean level.

On the other hand, a series containing a trend will not revert to a long-run level. Note that the trend can have deterministic and stochastic components. These components of the trend have important implications for the appropriate transformation necessary to attain a stationary series. The usual methods for eliminating the trend are **differencing** and **detrending.** Detrending entails regressing a variable on time and saving the residuals.[2] A series containing a unit root can be made stationary by differencing. In fact, we already know that the d-th difference of ARIMA (p, d, q) model is stationary. The aim of this section is to compare these two methods of isolating the trend.

Differencing

First consider the solution for the random walk plus drift model:

$$y_t = y_0 + a_0 t + \sum_{i=1}^{t} e_i$$

Taking the first difference, we obtain $\Delta y_t = a_0 + \varepsilon_t$. Clearly, the $\{\Delta y_t\}$ sequence—equal to a constant plus a white-noise disturbance—is stationary. Viewing Δy_t as the variable of interest, we have

$$E(\Delta y_t) = E(a_0 + \varepsilon_t) = a_0$$
$$\mathrm{Var}(\Delta y_t) \equiv E(\Delta y_t - a_0)^2 = E(\varepsilon_t)^2 = \sigma^2$$

and

$$\mathrm{Cov}(\Delta y_t, \Delta y_{t-s}) \equiv E[(\Delta y_t - a_0)(\Delta y_{t-s} - a_0)] = E(\varepsilon_t \varepsilon_{t-s}) = 0$$

Since the mean and variance are constants and the covariance between Δy_t and Δy_{t-s} depends solely on s, the $\{\Delta y_t\}$ sequence is stationary.

The random walk plus noise model is an interesting case study. In first differences the model can be written as $\Delta y_t = \varepsilon_t + \Delta \eta_t$. In this form, it is easy to show that Δy_t is stationary. Clearly, the mean is zero because

$$E\Delta y_t = E(\varepsilon_t + \Delta \eta_t) = 0$$

Moreover, the variance and all autocovariances are constant and time-invariant because

$$\mathrm{Var}(\Delta y_t) = E[(\Delta y_t)^2] = E[(\varepsilon_t + \Delta \eta_t)^2]$$
$$= E[(\varepsilon_t)^2 + 2\varepsilon_t \Delta \eta_t + (\Delta \eta_t)^2]$$
$$= \sigma^2 + 2E[\varepsilon_t \Delta \eta_t] + E[(\eta_t)^2 - 2\eta_t \eta_{t-1} + (\eta_{t-1})^2] = \sigma^2 + 2\sigma_\eta^2$$

$$\mathrm{Cov}(\Delta y_t, \Delta y_{t-1}) = E[(\varepsilon_t + \eta_t - \eta_{t-1})(\varepsilon_{t-1} + \eta_{t-1} - \eta_{t-2})] = -\sigma_\eta^2$$

and

$$\mathrm{Cov}(\Delta y_t, \Delta y_{t-s}) = E[(\varepsilon_t + \eta_t - \eta_{t-1})(\varepsilon_{t-s} + \eta_{t-s} - \eta_{t-s-1})] = 0 \qquad \text{for } s \geq 1$$

If we set $s = 1$, the correlation coefficient between Δy_t and Δy_{t-1} is

$$\rho_1 = \frac{\mathrm{cov}(\Delta y_t, \Delta y_{t-1})}{\mathrm{var}(\Delta y_t)} = \frac{-\sigma_\eta^2}{\sigma^2 + 2\sigma_\eta^2}$$

Examination reveals $-0.5 \leq \rho_1 \leq 0$ and that all other correlation coefficients are zero. Since the first difference of y_t acts exactly as an MA(1) process, the random walk plus noise model is ARIMA(0, 1, 1). Since adding a constant to a series has no effect on the correlogram, it additionally follows that the trend plus noise model of (4.8) also acts as an ARIMA(0, 1, 1) process.

Now consider the general class of ARIMA(p, d, q) models:

$$A(L)y_t = B(L)\varepsilon_t \tag{4.10}$$

where $A(L)$ and $B(L)$ are polynomials of orders p and q in the lag operator L.[3]

First suppose that $A(L)$ has a single unit root and that $B(L)$ has all roots outside the unit circle.[4] We can factor $A(L)$ into two components $(1 - L)A^*(L)$ where $A^*(L)$ is a polynomial of order $p - 1$. Since $A(L)$ has only one unit root, it follows that all roots of $A^*(L)$ are outside of the unit circle. Thus, we can write (4.10) as

$$(1 - L)A^*(L)\, y_t = B(L)\varepsilon_t$$

Now define $y_t^* = \Delta y_t$ so that

$$A^*(L)y_t^* = B(L)\varepsilon_t \tag{4.11}$$

The $\{y_t^*\}$ sequence is stationary since all roots of $A^*(L)$ lie outside the unit circle. The point is that the first difference of a unit root process is stationary. If $A(L)$ has two unit roots, the same argument can be used to show that the second difference of $\{y_t\}$ is stationary. *The general point is that the d-th difference of a process with d unit roots is stationary.* An ARIMA(p, d, q) model has d unit roots; the d-th difference of such a model is a stationary ARMA(p, q) process. Such a sequence is integrated of order d and is denoted by $I(d)$.

Detrending

We have shown that differencing can sometimes be used to transform a nonstationary model into a stationary model with an ARMA representation. This does not mean that all nonstationary models can be transformed into well-behaved ARMA models by appropriate differencing. Consider, for example, a model that is the sum of a deterministic trend and a pure noise component:

$$y_t = y_0 + a_1 t + \varepsilon_t$$

The first difference of y_t is not well-behaved because

$$\Delta y_t = a_1 + \varepsilon_t - \varepsilon_{t-1}$$

Here Δy_t is not *invertible* in the sense that Δy_t cannot be expressed in the form of an autoregressive process. Recall that invertibility of a stationary process requires that the MA component does not have a unit root.

Instead, an appropriate way to transform this model is to estimate the regression equation $y_t = a_0 + a_1 t + \varepsilon_t$. Subtracting the estimated values of y_t from the observed series yields estimated values of the $\{\varepsilon_t\}$ series. More generally, a time series may have the polynomial trend as

$$y_t = a_0 + a_1 t + a_2 t^2 + a_3 t^3 + \ldots + a_n t^n + e_t$$

where $\{e_t\}$ = a stationary process.

Detrending is accomplished by regressing $\{y_t\}$ on a deterministic polynomial time trend, as in (4.1). The appropriate degree of the polynomial can be determined by standard t-tests, F-tests, and/or using statistics such as the AIC or SBC. The common practice is to estimate the regression equation using the largest value of n deemed reasonable. If the t-statistic for a_n is zero, consider a polynomial trend of order $n - 1$. Continue to pare down the order of the polynomial trend until a nonzero coefficient is found. F-tests can be used to determine whether a group of coefficients, say, a_{n-i} through a_n, is statistically different from zero. The AIC and SBC statistics can be used to reconfirm the appropriate degree of the polynomial.

The difference between the estimated values of the $\{y_t\}$ sequence from the actual values yields an estimate of the stationary sequence $\{e_t\}$. The detrended process can then be modeled using traditional methods (such as ARMA estimation).

Difference versus Trend Stationary Models

We have encountered two ways to eliminate a trend. A trend stationary series can be transformed into a stationary series by removing the deterministic trend. A series with a unit root, sometimes called a **difference stationary** (DS) series, can be transformed into a stationary series by differencing. A serious problem is encountered when the inappropriate method is used to eliminate trend. We saw an example of the problem in attempting to difference the equation $y_t = y_0 + a_1 t + \varepsilon_t$. Consider a more general trend stationary process of the form

$$A(L)y_t = a_0 + a_1 t + e_t$$

where the characteristic roots of the polynomial $A(L)$ are all outside the unit circle and the expression e_t is allowed to have the form $e_t = B(L)\varepsilon_t$. Subtracting an estimate of the deterministic time trend yields a stationary and invertible ARMA model. However, if we use the notation of (4.11), the first difference of such a model yields

$$A(L)y_t^* = a_1 + (1 - L)B(L)\varepsilon_t$$

First-differencing the *TS* process has introduced a noninvertible unit root process into the MA component of the model. Of course, the same problem is encountered in a model with a polynomial time trend.

In the same way, subtracting a deterministic time trend from a difference stationary process is also inappropriate. For example, in the general trend plus irregular model of (4.9), subtracting $y_0 + a_0 t$ from each observation does not result in a stationary series since the stochastic portion of the trend is not eliminated.

Are There Business Cycles?

Traditional business cycle research decomposed real macroeconomic variables into a long-run (secular) trend and a cyclical component. The typical decomposition is illustrated by the hypothetical data in Figure 4.4. The secular trend, portrayed by the straight line, was deemed to be in the domain of growth theory. The slope of the trend line was thought to be determined by long-run factors such as technological growth, fertility, and educational attainment levels.

One source of the deviations from trend occurs because of the wavelike motion of real economic activity called the **business cycle.** Although the actual period of the cycle was never thought to be as regular as that depicted in the figure, the periods of prosperity and recovery were regarded to be as inevitable as the tides. The goal of monetary and fiscal policy was to reduce the amplitude of the cycle (measured by distance *ab*). In terms of our previous discussion, the trend is the nonstationary component and the cyclical and irregular components are stationary.

Although there have been recessions and periods of high prosperity, the post-World War II experience taught us that business cycles do not have a regular period. Even so, there is a widespread belief that over the long run, macroeconomic variables grow at a constant trend rate and that any deviations from trend are eventually eliminated by the *invisible hand*. The belief that trend is unchanging over time leads to the

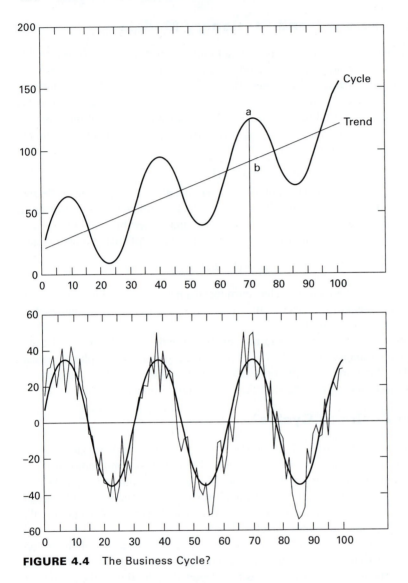

FIGURE 4.4 The Business Cycle?

common practice of *detrending* macroeconomic data using a linear (or polynomial) deterministic regression equation.

Nelson and Plosser (1982) challenged the traditional view by demonstrating that important macroeconomic variables tend to be DS rather than TS processes. They obtained time-series data for thirteen important macroeconomic time series: real GNP, nominal GNP, industrial production, employment, unemployment rate, GNP deflator, consumer prices, wages, real wages, money stock, velocity, bond yields, and an index of common stock prices. The sample began as early as 1860 for consumer prices to as late as 1909 for GNP data and ended in 1970 for all of the series. Some of their findings are reported in Table 4.1. The first two columns report the first- and second-order autocorrelations of real and nominal GNP, industrial production, and the unemployment rate. Notice that the autocorrelations of the first three of the series are strongly indicative of a unit root process. Although ρ_1 for the unemployment rate is 0.75, the second-order autocorrelation is less than 0.5.

First differences of the series yield the first- and second-order sample autocorrelations $r(1)$ and $r(2)$, respectively. Sample autocorrelations of the first differences are indicative of stationary processes. The evidence supports the claim that the data are generated from DS processes. Nelson and Plosser point out that the positive autocorrelation of differenced real and nominal GNP at lag 1 only is suggestive of an MA(1) process. To further strengthen the argument for DS processes, recall that differencing a TS process yields a noninvertible moving-average process. None of the differenced series reported by Nelson and Plosser appear to have a unit root in the MA terms.

The results from fitting a linear trend to the data and forming sample autocorrelations of the residuals are shown in the last two columns of the table. An interesting feature of the data is that the sample autocorrelations of the detrended data are reasonably high. This is consistent with the fact that detrending a DS series will not eliminate the nonstationarity. Notice that detrending the unemployment rate has *no effect* on the autocorrelations. The implication is that macroeconomic variables do not grow at a smooth long-run rate. Some macroeconomic shocks are of a permanent nature; the effects of such shocks are never eliminated.

The Trend in Real GDP

Another way to make the same point is to note that the real GDP series shown in Figure 4.1 has a clear trend. However, the tight fit of the estimated model might fool a researcher into thinking the series is actually stationary around the cubic trend line shown in Figure 4.1. Our eyes can be deceived because such trend lines are fit so as to make the observed residuals as small as possible. The ACF and PACF of the residuals from (4.1) are shown in Panel (*a*) of Figure 4.5. You can see that the ACF decays slowly

Table 4.1 Selected Autocorrelations from Nelson and Plosser

	ρ_1	ρ_2	$r(1)$	$r(2)$	$d(1)$	$d(2)$
Real GNP	.95	.90	.34	.04	.87	.66
Nominal GNP	.95	.89	.44	.08	.93	.79
Industrial production	.97	.94	.03	−.11	.84	.67
Unemployment rate	.75	.47	.09	−.29	.75	.46

Notes:

1. Full details of the correlogram can be obtained from Nelson and Plosser (1982), who report the first six sample autocorrelations.

2. Respectively, ρ_i, $r(i)$, and $d(i)$ refer to the i-th-order autocorrelation coefficient for each series, for the first difference of the series, and for the detrended values of the series.

FIGURE 4.5 ACF and PACF

while the PACF cuts to zero after one lag. In fact, this type of slow decay in the ACF might mimic that of a series with a stochastic trend. Thus, detrending the data does not seem to result in a stationary series. Panel (b) shows the ACF and PACF of the logarithmic change in real GDP. The ACF and PACF quickly converge to zero; after two lags, all autocorrelations and partial autocorrelations are not statistically different from zero. The estimated model for logarithmic change in real GDP ($\Delta lrgdp$) is

$$\Delta lrgdp_t = 0.0050 + 0.256\Delta lrgdp_{t-1} + 0.1496\Delta lrgdp_{t-2}$$
$$(5.03) \quad (3.30) \quad\quad\quad (1.94)$$

Unlike the model of the deterministic trend, the residuals from this model all appear to be white noise. Thus, differencing is sufficient to remove the trend.

Rather than rely solely on an analysis of correlograms, it is possible to formally test whether a series is stationary. We examine such tests in the next several sections. The testing procedure is not as straightforward as it may seem. We cannot use the usual testing techniques because classical procedures all presume that the data are stationary. For now, it suffices to say that Nelson and Plosser are not able to reject the null hypothesis of a unit root. However, before we examine the tests for a unit root, it is important to note that the issue of nonstationarity also arises quite naturally in the context of the standard regression model.

3. UNIT ROOTS AND REGRESSION RESIDUALS

Consider the regression equation[5]

$$y_t = a_0 + a_1 z_t + e_t \qquad (4.12)$$

The assumptions of the classical regression model necessitate that both the $\{y_t\}$ and $\{z_t\}$ sequences be stationary and that the errors have a zero mean and a finite variance. In the presence of nonstationary variables, there might be what Granger and Newbold (1974) call a **spurious regression.** A spurious regression has a high R^2 and t-statistics that appear to be significant, but the results are without any economic meaning. The regression output "looks good" because the least-squares estimates are not consistent and the customary tests of statistical inference do not hold. Granger and Newbold (1974) provide a detailed examination of the consequences of violating the stationarity assumption by generating two sequences, $\{y_t\}$ and $\{z_t\}$, as *independent* random walks using the formulas

$$y_t = y_{t-1} + \varepsilon_{yt} \tag{4.13}$$

and

$$z_t = z_{t-1} + \varepsilon_{zt} \tag{4.14}$$

where ε_{yt} and ε_{zt} are white-noise processes that are independent of each other.

Granger and Newbold generated many such samples and for each sample estimated a regression in the form of (4.12). Since the $\{y_t\}$ and $\{z_t\}$ sequences are independent of each other, (4.12) is necessarily meaningless; any relationship between the two variables is spurious. Surprisingly, at the 5 percent significance level, they were able to reject the null hypothesis $a_1 = 0$ in approximately 75 percent of the cases. Moreover, the regressions usually had very high R^2 values and the estimated residuals exhibited a high degree of autocorrelation.

To explain the Granger and Newbold findings, note that the regression equation (4.12) is necessarily meaningless if the residual series $\{e_t\}$ is nonstationary. Obviously, if the $\{e_t\}$ sequence has a stochastic trend, any error in period t never decays so that any deviation from the model is permanent. It is hard to imagine attaching any importance to an economic model having permanent errors. The simplest way to examine the properties of the $\{e_t\}$ sequence is to abstract from the intercept term a_0 and rewrite (4.12) as

$$e_t = y_t - a_1 z_t$$

If y_t and z_t are generated by (4.13) and (4.14), we can impose the initial conditions $y_0 = z_0 = 0$ so that

$$e_t = \sum_{i=1}^{t} \varepsilon_{yi} - a_1 \sum_{i=1}^{t} \varepsilon_{zi} \tag{4.15}$$

Clearly, the variance of the error becomes infinitely large as t increases. Moreover, the error has a permanent component in that $E_t e_{t+i} = e_t$ for all $i \geq 0$. Hence, the assumptions embedded in the usual hypothesis tests are violated so that any t-test, F-test, or R^2 values are unreliable. It is easy to see why the estimated residuals from a spurious regression will exhibit a high degree of autocorrelation. Updating (4.15), you should be able to demonstrate that the theoretical value of the correlation coefficient between e_t and e_{t+1} goes to unity as t increases.

Under the null hypothesis that $a_1 = 0$, the data-generating process in (4.12) is $y_t = a_0 + e_t$. Given that $\{y_t\}$ is integrated of order one [i.e., $I(1)$], it follows that $\{e_t\}$

is $I(1)$ under the null hypothesis. Yet the assumption that the error term is a unit root process is inconsistent with the distributional theory underlying the use of OLS. This problem will not disappear in large samples. In fact, Phillips (1986) proves that the larger the sample, the more likely you are to falsely conclude that $a_1 \neq 0$.

Worksheet 4.1 illustrates the problem of spurious regressions. The top two graphs show 100 realizations of the $\{y_t\}$ and $\{z_t\}$ sequences generated according to (4.13) and (4.14). Although $\{\varepsilon_{yt}\}$ and $\{\varepsilon_{zt}\}$ are drawn from white-noise distributions, the realizations of the two sequences are such that y_{100} is positive and z_{100} is negative.

You can see that the regression of y_t on z_t captures the *within-sample* tendency of the sequences to move in opposite directions. The straight line shown in the scatter plot is the OLS regression line $y_t = -0.31 - 0.46z_t$. The correlation coefficient between $\{y_t\}$ and $\{z_t\}$ is -0.372. The residuals from this regression have a unit root; as such, the coefficients -0.31 and -0.46 are spurious. Worksheet 4.2 illustrates the same problem using two simulated random walk plus drift sequences: $y_t = 0.2 + y_{t-1} + \varepsilon_{yt}$ and $z_t = -0.1 + z_{t-1} + \varepsilon_{zt}$. The drift terms dominate so that for small values of t, it appears that $y_t = -2z_t$. As sample size increases, however, the cumulated sum of the errors (i.e., Σe_t) will pull the relationship further and further from -2.0. The scatter plot of the two sequences suggests that the R^2 statistic will be close to unity; in fact, R^2 is almost 0.97. However, as you can see in the last panel of Worksheet 4.2, the residuals from the regression equation are nonstationary. All departures from this relationship are necessarily permanent.

The point is that the econometrician has to be very careful in working with non-stationary variables. In terms of (4.12), there are four cases to consider:

CASE 1

Both $\{y_t\}$ and $\{z_t\}$ are stationary. When both variables are stationary, the classical regression model is appropriate.

CASE 2

The $\{y_t\}$ and $\{z_t\}$ sequences are integrated of different orders. Regression equations using such variables are meaningless. For example, replace (4.14) with the stationary process $z_t = \rho z_{t-1} + \varepsilon_{zt}$ where $|\rho| < 1$. Now (4.15) is replaced by $e_t = \Sigma \varepsilon_{yi} - a_1 \Sigma \rho^i \varepsilon_{zt-i}$. Although the expression $\Sigma \rho^i \varepsilon_{zt-i}$ is convergent, the $\{e_t\}$ sequence still contains a trend component.[6]

CASE 3

The nonstationary $\{y_t\}$ and $\{z_t\}$ sequences are integrated of the same order and the residual sequence contains a stochastic trend. This is the case in which the regression is spurious. The results from such spurious regressions are meaningless in that all errors are permanent. In this case, it is often recommended that

WORKSHEET *4.1*

SPURIOUS REGRESSIONS: EXAMPLE 1

Consider the two random walk processes:

$$y_t = y_{t-1} + \varepsilon_{yt}$$

$$z_t = z_{t-1} + \varepsilon_{zt}$$

Since the $\{\varepsilon_{yt}\}$ and $\{\varepsilon_{zt}\}$ sequences are independent, the regression of y_t on z_t is spurious. Given the realizations of the random disturbances, it appears as if the two sequences are related. In the scatter plot of y_t against z_t, you can see that y_t tends to rise as z_t decreases. A regression equation of y_t on z_t will capture this tendency. The correlation coefficient between y_t and z_t is -0.372 and a linear regression yields $y_t = -0.46z_t - 0.31$. However, the residuals from the regression equation are nonstationary.

Scatter plot of y_t and z_t

Regression residuals

+ Scatter plot
— Regression line

the regression equation be estimated in first differences. Consider the first difference of (4.12):

$$\Delta y_t = a_1 \Delta z_t + \Delta e_t$$

Since y_t, z_t, and e_t each contain unit roots, the first difference of each is stationary. Hence, the usual asymptotic results apply. Of course, if one of the trends is deterministic and the other is stochastic, first-differencing each is not appropriate.

WORKSHEET *4.2*

SPURIOUS REGRESSIONS: EXAMPLE 2

Consider the two random walk plus drift processes:

$y_t = 0.2 + y_{t-1} + \varepsilon_{yt}$

$z_t = -0.1 + z_{t-1} + \varepsilon_{zt}$

Again, the $\{\varepsilon_{yt}\}$ and $\{\varepsilon_{zt}\}$ sequences are independent so that the regression of y_t on z_t is spurious. The scatter plot of y_t against z_t strongly suggests that the two series are related. It is the deterministic time trend that causes the sustained increase in y_t and the sustained fall in z_t. The residuals from the regression equation $y_t = -2z_t + e_t$ are nonstationary.

Scatter plot of y_t and z_t

Regression residuals

CASE 4

The nonstationary $\{y_t\}$ and $\{z_t\}$ sequences are integrated of the same order and the residual sequence is stationary. In this circumstance, $\{y_t\}$ and $\{z_t\}$ are **cointegrated**. A trivial example of a cointegrated system occurs if ε_{zt} and ε_{yt} are perfectly correlated. If $\varepsilon_{zt} = \varepsilon_{yt}$, then (4.15) can be set equal to zero (which is stationary) by setting $a_1 = 1$. To consider a more interesting example, suppose that both z_t and y_t are the random walk plus noise processes:

$$y_t = \mu_t + \varepsilon_{yt}$$
$$z_t = \mu_t + \varepsilon_{zt}$$

where ε_{yt} and ε_{zt} are white-noise processes and μ_t is the random walk process $\mu_t = \mu_{t-1} + \varepsilon_t$. Note that both $\{z_t\}$ and $\{y_t\}$ are $I(1)$ processes but that $y_t - z_t = \varepsilon_{yt} - \varepsilon_{zt}$ is stationary.

All of Chapter 6 is devoted to the issue of cointegrated variables. For now it is sufficient to note that pretesting the variables in a regression for nonstationarity is extremely important. Estimating a regression in the form of (4.12) is meaningless if cases 2 or 3 apply. If the variables are cointegrated, the results of Chapter 6 apply. The remainder of this chapter considers the formal test procedures for the presence of unit roots and/or deterministic time trends.

4. THE MONTE CARLO METHOD

As an applied researcher, you need to know whether a data series contains a trend and the best way to estimate the trend. You also need to avoid several critical mistakes. Clearly, you do not want to difference or detrend a stationary series. Moreover, you do not want to detrend a unit root process or difference a trend stationary process. Although the properties of a sample correlogram are useful tools for detecting the possible presence of unit roots or deterministic trends, the method is necessarily imprecise. What may appear as a unit root to one observer may appear as a stationary process to another. The problem is difficult because a near-unit root process will have the same shaped ACF as that of a process containing a trend. For example, the correlogram of a stationary AR(1) process such that $\rho_1 = 0.99$ will exhibit the type of gradual decay indicative of a nonstationary process. To illustrate some of the issues involved, suppose that we know a series is generated from the following first-order process:[7]

$$y_t = a_1 y_{t-1} + \varepsilon_t \tag{4.16}$$

where $\{\varepsilon_t\}$ is white noise.

First, suppose that we wish to test the null hypothesis that $a_1 = 0$. Under the maintained null hypothesis of $a_1 = 0$, we can estimate (4.16) using OLS. The fact that ε_t is a white-noise process and that $|a_1| < 1$ guarantees that the $\{y_t\}$ sequence is stationary and that the estimate of a_1 is efficient. Calculating the standard error of the estimate of a_1, the researcher can use a t-test to determine whether a_1 is significantly different from zero.

The situation is quite different if we want to test the hypothesis $a_1 = 1$. Now, under the null hypothesis, the $\{y_t\}$ sequence is generated by the nonstationary process:

$$y_t = y_0 + \sum_{i=1}^{t} \varepsilon_i \tag{4.17}$$

Thus, if $a_1 = 1$, the variance becomes infinitely large as t increases. Under the null hypothesis, it is inappropriate to use classical statistical methods to estimate and perform significance tests on the coefficient a_1. If the $\{y_t\}$ sequence is generated as in (4.17), it is simple to show that the OLS estimate of (4.16) will yield a biased estimate of a_1. In Section 1, it was shown that the first-order autocorrelation coefficient in a random walk model is

$$\rho_1 = [(t-1)/t]^{0.5} < 1$$

Since the estimate of a_1 is directly related to the value of ρ_1, the estimated value of a_1 is biased to be below its true value of unity. The estimated model will mimic that of a stationary AR(1) process with a near unit root. Hence, the usual t-test cannot be used to test the hypothesis $a_1 = 1$.

Figure 4.6 shows the sample correlogram for a simulated random walk process. One hundred normally distributed random deviates were obtained so as to mimic the $\{\varepsilon_t\}$ sequence. Assuming $y_0 = 0$, the next 100 values in the $\{y_t\}$ sequence were calculated as $y_t = y_{t-1} + \varepsilon_t$. This particular correlogram is characteristic of most sample correlograms constructed from nonstationary data. The estimated value of ρ_1 is close to unity and the sample autocorrelations die out slowly. If we did not know the way in which the data were generated, inspection of Figure 4.6 might lead us to falsely conclude that the data was generated from a stationary process. With this particular data, estimates of an AR(1) model with and without an intercept yield (standard errors are in parentheses):

$$y_t = 0.9546y_{t-1} + \varepsilon_t \qquad\qquad R^2 = 0.860 \qquad\qquad (4.18)$$
$$(0.030)$$

$$y_t = 0.164 + 0.9247y_{t-1} + \varepsilon_t \qquad R^2 = 0.864 \qquad\qquad (4.19)$$
$$(0.037)$$

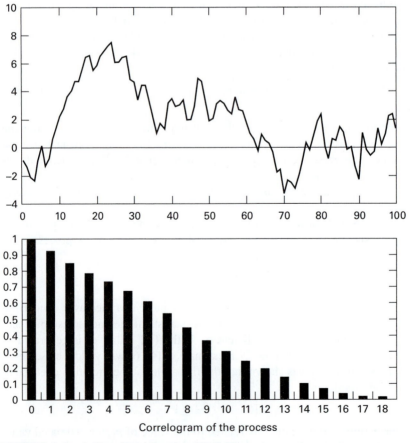

Correlogram of the process

FIGURE 4.6   A Simulated Random Walk Process

Examining (4.18), a careful researcher would not be willing to dismiss the possibility of a unit root since the estimated value of a_1 is only 1.5133 standard deviations from unity. We might correctly recognize that, under the null hypothesis of a unit root, the estimate of a_1 will be biased below unity. If we knew the true distribution of a_1 under the null of a unit root, we could perform such a significance test. Of course, if we did not know the true data-generating process, we might estimate the model with an intercept. In (4.19), the estimate of a_1 is more than two standard deviations from unity: $(1 - 0.9247) / 0.037 = 2.035$. However, it would be wrong to use this information to reject the null of a unit root. After all, the point of this section has been to indicate that such t-tests are inappropriate under the null of a unit root.

Fortunately, Dickey and Fuller (1979, 1981) devised a procedure to formally test for the presence of a unit root. Their methodology is similar to that used in constructing the data reported in Figure 4.6. Suppose that we generated thousands of such random walk sequences and that for each we calculated the estimated value of a_1. Although most of the estimates would be close to unity, some would be further from unity than others. In performing this experiment, Dickey and Fuller found that in the presence of an intercept:

- 90 percent of the estimated values of a_1 are less than 2.58 standard errors from unity;
- 95 percent of the estimated values of a_1 are less than 2.89 standard errors from unity;
- 99 percent of the estimated values of a_1 are less than 3.51 standard errors from unity.[8]

The application of these Dickey–Fuller *critical values* to tests for unit roots is straightforward. Suppose we did not know the true data-generating process and were trying to ascertain whether the data used in Figure 4.6 contained a unit root. Using these Dickey–Fuller statistics, we would not reject the null of a unit root in (4.19). The estimated value of a_1 is only 2.035 standard deviations from unity. In fact, if the true value of a_1 does equal unity, we should find the estimated value to be within 2.58 standard deviations from unity 90 percent of the time.

Be aware that stationarity necessitates $-1 < a_1 < 1$ or, equivalently, $a_1^2 < 1$. Thus, if the estimated value of a_1 is close to -1, you should also be concerned about nonstationarity. If we define $\gamma = a_1 - 1$, the equivalent restriction is: $-2 < \gamma < 0$. In conducting a Dickey–Fuller test, *it is possible to check that the estimated value of γ is greater than -2*.[9]

Monte Carlo Experiments

The procedure that Dickey and Fuller (1979, 1981) used to obtain their critical values is typical of that found in the modern time-series literature. Hypothesis tests concerning the coefficients of nonstationary variables cannot be conducted using traditional t-tests or F-tests. The distributions of the appropriate test statistics are nonstandard and cannot be analytically evaluated. However, given the trivial cost of computer time, the nonstandard distributions can easily be derived using a Monte Carlo simulation.

A Monte Carlo experiment attempts to replicate an actual data-generating process (DGP) on a computer. To be more specific, you simulate a data set with the essential characteristics of the actual data in question. A Monte Carlo experiment generates a random sample of size T and the parameters and/or sample statistics of interest are calculated. This process is repeated N times (where N is a large number) so that the distribution of the desired parameters and/or sample statistics can be tabulated. These empirical distributions are used as estimates of the actual distributions.

All major statistical software packages have a built-in random number generator. The first step in a Monte Carlo experiment is to computer generate a set of random numbers (sometimes called pseudo-random numbers) from a given distribution. Of course, the numbers cannot be entirely random since all computer algorithms rely on a deterministic number-generating mechanism. However, the numbers are drawn so as to mimic a random process having some specified distribution. Usually, the numbers are designed to be normally distributed and serially uncorrelated. The idea is to use these numbers to represent one replication of the entire $\{\varepsilon_t\}$ sequence.

The second step is to specify the parameters and initial conditions of the $\{y_t\}$ sequence. Using these parameters, initial conditions and random numbers, the $\{y_t\}$ sequence can be constructed. For example, Dickey and Fuller (1979, 1981) obtained 100 values for $\{\varepsilon_t\}$, set $a_1 = 1$, $y_0 = 0$ and calculated 100 values for $\{y_t\}$ according to (4.16). Once a series has been generated, the third step is to estimate the parameters of interest (such as the estimate of a_1 or the in-sample variance of the $\{y_t\}$ series).

The beauty of the method is that all important attributes of the constructed $\{y_t\}$ sequence are known to the researcher. For this reason, a Monte Carlo simulation is often referred to as an "experiment." The only problem is that the set of random numbers drawn is just one possible outcome. Obviously, the estimates in (4.18) and (4.19) are dependent on the values of the simulated $\{\varepsilon_t\}$ sequence. Different outcomes for $\{\varepsilon_t\}$ will yield different values of the simulated $\{y_t\}$ sequence.

This is why Monte Carlo studies perform many replications of the process outlined above. The fourth step is to replicate steps 1 and 3 thousands of times. The goal is to ensure that the statistical properties of the constructed $\{y_t\}$ sequence are in accord with the true distribution. Thus, for each replication, the parameters of interest are tabulated and critical values (or confidence intervals) obtained. As such, the properties of your data can be compared to the properties of the simulated data so that hypothesis tests can be performed.

For our purposes, it suffices to say that the use of the Monte Carlo method is warranted by the Law of Large Numbers. Consider the simplest case where v_t is an identically and independently distributed (*i.i.d.*) random number with mean μ and variance σ^2 so that

$$v_t \sim (\mu, \sigma^2)$$

The sample mean constructed by using T observations of the $\{v_t\}$ sequence is

$$\bar{v} = (1/T)\sum_{t=1}^{T} v_t$$

By the Law of Large Numbers, as the sample size T grows sufficiently large, $\bar{v}$ converges to the true mean μ. Hence, the sample mean $\bar{v}$ is an unbiased estimate of the population mean. This is the justification for using the Dickey–Fuller critical values to test the hypothesis $a_1 = 1$. Moreover, if the draws are independent, and the sample size T grows sufficiently large, the distribution of $\bar{v}$ approaches a normal distribution with mean μ and variance σ^2/T.[10]

An important limitation of a Monte Carlo experiment is that the results are specific to the assumptions used to generate the simulated data. If you change the sample size, include (or delete) an additional parameter in the data-generating process, or use alternative initial conditions, an entirely new simulation needs to be performed. Moreover, the precision of your estimates depends on the number of replications you use. Oftentimes you do not need many replications to obtain a good estimate of a population mean. However, it is necessary to use many thousands of replications to obtain good estimates of critical values. Nevertheless, you should be able to envision many applications of Monte Carlo experiments. As discussed in Hendry, Neale, and Ericsson (1990), they are particularly helpful for studying the small sample properties of time-series data. As you will see shortly, Monte Carlo experiments are the workhorse of many tests used in modern time-series analysis.

Example of the Monte Carlo Method

Suppose you did not know the probability distribution for the sum of the roll of two dice. One way to calculate the probability distribution would be to buy a pair of dice and roll them several thousand times. If the dice were fair, you would find that a sum on your rolls would approximate this result:

sum	2	3	4	5	6	7	8	9	10	11	12
percent	1/36	2/36	3/36	4/36	5/36	6/36	5/36	4/36	3/36	2/36	1/36

Instead of actually rolling the dice, you can easily replicate the experiment on a computer. You could draw a random number from a uniform [0, 1] distribution to replicate the roll of the first die. If the computer-generated number falls within the interval [0, 1/6], set the variable $r_1 = 1$. Similarly, if the number falls within the interval (1/6, 2/6], set $r_1 = 2$, and so on. In this way, r_1 will be some integer 1 through 6, each with a probability 1/6. Next, draw a second number from the same uniform [0, 1] distribution to represent the roll of die 2 (r_2). You complete your first Monte Carlo replication by computing the sum $r_1 + r_2$. If you compute several thousand such sums, the sample distribution of the sums will approximate the true distribution.

Of course, more complicated experiments are possible. It is interesting to note that this method was used to reform a standard recommendation at the blackjack tables. At one time, the recommendation was to "stick" if the dealer shows a 2 or a 3 and you held a 12. Monte Carlo experiments of a game of blackjack showed that this recommendation was incorrect. Now, a sharp blackjack player will take another card in these circumstances.

Generating the Dickey–Fuller Distribution

We need to modify the procedure above only slightly to obtain the Dickey and Fuller (1979) distribution. To generate the distribution for a sample size of 100, we can perform the following steps:

STEP 1: First, we need a set of random numbers to represent the $\{\varepsilon_t\}$ sequence. If we use the usual set of assumptions, we can draw a set of 100 random numbers from a standard normal distribution. Of course, the Monte Carlo method would allow us to experiment with other distributions.

STEP 2: We need to generate the sequence $y_t = y_{t-1} + \varepsilon_t$. Note that we need to initialize the value of y_0. Once we draw the value of ε_1, we cannot construct y_1 without positing some value for y_0. However, we do not want the results to be sensitive to the initial value chosen for the series. Two slightly different procedures are used to purge the effects of the initial condition from the Monte Carlo results. First, you can initialize the value of y_0 to equal the unconditional mean of the $\{y_t\}$ sequence. Alternatively, suppose you want to generate T values of the $\{y_t\}$ sequence. You can pick an initial condition for y_0 and then generate the next $T + 50$ realizations. Discard the first 50 realizations and use only the last T values. The idea is that the effect of the initial condition will dissipate after 50 periods.

STEP 3: We need to estimate the model under the alternative hypothesis. As such, we estimate an equation of the form $\Delta y_t = a_0 + \gamma y_{t-1} + \varepsilon_t$. Obtain the t-statistic for the null hypothesis $\gamma = 0$. Note that the data are generated under the null hypothesis of a unit root and estimated under the alternative hypothesis.

STEP 4: Repeat steps $1 - 3$ 10,000 or more times. If you use a sample size such that $T = 100$, you should obtain something very similar to the Dickey–Fuller τ_μ distribution plotted in Figure 4.7. Of course, you will not obtain the exact numbers used in the figure since you will be using a different set of random numbers.

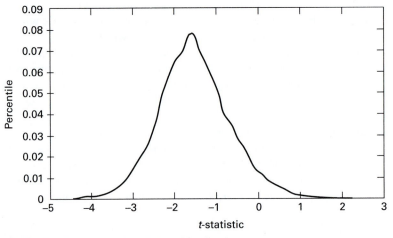

FIGURE 4.7 The Dickey–Fuller Distribution

The data used to draw Figure 4.7 contains 10,000 replications. Additional replications would reveal a somewhat smoother probability distribution. As you might expect, the mean of the distribution is far below zero. The mean of the t-statistics shown in the figure is -1.53. The distribution of t-statistics for the null hypothesis $\gamma = 0$ is only slightly different from those reported by Dickey and Fuller; about 95 percent are less than -2.89 and 99 percent are less than -3.51. Hence, if you estimate a model in the form $\Delta y_t = a_0 + \gamma y_{t-1} + \varepsilon_t$ and find that the t-statistic for the null hypothesis $\gamma = 0$ is -3.00, you can reject the null hypothesis of a unit root at the 5 percent, but not at the 1 percent, level of significance. We will encounter a number of additional applications of Monte Carlo experiments throughout the text. Additional details of the methodology are discussed in the appendix to this chapter and in the Programming Manual that accompanies this text.

An important limitation of a Monte Carlo experiment is that it is specific to the assumptions used to generate the simulated data. For the Monte Carlo analysis to be complete, we need to know if the results are sensitive to the assumptions used to generate the data. Obviously, the sample size is important. However, it turns out that the magnitude of a_0 is unimportant for the Dickey–Fuller test. In this case, changing the magnitude of the intercept has no effect on the estimates of the slope coefficient. Similarly, we could draw the $\{\varepsilon_t\}$ sequence from a distribution other than normal distribution.

5. DICKEY–FULLER TESTS

The last section outlined a simple procedure to determine whether $a_1 = 1$ in the model $y_t = a_1 y_{t-1} + \varepsilon_t$. Begin by subtracting y_{t-1} from each side of the equation in order to write the equivalent form: $\Delta y_t = \gamma y_{t-1} + \varepsilon_t$ where $\gamma = a_1 - 1$. Of course, testing the hypothesis $a_1 = 1$ is equivalent to testing the hypothesis $\gamma = 0$. Dickey and Fuller (1979) actually consider three different regression equations that can be used to test for the presence of a unit root:

$$\Delta y_t = \gamma y_{t-1} + \varepsilon_t \tag{4.20}$$

$$\Delta y_t = a_0 + \gamma y_{t-1} + \varepsilon_t \tag{4.21}$$

$$\Delta y_t = a_0 + \gamma y_{t-1} + a_2 t + \varepsilon_t \tag{4.22}$$

The difference between the three regressions concerns the presence of the deterministic elements a_0 and $a_2 t$. The first is a pure random walk model, the second adds an intercept or *drift* term, and the third includes both a drift and a linear time trend.

The parameter of interest in all the regression equations is γ; if $\gamma = 0$, the $\{y_t\}$ sequence contains a unit root. The test involves estimating one (or more) of the equations above using OLS in order to obtain the estimated value of γ and the associated standard error. Comparing the resulting t-statistic with the appropriate value reported in the Dickey–Fuller tables allows the researcher to determine whether to accept or reject the null hypothesis $\gamma = 0$.

Recall that in (4.18), the estimate of $y_t = a_1 y_{t-1} + \varepsilon_t$ was such that $a_1 = 0.9546$ with a standard error of 0.030. Clearly, the OLS regression in the form $\Delta y_t = \gamma y_{t-1} + \varepsilon_t$ will yield an estimate of γ equal to –0.0454 with the same standard error of 0.030. Hence, the associated t-statistic for the hypothesis $\gamma = 0$ is –1.5133 (–0.0454/.03 = –1.5133).

The methodology is precisely the same regardless of which of the three forms of the equations is estimated. However, be aware that the critical values of the t-statistics do depend on whether an intercept and/or time trend is included in the regression equation. In their Monte Carlo study, Dickey and Fuller (1979) found that the critical values for $\gamma = 0$ depend on the form of the regression and on sample size. The statistics labeled τ, τ_μ, and τ_τ are the appropriate statistics to use for equations (4.20), (4.21), and (4.22), respectively.

Now, look at Table A at the end of this book. With 100 observations, there are three different critical values for the t-statistic $\gamma = 0$. For a regression without the intercept and trend terms ($a_0 = a_2 = 0$), use the section labeled τ. With 100 observations, the critical values for the t-statistic are –1.61, –1.95, and –2.60 at the 10 percent, 5 percent, and 1 percent significance levels, respectively. Thus, in the hypothetical example with $\gamma = -0.0454$ and a standard error of 0.03 (so that $t = -1.5133$), it is not possible to reject the null of a unit root at conventional significance levels. Note that the appropriate critical values depend on sample size. As in most hypothesis tests, for any given level of significance, the critical values of the t-statistic decrease as sample size increases.

Including an intercept term but not a trend term (only $a_2 = 0$) necessitates the use of the critical values in the section labeled τ_μ. Estimating (4.19) in the form $\Delta y_t = a_0 + \gamma y_{t-1} + \varepsilon_t$ necessarily yields a value of γ equal to $(0.9247 - 1) = -0.0753$ with a standard error of 0.037. The appropriate calculation for the t–statistic yields –0.0753/0.037 = –2.035. If we read from the appropriate row of Table A, with the same 100 observations, the critical values are –2.58, –2.89, and –3.51 at the 10 percent, 5 percent, and 1 percent significance levels, respectively. Again, the null of a unit root cannot be rejected at conventional significance levels. Finally, with both intercept and trend, use the critical values in the section labeled τ_τ; now the critical values are –3.45 and –4.04 at the 5 percent and 1 percent significance levels, respectively. The equation was not estimated using a time trend; inspection of Figure 4.5 indicates there is little reason to include a deterministic trend in the estimating equation.

As discussed in Section 7, these critical values are unchanged if (4.20), (4.21), and (4.22) are replaced by the autoregressive processes:[11]

$$\Delta y_t = \gamma y_{t-1} + \sum_{i=2}^{p} \beta_i \Delta y_{t-i+1} + \varepsilon_t \qquad (4.23)$$

$$\Delta y_t = a_0 + \gamma y_{t-1} + \sum_{i=2}^{p} \beta_i \Delta y_{t-i+1} + \varepsilon_t \qquad (4.24)$$

$$\Delta y_t = a_0 + \gamma y_{t-1} + a_2 t + \sum_{i=2}^{p} \beta_i \Delta y_{t-i+1} + \varepsilon_t \qquad (4.25)$$

The same τ, τ_{μ} and τ_{τ} statistics are all used to test the hypotheses $\gamma = 0$. Dickey and Fuller (1981) provide three additional F-statistics (called ϕ_1, ϕ_2, and ϕ_3) to test **joint** hypotheses on the coefficients. Using (4.21) or (4.24), the null hypothesis $\gamma = a_0 = 0$ is tested using the ϕ_1 statistic. Including a time trend in the regression—so that (4.22) or (4.25) is estimated—the joint hypothesis $a_0 = \gamma = a_2 = 0$ is tested using the ϕ_2 statistic and the joint hypothesis $\gamma = a_2 = 0$ is tested using the ϕ_3 statistic.

The ϕ_1, ϕ_2, and ϕ_3 statistics are constructed in exactly the same way as ordinary F-tests:

$$\phi_i = \frac{[SSR(\text{restricted}) - SSR(\text{unrestricted})] / r}{SSR(\text{unrestricted}) / (T - k)}$$

where: SSR(restricted) and SSR(unrestricted) = the sums of the squared residuals from the restricted and unrestricted models

r = number of restrictions

T = number of usable observations

k = number of parameters estimated in the unrestricted model

Hence, $T - k$ = degrees of freedom in the unrestricted model.

Comparing the calculated value of ϕ_i to the appropriate value reported in Dickey and Fuller (1981) allows you to determine the significance level at which the restriction is binding. The null hypothesis is that the data are generated by the restricted model and the alternative hypothesis is that the data are generated by the unrestricted model. If the restriction is not binding SSR(restricted) should be close to SSR(unrestricted) and ϕ_i should be small; hence, large values of ϕ_i suggest a binding restriction and a rejection of the null hypothesis. Thus, if the calculated value of ϕ_i is smaller than that reported by Dickey and Fuller, you can accept the restricted model (i.e., you do not reject the null hypothesis that the restriction is not binding). If the calculated value of ϕ_i is larger than that reported by Dickey and Fuller, you can reject the null hypothesis and conclude that the restriction is binding. The critical values of the three ϕ_i statistics are reported in Table B at the end of this text. The complete set of test statistics and their critical values for a sample size of 100 is summarized in Table 4.2.

Table 4.2   Summary of the Dickey–Fuller Tests

Model	Hypothesis	Test Statistic	Critical Values for 95% and 99% Confidence Intervals
$\Delta y_t = a_0 + \gamma y_{t-1} + a_2 t + \varepsilon_t$	$\gamma = 0$	τ_τ	−3.45 and −4.04
	$\gamma = a_2 = 0$	ϕ_3	6.49 and 8.73
	$a_0 = \gamma = a_2 = 0$	ϕ_2	4.88 and 6.50
$\Delta y_t = a_0 + \gamma y_{t-1} + \varepsilon_t$	$\gamma = 0$	τ_μ	−2.89 and −3.51
	$a_0 = \gamma = 0$	ϕ_1	4.71 and 6.70
$\Delta y_t = \gamma y_{t-1} + \varepsilon_t$	$\gamma = 0$	τ	−1.95 and −2.60

Note: Critical values are for a sample size of 100.

An Example

To illustrate the use of the various test statistics, Dickey and Fuller (1981) use quarterly values of the logarithm of the Federal Reserve Board's Production Index over the 1950:I – 1977:IV period to estimate the following three equations:

$$\Delta y_t = 0.52 + 0.00120t - 0.119y_{t-1} + 0.498\Delta y_{t-1} + \varepsilon_t \quad SSR = 0.056448 \quad (4.26)$$
$$(0.15) \ (0.00034) \ (0.033) \quad (0.081)$$

$$\Delta y_t = 0.0054 + 0.447\Delta y_{t-1} + \varepsilon_t \quad\quad\quad\quad SSR = 0.063211 \quad (4.27)$$
$$(0.0025) \ (0.083)$$

$$\Delta y_t = 0.511\Delta y_{t-1} + \varepsilon_t \quad\quad\quad\quad\quad\quad\quad SSR = 0.065966 \quad (4.28)$$
$$(0.079)$$

where SSR = sum of squared residuals, and standard errors are in parentheses.

To test the null hypothesis that the data are generated by (4.28) against the alternative that (4.26) is the "true" model, use the ϕ_2 statistic. Dickey and Fuller test the null hypothesis $a_0 = a_2 = \gamma = 0$ as follows. Note that the residual sums of squares of the restricted and unrestricted models are 0.065966 and 0.056448 and that the null hypothesis entails three restrictions. With 110 usable observations and four estimated parameters, the unrestricted model contains 106 degrees of freedom. Since 0.056448/106 = 0.000533, the ϕ_2 statistic is given by

$$\phi_2 = (0.065966 - 0.056448) / [3(0.000533)] = 5.95$$

With 110 observations, the critical value of ϕ_2 calculated by Dickey and Fuller is 5.59 at the 2.5 percent significance level. Hence, it is possible to reject the null hypothesis of a random walk against the alternative that the data contain an intercept and/or a unit root and/or a deterministic time trend (i.e., rejecting $a_0 = a_2 = \gamma = 0$ means that one or more of these parameters does not equal zero).

Dickey and Fuller also test the null hypothesis $a_2 = \gamma = 0$ given the alternative of (4.26). If we now view (4.27) as the restricted model and (4.26) as the unrestricted model, the ϕ_3 statistic is calculated as

$$\phi_3 = (0.063211 - 0.056448) / [2(0.000533)] = 6.34$$

With 110 observations, the critical value of ϕ_3 is 6.49 at the 5 percent significance level and 5.47 at the 10 percent significance level.[12] At the 10 percent level, they reject the null hypothesis and accept the alternative that the series is trend stationary. However, at the 5 percent level, the calculated value of ϕ_3 is smaller than the critical value of 6.49; at this significance level, they do not reject the null hypothesis. Hence, at the 5 percent significance level, they maintain the hypothesis that the series contains a unit root and/or a deterministic time trend.

To compare with the τ_τ test (i.e., the hypothesis that only $\gamma = 0$), note that

$$\tau_\tau = -0.119/0.033 = -3.61$$

which rejects the null of a unit root at the 5 percent level.

6. EXAMPLES OF THE DICKEY–FULLER TEST

Section 2 reviewed the evidence reported by Nelson and Plosser (1982) suggesting that macroeconomic variables are difference stationary rather than trend stationary. We are now in a position to consider their formal tests of the hypothesis. For each series under study, Nelson and Plosser estimated the regression

$$\Delta y_t = a_0 + a_2 t + \gamma y_{t-1} + \sum_{i=2}^{p} \beta_i \Delta y_{t-i+1} + \varepsilon_t$$

The chosen lag lengths are reported in the column labeled p in Table 4.3. The estimated values a_0, a_2, and γ are reported in columns 3, 4, and 5, respectively.

Recall that the traditional view of business cycles maintains that GNP and production levels are trend stationary rather than difference stationary. An adherent to this view must assert that γ is different from zero; if $\gamma = 0$, the series has a unit root and is difference stationary. Given the sample sizes used by Nelson and Plosser (1982), at the 0.05 level, the critical value of the t-statistic for the null hypothesis $\gamma = 0$ is -3.45. Thus, only if the estimated value of γ is more than 3.45 standard deviations from zero is it possible to reject the hypothesis that $\gamma = 0$. As can be seen from inspection of Table 4.3, the estimated values of γ for real GNP, nominal GNP, and industrial production are not statistically different from zero. Only the unemployment rate has an estimated value of γ that is significantly different from zero at the 0.05 level.

Table 4.3   Nelson and Plosser's Tests for Unit Roots

	p	a_0	a_2	γ	$\gamma + 1$
Real GNP	2	0.819	0.006	−0.175	0.825
		(3.03)	(3.03)	(−2.99)	
Nominal GNP	2	1.06	0.006	−0.101	0.899
		(2.37)	(2.34)	(−2.32)	
Industrial production	6	0.103	0.007	−0.165	0.835
		(4.32)	(2.44)	(−2.53)	
Unemployment rate	4	0.513	−0.000	−0.294*	0.706
		(2.81)	(−0.23)	(−3.55)	

Notes:

1. p is the chosen lag length. Coefficients divided by their standard errors are in parentheses. Thus, entries in parentheses represent the t-test for the null hypothesis that a coefficient is equal to zero. Under the null of nonstationarity, it is necessary to use the Dickey–Fuller critical values. At the 0.05 significance level, the critical value for the t-statistic is -3.45.

2. A (*) denotes significance at the 0.05 level. For real and nominal GNP and for industrial production, it is not possible to reject the null hypothesis $\gamma = 0$ at the 0.05 level. Hence, the unemployment rate appears to be stationary.

3. The expression $\gamma + 1$ is the estimate of the partial autocorrelation between y_t and y_{t-1}.

Unit Roots and Purchasing Power Parity

Purchasing Power Parity (PPP) is a simple relationship linking national price levels and exchange rates. In its simplest form, PPP asserts that the rate of currency depreciation is approximately equal to the difference between domestic and foreign inflation rates. If p_t and p_{ft} denote the logarithms of U.S. and foreign price levels and e denotes the logarithm of the dollar price of foreign exchange, PPP implies

$$e_t = p_t - p_{ft} + d_t$$

where d_t represents the deviation from PPP in period t.

In applied work, p_t and p_{ft} usually refer to national price indices in t relative to a base year, so that e_t refers to an index of the domestic currency price of foreign exchange relative to a base year. For example, if the U.S. inflation rate is 10 percent while the foreign inflation rate is 15 percent, the dollar price of foreign exchange should fall by approximately 5 percent. The presence of the term d_t allows for short-run deviations from PPP.

Because of its simplicity and intuitive appeal, PPP has been used extensively in theoretical models of exchange rate determination. However, as in the well-known Dornbusch (1976) "overshooting" model, real economic shocks, such as productivity or demand shocks, can cause permanent deviations from PPP. For our purposes, the theory of PPP serves as an excellent vehicle to illustrate many time-series testing procedures. One test of long-run PPP is to determine whether d_t is stationary. After all, if the deviations from PPP are nonstationary (i.e., if the deviations are permanent in nature), we can reject the theory. Note that PPP does allow for persistent deviations; the autocorrelations of the $\{d_t\}$ sequence need not be zero. One popular testing procedure is to define the "real" exchange rate in period t:

$$r_t \equiv e_t + p_{ft} - p_t$$

Long-run PPP is said to hold if the $\{r_t\}$ sequence is stationary. For example, in Enders (1988), I constructed real exchange rates for three major U.S. trading partners: Germany, Canada, and Japan. The data were divided into two periods: January 1960 to April 1971 (representing the fixed exchange rate period) and January 1973 to November 1986 (representing the flexible exchange rate period). Each nation's Wholesale Price Index (WPI) was multiplied by an index of the U.S. dollar price of the foreign currency and then divided by the U.S. WPI. The log of the constructed series is the $\{r_t\}$ sequence.

A critical first step in any econometric analysis is to visually inspect the data. The plots of the three real exchange rate series during the flexible exchange rate period are shown in Figure 4.8.[13] Each series seems to meander in a fashion characteristic of a random walk process. Notice that there is little visual evidence of explosive behavior or of a deterministic time trend. The autocorrelation function for all of the series in the analysis look similar to that in Figure 4.6. In particular, the autocorrelation functions show little tendency to decay while the autocorrelations of the first differences display the classic pattern of a stationary series.

To formally test for the presence of a unit root in the real exchange rates, augmented Dickey–Fuller tests of the form given by (4.24) were conducted. The

FIGURE 4.8 Real Exchange Rates

regression $\Delta r_t = a_0 + \gamma r_{t-1} + \beta_2 \Delta r_{t-1} + \beta_3 \Delta r_{t-2} + \ldots + \varepsilon_t$ was estimated based on the following considerations:

1. The theory of PPP does not allow for a deterministic time trend. Any such findings would refute the theory as posited. Given that the series all decline throughout the early 1980s and all rise during the middle to late 1980s, there is no reason to entertain the notion of trend stationarity. As such, the expression $a_2 t$ was not included in the estimating equation.

2. In both time periods, F-tests and the SBC indicated that β_3 through β_{24} could be set equal to zero. For Germany and Japan during the flexible rate period, β_2 was statistically different from zero; in the other four instances, β_2 could be set equal to zero. In spite of these findings, with monthly data it is always important to entertain the possibility of a lag length no shorter than 12 months. As such, tests were conducted using the short lags selected by the F-tests and the SBC and using a lag length of 12 months.

For the Canadian case during the 1973 to 1986 period, the t-statistic for the null hypothesis that $\gamma = 0$ is -1.42 using no lags and -1.51 using all 12 lags. Given the critical value of the τ_μ statistic, it is not possible to reject the null of a unit root in the Canadian/U.S. real exchange rate series. Hence, PPP fails for these two nations. In the 1960 to 1971 period, the calculated value of the t-statistic is -1.59; again it is possible to conclude that PPP fails.

Table 4.4 reports the results of all six estimations using the short lag lengths suggested by the F-tests and the SBC. Notice the following properties of the estimated models:

1. For all six models, it is not possible to reject the null hypothesis that PPP fails. As can be seen from the third column of Table 4.4, the absolute value of the t-statistic for the null $\gamma = 0$ is never more than 1.59. The economic interpretation is that real productivity and/or demand shocks have had a permanent influence on real exchange rates.

2. As measured by the sample standard deviation (SD), real exchange rates were far more volatile in the 1973 to 1986 period than in the 1960 to 1971 period. Moreover, as measured by the standard error of the estimate (SEE), real exchange rate volatility is associated with unpredictability. The SEE during the flexible exchange rate period is several hundred times that of the fixed rate period. It seems reasonable to conclude that the change in the exchange rate regime (i.e., the end of Bretton Woods) affected the volatility of the real exchange rate.

3. Care must be taken to keep the appropriate null hypothesis in mind. Under the null of a unit root, classical test procedures are inappropriate and we resort to the statistics tabulated by Dickey and Fuller. However, classical test procedures (which assume stationary variables) are appropriate under

Table 4.4   Real Exchange Rate Estimation

	γ^1	$H_0: \gamma = 0^2$	a_1	a_2	Mean[3]	ρ/DW	F	SD/SEE
1973–1986								
Canada	−0.022	$t = -1.42$	0.978		1.05	0.059	0.194	5.47
	(.0155)					1.88		1.16
Japan	−0.047	$t = -0.635$	1.25	−0.297	1.01	−0.007	0.226	10.44
	(0.074)					2.01		2.81
Germany	−0.027	$t = -0.280$	1.22	−0.247	1.11	−0.014	0.858	20.68
	(0.076)					2.04		3.71
1960–1971								
Canada	−0.031	$t = -1.59$	0.969		1.02	−0.107	0.434	.014
	(0.019)					2.21		.004
Japan	−0.030	$t = -1.04$	0.970		0.980	0.046	0.330	.017
	(0.028)					1.98		.005
Germany	−0.016	$t = -1.23$	0.984		1.01	0.038	0.097	.026
	(0.012)					1.93		.004

Notes:

1. Standard errors are in parentheses.

2. Entries are the t-statistic for the hypothesis $\gamma = 0$.

3. Mean is the estimated value of $a_0/(1 - a_1 - a_2)$. SD is the standard deviation of the real exchange rate. SEE is the estimated standard deviation of the residuals (i.e., the standard error of the estimate). F is the significance level of the test that lags 2 (or 3) through 12 can be excluded. DW is the Durbin–Watson statistic for first-order serial correlation and ρ is the estimated autocorrelation coefficient.

the null that the real rates are stationary. Thus, the following possibility arises: Suppose that the *t*-statistic in the Canadian case happened to be –2.16 instead of –1.42. If you used the Dickey–Fuller critical values, you would not reject the null of a unit root. Hence, you could conclude that PPP fails. However, under the null of stationarity (where we can use classical procedures), γ is more than two standard deviations from zero and you would *not reject the null of stationarity*.

This apparent dilemma commonly occurs when analyzing series with roots close to unity in absolute value. Unit root tests do not have much power in discriminating between characteristic roots close to unity and actual unit roots. The dilemma is only apparent since the two null hypotheses are quite different. It is perfectly consistent to maintain a null that PPP holds and not be able to reject a null that PPP fails! Notice that this dilemma does not arise for any of the other series reported in Table 4.4; for each, it is not possible to reject a null of $\gamma = 0$ at conventional significance levels.

In some circumstances, you might need to test the null hypothesis of stationarity against the alternative of nonstationarity. Kwiatowski, Phillips, Schmidt and Shin (1992) show how to perform this type of test.

4.   Looking at some of the diagnostic statistics, the *F*-statistics all indicate that it appropriate to exclude lags 2 (or 3) through 12 from the regression equation. To reinforce the use of short lags, notice that the first-order correlation coefficient of the residuals (ρ) is low and that the Durbin–Watson statistic is close to two. It is interesting that the point estimates of the characteristic roots all indicate that real exchange rates are convergent. To obtain the characteristic roots, rewrite the estimated equations in the autoregressive form $r_t = a_0 + a_1 r_{t-1}$ or $r_t = a_0 + a_1 r_{t-1} + a_2 r_{t-2}$. For the four AR(1) models, the point estimates of the slope coefficients are all less than unity. In the post–Bretton Woods period (1973–1986), the point estimates of the characteristic roots of Japan's second-order process are 0.931 and 0.319; for Germany, the roots are 0.964 and 0.256. Yet, this is precisely what we would expect if PPP fails; under the null of a unit root, we know that γ is biased downward.

To update the study, the file PANEL.XLS contains quarterly values of the real effective exchange rates (CPI based) for Australia, Canada, France, Germany, Japan, the Netherlands, the United Kingdom, and the United States over the 1980:Q1 to 2002:Q2 period. These are multilateral (not bilateral) real exchange rates. The rates for the United Stares, Canada, and Germany are shown in Figure 5 of Chapter 3. As an exercise, you should use this data to verify that very little has changed. You should find that only for the Netherlands is it possible to reject a unit root in the real exchange rate at the 5 percent significance level. Try not to peek; however, for each country, the estimated value of γ and the appropriate lag length is reported in Table 4.8.

7. EXTENSIONS OF THE DICKEY–FULLER TEST

Not all time-series variables can be well represented by the first-order autoregressive process $\Delta y_t = a_0 + \gamma y_{t-1} + a_2 t + \varepsilon_t$. It is possible to use the Dickey–Fuller tests in higher-order equations such as (4.23), (4.24), and (4.25). Consider the p-th order autoregressive process:

$$y_t = a_0 + a_1 y_{t-1} + a_2 y_{t-2} + a_3 y_{t-3} + \ldots + a_{p-2} y_{t-p+2} + a_{p-1} y_{t-p+1} + a_p y_{t-p} + \varepsilon_t$$

To best understand the methodology of the **augmented Dickey–Fuller** (ADF) test, add and subtract $a_p y_{t-p+1}$ to obtain

$$y_t = a_0 + a_1 y_{t-1} + a_2 y_{t-2} + a_3 y_{t-3} + \ldots + a_{p-2} y_{t-p+2} + (a_{p-1} + a_p) y_{t-p+1} - a_p \Delta y_{t-p+1} + \varepsilon_t$$

Next, add and subtract $(a_{p-1} + a_p) y_{t-p+2}$ to obtain:

$$y_t = a_0 + a_1 y_{t-1} + a_2 y_{t-2} + a_3 y_{t-3} + \ldots - (a_{p-1} + a_p) \Delta y_{t-p+2} - a_p \Delta y_{t-p+1} + \varepsilon_t$$

Continuing in this fashion, we obtain

$$\Delta y_t = a_0 + \gamma y_{t-1} + \sum_{i=2}^{p} \beta_i \Delta y_{t-i+1} + \varepsilon_t \tag{4.29}$$

where: $\quad \gamma = -\left(1 - \sum_{i=1}^{p} a_i\right)$

$$\beta_i = -\sum_{j=i}^{p} a_j$$

In (4.29), the coefficient of interest is γ; if $\gamma = 0$, the equation is entirely in first differences and so has a unit root. We can test for the presence of a unit root using the same Dickey–Fuller statistics discussed above. Again, the appropriate statistic to use depends on the deterministic components included in the regression equation. Without an intercept or trend, use the τ statistic; with only the intercept, use the τ_μ statistic; and with both intercept and trend, use the τ_τ statistic. It is worthwhile pointing out that the results here are perfectly consistent with our study of difference equations in Chapter 1. If the coefficients of a difference equation sum to 1, *at least* one characteristic root is unity. Here, if $\Sigma a_i = 1$, $\gamma = 0$ and the system has a unit root.

Note that the Dickey–Fuller tests assume that the errors are independent and have a constant variance. This raises six important problems related to the fact that we do not know the true data-generating process:

1. The DGP may contain both autoregressive and moving average components. We need to know how to conduct the test if the order of the moving average terms (if any) is unknown.
2. We cannot properly estimate γ and its standard error unless all of the autoregressive terms are included in the estimating equation. Clearly, the simple regression $\Delta y_t = a_0 + \gamma y_{t-1} + \varepsilon_t$ is inadequate to this task if (4.29) is the true data-generating process. Since the true order of the autoregressive process is unknown, the problem is to select the appropriate lag length.
3. The Dickey–Fuller test considers only a single unit root. However, a p-th order autoregression has p characteristic roots; if there are $m \leq p$ unit roots, the series needs to be differenced m times to achieve stationarity.

4. As we saw in Chapter 2, there may be roots that require first differences and others that necessitate seasonal differencing. We need to develop a method that can distinguish between these two types of unit root processes.

5. There might be structural breaks in the data (see Section 8). Such breaks can impart an apparent trend to the data.

6. It might not be known whether an intercept and/or time trend belongs in (4.29). Section 9 is concerned with the issue of the appropriate deterministic regressors.

Since an invertible MA model can be transformed into an autoregressive model, the procedure can be generalized to allow for moving average components. Let the $\{y_t\}$ sequence be generated from the mixed autoregressive/moving-average process:

$$A(L)y_t = C(L)\varepsilon_t$$

where $A(L)$ and $C(L)$ are polynomials of orders p and q, respectively.

If the roots of $C(L)$ are outside the unit circle, we can write the $\{y_t\}$ sequence as the autoregressive process:

$$A(L)y_t / C(L) = \varepsilon_t$$

or, defining $D(L) = A(L)/C(L)$, we can write the process as

$$D(L)y_t = \varepsilon_t$$

Even though $D(L)$ will generally be an infinite-order polynomial, in principle we can use the same technique as used to obtain (4.29) to form the infinite-order autoregressive model

$$\Delta y_t = \gamma y_{t-1} + \sum_{i=2}^{\infty} \beta_i \, \Delta y_{t-i+1} + \varepsilon_t \tag{4.30}$$

As it stands, (4.30) is an infinite-order autoregression that cannot be estimated using a finite data set. Fortunately, Said and Dickey (1984) have shown that an unknown ARIMA(p, 1, q) process can be well approximated by an ARIMA(n, 1, 0) autoregression of order n where $n \leq T^{1/3}$. Thus, we can solve the first problem by using a finite-order autoregression to approximate (4.30). The test for $\gamma = 0$ can be conducted using the aforementioned Dickey–Fuller τ, τ_{μ} or τ_τ test statistics.

Selection of the Lag Length

Now the second problem concerning the appropriate lag length arises. Too few lags means that the regression residuals do not behave like white-noise processes. The model will not appropriately capture the actual error process so that γ and its standard error will not be well-estimated. Including too many lags reduces the power of the test to reject the null of a unit root since the increased number of lags necessitates the estimation of additional parameters and a loss of degrees of freedom. The degrees of freedom decrease since the number of parameters estimated has increased and the number of usable observations has decreased. (We lose one observation for each additional lag included in the autoregression). As such, the presence of unnecessary lags will reduce the power of the Dickey–Fuller test to detect a unit root. In fact, an augmented Dickey–Fuller test may indicate a unit root for some lag lengths but not for others.

How does a careful researcher select the appropriate lag length in such circumstances? One approach is to start with a relatively long lag length and pare down the model by the usual t-test and/or F-tests. For example, one could estimate equation (4.29) using a lag length of p^*. If the t-statistic on lag p^* is insignificant at some specified critical value, re-estimate the regression using a lag length of $p^* - 1$. Repeat the process until the lag is significantly different from zero. In the pure autoregressive case, such a procedure will yield the true lag length with an asymptotic probability of unity, provided the initial choice of lag length includes the true length. Using seasonal data, the process is a bit different. For example, using quarterly data, one could start with three years of lags ($p = 12$). If the t-statistic on lag twelve is insignificant at some specified critical value, and if an F-test indicates that lags 9–12 are also insignificant, move to lags 1–8. Repeat the process for lag 8 and lags 5–8 until a reasonable lag length has been determined.

Once a tentative lag length has been determined, diagnostic checking should be conducted. As always, plotting the residuals is a most important diagnostic tool. There should not appear to be any strong evidence of structural change or serial correlation. Moreover, the correlogram of the residuals should appear to be white noise. The Ljung–Box Q-statistic should not reveal any significant autocorrelations among the residuals. It is inadvisable to use the alternative procedure of beginning with the most parsimonious model and continuing to add lags until the first insignificant lag is found. Monte Carlo studies show that this procedure is biased towards selecting a value of p that is less than the true value.

As long as the regression equation does not omit a deterministic regressor present in the data-generating process, it is possible to perform lag length tests using t-tests or F-tests. The rationale follows from an important result proved by Sims, Stock, and Watson (1990). We will have cause to refer to several of the results of their paper. Here is the first finding of interest:

> **Rule 1:** Consider a regression equation containing a mixture of $I(1)$ and $I(0)$ variables such that the residuals are white noise. If the model is such that the coefficient of interest can be written as a coefficient on zero-mean stationary variables, then asymptotically, the OLS estimator converges to a normal distribution. As such, a t-test is appropriate.

Although this rule refers to any regression equation estimated by OLS, it applies directly to unit root tests. As shown above, the p-th order autoregressive process:

$$y_t = a_0 + a_1 y_{t-1} + a_2 y_{t-2} + a_3 y_{t-3} + \ldots + a_{p-2} y_{t-p+2} + a_{p-1} y_{t-p+1} + a_p y_{t-p} + \varepsilon_t$$

can be written as

$$\Delta y_t = \gamma y_{t-1} + \beta_2 \Delta y_{t-1} + \beta_3 \Delta y_{t-2} + \ldots + \beta_p \Delta y_{t-p+1} + \varepsilon_t \qquad (4.31)$$

From Rule 1, all the coefficients on the expressions Δy_{t-i} converge to t-distributions. As such, groups of these coefficients will converge to an F-distribution. Hence, you can perform a test of the form $\beta_i = \beta_{i+1} = \ldots = \beta_p = 0$ using an F-test. Nevertheless, under the null hypothesis of a unit root, the value of γ multiplies a nonstationary variable. As such, a test of $\gamma = 0$ *cannot* be conducted using a standard t-test.

In addition to the use of F-tests and t-tests, it is also possible to determine the lag length using an information criterion such as the AIC or the SBC. Of course, in very large samples with normally distributed errors, the methods should all select the same lag length. In practice, the SBC will select a more parsimonious model than will either the AIC or t-tests. Nevertheless, whichever method is used, the researcher must ensure that residuals act as white-noise processes.

An Example: In order to illustrate the various procedures to select the lag-length for an augmented Dickey–Fuller test, 200 realizations of the following unit root process were generated:

$$\Delta y_t = 0.5 + 0.5\Delta y_{t-1} + 0.2\Delta y_{t-3} + \varepsilon_t$$

Notice that the sequence contains a single unit-root and that the appropriate value of p is 3. The drift parameter gives the series the decidedly increasing pattern shown in Figure 4.9. Pretend that you do not know the actual DGP. As such, the time path of the sequence allows for two possible DGP; the series may be trend stationary or a unit root process containing a drift term. Hence, the null hypothesis is that of a unit root process containing a drift against the alternative of a trend stationary process. The appropriate way to proceed is to estimate the series under the alternative hypothesis; hence, we estimate a regression equation of the form

$$\Delta y_t = a_0 + \gamma y_{t-1} + a_2 t + \sum_{i=1}^{p} \beta_i \Delta y_{t-i} + \varepsilon_t$$

If it is possible to reject the null hypothesis $\gamma = 0$, the process is trend stationary. The problem is to determine the appropriate value for p. Toward this end, the equation was estimated for lag lengths of 1 through 4. As shown in Table 4.5, the AIC selects a lag length of three and the SBC selects a lag length of two. Nevertheless, in this instance, the lag length seems not to make a difference; at the 5 percent significance level, the critical value for the null hypothesis $\gamma = 0$ is -3.43.

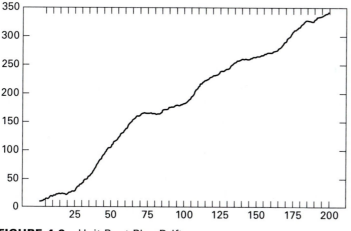

FIGURE 4.9   Unit Root Plus Drift

Table 4.5 Dickey–Fuller Tests and Lag Length

p	AIC	SBC	γ	t-statistic	ϕ_2	ϕ_3
1	1038.69823	1051.79023	−0.00750	−1.46988	8.37517	1.33466
2	1031.37934	1047.74434	−0.00924	−1.83843	5.68846	1.86303
3	1029.33567	1048.97367	−0.01072	−2.12571	4.94318	2.40975
4	1031.04937	1053.96037	−0.01114	−2.17744	4.75005	2.51896

As such, the lag lengths selected by the AIC and the SBC are such that the null hypothesis of a unit root is not rejected. We can conclude that the sequence is not trend stationary.

The ϕ_3 allows us to test the null hypothesis $\gamma = a_2 = 0$; at the 5 percent significance level, the critical value is 6.49. As such, for any lag length, we would not reject the null hypothesis and conclude that the sequence has a stochastic trend. However, at the 5 percent significance level, the critical value for the null hypothesis $a_0 = \gamma = a_2 = 0$ (i.e., the critical value of the ϕ_2 statistic) is 4.88. For the lag lengths selected by the AIC and the SBC, this null hypothesis is rejected.

It is also possible to use t-tests and F-tests to determine the lag length. Estimating the equation using the lag length $p = 4$ yields

$$\Delta y_t = 0.542 - 0.011 y_{t-1} + 0.018t + 0.498\Delta y_{t-1} + 0.136\Delta y_{t-2} + 0.123\Delta y_{t-3} + 0.038\Delta y_{t-4} + \varepsilon_t$$
$$\quad (2.78)(-2.18) \quad\ (2.08)\ \ (6.89) \qquad (1.70) \qquad\quad (1.53) \qquad\quad (0.53)$$

A t-test for the coefficient on Δy_{t-4} suggests a lag length no greater than 3. Moreover, the F-statistic for the null hypothesis $\beta_3 = \beta_4 = 0$ is 2.11 with a $prob$-value of 0.124. As such, we can eliminate lags 3 and 4. Moreover, the F-statistic for the null hypothesis $\beta_2 = \beta_3 = \beta_4 = 0$ is 4.45 with a $prob$-value of 0.004. Hence, the F-tests select a model with two lags.

The results also show that too many lags can reduce the power of the test. Had we mistakenly used $p = 4$, the null hypothesis $a_0 = \gamma = a_2 = 0$ (i.e., the ϕ_2 test) would not have been rejected even though the true value of a_0 is 0.5.

Multiple Roots

Dickey and Pantula (1987) suggest a simple extension of the basic procedure if more than one unit root is suspected. In essence, the methodology entails nothing more than performing Dickey–Fuller tests on successive differences of $\{y_t\}$. When exactly one root is suspected, the Dickey–Fuller procedure is to estimate an equation such as $\Delta y_t = a_0 + \gamma y_{t-1} + \varepsilon_t$. In contrast, if two roots are suspected, estimate the equation

$$\Delta^2 y_t = a_0 + \beta_1 \Delta y_{t-1} + \varepsilon_t \qquad (4.32)$$

Use the appropriate statistic (i.e., τ, τ_μ, or τ_τ depending on the deterministic elements actually included in the regression) to determine whether β_1 is significantly different from zero. If you cannot reject the null hypothesis that $\beta_1 = 0$, conclude that the $\{y_t\}$ sequence is $I(2)$. If β_1 does differ from zero, go on to determine whether there is a single unit root by estimating

$$\Delta^2 y_t = a_0 + \beta_1 \Delta y_{t-1} + \beta_2 y_{t-1} + \varepsilon_t \qquad (4.33)$$

Since there are not two unit roots, you should find that β_1 and/or β_2 differ from zero. Under the null hypothesis of a single unit root, $\beta_1 < 0$ and $\beta_2 = 0$; under the alternative hypothesis $\{y_t\}$ is stationary so that β_1 and β_2 are both negative. Thus, estimate (4.33) and use the Dickey–Fuller critical values to test the null hypothesis $\beta_2 = 0$. If you reject this null hypothesis, conclude that $\{y_t\}$ is stationary.

As a rule of thumb, economic series do not need to be differenced more than two times. However, in the odd case in which *at most* r unit roots are suspected, the procedure is to first estimate

$$\Delta^r y_t = a_0 + \beta_1 \Delta^{r-1} y_{t-1} + \varepsilon_t$$

If $\Delta^r y_t$ is stationary, you should find that $-2 < \beta_1 < 0$. If the Dickey–Fuller critical values for β_1 are such that it is not possible to reject the null of a unit root, you accept the hypothesis that $\{y_t\}$ contains r unit roots. If we reject this null of exactly r unit roots, the next step is to test for $r - 1$ roots by estimating

$$\Delta^r y_t = a_0 + \beta_1 \Delta^{r-1} y_{t-1} + \beta_2 \Delta^{r-2} y_{t-1} + \varepsilon_t$$

If both β_1 and β_2 differ from zero, reject the null hypothesis of $r - 1$ roots. You can use the Dickey–Fuller statistics to test the null of exactly $r - 1$ unit roots if the t-statistics for β_1 *and* β_2 are both statistically different from zero. If you can reject this null, the next step is to form

$$\Delta^r y_t = a_0 + \beta_1 \Delta^{r-1} y_{t-1} + \beta_2 \Delta^{r-2} y_{t-1} + \beta_3 \Delta^{r-3} y_{t-1} + \varepsilon_t$$

As long as it is possible to reject the null hypothesis that the various values of the β_i are nonzero, continue towards the equation

$$\Delta^r y_t = a_0 + \beta_1 \Delta^{r-1} y_{t-1} + \beta_2 \Delta^{r-2} y_{t-1} + \beta_3 \Delta^{r-3} y_{t-1} + \ldots + \beta_r y_{t-1} + \varepsilon_t$$

Continue in this fashion until it is not possible to reject the null of a unit root or until the $\{y_t\}$ series is shown to be stationary. Notice that this procedure is quite different from the sequential testing for successively greater numbers of unit roots. It might seem tempting to test for a single unit root and, if the null cannot be rejected, go on to test for the presence of a second root. In repeated samples, this method tends to select too few roots.

Seasonal Unit Roots

You will recall that the best-fitting model for U.S. money supply data used in Chapter 2 had the form

$$(1 - L^4)(1 - L)(1 - a_1 L) y_t = (1 + \beta_4 L^4) \varepsilon_t$$

The money supply has a unit root and a seasonal unit root. Since seasonality is a key feature of many economic series, a sizable literature has been developed to test for seasonal unit roots. Before proceeding, note that the first difference of a seasonal unit root process will not be stationary. To keep matters simple, suppose that the quarterly observations of $\{y_t\}$ are generated by

$$y_t = y_{t-4} + \varepsilon_t$$

Here the seasonal difference of $\{y_t\}$ is stationary; using the notation of Chapter 2, we can write $\Delta_4 y_t = \varepsilon_t$. Given the initial condition $y_0 = y_{-1} = \ldots = 0$, the solution for y_t is

$$y_t = \varepsilon_t + \varepsilon_{t-4} + \varepsilon_{t-8} + \ldots$$

so that

$$y_t - y_{t-1} = \sum_{i=0}^{t/4} \varepsilon_{4i} - \sum_{i=0}^{t/4} \varepsilon_{4i-1}$$

Hence, Δy_t equals the difference between two stochastic trends. Since each shock has a permanent effect on the level of Δy_t, the sequence is not mean reverting. However, the seasonal difference of a unit root process may be stationary. For example, if $\{y_t\}$ is generated by $y_t = y_{t-1} + \varepsilon_t$, the fourth difference (i.e., $\Delta_4 y_t = \varepsilon_t + \varepsilon_{t-1} + \varepsilon_{t-2} + \varepsilon_{t-3}$) is stationary. The point is that the Dickey–Fuller procedure must be modified in order to test for seasonal unit roots and to distinguish between seasonal versus nonseasonal roots.

There are several alternative ways to treat seasonality in a nonstationary sequence. The most direct method occurs when the seasonal pattern is purely deterministic. For example, let D_1, D_2, and D_3 represent quarterly seasonal dummy variables such that the value of D_i is unity in season i and zero otherwise. Estimate the regression equation

$$\Delta y_t = a_0 + a_1 D_1 + a_2 D_2 + a_3 D_3 + \gamma y_{t-1} + \sum_{i=2}^{p} \beta_i \Delta y_{t-i+1} + \varepsilon_t \qquad (4.34)$$

The null hypothesis of a unit root (i.e., $\gamma = 0$) can be tested using the Dickey–Fuller τ_μ statistic. (Note that you use the τ_μ statistic since the original data contains an intercept). Rejecting the null hypothesis is equivalent to accepting the alternative that the $\{y_t\}$ sequence is stationary. The test is possible as Dickey, Bell, and Miller (1986) show that the limiting distribution for γ is not affected by the removal of the deterministic seasonal components. If you want to include a time trend in (4.34), use the τ_τ statistic.

Notice that the specification in (4.34) makes it difficult to test hypothesis concerning a_0. Since the mean of each D_i series is 1/4, the presence of the seasonals affect the magnitude of the drift term a_0. To correct for this, it is common to use **centered** seasonal dummy variables. Simply let $D_i = 0.75$ in season i and -0.25 in each of the other three quarters of the year. Hence, the mean of $D_i = 0$ so that the magnitude of a_0 is unchanged.

If you suspect a seasonal unit root, it is necessary to use an alternative procedure. To keep the notation simple, suppose you have quarterly observations on the $\{y_t\}$ sequence and want to test for the presence of a seasonal unit root. To explain the methodology, note that the polynomial $(1 - \gamma L^4)$ can be factored such that there are four distinct characteristic roots:

$$(1 - \gamma L^4) = (1 - \gamma^{1/4}L)(1 + \gamma^{1/4}L)(1 - i\gamma^{1/4}L)(1 + i\gamma^{1/4}L) \qquad (4.35)$$

If y_t has a seasonal unit root, $\gamma = 1$. Equation (4.35) is a bit restrictive in that it only allows for a unit root at an annual frequency. Hylleberg, et al. (1990) develop a clever technique that allows you to test for unit roots at various frequencies; you can test for a unit root (i.e., a root at a zero frequency), a unit root at a semiannual frequency, or a seasonal unit root. To understand the HEGY test (named after the four authors of the paper), suppose y_t is generated by

$$A(L)y_t = \varepsilon_t$$

where $A(L)$ is a fourth order polynomial such that

$$(1 - a_1 L)(1 + a_2 L)(1 - a_3 iL)(1 + a_4 iL)y_t = \varepsilon_t \tag{4.36}$$

Now, if $a_1 = a_2 = a_3 = a_4 = 1$, (4.36) is equivalent to setting $\gamma = 1$ in (4.35). Hence, if $a_1 = a_2 = a_3 = a_4 = 1$, there is a seasonal unit root. Consider some of the other possible cases:

CASE 1

If $a_1 = 1$, one homogeneous solution to (4.36) is $y_t = y_{t-1}$. As such, the $\{y_t\}$ sequence will act as a random walk in that it tends to repeat itself each and every period. This is the case of a nonseasonal unit root; the appropriate period of differencing is Δy_t.

CASE 2

If $a_2 = 1$, one homogeneous solution to (4.36) is $y_t + y_{t-1} = 0$. In this instance, the sequence tends to replicate itself at 6-month intervals so that there is a semiannual unit root. For example, if $y_t = 1$, it follows that $y_{t+1} = -1, y_{t+2} = +1, y_{t+3} = -1, y_{t+4} = 1$, and so forth.

CASE 3

If either a_3 or a_4 is equal to unity, the $\{y_t\}$ sequence has an annual cycle. For example, if $a_3 = 1$, a homogeneous solution to (4.36) is $y_t = iy_{t-1}$. Thus, if $y_t = 1$, $y_{t+1} = i, y_{t+2} = i^2 = -1, y_{t+3} = -i$, and $y_{t+4} = -i^2 = 1$ so that the sequence replicates itself every fourth period. The appropriate degree of differencing is $\Delta_4 y_t = (1 - L^4)y_t$.

To develop the test, view (4.36) as function of a_1, a_2, a_3, and a_4 and take a Taylor series approximation of $A(L)$ around the point $a_1 = a_2 = a_3 = a_4 = 1$. Although the details of the expansion are messy, first take the partial derivative:

$$\partial A(L)/\partial a_1 = \partial(1 - a_1 L)(1 + a_2 L)(1 - a_3 iL)(1 + a_4 iL)/\partial a_1$$
$$= -(1 + a_2 L)(1 - a_3 iL)(1 + a_4 iL)L$$

Evaluating this derivative at the point $a_1 = a_2 = a_3 = a_4 = 1$ yields

$$-L(1 + L)(1 - iL)(1 + iL) = -L(1 + L)(1 + L^2) = -L(1 + L + L^2 + L^3)$$

Next, form

$$\partial A(L)/\partial a_2 = \partial(1 - a_1L)(1 + a_2L)(1 - a_3iL)(1 + a_4iL)/\partial a_2$$
$$= (1 - a_1L)(1 - a_3iL)(1 + a_4iL)L$$

Evaluating at the point $a_1 = a_2 = a_3 = a_4 = 1$ yields $(1 - L + L^2 - L^3)L$. It should not take too long to convince yourself that evaluating $\partial A(L)/\partial a_3$ and $\partial A(L)/\partial a_4$ at the point $a_1 = a_2 = a_3 = a_4 = 1$ yields

$$\partial A(L)/\partial a_3 = -(1 - L^2)(1 + iL)iL$$

and

$$\partial A(L)/\partial a_4 = (1 - L^2)(1 - iL)iL$$

Since $A(L)$ evaluated at $a_1 = a_2 = a_3 = a_4 = 1$ is $(1 - L^4)$, it is possible to approximate (4.36) by

$$[(1 - L^4) - L(1 + L + L^2 + L^3)(a_1-1) + (1 - L + L^2 - L^3)L(a_2-1)$$
$$-(1 - L^2)(1 + iL)iL(a_3 - 1) + (1 - L^2)(1 - iL)iL(a_4 - 1)]y_t = \varepsilon_t$$

Define γ_i such that $\gamma_i = (a_i - 1)$ and note that $(1 + iL)i = i - L$ and $(1 - iL)i = i + L$; hence,

$$(1 - L^4)y_t = \gamma_1(1 + L + L^2 + L^3)y_{t-1} - \gamma_2(1 - L + L^2 - L^3)y_{t-1}$$
$$+ (1 - L^2)[\gamma_3(i - L) - \gamma_4(i + L)]y_{t-1} + \varepsilon_t$$

so that

$$(1 - L^4)y_t = \gamma_1(1 + L + L^2 + L^3)y_{t-1} - \gamma_2(1 - L + L^2 - L^3)y_{t-1}$$
$$+ (1 - L^2)[(\gamma_3 - \gamma_4)i - (\gamma_3 + \gamma_4)L]y_{t-1} + \varepsilon_t \qquad (4.37)$$

To purge the imaginary numbers from this expression, define γ_5 and γ_6 such that $2\gamma_3 = -\gamma_6 - i\gamma_5$ and $2\gamma_4 = -\gamma_6 + i\gamma_5$. Hence, $(\gamma_3 - \gamma_4)i = \gamma_5$ and $\gamma_3 + \gamma_4 = \gamma_6$. Substituting into (4.37) yields

$$(1 - L^4)y_t = \gamma_1(1 + L + L^2 + L^3)y_{t-1} - \gamma_2(1 - L + L^2 - L^3)y_{t-1}$$
$$+ (1 - L^2)(\gamma_5 - \gamma_6L)y_{t-1} + \varepsilon_t$$

Fortunately, many software packages can perform the test directly on quarterly and monthly data. However, to understand the mechanics necessary to implement the procedure, use the following steps:

STEP 1: For quarterly data form the following variables:

$$y_{1t-1} = (1 + L + L^2 + L^3)y_{t-1} = y_{t-1} + y_{t-2} + y_{t-3} + y_{t-4}$$
$$y_{2t-1} = (1 - L + L^2 - L^3)y_{t-1} = y_{t-1} - y_{t-2} + y_{t-3} - y_{t-4}$$
$$y_{3t-1} = (1 - L^2)y_{t-1} = y_{t-1} - y_{t-3} \qquad \text{so that } y_{3t-2} = y_{t-2} - y_{t-4}$$

STEP 2: Estimate the regression:

$$(1-L^4)y_t = \gamma_1 y_{1t-1} - \gamma_2 y_{2t-1} + \gamma_5 y_{3t-1} - \gamma_6 y_{3t-2} + \varepsilon_t$$

You might want to modify the form of the equation by including an intercept, deterministic seasonal dummies, and a linear time trend. As in the augmented form of the Dickey–Fuller test, lagged values of $(1 - L^4)y_{t-i}$ may also be included. Perform the appropriate diagnostic checks to ensure that the residuals from the regression equation approximate a white-noise process.

STEP 3: Form the t-statistic for the null hypothesis $\gamma_1 = 0$; the appropriate critical values are reported in Hylleberg, et al. (1990). If you do not reject the hypothesis $\gamma_1 = 0$, conclude that $a_1 = 1$ so that there is a nonseasonal unit root. Next form the t-test for the hypothesis $\gamma_2 = 0$. If you do not reject the null hypothesis, conclude that $a_2 = 1$ and that there is a unit root with a semiannual frequency. Finally, perform the F-test for the hypothesis $\gamma_5 = \gamma_6 = 0$. If the calculated value is less than the critical value reported in Hylleberg, et al. (1990), conclude that γ_5 and/or γ_6 is zero so that there is a seasonal unit root. Be aware that the three null hypotheses are not alternatives; a series may have nonseasonal, semiannual, and a seasonal unit roots.

At the 5 percent significance level, Hylleberg, et al. (1990) report that the critical values using 100 observations are

	$\gamma_1 = 0$	$\gamma_2 = 0$	$\gamma_5 = \gamma_6 = 0$
Intercept	−2.88	−1.95	3.08
Intercept plus Seasonal Dummies	−2.95	−2.94	6.57
Intercept plus Seasonal Dummies plus time	−3.53	−2.94	6.60

An Example: In Chapter 2, we took the nonseasonal and the seasonal differences of the U.S. money supply and estimated a model of the form:

$$m_t = a_0 + a_1 m_{t-1} + \varepsilon_t + \beta_4 \varepsilon_{t-4}$$

where

$$m_t = (1 - L)(1 - L^4)y_t$$

and y_t is the logarithm of U.S. money supply as measured by M1.

We can use the HEGY test to determine if it is appropriate to use the seasonal and nonseasonal differences. Since it is clear that the money supply series has a sustained upward movement, (see Section 11 in Chapter 2), we want to allow for the possibility that the series is trend stationary. Hence, we include a deterministic trend and an intercept in the regression. Consider the following regression:

$$(1 - L^4)y_t = 0.107 + 0.0003t - 0.006y_{1t-1}$$
$$(2.22)\quad(2.03)\quad\;\;(-2.13)$$

$$-0.094y_{2t-1} - 0.084y_{3t-1} - 0.187y_{3t-2} + \sum_{i=1}^{9}\beta_i(1 - L^4)\Delta y_{t-i+1}$$
$$(-1.66)\qquad(-1.21)\qquad(-2.83)$$

where the lag length of nine was chosen by F-tests on the various β_i, and $y_{1t-1}, y_{2t-1}, y_{3t-1}$, and y_{3t-2} are defined above.

The coefficient on y_{1t-1} has a t-statistic of −2.13. Given the 5 percent critical value, we cannot reject the null hypothesis of a nonseasonal unit root. The sample F-statistic for the null hypothesis that the coefficients on y_{3t-1} and y_{3t-2} jointly equal zero is 2.62. Hence, there is a unit root at the annual frequency; hence, seasonal differencing is appropriate. Thus, we were quite correct to use both seasonal and nonseasonal differences to model the money supply series.

8. STRUCTURAL CHANGE

In performing unit root tests, special care must be taken if it is suspected that structural change has occurred. When there are structural breaks, the various Dickey–Fuller test statistics are biased towards the nonrejection of a unit root. To explain, consider the situation in which there is a one-time change in the mean of an otherwise stationary sequence. In the top graph of Figure 4.10, the $\{y_t\}$ sequence was constructed so as to be stationary around a mean of zero for $t = 0, \ldots, 50$ and then to fluctuate around a mean of 6 for $t = 51, \ldots, 100$. The sequence was formed by drawing 100 normally and

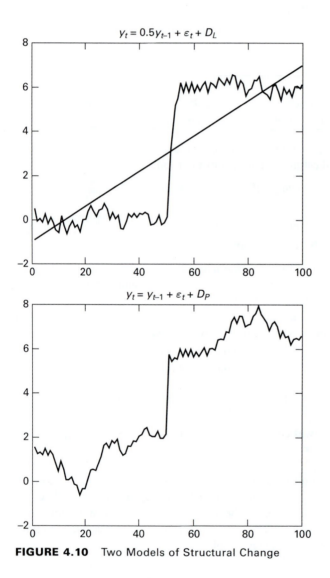

FIGURE 4.10 Two Models of Structural Change

independently distributed values for the $\{\varepsilon_t\}$ sequence. Setting $y_0 = 0$, the next 100 values in the sequence were generated using the formula:

$$y_t = 0.5y_{t-1} + \varepsilon_t + D_L \qquad (4.38)$$

where D_L is a dummy variable such that $D_L = 0$ for $t = 1, \ldots, 50$ and $D_L = 3$ for $t = 51$, $\ldots, 100$. The subscript L is designed to indicate that the *level* of the dummy changes. At times it will be convenient to refer to the value of the dummy variable in period t as $D_L(t)$; in the example at hand, $D_L(50) = 0$ and $D_L(51) = 3$.

In practice, the structural change may not be as apparent as the break shown in the figure. However, the large simulated break is useful for illustrating the problem of using a Dickey–Fuller test in such circumstances. The straight line shown in the figure highlights the fact that the series appears to have a deterministic trend. In fact, the straight line is the best-fitting OLS equation:

$$y_t = a_0 + a_2 t + e_t$$

In the figure, you can see that the fitted value of a_0 is negative and the fitted value of a_2 is positive. The proper way to estimate (4.38) is to fit a simple AR(1) model and allow the intercept to change by including the dummy variable D_L. However, suppose that we unsuspectingly fit the regression equation:

$$y_t = a_0 + a_1 y_{t-1} + e_t \qquad (4.39)$$

As you can infer from Figure 4.10, the estimated value of a_1 is necessarily biased toward unity. The reason for this upward bias is that the estimated value of a_1 captures the property that "low" values of y_t (i.e., those fluctuating around zero) are followed by other "low" values, and "high" values (i.e., those fluctuating around a mean of six) are followed by other "high" values. For a formal demonstration, note that as a_1 approaches unity, (4.39) approaches a random walk plus drift. We know that the solution to the random walk plus drift model includes a deterministic trend; that is,

$$y_t = y_0 + a_0 t + \sum_{i=1}^{t} \varepsilon_i$$

Thus, the misspecified equation (4.39) will tend to mimic the trend line shown in Figure 4.10 by biasing a_1 towards unity. This bias in a_1 means that the Dickey–Fuller test is biased toward accepting the null hypothesis of a unit root *even though the series is stationary within each of the subperiods.*

Of course, a unit root process can also exhibit a structural break. The lower portion of Figure 4.10 simulates a random walk process with a structural change occurring at $t = 51$. This second simulation used the same 100 realizations for the $\{\varepsilon_t\}$ sequence and the initial condition $y_0 = 2$. The 100 realizations of the $\{y_t\}$ sequence were constructed as

$$y_t = y_{t-1} + \varepsilon_t + D_P$$

where $D_P(51) = 4$ and all other values of $D_P = 0$.

Here, the subscript P refers to the fact that there is a single *pulse* in the dummy variable. In a unit root process, a single pulse in the dummy will have a permanent effect on the level of the $\{y_t\}$ sequence. In $t = 51$, the pulse in the dummy is equivalent to an ε_{t+51} shock of 4 extra units. Hence, the *one-time* shock to $D_P(51)$ has a *permanent* effect on the mean value of the sequence for $t \geq 51$. In the figure, you can see that the level of the process takes a discrete jump in $t = 51$, never exhibiting any tendency to return to the prebreak level.

This bias in the Dickey–Fuller tests was confirmed in a Monte Carlo experiment. Perron (1989) generated 10,000 replications of a process like that of (4.38). Each replication was formed by drawing 100 normally and independently distributed values for the $\{\varepsilon_t\}$ sequence. For each of the 10,000 replicated series, he used OLS to estimate a regression in the form of (4.39).[14] As could be anticipated from our earlier discussion, Perron found that the estimated values of a_1 were biased towards unity. Moreover, the bias became more pronounced as the magnitude of the break increased.

Testing for Structural Change

Returning to the two graphs of Figure 4.10, there may be instances in which the unaided eye cannot easily detect the difference between the alternative types of sequences. One econometric procedure to test for unit roots in the presence of a structural break involves splitting the sample into two parts and using Dickey–Fuller tests on each part. The problem with this procedure is that the degrees of freedom for each of the resulting regressions are diminished. Moreover, you may not know when the breakpoint actually occurs. It is preferable to have a single test based on the full sample.

Perron (1989) goes on to develop a formal procedure to test for unit roots in the presence of a structural change at time period $t = \tau + 1$. Consider the null hypothesis of a one-time jump in the level of a unit root process against the alternative of a one-time change in the intercept of a trend stationary process. Formally, let the null and alternative hypotheses be

$$H_1: y_t = a_0 + y_{t-1} + \mu_1 D_P + \varepsilon_t \qquad (4.40)$$

$$A_1: y_t = a_0 + a_2 t + \mu_2 D_L + \varepsilon_t \qquad (4.41)$$

where D_P represents a *pulse* dummy variable such that $D_P = 1$ if $t = \tau + 1$ and zero otherwise, and D_L represents a *level* dummy variable such that $D_L = 1$ if $t > \tau$ and zero otherwise.

Under the null hypothesis, $\{y_t\}$ is a unit root process with a one-time jump in the level of the sequence in period $t = \tau + 1$. Under the alternative hypothesis, $\{y_t\}$ is trend stationary with a one-time jump in the intercept. Figure 4.11 can help you to visualize the two hypotheses. Simulating (4.40) by setting $a_0 = 1$ and using 100 realizations for the $\{\varepsilon_t\}$ sequence, the erratic line in the figure depicts the time path of $\{y_t\}$ under the null hypothesis. You can see the one-time jump in the level of the process occurring in period 51. Thereafter, the $\{y_t\}$ sequence continues the original random walk plus drift process. The alternative hypothesis posits that the $\{y_t\}$ sequence is stationary around the broken trend line. Up to $t = \tau$, $\{y_t\}$ is stationary around $a_0 + a_2 t$, and beginning at $\tau + 1$, y_t is stationary around $a_0 + a_2 t + \mu_2$. As illustrated by the broken line, there is a one-time increase in the intercept of the trend if $\mu_2 > 0$.

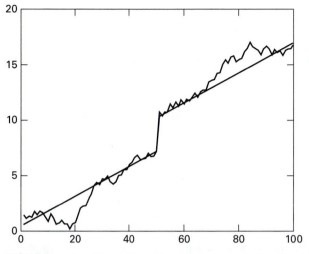

FIGURE 4.11   Alternative Representation of Structural Change

The econometric problem is to determine whether an observed series is best modeled by (4.40) or (4.41). The implementation of Perron's (1989) technique is straightforward:

STEP 1: Detrend the data by estimating the model under the alternative hypothesis and calling the residuals $\hat{y}_t$. Hence, each value of $\hat{y}_t$ is the residual from the regression $y_t = a_0 + a_2 t + \mu_2 D_L + \hat{y}_t$.

STEP 2: Estimate the regression:

$$\hat{y}_t = a_1 \hat{y}_{t-1} + \varepsilon_t$$

Under the null hypothesis of a unit root, the theoretical value of a_1 is unity. Perron (1989) shows that when the residuals are identically and independently distributed, the distribution of a_1 depends on the proportion of observations occurring prior to the break. Denote this proportion by $\lambda = \tau/T$ where T = total number of observations.

STEP 3: Perform diagnostic checks to determine if the residuals from Step 2 are serially uncorrelated. If there is serial correlation, use the augmented form of the regression:

$$\hat{y}_t = a_1 \hat{y}_{t-1} + \sum_{i=1}^{k} \beta_i \Delta \hat{y}_{t-i} + \varepsilon_t$$

STEP 4: Calculate the t-statistic for the null hypothesis $a_1 = 1$. This statistic can be compared to the critical values calculated by Perron. Perron generated 5,000 series according to H_1 using values of λ ranging from 0 to 1 by increments of 0.1. For each value of λ, he estimated the regressions $\hat{y}_t = a_1 \hat{y}_{t-1} + \varepsilon_t$ and calculated the sample distribution of a_1. Naturally the critical values are identical to the Dickey–Fuller statistics when $\lambda = 0$ and $\lambda = 1$; in effect, there is no structural change unless $0 < \lambda < 1$. The maximum difference between the two statistics occurs when $\lambda = 0.5$. For $\lambda = 0.5$, the critical value of the t-statistic at the 5 percent level of significance is -3.76 (which is larger in absolute than the corresponding Dickey–Fuller statistic of -3.41). If you find a t-statistic greater than the critical value calculated by Perron, it is possible to reject the null hypothesis of a unit root.

Of course, it is possible to incorporate Step 1 directly into Steps 2 or 3. To combine Steps 1 and 3, simply estimate the equation:

$$y_t = a_0 + a_1 y_{t-1} + a_2 t + \mu_2 D_L + \sum_{i=1}^{k} \beta_i \Delta y_{t-i} + \varepsilon_t$$

The t-statistic for the null hypothesis $a_1 = 1$ can then be compared to the appropriate critical value calculated by Perron. In addition, the methodology is quite general in that it can also allow for a one-time change in the drift or a one-time change in both the mean and the drift. For example, it is possible to test the null hypothesis of a permanent change in the drift term versus the alternative of a change in the slope of the trend. Here the null hypothesis is

$$H_2: y_t = a_0 + y_{t-1} + \mu_2 D_L + \varepsilon_t$$

where $D_L = 1$ if $t > \tau$ and zero otherwise. With this specification, the $\{y_t\}$ sequence is generated by $\Delta y_t = a_0 + \varepsilon_t$ up to period τ and by $\Delta y_t = a_0 + \mu_2 + \varepsilon_t$ thereafter. If $\mu_2 > 0$, the magnitude of the drift increases for $t > \tau$. Similarly, a reduction in the drift occurs if $\mu_2 < 0$.

The alternative hypothesis posits a trend stationary series with a change in the slope of the trend for $t > \tau$

$$A_2: y_t = a_0 + a_2 t + \mu_3 D_T + \varepsilon_t$$

where $D_T = t - \tau$ for $t > \tau$ and zero otherwise.

For example, suppose that the break occurs in period 51 so that $\tau = 50$. Thus, $D_T(1)$ through $D_T(50)$ are all zero, so that for the first 50 periods, $\{y_t\}$ evolves as $y_t = a_0 + a_2 t + \varepsilon_t$. Beginning with period 51, $D_T(51) = 1$, $D_T(52) = 2$, ... so that for $t > \tau$, $\{y_t\}$ evolves as: $y_t = a_0 + a_2 t + \mu_3(t - 50) + \varepsilon_t = a_0 + (a_2 + \mu_3)t - 50\mu_3 + \varepsilon_t$. Hence, D_T changes the slope of the deterministic trend line. The slope of the trend is a_2 for $t \leq \tau$ and $a_2 + \mu_3$ for $t > \tau$.

To be even more general, it is possible to combine the two null hypotheses H_1 and H_2. A change in both the level and drift of a unit root process can be represented by

$$H_3: y_t = a_0 + y_{t-1} + \mu_1 D_P + \mu_2 D_L + \varepsilon_t$$

where D_P and D_L are the pulse and level dummies defined above.

The appropriate alternative for this case is

$$A_3: y_t = a_0 + a_2 t + \mu_2 D_L + \mu_3 D_T + \varepsilon_t$$

Again, the procedure entails estimating the regression A_2 or A_3. Next, using the residuals $\hat{y}_t$, estimate the regression

$$\hat{y}_t = a_1 \hat{y}_{t-1} + e_t$$

If the errors from this second regression equation do not appear to be white noise, estimate the equation in the form of an augmented Dickey–Fuller test. The t-statistic for the null hypothesis $a_1 = 1$ can be compared to the critical values calculated by Perron (1989). For $\lambda = 0.5$, Perron reports the critical value of the t-statistic at the 5 percent significance level to be -3.96 for H_2 and -4.24 for H_3.

Perron's Test for Structural Change

Perron (1989) used his analysis of structural change to challenge the findings of Nelson and Plosser (1982). With the same variables, his results indicate that most macroeconomic variables are *not* characterized by unit root processes. Instead, the variables appear to be TS processes coupled with structural breaks. According to Perron (1989), the stock market crash of 1929 and the dramatic oil price increase of 1973 were exogenous shocks having permanent effects on the mean of most macroeconomic variables. The crash induced a one-time fall in the mean. Otherwise, macroeconomic variables appear to be trend stationary.

All variables in Perron's study (except real wages, stock prices and the stationary unemployment rate) appeared to have a trend with a constant slope and exhibited a major change in the level around 1929. In order to entertain various hypotheses concerning the effects of the stock market crash, consider the regression equation:

$$y_t = a_0 + \mu_1 D_L + \mu_2 D_P + a_2 t + a_1 y_{t-1} + \sum_{i=1}^{k} \beta_i \, \Delta y_{t-i} + \varepsilon_t$$

where: $D_P(1930) = 1$ and zero otherwise
$\quad\quad\quad$ $D_L = 1$ for all t beginning in 1930 and zero otherwise

Under the presumption of a one-time change in the level of a unit root process, $a_1 = 1$, $a_2 = 0$, and $\mu_2 \neq 0$. Under the alternative hypothesis of a permanent one-time break in the trend stationary model, $a_1 < 1$ and $\mu_1 \neq 0$. Perron's (1989) results using real GNP, nominal GNP, and industrial production are reported in Table 4.6. Given

Table 4.6   Retesting Nelson and Plosser's Data for Structural Change

	T	λ	k	a_0	μ_1	μ_2	a_2	a_1
Real GNP	62	0.33	8	3.44	−0.189	−0.018	0.027	0.282
				(5.07)	(−4.28)	(−0.30)	(5.05)	(−5.03)
Nominal GNP	62	0.33	8	5.69	−3.60	0.100	0.036	0.471
				(5.44)	(−4.77)	(1.09)	(5.44)	(−5.42)
Industrial production	111	0.66	8	0.120	−0.298	−0.095	0.032	0.322
				(4.37)	(−4.56)	(−.095)	(5.42)	(−5.47)

Notes:

1. T = number of observations; λ = proportion of observations occurring before the structural change; k = lag length.

2. The appropriate t-statistics are in parentheses. For a_0, μ_1, μ_2, and a_2, the null is that the coefficient is equal to zero. For a_1, the null hypothesis is $a_1 = 1$. Note that all estimated values of a_1 are significantly different from unity at the 1% level.

the length of each series, the 1929 crash means that λ is 1/3 for both real and nominal GNP and equal to 2/3 for industrial production. Lag lengths (i.e., the values of k) were determined using t-tests on the coefficients β_i. The value k was selected if the t-statistic on β_k was greater than 1.60 in absolute value and the t-statistic on β_i for $i > k$ was less than 1.60.

First consider the results for real GNP. When you examine the last column of the table, it is clear that there is little support for the unit root hypothesis; the estimated value of $a_1 = 0.282$ is significantly different from unity at the 1 percent level. Instead, real GNP appears to have a deterministic trend (a_2 is estimated to be over five standard deviations from zero). Also note that the point estimate $\mu_1 = -0.189$ is significantly different from zero at conventional levels. Thus, the stock market crash is estimated to have induced a permanent one-time decline in the intercept of real GNP.

These findings receive additional support since the estimated coefficients and their t-statistics are quite similar across the three equations. All values of a_1 are about five standard deviations from unity and the coefficients of the deterministic trends (a_2) are all over five standard deviations from zero. Since all estimated values of μ_1 are significant at the 1 percent level and negative, the data seem to support the contention that real macroeconomic variables are TS, except for a structural break resulting from the stock market crash.

Tests with Simulated Data

To further illustrate the procedure, 100 random numbers were drawn to represent the $\{\varepsilon_t\}$ sequence. By setting $y_0 = 0$, the next 100 values in the $\{y_t\}$ sequence were drawn as

$$y_t = 0.5y_{t-1} + \varepsilon_t + D_L$$

where: $D_L = 0$ for $t = 1, \ldots, 50$
$D_L = 1$ for $t = 51, \ldots, 100$

Thus, the simulation is identical to (4.38) except that the magnitude of the structural break is diminished. This simulated series is in the data file labeled BREAK.XLS; you should try to reproduce the following results. If you were to plot the data, you would see the same pattern as in Figure 4.10. However, if you did not plot the data or were otherwise unaware of the break, you might easily conclude that the $\{y_t\}$ sequence had a unit root. The ACF of the $\{y_t\}$ sequence suggests a unit root process; for example, the first 6 autocorrelations are

Lag:	1	2	3	4	5	6
	0.94	0.88	0.84	0.81	0.77	0.72

and the ACF of the first differences is

Lag:	1	2	3	4	5	6
	−0.002	−0.201	−0.117	0.038	−0.035	−0.054

Dickey–Fuller tests yield

$\Delta y_t = -0.0233 y_{t-1} + \varepsilon_t$ t-statistic for $\gamma = 0$: -0.98495
$\Delta y_t = 0.0661 - 0.0566 y_{t-1} + \varepsilon_t$ t-statistic for $\gamma = 0$: -1.70630
$\Delta y_t = -0.0488 - 0.1522 y_{t-1} + 0.004t + \varepsilon_t$ t-statistic for $\gamma = 0$: -2.73397

Diagnostic tests indicate that longer lags are not needed. Regardless of the presence of the constant or the trend, the $\{y_t\}$ sequence appears to be difference stationary. Of course, the problem is that the structural break biases the data toward suggesting a unit root.

Now, using the Perron procedure, the first step is to estimate the model $y_t = a_0 + a_2 t + \mu_2 D_L + \hat{y}_t$. The residuals from this equation are the detrended $\{\hat{y}_t\}$ sequence. The second step is to test for a unit root in the residuals by estimating $\hat{y}_t = a_1 \hat{y}_{t-1} + \varepsilon_t$. The resulting regression is

$$\hat{y}_t = 0.4843 \hat{y}_{t-1} + \varepsilon_t$$

In the third step, all of the diagnostic statistics indicate that $\{\varepsilon_t\}$ approximates a white-noise process. Finally, the t-statistic for $a_1 = 1$ is 5.396. Hence, we can reject the null of a unit root and conclude that the simulated data are stationary around a break point at $t = 51$.

Some care must be exercised in using Perron's procedure since it assumes that the date of the structural break is known. In your own work, if the date of the break is uncertain, you should consult Perron and Vogelsang (1992), Zivot and Andrews (2002), Perron (1997) or Vogelsang and Perron (1998). The entire issue of the July 1992 *Journal of Business and Economic Statistics* is devoted to breakpoints and unit roots. An interesting application is found in Ben-David and Papell (1995). They consider a long span (of up to 130 years) of GDP data for 16 countries. Allowing for breaks, they reject the null of a unit root in approximately half of the cases.

9. POWER AND THE DETERMINISTIC REGRESSORS

Tests for unit roots are not especially good at distinguishing between a series with a characteristic root that is close to unity and a true unit root process. Part of the problem concerns the power of the test and the presence of the deterministic regressors in the estimating equations. Although many details are beyond the level of this text, it is important to be aware of some of the difficulties entailed in testing for the presence of a trend (either deterministic or stochastic) in the data-generating process.

Power

Formally, the **power** of a test is equal to the probability of rejecting a false null hypothesis (i.e., one minus the probability of a type II error). Monte Carlo simulations have shown that the power of the various Dickey–Fuller tests can be very low. As such, these tests will too often indicate that a series contains a unit root. Moreover, they have little power to distinguish between trend stationary and drifting processes.

In finite samples, any trend stationary process can be arbitrarily well approximated by a unit root process, and a unit root process can be arbitrarily well approximated by a trend stationary process. These results should not be too surprising after examining Figure 4.12. The top graph of the figure shows a stationary process and a unit root process that were constructed from the equations:

$$y_t = 1.1y_{t-1} - 0.1y_{t-2} + \varepsilon_t$$
$$z_t = 1.1z_{t-1} - 0.15z_{t-2} + \varepsilon_t$$

where $y_0 = y_1 = z_0 = z_1 = 0$ and the same simulated values for $\{\varepsilon_t\}$ were used to construct the $\{y_t\}$ and $\{z_t\}$ sequences.

The $\{y_t\}$ sequence has a unit root; the roots of the $\{z_t\}$ sequence are 0.9405 and 0.1594. Although $\{z_t\}$ is stationary, it can be called a near-unit root process. If you

FIGURE 4.12   Stationary and Unit Root Processes

didn't know the actual data-generating processes, it would be difficult to tell that only $\{z_t\}$ is stationary.

Similarly, as illustrated in the lower graph of Figure 4.12, it can be quite difficult to distinguish between a trend stationary and a unit root plus drift process. Still using the same 100 values for $\{\varepsilon_t\}$, two other sequences were constructed using the equations:

$$w_t = 1 + 0.02t + \varepsilon_t$$
$$x_t = 0.02 + x_{t-1} + (1/3)\varepsilon_t$$

where $x_0 = 1$.

Here the trend and the drift terms dominate the time paths of the two sequences. Again, it is very difficult to distinguish between the sequences. This is especially true since dividing each realization of ε_t by 3 acts to smooth out the $\{x_t\}$ sequence. Just as it is difficult for the naked eye to perceive the differences in the sequences, it is also difficult for the Dickey–Fuller test to select the correct specification.

It is easy to show that a trend stationary process can be made to mimic a unit root process arbitrarily well. A drift term can be included in the random walk plus noise process so that

$$\Delta y_t = a_0 + \varepsilon_t + \Delta \eta_t \qquad (4.42)$$

If $\text{var}(\varepsilon_t) \neq 0$, (4.42) is clearly a unit root process. However, if $\text{var}(\varepsilon_t) = 0$, we can set all values of $\{\varepsilon_t\} = 0$. If we now let y_0 denote the initial value of the series, it follows that $\{y_t\}$ is the trend stationary process

$$y_t = y_0 + a_0 t + \eta_t \qquad (4.43)$$

Thus, the difference between the difference stationary process of (4.42) and the trend process of (4.43) concerns the variance of ε_t. Having observed the composite effects of the two shocks—but not the individual components η_t and ε_t—there is no simple way to determine whether $\text{var}(\varepsilon_t) \equiv \sigma^2$ is *exactly* equal to zero. This is particularly true if the data-generating process is such that σ_η^2 is large relative to σ^2. In a finite sample, arbitrarily increasing σ_η^2 will make it virtually impossible to distinguish between a TS and a DS series. It also follows that a trend stationary process can arbitrarily well approximate a unit root process. If the stochastic portion of the trend stationary process has sufficient variance, it will not be possible to distinguish between the unit root and trend stationary hypotheses.

It is simple to conduct a Monte Carlo experiment that determines the power of the Dickey–Fuller test. To be more specific, suppose that the true data-generating process for a series is $y_t = a_0 + a_1 y_{t-1} + \varepsilon_t$ where $|a_1| < 1$. Since you do not know the actual data-generating process, you might test the series for a unit root using a Dickey–Fuller test. Of course, the series is actually stationary so that an ordinary t-statistic is appropriate. The question at hand is: How often will the Dickey–Fuller test fail to detect that the series is actually stationary? Since the confidence intervals for the t-statistics of the Dickey–Fuller test exceed those for the usual t-test, it is to be expected that the power of the Dickey–Fuller test is low. To find out the exact answer to the question, we can generate 10,000 stationary series and apply a Dickey–Fuller test to each. We can then calculate the percentage of the times that the test correctly identifies a truly stationary process.

The ability of the test to properly detect that the series is stationary will depend on the value of a_1. We would expect the test to have the least power when $|a_1|$ is close to unity. Thus, it makes sense to examine how the magnitude of a_1 affects the power of the test. We first construct 100 observations of the series $y_t = a_0 + a_1 y_{t-1} + \varepsilon_t$ using a value of $a_1 = 0.8$ and an $\{\varepsilon_t\}$ sequence drawn from a standardized normal distribution. The magnitude of a_0 is unimportant and so is set equal to zero. The initial value of y_0 is set equal to the unconditional mean of zero. Next, the simulated series is estimated in the form $\Delta y_t = a_0 + \gamma y_{t-1} + \varepsilon_t$. The Dickey–Fuller τ_μ statistics are used to determine whether the null hypothesis that $\gamma = 0$ can be rejected at the 10 percent, 5 percent, and 1 percent significance levels. The experiment is repeated 10,000 times and the proportion of the instances in which the null hypothesis is correctly rejected is recorded. Finally, the entire experiment is repeated for other values of a_1. Consider the following table of proportions:

a_1	10%	5%	1%
0.80	95.9	87.4	51.4
0.90	52.1	33.1	9.0
0.95	23.4	12.7	2.6
0.99	10.5	5.8	1.3

When the true value of $a_1 = 0.8$, the test does reasonably well. For example, at the 5 percent significance level, the false null hypothesis of a unit root is rejected in 87.4 percent of the Monte Carlo replications. However, when $a_1 = 0.95$, the probability of correctly rejecting the null hypothesis of a unit root is estimated to be only 12.7 percent at the 5 percent significance level and 2.6 percent at the 1 percent level. Thus, the test has very low power to detect near unit root series.

Does it matter that it is often impossible to distinguish between borderline stationary, trend stationary, and unit root processes? The realistic answer is that it depends on the question at hand. In borderline cases, the short-run forecasts from the alternative models may have nearly identical forecasting performance. In fact, Monte Carlo studies indicate that when the true data-generating process is stationary but has a root close to unity, the one-step-ahead forecasts from a differenced model are usually superior to the forecasts from a stationary model. However, the long-run forecasts of a model with a deterministic trend will be quite different from those of other models.[15]

Determination of the Deterministic Regressors

Unless the researcher knows the actual data-generating process, there is a question concerning whether it is most appropriate to estimate (4.20), (4.21), or (4.22). It might seem reasonable to test the hypothesis $\gamma = 0$ using the most general of the models:

$$\Delta y_t = a_0 + \gamma y_{t-1} + a_2 t + \sum_{i=2}^{p} \beta_i \Delta y_{t-i+1} + \varepsilon_t \qquad (4.44)$$

After all, if the true process is a random walk process, this regression should find that $a_0 = \gamma = a_2 = 0$. One problem with this line of reasoning is that the presence of the additional parameters reduces degrees of freedom and the power of the test. Reduced power means that the researcher will not be able to reject the null of a unit root when, in fact, no unit root is present. The second problem is that the appropriate statistic (i.e., τ, τ_μ, and τ_τ) for testing $\gamma = 0$ depends on which regressors are included in the model. As you can see by examining the three Dickey–Fuller tables, for a given significance level, the confidence intervals around $\gamma = 0$ dramatically expand if a drift and a time trend are included in the model. This is quite different from the case in which $\{y_t\}$ is stationary. When $\{y_t\}$ is stationary, the distribution of the t-statistic does not depend on the presence of the other regressors.

The point is that it is important to use a regression equation that mimics the actual data-generating process. Inappropriately omitting the intercept or time trend can cause the power of the test to go to zero.[16] For example, if as in (4.44) the data-generating process includes a trend, omitting the term $a_2 t$ imparts an upward bias in the estimated value of γ. On the other hand, extra regressors increase the critical values so that you may fail to reject the null of a unit root.

How do you know whether to include a drift or time trend in performing the tests? The key problem is that *the tests for unit roots are conditional on the presence of the deterministic regressors and tests for the presence of the deterministic regressors are conditional on the presence of a unit root.*

Campbell and Perron (1991) report the following results concerning unit root tests:

1. When the estimated regression includes *at least* all of the deterministic elements in the actual data-generating process, the distribution of γ is nonnormal under the null of a unit root. The distribution itself varies with the set of parameters included in the estimating equation.

2. If the estimated regression includes deterministic regressors that are not in the actual data-generating process, the power of the unit root test against a stationary alternative decreases as additional deterministic regressors are added. Hence, you do not want to include regressors that are not in the data-generating process.

3. If the estimated regression omits an important deterministic trending variable present in the true data-generating process—such as the expression $a_2 t$ in (4.44)—the power of the t-statistic test goes to zero as sample size increases. If the estimated regression omits a nontrending variable (such as an intercept), the t-statistic is consistent, but the finite sample power is adversely affected and decreases as the magnitude of the coefficient on the omitted component increases. Hence, you do not want to omit regressors that are in the data-generating process.

The direct implication of these findings is that the researcher may fail to reject the null hypothesis of a unit root because of a misspecification concerning the deterministic part of the regression. Too few or too many regressors may cause a failure of the test to reject the null of a unit root. Although we can never be sure that we are including the appropriate deterministic regressors in our econometric model, there are some useful guidelines.

1. *Always plot your data.* Visual inspection can help you determine whether there is a clear trend in the data.

2. *Be clear about the appropriate null hypothesis and the alternative hypothesis.* When you perform a Dickey–Fuller test, always estimate the

model under the alternative hypothesis and impose the restriction implied by the null hypothesis. Since the null hypothesis is that the series has a unit root, always estimate the series as if it were stationary or TS. For example, the real GDP series shown in Figure 4.1 moves decidedly upward over time. The issue is whether the series is trend stationary or contains a unit root plus a drift term. As such, the appropriate model to estimate has the form $\Delta y_t = a_0 + \gamma y_{t-1} + a_2 t + \Sigma \beta_i \Delta y_{t-i} + \varepsilon_t$. You then test the restrictions $\gamma = 0$ and/or $\gamma = a_2 = 0$. There is no need to estimate a model without $a_2 t$ since the alternative hypothesis is not represented in such a specification.

3. *You do not want to reject the null hypothesis when the series actually has a unit root (a Type I error) or incorrectly accept the null of a unit root when the series is stationary or TS (a Type II error).* Nevertheless, any test involves the possibility of making such errors. As such, you do not want to perform needless tests. In the example of real GDP, there is little point in testing the restriction $a_0 = \gamma = a_2 = 0$ since real GDP clearly increases over time.

4. *Testing a restriction on a model that has already been restricted creates the possibility of compounding your errors.* Suppose that a test for the presence of the time trend allows you to set $a_2 = 0$. A subsequent test of the restriction $a_0 = \gamma = 0$ in the model $\Delta y_t = a_0 + \gamma y_{t-1} + \Sigma \beta_i \Delta y_{t-i} + \varepsilon_t$ is conditional on whether the first test was correct in allowing you to exclude the deterministic trend.

Sometimes it is hard to follow the guidelines since the appropriate null and alternative hypotheses are unclear. You do not want to lose power by including a superfluous deterministic regressor in a unit root test. However, omitting a regressor that is actually in the data-generating process leads to a misspecification error. Fortunately, Sims, Stock and Watson (1990) provide a second rule that is helpful in selecting the appropriate set of regressors:

> **Rule 2:** If the data-generating process contains any deterministic regressors (i.e., an intercept or a time trend) and the estimating equation contains these deterministic regressors, inference on all coefficients can be conducted using a t-test or an F-test. This is because a test involving a single restriction across parameters with different rates of convergence is dominated asymptotically by the parameters with the slowest rates of convergence.

While the proof is beyond the scope of this text, the point is that the nonstandard Dickey–Fuller distributions are needed only when you include deterministic regressors not in the actual data-generating process. Hence, if the DGP is known to contain a trend, the null hypothesis $\gamma = 0$ can be tested using the standardized normal distribution if you estimate the model in the form of (4.25). As such, Dolado, Jenkinson, and Sosvilla–Rivero (1990) suggest the following procedure to test for a unit root when the form of the data-generating process is *completely* unknown. The following is a straightforward modification of their method:

STEP 1: As shown in Figure 4.13, start with the least restrictive of the plausible models (which will generally include a trend and drift) and use the τ_τ statistic to test the null hypothesis $\gamma = 0$. Unit root tests have low power to reject the null hypothesis; hence, if the null hypothesis of a unit root is *rejected*, there is no need to proceed. Conclude that the $\{y_t\}$ sequence does not contain a unit root.

STEP 2: If the null hypothesis is *not rejected*, it is necessary to determine whether too many deterministic regressors were included in Step 1 above.[17] The presence of these regressors may have reduced the power of the test. As such, you can test for the significance of the trend term by testing the hypothesis $a_2 = \gamma = 0$ using the ϕ_3 statistic. If the trend is not significant,

Estimate $\Delta y_t = a_0 + \gamma y_{t-1} + a_2 t + \Sigma \beta_i \Delta y_{t-i} + \varepsilon_t$

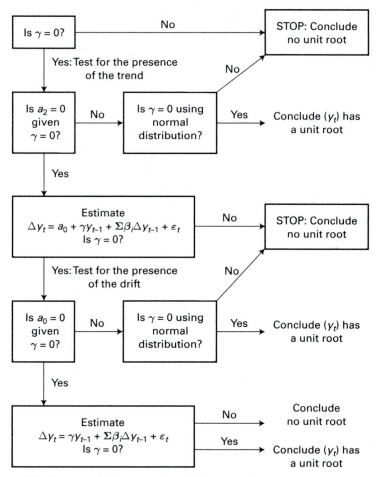

FIGURE 4.13   A Procedure to Test for Unit Roots

proceed to Step 3. Otherwise, if the trend is significant, retest for the presence of a unit root using the standardized normal distribution. After all, if a trend is actually present in the GDP, the limiting distribution of γ is the standardized normal. If the null of a unit root is rejected, proceed no further; conclude that the $\{y_t\}$ sequence does not contain a unit root. Otherwise, conclude that the $\{y_t\}$ sequence contains a unit root.

STEP 3: Estimate the model without the trend [i.e., estimate a model in the form of (4.24)]. Test for the presence of a unit root using the τ_μ statistic. If the null is rejected, conclude that the model does not contain a unit root. If the null hypothesis of a unit root is not rejected, test for the significance of the constant by testing the hypothesis $a_0 = \gamma = 0$ using the ϕ_1 statistic. If the drift is not significant, estimate an equation in the form of (4.24) and proceed to Step 4. If the drift is significant, test for the presence of a unit root using the standardized normal. If the null hypothesis of a unit root is rejected, conclude that the $\{y_t\}$ sequence does not contain a unit root. Otherwise, conclude that the $\{y_t\}$ sequence contains a unit root.

STEP 4: Estimate (4.44) without the trend or drift; i.e., estimate a model in the form of (4.23). Use τ to test for the presence of a unit root. If the null hypothesis of a unit root is rejected, conclude that the $\{y_t\}$ sequence does not contain a unit root. Otherwise, conclude that the $\{y_t\}$ sequence contains a unit root.

Remember, no procedure can be expected to work well if it is used in a completely mechanical fashion. Plotting the data is usually an important indicator of the presence of deterministic regressors. The interest rate series shown in Figure 4.2 can hardly be said to contain a deterministic trend. Moreover, theoretical considerations might suggest the appropriate regressors. The efficient market hypothesis is inconsistent with the presence of a deterministic trend in an asset's return. Similarly, in testing for PPP you should not begin using a deterministic time trend. However, the procedure is a sensible way to test for unit roots when the form of the data-generating process is completely unknown.

GDP and Unit Roots

Although the methodology outlined in Figure 4.13 can be very useful, it does have its problems. Each step in the procedure involves a test that is conditioned on all the previous tests being correct; the significance level of each of the cascading tests is impossible to ascertain.

The procedure and its inherent dangers are nicely illustrated by trying to determine if the real GDP data shown in Figure 4.1 has a unit root. It is a good idea to replicate the results reported below using the data in QUARTERLY.XLS. Using quarterly data over the 1960:1 – 2002:1 period, the correlogram of the logarithm of real GDP exhibits slow decay. At the end of Section 2, the logarithmic first difference of the series was estimated as

$$\Delta lrgdp_t = 0.0050 + 0.256\Delta lrgdp_{t-1} + 0.1496\Delta lrgdp_{t-2}$$
$$(5.03) \quad (3.30) \quad\quad\quad (1.94)$$

The model is well estimated in that the residuals appear to be white noise and all coefficients are of high quality. For our purposes, the interesting point is that the

$\{\Delta lrgdp_t\}$ series appears to be a stationary process. Integrating suggests that $\{lrgdp_t\}$ has a stochastic and a deterministic trend. The issue here is to determine whether it was appropriate to difference the log of real GDP. Towards this end, consider the augmented Dickey–Fuller equation with t-statistics in parentheses:

$$\Delta lrgdp_t = 0.0635 + 0.00048t - 0.0629\ lrgdp_{t-1}$$
$$(3.72) \quad (3.27) \quad (-3.37)$$
$$+\ 0.256\Delta lrgdp_{t-1} + 0.1486\Delta lrgdp_{t-2} \qquad (4.45)$$
$$(3.39) \qquad\qquad (2.45)$$

As in Step 1, we estimate the least restrictive model; as such, (4.45) contains an intercept and a deterministic trend. The point estimates of (4.45) suggest that the real GDP is trend stationary. However, the issue is to formally test the statistical significance of the null hypothesis $\gamma = 0$. The t-statistic for the null hypothesis $\gamma = 0$ is -3.37. Critical values with 166 usable observations are not reported in the Dickey–Fuller table.[18] However, with 100 observations, the critical value of τ_τ at the 10 percent and 5 percent significance levels are -3.15 and -3.45, respectively. If you are comfortable using the 10 percent significance level, there is no need to proceed further; conclude that there is not a unit root. At the 5 percent level, we cannot reject the null of a unit root. However, the power of the test may have been reduced due to the presence of an unnecessary time trend and/or drift term. In Step 2, test for the presence of the time trend, given the presence of a unit root. In (4.45), the t-statistic for the null hypothesis $a_2 = 0$ is 3.27. Don't let this large value fool you into thinking that a_2 is significantly different from zero. Instead, we can use the ϕ_3 statistic to test the joint hypothesis $a_2 = \gamma = 0$. The sample value of F for the restriction is 6.14. Since the critical value of ϕ_3 is 6.49 at the 5 percent significance level, it is possible to conclude that the restriction $a_2 = \gamma = 0$ is not binding. Thus, we can proceed to Step 3 and estimate the model without the trend. Consider the following model:

$$\Delta lrgdp_t = 0.0084 - 0.0021\ lrgdp_{t-1} + 0.248\Delta lrgdp_{t-1} + 0.145\Delta lrgdp_{t-2} \quad (4.46)$$
$$(2.80) \quad (-1.22) \qquad\qquad (3.20) \qquad\qquad (1.88)$$

In (4.46), the t-statistic for the null hypothesis $\gamma = 0$ is -1.22. Since the critical value of the τ_μ statistic is -2.89 at the 5 percent significance level, the null hypothesis of a unit root is not rejected at conventional significance levels. Again, the power of this test will have been reduced if the drift term does not belong in the model. To test for the presence of the drift, use the ϕ_1 statistic. The sample value of F for the restriction $a_0 = \gamma = 0$ is 13.43. Since 13.43 exceeds the critical value of 4.71, we conclude that the restriction is binding. Since we do not reject $a_0 = 0$, we can test $\gamma = 0$ using a standard normal distribution. In (4.46), the test for γ is not statistically different from zero. Hence, we can conclude that the series has a unit root and a drift term.

10. TRENDS AND UNIVARIATE DECOMPOSITIONS

Nelson and Plosser's (1982) findings suggest that many economic time series have a stochastic trend plus a stationary component. Having observed a series, but not the individual components, is there any way to decompose the series into its constituent parts? Numerous economic theories suggest it is important to distinguish between temporary and permanent movements in a series. A sale (i.e., a temporary price decline) is designed to induce us to purchase now, rather than in the future. Labor economists argue that "hours supplied" is more responsive to a temporary wage increase than to a permanent increase. The idea is that workers will temporarily substitute income for leisure time. Certainly, modern theories of the consumption function that classify an individual's income into permanent and transitory components highlight the importance of such as decomposition.

Any such decomposition is straightforward if it is known that the trend in $\{y_t\}$ is purely deterministic. For example, a linear time trend induces a fixed change in each and every period. This deterministic trend can be subtracted from the actual value of y_t to obtain the stationary component.

A difficult conceptual issue arises if the trend is stochastic. For example, suppose you are asked to measure the current phase of the business cycle. If the trend in GDP is stochastic, how is it possible to tell if GDP is above or below trend? The traditional measurement of a recession by consecutive quarterly declines in real GDP is not helpful. After all, if GDP has a deterministic trend component, a negative realization for the stationary component may be outweighed by the positive deterministic trend component.

If it is possible to decompose a sequence into its separate permanent and stationary components, the issue can be solved. To better understand the nature of stochastic trends, note that—in contrast to a deterministic trend—a stochastic trend increases *on average* by a fixed amount each period. For example, consider the random walk plus drift model:

$$y_t = y_{t-1} + a_0 + \varepsilon_t$$

Since $E\varepsilon_t = 0$, the *average* change in y_t is the deterministic constant a_0. Of course, in any period t, the actual change will differ from a_0 by the stochastic quantity ε_t. Yet each sequential change in $\{y_t\}$ adds to its level regardless of whether the change results from the deterministic or the stochastic component. As we saw in (4.5), the random walk plus drift model has no stationary component; hence, it is a model of pure trend.

The idea that a random walk plus drift is a pure trend has proven especially useful in time-series analysis. Beveridge and Nelson (1981) show how to decompose any ARIMA(p, 1, q) model into the sum of a random walk plus drift and a stationary component (i.e., the general trend plus irregular model). Before considering the general case, begin with the simple example of an ARIMA(0, 1, 2) model:

$$y_t = y_{t-1} + a_0 + \varepsilon_t + \beta_1\varepsilon_{t-1} + \beta_2\varepsilon_{t-2} \qquad (4.47)$$

If $\beta_1 = \beta_2 = 0$, (4.47) is nothing more than the pure random walk plus drift model. The introduction of the two moving average terms adds a stationary component to the $\{y_t\}$ sequence. The first step in understanding the Beveridge and Nelson (1981) procedure is to obtain the forecast function. For now, keep the issue simple by defining $e_t = \varepsilon_t + \beta_1\varepsilon_{t-1} + \beta_2\varepsilon_{t-2}$ so that we can write $y_t = y_{t-1} + a_0 + e_t$. Given an initial condition for y_0, the general solution for y_t is[19]

$$y_t = a_0 t + y_0 + \sum_{i=1}^{t} e_i \qquad (4.48)$$

Updating by s periods, we obtain

$$y_{t+s} = a_0(t+s) + y_0 + \sum_{i=1}^{t+s} e_i \qquad (4.49)$$

Substituting (4.48) into (4.49) so as to eliminate y_0 yields

$$y_{t+s} = a_0 s + y_t + \sum_{i=1}^{s} e_{t+i} \qquad (4.50)$$

To express the solution for y_{t+s} in terms of $\{\varepsilon_t\}$ rather than $\{e_t\}$, note that

$$\sum_{i=1}^{s} e_{t+i} = \sum_{i=1}^{s} \varepsilon_{t+i} + \beta_1 \sum_{i=1}^{s} \varepsilon_{t-1+i} + \beta_2 \sum_{i=1}^{s} \varepsilon_{t-2+i} \qquad (4.51)$$

so that the solution for y_{t+s} can be written as

$$y_{t+s} = a_0 s + y_t + \sum_{i=1}^{s} \varepsilon_{t+i} + \beta_1 \sum_{i=1}^{s} \varepsilon_{t-1+i} + \beta_2 \sum_{i=1}^{s} \varepsilon_{t-2+i} \qquad (4.52)$$

Now consider the forecast of y_{t+s} for various values of s. Since all values of $E_t \varepsilon_{t+i} = 0$ for $i > 0$, it follows that

$$E_t y_{t+1} = a_0 + y_t + \beta_1 \varepsilon_t + \beta_2 \varepsilon_{t-1}$$
$$E_t y_{t+2} = 2a_0 + y_t + (\beta_1 + \beta_2)\varepsilon_t + \beta_2 \varepsilon_{t-1}$$
$$\cdots$$
$$E_t y_{t+s} = sa_0 + y_t + (\beta_1 + \beta_2)\varepsilon_t + \beta_2 \varepsilon_{t-1} \qquad (4.53)$$

Here, the forecasts for all $s > 1$ are equal to the expression $sa_0 + y_t + (\beta_1 + \beta_2)\varepsilon_t + \beta_2 \varepsilon_{t-1}$. Thus, the forecast function converges to a linear function of the forecast horizon s; the slope of the function equals a_0 and the level equals $y_t + (\beta_1 + \beta_2)\varepsilon_t + \beta_2 \varepsilon_{t-1}$. This stochastic level can be called the value of the stochastic trend at t and is denoted by μ_t. This trend plus the deterministic value $a_0 s$ constitutes the forecast $E_t y_{t+s}$. There are several interesting points to note:

1. The trend is defined to be the conditional expectation of the limiting value of the forecast function. In lay terms, the trend is the "long-term" forecast. This forecast will differ at each period t as additional realizations of $\{\varepsilon_t\}$ become available. At any period t, the stationary component of the series is the difference between y_t and the trend μ_t. Hence, the stationary component of the series is

$$y_t - \mu_t = -(\beta_1 + \beta_2)\varepsilon_t - \beta_2 \varepsilon_{t-1} \qquad (4.54)$$

   At any point in time, the trend and the stationary components are perfectly correlated (the correlation coefficient being -1).

2. By definition, ε_t is the innovation in y_t and the variance of the innovation is σ^2. Since the change in the trend resulting from a change in ε_t is $1 + \beta_1 + \beta_2$, the variance of the innovation in the trend can exceed the variance of y_t itself. If $(1 + \beta_1 + \beta_2)^2 > 1$, the trend is more volatile than y_t since the negative correlation between μ_t and the stationary component act to smooth the $\{y_t\}$ sequence.

3. The trend is a random walk plus drift. Since the trend at t is μ_t, it follows that $\mu_t = y_t + (\beta_1 + \beta_2)\varepsilon_t + \beta_2\varepsilon_{t-1}$. Hence,

$$\Delta\mu_t = \Delta y_t + (\beta_1 + \beta_2)\Delta\varepsilon_t + \beta_2\Delta\varepsilon_{t-1}$$
$$= (y_t - y_{t-1}) + (\beta_1 + \beta_2)\varepsilon_t - \beta_1\varepsilon_{t-1} - \beta_2\varepsilon_{t-2}$$

Since $y_t - y_{t-1} = a_0 + \varepsilon_t + \beta_1\varepsilon_{t-1} + \beta_2\varepsilon_{t-2}$,

$$\Delta\mu_t = a_0 + (1 + \beta_1 + \beta_2)\varepsilon_t$$

Thus, $\mu_t = \mu_{t-1} + a_0 + (1 + \beta_1 + \beta_2)\varepsilon_t$, so that the trend at t is composed of the drift term a_0 plus the white-noise innovation $(1 + \beta_1 + \beta_2)\varepsilon_t$.

Beveridge and Nelson show how to recover the trend and stationary components from the data. In the example at hand, estimate the $\{y_t\}$ series using the Box–Jenkins technique. After differencing the data, an appropriately identified and estimated ARMA model will yield high-quality estimates of a_0, β_1, and β_2. Next, obtain ε_t and ε_{t-1} as the one-step-ahead forecast errors of y_t and y_{t-1}, respectively. To obtain these values, use the estimated ARMA model to make in-sample forecasts of each observation of y_{t-1} and y_t. The resulting forecast errors become ε_t and ε_{t-1}. Combining the estimated values of β_1, β_2, ε_t, and ε_{t-1} as in (4.54) yields the irregular component. Repeating for each value of t yields the entire irregular sequence. From (4.54), this irregular component is y_t minus the value of the trend; hence, the permanent component can be obtained directly.

The General ARIMA (*p*, 1, *q*) Model

The first difference of any ARIMA(p, 1, q) series has the stationary infinite-order moving average representation:

$$y_t - y_{t-1} = a_0 + \varepsilon_t + \beta_1\varepsilon_{t-1} + \beta_2\varepsilon_{t-2} + \dots$$

As in the earlier example, it is useful to define $e_t = \varepsilon_t + \beta_1\varepsilon_{t-1} + \beta_2\varepsilon_{t-2} + \beta_3\varepsilon_{t-3} + \dots$, so that it is possible to write the solution for y_{t+s} in the same form as (4.50):

$$y_{t+s} = y_t + a_0 s + \sum_{i=1}^{s} e_{t+i}$$

The next step is to express the $\{e_t\}$ sequence in terms of the various values of the $\{\varepsilon_t\}$ sequence. In this general case, (4.51) becomes

$$\sum_{i=1}^{s} e_{t+i} = \sum_{i=1}^{s} \varepsilon_{t+i} + \beta_1 \sum_{i=1}^{s} \varepsilon_{t-1+i} + \beta_2 \sum_{i=1}^{s} \varepsilon_{t-2+i} + \beta_3 \sum_{i=1}^{s} \varepsilon_{t-3+i} + \dots \quad (4.55)$$

Since $E_t\varepsilon_{t+i} = 0$, it follows that the forecast function can be written as

$$E_t\, y_{t+s} = y_t + a_0 s + \left(\sum_{i=1}^{s} \beta_i\right)\varepsilon_t + \left(\sum_{i=2}^{s+1} \beta_i\right)\varepsilon_{t-1} + \left(\sum_{i=3}^{s+2} \beta_i\right)\varepsilon_{t-2} + \dots \quad (4.56)$$

Now, to find the stochastic trend, take the limiting value of the forecast $E_t(y_{t+s} - a_0 s)$ as s becomes infinitely large. As such, the stochastic trend is[20]

$$y_t + \left(\sum_{i=1}^{\infty} \beta_i\right)\varepsilon_t + \left(\sum_{i=2}^{\infty} \beta_i\right)\varepsilon_{t-1} + \left(\sum_{i=3}^{\infty} \beta_i\right)\varepsilon_{t-2} + \dots$$

The key to operationalizing the decomposition is to recognize that y_{t+s} can be written as

$$y_{t+s} = \Delta y_{t+s} + \Delta y_{t+s-1} + \Delta y_{t+s-2} + \dots + \Delta y_{t+1} + y_t$$

As such, the trend can always be written as the current value of y_t plus the sum of all of the forecasted changes in the sequence. Abstracting from $a_0 s$, the stochastic portion of the trend is

$$\lim_{s \to \infty} E_t y_{t+s} = \lim_{s \to \infty} E_t[(y_{t+s} - y_{t+s-1}) + (y_{t+s-1} - y_{t+s-2})$$
$$+ \dots + (y_{t+2} - y_{t+1}) + (y_{t+1} - y_t)] + y_t$$
$$= \lim_{s \to \infty} E_t(\Delta y_{t+s} + \Delta y_{t+s-1} + \dots + \Delta y_{t+2} + \Delta y_{t+1}) + y_t \quad (4.57)$$

The useful feature of (4.57) is that the Box–Jenkins method allows you to calculate each value of $E_t \Delta y_{t+s}$. For each observation in your data set, find all s-step-ahead forecasts and construct the sum given by (4.57). Since the irregular component is y_t minus the sum of the deterministic and stochastic trends, the irregular component can be constructed as

$$y_t - \lim_{s \to \infty} (E_t y_{t+s} + a_0 s) = - \lim_{s \to \infty} E_t(\Delta y_{t+s} + \Delta y_{t+s-1} + \dots + \Delta y_{t+2} + \Delta y_{t+1}) - a_0 s$$

Thus, to use the Beveridge and Nelson (1981) technique:

STEP 1: Estimate the first difference of the series using the Box–Jenkins technique. Select the best-fitting ARMA(p, q) model of the $\{\Delta y_t\}$ sequence.

STEP 2: Using the best fitting ARMA model, for each time period $t = 1, \dots, T$, find the one-step-ahead, two-step-ahead, …, s-step-ahead forecasts; that is, find $E_t \Delta y_{t+s}$ for each value of t and s. For each value of t, use these forecasted values to construct the sums: $E_t[\Delta y_{t+s} + \Delta y_{t+s-1} + \dots + \Delta y_{t+1}] + y_t$. In practice, it is necessary to find a reasonable approximation to (4.57); in their own work, Beveridge and Nelson let $s = 100$. For example, for the first usable observation (i.e., $t = 1$), find the sum

$$\mu_1 = E_1(\Delta y_{101} + \Delta y_{100} + \dots + \Delta y_2) + y_1$$

The value of y_1 plus the sum of these forecasted changes equals $E_1 y_{101}$; the stochastic portion of trend in period 1 is $E_1 y_{101} - a_0 s$ and the deterministic portion is $a_0 s$. Similarly, for $t = 2$, construct

$$\mu_2 = E_2(\Delta y_{102} + \Delta y_{101} + \dots + \Delta y_3) + y_2$$

If there are T observations in your data set, the trend component for the last period is

$$\mu_T = E_T(\Delta y_{T+100} + \Delta y_{T+99} + \dots + \Delta y_{T+1}) + y_T$$

The entire sequence of constructed trends (i.e., $\mu_1, \mu_2, \ldots, \mu_T$) constitutes the $\{\mu_t\}$ sequence.

STEP 3: Form the irregular component at t by subtracting the stochastic portion of the trend at t from the value of y_t. Thus, for each observation t, the irregular component is $-E_t(\Delta y_{t+100} + \Delta y_{t+99} + \ldots + \Delta y_1)$.

Note that for many series the value of s can be quite small. For example, in the ARIMA(0, 1, 2) model of (4.47), the value of s can be set equal to 2 since all forecasts for $s > 2$ are equal to zero. If the ARMA model that is estimated in Step 1 has slowly decaying autoregressive components, the value of s should be large enough that the s-step-ahead forecasts converge to the deterministic change a_0.

Two Examples: The file PANEL.XLS contains quarterly values of the real Canadian dollar for the 1980:1 through 2002:2 period. As you can verify, the log of the series can be well estimated by the ARIMA(0, 1, 1) process

$$\Delta y_t = -0.0018 + \varepsilon_t + 0.363\varepsilon_{t-1}$$

where Δy_t is the logarithmic change in the real Canadian dollar.

Step 2 requires that for each observation, we form the one-step-ahead through s-step-ahead forecasts. For this model, the mechanics are trivial since for each period t, the one-step-ahead forecast is

$$E_t\Delta y_{t+1} = -0.0018 + 0.363\varepsilon_t$$

and all other s-step-ahead forecasts are -0.0018.

Thus, for each observation t, the summation $E_t(\Delta y_{t+100} + \Delta y_{t+99} + \ldots + \Delta y_{t+1})$ is equal to $-100(0.0018) + 0.363\varepsilon_t$. For example, for 1980:Q2 (the first usable observation in the sample), the *stochastic* portion of the trend is $y_{1980:Q2} + 0.363\varepsilon_{1980:Q2}$ and the temporary portion of $y_{1980:Q2}$ is $-0.363\varepsilon_{1980:Q2}$. Repeating for each point in the data set yields the irregular and permanent components of the sequence. The estimated ARIMA(0, 1, 1) model is the special case of (4.47) in which β_2 is set equal to zero. As such, you should be able to write the equivalent of (4.48) – (4.54) for the real Canadian dollar.

We have verified that the real U.S. GDP is a unit root process. If you estimate (4.46) without the lagged value $lrgdp_{t-1}$, you will obtain

$$\Delta lrgdp_t = 0.0050 + 0.256\Delta lrgdp_{t-1} + 0.150\Delta lrgdp_{t-2}$$
$$(5.03) \quad (3.03) \quad\quad\quad (1.94)$$

Now it is more difficult to calculate the sum of the forecasted changes. Nevertheless, it is worthwhile to illustrate the process for the first few values. In 1960:2 and 1960:3, the values of $\Delta lrgdp_t$ were -0.004947 and 0.001848, respectively. Thus, conditional on the information available in 1960:3, the one-step-ahead forecast for 1960:4 is -0.0002691 [$= (0.256)(0.001848) + (0.150)(-0.004947)$] and the two-step-ahead forecast is 0.0002083 [$= (0.256)(-0.0002691) + (0.150)(0.001848)$]. The forecasts quickly converge to zero after a few periods. Adding up all such forecasted changes, you should obtain 1.2848 E–5. If you add this sum to the $lrgdp_{1960:3}$ ($= 3.38$) and take the anti-log, you find the permanent component of real GDP for 1960:3. Since the sum of the forecasted changes is so close to zero, the actual value and the permanent component are virtually identical.

Repeating this process for all observations in the data set yields the time path of the trend component of real GDP. If you were to plot the trend along with the actual values, you would find that the two series virtually overlap. Since the autoregressive coefficients (i.e., 0.256 and 0.150) are so small, virtually all of the movements in the trend component of the real GDP series are permanent.

An Alternative Decomposition

The Beveridge and Nelson (1981) decomposition has proven especially useful in that it provides a straightforward method to decompose any ARIMA(p, 1, q) process into a temporary and a permanent component. However, it is important to note that *the Beveridge and Nelson decomposition is not unique.* Equations (4.53) and (4.54) provide an example in which the Beveridge and Nelson decomposition forces the innovation in the trend and the stationary components to be perfectly correlated.

In fact, this result applies to the more general ARIMA(p, 1, q) model. Obtaining the irregular component as the difference between y_t and its trend forces the correlation coefficient between the innovations to equal -1. However, there is no reason to constrain the two innovations in the two components to be perfectly correlated. To illustrate the point using a specific example, consider the general trend plus noise model:

$$y_t = y_0 + a_0 t + \sum_{i=1}^{t} \varepsilon_i + \eta_t$$

The deterministic portion of the trend is $y_0 + a_0 t$, the stochastic trend is $\Sigma \varepsilon_i$ and the irregular component is η_t. The stochastic trend and the noise components are uncorrelated because $E(\varepsilon_i \eta_t) = 0$. Thus, the Beveridge and Nelson methodology would incorrectly identify the trend and the irregular components because it would force the two innovations to be perfectly correlated.

Now consider the correct way to identify the two components of the sequence. In Section 2, this general trend plus noise model was shown to have an equivalent ARIMA(0, 1, 1) representation such that

$$E\Delta y_t = 0; \quad \text{var}(\Delta y_t) = \sigma^2 + 2\sigma_\eta^2, \text{ and } \text{cov}(\Delta y_t, \Delta y_{t-1}) = -\sigma_\eta^2 \quad (4.58)$$

Hence, it is possible to represent the first difference of the trend plus noise model as the MA(1) process

$$\Delta y_t = a_0 + e_t + \beta_1 e_{t-1} \quad (4.59)$$

where e_t is an independent white-noise disturbance. The notation e_t is designed to indicate that shocks to Δy_t come from two sources: ε_t and η_t. The problem is to decompose the estimated values of $\{e_t\}$ into these two source components.

In this instance, it is possible to recover, or *identify*, the individual $\{\varepsilon_t\}$ and $\{\eta_t\}$ shocks from the estimation of (4.59). The appropriate use of the Box–Jenkins methodology will yield estimates of a_0, β_1, and the elements of the $\{e_t\}$ sequence. Given the coefficient estimates, it is possible to form

$$\text{Var}(\Delta y_t) = \text{var}(e_t + \beta_1 e_{t-1}) = (1 + \beta_1)^2 \text{var}(e_t)$$

and

$$\text{Cov}(\Delta y_t, \Delta y_{t-1}) = \beta_1 \text{var}(e_t)$$

However, these estimates of the variance and covariance are not arbitrary; for (4.59) to satisfy the restrictions of (4.58) it must be the case that

$$(1 + \beta_1)^2 \text{var}(e_t) = \sigma^2 + 2\sigma_\eta^2$$

and

$$\beta_1 \text{var}(e_t) = -\sigma_\eta^2$$

Now that we have estimated β_1 and var(e_t), it is possible to recover σ^2 and σ_η^2 from the data. The individual values of the $\{\varepsilon_t\}$ and $\{\eta_t\}$ sequences can be recovered as well. From the forecast function, $E_t y_{t+1} = y_t + a_0 - \eta_t$. Hence, it is possible to use one-step-ahead forecasts from (4.59) to find $E_t \Delta y_{t+1} = a_0 + \beta_1 e_t$, so that $E_t y_{t+1} = y_t + a_0 + \beta_1 e_t$. Since the two forecasts must be equivalent, it follows that

$$\beta_1 e_t = -\eta_t$$

Thus, the estimated values of $\beta_1 e_t$ can be used to identify the entire $\{\eta_t\}$ sequence. Given $\{e_t\}$ and $\{\eta_t\}$, the values of $\{\varepsilon_t\}$ can be obtained from $\Delta y_t = a_0 + \varepsilon_t + \Delta \eta_t$. For each value of t, form $\varepsilon_t = \Delta y_t - a_0 - \Delta \eta_t$ using the known values of Δy_t and the estimated values of a_0 and $\Delta \eta_t$.

The point is that it is possible to decompose a series such that the correlation between the trend and irregular components is zero. The example illustrates an especially important point. To decompose a series into a random walk plus drift and a stationary irregular component, it is necessary to specify the correlation coefficient between innovations in the trend and the irregular components. We have seen two ways to decompose an ARIMA(0, 1, 1) model. In terms of (4.58) and (4.59), the Beveridge and Nelson technique adds the restriction that

$$E\varepsilon_t \eta_t / \sigma \sigma_\eta = 1$$

so that the innovations are perfectly correlated, while the second decomposition adds the restriction

$$E\varepsilon_t \eta_t = 0$$

In fact, the correlation coefficient between the two components can be any number in the interval -1 to $+1$. Without the extra restriction concerning the correlation between the innovations, the trend and stationary components cannot be identified; in a sense, we are an equation short. This result carries over to more complicated models since it is always necessary to "cleave" or "partition" the contemporaneous movement of a series into its two constituent parts. The problem is important because economic theory does not always provide the relationship between the two innovations. Yet, *without a priori knowledge of the relationship between innovations in the trend and stationary components, the decomposition of a series into a random walk plus drift and a stationary component is not unique.*

What if ε_t and η_t are uncorrelated but you incorrectly use a Beveridge and Nelson (1981) decomposition to obtain the temporary and permanent components? Clearly, the fitted values are invariant to the form of the decomposition. Equation (4.54) has an ARIMA(0, 1, 1) representation that you should properly capture using Step 1 of the Beveridge and Nelson method. As such, there is no way for you to determine that the assumption of perfectly correlated innovations is incorrect. The issue has nothing to do with the correct form of the ARIMA model; rather, the problem is the way in which the innovations in the trend and irregular components are partitioned.

What will the researcher incorrectly partitioning the variances find? Using a Beveridge and Nelson decomposition for an ARIMA(0, 1, 1) model—see (4.54) with $\beta_2 = 0$—the researcher will set the irregular component equal to $-\beta_1$ multiplied by the entire innovation in y_t (i.e., $\varepsilon_t + \eta_t$). If, in fact, the innovations are uncorrelated, the actual value of the irregular component at t is η_t. The dilemma is that there is no way to identify the "true" model using sample data. Any univariate decomposition necessitates that the researcher arbitrarily specify the correlation between the two innovations.

Watson (1986) decomposes the logarithm of GNP under the two alternative assumptions concerning the innovations in the trend and the irregular. Using a Beveridge and Nelson decomposition, he estimates the ARIMA(1, 1, 0) model (with standard errors in parenthesis):

$$\Delta y_t = 0.005 + 0.406\Delta y_{t-1} + \varepsilon_t \qquad \sigma = 0.0103$$
$$(0.001) \qquad (0.077)$$

Assuming that innovations in the trend and irregular components are uncorrelated, Watson estimates $y_t = \mu_t + A(L)\eta_t$:[21]

$$\Delta\mu_t = 0.008 + \varepsilon_t \qquad\qquad \sigma = 0.0057$$
$$(0.001)$$

$$A(L)\eta_t = (1 - 1.501L + 0.577L^2)\eta_t \quad \sigma_\eta = 0.0076$$
$$(0.121) \quad (0.125)$$

The short-term forecasts of the two models are quite similar. The standard error of the one-step-ahead forecast of this second model is slightly smaller than that of the first: $(\sigma^2 + \sigma_\eta^2)^{1/2} \cong 0.0095$ is slightly smaller than 0.0103. However, the long-run properties of the two models are quite different. For example, writing $\Delta y_t = (0.005 + \varepsilon_t)/(1-0.406L)$ yields the impulse response function using Beveridge and Nelson decomposition. The sum of the coefficients for this impulse response function is 1.68. Hence, a one-unit innovation will eventually increase log(GNP) by a full 1.68 units. Since all coefficients are positive, following the initial shock, y_t steadily increases to its new level. In contrast, the sum of the impulse response coefficients in the second model is about 0.57. All coefficients beginning with lag 4 are negative. As such, a one-unit innovation in y_t has a larger effect in the short run than in the long run.

The Hodrick–Prescott Decomposition

Another method of decomposing a series into a trend and a stationary component has been developed by Hodrick and Prescott (1997). Suppose you observe the values y_1

through y_T and want to decompose the series into a trend $\{\mu_t\}$ and a stationary component $y_t - \mu_t$. Consider the sum of squares

$$\frac{1}{T}\sum_{t=1}^{T}(y_t - \mu_t)^2 + \frac{\lambda}{T}\sum_{t=2}^{T-1}[(\mu_{t+1} - \mu_t) - (\mu_t - \mu_{t-1})]^2$$

where λ is a constant and T is the number of usable observations.

The problem is to select the $\{\mu_t\}$ sequence so as to minimize this sum of squares. In the minimization problem λ is an arbitrary constant reflecting the "cost" or penalty of incorporating fluctuations into the trend. In many applications, including Hodrick and Prescott (1984) and Farmer (1993), λ is set equal to 1,600. Increasing the value of λ acts to "smooth out" the trend. If $\lambda = 0$, the sum of squares is minimized when $y_t = \mu_t$; the trend is equal to y_t itself. As $\lambda \to \infty$, the sum of squares is minimized when $(\mu_{t+1} - \mu_t) = (\mu_t - \mu_{t-1})$. As such, as $\lambda \to \infty$, the change in the trend is constant; the result is that there is a linear time trend. Intuitively, for large values of λ, the Hodrick–Prescott (HP) decomposition forces the change in the trend (i.e., $\Delta\mu_{t+1} - \Delta\mu_t$) to be as small as possible. This occurs when the trend is linear.

The benefit of the Hodrick–Prescott decomposition is that it uses the same method to extract the trend from a set of variables. For example, many real business cycle models indicate that all variables will have the same stochastic trend. A Beveridge and Nelson decomposition separately applied to each variable will not yield the same trend for each. Figure 4.14 shows a HP decomposition applied to real U.S. GDP, consumption, and investment. You can see that the smoothed lines

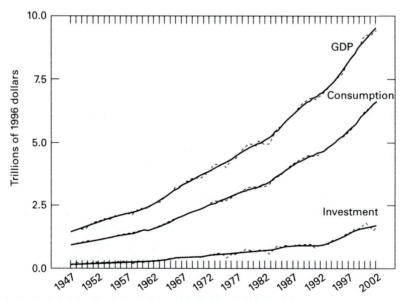

FIGURE 4.14   Real GDP, Consumption and Investment

(representing the trends extracted by the HP decomposition) are such that the permanent components of each series account for the majority of the variation. However, a word of warning is in order. Since the HP filter is a function that smoothes the trend, it has been shown to introduce spurious fluctuations into the irregular component of a series.

11. PANEL UNIT ROOT TESTS

Section 6 presented some strong evidence that the three real exchange rate series shown in Figure 4.8 are unit root processes. Of course, it is possible that the series are mean reverting but the Dickey–Fuller tests have little power to detect the fact that the series are stationary. One way to obtain a more powerful test is to pool the estimates from a number of separate series and then test the pooled value. The theory underlying the test is very simple: if you have n independent and unbiased estimates of a parameter, the mean of the estimates is also unbiased. More importantly, so long as the estimates are independent, the central limit theory suggests that the sample mean will be normally distributed around the true mean.

Im, Pesaran, and Shin (2002) show how to use this result to construct a test for a unit root when you have a number of similar time-series variables (i.e., a panel). The only complicating factor is that the OLS estimates for γ in the Dickey–Fuller test are biased downward. Suppose you have n series each containing T observations. For each series, perform an ADF test of the form

$$\Delta y_{it} = a_{i0} + \gamma_i y_{it-1} + a_{i2}t + \sum_{j=1}^{p_i} \beta_{ij}\Delta y_{it-j} + \varepsilon_{it} \quad i = 1, \cdots, n \qquad (4.60)$$

Because the lag lengths can differ across equations, you should perform separate lag length tests for each equation. Moreover, you may choose to exclude the deterministic time trend. However, if the trend is included in one equation, it should be included in all. Once you have estimated the various γ_i, obtain the t-statistic or the null hypothesis $\gamma_i = 0$. In a traditional Dickey–Fuller test, each of these t-statistics—denoted by t_i—would be compared to the appropriate critical value reported in Table A. However, for the panel unit root test, form the sample mean of the t-statistics as

$$\bar{t} = (1/n)\sum_{i=1}^{n} t_i \qquad (4.61)$$

It is straightforward to construct the statistic Z_{tbar} as

$$Z_{\text{tbar}} = \frac{\sqrt{n}\left[\bar{t} - E(\bar{t})\right]}{\sqrt{\text{var}(\bar{t})}}$$

where $E\bar{t}$ and $\text{var}(\bar{t})$ denote the theoretical mean and variance of $\bar{t}$. If the OLS estimates of the individual t_i were unbiased, the value of $E\bar{t}$ would be zero. However, to correct for the bias, the values $E\bar{t}$ and $\text{var}(\bar{t})$ can be calculated by Monte Carlo simulation. Im, Pesaran, and Shin (IPS) report these values as follows:

T	6	8	10	15	20	50	100	500
$E\bar{t}$	−1.52	−1.50	−1.50	−1.51	−1.52	−1.53	−1.53	−1.53
$\text{var}(\bar{t})$	1.75	1.23	1.07	0.92	0.85	0.76	0.74	0.72

Im, Pesaran, and Shin show that Z_{tbar} has an asymptotic standardized normal distribution.[22] This fact should not be too surprising. If each of the estimated values of the various t_i are independent, the central limit theorem indicates that deviation of the sample average from the true mean will have a normal distribution. Rejecting the null hypothesis $Z_{tbar} = 0$ is equivalent to accepting the alternative hypothesis that *at least* one value of the γ_i differs from zero. After all, if the sample average of the t-statistics is significantly different at least one of the values of γ_i is statistically different from zero.

The proof that Z_{tbar} has a normal distribution relies on very large samples. For the sample sizes typically used by applied econometricians, it is preferable to use the critical values contained in Table 4.7. Notice that the critical values depend on n, T and whether a time trend is included in (4.60). For example, if you have seven series each containing 50 observations and you include a time trend in (4.60), the 5 percent critical value for $\bar{t}$ is −2.67. If you had used the Dickey–Fuller test, the corresponding critical value for each of the seven values of t_i would be −3.50 (see Table A). Note that is necessary to have values of T and n that are greater than 4. Large values of T are standard in time-series econometrics. However, if n is too small, the calculation of $\bar{t}$ will not be meaningful.

Table 4.7   Selected Critical Values for the IPS Panel Unit Root Test

N/T	25			50			70		
	10%	5%	1%	10%	5%	1%	10%	5%	1%
				No Time Trend					
5	−2.04	−2.18	−2.46	−2.02	−2.15	−2.42	−2.02	−2.15	−2.40
7	−1.95	−2.08	−2.32	−1.95	−2.06	−2.28	−1.95	−2.06	−2.28
10	−1.88	−1.99	−2.19	−1.88	−1.98	−2.16	−1.88	−1.98	−2.16
25	−1.75	−1.82	−1.94	−1.75	−1.81	−1.93	−1.75	−1.81	−1.93
50	−1.69	−1.73	−1.82	−1.68	−1.73	−1.81	−1.68	−1.73	−1.73
				Time Trend					
5	−2.65	−2.80	−3.09	−2.62	−2.76	−3.02	−2.62	−2.75	−3.00
7	−2.58	−2.70	−2.94	−2.56	−2.67	−2.88	−2.55	−2.66	−2.67
10	−2.51	−2.62	−2.82	−2.50	−2.59	−2.77	−2.49	−2.58	−2.75
25	−2.39	−2.45	−2.58	−2.38	−2.44	−2.55	−2.38	−2.44	−2.54
50	−2.33	−2.37	−2.45	−2.32	−2.36	−2.44	−2.32	−2.36	−2.44

As mentioned in Section 6, the file PANEL.XLS contains quarterly values of the real effective exchange rates (CPI based) for Australia, Canada, France, Germany, Japan, the Netherlands, the United Kingdom, and the United States over the 1980:$Q1$ to 2002:$Q2$ period. Since Purchasing Power Parity (PPP) does not allow for a deterministic time trend, each was estimated in the form of (4.60) but without the trend. The results of the individual Dickey–Fuller tests for the logarithmic values of the real rates are shown in the first three columns of Table 4.8. For example, the Australian equation used five lags of $\{\Delta y_{it}\}$ and the estimated value of γ_i was –0.083. Notice that the eight t-statistics for the null hypothesis $\gamma_i = 0$ have an average value of –1.967. Since each series has 90 observations ($T = 90$), the critical values at the 10 percent and 5 percent significance levels are about –1.95 and –2.06, respectively. Hence, at the 10 percent significance level, it is possible to reject the null hypothesis that all values of $\gamma_i = 0$. If the Netherlands is excluded, the average falls to –1.833 and the null hypothesis cannot be rejected at any conventional significance level.

One problem with the results is that the residuals from the individual equation are contemporaneously correlated in the $E\varepsilon_{it}\varepsilon_{ji} \neq 0$. For example, the correlation coefficient between the residuals from the French and German equations is 0.585. The explanation is that the shocks that affect the French real rate are likely to affect the German real rate. In this circumstance, a common strategy is to subtract a common time effect from each observation. At time period t, the mean value of each series is

$$\bar{y}_t = (1/n)\sum_{i=1}^{n} y_{it}$$

The method is to subtract this common mean from each observation (i.e., form $y_{it}^* = y_{it} - \bar{y}_t$) and estimate (4.60) using the values of y_{it}^*. In the example at hand, y_{it} is the logarithm of real rate i at period t; hence, for each time period t, the average of these logarithmic values was subtracted from y_{it}. The last three columns of Table 4.8

Table 4.8 The Panel Unit Root Tests for Real Exchange Rates

	Lags	Estimated γ_i	t-statistic	Lags	Estimated γ_i	t-statistic
		Log of the Real Rate			Minus the Common Time Effect	
Australia	5	–0.083	–2.324	5	–0.087	–2.279
Canada	1	–0.019	–0.952	1	–0.079	–0.912
France	1	–0.086	–2.402	1	–0.093	–2.463
Germany	6	–0.056	–1.251	6	–0.055	–1.390
Japan	3	–0.047	–1.882	3	–0.042	–1.780
Netherlands	6	–0.134	–2.902	6	–0.112	–2.137
U.K.	1	–0.074	–2.233	1	–0.081	–2.117
U.S.	3	–0.047	–1.787	3	–0.053	–1.883

show the test results for the $\{y_{it}^*\}$ sequences. Notice that the lag lengths have not changed but the average value of the t-statistics is -1.870. As such, it is not possible to reject the null hypothesis that the real rates are mean reverting.

Limitations of the Panel Unit Root Test

1. The null hypothesis for the IPS test is $\gamma_i = \gamma_2 = \ldots = \gamma_n = 0$. Rejection of the null hypothesis means that *at least* one of the γ_i's differs from zero. Thus, it is possible for only one or two values of the γ_i to differ from zero and still reject the null hypothesis. Unfortunately, there is no particular way of knowing which of the γ_i are statistically different from zero. As illustrated by the Netherlands, the results of a panel unit root test may be dependent on the choice of the time-series variables included in the panel.

2. At this point, there is substantial disagreement about the asymptotic theory underlying the test. Sample size can approach infinity by increasing n for a given T, increasing T for a given n, or by simultaneously increasing n and T. Unfortunately, many of the important findings about the various tests are sensitive to this seemingly innocuous choice among the various assumptions. For example, the critical values reported in Table 4.7 are invariant to augmenting (4.60) with lagged changes for large T. However, for small T and large n, the critical values are dependent on the magnitudes of the various β_{ij}.

3. The test requires that that the error terms from (4.60) be serially uncorrelated and contemporaneously uncorrelated. You need to determine the values of p_i to ensure that the autocorrelations of $\{\varepsilon_{it}\}$ are zero. Nevertheless, the errors may be contemporaneously correlated in that $E\varepsilon_{it}\varepsilon_{jt} \neq 0$. If the regression residuals are correlated across equations, the critical values in Table 4.7 are not applicable. The example above illustrates a common technique to correct for correlation across equations. As in the example, you can subtract a common time effect from each observation. However, there is no assurance that this correction will completely eliminate the correlation. Moreover, it is quite possible that $\{\bar{y}_t\}$ is nonstationary. Subtracting a nonstationary component from each sequence is clearly at odds with the notion that the variables are stationary. As an alternative, many researchers would generate their own critical values by bootstrapping the value of $\bar{t}$. Some of the details are described in the appendix.

There are a number of other panel unit root tests in the literature. The Maddala–Wu (1999) test is similar to the IPS test but requires that you bootstrap your own critical values. The Levin–Lin–Chu (2002) test has the more restrictive alternative hypothesis $\gamma_1 = \gamma_2 = \ldots = \gamma_n$. Nevertheless, the cautions listed above are applicable to all of the panel unit root tests. An interesting comparison of the tests can be found in the August 2001 issue of the *Journal of Money Credit and Banking*. Three different articles perform various panel unit roots for a number of real exchange rate series.

12. SUMMARY AND CONCLUSIONS

The trend in a series can contain both stochastic and deterministic components. Differencing can remove a stochastic trend and detrending can eliminate a deterministic trend. However, it is inappropriate to difference a trend-stationary series and to detrend a series containing a stochastic trend. The resultant irregular component of the series can be estimated using Box–Jenkins techniques.

In contrast to traditional theory, the consensus view is that most macroeconomic time series contain a stochastic trend. In finite samples, the correlogram of a unit root process will decay slowly. As such, a slowly decaying ACF can be indicative of a unit root or a near-unit root process. The issue is especially important since many economic time series appear to have a nonstationary component. When you encounter such a time-series, do you detrend, do you first-difference, or do you do nothing since the series might be stationary?

Adherents of the Box–Jenkins methodology recommend differencing a nonstationary variable or a variable with a near-unit root. For very short-term forecasts, the form of the trend is nonessential. Differencing also reveals the pattern of the other autoregressive and moving average coefficients. However, as the forecast horizon expands, the precise form of the trend becomes increasingly important. Stationarity implies the absence of a trend and long-run mean reversion. A deterministic trend implies steady increases (or decreases) into the infinite future. Forecasts of a series with a stochastic trend converge to a steady level. As illustrated by the distinction between real business cycles and the more traditional formulations, the nature of the trend may have important theoretical implications.

The usual t-statistics and F-statistics are not applicable to determine whether or not a sequence has a unit root. Dickey and Fuller (1979, 1981) provide the appropriate test statistics to determine whether a series contains a unit root, a unit root plus drift, and/or a unit root plus drift plus a time trend. The tests can also be modified to account for seasonal unit roots. Structural breaks will bias the Dickey–Fuller test towards the nonrejection of a unit root. Perron (1989) shows how it is possible to incorporate a known structural change into the tests for unit roots. Caution needs to be exercised because it is always possible to argue that structural change has occurred; each year has something different about it than the previous year. In an interesting extension, Perron and Vogelsang (1992) and Vogelsang and Perron (1998) show how to test for a unit root when the precise date of the structural break is unknown. If the residuals of a unit root process are heterogeneous or weakly dependent, the alternative Phillips–Perron (1988) test can be used.

All the aforementioned tests have very low power to distinguish between a unit root and a near-unit root process. A trend stationary process can be arbitrarily well approximated by a unit root process and a unit root process can be arbitrarily well approximated by a trend-stationary process. Moreover, the testing procedure is confounded by the presence of the deterministic regressors (i.e., the intercept and the deterministic trend). Too many or too few regressors reduce the power of the tests. Panel unit root tests can be used to increase the power of a unit root test.

An alternative is to take a Bayesian approach and to avoid specific hypothesis testing altogether. West and Harrison (1989) provide an accessible introduction to Bayesian analysis in the context of regression analysis. Zellner (1988) discusses some of the philosophical underpinnings of the approach and Leamer (1986) provides a straightforward application to estimating the determinants of inflation. Sims (1988) is the standard reference for the Bayesian approach to unit roots.

Decomposing real GNP into its permanent and temporary components, as in Beveridge and Nelson (1981), indicates that innovations in the stochastic trend account for a sizable proportion of the period-to-period movements. However, the Beveridge and Nelson decomposition is not unique in that it forces the correlation coefficient between innovations in the trend and irregular components to be unity. In Chapter 5 you will be shown a multivariate technique that allows for a unique decomposition of a series into its temporary and permanent components.

QUESTIONS AND EXERCISES

1. Given an initial condition for y_0, find the solution for y_t. Also find the s-step-ahead forecast $E_t y_{t+s}$.

    a. $y_t = y_{t-1} + \varepsilon_t + 0.5\varepsilon_{t-1}$ **b.** $y_t = 1.1y_{t-1} + \varepsilon_t$

    c. $y_t = y_{t-1} + 1 + \varepsilon_t$ **d.** $y_t = y_{t-1} + t + \varepsilon_t$

    e. $y_t = \mu_t + \eta_t + 0.5\eta_{t-1}$, where $\mu_t = \mu_{t-1} + \varepsilon_t$

    f. $y_t = \mu_t + \eta_t + 0.5\eta_{t-1}$, where $\mu_t = 0.5 + \mu_{t-1} + \varepsilon_t$

    g. How can you make the models of parts b and d stationary?

    h. Does model e have an ARIMA(p, 1, q) representation?

2. Given the initial condition y_0, find the general solution and the forecast function (i.e., $E_t y_{t+s}$) for the following variants of the trend plus irregular model:

    a. $y_t = \mu_t + v_t$, where $u_t = u_{t-1} + \varepsilon_t$, $v_t = (1 + \beta_1 L)\eta_t$ and $E\varepsilon_t \eta_t = 0$

    b. $y_t = \mu_t + v_t$, where $u_t = u_{t-1} + \varepsilon_t$ and $v_t = (1 + \beta_1 L)\eta_t$ and the correlation between ε_t and η_t equals unity.

    c. Find the ARIMA representation of each model.

3. Monte Carlo experiments allow you to replicate a random process so as to calculate the probability of a particular type of outcome. In a properly designed experiment, you can obtain the entire probability distribution. Consider each of the following:

    a. Suppose you toss a coin and a tetrahedron. For the coin, you get 1 point for a tail and 2 points for a head. The faces of the tetrahedron are labeled 1 through 4. For the tetrahedron, you get the number of points shown on the downward face. Your total score equals the number of points received for the coin and the tetrahedron. Of course, it is impossible to have a score of zero or 1. It is straightforward to calculate that the probabilities of scores 3, 4, and 5 equal 0.25 while the probabilities of scores 2 and 6 equal 0.125.

        i. Describe how you can design a Monte Carlo experiment to calculate these probabilities.

        ii. If your software package allows you to program such an experiment, find out how close the calculated probabilities come to the actual probabilities using 100 replications. How does your answer change if you use 1,000 replications?

    b. Replicate the Monte Carlo results that were reported in Section 4 for the t-distribution of a unit root.

    c. Suppose that a series is generated by the equation $\Delta y_t = a_0 + a_2 t + \varepsilon_t$. A researcher unaware of the actual nature of the series estimates the equation in the form $\Delta y_t = a_0 + \rho y_{t-1} + a_2 t + \varepsilon_t$. Since there is a trend and an intercept in the DGP, Figure 4.13 indicates that it is appropriate to test the null hypothesis $\rho = 0$ using a normal distribution.

        i. Perform the following Monte Carlo experiment to verify this result.

            First, select values of a_0 and a_2. If the assertion is correct, you must be able to select any nonzero values for these two coefficients. Generate a series of 100 observations using the equation $y_t = a_0 + y_{t-1} + a_2 t + \varepsilon_t$. Let the initial value of the series be a_0.

Second, estimate the series in the form $\Delta y_t = a_0 + \rho y_{t-1} + a_2 t + \varepsilon_t$ and obtain the t-statistic for the null hypothesis $\rho = 0$.

Third, repeat the first two steps 2000 times. Obtain the distribution for the calculated t-statistics.

ii. John obtained the following results using 10,000 Monte Carlo replications:

First percentile:	−2.38	Ninetieth percentile:	1.29
Fifth percentile:	−1.67	Ninety-fifth percentile:	1.67
Tenth percentile:	−1.30	Ninety-ninth percentile:	2.33
Twenty-fifth percentile:	−0.66		

Explain how John's findings are consistent with the claim that it is appropriate to test the null hypothesis $\rho = 0$ using a normal distribution.

d. In contrast to part c, suppose that a series is generated by the equation $\Delta y_t = \varepsilon_t$. A researcher unaware of the actual nature of the series estimates the equation in the form $\Delta y_t = a_0 + \rho y_{t-1} + a_2 t + \varepsilon_t$. Repeat steps 1 to 3 above using $a_0 = a_2 = 0$. How close do your results come to the Dickey–Fuller τ_τ-statistic?

4. The columns in the file REAL.XLS contain the logarithms of the real exchange rates for Canada, Japan, Germany, and the U.K. The four series are called RCAN, RGER, RJAP, and RUK, respectively. As described in Section 6, each series is constructed as $r_t = e_t + p_{ft} - p_t$ where $r = $ log of the real exchange rate, $e = $ log of the dollar price of foreign exchange, $p_{ft} = $ log of the foreign wholesale price index, and $p = $ log of the U.S. wholesale price index. All series run from February 1973 through December 1989 and each is expressed as an index number such that February 1973 $= 1.00$.

a. For each sequence, find the ACF and PACF of (i) the level of the real exchange rate; (ii) the first difference of the real exchange rate; and (iii) the detrended real exchange rate. For example, for Canada you should find

ACF

Lags 1–12:	0.951	0.917	0.897	0.869	0.847	0.819
	0.797	0.779	0.754	0.729	0.700	0.658

ACF of the First Difference

Lags 1–12:	−0.156	−0.153	0.044	−0.015	0.105	−0.074
	−0.047	0.060	−0.026	0.014	0.181	−0.115

b. Explain why is it not possible to determine whether the sequence is stationary or nonstationary by the simple examination of the ACF and PACF.

c. Including a constant, use Dickey–Fuller and Augmented Dickey–Fuller tests (with 12 monthly lags) to test whether the series are unit root processes. You should find that the t-statistics for $\gamma = 0$ are

Series	No lags	12 lags	Trend + 12 lags
RCAN:	−1.81305	−1.50810	−0.85650
RJAP:	−1.81978	−2.30579	−2.61854
RGER:	−1.64297	−2.10719	−2.09955
RUK:	−1.55877	−2.51668	−2.57493

i. The last entry in the table means that γ is more than 2.57 standard deviations from zero. A t–table indicates that at the 95 percent significance level, critical value is about 1.96 standard deviations. Why is it incorrect to conclude that the null hypothesis of a unit root can be *rejected* since the calculated *t*-statistic is more than 1.96 standard deviations from zero?

    ii. For each entry reported in the table what are the appropriate statistics to use (τ, τ_μ, or τ_τ) in order to test the null hypothesis of a unit root?

d. Determine whether an intercept term belongs in the regression equations. Determine whether the time trend should be included in the equations. Determine whether the intercept *and* the time trend belong in the equations.

e. Use the Japanese data to show that you can reject the null hypothesis of two unit roots.

5. The file QUARTERLY.XLS contains the M1NSA series used to illustrate the test for seasonal unit roots. Make the appropriate data transformations and verify the results concerning seasonal unit roots presented in Section 7.

6. The second column in the file BREAK.XLS contains the simulated data used in Section 8.

    a. Plot the data to see if you can recognize the effects of the structural break.

    b. Verify the results reported in Section 8.

    c. The third column in the file BREAK.XLS contains another simulated data series called $\{y2_t\}$ with a structural break at $t = 51$. Plot the series and compare your graph to those of Figures 4.10 and 4.11.

    d. Obtain the ACF and PACF of the $\{y2_t\}$ sequence and of the first difference of the sequence. Does the data appear to be difference stationary?

    e. If you perform a Dickey–Fuller test including a constant and a trend, you should obtain

Variable	Coeff	Standard Error	t-statistic	Significance
Constant	0.072445666	0.071447971	1.01396	0.3131
TREND	-0.000101438	0.002120465	-0.04784	0.9619
$y2_{t-1}$	-0.022398360	0.034013944	-0.65851	0.5118

    In what ways is this regression equation inadequate? What diagnostic checks would you want to perform?

    f. Estimate the equation $y2_t = a_0 + a_2 t + \mu_2 D_L$ and save the residuals. Perform a Dickey–Fuller test on the saved residuals. Perform the appropriate diagnostic tests on this regression to ensure that the residuals approximate white noise. You should conclude that the series is a unit root process with a one-time pulse at $t = 51$.

    g. Reestimate the model without the insignificant time trend. How is your answer affected?

7. The file QUARTERLY.XLS contains the real GDP data that was used to estimate (4.45).

    a. Use the series to replicate the results in Section 9.

    b. It is often argued that the oil price shock in 1973 reduced the trend growth rate of real U.S. GDP. Perform the Perron test to determine whether the series is trend stationary with a break occurring in mid-1973.

    c. Decompose the real GDP series into the temporary and permanent components using the HP filter and the Beveridge–Nelson decomposition. Plot the transitory component that you obtain from the HP filter and the one you obtain from the Beveridge–Nelson decomposition. In what ways are the two series different?

    d. Suppose that real GDP is trend stationary with a break occurring in mid-1973. Let the deviations from trend constitute the transitory component of the series. How does this transitory component compare with your answers found in part c?

8. The file PANEL.XLS contains the real exchange rate series used to perform the panel unit root tests reported in Section 11.
   a. Replicate the results of Section 11.
   b. In what way do the results of the test change if Germany and Canada are excluded from the panel? Why is it inappropriate to exclude the countries with the lowest t-statistics?
   c. Suppose that you mistakenly included a time trend in the augmented Dickey–Fuller tests. Determine how the results reported in Section 11 change.

9. Section 5 of Chapter 4 in the Programming Manual that accompanies this text illustrates a number of Monte Carlo experiments. If you have not already done so, download the manual from the Wiley Web site.
   a. Program 4.5 performs the modified coin-tossing problem using a coin and a tetrahedron. How would you modify the program so that you toss two tetrahedra?
   b. Program 4.6 shows the downward bias for the first-order AR coefficient in a sample of 100 observations. Modify the program to calculate the extent of the bias in a smaller sample.
   c. Program 4.7 calculates the Dickey–Fuller critical values for τ_μ using a sample size of 100. How would you modify the program to obtain the critical values of the τ_τ statistic?
   d. Program 4.7 also calculates the power of the τ_μ statistic. How would you modify the program to obtain the power of the τ_τ statistic?

10. Section 7 of Chapter 4 of the Programming Manual that accompanies this text contains a discussion of bootstrapping. In particular, Program 4.14 provides an example of bootstrapping regression coefficients.
   a. Use the data in MONEY_DEM.XLS to estimate the logarithmic change in real GDP ($dlrgdp_t$) as an AR(2) process. You should obtain

   $$dlrgdp_t = 0.005 + 0.251 dlrgdp_{t-1} + 0.136 dlrgdp_{t-2} + \varepsilon_t$$

   As shown in the program, construct the 95 percent confidence interval for the AR(2) coefficient 0.0136.
   b. Follow the program to obtain the bootstrap 95 percent confidence interval for the coefficient.
   c. How would you modify the program so as to obtain the bootstrap 95 percent confidence interval for the AR(1) coefficient?

ENDNOTES

1. Many treatments use the representation y_t = trend + seasonal + cyclical + noise. In this text, the term *cyclical* is avoided because it implies that cyclical economic components are deterministic.
2. A linguist might want to know why detrending entails removing the deterministic trend and not the stochastic trend. The reason is purely historical; originally, trends were viewed as deterministic. Today, subtracting the deterministic time trend is still called *detrending*.
3. If $B(L)$ is of infinite order, it is assumed that $\Sigma \beta_i^2$ is finite.
4. If only $B(L)$ has a unit root, the process is not invertible. The $\{y_t\}$ sequence may be stationary, but the usual estimation techniques are inappropriate. If both $A(L)$ and $B(L)$ have unit roots, there is the *common factor problem* discussed in Chapter 2. The unit root can be factored from $A(L)$ and $B(L)$.
5. Here we use the notation e_t, rather than ε_t, to highlight that the residuals from such a regression will generally not be white noise.
6. For the same reason, it is also inappropriate to use one variable that is trend stationary and another that is difference stationary. In such instances, "time" can be included as a so-called *explanatory* variable, or the variable in question can be detrended.

6. For the same reason, it is also inappropriate to use one variable that is trend stationary and another that is difference stationary. In such instances, "time" can be included as a so-called *explanatory* variable, or the variable in question can be detrended.

7. Issues concerning higher order equations, longer lag lengths, serial correlation in the residuals, structural change, and the presence of deterministic components are temporarily ignored.

8. The Dickey–Fuller critical values are all reported in Table A at the end of this text.

9. Suppose that the estimated value of γ is -1.9 (so that the estimate of a_1 is -0.9) with a standard error of 0.04. Since the estimated value of γ is 2.5 standard errors from -2 [$(2 - 1.9)/.04 = 2.5$], the Dickey–Fuller statistics indicate that we cannot reject the null hypothesis $a_1 = -2$ at the 95 percent significance level. Unless stated otherwise, the discussion in this text assumes that a_1 is positive. Also note that if there is no prior information concerning the sign of a_1, a two-tailed test can be conducted.

10. When the distribution for v_t is more complicated, the distribution of the mean may not be normal with variance σ^2/T.

11. Tests using lagged changes in the $\{\Delta y_t\}$ sequence are called augmented Dickey–Fuller tests.

12. In their simulations, Dickey and Fuller (1981) found that 90 percent of the calculated ϕ_3 statistics were 5.47 or less and that 95 percent were 6.49 or less when the actual data were generated according to the null hypothesis.

13. To give you the chance to practice (see Question 4 of the Questions and Exercises), the data of the graph and the data set runs through 1989.

14. Perron's Monte Carlo study allows for a drift and a deterministic trend. Nonetheless, the value of a_1 is biased towards unity in the presence of the deterministic trend.

15. Moreover, Evans and Savin (1981) find that for an AR(1) model, the limiting distribution of the autoregressive parameter has a normal asymptotic distribution. However, when the parameter is near one, the unit root distribution is a better finite sample approximation than the asymptotic correct distribution.

16. Campbell and Perron (1991) report that omitting a variable that is growing at least as fast as any other of the appropriately included regressors causes the power of the tests to approach zero.

17. Using the most general model in Step 1 is meant to address the problem of omitting important deterministic regressors.

18. The sample period 1960:1 to 2002:1 contains 169 total observations. Three observations are lost by creating the two lagged changes.

19. Also assume that all values of ε_i are zero for $i < 1$.

20. As an exercise, prove that the first–difference of the trend acts as a random walk plus drift. Show that $\mu_t - \mu_{t-1}$ has the intercept a_0 plus a serially uncorrelated error.

21. The assumption that ε_t and η_t are uncorrelated places restrictions on the autoregressive and moving average coefficients of Δy_t. For example, in the pure random walk plus noise model, β_1 must be negative. To avoid estimating a constrained ARIMA model, Watson estimates the trend and the irregular terms as unobserved components. Many software packages are capable of estimating such equations as time varying parameter models. Details of the procedure can be obtained in Harvey (1989).

22. The result holds for very large values of n and T.

APPENDIX: THE BOOTSTRAP

Bootstrapping is similar to a Monte Carlo experiment with one essential difference. In a Monte Carlo study, you generate the random variables from a given distribution such as the Normal. The bootstrap takes a different approach—the random variables are drawn from their observed distribution. In essence, the bootstrap uses the **plug-in principle**—the observed distribution of the random variables is the best estimate of their actual distribution.

The idea of the bootstrap was developed in Efron (1979). The key point made by Efron is that the observed data set is a random sample of size T drawn from the actual probability distribution generating the data. In a sense, the empirical distribution of the data is the best estimate of the actual distribution of the data. As such, the empirical distribution function is defined to be the discrete distribution that places a probability of $1/T$ on each of the observed values. It is the empirical distribution function—and not some prespecified distribution such as the Normal—that is used to generate the random variables. The **bootstrap sample** is a random sample of size T drawn *with* replacement from the observed data putting a probability of $1/T$ on each of the observed values.

Example: To be more specific, suppose that we have the following 10 values of x_t:

t	1	2	3	4	5	6	7	8	9	10
x_t	0.8	3.5	0.5	1.7	7.0	0.6	1.3	2.0	1.8	−0.5

The sample mean is 1.87 and the standard deviation is 2.098. The data below show three different bootstrap samples. Each bootstrap sample consists of 10 randomly selected values of x_t drawn with replacement—each of the 10 values listed above is drawn with a probability of 0.1. It might seem that this resampling repeatedly selects the same sample. However, by sampling with replacement, some elements of x_t will appear more than once in the bootstrap sample. The first three bootstrap samples might look like this:

t	1	2	3	4	5	6	7	8	9	10	μ_i^*
x_1^*	3.5	1.7	−0.5	0.5	1.8	2.0	1.7	0.6	0.6	7.0	1.89
x_2^*	−0.5	0.6	0.6	0.8	1.7	7.0	1.8	3.5	1.8	0.8	1.81
x_3^*	0.5	0.6	7.0	1.3	1.3	7.0	1.3	1.8	3.5	0.6	2.49

where x_i^* denotes bootstrap sample i and μ_i^* is the sample mean.

Notice that 0.6 and 1.7 appear twice in the first bootstrap sample, 0.6, 0.8, and 1.8 appear twice in the second and 1.3 appears three times in the third bootstrap sample. Unless there is a large outlier, Efron (1979) shows that the moments of the bootstrap samples converge to the population moments as the number of bootstrap samples goes to infinity.

Bootstrapping Regression Coefficients

Suppose you have a data set with T observations and want to estimate the effects of variable x on variable y. Towards this end, you might estimate the linear regression:

$$y_t = a_0 + a_1 x_t + \varepsilon_t$$

Although the properties of the estimators are well known, you might not be confident about using standard t-tests if the estimated residuals do not appear to be normally distributed. You could perform a Monte Carlo study concerning the statistical properties of $\hat{a}_0$ and $\hat{a}_1$. However, instead of selecting various values of ε_t from a normal distribution, you can use the actual regression residuals. The technique is called the method of **bootstrapped residuals**.[1] To use the procedure, perform the following steps:

STEP 1: Estimate the model and calculate the residuals as

$$e_t = y_t - \hat{a}_0 - \hat{a}_1 x_t$$

STEP 2: Generate a bootstrap sample of the error terms containing the elements e_1^*, e_2^*, ..., e_T^*. Use the bootstrap sample to calculate a bootstrapped y series (called y^*). For each value of t running from 1 to T, calculate y_t^* as

$$y_t^* = \hat{a}_0 + \hat{a}_1 x_t + e_t^*$$

Note that the estimated values of the coefficients are treated as fixed. Moreover, the values of x_t are treated as fixed quantities so that they remain the same in the bootstrap sample.

STEP 3: Use the bootstrap sample to estimate new values of a_0 and a_1 calling the resulting values a_0^* and a_1^*.

STEP 4: Repeat Steps 2 and 3 many times and calculate the sample statistics for a_0^* and a_1^*. These should be distributed in the same way as $\hat{a}_0$ and $\hat{a}_1$. For example, you can find the 95 percent confidence interval for $\hat{a}_1$ as the interval between the lowest 2.5 percent and the highest 97.5 percent of the values of a_1^*.

Step 2 needs to be modified for a time series model due to the presence of lagged dependent variables. As such, the bootstrap $\{y_t^*\}$ sequence is constructed in a slightly different manner. Consider the simple AR(2) model:

$$y_t = a_0 + a_1 y_{t-1} + a_2 y_{t-2} + \varepsilon_t$$

As in Step 2, we can construct a bootstrap sample of the error terms containing the elements e_1^*, e_2^*, ..., e_T^*. Now, construct the bootstrap $\{y_t^*\}$ sequence using this sample of error terms. In particular, given the estimates of a_0, a_1, and a_2 and two initial conditions for y_1^* and y_2^*, the remaining values of the $\{y_t^*\}$ sequence can be constructed using

$$y_t^* = \hat{a}_0 + \hat{a}_1 y_{t-1}^* + \hat{a}_2 y_{t-2}^* + e_t^*$$

For an AR(p) model, the initial conditions for y_1^* through y_p^* are usually selected by random draws from the actual $\{y_t\}$ sequence.[2] To avoid problems concerning the selection of the initial condition, it is typical to construct a bootstrap sample with $T + 50$ elements and to discard the first 50.

Example 1: In Sections 2 and 9, the logarithmic change in real U.S. GDP was estimated as

$$\Delta lrgdp_t = 0.0050 + 0.256 \Delta lrgdp_{t-1} + 0.1496 \Delta lrgdp_{t-2}$$
$$(5.03) \quad (3.30) \quad\quad\quad (1.94)$$

The t-statistic on the AR(2) coefficient is just on the border of a 95 percent confidence interval obtained from a t-distribution. In fact, a two standard deviation confidence interval runs from -0.00161 to 0.30071. However, the residuals do not appear to be normally distributed so that the t-distribution may not be appropriate.[3] As such, we may want to construct bootstrap confidence intervals for the coefficient 0.1496. For Step 2, we need to generate a bootstrap sample of the regression residuals. This series, denoted by $\{e_t^*\}$, consists of 166 randomly drawn values from the actual residual sequence. We also need two initial conditions; we can draw two consecutive values of the $\{\Delta lrgdp_t\}$ sequence to serve as the initial conditions. As such, we can create the following bootstrap sequence for $\{y_t^*\}$ containing a total of 168 observations

$$y_t^* = 0.0050 + 0.256 y_{t-1}^* + 0.1496 y_{t-2}^* + e_t^*$$

For Step 3, we pretend that we do not know the actual data-generating process for $\{y_t^*\}$ and estimate the series as an AR(2). Suppose you find that the estimated AR(2) coefficient is 0.21. This estimate is the first value of a_2^*. Repeat this process several thousand times to obtain the distribution of a_2^*. After performing the 10,000 replications of the experiment, you should find that approximately 2.5 percent of the estimates lie below –0.0089 and 2.5 percent lie above 0.277. These values serve as a 95 percent confidence interval. In this case, it turns out that the bootstrap confidence interval is similar to that obtained using a t-distribution.

Example 2: Equation (4.45) was used to perform a Dickey–Fuller test on the real GDP series. Recall that the estimated model was

$$\Delta lrgdp_t = 0.0635 + 0.00048t - 0.0629\ lrgdp_{t-1} + 0.256\Delta lrgdp_{t-1} + 0.1486\Delta lrgdp_{t-2}$$

The t-statistic for γ (i.e., the coefficient on $lrgdp_{t-1}$) of –3.37 is significant at the 10 percent, but not the 5 percent, significance level. Again, a concern is that the residuals from model are not normally distributed. Moreover, only in large samples do the coefficients of the augmented terms have no bearing on the appropriate critical values. Hence, it seems reasonable to bootstrap the τ_τ-statistic for (4.45). If we bootstrap the series under the null hypothesis of no deterministic time trend and $\gamma = 0$, we need only construct the bootstrap series

$$y_t^* = 0.0050 + 0.256 y_{t-1}^* + 0.1496 y_{t-2}^* + e_t^*$$

Since y_t^* represents a first difference, it is necessary to create the level of the series as $Y_t^* = Y_{t-1}^* + y_t^*$. Now, for Step 3, estimate the bootstrap series in the form

$$y_t^* = a_0^* + \gamma^* Y_{t-1}^* + \lambda^* t + a_1^* y_{t-1}^* + a_2^* y_{t-2}^*$$

Replicate the experiment many times; on each trial, record the t-statistic for the null hypothesis $\gamma^* = 0$. The value of the t-statistic marking the fifth percentile of all of the bootstrapped t-statistics is the 5 percent critical value. In addition, to obtain the bootstrap ϕ_3-statistic, we can obtain the sample values of F for the null hypothesis $\gamma^* = \lambda^* = 0$.

You can select the initial value of Y_1^* as $\log(GDP_1)$ plus an error term. However, as mentioned above, most researchers would actually construct a series with an extra 50 observations and then discard the first 50 of the realizations. When this process was repeated 10,000 times, only 500 (i.e., 5 percent) of the t-statistics for the null hypothesis $\gamma^* = 0$ had values below –3.43. Given the actual value of the t-statistic of –3.37, we cannot reject the null hypothesis $\gamma = 0$ at the 5 percent significance level. Moreover, 95 percent of the F-statistics for the null hypothesis $\gamma^* = \lambda^* = 0$ were less than 6.48. Recall that the sample value ϕ_3 from equation (4.45) was only 6.14. Hence, at the 5 percent significance level, we cannot reject the null hypothesis $\gamma = \lambda = 0$.

Example 3: If the residuals from a panel unit root test are highly correlated across equations, you should use bootstrapped critical values. The only modification needed from Example 2 is that in a panel unit root test, you estimate a vector of equations. The essential requirement is that the residuals need to be sampled in such a way that preserves the contemporaneous correlations present in the data. Let $\{e_{it}\}$ denote the regression residual from (4.60) for regression i for time period t. If e_t denotes the vector of residuals for time period t, we can write

$$e_1 = (e_{11}, e_{21}, e_{31}, \ldots, e_{n1})$$
$$e_2 = (e_{12}, e_{22}, e_{32}, \ldots, e_{n2})$$
$$e_3 = (e_{13}, e_{23}, e_{33}, \ldots, e_{n3})$$
$$\ldots$$
$$e_T = (e_{1T}, e_{2T}, e_{3T}, \ldots, e_{nT})$$

Thus, the first bootstrap sample of the residuals might be

$$e_1^* = (e_{13}, e_{23}, e_{33}, \ldots, e_{n3})$$
$$e_2^* = (e_{15}, e_{25}, e_{35}, \ldots, e_{n5})$$
$$\ldots$$
$$e_T^* = (e_{12}, e_{22}, e_{32}, \ldots, e_{n2})$$

The point is that you resample in such a way as to maintain the contemporaneous relationships among the regression residuals. As in Example 2, construct a bootstrap series using the resampled values of $\{e_t^*\}$. Once you obtain the average value of the t-statistics for the first bootstrap sample, repeat the entire process several thousand times.

Efron and Tibshirani (1993) is an extremely accessible treatment of bootstrapping. You may also download a programming manual that illustrates some bootstrapping techniques (at no charge) from the Wiley Web site for this text.

ENDNOTES

1. Another possibility discussed by Efron is to resample the paired (y_i, x_i) combinations.
2. A second, although less common, bootstrapping technique used in time series models is called "Moving Blocks." For an AR(p) process, select a length L that is longer than p; L is the length of the block. To construct the bootstrap y^* series, randomly select a group of L adjacent data points to represent the first L observations of the bootstrap sample. In total, you need to select T/L of these samples to form a bootstrap sample with T observations. The idea of selecting a block is to preserve the time–dependence of the data. However, observations more than L apart will be nearly independent. Use this bootstrap sample to estimate the bootstrap coefficients a_0^* and a_1^*.
3. The value of the Jarque–Bera test statistic for normality is 15.51; hence, normality can be rejected at the 0.00042856 significance level.

CHAPTER 5

MULTIEQUATION TIME-SERIES MODELS

As we have seen in previous chapters, you can capture many interesting dynamic relationships using single equation time-series methods. In the recent past, many time-series texts would end with nothing more than a brief discussion of multiequation models. Yet, one of the most fertile areas of contemporary time-series research concerns multiequation models. This chapter has four specific aims:

1. Introduce **intervention analysis** and **transfer function analysis.** These two techniques generalize the univariate methodology by allowing the time path of the *dependent* variable to be influenced by the time path of an *independent* or *exogenous* variable. If it is known that there is no feedback, intervention and transfer function analysis can be very effective tools for forecasting and hypothesis testing.

2. Introduce the concept of a vector autoregression (VAR). The major limitation of intervention and transfer function models is that many economic systems do exhibit feedback. In practice, it is not always known if the time path of a series designated to be the *independent* variable has been unaffected by the time path of the *dependent* variable. The most basic form of a VAR treats all variables symmetrically without making reference to the issue of dependence versus independence.

3. Show that tools employed by VAR analysis—Granger causality, impulse response analysis, and variance decompositions—can be helpful in understanding the interrelationships among economic variables and in the formulation of a more structured economic model. These tools are illustrated using examples concerning the fight against transnational terrorism.

4. Develop two new techniques, **structural VARs** and **multivariate decompositions,** that blend economic theory and multiple time-series analysis. Economic theories contain behavioral, structural, and/or reduced-form relationships that can be incorporated into a VAR analysis. In a structural VAR, the restrictions of a particular economic model are imposed on the contemporaneous relationship among the variables. The dynamic response of each variable to various economic shocks can be obtained and the restrictions of the model tested. Similarly, long-run neutrality restrictions can aid in decomposing a series into its temporary and permanent components. As

opposed to the class of univariate decompositions considered in Chapter 4, decompositions in a VAR framework can be exactly identified.

1. INTERVENTION ANALYSIS

Although the events of September 11, 2001, brought terrorism to the world's attention, the international community experienced a sharp increase in transnational terrorism beginning in the late 1960s. Terrorists engage in a wide variety of operations, including assassinations, armed attacks, bombings, kidnappings, and skyjackings. Such incidents are particularly heinous because they are often directed at innocent victims who are not part of the decision-making apparatus that the terrorists seek to influence. Figure 5.1 shows the total number of transnational terrorist incidents, along with the number of bombing incidents, that have occurred since 1968. Note that bombings are a large proportion of the total incident series. It is also interesting to note that the number of incidents has steadily declined since the mid-1990s.

The skyjackings on September 11 and the skyjacking of Pan Am flight 103 over Lockerbie, Scotland, on December 21, 1988, captured the attention of the international community. However, skyjacking incidents have actually been quite numerous. The United States launched a critical response to the rise in skyjackings when it began to install metal detectors in all U.S. airports in January 1973. Other international authorities soon followed suit.

The quarterly totals of all transnational and U.S. domestic skyjackings are shown in Figure 5.2. Although the number of skyjacking incidents appears to take a sizable and permanent decline at this date, we might be interested in actually measuring the

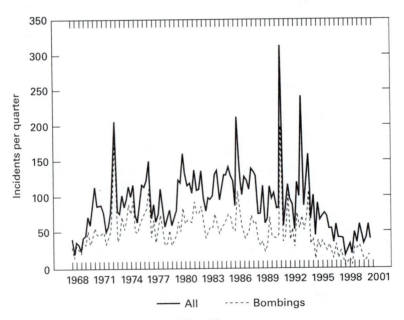

FIGURE 5.1   All Incidents and Bombings

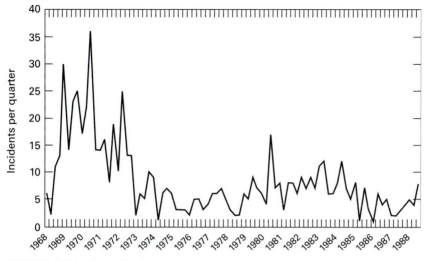

FIGURE 5.2 Skyjackings

effects of installing the metal detectors. If $\{y_t\}$ represents the quarterly total of sky-jackings, one might try to take the mean value of $\{y_t\}$ for all $t < 1973{:}1$ and compare it to the mean value of $\{y_t\}$ for all $t \geq 1973{:}1$. However, such a test is poorly designed because successive values of y_t are serially correlated. As such, some of the effects of the pre-metal detector regime could "carry over" to the post-intervention date. For example, some planned skyjacking incidents already in the pipeline might not be deterred as readily as others.

Intervention analysis allows for a formal test of a change in the mean of a time series. Consider the model used in Enders, Sandler, and Cauley (1990) to study the impact of metal detector technology on the number of skyjacking incidents:

$$y_t = a_0 + a_1 y_{t-1} + c_0 z_t + \varepsilon_t, \; |a_1| < 1 \qquad (5.1)$$

where: z_t = the intervention (or dummy) variable that takes on the value of zero prior to 1973:1 and unity beginning in 1973:1

ε_t = a white-noise disturbance

To explain the nature of the model, notice that for $t < 1973{:}1$, the value z_t is zero.[1] As such, the intercept term is a_0 and the long-run mean of the series is $a_0/(1 - a_1)$. Beginning in 1973, the intercept term jumps to $a_0 + c_0$ (since $z_{1973{:}1}$ jumps to unity). Thus, the initial or **impact effect** of the metal detectors is given by the magnitude of c_0. The statistical significance of c_0 can be tested using a standard t-test. We would conclude that metal detectors reduced the number of skyjacking incidents if c_0 is negative and statistically different from zero.

The long-run effect of the intervention is given by $c_0/(1 - a_1)$, which is equal to the new long-run mean $(a_0 + c_0)/(1 - a_1)$ minus the value of the original mean $a_0/(1 - a_1)$. The various transitional effects can be obtained from the impulse response function. Using lag operators, rewrite (5.1) as

$$(1 - a_1 L)y_t = a_0 + c_0 z_t + \varepsilon_t$$

so that

$$y_t = a_0 /(1 - a_1) + c_0 \sum_{i=0}^{\infty} a_1^i z_{t-i} + \sum_{i=0}^{\infty} a_1^i \varepsilon_{t-i} \tag{5.2}$$

Equation (5.2) is an impulse response function; the interesting twist added by the intervention variable is that we can obtain the responses of the $\{y_t\}$ sequence to the intervention. To trace out the effects of metal detectors on skyjackings, suppose that $t = 1973{:}1$ (so that $t + 1 = 1973{:}2$, $t + 2 = 1973{:}3$, etc.). For time period t, the impact of z_t on y_t is given by the magnitude of the coefficient c_0. The simplest way to derive the remaining impulse responses is to recognize that (1) $dy_t/dz_{t-i} = dy_{t+i}/dz_t$ and (2) $z_{t+i} = z_t = 1$ for all $i > 0$.

Hence, differentiate (5.2) with respect to z_{t-1} and update by one period so that

$$dy_{t+1}/dz_t = c_0 + c_0 a_1$$

The presence of the term c_0 reflects the direct impact of z_{t+1} on y_{t+1}, and the second term $c_0 a_1$ reflects the effect of z_t on y_t $(= c_0)$ multiplied by the effect of y_t on y_{t+1} $(= a_1)$. Continuing in this fashion, we can trace out the entire impulse response function as

$$dy_{t+j}/dz_t = c_0[1 + a_1 + \ldots + (a_1)^j]$$

since $z_{t+1} = z_{t+2} = \ldots = 1$.

Taking limits as $j \to \infty$, we can reaffirm that the long-run impact is given by $c_0/(1 - a_1)$. If it is assumed that $0 < a_1 < 1$, the absolute value of the magnitude of the impacts is an increasing function of j. As we move further away from the date on which the policy was introduced, the greater is the absolute value of the magnitude of the policy response. If $-1 < a_1 < 0$, the policy has a damped oscillating effect on the $\{y_t\}$ sequence. After the initial jump of c_0, the successive values of $\{y_t\}$ oscillate toward the long-run level of $c_0/(1 - a_1)$.

There are several important extensions to the intervention example provided here. Of course, the model need not be a first-order autoregressive process. A more general ARMA(p, q) intervention model has the form

$$y_t = a_0 + A(L)y_{t-1} + c_0 z_t + B(L)\varepsilon_t$$

where $A(L)$ and $B(L)$ are polynomials in the lag operator L.

Also, the intervention need not be the pure jump illustrated in Panel (a) of Figure 5.3. In our study, the value of the intervention sequence jumps from zero to unity in 1973:1. However, there are several other possible ways to model the intervention function:

1. *Pulse function.* As shown in Panel (b) of the figure, the function z_t is zero for all periods, except in one particular period in which z_t is unity. This pulse function best characterizes a purely temporary intervention. Of course, the effects of the single impulse may last many periods due to the autoregressive nature of the $\{y_t\}$ series.

2. *Gradually changing function.* An intervention may not reach its full force immediately. Although the U.S. began installing metal detectors in airports

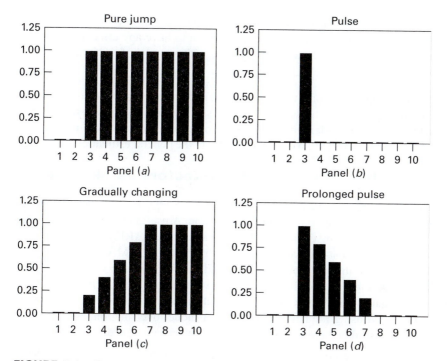

FIGURE 5.3 Typical Intervention Functions

in January 1973, it took almost a full year for installations to be completed at some major international airports. Our intervention study of the impact of metal detectors on quarterly skyjackings also modeled the z_t series as 1/4 in 1973:1, 1/2 in 1973:2, 3/4 in 1973:3, and 1.0 in 1973:4 and all subsequent periods. This type of intervention function is shown in Panel (c) of the figure.

3. *Prolonged impulse function.* Rather than a single pulse, the intervention may remain in place for one or more periods and then begin to decay. For a short time, sky marshals were put on many U.S. flights to deter skyjackings. Since the sky marshal program was allowed to terminate, the $\{z_t\}$ sequence for sky marshals might be represented by the decaying function shown in Panel (d) of Figure 5.3.

Be aware that the effects of these interventions change if $\{y_t\}$ has a unit root. From the discussion of Perron (1989) in Chapter 4, you should recall that a pulse intervention will have a permanent effect on the level of a unit root process. Similarly, if $\{y_t\}$ has a unit root, a pure jump intervention will act as a drift term. As indicated in Question 1 at the end of this chapter, an intervention will have a temporary effect on a unit root process if all values of $\{z_t\}$ sum to zero (e.g., $z_t = 1, z_{t+1} = -0.5, z_{t+2} = -0.5$, and all other values of the intervention variable equal zero).

Also be aware that the intervention may affect the variable of interest with a delay. Suppose that it takes d periods for z_t to begin to have any effect on the series of interest. It is possible to capture this behavior with a model of the form

$$y_t = a_0 + A(L)y_{t-1} + c_0 z_{t-d} + B(L)\varepsilon_t$$

Often, the shape of the intervention function and the delay factor d are clear from a priori reasoning. When there is an ambiguity, estimate the plausible alternatives and then use the standard Box–Jenkins model selection criteria to choose the most appropriate model. The following two examples illustrate the general estimation procedure.

Estimating the Effect of Metal Detectors on Skyjackings

The linear form of the intervention model $y_t = a_0 + A(L)y_{t-1} + c_0 z_t + B(L)\varepsilon_t$ assumes that the coefficients are invariant to the intervention. A useful check of this assumption is to pretest the data by estimating the most appropriate ARIMA(p, d, q) models for both the pre- and post-intervention periods. If the two ARIMA models are quite different, it is likely that the autoregressive and moving average coefficients have changed. Usually there are not enough pre-intervention and post-intervention observations to estimate two separate models. In such instances, the researcher must be content to proceed using the best-fitting ARIMA model over the longest data span. The procedure described below is typical of most intervention studies.

STEP 1: Use the longest data span (i.e., either the pre- or the post-intervention observations) to find a plausible set of ARIMA models.

You should be careful to ensure that the $\{y_t\}$ sequence is stationary. If you suspect nonstationarity, you can perform unit root tests on the longest span of data. Alternatively, you can use the Perron (1989) test for structural change discussed in Chapter 4. In the presence of d unit roots, estimate the intervention model using the d-th difference of y_t (i.e., $\Delta^d y_t$).

In our study, we were interested in the effects of metal detectors on U.S. domestic skyjackings, transnational skyjackings (including those involving the United States), and all other skyjackings. Call each of these time series $\{DS_t\}$, $\{TS_t\}$, and $\{OS_t\}$, respectively. Since there are only five years of data (i.e., 20 observations) for the preintervention period, we estimated the best-fitting ARIMA model over the 1973:1 to 1988:4 period. Using the various criteria discussed in Chapter 2 (including diagnostic checks of the residuals), we selected an AR(1) model for the $\{TS_t\}$ and $\{OS_t\}$ sequences and a pure noise model (i.e., all autoregressive and moving average coefficients equal to zero) for the $\{DS_t\}$ sequence.

STEP 2: Estimate the various models over the entire sample period, including the effect of the intervention.

The installation of metal detectors was tentatively viewed as an immediate and permanent intervention. As such, we set $z_t = 0$ for $t < 1973{:}1$ and $z_t = 1$ beginning in 1973:1. The results of the estimations over the entire sample period are reported in Table 5.1. As you can see, the installation of metal detectors reduced each of the three types of skyjacking incidents. The

Table 5.1 Metal Detectors and Skyjackings

	Pre-Intervention Mean	a_1	Impact Effect (c_0)	Long-Run Effect
Transnational (TS_t)	3.032	0.276	−1.29	−1.78
	(5.96)	(2.51)	(−2.21)	
U.S. Domestic (DS_t)	6.70		−5.62	−5.62
	(12.02)		(−8.73)	
Other Skyjackings (OS_t)	6.80	0.237	−3.90	−5.11
	(7.93)	(2.14)	(−3.95)	

Notes:
1. t-statistics are in parentheses.
2. The long-run effect is calculated as $c_0/(1 - a_1)$.

most pronounced effect was that U.S. domestic skyjackings immediately fell by more than 5.6 incidents per quarter. All effects are immediate because the estimate of a_1 is zero. The situation is somewhat different for the $\{TS_t\}$ and $\{OS_t\}$ sequences because the estimated autoregressive coefficients are different from zero. On impact, transnational skyjackings and other types of skyjacking incidents fell by 1.29 and 3.9 incidents per quarter. The long-run effects on $\{TS_t\}$ and $\{OS_t\}$ are estimated to be −1.78 and −5.11 incidents per quarter, respectively.

STEP 3: Perform diagnostic checks of the estimated equations.

Diagnostic checking is particularly important since we have merged the observations from the pre- and post-intervention periods. To reiterate the discussion of ARIMA models, a well-estimated intervention model will have the following characteristics:

1. The estimated coefficients should be of "high quality." All coefficients should be statistically significant at conventional levels. As in all ARIMA modeling, we wish to use a parsimonious model. If any coefficient is not significant, an alternative model should be considered. Moreover, the autoregressive coefficients should imply that the $\{y_t\}$ sequence is convergent.

2. The residuals should approximate white noise. If the residuals are serially correlated, the estimated model does not mimic the actual data-generating process. Forecasts from the estimated model cannot possibly make use of all available information. If the residuals do not approximate a normal distribution, the usual tests of statistical inference are not appropriate in small samples. If the errors appear to be ARCH, the entire intervention model can be reestimated as an ARCH process.

3. The tentative model should outperform plausible alternatives. Of course, no one model can be expected to dominate all others in all

possible criteria. However, it is good practice to compare the results of the maintained model to those of reasonable rivals. In the skyjacking example, a plausible alternative was to model the intervention as a gradually increasing process. This is particularly true because the impact effect was immediate for U.S. domestic flights and convergent for transnational and other domestic flights. Our conjecture was that metal detectors were gradually installed in non–U.S. airports and, even when installed, the enforcement was sporadic. As a check, we modeled the intervention as gradually increasing over the year 1973. Although the coefficients were nearly identical to those reported in Table 5.1, the AIC and SBC were slightly lower (indicating a better fit) using the gradually increasing process. Hence, it is reasonable to conclude that metal detector adoption was more gradual outside of the United States.

Estimating the Effect of the Libyan Bombing

We also considered the effects of the U.S. bombing of Libya on the morning of April 15, 1986. The stated reason for the attack was Libya's alleged involvement in the terrorist bombing of the La Belle Discotheque in West Berlin. Since 18 of the F-111 fighter-bombers were deployed from British bases at Lakenheath and Upper Heyford, England, the United Kingdom implicitly assisted in the raid. The remaining U.S. planes were deployed from aircraft carriers in the Mediterranean Sea. Now let y_t denote all transnational terrorist incidents directed against the United States and the United Kingdom during month t. A plot of the $\{y_t\}$ sequence exhibits a large positive spike immediately after the bombing; the immediate effect seemed to be a wave of anti-U.S. and anti-U.K. attacks to protest the retaliatory strike. You can see this spike in each of the two series shown in Figure 5.1.

Preliminary estimates of the monthly data from January 1968 to March 1986 indicated that the $\{y_t\}$ sequence could be estimated as a purely autoregressive model with significant coefficients at lags 1 and 5. We were surprised by a significant coefficient at lag 5, but the AIC and SBC both indicated that the fifth lag is important. Nevertheless, we estimated versions of the model with and without the fifth lag. In addition, we considered two possible patterns for the intervention series. For the first, $\{z_t\}$ was modeled as 0 until April 1986 and 1 in all subsequent periods. Using this specification, we obtained the following estimates (with t-statistics in parentheses):

$$y_t = 5.58 + 0.336y_{t-1} + 0.123y_{t-5} + 2.65z_t$$
$$(5.56) \quad (3.26) \quad (0.84)$$
$$\text{AIC} = 1656.03 \quad \text{SBC} = 1669.95$$

Note that the coefficient of z_t has a t-statistic of 0.84 (which is not significant at the 0.05 level). Alternatively, when z_t was allowed to be 1 only in the month of the attack, we obtained

$$y_t = 3.79 + 0.327y_{t-1} + 0.157y_{t-5} + 38.9z_t$$
$$(5.53) \quad (2.59) \quad (6.09)$$
$$\text{AIC} = 1608.68 \quad \text{SBC} = 1626.06$$

In comparing the two estimates, it is clear that magnitudes of the autoregressive coefficients are similar. Although Q-tests indicated that the residuals from both models approximate white noise, the second model is preferable. The coefficient on the pulse term is highly significant, and the AIC and SBC both select the second specification. Our conclusion was that the Libyan bombing did not have the desired effect of reducing terrorist attacks against the United States and the United Kingdom. Instead, the bombing caused an immediate increase of more than 38 attacks. Subsequently, the number of attacks declined; 0.327 of these attacks are estimated to have persisted for one period ($0.327 \cdot 38.9 = 12.7$). Since the autoregressive coefficients imply convergence, the long-run consequences of the raid were estimated to be zero.

2. TRANSFER FUNCTION MODELS

A natural extension of the intervention model is to allow the $\{z_t\}$ sequence to be something other than a deterministic dummy variable. Consider the following generalization of the intervention model:

$$y_t = a_0 + A(L)y_{t-1} + C(L)z_t + B(L)\varepsilon_t \qquad (5.3)$$

where $A(L)$, $B(L)$, and $C(L)$ are polynomials in the lag operator L.

In a typical transfer function analysis, the researcher will collect data on the endogenous variable $\{y_t\}$ and on the exogenous variable $\{z_t\}$. The goal is to estimate the parameter a_0 and the parameters of the polynomials $A(L)$, $B(L)$, and $C(L)$. The major difference between (5.3) and the intervention model is that $\{z_t\}$ is not constrained to have a particular deterministic time path. In a sense, the intervention variable is allowed to be any exogenous process. The polynomial $C(L)$ is called the **transfer function** in that it shows how a movement in the exogenous variable z_t affects the time path of (i.e., is transferred to) the endogenous variable $\{y_t\}$. The coefficients of $C(L)$, denoted by c_i, are called transfer function weights.

It is critical to note that transfer function analysis assumes that $\{z_t\}$ is an exogenous process that evolves independently of the $\{y_t\}$ sequence. Innovations in $\{y_t\}$ are assumed to have no effect on the $\{z_t\}$ sequence so that $Ez_t\varepsilon_{t-s} = 0$ for all values of s and t. Since z_t can be observed and is uncorrelated with the current innovation in y_t (i.e., the disturbance term ε_t), the current and lagged values of z_t are explanatory variables for y_t. Let $C(L)$ be $c_0 + c_1L + c_2L^2 + \dots$ If $c_0 = 0$, the contemporaneous value of z_t does not directly affect y_t. As such, $\{z_t\}$ is called a **leading indicator** in that the observations z_t, $z_{t-1}, z_{t-2}, \dots$ can be used in predicting future values of the $\{y_t\}$ sequence.[2]

It is easy to conceptualize numerous applications for (5.3). After all, a large part of dynamic economic analysis concerns the effects of an "exogenous" or "independent" sequence $\{z_t\}$ on the time path of an endogenous sequence $\{y_t\}$. For example, much of the current research in agricultural economics centers on the effects of the macroeconomy on the agricultural sector. Using (5.3), farm output $\{y_t\}$ is affected by its own past as well as by the current and past state of the macroeconomy $\{z_t\}$. The effects of macroeconomic fluctuations on farm output can be represented by the coefficients of $C(L)$. Here, $B(L)\varepsilon_t$ represents the unexplained portion of farm output. Alternatively, the level of ozone in the atmosphere $\{y_t\}$ is a naturally evolving process; hence, in the absence of other outside influences, we should expect the ozone level to be well represented by an ARIMA model. However, many have argued that the use of fluorocarbons has damaged the ozone layer. Because of a cumulative effect, it is argued that current and past values of fluorocarbon usage affect the value of y_t. Letting z_t denote fluorocarbon usage in t, it is possible to model the effects of fluorocarbon usage on the ozone layer using a model in the form of (5.3). The natural dissipation of ozone is captured through the coefficients of $A(L)$. Stochastic shocks to the ozone layer, possibly due to electrical storms and the presence of measurement errors, are captured by $B(L)\varepsilon_t$. The contemporaneous effect of fluorocarbons on the ozone layer is captured by the coefficient c_0, and the lagged effects are captured by the other transfer function weights (i.e., the values of the various c_i).

In contrast to the pure intervention model, there is no pre- versus post-intervention period so that we cannot estimate a transfer function in the same fashion in which we estimated an intervention model. However, the methods are very similar in that the goal is to estimate a parsimonious model. The procedure involved in fitting a transfer function model is easiest to explain by considering a simple case of (5.3). To begin, suppose $\{z_t\}$ is generated by a white-noise process that is uncorrelated with ε_t at all leads and lags. Also suppose that the realization of z_t affects the $\{y_t\}$ sequence with a lag of unknown duration. Specifically, let

$$y_t = a_1 y_{t-1} + c_d z_{t-d} + \varepsilon_t \qquad (5.4)$$

where $\{z_t\}$ and $\{\varepsilon_t\}$ are white-noise processes such that $E(z_t \varepsilon_{t-i}) = 0$; a_1 and c_d are unknown coefficients; and d is the "delay" or lag duration to be determined by the econometrician.

Since $\{z_t\}$ and $\{\varepsilon_t\}$ are assumed to be independent white-noise processes, it is possible to separately model the effects of each type of shock. Since we can observe the various z_t values, the first step is to calculate the **cross-correlations** between y_t and the various z_{t-i}. The cross-correlation between y_t and z_{t-i} is defined to be

$$\rho_{yz}(i) \equiv \text{cov}(y_t, z_{t-i})/(\sigma_y \sigma_z) \qquad (5.5)$$

where σ_y and $\sigma_z =$ the standard deviations of y_t and z_t, respectively. The standard deviation of each sequence is assumed to be time-independent.

Plotting each value of $\rho_{yz}(i)$ yields the cross-correlation function (CCF) or **cross-correlogram.** In practice, we must use the cross-correlations calculated using sample data because we do not know the true covariances or standard deviations. The key point is that the examination of the sample cross-correlations provides the same type of information as the ACF in an ARMA model. To explain, solve (5.4) to obtain

$$y_t = c_d z_{t-d}/(1 - a_1 L) + \varepsilon_t/(1 - a_1 L)$$

Use the properties of lag operators to expand the expression $c_d z_{t-d}/(1 - a_1 L)$:

$$y_t = c_d(z_{t-d} + a_1 z_{t-d-1} + a_1^2 z_{t-d-2} + a_1^3 z_{t-d-3} + \ldots) + \varepsilon_t/(1 - a_1 L)$$

Analogously to our derivation of the Yule-Walker equations, we can obtain the
cross-covariances by the successive multiplication of y_t by $z_t, z_{t-1}, \ldots$ to form

$$y_t z_t = c_d(z_t z_{t-d} + a_1 z_t z_{t-d-1} + a_1^2 z_t z_{t-d-2}$$
$$+ a_1^3 z_t z_{t-d-3} + \ldots) + z_t \varepsilon_t / (1 - a_1 L)$$

$$y_t z_{t-1} = c_d(z_{t-1} z_{t-d} + a_1 z_{t-1} z_{t-d-1} + a_1^2 z_{t-1} z_{t-d-2}$$
$$+ a_1^3 z_{t-1} z_{t-d-3} + \ldots) + z_{t-1} \varepsilon_t / (1 - a_1 L)$$

$$\ldots$$

$$y_t z_{t-d} = c_d(z_{t-d} z_{t-d} + a_1 z_{t-d} z_{t-d-1} + a_1^2 z_{t-d} z_{t-d-2}$$
$$+ a_1^3 z_{t-d} z_{t-d-3} + \ldots) + z_{t-d} \varepsilon_t / (1 - a_1 L)$$

$$y_t z_{t-d-1} = c_d(z_{t-d-1} z_{t-d} + a_1 z_{t-d-1} z_{t-d-1} + a_1^2 z_{t-d-1} z_{t-d-2}$$
$$+ a_1^3 z_{t-d-1} z_{t-d-3} + \ldots) + z_{t-d-1} \varepsilon_t / (1 - a_1 L)$$

$$\ldots$$

Now take the expected value of each of the above equations. If we continue to
assume that $\{z_t\}$ and $\{\varepsilon_t\}$ are independent white-noise disturbances, it follows that

$$Ey_t z_t = 0$$
$$Ey_t z_{t-1} = 0$$
$$\ldots$$

$$Ey_t z_{t-d} = c_d \sigma_z^2$$
$$Ey_t z_{t-d-1} = c_d a_1 \sigma_z^2$$
$$Ey_t z_{t-d-2} = c_d a_1^2 \sigma_z^2$$
$$\ldots$$

so that in compact form,

$$Ey_t z_{t-i} = 0 \text{ for all } i < d$$
$$= c_d a_1^{i-d} \sigma_z^2 \text{ for } i \geq d \qquad (5.6)$$

Dividing each value of $Ey_t z_{t-i} = \text{cov}(y_t, z_{t-i})$ by $\sigma_y \sigma_z$ yields the CCF. Note that
the cross-correlogram consists of zeroes until lag d. The absolute value of height of
the first nonzero cross-correlation is positively related to the magnitudes of c_d and a_1.
Thereafter, the cross-correlations decay at the rate a_1. The decay of the correlogram
matches the autoregressive patterns of the $\{y_t\}$ sequence.

The pattern exhibited by (5.6) is easily generalized. Suppose we allow both z_{t-d}
and z_{t-d-1} to directly affect y_t:

$$y_t = a_1 y_{t-1} + c_d z_{t-d} + c_{d+1} z_{t-d-1} + \varepsilon_t$$

Solving for y_t, we obtain

$$y_t = (c_d z_{t-d} + c_{d+1} z_{t-d-1})/(1 - a_1 L) + \varepsilon_t /(1 - a_1 L)$$

$$= c_d(z_{t-d} + a_1 z_{t-d-1} + a_1^2 z_{t-d-2} + a_1^3 z_{t-d-3} + \cdots)$$

$$+ c_{d+1}(z_{t-d-1} + a_1 z_{t-d-2} + a_1^2 z_{t-d-3} + a_1^3 z_{t-d-4} + \cdots) + \varepsilon_t /(1 - a_1 L)$$

so that

$$y_t = c_d z_{t-d} + (c_d a_1 + c_{d+1}) z_{t-d-1} + a_1(c_d a_1 + c_{d+1}) z_{t-d-2}$$

$$+ a_1^2(c_d a_1 + c_{d+1}) z_{t-d-3} + \cdots + \varepsilon_t /(1 - a_1 L)$$

Given that we are assuming $Ez_t = 0$, the cross-covariances are $Ey_t z_{t-i}$ and the cross-correlations are $Ey_t z_{t-i}/ \sigma_y \sigma_z$. In the literature, it is also common to work with the standardized cross-covariances denoted by $Ey_t z_{t-i}/ \sigma_z^2$. The choice between the two is a matter of indifference since the CCF and the standardized cross-covariance function (CCVF) are proportional to each other. In the example at hand, the CCVF reveals the following pattern:[3]

$$
\begin{aligned}
\gamma_{yz}(i) &= 0 && \text{for } i < d \\
&= c_d && \text{for } i = d \\
&= c_d a_1 + c_{d+1} && \text{for } i = d + 1 \\
&= a_1^{j-1}(c_d a_1 + c_{d+1}) && \text{for } i = d + j \; (j > 0)
\end{aligned}
$$

Panel (a) of Figure 5.4 shows the shape of the standardized cross-covariances for $d = 3$, $c_d = 1$, $c_{d+1} = 1.5$, and $a_1 = 0.8$. Note that there are distinct spikes at lags 3 and 4 corresponding to the nonzero values of c_3 and c_4. Thereafter the CCVF decays at the rate a_1. Panel (b) of the figure replaces c_4 with the value -1.5. Again, all cross-covariances are zero until lag 3; since $c_3 = 1$, the standardized value of $\gamma_{yz}(3) = 1$. To find the standardized value of $\gamma_{yz}(4)$, form $\gamma_{yz}(4) = 0.8 - 1.5 = -0.7$. The subsequent values of $\gamma_{yz}(i)$ decay at the rate 0.8. The pattern illustrated by these two examples generalizes to any intervention model of the form

$$y_t = a_0 + a_1 y_{t-1} + C(L)z_t + B(L)\varepsilon_t \tag{5.7}$$

The theoretical CCVF (and CCF) has a shape with the following characteristics:

1. All $\gamma_{yz}(i)$ will be zero until the first nonzero element of the polynomial $C(L)$.
2. The form of $B(L)$ is immaterial to the *theoretical* CCVF. Since z_t is uncorrelated with ε_t at all leads and lags, the form of the polynomial $B(L)$ will not affect any of the theoretical cross-covariances $\gamma_{yz}(i)$. Obviously, the intercept term a_0 does not affect any of the cross-covariances.
3. A spike in the CCVF indicates a nonzero element of $C(L)$. Thus, a spike at lag d indicates that z_{t-d} directly affects y_t.
4. All spikes decay at the rate a_1; convergence implies that the absolute value of a_1 is less than unity. If $0 < a_1 < 1$, decay in the cross-covariances will be direct whereas if $-1 < a_1 < 0$, the decay pattern will be oscillatory.

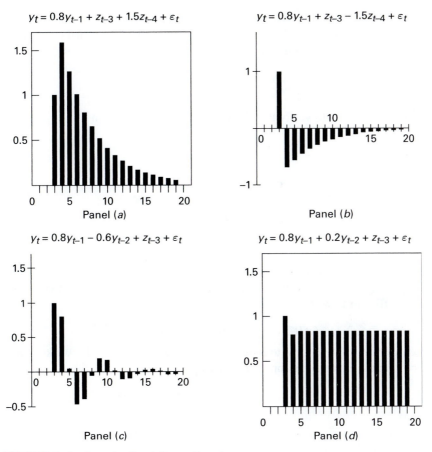

FIGURE 5.4   Standardized Cross-Correlograms

Only the nature of the decay process changes if we generalize equation (5.7) to include additional lags of y_{t-i}. In the general case of (5.3), the *decay pattern in the cross-covariances* is determined by the characteristic roots of the polynomial $A(L)$; the shape is precisely that suggested by the autocorrelations of a pure ARMA model. This should not come as a surprise; in the examples of (5.4) and (5.7), the decay factor was simply the first-order coefficient a_1. We know that there will be decay since all characteristic roots of $1 - A(L)$ must be outside the unit circle for the process to be stationary. Convergence will be direct if the roots are positive and will tend to oscillate if a root is negative. Imaginary roots impart a sine-wave pattern to the decay process.

The Cross-Covariances of a Second-Order Process

To use another example, consider the transfer function:

$$y_t = a_1 y_{t-1} + a_2 y_{t-2} + c_d z_{t-d} + \varepsilon_t$$

Using lag operators to solve for y_t is inconvenient since we do not know the numerical values of a_1 and a_2. Instead, use the method of undetermined coefficients and form the **challenge solution:**

$$y_t = \sum_{i=0}^{\infty} W_i z_{t-i} + \sum_{i=0}^{\infty} V_i \varepsilon_{t-i}$$

You should be able to verify that the values of the W_i are given by

$$W_0 = 0$$

$$\ldots$$

$$W_d = c_d$$
$$W_{d+1} = c_d a_1$$
$$W_{d+2} = c_d(a_1^2 + a_2)$$
$$W_{d+3} = a_1 W_{d+2} + a_2 W_{d+1}$$
$$W_{d+4} = a_1 W_{d+3} + a_2 W_{d+2}$$

$$\ldots$$

Thus, for all $i > d + 1$, the successive coefficients satisfy the difference equation $W_i = a_1 W_{i-1} + a_2 W_{i-2}$. At this stage we are not interested in the values of the various V_i, so it is sufficient to write the solution for y_t as

$$y_t = c_d z_{t-d} + c_d a_1 z_{t-d-1} + c_d(a_1^2 + a_2) z_{t-d-2} + \ldots + \Sigma V_i \varepsilon_{t-i}$$

Next, use this solution for y_t to form all covariances using the Yule–Walker equations. Forming the expressions for $\gamma_{yz}(i)$ as $E y_t z_{t-i} / \sigma_z^2$

$$\gamma_{yz}(i) = 0 \text{ for } i < d \qquad [\text{since } E z_t z_{t-i} = 0 \text{ for } i < d]$$
$$\gamma_{yz}(d) = c_d$$
$$\gamma_{yz}(d-1) = a_1 c_d$$
$$\gamma_{yz}(d-2) = c_d(a_1^2 + a_2)$$

$$\ldots$$

Thus, there is an initial spike at lag d reflecting the nonzero value of c_d. After one period, a_1 percent of c_d remains. After two periods, the decay pattern in the standardized cross-covariances begins to satisfy the difference equation:

$$\gamma_{yz}(i) = a_1 \gamma_{yz}(i-1) + a_2 \gamma_{yz}(i-2)$$

Panel (c) of Figure 5.4 shows the shape of the CCVF for the case of $d = 3$, $c_d = 1$, $a_1 = 0.8$, and $a_2 = -0.6$. The oscillatory pattern reflects the fact that the characteristic roots of the process are imaginary. For purposes of comparison, Panel (d) shows the CCVF of a unit root process. The fact that one of the characteristic roots is equal to unity means that a z_{t-3} shock has a permanent effect on the $\{y_t\}$ sequence.[4]

Higher-Order Input Processes

The econometrician will rarely be so fortunate as to work with a $\{z_t\}$ series that is white noise. We need to further generalize our discussion of transfer functions to consider the case in which the $\{z_t\}$ sequence is a stationary ARMA process. As discussed next, the estimation of the transfer function becomes more difficult in this case.

However, the extra difficulty is worthwhile because a rich set of interactions between the variables is possible. For a moment, we can abstract from the estimation problem and consider the system of equations represented by (5.3)—reproduced for your convenience—and the $\{z_t\}$ process:

$$y_t = a_0 + A(L)y_{t-1} + C(L)z_t + B(L)\varepsilon_t$$

$$D(L)z_t = E(L)\varepsilon_{zt} \tag{5.8}$$

where $D(L)$ and $E(L)$ are polynomials in the lag operator L and ε_{zt} is white noise. The roots of $D(L)$ and $E(L)$ are such that the $\{z_t\}$ sequence is a stationary and invertible ARMA process. Since $\{z_t\}$ is independent of $\{y_t\}$, shocks to the $\{y_t\}$ sequence cannot influence $\{z_t\}$. As such, it must be the case that $E\varepsilon_t\varepsilon_{zt} = 0$.

Once the coefficients of the two equations have been properly estimated, it is possible to trace out two separate impulse response functions. As in a standard Box–Jenkins model, it is possible to trace out the effects of a one-unit shock to ε_t on the entire y_t sequence. Holding all values of z_t constant, the impulse responses are given by the coefficients of the polynomial $[B(L)/(1 - A(L))]$. More importantly, it is possible to show how shocks to the input series $\{z_t\}$ are transferred to the output series $\{y_t\}$. A one-unit shock to ε_{zt} directly affects z_t by one unit and y_t by $c_0\varepsilon_{zt}$ units. It is relatively straightforward for a computer to trace out the effects of the ε_{zt} shock on the entire $\{z_t\}$ and $\{y_t\}$ sequences. Formally, the impulse responses of ε_{zt} shocks on the $\{y_t\}$ sequence are given by combining (5.3) and (5.8) such that

$$y_t = a_0 + A(L)y_{t-1} + C(L)E(L)\varepsilon_{zt}/D(L) + B(L)\varepsilon_t$$

If you solve for y_t, it will be clear that the impulse responses are the coefficients of $C(L)E(L)/[(D(L)(1 - A(L)L)]$. Similarly, transfer functions are useful because they are conducive to multi-step-ahead forecasting. Since $\{z_t\}$ is an independent process, you can use (5.8) to forecast using the techniques developed in Chapter 2. As such, if you have T observations, you can use (5.8) to form the forecasts $E_T z_{T+1}, E_T z_{T+2}, \ldots$. These forecasts are used in the multi-step-ahead forecasts for y_{T+i}. For example, suppose that $z_t = d_1 z_{t-1} + \varepsilon_{zt}$ and $y_t = a_1 y_{t-1} + c_1 z_t + \varepsilon_t$. Since the j-step-ahead forecasts for z_{T+j} are $(d_1)^j z_T$, the multi-step-ahead forecasts for y_{T+j} are

$$E_{TY\,T+1} = a_1 y_T + c_1 E_T z_{T+1} = a_1 y_T + c_1 d_1 z_T$$
$$E_{TY\,T+2} = (a_1)^2 y_T + c_1 d_1 (a_1 + d_1) z_T$$
$$\cdots$$

Identification and Estimation

Since $\{z_t\}$ evolves independently of $\{y_t\}$, we can use the methodology developed in Chapter 2 to estimate $\{z_t\}$ as the ARMA process given by (5.8). The residuals from such a model, denoted by $\{\hat{\varepsilon}_{zt}\}$, should be white noise. The idea is to estimate the *innovations* in the $\{z_t\}$ sequence even though the sequence itself is not a white-noise process.

Once (5.8) has been estimated, you can choose between two techniques to estimate the transfer function. The first is to simply estimate the regression equation

$$y_t = a_0 + \sum_{i=1}^{p} a_i y_{t-i} + \sum_{i=0}^{n} c_i z_{t-i} + \varepsilon_t \tag{5.9}$$

Instead of estimating (5.3), the $\{y_t\}$ series represented by (5.9) is estimated as an AR(p) process that is affected by current and lagged values of $\{z_t\}$. This specification is called an autoregressive distributed lag (ADL) model. Unlike the standard Box–Jenkins approach, begin estimating an ADL using the largest values of p and n deemed feasible. Then, F-tests and t-tests can be used to pare down the model by eliminating unnecessary coefficients. You could also use the AIC or the SBC to find the lag lengths yielding the best fit. As in any time-series estimation, it is crucial to perform the appropriate diagnostic checks to ensure that the residuals are white noise. The benefit of this method is that it is simple to perform. However, you can easily end up with an overly parameterized model. As you know, there might be an ARMA model for $\{y_t\}$ that is more parsimonious than an AR representation. Moreover, since z_t and z_{t-i} are correlated, it is not always straightforward to use t-tests to pare down the coefficients of the transfer function. Nevertheless, the method is quite common and is consistent with the vector-autoregressive methodology discussed in Sections 5 to 13. A fairly detailed example of estimating an ADL is presented in Chapter 6.

The second method estimates (5.3) directly. Although identifying the coefficients of $B(L)$ can be difficult, it can yield a parsimonious model. Just as an ARMA process can approximate high-order AR process, (5.3) can provide a parsimonious representation of (5.9). As in the case where $\{z_t\}$ is white noise, the idea is to use the cross-correlations to obtain the pattern of the coefficients as they appear in the transfer function. It is tempting to think that we should form the cross-correlations between the $\{y_t\}$ sequence and $\{\hat\varepsilon_{zt-i}\}$. However, this procedure would be inconsistent with the maintained hypothesis that the structure of the transfer function is given by (5.3). The reason is that $z_t, z_{t-1}, z_{t-2},$ ... (and not simply the innovations) directly affect the value of y_t. Cross-correlations between y_t and the various ε_{zt-i} would not reveal the pattern of the coefficients in $C(L)$.

The appropriate methodology is to **filter** the $\{y_t\}$ sequence by multiplying (5.3) by the previously estimated polynomial $D(L)/E(L)$. As such, the filtered value of y_t is $D(L)y_t/E(L)$ and is denoted by y_{ft}. The cross-correlations of $\hat\varepsilon_{zt}$ and y_{ft} reveal the form of the transfer function. To explain, multiply (5.3) by $D(L)/E(L)$ to obtain

$$D(L)y_t/E(L) = D(L)a_0/E(L) + D(L)A(L)y_{t-1}/E(L)$$
$$+ C(L)D(L)z_t/E(L) + B(L)D(L)\varepsilon_t/E(L)$$

Given that $D(L)y_t/E(L) = y_{ft}$, $D(L)y_{t-1}/E(L) = y_{ft-1}$ and $D(L)z_t/E(L) = \varepsilon_{zt}$, this is equivalent to

$$y_{ft} = D(L)a_0/E(L) + A(L)y_{ft-1} + C(L)\varepsilon_{zt} + B(L)D(L)\varepsilon_t/E(L) \qquad (5.10)$$

Although you could construct the sequence $D(L)y_t/E(L)$, most software packages can make the appropriate transformations automatically. Now compare (5.3) and (5.10). You can see that y_t and z_t in (5.3) will have the same cross-covariances as y_{ft} and ε_{zt} in (5.10). As in the previous case in which $\{z_t\}$ is white noise, we can examine the CCVF between y_{ft} and ε_{zt} to determine the spikes and the decay pattern.

Again, consider the example where $z_t = d_1 z_{t-1} + \varepsilon_{zt}$ and $y_t = a_1 y_{t-1} + c_1 z_t + \varepsilon_t$. Given that you can never actually observe the form of the transfer function, you might not be able to deduce that only z_t has a direct effect on y_t. In fact, substitution for z_t yields $y_t = a_1 y_{t-1} + c_1(d_1 z_{t-1} + \varepsilon_{zt}) + \varepsilon_t$. As such, you might be fooled into estimating an equation of the form

$$y_t = a_1 y_{t-1} + a_2 z_{t-1} + \varepsilon_{1t}$$

Although there is nothing "wrong" with this equation, the interpretation is such that z_t affects the $\{y_t\}$ sequence with a one-period lag. It should also be clear that $\text{var}(\varepsilon_{1t}) = \text{var}(c_1\varepsilon_{zt} + \varepsilon_t)$. Hence, the estimated transfer function will have a larger variance than that from $y_t = a_1 y_{t-1} + c_1 z_t + \varepsilon_t$. The proper way to identify the form of the transfer function is to filter the values of y_t such that

$$y_{ft} = (1 - d_1 L)y_t = y_t - d_1 y_{t-1}$$

Now multiply each side of the transfer function by $(1 - d_1 L)$ to obtain

$$(1 - d_1 L)y_t = a_1(1 - d_1 L)y_{t-1} + c_1(1 - d_1 L)z_t + (1 - d_1 L)\varepsilon_t$$

or

$$y_{ft} = a_1 y_{ft-1} + c_1\varepsilon_{zt} + \varepsilon_t - d_1\varepsilon_{t-1}$$

Clearly, the covariances between y_{ft} and ε_{zt} will have the same pattern as those between y_t and z_t. In summary, the full procedure for fitting a transfer function entails:

STEP 1: Fit an ARMA model to the z_t sequence. The technique used at this stage is precisely that for estimating any ARMA model. A properly estimated ARMA model should approximate the data-generating process for the $\{z_t\}$ sequence. The calculated residuals $\{\hat{\varepsilon}_{zt}\}$ are called the *filtered* values of the $\{z_t\}$ series. These filtered values can be interpreted as the pure innovations in the $\{z_t\}$ sequence. Calculate and store the $\{\hat{\varepsilon}_{zt}\}$ sequence.

STEP 2: Obtain the filtered $\{y_t\}$ sequence by applying the filter $D(L)/E(L)$ to each value of $\{y_t\}$; that is, use the results of Step 1 to obtain $D(L)/E(L)y_t \equiv y_{ft}$. Form the CCF (or CCVF) between y_{ft} and $\hat{\varepsilon}_{zt-i}$. Of course, the sample cross-covariances will not precisely conform to their theoretical values. Under the null hypothesis that the cross-correlations are all zero, the *sample* variance of cross-correlation coefficient i asymptotically converges to $(T - i)^{-1}$ where $T =$ number of usable observations. Let $r_{yz}(i)$ denote the sample cross-correlation coefficient between y_t and z_{t-i}. Under the null hypothesis that the true values of $\rho_{yz}(i)$ all equal zero, the variance of $r_{yz}(i)$ converges to

$$\text{Var}[r_{yz}(i)] = (T - i)^{-1}$$

For example, with 100 usable observations, the standard deviation of the cross-correlation coefficient between y_t and z_{t-1} is approximately equal to 0.10. If the calculated value of $r_{yz}(1)$ exceeds 0.2 (or is less than -0.2), the null hypothesis can be rejected. Significant cross-correlations at lag i indicate that an innovation in z_t affects the value of y_{t+i}. To test the significance of the first k cross-correlations, use the statistic

$$Q = T(T + 2)\sum_{i=0}^{k} r_{yz}^2(i) / (T - k)$$

Asymptotically, Q has a χ^2 distribution with $(k - p_1 - p_2)$ degrees of freedom where p_1 and p_2 denote the number of nonzero coefficients in $A(L)$ and $C(L)$, respectively.

STEP 3: Examine the pattern of the cross-correlogram (or CCVF). Just as the ACF can be used as a guide in identifying an ARMA model, the cross-correlogram can help identify the form of $A(L)$ and $C(L)$. This can be difficult since you try to infer the form of both functions from the cross-correlations. Remember that spikes in the cross-correlogram indicate nonzero values of c_i. The decay pattern of the cross-correlations suggests plausible candidates for coefficients of $A(L)$. For example, geometric decay after a single spike at lag d suggests the model $y_t = a_0 + a_1 y_{t-1} + c_d z_{t-d} + \varepsilon_t$. As illustrated by the CCVF in Figure 5.4, this decay pattern is perfectly analogous to the ACF in a traditional ARMA model. In practice, examination of the cross-correlogram will suggest several plausible transfer functions. Estimate each of these plausible models and select the "best-fitting" model. Regress y_t (not y_{ft}) on its own lags and the selected values of $\{z_t\}$. At this point, you will have estimated a model of the form

$$[1 - a(L)L] y_t = C(L)z_t + e_t$$

where e_t denotes the error term, which is not necessarily white noise.

STEP 4: The $\{e_t\}$ sequence obtained in Step 3 is an approximation of $B(L)\varepsilon_t$. As such, the ACF of these residuals can suggest the appropriate form for the $B(L)$ function. If the $\{e_t\}$ sequence appears to be white noise, your task is complete. However, the correlogram of the $\{e_t\}$ sequence will usually suggest a number of plausible forms for $B(L)$. Use the $\{e_t\}$ sequence to estimate the various forms of $B(L)$ and select the "best" model for the $B(L)e_t$.

STEP 5: Combine the results of Steps 3 and 4 to estimate the full equation. At this stage, you will estimate $A(L)$, $B(L)$, and $C(L)$ simultaneously. The properties of a well-estimated model are such that the coefficients are of high quality, the model is parsimonious, the residuals conform to a white-noise process, and the forecast errors are small. You should compare your estimated model to the other plausible candidates from Steps 3 and 4.

There is no doubt that estimating a transfer function involves judgment on the part of the researcher. Experienced econometricians would agree that the procedure is a blend of skill, art, and perseverance that is developed through practice. Keep in mind that the goal is to find a parsimonious representation of a potentially complicated interaction among the variables. As in an ARMA process, different models can have similar economic implications and yield similar forecasts. Nevertheless, there are some hints that can be quite helpful.

1. After estimating the full model in Step 5, any remaining autocorrelation in the residuals probably means that $B(L)$ is misspecified. Return to Step 4 and reformulate the form of $B(L)$ so as to capture the remaining explanatory power of the residuals.

2. After estimating the full model in Step 5, if the residuals are correlated with $\{z_t\}$, the $C(L)$ function is probably misspecified. Return to Step 3 and reformulate the specifications of $A(L)$ and $C(L)$.

3. Instead of estimating $\{e_t\}$ as a pure autoregressive process in Step 4, you can estimate $B(L)$ as an ARMA process. Thus, $e_t = B(L)\varepsilon_t$ is allowed to have the form $e_t = G(L)\varepsilon_t/H(L)$. Here, $G(L)$ and $H(L)$ are low-order polynomials in the lag operator L. The benefit is that a high-order autoregressive process can often be approximated by a low-order ARMA model.

4. The sample cross-correlations are not meaningful if $\{y_t\}$ and/or $\{z_t\}$ are not stationary. You can test each for a unit root using the procedures discussed

in Chapter 4. In the presence of unit roots, Box and Jenkins (1976) recommend differencing each variable until it is stationary. The next chapter considers unit roots in a multivariate context. For now, it is sufficient to note that this recommendation can lead to overdifferencing.

The interpretation of the transfer function depends on the type of differencing performed. Consider the following three specifications and assume that $|a_1| < 1$:

$$y_t = a_1 y_{t-1} + c_0 z_t + \varepsilon_t \qquad (5.11)$$

$$\Delta y_t = a_1 \Delta y_{t-1} + c_0 z_t + \varepsilon_t \qquad (5.12)$$

$$\Delta y_t = a_1 \Delta y_{t-1} + c_0 \Delta z_t + \varepsilon_t \qquad (5.13)$$

In (5.11), a one-unit shock in z_t has the initial effect of increasing y_t by c_0 units. This initial effect decays at the rate a_1. In (5.12), a one-unit shock in z_t has the initial effect of increasing *the change in* y_t by c_0 units. The effect on the *change* decays at the rate a_1 but the effect on the *level* of the $\{y_t\}$ sequence never decays. In (5.13), only the change in z_t affects the change in y_t. Here, a pulse in the $\{z_t\}$ sequence will have a temporary effect on the level of $\{y_t\}$. Questions 2 and 3 at the end of this chapter are intended to help you gain familiarity with the different specifications.

3. ESTIMATING A TRANSFER FUNCTION

The clustering of high-profile terrorist events (e.g., the hijacking of TWA flight 847 on June 14, 1985; the hijacking of the *Achille Lauro* cruise ship on October 7, 1985; and the Abu Nidal attacks on the Vienna and Rome airports on December 27, 1985) caused much speculation in the press about tourists changing their travel plans. Similarly, the tourism industry was especially hard-hit after the attacks on September 11, 2001. Although opinion polls of prospective tourists suggest that terrorism affects tourism, the true impact, if any, can best be discovered through the application of statistical techniques. Polls conducted in the aftermath of significant incidents cannot indicate whether respondents actually rebooked trips. Moreover, polls cannot account for tourists not surveyed who may have been induced to take advantage of offers designed to entice tourists back to a troubled spot.

To measure the impact of terrorism on tourism, Enders, Sandler, and Parise (1992) constructed the quarterly values of total receipts from tourism for twelve countries.[6] The logarithmic share of each nation's revenues was treated as the dependent variable $\{y_t\}$, and the number of transnational terrorist incidents occurring within each nation was treated as the independent variable $\{z_t\}$. The crucial assumption for the use of intervention analysis is that there is no feedback from tourism to terrorism. This assumption would be violated if changes in tourism induced terrorists to change their activities.

Consider a transfer function in the form of (5.3):

$$y_t = a_0 + A(L)y_{t-1} + C(L)z_t + B(L)\varepsilon_t$$

where: y_t = the logarithmic share of a nation's tourism revenues in quarter t

z_t = the number of transnational terrorist incidents within that country during quarter t[5]

Using the methodology developed in the previous section, the first step in fitting a transfer function is to fit an ARMA model to the $\{z_t\}$ sequence. For illustrative purposes, it is helpful to consider the Italian case since terrorism in Italy appeared to be white noise (with a constant mean of 4.20 incidents per quarter). Let $\rho_z(i)$ denote the autocorrelations between z_t and z_{t-i}. The correlogram for terrorist attacks in Italy is

Correlogram for Terrorist Attacks in Italy

$\rho_z(0)$	$\rho_z(1)$	$\rho_z(2)$	$\rho_z(3)$	$\rho_z(4)$	$\rho_z(5)$	$\rho_z(6)$	$\rho_z(7)$	$\rho_z(8)$
1	0.13	0.02	−0.06	−0.04	0.11	−0.01	0.00	−0.13

Each value of $\rho_z(i)$ is less than two standard deviations from unity. The Ljung–Box Q-statistics for the significance of the first 4, 8, 12, and 16 lags are

$$Q(4) = 2.06, \quad \text{significance level} = 0.725$$
$$Q(8) = 4.52, \quad \text{significance level} = 0.807$$
$$Q(12) = 7.02, \quad \text{significance level} = 0.855$$
$$Q(16) = 8.06, \quad \text{significance level} = 0.947$$

Since terrorist incidents appear to be a white-noise process, we can skip Step 1; there is no need to fit an ARMA model to the series or to filter the $\{v_t\}$ sequence for Italy. At this point, we conclude that terrorists randomize their acts so that the number of incidents in quarter t is uncorrelated with the number of incidents in previous periods.

Step 2 calls for obtaining the cross-correlogram between tourism and terrorism. The cross-correlogram is

Cross-Correlogram Between Terrorism and Tourism in Italy

$\rho_{yz}(0)$	$\rho_{yz}(1)$	$\rho_{yz}(2)$	$\rho_{yz}(3)$	$\rho_{yz}(4)$	$\rho_{yz}(5)$	$\rho_{yz}(6)$	$\rho_{yz}(7)$	$\rho_{yz}(8)$
−0.18	−0.23	−0.24	−0.05	0.04	0.13	0.04	0.00	0.10

There are several interesting features of the cross-correlogram:

1. With T observations and i lags, the theoretical value of the standard deviation of each value of $\rho_{yz}(i)$ is $(T - i)^{-1/2}$. With 73 observations, $T^{-1/2}$ is approximately equal to 0.117. At the 5 percent significance level (i.e., two standard deviations), the sample value of $\rho_{yz}(0)$ is not significantly different from zero, and $\rho_{yz}(1)$ and $\rho_{yz}(2)$ are just on the margin. However, the Q-statistic for $\rho_{yz}(0) = \rho_{yz}(1) = \rho_{yz}(2) = 0$ is significant at the 0.01 level. Thus, there appears to be a strong negative relationship between terrorism and tourism beginning at lag 1 or at lag 2.

2. It is good practice to examine the cross-correlations between y_t and leading values of z_{t+i}. If the current value of y_t tends to be correlated with *future* values of z_{t+i}, it might be that the assumption of no feedback is violated. The presence of a significant cross-correlation between y_t and leads of z_t might be due to the effect of the current realization of y_t on future values of the $\{z_t\}$ sequence.

3. Since $\rho_{yz}(0)$ is not significantly different from zero at the 5 percent level, it is likely that the delay factor is one quarter; it takes at least one quarter for tourists to significantly revise their travel plans. However, there is no obvious

pattern to the cross-correlation function. It is wise to entertain the possibility of several plausible models at this point in the process.

Step 3 entails examining the cross-correlogram and estimating each of the plausible models. Based on the ambiguous evidence of the cross-correlogram, several different models for the transfer function were estimated. We experimented using delay factors of 0, 1, and 2 quarters. Since the decay pattern of the cross-correlogram is also ambiguous, we allowed $A(L)$ to have the form $a_1 y_{t-1}$ and $a_1 y_{t-1} + a_2 y_{t-2}$. Some of our estimates are reported in Table 5.2.

Model 1 has the form $y_t = a_0 + a_1 y_{t-1} + a_2 y_{t-2} + c_1 z_{t-1} + e_t$. The problem with this specification is that the intercept term a_0 is not significantly different from zero. Eliminating this coefficient yields Model 2. Notice that all coefficients in Model 2 are significant at conventional levels and that the magnitude of each is quite reasonable. The estimated value of c_1 is such that a terrorist incident reduces the logarithmic share of Italy's tourism by 0.003 in the following period. The point estimates of the autoregressive coefficients imply imaginary characteristic roots (the roots are 0.434 $\pm$ 0.69i). Since these roots lie inside the unit circle, the effect of any incident decays in a sine-wave pattern.

Model 3 changes the delay so as to allow a contemporaneous effect of z_t on y_t. The point estimates of the coefficients are reasonable and all are more than two standard deviations from zero. However, the AIC and SBC both select Model 2 over Model 3. The appropriate delay seems to be one quarter.

Since the cross-correlogram seems to have two spikes and exhibits little decay, we allowed both z_{t-1} and z_{t-2} to directly affect y_t. You can see from the table that Models 4 and 5 are inadequate in nearly all respects. Thus, we tentatively selected Model 2 as the "best" model.

For Step 4, we obtained the $\{e_t\}$ sequence from the residuals of Model 2. Hence,

$$e_t = y_t - [-0.003 z_{t-1} / (1 - 0.868L + 0.696L^2)]$$

Table 5.2   Terrorism and Tourism in Italy (Estimates from Step 3)

	a_0	a_1	a_2	c_0	c_1	c_2	AIC/ SBC
Model 1	0.0249 (1.25)	0.795 (2.74)	−0.469 (−1.63)		−0.0046 (−2.34)		−5.09/ 4.01
Model 2		.868 (4.52)	−0.696 (−3.44)		−0.0030 (−2.23)		−5.54/ 1.28
Model 3		1.09 (4.51)	−0.683 (−2.96)	−0.0025 (−2.10)			−4.94/ 1.89
Model 4					−0.0025 (−1.15)	−0.0019 (−0.945)	−4.84/ 3.27
Model 5		−0.217 (−0.221)			−.0025 (−1.16)	−.0027 (−.080)	−2.93/ 3.89

Note: The numbers in parentheses are the t-statistics for the null hypothesis of a zero coefficient.

The correlogram of the residuals is

$\rho(0)$	$\rho(1)$	$\rho(2)$	$\rho(3)$	$\rho(4)$	$\rho(5)$	$\rho(6)$	$\rho(7)$	$\rho(8)$
1.0	0.621	0.554	0.431	0.419	0.150	0.066	0.021	−0.00

The residuals were then estimated as an ARMA process using standard Box–Jenkins methods. Without going into details, the best-fitting ARMA model of the residuals is

$$e_t = 0.485e_{t-1} + 0.295e_{t-2} + (1 + 0.238L^4)\varepsilon_t$$

where the t-statistics for the coefficients are 4.08, 2.33, and 1.83 (significant at the 0.000, 0.023, and 0.071 levels), respectively.

At this point, our tentative transfer function is

$$y_t = -\frac{0.003z_{t-1}}{1-0.868L+0.696L^2} + \frac{(1+0.238L^4)\,\varepsilon_t}{1-0.485L-0.295L^2} \qquad (5.14)$$

The problem with (5.14) is that the coefficients in the first expression were estimated separately from the coefficients in the second expression. In Step 5, we estimated all coefficients simultaneously and obtained

$$y_t = \frac{-0.0022z_{t-1}}{1-0.876L+0.749L^2} + \frac{(1+0.293L^4)\varepsilon_t}{1-0.504L-0.245L^2} \qquad (5.15)$$

Note that the coefficients of (5.15) are similar to those of (5.14). The t-statistics for the two numerator coefficients are −2.17 and 2.27, and the t-statistics for the four denominator coefficients are −7.78, 5.20, −4.31, and −1.94, respectively. The roots of the inverse characteristic equation for z_{t-1} are imaginary and outside the unit circle (the inverse characteristic roots are $0.585 \pm 0.996i$ so that the characteristic roots are $0.438 \pm 0.246i$). As in Model 2, the effects of a terrorist incident decay in a sine-wave pattern. The roots of the inverse characteristic equation for ε_t are −3.29 and 1.238 so that the characteristic roots are −0.303 and 0.807. As an aside, note that you can obtain the original form of the model given in (5.3) by multiplying (5.15) by the two denominator coefficients.

The Ljung–Box Q-statistics indicate that the residuals of (5.15) appear to be white noise. For example, $Q(8) = 6.54$ and $Q(16) = 12.67$ with significance levels of 0.587 and 0.696, respectively. Additional diagnostic checking included excluding the MA(4) term in the numerator (since the significance level was 5.5 percent) and estimating other plausible forms of the transfer functions. All other models had insignificant coefficients and/or larger values of the AIC and SBC and/or Q-statistics indicating significant correlation in the estimated residuals. Hence, we concluded that (5.15) best captures the effects of terrorism on tourism in Italy.

Our ultimate aim was to use the estimated transfer function to simulate the effects of a typical terrorist incident. Initializing the system such that all values of $y_0 = y_1 = y_2 = y_3 = 0$ and setting all $\{\varepsilon_t\} = 0$, we let the value of $z_t = 1$. Figure 5.5 shows the *impulse response function* for this one unit change in the $\{z_t\}$ sequence. As you can see from the figure, after a one-period delay, tourism in Italy declines sharply. After a sustained decline, tourism returns to its initial value in approximately one year. The system has a memory, and tourism again falls; notice the oscillating decay pattern.

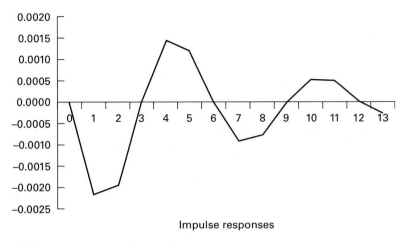

Impulse responses

FIGURE 5.5 Italy's Share of Tourism

Integrating over time and over all incidents allowed us to estimate Italy's total losses to tourism. The undiscounted losses exceeded 600 million SDR; using a 5 percent real interest rate, the total value of the losses exceeded 861 million 1988 SDRs (equal to 6 percent of Italy's annual revenues).

4. LIMITS TO STRUCTURAL MULTIVARIATE ESTIMATION

There are two important difficulties involved in fitting a multivariate equation such as a transfer function. The first concerns the goal of fitting a parsimonious model. Obviously, a parsimonious model is preferable to an overparameterized model. In the relatively small samples usually encountered in economic data, estimating an unrestricted model may so severely limit degrees of freedom as to render forecasts useless. Moreover, the possible inclusion of large but insignificant coefficients will add variability to the model's forecasts. However, in paring down the form of the model, two equally skilled researchers will likely arrive at two different transfer functions. Although one model may have a better "fit" (in terms of the AIC or SBC), the residuals of the other may have better diagnostic properties. There is substantial truth to the consensus opinion that fitting a transfer function model has many characteristics of an "art form." There is a potential cost to using a parsimonious model. Suppose you simply estimate the equation $y_t = A(L)y_{t-1} + C(L)z_t + B(L)\varepsilon_t$ using long lags for $A(L)$, $B(L)$, and $C(L)$. As long as $\{z_t\}$ is exogenous, the estimated coefficients and forecasts are unbiased even though the model is overparameterized. Such is *not* the case if the researcher improperly imposes zero restrictions on any of the polynomials in the model.

The second problem concerns the assumption of no feedback from the $\{y_t\}$ sequence to the $\{z_t\}$ sequence. For the coefficients of $C(L)$ to be unbiased estimates of the impact effects of $\{z_t\}$ on the $\{y_t\}$ sequence, z_t must be uncorrelated with $\{\varepsilon_t\}$ at all leads and lags. Although certain economic models may assert that policy variables (such as money supply or government spending) are exogenous, there may be feedback such that the policy variables are set with specific reference to the state of other variables in the system. To understand the problem of feedback, suppose that you were trying to keep a constant 70°F temperature inside your apartment by turning the thermostat up or down. Of course, the "true" model is that turning up the heat (the intervention variable z_t) warms up your apartment (the $\{y_t\}$ sequence). However, intervention analysis cannot adequately capture the true relationship in the presence of feedback. Clearly, if you perfectly controlled the inside temperature, there would be no correlation between the *constant* value of the inside temperature and the movement of the thermostat. Alternatively, you might listen to the weather forecast and turn up the thermostat whenever you expected it to be cold. If you underreacted by not turning the heat high enough, the cross-correlogram between the two variables would tend to show a negative spike reflecting the drop in room temperature with the upward movement in the thermostat setting. Instead, if you overreacted by greatly increasing the thermostat setting, both room temperature and the thermostat setting would rise together. Only if you moved the thermostat setting without reference to room temperature would we expect to uncover the actual model.

The need to restrict the form of the transfer function and the problem of feedback or "reverse causality" led Sims (1980) to propose a nonstructural estimation strategy. To best understand the vector autoregression approach, it is useful to consider the state of macroeconometric modeling that led Sims to his then-radical ideas.

Multivariate Macroeconometric Models: Some Historical Background

Traditionally, macroeconometric hypothesis tests and forecasts were conducted using large-scale macroeconometric models. Usually a complete set of structural equations was estimated, one equation at a time. Then all equations were aggregated in order to form overall macroeconomic forecasts. Consider two of the equations from the Brookings Quarterly Econometric Model of the United States, as reported by Suits and Sparks (p. 208, 1965):

$$C_{NF} = 0.0656Y_D - 10.93(P_{CNF}/P_C)_{t-1} + 0.1889(N + N_{ML})_{t-1}$$
$$\phantom{C_{NF} = }(0.0165) \quad\ (2.49) \qquad\qquad\qquad (0.0522)$$

$$C_{NEF} = 4.2712 + 0.1691Y_D - 0.0743(ALQD_{HH}/P_C)_{t-1}$$
$$\phantom{C_{NEF} = 4.2712 + }(0.0127) \qquad\quad (0.0213)$$

where: $\quad C_{NF}$ = personal consumption expenditures on food
$\qquad\quad Y_D$ = disposable personal income
$\qquad P_{CNF}$ = implicit price deflator for personal consumption expenditures on food
$\qquad\quad P_C$ = implicit price deflator for personal consumption expenditures
$\qquad\qquad N$ = civilian population
$\qquad\ N_{ML}$ = military population including armed forces overseas
$\qquad C_{NEF}$ = personal consumption expenditures for nondurables other than food
$\quad ALQD_{HH}$ = end-of-quarter stock of liquid assets held by households
and standard errors are in parentheses.

The remaining portions of the model contain estimates for the other components of aggregate consumption, investment spending, government spending, exports, imports, the financial sector, various price determination equations, and so on. Note that food expenditures, but not expenditures on other nondurables, are assumed to depend on relative price and population. However, expenditures for other nondurables are assumed to depend on real liquid assets held by households in the previous quarter.

Are such ad hoc behavioral assumptions consistent with economic theory? Sims (p.3, 1980) considers such multiequation models and argues that

> ... what 'economic theory' tells us about them is mainly that any variable that appears on the right-hand side of one of these equations belongs in principle on the right-hand side of all of them. To the extent that models end up with very different sets of variables on the right-hand side of these equations, they do so not by invoking economic theory, but (in the case of demand equations) by invoking an intuitive econometrician's version of psychological and sociological theory, since constraining utility functions is what is involved here. Furthermore, unless these sets of equations are considered as a system in the process of specification, the behavioral implications of the restrictions on all equations taken together may be less reasonable than the restrictions on any one equation taken by itself.

On the other hand, many of the monetarists used **reduced-form** equations to ascertain the effects of government policy on the macroeconomy. As an example, consider the following form of the *St. Louis model* estimated by Anderson and Jordan (1968). Using U.S. quarterly data from 1952 to 1968, they estimated the following reduced-form GNP determination equation:

$$\Delta Y_t = 2.28 + 1.54\Delta M_t + 1.56\Delta M_{t-1} + 1.44\Delta M_{t-2} + 1.29\Delta M_{t-3}$$
$$+ 0.40\Delta E_t + 0.54\Delta E_{t-1} - 0.03\Delta E_{t-2} - 0.74\Delta E_{t-3} \qquad (5.16)$$

where: ΔY_t = change in nominal GNP
ΔM_t = change in the monetary base
ΔE_t = change in "high employment" budget deficit

In their analysis, Anderson and Jorden used base money and the high employment budget deficit because these are the variables under the control of the monetary and fiscal authorities, respectively. The St. Louis model was an attempt to demonstrate the monetarist policy recommendations that changes in the money supply, but not changes in government spending or taxation, affected GNP. The t-tests for the individual coefficients are misleading because of the substantial multicollinearity between each variable and its lags. However, testing whether the sum of the monetary base coefficients (i.e., $1.54 + 1.56 + 1.44 + 1.29 = 5.83$) differs from zero yields a t-value of 7.25. Hence, they concluded that changes in the money base translate into changes in nominal GNP. Since all the coefficients are positive, the effects of monetary policy are cumulative. On the other hand, the test that the sum of the fiscal coefficients ($0.40 + 0.54 - 0.03 - 0.74 = 0.17$) equals zero yields a t-value of 0.54. According to Anderson and Jordan, the results support "lagged crowding out" in the sense that an increase in the budget deficit initially stimulates the economy. Over time, however, changes in interest rates and other macro-economic variables lead to reductions in private sector expenditures. The cumulated effects of the fiscal stimulus are not statistically different from zero.

Sims (1980) also points out several problems with this type of analysis. Sims's criticisms are easily understood by recognizing that (5.16) is a transfer function with two independent variables $\{M_t\}$ and $\{E_t\}$ and no lags of the dependent variable. As with any type of transfer function analysis we must be concerned with two things:

1. *Ensuring that lag lengths are appropriate.* Serially correlated residuals in the presence of lagged dependent variables lead to biased coefficient estimates.

2. *Ensuring that there is no feedback between GNP and the money base or the budget deficit.* However, the assumption of no feedback is unreasonable if the monetary or fiscal authorities deliberately attempt to alter nominal GNP. As in the thermostat example, if the monetary authority attempts to control the economy by changing the money base, we cannot identify the "true" model. In the jargon of time-series econometrics, changes in GNP would "cause" changes in the money supply. One appropriate strategy would be to simultaneously estimate the GNP determination equation *and* the money supply feedback rule.

Comparing the two types of models, Sims (pp. 14–15, 1980) states:

> Because existing large models contain too many incredible restrictions, empirical research aimed at testing competing macroeconomic theories too often proceeds in a single- or few-equation framework. For this reason alone, it appears worthwhile to investigate the possibility of building large models in a style which does not tend to accumulate restrictions so haphazardly.... It should be feasible to estimate large-scale macromodels as unrestricted reduced forms, treating all variables as endogenous.

5. INTRODUCTION TO VAR ANALYSIS

When we are not confident that a variable is actually exogenous, a natural extension of transfer function analysis is to treat each variable symmetrically. In the two variable case, we can let the time path of $\{y_t\}$ be affected by current and past realizations of the $\{z_t\}$ sequence *and* let the time path of the $\{z_t\}$ sequence be affected by current and past realizations of the $\{y_t\}$ sequence. Consider the simple bivariate system:

$$y_t = b_{10} - b_{12}z_t + \gamma_{11}y_{t-1} + \gamma_{12}z_{t-1} + \varepsilon_{yt} \qquad (5.17)$$

$$z_t = b_{20} - b_{21}y_t + \gamma_{21}y_{t-1} + \gamma_{22}z_{t-1} + \varepsilon_{zt} \qquad (5.18)$$

where it is assumed that (1) both y_t and z_t are stationary; (2) ε_{yt} and ε_{zt} are white-noise disturbances with standard deviations of σ_y and σ_z, respectively; and (3) $\{\varepsilon_{yt}\}$ and $\{\varepsilon_{zt}\}$ are uncorrelated white-noise disturbances.

Equations (5.17) and (5.18) constitute a *first-order* vector autoregression (VAR) because the longest lag length is unity. This simple two-variable first-order VAR is useful for illustrating the multivariate higher order systems that are introduced in Section 8. The structure of the system incorporates feedback because y_t and z_t are allowed to affect each other. For example, $-b_{12}$ is the contemporaneous effect of a unit change of z_t on y_t and γ_{12} is the effect of a unit change in z_{t-1} on y_t. Note that the terms ε_{yt} and ε_{zt} are pure innovations (or shocks) in y_t and z_t, respectively. Of course, if b_{21} is not equal to zero, ε_{yt} has an indirect contemporaneous effect on z_t, and if b_{12} is not equal to zero, ε_{zt} has an indirect contemporaneous effect on y_t. Such a system could be used to capture the feedback effects in our temperature-thermostat example. The first equation allows current and past values of the thermostat setting to affect the time path of the temperature; the second allows for feedback between current and past values of the temperature and the thermostat setting.[7]

Equations (5.17) and (5.18) are not reduced-form equations since y_t has a contemporaneous effect on z_t and z_t has a contemporaneous effect on y_t. Fortunately, it is possible to transform the system of equations into a more usable form. Using matrix algebra, we can write the system in the compact form:

$$\begin{bmatrix} 1 & b_{12} \\ b_{21} & 1 \end{bmatrix}\begin{bmatrix} y_t \\ z_t \end{bmatrix} = \begin{bmatrix} b_{10} \\ b_{20} \end{bmatrix} + \begin{bmatrix} \gamma_{11} & \gamma_{12} \\ \gamma_{21} & \gamma_{22} \end{bmatrix}\begin{bmatrix} y_{t-1} \\ z_{t-1} \end{bmatrix} + \begin{bmatrix} \varepsilon_{yt} \\ \varepsilon_{zt} \end{bmatrix}$$

or

$$Bx_t = \Gamma_0 + \Gamma_1 x_{t-1} + \varepsilon_t$$

where

$$B = \begin{bmatrix} 1 & b_{12} \\ b_{21} & 1 \end{bmatrix}, \quad x_t = \begin{bmatrix} y_t \\ z_t \end{bmatrix}, \quad \Gamma_0 = \begin{bmatrix} b_{10} \\ b_{20} \end{bmatrix},$$

$$\Gamma_1 = \begin{bmatrix} \gamma_{11} & \gamma_{12} \\ \gamma_{21} & \gamma_{22} \end{bmatrix}, \quad \varepsilon_t = \begin{bmatrix} \varepsilon_{yt} \\ \varepsilon_{zt} \end{bmatrix}$$

Premultiplication by B^{-1} allows us to obtain the VAR model in *standard* form

$$x_t = A_0 + A_1 x_{t-1} + e_t \tag{5.19}$$

where: $A_0 = B^{-1}\Gamma_0$
$A_1 = B^{-1}\Gamma_1$
$e_t = B^{-1}\varepsilon_t$

For notational purposes, we can define a_{i0} as element i of the vector A_0, a_{ij} as the element in row i and column j of the matrix A_1, and e_{it} as the element i of the vector e_t. Using this new notation, we can rewrite (5.19) in the equivalent form:

$$y_t = a_{10} + a_{11}y_{t-1} + a_{12}z_{t-1} + e_{1t} \tag{5.20}$$

$$z_t = a_{20} + a_{21}y_{t-1} + a_{22}z_{t-1} + e_{2t} \tag{5.21}$$

To distinguish between the systems represented by (5.17) and (5.18) versus (5.20) and (5.21), the first is called a structural VAR or the primitive system and the second is called a VAR in standard form. It is important to note that the error terms (i.e., e_{1t} and e_{2t}) are composites of the two shocks ε_{yt} and ε_{zt}. Since $e_t = B^{-1}\varepsilon_t$, we can compute e_{1t} and e_{2t} as

$$e_{1t} = (\varepsilon_{yt} - b_{12}\varepsilon_{zt})/(1 - b_{12}b_{21}) \tag{5.22}$$

$$e_{2t} = (\varepsilon_{zt} - b_{21}\varepsilon_{yt})/(1 - b_{12}b_{21}) \tag{5.23}$$

Since ε_{yt} and ε_{zt} are white-noise processes, it follows that both e_{1t} and e_{2t} have zero means, constant variances, and are individually serially uncorrelated. To find the properties of $\{e_{1t}\}$, first take the expected value of (5.22):

$$Ee_{1t} = E(\varepsilon_{yt} - b_{12}\varepsilon_{zt})/(1 - b_{12}b_{21}) = 0$$

The variance of e_{1t} is given by

$$Ee_{1t}^2 = E[(\varepsilon_{yt} - b_{12}\varepsilon_{zt})/(1 - b_{12}b_{21})]^2$$
$$= (\sigma_y^2 + b_{12}^2\sigma_z^2)/(1 - b_{12}b_{21})^2 \qquad (5.24)$$

Thus, the variance of e_{1t} is time-independent. The autocorrelations of e_{1t} and e_{1t-i} are

$$Ee_{1t}e_{1t-i} = E[(\varepsilon_{yt} - b_{12}\varepsilon_{zt})(\varepsilon_{yt-i} - b_{12}\varepsilon_{zt-i})]/(1 - b_{12}b_{21})^2 = 0 \qquad \text{for } i \neq 0$$

Similarly, (5.23) can be used to demonstrate that e_{2t} is a stationary process with zero mean, constant variance, and all autocovariances equal to zero. A critical point to note is that e_{1t} and e_{2t} are correlated. The covariance of the two terms is

$$Ee_{1t}e_{2t} = E[(\varepsilon_{yt} - b_{12}\varepsilon_{zt})(\varepsilon_{zt} - b_{21}\varepsilon_{yt})]/(1 - b_{12}b_{21})^2$$
$$= -(b_{21}\sigma_y^2 + b_{12}\sigma_z^2)/(1 - b_{12}b_{21})^2 \qquad (5.25)$$

In general, (5.25) will not be zero so that the two shocks will be correlated. In the special case where $b_{12} = b_{21} = 0$ (i.e., if there are no contemporaneous effects of y_t on z_t and z_t on y_t), the shocks will be uncorrelated. It is useful to define the variance/covariance matrix of the e_{1t} and e_{2t} shocks as

$$\Sigma = \begin{bmatrix} \text{var}(e_{1t}) & \text{cov}(e_{1t}, e_{2t}) \\ \text{cov}(e_{1t}, e_{2t}) & \text{var}(e_{2t}) \end{bmatrix}$$

Since all elements of Σ are time-independent, we can use the more compact form

$$\Sigma = \begin{bmatrix} \sigma_1^2 & \sigma_{12} \\ \sigma_{21} & \sigma_2^2 \end{bmatrix} \qquad (5.26)$$

where $\text{var}(e_{it}) = \sigma_i^2$ and $\text{cov}(e_{1t}, e_{2t}) = \sigma_{12} = \sigma_{21}$.

Stability and Stationarity

In the first-order autoregressive model $y_t = a_0 + a_1 y_{t-1} + \varepsilon_t$, the stability condition is that a_1 be less than unity in absolute value. There is a direct analogue between this stability condition and the matrix A_1 in the first-order VAR model of (5.19). Using the brute force method to solve the system, iterate (5.19) backwards to obtain

$$x_t = A_0 + A_1(A_0 + A_1 x_{t-2} + e_{t-1}) + e_t$$
$$= (I + A_1)A_0 + A_1^2 x_{t-2} + A_1 e_{t-1} + e_t$$

where $I = 2 \cdot 2$ identity matrix.

After n iterations,

$$x_t = (I + A_1 + \ldots + A_1^n)A_0 + \sum_{i=0}^{n} A_1^i e_{t-i} + A_1^{n+1} x_{t-n-1}$$

If we continue to iterate backward, it is clear that convergence requires that the expression A_1^n vanish as n approaches infinity. As shown below, stability requires that the roots of $(1 - a_{11}L)(1 - a_{22}L) - (a_{12}a_{21}L^2)$ lie outside the unit circle (the stability condition for higher-order systems is derived in Appendix 2 to the next chapter). For the time being, assuming the stability condition is met, we can write the particular solution for x_t as

$$x_t = \mu + \sum_{i=0}^{\infty} A_1^i e_{t-i} \tag{5.27}$$

where $\mu = [\bar{y} \ \bar{z}]'$

and

$$\bar{y} = [a_{10}(1 - a_{22}) + a_{12} a_{20}]/\Delta; \quad \bar{z} = [a_{20}(1 - a_{11}) + a_{21} a_{10}]/\Delta$$
$$\Delta = (1 - a_{11})(1 - a_{22}) - a_{12}a_{21}$$

If we take the expected value of (5.27), the unconditional mean of x_t is μ; hence, the unconditional means of y_t and z_t are $\bar{y}$ and $\bar{z}$, respectively. The variances and covariances of y_t and z_t can be obtained as follows. First, form the variance/covariance matrix as

$$E(x_t - \mu)^2 = E \left| \sum_{i=0}^{\infty} A_1^i e_{t-i} \right|^2$$

Next, using (5.26) note that

$$Ee_t^2 = E \begin{bmatrix} e_{1t} \\ e_{2t} \end{bmatrix} [e_{1t}, e_{2t}]$$
$$= \Sigma$$

Since $Ee_t e_{t-i} = 0$ for $i \neq 0$, it follows that

$$E(x_t - \mu)^2 = (I + A_1^2 + A_1^4 + A_1^6 + \ldots)\Sigma$$
$$= [I - A_1^2]^{-1}\Sigma$$

where it is assumed that the stability condition holds, so A_1^n approaches zero as n approaches infinity.

If we can abstract from an initial condition, the $\{y_t\}$ and $\{z_t\}$ sequences will be jointly covariance stationary if the stability condition holds. Each sequence has a finite and time-invariant mean, and a finite and time-invariant variance.

In order to get another perspective on the stability condition, use lag operators to rewrite the VAR model of (5.20) and (5.21) as

$$y_t = a_{10} + a_{11}Ly_t + a_{12}Lz_t + e_{1t}$$
$$z_t = a_{20} + a_{21}Ly_t + a_{22}Lz_t + e_{2t}$$

or

$$(1 - a_{11}L)y_t = a_{10} + a_{12}Lz_t + e_{1t}$$
$$(1 - a_{22}L)z_t = a_{20} + a_{21}Ly_t + e_{2t}$$

If we use this last equation to solve for z_t, it follows that Lz_t is

$$Lz_t = L(a_{20} + a_{21}Ly_t + e_{2t})/(1 - a_{22}L)$$

so that

$$(1 - a_{11}L)y_t = a_{10} + a_{12}L[(a_{20} + a_{21}Ly_t + e_{2t})/(1 - a_{22}L)] + e_{1t}$$

Notice that we have transformed the first-order VAR in the $\{y_t\}$ and $\{z_t\}$ sequences into a second-order stochastic difference equation in the $\{y_t\}$ sequence. Explicitly solving for y_t, we get

$$y_t = \frac{a_{10}(1 - a_{22}) + a_{12}a_{20} + (1 - a_{22}L)e_{1t} + a_{12}e_{2t-1}}{(1 - a_{11}L)(1 - a_{22}L) - a_{12}a_{21}L^2} \tag{5.28}$$

In the same fashion, you should be able to demonstrate that the solution for z_t is

$$z_t = \frac{a_{20}(1 - a_{11}) + a_{21}a_{10} + (1 - a_{11}L)e_{2t} + a_{21}e_{1t-1}}{(1 - a_{11}L)(1 - a_{22}L) - a_{12}a_{21}L^2} \tag{5.29}$$

Equations (5.28) and (5.29) both have the same characteristic equation; convergence requires that the roots of the polynomial $(1 - a_{11}L)(1 - a_{22}L) - a_{12}a_{21}L^2$ must lie outside the unit circle. (If you have forgotten the stability conditions for second-order difference equations, you might want to refresh your memory by reexamining Chapter 1.) Just as in any second-order difference equation, the roots may be real or complex and may be convergent or divergent. Notice that both y_t and z_t have the same characteristic equation; as long as a_{12} and a_{21} do not both equal zero, the solutions for the two sequences have the same characteristic roots. Hence, both will exhibit similar time paths.

Dynamics of a VAR Model

Figure 5.6 shows the time paths of four simple systems. For each system, 100 sets of normally distributed random numbers representing the $\{e_{1t}\}$ and $\{e_{2t}\}$ sequences were drawn. The initial values of y_0 and z_0 were set equal to zero and $\{y_t\}$ and $\{z_t\}$ sequences were constructed as in (5.20) and (5.21). Panel (a) uses the values

$$a_{10} = a_{20} = 0; \ a_{11} = a_{22} = 0.7; \ \text{and} \ a_{12} = a_{21} = 0.2$$

When we substitute these values into (5.27), it is clear that the mean of each series is zero. From the quadratic formula, the two roots of the inverse characteristic equation $(1 - a_{11}L)(1 - a_{22}L) - a_{12}a_{21}L^2$ are 1.111 and 2.0. Since both are outside the unit circle, the system is stationary; the two characteristic roots of the solution for $\{y_t\}$ and $\{z_t\}$ are 0.9 and 0.5. Since these roots are positive, real, and less than unity, convergence will be direct. As you can see in the figure, there is a tendency for the sequences to move together. Since a_{21} is positive, a large realization in y_t induces a large realization of z_{t+1}; since a_{12} is positive, a large realization of z_t induces a large realization of y_{t+1}. The cross-correlations between the two series are positive.

Panel (b) illustrates a stationary process with $a_{10} = a_{20} = 0$; $a_{11} = a_{22} = 0.5$; and $a_{12} = a_{21} = -0.2$. Again, the mean of each series is zero and the characteristic roots are 0.7 and 0.3. However, in contrast to the previous case, a_{21} and a_{12} are both neg-

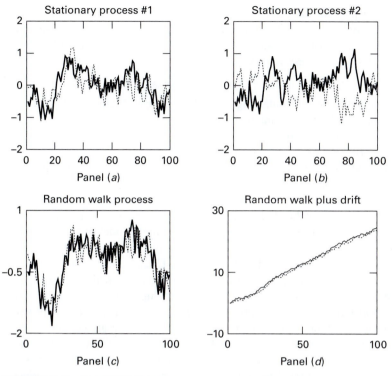

FIGURE 5.6 Four VAR Processes

ative so that positive realizations of y_t can be associated with negative realizations of z_{t+1} and vice versa. As can be seen from comparing the second panel, the two series appear to be negatively correlated.

In contrast, Panel (c) shows a process possessing a unit root; here, $a_{11} = a_{22} = a_{12} = a_{21} = 0.5$. You should take a moment to find the characteristic roots. Undoubtedly, there is little tendency for either of the series to revert to a constant long-run value. Here, the intercept terms a_{10} and a_{20} are equal to zero so that Panel (c) represents a multivariate generalization of the random walk model. You can see how the series seem to meander together. In Panel (d), the VAR process of Panel (c) also contains a nonzero intercept term ($a_{10} = .5$ and $a_{20} = 0$) that takes the role of a "drift." As you can see from Panel (d), the two series appear to move closely together. The drift term adds a deterministic time trend to the nonstationary behavior of the two series. Combined with the unit characteristic root, the $\{y_t\}$ and $\{z_t\}$ sequences are joint random walk plus drift processes. Notice that the presence of the drift dominates the long-run behavior of the series.

6. ESTIMATION AND IDENTIFICATION

One explicit aim of the Box–Jenkins approach is to provide a methodology that leads to parsimonious models. The ultimate objective of making accurate short-term forecasts is best served by purging insignificant parameter estimates from the model. Sims's (1980) criticisms of the "incredible identification restrictions" inherent in structural models argue for an alternative estimation strategy. Consider the following multivariate generalization of an autoregressive process:

$$x_t = A_0 + A_1 x_{t-1} + A_2 x_{t-2} + \ldots + A_p x_{t-p} + e_t \qquad (5.30)$$

where: x_t = an $(n \cdot 1)$ vector containing each of the n variables included in the VAR
A_0 = an $(n \cdot 1)$ vector of intercept terms
A_i = $(n \cdot n)$ matrices of coefficients
e_t = an $(n \cdot 1)$ vector of error terms

Sims's methodology entails little more than a determination of the appropriate variables to include in the VAR and a determination of the appropriate lag length. The variables to be included in the VAR are selected according to the relevant economic model. Lag length tests (to be discussed below) select the appropriate lag length. Otherwise, no explicit attempt is made to "pare down" the number of parameter estimates. The matrix A_0 contains n parameters and each matrix A_i contains n^2 parameters; hence, $n + pn^2$ coefficients need to be estimated. Unquestionably, a VAR will be *overparameterized* in that many of these coefficient estimates will be insignificant. However, the goal is to find the important interrelationships among the variables and not to make short-term forecasts. Improperly imposing zero restrictions may waste important information. Moreover, the regressors are likely to be highly colinear so that the *t*-tests on individual coefficients are not reliable guides for paring down the model.

Note that the right-hand side of (5.30) contains only predetermined variables and that the error terms are assumed to be serially uncorrelated with constant variance. Hence, *each equation in the system can be estimated using OLS.* Moreover, OLS estimates are consistent and asymptotically efficient. Even though the errors are correlated across equations, seemingly unrelated regressions (SUR) do not add to the efficiency of the estimation procedure since all regressions have identical right-hand-side variables.

There is an issue of whether the variables in a VAR need to be stationary. Sims (1980) and Sims, Stock, and Watson (1990) recommend against differencing *even if the variables contain a unit root.* They argue that the goal of a VAR analysis is to determine the interrelationships among the variables, *not* to determine the parameter estimates. The main argument against differencing is that it "throws away" information concerning the comovements in the data (such as the possibility of cointegrating relationships). Similarly, it is argued that the data need not be detrended. In a VAR, a trending variable will be well approximated by a unit root plus drift. However, the majority view is that the form of the variables in the VAR should mimic the true data-generating process. This is particularly true if the aim is to estimate a structural model. We return to these issues in the next chapter; for now, it is assumed that all variables are stationary. Questions 7 and 8 at the end of this chapter ask you to compare a VAR in levels to a VAR in first differences.

Identification

To illustrate the identification procedure, return to the two-variable/first-order VAR of the previous section. Due to the feedback inherent in a VAR process, the primitive equations (5.17) and (5.18) cannot be estimated directly. The reason is that z_t is correlated with the error term ε_{yt} *and* that y_t is correlated with the error term ε_{zt}. Standard estimation techniques require that the regressors be uncorrelated with the error term. Note that there is no such problem in estimating the VAR system in the form of (5.20) and (5.21). OLS can provide estimates of the two elements of A_0 and of the four elements of A_1. Moreover, obtaining the residuals from the two regressions, it is possible to calculate estimates of the variance of e_{1t}, e_{2t}, and of the covariance between e_{1t} with e_{2t}. The issue is whether it is possible to recover all of the information present in the primitive system given by (5.17) and (5.18). In other words, is the primitive system identifiable given the OLS estimates of the VAR model in the form of (5.20) and (5.21)?

The answer to this question is, "No, unless we are willing to appropriately restrict the primitive system." The reason is clear if we compare the number of parameters of the primitive system with the number of parameters recovered from the estimated VAR model. Estimating (5.20) and (5.21) yields six coefficient estimates (a_{10}, a_{20}, a_{11}, a_{12}, a_{21}, and a_{22}) and the calculated values of var(e_{1t}), var(e_{2t}), and cov(e_{1t}, e_{2t}). However, the primitive system (5.17) and (5.18) contains ten parameters. In addition to the two intercept coefficients b_{10} and b_{20}, the four autoregressive coefficients γ_{11}, γ_{12}, γ_{21}, and γ_{22}, and the two feedback coefficients b_{12} and b_{21}, there are the two standard deviations σ_y and σ_z. In all, the primitive system contains ten parameters whereas the VAR estimation yields only nine parameters. Unless one is willing to restrict one of the parameters, it is not possible to identify the primitive system; equations (5.17) and (5.18) are underidentified.

One way to identify the model is to use the type of **recursive** system proposed by Sims (1980). Suppose that you are willing to impose a restriction on the primitive system such that the coefficient b_{21} equal to zero. Writing (5.17) and (5.18) with the constraint imposed yields

$$y_t = b_{10} - b_{12}z_t + \gamma_{11}y_{t-1} + \gamma_{12}z_{t-1} + \varepsilon_{yt} \tag{5.31}$$

$$z_t = b_{20} + \gamma_{21}y_{t-1} + \gamma_{22}z_{t-1} + \varepsilon_{zt} \tag{5.32}$$

Similarly, we can rewrite the relationship between the pure shocks and the regression residuals given by (5.22) and (5.23) as

$$e_{1t} = \varepsilon_{yt} - b_{12}\varepsilon_{zt}$$
$$e_{2t} = \varepsilon_{zt}$$

The point is that forcing $b_{21} = 0$ means that z_t has a contemporaneous effect on y_t but y_t affects the $\{z_t\}$ sequence with a one-period lag. Nevertheless, it should be clear that this restriction (which might be suggested by a particular economic model) results in an exactly identified system. Imposing the restriction $b_{21} = 0$ means that B^{-1} is given by

$$B^{-1} = \begin{bmatrix} 1 & -b_{12} \\ 0 & 1 \end{bmatrix}$$

Now, premultiplication of the primitive system by B^{-1} yields

$$\begin{bmatrix} y_t \\ z_t \end{bmatrix} = \begin{bmatrix} 1 & -b_{12} \\ 0 & 1 \end{bmatrix}\begin{bmatrix} b_{10} \\ b_{20} \end{bmatrix} + \begin{bmatrix} 1 & -b_{12} \\ 0 & 1 \end{bmatrix}\begin{bmatrix} \gamma_{11} & \gamma_{12} \\ \gamma_{21} & \gamma_{22} \end{bmatrix}\begin{bmatrix} y_{t-1} \\ z_{t-1} \end{bmatrix} + \begin{bmatrix} 1 & -b_{12} \\ 0 & 1 \end{bmatrix}\begin{bmatrix} \varepsilon_{yt} \\ \varepsilon_{zt} \end{bmatrix}$$

or

$$\begin{bmatrix} y_t \\ z_t \end{bmatrix} = \begin{bmatrix} b_{10} - b_{12}b_{20} \\ b_{20} \end{bmatrix} + \begin{bmatrix} \gamma_{11} - b_{12}\gamma_{21} & \gamma_{12} - b_{12}\gamma_{22} \\ \gamma_{21} & \gamma_{22} \end{bmatrix} \begin{bmatrix} y_{t-1} \\ z_{t-1} \end{bmatrix} + \begin{bmatrix} \varepsilon_{yt} - b_{12}\varepsilon_{zt} \\ \varepsilon_{zt} \end{bmatrix} \quad (5.33)$$

Estimating the system using OLS yields the parameter estimates from

$$y_t = a_{10} + a_{11}y_{t-1} + a_{12}z_{t-1} + e_{1t}$$

$$z_t = a_{20} + a_{21}y_{t-1} + a_{22}z_{t-1} + e_{2t}$$

where: $a_{10} = b_{10} - b_{12}b_{20}$
$a_{11} = \gamma_{11} - b_{12}\gamma_{21}$
$a_{12} = \gamma_{12} - b_{12}\gamma_{22}$
$a_{20} = b_{20}$
$a_{21} = \gamma_{21}$
$a_{22} = \gamma_{22}$

Since $b_{21} = 0$, it follows that $e_{1t} = \varepsilon_{yt} - b_{12}\varepsilon_{zt}$ and $e_{2t} = \varepsilon_{zt}$. Hence,

$$\text{Var}(e_1) = \sigma_y^2 + b_{12}^2\sigma_z^2$$

$$\text{Var}(e_2) = \sigma_z^2$$

$$\text{Cov}(e_1, e_2) = -b_{12}\sigma_z^2$$

Thus, we have nine parameter estimates a_{10}, a_{11}, a_{12}, a_{20}, a_{21}, a_{22}, var(e_1), var(e_2), and cov(e_1, e_2) that can be substituted into the nine equations above in order to simultaneously solve for b_{10}, b_{12}, γ_{11}, γ_{12}, b_{20}, γ_{21}, γ_{22}, σ_y^2, and σ_z^2.

Note also that the estimates of the $\{\varepsilon_{yt}\}$ and $\{\varepsilon_{zt}\}$ sequences can be recovered. The residuals from the second equation (i.e., the $\{e_{2t}\}$ sequence) are estimates of the $\{\varepsilon_{zt}\}$ sequence. Combining these estimates along with the solution for b_{12} allows us to calculate the estimates of the $\{\varepsilon_{yt}\}$ sequence using the relationship $e_{1t} = \varepsilon_{yt} - b_{12}\varepsilon_{zt}$.

Take a minute to examine the restriction. In (5.32), the assumption $b_{21} = 0$ means that y_t does not have a contemporaneous effect on z_t. In (5.33), the restriction manifests itself such that both ε_{yt} and ε_{zt} shocks affect the contemporaneous value of y_t but only ε_{zt} shocks affect the contemporaneous value of z_t. The observed values of e_{2t} are completely attributed to pure shocks to the $\{z_t\}$ sequence. Decomposing the residuals in this triangular fashion is called a **Choleski** decomposition.

In fact, the result is quite general. In an n-variable VAR, B is an $n \cdot n$ matrix since there are n regression residuals and n structural shocks. As shown in Section 10, exact identification requires that $(n^2 - n)/2$ restrictions be placed on the relationship between the regression residuals and the structural innovations. Since the Choleski decomposition is triangular, it forces exactly $(n^2 - n)/2$ values of the B matrix to equal zero.

7. THE IMPULSE RESPONSE FUNCTION

Just as an autoregression has a moving average representation, a vector autoregression can be written as a vector moving average (VMA). In fact, equation (5.27) is the

VMA representation of (5.19) in that the variables (i.e., y_t and z_t) are expressed in terms of the current and past values of the two types of shocks (i.e., e_{1t} and e_{2t}). The VMA representation is an essential feature of Sims's (1980) methodology in that it allows you to trace out the time path of the various shocks on the variables contained in the VAR system. For illustrative purposes, continue to use the two-variable/first-order model analyzed in the previous two sections. Writing the two-variable VAR in matrix form,

$$\begin{bmatrix} y_t \\ z_t \end{bmatrix} = \begin{bmatrix} a_{10} \\ a_{20} \end{bmatrix} + \begin{bmatrix} a_{11} & a_{12} \\ a_{21} & a_{22} \end{bmatrix} \begin{bmatrix} y_{t-1} \\ z_{t-1} \end{bmatrix} + \begin{bmatrix} e_{1t} \\ e_{2t} \end{bmatrix} \tag{5.34}$$

or, using (5.27), we get

$$\begin{bmatrix} y_t \\ z_t \end{bmatrix} = \begin{bmatrix} \bar{y} \\ \bar{z} \end{bmatrix} + \sum_{i=0}^{\infty} \begin{bmatrix} a_{11} & a_{12} \\ a_{21} & a_{22} \end{bmatrix}^i \begin{bmatrix} e_{1t-i} \\ e_{2t-i} \end{bmatrix} \tag{5.35}$$

Equation (5.35) expresses y_t and z_t in terms of the $\{e_{1t}\}$ and $\{e_{2t}\}$ sequences. However, it is insightful to rewrite (5.35) in terms of the $\{\varepsilon_{yt}\}$ and $\{\varepsilon_{zt}\}$ sequences. From (5.22) and (5.23), the vector of errors can be written as

$$\begin{bmatrix} e_{1t} \\ e_{2t} \end{bmatrix} = \frac{1}{1 - b_{12}b_{21}} \begin{bmatrix} 1 & -b_{12} \\ -b_{21} & 1 \end{bmatrix} \begin{bmatrix} \varepsilon_{yt} \\ \varepsilon_{zt} \end{bmatrix} \tag{5.36}$$

so that (5.35) and (5.36) can be combined to form

$$\begin{bmatrix} y_t \\ z_t \end{bmatrix} = \begin{bmatrix} \bar{y} \\ \bar{z} \end{bmatrix} + \frac{1}{1 - b_{12}\,b_{21}} \sum_{i=0}^{\infty} \begin{bmatrix} a_{11} & a_{12} \\ a_{21} & a_{22} \end{bmatrix}^i \begin{bmatrix} 1 & -b_{12} \\ -b_{21} & 1 \end{bmatrix} \begin{bmatrix} \varepsilon_{yt-i} \\ \varepsilon_{zt-i} \end{bmatrix}$$

Since the notation is getting unwieldy, we can simplify by defining the $2 \cdot 2$ matrix ϕ_i with elements $\phi_{jk}(i)$:

$$\phi_i = \frac{A_1^i}{1 - b_{12}b_{21}} \begin{bmatrix} 1 & -b_{12} \\ -b_{21} & 1 \end{bmatrix}$$

Hence, the moving average representation of (5.35) and (5.36) can be written in terms of the $\{\varepsilon_{yt}\}$ and $\{\varepsilon_{zt}\}$ sequences:

$$\begin{bmatrix} y_t \\ z_t \end{bmatrix} = \begin{bmatrix} \bar{y} \\ \bar{z} \end{bmatrix} + \sum_{i=0}^{\infty} \begin{bmatrix} \phi_{11}(i) & \phi_{12}(i) \\ \phi_{21}(i) & \phi_{22}(i) \end{bmatrix} \begin{bmatrix} \varepsilon_{yt-i} \\ \varepsilon_{zt-i} \end{bmatrix}$$

or, more compactly,

$$x_t = \mu + \sum_{i=0}^{\infty} \phi_i\, \varepsilon_{t-i} \tag{5.37}$$

The moving average representation is an especially useful tool to examine the interaction between the $\{y_t\}$ and $\{z_t\}$ sequences. The coefficients of ϕ_i can be used to generate the effects of ε_{yt} and ε_{zt} shocks on the entire time paths of the $\{y_t\}$ and $\{z_t\}$ sequences. If you understand the notation, it should be clear that the four elements $\phi_{jk}(0)$ are **impact multipliers.** For example, the coefficient $\phi_{12}(0)$ is the instantaneous impact of a one-unit change in ε_{zt} on y_t. In the same way, the elements $\phi_{11}(1)$ and $\phi_{12}(1)$ are the one-period responses of unit changes in ε_{yt-1} and ε_{zt-1} on y_t, respectively. Updating by one period indicates that $\phi_{11}(1)$ and $\phi_{12}(1)$ also represent effects of unit changes in ε_{yt} and ε_{zt} on y_{t+1}.

The accumulated effects of unit impulses in ε_{yt} and/or ε_{zt} can be obtained by the appropriate summation of the coefficients of the impulse response functions. For example, note that after n periods, the effect of ε_{zt} on the value of y_{t+n} is $\phi_{12}(n)$. Thus, after n periods, the cumulated sum of the effects of ε_{zt} on the $\{y_t\}$ sequence is

$$\sum_{i=0}^{n} \phi_{12}(i)$$

Letting n approach infinity yields the **long-run multiplier.** Since the $\{y_t\}$ and $\{z_t\}$ sequences are assumed to be stationary, it must be the case that for all j and k,

$$\sum_{i=0}^{\infty} \phi_{jk}^2(i) \text{ is finite}$$

The four sets of coefficients $\phi_{11}(i)$, $\phi_{12}(i)$, $\phi_{21}(i)$, and $\phi_{22}(i)$ are called the **impulse response functions.** Plotting the impulse response functions [i.e., plotting the coefficients of $\phi_{jk}(i)$ against i] is a practical way to visually represent the behavior of the $\{y_t\}$ and $\{z_t\}$ series in response to the various shocks. In principle, it might be possible to know all of the parameters of the primitive system (5.17) and (5.18). With such knowledge, it would be possible to trace out the time paths of the effects of pure ε_{yt} or ε_{zt} shocks. However, this methodology is not available to the researcher since an estimated VAR is underidentified. As explained in the previous section, knowledge of the various a_{ij} and the variance/covariance matrix Σ is not sufficient to identify the primitive system. Hence, the econometrician must impose an additional restriction on the two-variable VAR system in order to identify the impulse responses.

One possible identification restriction is to use the Choleski decomposition such that y_t does not have a contemporaneous effect on z_t. Formally, this restriction is represented by setting $b_{21} = 0$ in the primitive system. In terms of (5.36), the error terms can be decomposed as follows:

$$e_{1t} = \varepsilon_{yt} - b_{12}\varepsilon_{zt} \tag{5.38}$$

$$e_{2t} = \varepsilon_{zt} \tag{5.39}$$

As already noted, if we use (5.39), all of the observed errors from the $\{e_{2t}\}$ sequence are attributed to ε_{zt} shocks. Given the calculated $\{\varepsilon_{zt}\}$ sequence, knowledge of the values of the $\{e_{1t}\}$ sequence and the correlation coefficient between e_{1t} and e_{2t} allows for the calculation of the $\{\varepsilon_{yt}\}$ sequence using (5.38). Although this Choleski decomposition constrains the system such that an ε_{yt} shock has no direct effect on z_t, there is an indirect effect in that lagged values of y_t affect the contemporaneous value of z_t. The key point is that the decomposition forces a potentially important asymmetry on the system since an ε_{zt} shock has contemporaneous effects on both y_t and z_t. For this reason, (5.38) and (5.39) are said to be an **ordering** of the variables. An ε_{zt} shock directly affects e_{1t} and e_{2t}, but an ε_{yt} shock does not affect e_{2t}. Hence, z_t is said to be "causally prior" to y_t.

Suppose that estimates of equations (5.20) and (5.21) yield the values: $a_{10} = a_{20} = 0$, $a_{11} = a_{22} = 0.7$, and $a_{12} = a_{21} = 0.2$. You will recall that this is precisely the model used in the simulation reported in Panel (a) of Figure 5.6. Also suppose that the elements of the Σ matrix are such that $\sigma_1^2 = \sigma_2^2$ and that $cov(e_{1t}, e_{2t})$ is such that the correlation coefficient between e_{1t} and e_{2t} (denoted by ρ_{12}) is 0.8. Hence, the decomposed errors can be represented by[8]

$$e_{1t} = \varepsilon_{yt} + 0.8\varepsilon_{zt} \tag{5.40}$$

$$e_{2t} = \varepsilon_{zt} \tag{5.41}$$

Panels (a) and (b) of Figure 5.7 trace out the effects of one-unit shocks to ε_{zt} and ε_{yt} on the time paths of the $\{y_t\}$ and $\{z_t\}$ sequences. As shown in Panel (a), a one-unit shock in ε_{zt} causes z_t to jump by one unit and y_t to jump by 0.8 units. [From (5.40), 80 percent of the ε_{zt} shock has a contemporaneous effect on e_{1t}]. In the next period, ε_{zt+1} returns to zero, but the autoregressive nature of the system is such that y_{t+1} and z_{t+1} do not immediately return to their long-run values. Since $z_{t+1} = 0.2y_t + 0.7z_t + \varepsilon_{zt+1}$, it follows that $z_{t+1} = 0.86$ $[0.2(0.8) + 0.7(1) = 0.86]$. Similarly, $y_{t+1} = 0.7y_t + 0.2z_t = 0.76$. As you can see from the figure, the subsequent values of the $\{y_t\}$ and $\{z_t\}$ sequences converge to their long-run levels. This convergence is assured by the stability of the system; as found earlier, the two characteristic roots are 0.5 and 0.9.

The effects of a one-unit shock in ε_{yt} are shown in Panel (b) of the figure. You can see the asymmetry of the decomposition immediately by comparing the two upper panels. A one-unit shock in ε_{yt} causes the value of y_t to increase by one unit; however, *there is no contemporaneous effect on the value of z_t* so that $y_t = 1$ and $z_t = 0$. In the subsequent period, ε_{yt+1} returns to zero. The autoregressive nature of the system is such that $y_{t+1} = 0.7y_t + 0.2z_t = 0.7$ and $z_{t+1} = 0.2y_t + 0.7z_t = 0.2$. The remaining points in the figure are the impulse responses for periods $t+2$ through $t+20$. Since the system is stationary, the impulse responses might ultimately decay.

Can you figure out the consequences of reversing the Choleski decomposition in such a way that b_{12}, rather than b_{21}, is constrained to equal zero? Since matrix A_1 is symmetric (i.e., $a_{11} = a_{22}$ and $a_{12} = a_{21}$), the impulse responses of an ε_{yt} shock would be similar to those in Panel (a) and the impulse responses of an ε_{zt} would be similar to those in Panel (b). The only difference would be that the solid line would represent the time path of the $\{z_t\}$ sequence and the hatched line would represent the time path of the $\{y_t\}$ sequence.

As a practical matter, how does the researcher decide which of the alternative decompositions is most appropriate? In some instances, there might be a theoretical reason to suppose that one variable has no contemporaneous effect on the other. In the terrorism/tourism example, knowledge that terrorist incidents affect tourism with a lag suggests that terrorism does not have a contemporaneous effect on tourism. Usually, there is no such a priori knowledge. Moreover, the very idea of imposing a

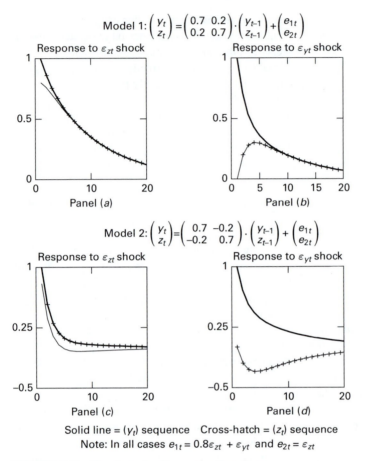

Model 1: $\begin{pmatrix} y_t \\ z_t \end{pmatrix} = \begin{pmatrix} 0.7 & 0.2 \\ 0.2 & 0.7 \end{pmatrix} \cdot \begin{pmatrix} y_{t-1} \\ z_{t-1} \end{pmatrix} + \begin{pmatrix} e_{1t} \\ e_{2t} \end{pmatrix}$

Response to ε_{zt} shock   Response to ε_{yt} shock

Panel (a)   Panel (b)

Model 2: $\begin{pmatrix} y_t \\ z_t \end{pmatrix} = \begin{pmatrix} 0.7 & -0.2 \\ -0.2 & 0.7 \end{pmatrix} \cdot \begin{pmatrix} y_{t-1} \\ z_{t-1} \end{pmatrix} + \begin{pmatrix} e_{1t} \\ e_{2t} \end{pmatrix}$

Response to ε_{zt} shock   Response to ε_{yt} shock

Panel (c)   Panel (d)

Solid line = (y_t) sequence   Cross-hatch = (z_t) sequence
Note: In all cases $e_{1t} = 0.8\varepsilon_{zt} + \varepsilon_{yt}$ and $e_{2t} = \varepsilon_{zt}$

FIGURE 5.7   Two Impulse Response Functions

structure on a VAR system seems contrary to the spirit of Sims's argument against "incredible identifying restrictions." Unfortunately, there is no simple way to circumvent the problem; identification necessitates imposing *some* structure on the system. The Choleski decomposition provides a minimal set of assumptions that can be used to identify the structural model.[9]

It is crucial to note that *the importance of the ordering depends on the magnitude of the correlation coefficient between e_{1t} and e_{2t}.* Let this correlation coefficient be denoted by ρ_{12} so that $\rho_{12} = \sigma_{12}/(\sigma_1 \sigma_2)$. Now suppose that the estimated model yields a value of Σ such that ρ_{12} is found to be equal to zero. In this circumstance, the ordering would be immaterial. Formally, (5.38) and (5.39) become $e_{1t} = \varepsilon_{yt}$ and $e_{2t} = \varepsilon_{zt}$. Since there is no correlation across equations, the residuals from the y_t and z_t equations are necessarily equivalent to the ε_{yt} and ε_{zt} shocks, respectively. The point is, if $Ee_{1t}e_{2t} = 0$, b_{12} and b_{21} can both be set equal to zero. At the other extreme, if ρ_{12} is found to be unity, there is a single shock that contemporarily affects both variables. Under the assumption $b_{21} = 0$,

(5.38) and (5.39) become $e_{1t} = \varepsilon_{zt}$ and $e_{2t} = \varepsilon_{zt}$ and under the alternative assumption $b_{12} = 0$, it follows that $e_{1t} = \varepsilon_{yt}$ and $e_{2t} = \varepsilon_{yt}$. Usually the researcher will want to test the significance of ρ_{12}. As in a univariate model, you can test the null hypothesis $\rho_{12} = 0$ using a normal distribution with a mean of zero and a standard deviation of $T^{-0.5}$. As such, with 100 usable observations, if $|\rho_{12}| > 0.2$, the correlation is deemed to be significant at conventional levels. If ρ_{12} is significant, the usual procedure is to obtain the impulse response function using a particular ordering. Compare the results to the impulse response function obtained by reversing the ordering. If the implications are quite different, additional investigation into the relationships between the variables is necessary.

The lower half of Figure 5.7, Panels (c) and (d), presents the impulse response functions for a second model; the sole difference between models 1 and 2 is the change in the values of a_{12} and a_{21} to -0.2. Notice that model was used in the simulation reported in Panel (b) of Figure 5.6. The negative off-diagonal elements of A_1 weaken the tendency for the two series to move together. Panel (c) traces out the effect of a one-unit ε_{zt} shock using ordering represented by (5.40) and (5.41). In period t, z_t rises by one unit and y_t rises by 0.8 units. In period $(t + 1)$, ε_{zt+1} returns to zero but the value of y_{t+1} is $0.7y_t - 0.2z_t = 0.36$ and the value of z_{t+1} is $-0.2y_t + 0.7z_t = 0.54$. The points represented by $t = 2$ through 20 show that the impulse responses converge to zero. Panel (d) traces the responses of a one-unit ε_{yt} shock. Since the value of z_t is unaffected by the shock, in period $(t + 1)$, $y_{t+1} = 0.7y_t - 0.2z_t = 0.7$ and $z_{t+1} = -0.2y_t + 0.7z_t = -0.2$. In the same way, $y_{t+2} = 0.7*0.7 - 0.2*(-0.2) = 0.53$ and $z_{t+2} = -0.2*(0.7) + 0.7*(-0.2) = -0.28$. Since the system is stable, both sequences eventually converge to zero.

Confidence Intervals and Impulse Responses

One key issue concerning the impulse response functions is that they are constructed using the estimated coefficients. Since each coefficient is estimated imprecisely, the impulse responses also contain error. The issue is to construct confidence intervals around the impulse responses that allow for the parameter uncertainty inherent in the estimation process. To illustrate the methodology, consider the following estimate of an $AR(1)$ model:

$$y_t = 0.60y_{t-1} + \varepsilon_t$$
$$(4.00)$$

Given the t-statistic of 4.00, the $AR(1)$ coefficient seems to be well-estimated. It is easy to form the impulse response function: for any given level of y_{t-1}, a one-unit shock to ε_t will increase y_t by one unit. In subsequent periods, y_{t+1} will be 0.60 and y_{t+2} will be $(0.60)^2$. As you can easily verify, the impulse response function can be written as $\phi(i) = (0.60)^i$.

Notice that the $AR(1)$ coefficient has an estimated mean of 0.6 and standard deviation of 0.15 ($0.15 = 0.60/4.00$). If we are willing to assume that the coefficient is normally distributed, there is a 95 percent chance that the actual value lies within the two-standard deviation interval 0.3 to 0.9. The problem is much more complicated in higher-order systems since the estimated coefficients will be correlated. Moreover, you may not want to assume normality (especially if you have nonstationary variables in your VAR). An alternative way to obtain the desired confidence intervals for the AR(p) process $y_t = a_0 + a_1 y_{t-1} + \ldots + a_p y_{t-p} + \varepsilon_t$ is to perform the following Monte Carlo study:

1. Estimate the coefficients a_0 through a_p using OLS and save the residuals. Let $\hat{a}_i$ denote the estimated value of a_i and let $\{\hat{\varepsilon}_i\}$ denote the estimated residuals.

2. For a sample size of T, draw T random numbers so as to represent the $\{\varepsilon_t\}$ sequence. Most software packages will draw the numbers using randomly selected values of $\hat{\varepsilon}_i$ (with replacement). In this way, they actually generate bootstrap confidence intervals. Thus, you will have a simulated series of length T, called ε_t^s, that should have the same properties as the true error process. Use these random numbers to construct the simulated $\{y_t^s\}$ sequence as

$$y_t^s = \hat{a}_0 + \hat{a}_1 y_{t-1}^s + \ldots + \hat{a}_p y_{t-p}^s + \varepsilon_t^s$$

Be sure that you appropriately initialize the series so as to eliminate the effects of the initial conditions.

3. Now act as if you did not know the values of the coefficient values used to generate the y_t^s series. Estimate y_t^s as an AR(p) process and obtain the impulse response function. If you repeat the process several thousand times, you can generate several thousand impulse response functions. You use these impulse response functions to construct the confidence intervals. For example, you can construct the interval that excludes the lowest 2.5 percent and highest 2.5 percent of the responses to obtain a 95 percent confidence interval.

The benefit of the method is that you do not need to make any special assumptions concerning the distribution of the autoregressive coefficients. The actual calculation of confidence intervals is only a bit more complicated in a VAR. Consider the two-variable system:

$$y_t = a_{11} y_{t-1} + a_{12} z_{t-1} + e_{1t}$$
$$z_t = a_{21} y_{t-1} + a_{22} z_{t-1} + e_{2t}$$

The complicating issue is that the regression residuals are correlated. As such, you need to draw e_{1t} and e_{2t} so as to maintain the appropriate error structure. Hence, you draw random numbers to represent the ε_{yt} and ε_{zt} sequences, making sure to take the correlation coefficient into account. If you use a Choleski decomposition such that $b_{21} = 0$, construct e_{1t} and e_{2t} using (5.38) and (5.39). Question 9 reports the confidence intervals from a three-variable VAR.

Variance Decomposition

Since unrestricted VARs are overparameterized, they are not particularly useful for short-term forecasts. However, understanding the properties of the forecast errors is exceedingly helpful in uncovering interrelationships among the variables in the system. Suppose that we knew the coefficients of A_0 and A_1 and wanted to forecast the various values of x_{t+i} conditional on the observed value of x_t. Updating (5.19) one period (i.e., $x_{t+1} = A_0 + A_1 x_t + e_{t+1}$) and taking the conditional expectation of x_{t+1}, we obtain

$$E_t x_{t+1} = A_0 + A_1 x_t$$

Note that the one-step-ahead forecast error is $x_{t+1} - E_t x_{t+1} = e_{t+1}$. Similarly, updating two periods, we get

$$\begin{aligned} x_{t+2} &= A_0 + A_1 x_{t+1} + e_{t+2} \\ &= A_0 + A_1(A_0 + A_1 x_t + e_{t+1}) + e_{t+2} \end{aligned}$$

If we take conditional expectations, the two-step-ahead forecast of x_{t+2} is

$$E_t x_{t+2} = (I + A_1)A_0 + A_1^2 x_t$$

The two-step-ahead forecast error (i.e., the difference between the realization of x_{t+2} and the forecast) is $e_{t+2} + A_1 e_{t+1}$. More generally, it is easily verified that the n-step-ahead forecast is

$$E_t x_{t+n} = (I + A_1 + A_1^2 + \ldots + A_1^{n-1})A_0 + A_1^n x_t$$

and that the associated forecast error is

$$e_{t+n} + A_1 e_{t+n-1} + A_1^2 e_{t+n-2} + \ldots + A_1^{n-1} e_{t+1} \tag{5.42}$$

We can also consider these forecast errors in terms of (5.37) (i.e., the VMA form of the structural model). Of course, the VMA and the VAR models contain exactly the same information but it is convenient (and a good exercise) to describe the properties of the forecast errors in terms of the $\{\varepsilon_t\}$ sequence. If we use (5.37) to conditionally forecast x_{t+1}, the one-step-ahead the forecast error is $\phi_0 \varepsilon_{t+1}$. In general,

$$x_{t+n} = \mu + \sum_{i=0}^{\infty} \phi_i \, \varepsilon_{t+n-i}$$

so that the n-period forecast error $x_{t+n} - E_t x_{t+n}$ is

$$x_{t+n} - E_t x_{t+n} = \sum_{i=0}^{n-1} \phi_i \, \varepsilon_{t+n-i}$$

Focusing solely on the $\{y_t\}$ sequence, we see that the n-step-ahead forecast error is

$$\begin{aligned} y_{t+n} - E_t y_{t+n} = {} & \phi_{11}(0) \, \varepsilon_{yt+n} + \phi_{11}(1) \, \varepsilon_{yt+n-1} + \ldots + \phi_{11}(n-1) \, \varepsilon_{yt+1} \\ & + \phi_{12}(0) \, \varepsilon_{zt+n} + \phi_{12}(1) \, \varepsilon_{zt+n-1} + \ldots + \phi_{12}(n-1) \, \varepsilon_{zt+1} \end{aligned}$$

Denote the n-step-ahead forecast error variance of y_{t+n} as $\sigma_y(n)^2$:

$$\begin{aligned} \sigma_y(n)^2 = {} & \sigma_y^2 [\phi_{11}(0)^2 + \phi_{11}(1)^2 + \ldots + \phi_{11}(n-1)^2] \\ & + \sigma_z^2 [\phi_{12}(0)^2 + \phi_{12}(1)^2 + \ldots + \phi_{12}(n-1)^2] \end{aligned}$$

Because all values of $\phi_{jk}(i)^2$ are necessarily nonnegative, the variance of the forecast error increases as the forecast horizon n increases. Note that it is possible to decompose the n-step-ahead forecast error variance into the proportions due to each shock. Respectively, the proportions of $\sigma_y(n)^2$ due to shocks in the $\{\varepsilon_{yt}\}$ and $\{\varepsilon_{zt}\}$ sequences are

$$\frac{\sigma_y^2 [\phi_{11}(0)^2 + \phi_{11}(1)^2 + \ldots + \phi_{11}(n-1)^2]}{\sigma_y(n)^2}$$

and

$$\frac{\sigma_z^2 [\phi_{12}(0)^2 + \phi_{12}(1)^2 + \ldots + \phi_{12}(n-1)^2]}{\sigma_y(n)^2}$$

The **forecast error variance decomposition** tells us the proportion of the movements in a sequence due to its "own" shocks versus shocks to the other variable. If ε_{zt} shocks explain none of the forecast error variance of $\{y_t\}$ at all forecast horizons, we can say that the $\{y_t\}$ sequence is exogenous. In this circumstance, $\{y_t\}$ evolves independently of the ε_{zt} shocks and of the $\{z_t\}$ sequence. At the other extreme, ε_{zt} shocks could explain all of the forecast error variance in the $\{y_t\}$ sequence at all forecast horizons, so that $\{y_t\}$ would be entirely endogenous. In applied research it is typical for a variable to explain almost all of its forecast error variance at short horizons and smaller proportions at longer horizons. We would expect this pattern if ε_{zt} shocks had little contemporaneous effect on y_t but acted to affect the $\{y_t\}$ sequence with a lag.

Note that the variance decomposition contains the same problem inherent in impulse response function analysis. In order to identify the $\{\varepsilon_{yt}\}$ and $\{\varepsilon_{zt}\}$ sequences, it is necessary to restrict the B matrix. The Choleski decomposition used in (5.38) and (5.39) necessitates that all of the one-period forecast error variance of z_t is due to ε_{zt}. If we use the alternative ordering, all of the one-period forecast error variance of y_t would be due to ε_{yt}. The dramatic effects of these alternative assumptions are reduced at longer forecasting horizons. In practice, it is useful to examine the variance decompositions at various forecast horizons. As n increases, the variance decompositions should converge. Moreover, if the correlation coefficient ρ_{12} is significantly different from zero, it is customary to obtain the variance decompositions under various orderings.

Nevertheless, impulse analysis and variance decompositions (together called **innovation accounting**) can be useful tools to examine the relationships among economic variables. If the correlations among the various innovations are small, the identification problem is not likely to be especially important. The alternative orderings should yield similar impulse responses and variance decompositions. Of course, the contemporaneous movements of many economic variables are highly correlated. Sections 10 through 13 consider two attractive methods that can be used to identify the structural innovations. Before examining these techniques, we consider hypothesis testing in a VAR framework and reexamine the interrelationships between terrorism and tourism.

8. TESTING HYPOTHESES

In principle, there is nothing to prevent you from incorporating a large number of variables in the VAR. It is possible to construct an n-equation VAR with each equation containing p lags of all n variables in the system. You will want to include those variables that have important economic effects on each other. As a practical matter, degrees of freedom are quickly eroded as more variables are included. For example, using monthly data with 12 lags, the inclusion of one additional variable uses an additional 12 degrees of freedom in each equation. A careful examination of the relevant theoretical model will help to select the set of variables to include in your VAR model.

An n-equation VAR can be represented by

$$\begin{bmatrix} x_{1t} \\ x_{2t} \\ \cdot \\ x_{nt} \end{bmatrix} = \begin{bmatrix} A_{10} \\ A_{20} \\ \cdot \\ A_{n0} \end{bmatrix} + \begin{bmatrix} A_{11}(L) & A_{12}(L) & \cdot & A_{1n}(L) \\ A_{21}(L) & A_{22}(L) & \cdot & A_{2n}(L) \\ \cdot & \cdot & \cdot & \cdot \\ A_{n1}(L) & A_{n2}(L) & \cdot & A_{nn}(L) \end{bmatrix} \begin{bmatrix} x_{1t-1} \\ x_{2t-1} \\ \cdot \\ x_{nt-1} \end{bmatrix} + \begin{bmatrix} e_{1t} \\ e_{2t} \\ \cdot \\ e_{nt} \end{bmatrix} \qquad (5.43)$$

where: A_{i0} = the parameters representing intercept terms

$A_{ij}(L)$ = the polynomials in the lag operator L

The individual coefficients of $A_{ij}(L)$ are denoted by $a_{ij}(1)$, $a_{ij}(2)$, ... Since all equations have the same lag length, the polynomials $A_{ij}(L)$ are all of the same degree. The terms e_{it} are white-noise disturbances that may be correlated. Again, designate the variance/covariance matrix by Σ, where the dimension of Σ is $(n \cdot n)$.

In addition to the determination of the set of variables to include in the VAR, it is important to determine the appropriate lag length. One possible procedure is to allow for different lag lengths for each variable in each equation. However, in order to preserve the symmetry of the system (and to be able to use OLS efficiently) it is common to use the same lag length for all equations. As indicated in Section 6, as long as there are identical regressors in each equation, OLS estimates are consistent and asymptotically efficient. If some of the VAR equations have regressors not included in the others, seemingly unrelated regressions (SUR) provide efficient estimates of the VAR coefficients. Hence, when there is a good reason to let lag lengths differ across equations, estimate the so-called **near-VAR** using SUR.

In a VAR, long lag lengths quickly consume degrees of freedom. If lag length is p, each of the n equations contains np coefficients plus the intercept term. Appropriate lag length selection can be critical. If p is too small, the model is misspecified; if p is too large, degrees of freedom are wasted. To check lag length, begin with the longest plausible length or the longest feasible length given degrees-of-freedom considerations. Estimate the VAR and form the variance/covariance matrix of the residuals. Using quarterly data, you might start with a lag length of 12 quarters based on the a priori notion that three years is sufficiently long to capture the system's dynamics. Call the variance/covariance matrix of the residuals from the 12-lag model Σ_{12}. Now suppose you want to determine whether 8 lags are appropriate. After all, restricting the model from 12 to 8 lags would reduce the number of estimated parameters by $4n$ in each equation.

Since the goal is to determine whether lag 8 is appropriate for all equations, an equation by equation F-test on lags 9 through 12 is not appropriate. Instead, the proper test for this **cross-equation** restriction is a likelihood ratio test. Reestimate the VAR *over the same sample period* using 8 lags and obtain the variance/covariance matrix of the residuals Σ_8. Note that Σ_8 pertains to a system of n equations with $4n$ restrictions in each equation for a total of $4n^2$ restrictions. The likelihood ratio statistic is

$$(T)(\log|\Sigma_8| - \log|\Sigma_{12}|)$$

However, given the sample sizes usually found in economic analysis, Sims (1980) recommends using

$$(T - c)(\log|\Sigma_8| - \log|\Sigma_{12}|)$$

where: $\quad T =$ number of usable observations

$\quad\quad c =$ number of parameters estimated in each equation of the unrestricted system

$\quad\quad \log|\Sigma_n| =$ the natural logarithm of the determinant of Σ_n

In the example at hand, $c = 1 + 12n$ since each equation of the unrestricted model has twelve lags for each variable terms plus an intercept.

This statistic has an asymptotic χ^2 distribution with degrees of freedom equal to the number of restrictions *in the system*. In the example under consideration, there are $4n$ restrictions in each equation for a total of $4n^2$ restrictions in the system. Clearly, if the restriction of a reduced number of lags is not binding, we would expect $\log|\Sigma_8|$ to be equal to $\log|\Sigma_{12}|$. Large values of this sample statistic indicate that only eight lags is a binding restriction; hence, a rejection of the null hypothesis that lag length = 8. If the calculated value of the statistic is less than χ^2 at a prespecified significance level, we will not be able to reject the null of only eight lags. At that point we could seek to determine whether four lags were appropriate by constructing

$$(T - c)(\log|\Sigma_4| - \log|\Sigma_8|)$$

Considerable care should be taken in paring down lag length in this fashion. Often this procedure will not reject the null hypotheses of eight versus twelve lags and four versus eight lags, although it will reject a null of four versus twelve lags. The problem with paring down the model is that you may lose a small amount of explanatory power at each stage. Overall, the total loss in explanatory power can be significant. In such circumstances, it is better to use the longer lag lengths.

This type of likelihood ratio test is applicable to any type of cross-equation restriction. Let Σ_u and Σ_r be the variance/covariance matrices of the unrestricted and restricted systems, respectively. If the equations of the unrestricted model contain different regressors, let c denote the maximum number of regressors contained in the longest equation. Sims' recommendation is to compare the test statistic

$$(T - c)(\log|\Sigma_r| - \log|\Sigma_u|) \tag{5.44}$$

to a χ^2 distribution with degrees of freedom equal to the number of restrictions in the system.

To take another example, suppose you wanted to capture seasonal effects by including three seasonal dummies in each of the n equations of a VAR. Estimate the unrestricted model by including the dummy variables and estimate the restricted model by excluding the dummies. The total number of restrictions in the system is $3n$. If lag length is p, the equations of the unrestricted model have $np + 4$ parameters (np lagged variables, the intercept, and the three seasonals). For T usable observations, set $c = np + 4$ and calculate the value of (5.44). If for some prespecified significance level, this calculated value χ^2 (with $3n$ degrees of freedom) exceeds the critical value, the restriction of no seasonal effects can be rejected.

The likelihood ratio test is based on asymptotic theory, which may not be very useful in the small samples available to time-series econometricians. Moreover, the likelihood ratio test is only applicable when one model is a restricted version of the other. Alternative test criteria are the multivariate generalizations of the AIC and SBC:

$$AIC = T \log|\Sigma| + 2N$$
$$SBC = T \log|\Sigma| + N \log(T)$$

where: $|\Sigma|$ = determinant of the variance/covariance matrix of the residuals

N = total number of parameters estimated *in all equations*

Thus, if each equation in an n-variable VAR has p lags and an intercept, $N = n^2p + n$; each of the n equations has np lagged regressors and an intercept.

Adding additional regressors will reduce $\log|\Sigma|$ at the expense of increasing N. As in the univariate case, select the model with the lowest AIC or SBC value. Make sure that you adequately compare the models by using the same number of observations in each. Note that the multivariate AIC and SBC cannot be used to *test* the statistical significance of alternative models. Instead, they are measures of the overall fit of the alternatives.

Granger Causality

One test of causality is whether the lags of one variable enter into the equation for another variable. In a two-equation model with p lags, $\{y_t\}$ does not **Granger cause** $\{z_t\}$ if and only if all of the coefficients of $A_{21}(L)$ are equal to zero. Thus, if $\{y_t\}$ does not improve the forecasting performance of $\{z_t\}$, then $\{y_t\}$ does not Granger cause $\{z_t\}$. *If all variables in the VAR are stationary*, the direct way to test Granger causality is to use a standard F-test of the restriction:

$$a_{21}(1) = a_{21}(2) = a_{21}(3) = \ldots = a_{21}(p) = 0$$

It is straightforward to generalize this notion to the n-variable case of (5.43). Since $A_{ij}(L)$ represents the coefficients of lagged values of variable j on variable i, variable j does not Granger cause variable i if all coefficients of the polynomial $A_{ij}(L)$ can be set equal to zero.

Note that Granger causality is something quite different from a test for exogeneity. For z_t to be exogenous, we would require that it not be affected by the contemporaneous value of y_t. However, Granger causality refers only to the effects of past values of $\{y_t\}$ on the current value of z_t. Hence, Granger causality actually measures whether current and past values of $\{y_t\}$ help to forecast future values of $\{z_t\}$. To illustrate the distinction in terms of a VMA model, consider the following equation for z_t:

$$z_t = \bar{z} + \phi_{21}(0)\varepsilon_{yt} + \sum_{i=0}^{\infty} \phi_{22}(i)\varepsilon_{zt-i}$$

If we forecast z_{t+1} conditional on the value of z_t, we obtain the forecast error $\phi_{21}(0)\varepsilon_{yt+1} + \phi_{22}(0)\varepsilon_{zt+1}$. Given the value of z_t, information concerning y_t does not aid in reducing the forecast error for z_{t+1}. In other words, for the model under consideration, $E_t(z_{t+1} \mid z_t) = E_t(z_{t+1} \mid z_t, y_t)$. The point is that the only additional information contained in y_t is the current and past values of $\{\varepsilon_{yt}\}$. However, such values do not affect z_t and so cannot improve on the forecasting performance of the z_t sequence. Thus, $\{y_t\}$ does not Granger cause $\{z_t\}$. On the other hand, since we are assuming that $\phi_{21}(0)$ is not zero, $\{z_t\}$ is not exogenous. Clearly, if $\phi_{21}(0)$ is not zero, pure shocks to y_{t+1} (i.e., ε_{yt+1}) affect the value of z_{t+1} even though the $\{y_t\}$ sequence does not Granger cause the $\{z_t\}$ sequence.

A **block exogeneity** test is useful for detecting whether to incorporate an additional variable into a VAR. Given the aforementioned distinction between causality and exogeneity, this multivariate generalization of the Granger causality test should actually be called a *block-causality* test. In any event, the issue is to determine whether lags of one variable—say, w_t—Granger cause any other of the variables in the system. In the three-variable case with w_t, y_t, and z_t, the test is whether lags of w_t Granger cause either y_t or z_t. In essence, the block exogeneity restricts all lags of w_t in the y_t and z_t to be equal to zero. This cross-equation restriction is properly tested using the likelihood ratio test given by (5.44). Estimate the y_t and z_t equations using lagged values of $\{y_t\}$, $\{z_t\}$, and $\{w_t\}$ and calculate Σ_u. Reestimate excluding the lagged values of $\{w_t\}$ and calculate Σ_r. Next, find the likelihood ratio statistic:

$$(T - c)(\log|\Sigma_r| - \log|\Sigma_u|)$$

As in (5.44), this statistic has a χ^2 distribution with degrees of freedom equal to the $2p$ (since p lagged values of $\{w_t\}$ are excluded from each equation). Here $c = 3p + 1$ because the unrestricted y_t and z_t equations contain p lags of $\{y_t\}$, $\{z_t\}$, and $\{w_t\}$ plus a constant.

Granger Causality and Money Supply Changes

The usefulness of Granger causality tests can be illustrated by a reconsideration of the type of time-series equation used in the St. Louis model. Through the late 1970s, the conventional wisdom was that fluctuations in money contained useful information about the future values of real income and prices. In fact, the argument in favor of conducting an active monetary policy is there exists a systematic relationship between current values of the money supply and future values of the price level and/or real income. However, there is a large literature indicating that this relationship broke down in the late 1970s. In an influential article, Friedman and Kuttner (1992) argue that the issue is whether fluctuations in money help predict future fluctuations in income that are not already predicted on the basis of income itself or other readily observable variables. Consider the VAR equation

$$\Delta y_t = \alpha + \sum_{i=1}^{4} \beta_i \Delta m_{t-i} + \sum_{i=1}^{4} \gamma_i \Delta g_{t-i} + \sum_{i=1}^{4} \delta_i \Delta y_{t-i} + \varepsilon_t$$

Notice how this equation differs from the St. Louis model given by (5.16). Here, the logarithmic change in nominal income (Δy_t) depends on its own past values, and past values of the logarithmic changes in the nominal money supply (Δm_t) and federal government expenditures (Δg_t).

The issue is simple; in the presence of past values of $\{\Delta y_t\}$ and $\{\Delta g_t\}$, does knowledge of the money supply series provide any information about future value of nominal income? Toward this end, Friedman and Kuttner (1992) used several measures of the money supply (e.g., the money base, $M1$, $M2$, and various short-term interest rates) and estimated a three-variable VAR over various sample periods. For the 1960:2 to 1979:2 period, the F-statistics for the null hypothesis that the money base does not Granger cause Δy_t is 3.68. At the 1 percent significance level, it is possible to conclude that money Granger causes $\{\Delta y_t\}$. However, for the 1970:3 to 1990:4 period, the F-statistic is only 0.82; hence, at any conventional significance level, money does not Granger cause income. The findings are quite robust to the other measures of the monetary variable. Until 1979:2, all of the monetary aggregates Granger cause nominal income at the 1 percent significance level. None of these aggregates Granger causes nominal income in the latter period.

To provide a better understanding of the interrelationships among the three variables, Friedman and Kuttner also report the results of the variance decompositions. For the 1960:2 to 1979:2 period, $M1$ explained 27 percent of the forecast error variance in $\{\Delta y_t\}$ at both the four- and eight-quarter forecast horizons. In contrast, for the 1970:3 to 1990:4 period, $M1$ explained about 10 percent of the forecast error variance in $\{\Delta y_t\}$ at both the four- and eight-quarter forecast horizons. These results are in striking contrast to those of the St. Louis equation. Undoubtedly, money supply changes have become less useful in predicting the future path of nominal income.

Tests with Nonstationary Variables

In Chapter 4, we saw that it possible to perform hypothesis tests on an individual equation when some of the regressors are stationary and others nonstationary. In particular, Rule 1 of Sims, Stock, and Watson (1990) was used to select the appropriate lag length in an augmented Dickey–Fuller test. The issue is particularly relevant to VARs since many of the regressors are likely to be nonstationary. Recall that a key finding of Sims, Stock, and Watson (1990) is: *If the coefficient of interest can be written as a coefficient on a stationary variable, then a t-test is appropriate.* If the sample size is large, you can use the normal approximation for the t-test. To take a specific example, consider the following equation from a two-variable VAR:

$$y_t = a_{11}y_{t-1} + a_{12}y_{t-2} + b_{11}z_{t-1} + b_{12}z_{t-2} + \varepsilon_t \tag{5.45}$$

First consider the case in which $\{y_t\}$ is $I(1)$ and $\{z_t\}$ is $I(0)$. Since b_{11} and b_{12} are coefficients on stationary variables, it is possible to use a t-test to test the hypothesis $b_{11} = 0$ or $b_{12} = 0$ and an F-test to test the hypothesis $b_{11} = b_{12} = 0$. Hence, lag lengths involving $\{z_t\}$ and the test to determine whether $\{z_t\}$ Granger causes $\{y_t\}$ can be performed using the t- or F-distributions.

Notice that it is possible to use a t-test for the restriction $a_{11} = 0$ or $a_{12} = 0$. You can perform both of these tests even though $\{y_t\}$ is not stationary. However, you cannot test the restriction $a_{11} = a_{12} = 0$ using an F-test. To make the point, add and subtract $a_{12}y_{t-1}$ to the right-hand side of (5.45) to obtain

$$y_t = a_{11}y_{t-1} + a_{12}y_{t-1} - a_{12}(y_{t-1} - y_{t-2}) + b_{11}z_{t-1} + b_{12}z_{t-2} + \varepsilon_t$$

and if we define $a_{11} + a_{12} = \gamma$, we can write

$$y_t = \gamma y_{t-1} - a_{12}\Delta y_{t-1} + b_{11}z_{t-1} + b_{12}z_{t-2} + \varepsilon_t$$

The coefficient a_{12} multiplies the stationary variable Δy_{t-1} so that it is permissible to test the null hypothesis $a_{12} = 0$ using a t-test. Alternatively, add and subtract $a_{11}y_{t-2}$ to the right-hand side of (5.45) to obtain

$$y_t = a_{11}\Delta y_{t-1} + \gamma y_{t-2} + b_{11}z_{t-1} + b_{12}z_{t-2} + \varepsilon_t$$

Thus, the null hypothesis $a_{11} = 0$ can similarly be tested using a t-statistic. It is important to recognize that the individual coefficients may have normal distributions, but the sum $a_{11} + a_{12} = \gamma$ does not have a normal distribution. It is impossible to isolate γ as the coefficient on a stationary variable.

Now suppose that $\{y_t\}$ and $\{z_t\}$ are both $I(1)$. It is easy to show that the coefficients a_{12} and b_{12} can be written as coefficients on stationary variables. Add and subtract both $a_{12}y_{t-1}$ and $b_{12}z_{t-1}$ to the right-hand side of (5.45) so that the equation becomes

$$y_t = (a_{11} + a_{12})y_{t-1} - a_{12}(y_{t-1} - y_{t-2}) + (b_{11} + b_{12})z_{t-1} - b_{12}(z_{t-1} - z_{t-2}) + \varepsilon_t$$

or

$$y_t = \gamma_1 y_{t-1} - a_{12}\Delta y_{t-1} + \gamma_2 z_{t-1} - b_{12}\Delta z_{t-1} + \varepsilon_t \qquad (5.46)$$

where $\gamma_1 = a_{11} + a_{12}$ and $\gamma_2 = b_{11} + b_{12}$.

Thus, it is possible to perform the lag length test $a_{12} = b_{12} = 0$ using an F-distribution. Equation (5.46) shows that it is possible to rewrite (5.45) in such a way that both coefficients multiply stationary variables. As such, an F-test can be used to test the joint restriction $a_{12} = b_{12} = 0$. However, the restriction that $\{z_t\}$ does not Granger cause $\{y_t\}$ involves the setting $\gamma_2 = b_{12} = 0$. Since γ_2 is a coefficient on a nonstationary variable, the test is nonstandard—a standard F-statistic is not appropriate. Only if you know that $\gamma_2 = 0$, can you perform a test to determine whether $\{z_t\}$ Granger causes $\{y_t\}$. Given that $\gamma_2 = 0$, (5.46) becomes

$$y_t = \gamma_1 y_{t-1} + a_{12}\Delta y_{t-1} + b_{12}\Delta z_{t-1} + \varepsilon_t$$

Now, it is possible to perform the causality test since only b_{12} needs to be restricted. In the same way, if it is known that $\gamma_1 = 1$, we can write[10]

$$\Delta y_t = a_{12}\Delta y_{t-1} + b_{12}\Delta z_{t-1} + \varepsilon_t$$

Now the VAR is entirely in first differences. As such, all coefficients multiply stationary variables. These results are quite general and hold for higher-order systems containing any number of lags. To summarize, in a VAR with stationary and nonstationary variables

1.   You can use t-tests or F-tests on the stationary variables.

2. You can perform a lag length test on any variable or any set of variables. This is true regardless of whether the variable in question is stationary.

3. You *may* be able to use an F-test to determine whether a nonstationary variable Granger causes another nonstationary variable. If the causal variable can be made to appear only in first differences, the test is permissible. For example, suppose y_t, z_t and x_t are all $I(1)$ and that it is possible to write the equation for $\{y_t\}$ as $y_t = \gamma_1 y_{t-1} + a_{12}\Delta y_{t-1} + a_{13}\Delta y_{t-2} + b_{12}\Delta z_{t-1} + b_{13}\Delta z_{t-2} + \gamma_3 x_{t-1} + c_{12}\Delta x_{t-1} + c_{13}\Delta x_{t-2} + \varepsilon_t$. It is possible to determine whether z_t Granger causes $\{y_t\}$ but not whether x_t Granger causes $\{y_t\}$. Similarly, you *cannot* test the joint restriction $\gamma_1 = a_{12} = 0$. (As shown in Chapter 6, if the variables are cointegrated, you cannot perform such causality tests.)

4. The issue of differencing is important. If the VAR can be written entirely in first differences, hypothesis tests can be performed on any equation or any set of equations using t-tests or F-tests. This follows because all of the variables are stationary. As you will see in the next chapter, it is possible to write the VAR in first differences if the variables are $I(1)$ and are *not* cointegrated. If the variables in question are cointegrated, the VAR cannot be written in first differences; hence, causality tests *cannot* be performed using t-tests or F-tests.

9. EXAMPLE OF A SIMPLE VAR: TERRORISM AND TOURISM IN SPAIN

In Enders and Sandler (1991), we used the VAR methodology to estimate the impact of terrorism on tourism in Spain during the period from 1970 to 1988. Most transnational terrorist incidents in Spain during this period were perpetrated by left-wing groups, which included the Anti-Fascist Resistance Group of October 1 (GRAPO), the ETA, the now-defunct International Revolutionary Armed Front (FRAP), and Iraultza. Most incidents are attributed to the ETA (Basque Fatherland and Liberty) and its splinter groups, such as the Autonomous Anti-Capitalist Commandos (CAA). Right-wing terrorist groups included the Anti-Terrorist Liberation Group (GAL), Anti-Terrorism ETA, and Warriors of Christ the King. Catalan independence groups, such as Free Land (Terra Lliure) and Catalan Socialist Party for National Liberation, were active in the late 1980s and often targeted U.S. businesses.

The transfer function model of Section 3 may not be appropriate because of feedback between terrorism and tourism. If high levels of tourism induce terrorist activities, the basic assumption of the transfer function methodology is violated. In fact, there is some evidence that the terrorist organizations in Spain target tourist hotels in the summer season. Since increases in tourism may generate terrorist acts, the VAR methodology allows us to examine the reactions of tourists to terrorism *and* the reactions of terrorists to tourism. We can gain some additional insights into the interrelation between the two series by performing Granger causality tests both of terrorism on tourism and of tourism on terrorism. Impulse response analysis can quantify and graphically depict the time path of the effects of a typical terrorist incident on tourism.

We assembled a time series of all publicly available transnational terrorist incidents that took place in Spain from 1970 through 1988. In total, there are 228 months of observation in the time series; each observation is the number of terrorist incidents occurring that month. The tourism data is taken from various issues of the National Statistics Institute's (Estadistic Institute Nacional) quarterly reports. In particular, we assemble a time series of the number of foreign tourists per month in Spain for the 1970–1988 period.

Empirical Methodology

Our basic methodology involves estimating tourism and terrorism in a vector autoregression (VAR) framework. Consider the following system of equations:

$$n_t = \alpha_{10} + A_{11}(L)n_{t-1} + A_{12}(L)i_{t-1} + e_{1t} \tag{5.47}$$

$$i_t = \alpha_{20} + A_{21}(L)n_{t-1} + A_{22}(L)i_{t-1} + e_{2t} \tag{5.48}$$

where: n_t = the number of tourists visiting Spain during time period t
  i_t = the number of transnational terrorist incidents in Spain during t
  α_{i0} = the vectors containing a constant, eleven seasonal (monthly) dummy
     variables, and a time trend
  A_{ij} = the polynomials in the lag operator L
  e_{it} = independent and identically distributed disturbance terms such that
     $E(e_{1t}e_{2t})$ is not necessarily zero

Although Sims (1980) recommends against the use of a deterministic time trend, we decided not to heed this advice. We experimented with several alternative ways to model the series; the model including the time trend had the best diagnostic statistics. Other variants included differencing (5.47) and (5.48) and simply eliminating the trend and letting the random walk plus drift terms capture any nonstationary behavior. Questions 7 and 8 at the end of this chapter ask you to compare these alternative ways of estimating a VAR.

The polynomials $A_{12}(L)$ and $A_{21}(L)$ in (5.47) and (5.48) are of particular interest. If all of the coefficients of $A_{21}(L)$ are zero, then knowledge of the tourism series does not reduce the forecast error variance of terrorist incidents. Formally, tourism would not Granger cause terrorism. Unless there is a contemporaneous response of terrorism to tourism, the terrorism series evolves independently of tourism. In the same way, if all of the coefficients of $A_{12}(L)$ are zero, then terrorism does not Granger cause tourism. The absence of a statistically significant contemporaneous correlation of the error terms would then imply that terrorism cannot affect tourism. If, instead, any of the coefficients in these polynomials differ from zero, there are interactions between the two series. In case of negative coefficients of $A_{12}(L)$, terrorism would have a negative effect on the number of foreign tourist visits to Spain.

Each equation was estimated using lag lengths of 24, 12, 6, and 3 months (i.e., for four estimations, we set $p = 24$, 12, 6, and 3). Because each equation has identical right-hand side variables, ordinary least squares (OLS) is an efficient estimation technique. Using χ^2 tests, we determined that a lag length of 12 months was most appropriate (reducing length from 24 to 12 months had a χ^2 value that was significant at the 0.56 level whereas reducing the lag length to 6 months had a χ^2 value that was significant at the 0.049 level). The AIC indicated that 12 lags were appropriate whereas the SBC suggested we could use only 6 lags. Since we were using monthly data, we decided to use the 12 lags.

To ascertain the importance of the interactions between the two series, we obtained the variance decompositions. The moving average representations of Equations (5.47) and (5.48) express n_t and i_t as dependent on the current and past values of both $\{e_{1t}\}$ and $\{e_{2t}\}$ sequences:

$$n_t = c_0 + \sum_{j=1}^{\infty} (c_{1j} e_{1t-j} + c_{2j} e_{2t-j}) + e_{1t} \qquad (5.49)$$

$$i_t = d_0 + \sum_{j=1}^{\infty} (d_{1j} e_{1t-j} + d_{2j} e_{2t-j}) + e_{2t} \qquad (5.50)$$

where c_0 and d_0 are vectors containing constants, the 11 seasonal dummies, and a trend; and c_{1j}, c_{2j}, d_{1j}, and d_{2j} are parameters.

Because we cannot estimate (5.49) and (5.50) directly, we used the residuals of (5.47) and (5.48) and then decomposed the variances of n_t and i_t into the percentages attributable to each type of innovation. We used the orthogonalized innovations obtained from a Choleski decomposition; the order of the variables in the factorization had no qualitative effects on our results (the contemporaneous correlation between e_{1t} and e_{2t} was -0.0176).

Empirical Results

The variance decompositions for a 24-month forecasting horizon, with significance levels in parentheses, are reported in Table 5.3. As expected, each time series explains the preponderance of its own past values; n_t explains over 91 percent of its forecast error variance, while i_t explains nearly 98 percent of its forecast error variance. It is interesting that terrorist incidents explain 8.7 percent of the forecast error variance of Spain's

Table 5.3 Variance Decomposition Percentage of 24-Month Variance

Percent of forecast error variance in	Typical shock in	
	n_t	i_t
n_t	91.3	8.7
	$(3 \times E - 15)$	(0.006)
i_t	2.2	97.8
	(17.2)	(93.9)

Note: The numbers in parentheses indicate the significance level for the joint hypothesis that all lagged coefficients of the variable in question can be set equal to zero.

tourism, while tourism explains only 2.2 percent of the forecast error variance of terrorist incidents. More important, Granger causality tests indicate that the effects of terrorism on tourism are significant at the 0.006 level, whereas the effects of tourism on terrorism are not significant at conventional levels. Thus, causality is unidirectional: Terrorism affects tourism but not the reverse. We also note that the terrorism series appears to be autonomous in the sense that neither series significantly explains the forecast error variance of i_t. This result is consistent with the notion that terrorists randomize their incidents so that any one incident is not predictable on a month-to-month basis.

Forecasts from an unrestricted VAR are known to suffer from overparameterization. Given the results of the variance decompositions and the Granger causality tests, we reestimated (5.47) and (5.48) restricting all of the coefficients of $A_{21}(L)$ to equal zero. Because the right-hand variables were no longer identical, we reestimated the equations with seemingly unrelated regressions (SUR). From the resulting coefficients from the SUR estimates, the effects of a typical terrorist incident on Spain's tourism can be depicted. In terms of the restricted version of (5.50), we set all e_{1t-j} and e_{2t-j} equal to zero for $j > 0$. We then simulated the time paths resulting from the effects of a one-unit shock to e_{2t}. The time path is shown in Figure 5.8, where the vertical axis measures the monthly impact on the number of foreign tourists and the horizontal axis the months following the shock. To smooth out the series, we present the time path of a three-month moving average of the simulated tourism response function.

After a "typical" terrorist incident, tourism to Spain begins to decline in the third month. After the sixth month, tourism begins to revert to its original level. There does appear to be a rebound in months eight and nine. There follows another drop in tourism in month nine, reaching the maximum decline about one year after the original incident. Obviously, some of this pattern is due to the seasonality in the series. However, tourism slowly recovers and generally remains below its preincident level for a substantial period of time. Aggregating all 36 monthly impacts, we estimate that the combined effects of a typical transnational terrorist incident in Spain are to decrease the total number of foreign visits by 140,847 people. By comparison, a total of 5,392,000 tourists visited Spain in 1988 alone.

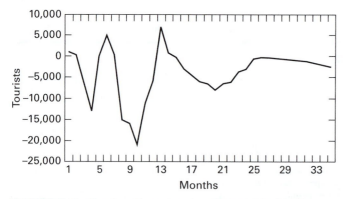

FIGURE 5.8   Tourism Response to a Terrorist Incident

10. STRUCTURAL VARS

Sims's (1980) VAR approach has the desirable property that all variables are treated symmetrically so that the econometrician does not rely on any "incredible identification restrictions." A VAR can be quite helpful in examining the relationship among a set of economic variables. Moreover, the resulting estimates can be used for forecasting purposes. Consider a first-order VAR system of the type represented by (5.19):

$$x_t = A_0 + A_1 x_{t-1} + e_t$$

Although the VAR approach yields only estimated values of A_0 and A_1, for exposition purposes, it is useful to treat each as being known. As we saw in (5.42), the n-step-ahead forecast error is

$$x_{t+n} - E_t x_{t+n} = e_{t+n} + A_1 e_{t+n-1} + A_1^2 e_{t+n-2} + \ldots + A_1^{n-1} e_{t+1} \quad (5.51)$$

Even though econometric analysis will never reveal the actual values of A_0 and A_1, an appropriately specified model will have forecasts that are unbiased and have minimum variance. Of course, if we had a priori information concerning any of the coefficients, it would be possible to improve the precision of the estimates and reduce the forecast-error variance. A researcher interested only on forecasting might want to trim down the overparameterized VAR model. Nonetheless, it should be clear that forecasting with a VAR is a multivariate extension of forecasting using a simple autoregression.

The VAR approach has been criticized as being devoid of any economic content. The sole role of the economist is to suggest the appropriate variables to include in the VAR. From that point on, the procedure is almost mechanical. Since there is so little economic input in a VAR, it should not be surprising that there is little economic content in the results. Of course, innovation accounting does require an ordering of the variables, but the selection of the ordering is generally ad hoc.

Unless the underlying structural model can be identified from the reduced-form VAR model, the innovations in a Choleski decomposition do not have a direct economic interpretation. Reconsider the two-variable VAR of (5.17) and (5.18):

$$y_t + b_{12} z_t = b_{10} + \gamma_{11} y_{t-1} + \gamma_{12} z_{t-1} + \varepsilon_{yt}$$
$$b_{21} y_t + z_t = b_{20} + \gamma_{21} y_{t-1} + \gamma_{22} z_{t-1} + \varepsilon_{zt}$$

so that it is possible to write the model in the form of (5.20) and (5.21):

$$y_t = a_{10} + a_{11} y_{t-1} + a_{12} z_{t-1} + e_{1t}$$
$$z_t = a_{20} + a_{21} y_{t-1} + a_{22} z_{t-1} + e_{2t}$$

where the various a_{ij} are defined as in (5.19). For our purposes, the important point to note is that the two error terms e_{1t} and e_{2t} are actually composites of the underlying shocks ε_{yt} and ε_{zt}. From (5.22) and (5.23),

$$\begin{bmatrix} e_{1t} \\ e_{2t} \end{bmatrix} = \frac{1}{1 - b_{12} b_{21}} \begin{bmatrix} 1 & -b_{12} \\ -b_{21} & 1 \end{bmatrix} \begin{bmatrix} \varepsilon_{yt} \\ \varepsilon_{zt} \end{bmatrix}$$

Although these composite shocks are the one-step-ahead forecast errors in y_t and z_t, they do not have a structural interpretation. Hence, there is an important difference between using VARs for forecasting and using VARs for economic analysis. In (5.51), e_{1t} and e_{2t} are forecast errors. If we are interested only in forecasting, the components of the forecast errors are unimportant. Given the economic model of (5.17) and (5.18), ε_{yt} and ε_{zt} are the autonomous changes in y_t and z_t in period t, respectively. If we want to obtain the impulse response functions or the variance decompositions, it is necessary to use the structural shocks (i.e., ε_{yt} and ε_{zt}), not the forecast errors. The aim of a structural VAR is to use economic theory (rather than the Choleski decomposition) to recover the structural innovations from the residuals $\{e_{1t}\}$ and $\{e_{2t}\}$.

The Choleski decomposition actually makes a strong assumption about the underlying structural errors. Suppose, as in (5.32), we select an ordering such that $b_{21} = 0$. With this assumption, the two pure innovations can be recovered as

$$\varepsilon_{zt} = e_{2t}$$

and

$$\varepsilon_{yt} = e_{1t} + b_{12}e_{2t}$$

Forcing $b_{21} = 0$ is equivalent to assuming that an innovation in y_t does not have a contemporaneous effect of z_t. Unless there is a theoretical foundation for this assumption, the underlying shocks are improperly identified. As such, the impulse responses and variance decompositions resulting from this improper identification can be quite misleading.

If the correlation coefficient between e_{1t} and e_{2t} is low, the ordering is not likely to be important. However, in a VAR with several variables, it is improbable that all correlations will be small. After all, in selecting the variables to include in a model, you are likely to choose variables that exhibit strong comovements. When the residuals of a VAR are correlated, it is not practical to try all alternative orderings. With a four-variable model, there are 24 (i.e., 4!) possible orderings. Sims (1986) and Bernanke (1986) propose modeling the innovations using economic analysis. The basic idea is to estimate the relationships among the structural shocks using an economic model. To understand the procedure, it is useful to examine the relationship between the forecast errors and the structural innovations in an n-variable VAR. Since this relationship is invariant to lag length, consider the first-order model with n variables:

$$\begin{bmatrix} 1 & b_{12} & b_{13} & \cdots & b_{1n} \\ b_{21} & 1 & b_{23} & \cdots & b_{2n} \\ \cdot & \cdot & \cdot & \cdots & \cdot \\ b_{n1} & b_{n2} & b_{n3} & \cdots & 1 \end{bmatrix} \begin{bmatrix} x_{1t} \\ x_{2t} \\ \cdots \\ x_{nt} \end{bmatrix} = \begin{bmatrix} b_{10} \\ b_{20} \\ \cdots \\ b_{n0} \end{bmatrix} + \begin{bmatrix} \gamma_{11} & \gamma_{12} & \gamma_{13} & \cdots & \gamma_{1n} \\ \gamma_{21} & \gamma_{22} & \gamma_{23} & \cdots & \gamma_{2n} \\ \cdot & \cdot & \cdot & \cdots & \cdot \\ \gamma_{n1} & \gamma_{n2} & \gamma_{n3} & \cdots & \gamma_{nn} \end{bmatrix} \begin{bmatrix} x_{1t-1} \\ x_{2t-1} \\ \cdots \\ x_{nt-1} \end{bmatrix} + \begin{bmatrix} \varepsilon_{1t} \\ \varepsilon_{2t} \\ \cdots \\ \varepsilon_{nt} \end{bmatrix}$$

or in compact form:

$$Bx_t = \Gamma_0 + \Gamma_1 x_{t-1} + \varepsilon_t$$

The multivariate generalization of (5.19) is obtained by premultiplying by B^{-1} so that

$$x_t = B^{-1}\Gamma_0 + B^{-1}\Gamma_1 x_{t-1} + B^{-1}\varepsilon_t$$

Defining $A_0 = B^{-1} \Gamma_0$, $A_1 = B^{-1} \Gamma_1$, and $e_t = B^{-1} \varepsilon_t$ yields (5.19). The problem, then, is to take the observed values of e_t and to restrict the system so as to recover ε_t as $\varepsilon_t = Be_t$. However, the selection of the various b_{ij} cannot be completely arbitrary. The issue is to restrict the system so as to (1) recover the various $\{\varepsilon_{it}\}$ and (2) to preserve the assumed error structure concerning the independence of the various $\{\varepsilon_{it}\}$ shocks. To solve this identification problem, simply count equations and unknowns. Using OLS, we can obtain the variance/covariance matrix Σ:

$$\Sigma = \begin{bmatrix} \sigma_1^2 & \sigma_{12} & \cdots & \sigma_{1n} \\ \sigma_{21} & \sigma_2^2 & \cdots & \sigma_{2n} \\ \cdot & \cdot & \cdot & \cdot \\ \sigma_{n1} & \sigma_{n2} & \cdots & \sigma_n^2 \end{bmatrix}$$

where each element of Σ is constricted as the sum:

$$\sigma_{ij} = (1/T) \sum_{t=1}^{T} e_{it}\, e_{jt}$$

Since Σ is symmetric, it contains only $(n^2 + n)/2$ distinct elements. There are n elements along the principal diagonal, $(n-1)$ along the first off-diagonal, $(n-2)$ along the next off-diagonal, ..., and one corner element for a total of $(n^2 + n)/2$ free elements. Given that the diagonal elements of B are all unity, B contains $n^2 - n$ unknown values. In addition, there are the n unknown values var(ε_{it}) for a total of n^2 unknown values in the structural model [i.e., the $n^2 - n$ values of B plus the n values var(ε_{it})]. Now the answer to the identification problem is simple; in order to identify the n^2 unknowns from the known $(n^2 + n)/2$ independent elements of Σ, it is necessary to impose an additional $n^2 - [(n^2 + n)/2] = (n^2 - n)/2$ restrictions on the system. This result generalizes to a model with p lags: *To identify the structural model from an estimated VAR, it is necessary to impose $(n^2 - n)/2$ restrictions on the structural model.*

Take a moment to count the number of restrictions in a Choleski decomposition. In the system above, the Choleski decomposition requires all elements above the principal diagonal to be zero:

$$b_{12} = b_{13} = b_{14} = \ldots = b_{1n} = 0$$
$$b_{23} = b_{24} = \ldots = b_{2n} = 0$$
$$b_{34} = \ldots = b_{3n} = 0$$
$$\ldots$$
$$b_{n-1n} = 0$$

Hence, there are a total of $(n^2 - n)/2$ restrictions; the system is exactly identified. To take a specific example, consider the following Choleski decomposition in a three-variable VAR:

$$e_{1t} = \varepsilon_{1t}$$
$$e_{2t} = c_{21}\varepsilon_{1t} + \varepsilon_{2t}$$
$$e_{3t} = c_{31}\varepsilon_{1t} + c_{22}\varepsilon_{2t} + \varepsilon_{3t}$$

From the previous discussion, you should be able to demonstrate that ε_{1t}, ε_{2t}, and ε_{3t} can be identified from the estimates of e_{1t}, e_{2t}, e_{3t}, and variance/covariance matrix Σ. In terms of our previous notation, define matrix $C = B^{-1}$ with elements c_{ij}. Hence, $e_t = C\varepsilon_t$. An alternative way to model the relationship between the forecast errors and the structural innovations is

$$
\begin{aligned}
e_{1t} &= \varepsilon_{1t} + c_{13}\varepsilon_{3t} \\
e_{2t} &= c_{21}\varepsilon_{1t} + \varepsilon_{2t} \\
e_{3t} &= c_{31}\varepsilon_{2t} + \varepsilon_{3t}
\end{aligned}
$$

Notice the absence of a triangular structure. Here, the forecast error of each variable is affected by its own structural innovation and the structural innovation in one other variable. Given the $(9-3)/2 = 3$ restrictions on C, the *necessary* condition for the exact identification of B and ε_t is satisfied. However, as illustrated in the next section, imposing $(n^2 - n)/2$ restrictions is not a sufficient condition for exact identification. Unfortunately, the presence of nonlinearities means there are no simple rules that guarantee exact identification.

For those wanting a bit more formality, write the variance/covariance matrix of the regression residuals as

$$
Eee' = \Sigma = \begin{pmatrix} \sigma_1^2 & \sigma_{12} \\ \sigma_{21} & \sigma_2^2 \end{pmatrix}
$$

Given that $e_t = B^{-1}\varepsilon_t$, it must be the case that

$$
Ee_te_t' = EB^{-1}\varepsilon_t\varepsilon_t'(B^{-1})' = B^{-1}\ E(\varepsilon_t\varepsilon_t')(B^{-1})' \tag{5.52}
$$

Note that $E(\varepsilon_t\varepsilon_t')$ is the variance/covariance matrix of the structural innovations (Σ_ε). Since the covariance between the structural shocks is zero, we can write Σ_ε as

$$
\Sigma_\varepsilon = \begin{bmatrix} \mathrm{var}(\varepsilon_1) & 0 \\ 0 & \mathrm{var}(\varepsilon_2) \end{bmatrix}
$$

To find the relationship between the structural innovations and the regression residuals, substitute Σ and Σ_ε into (5.52) to obtain

$$
\begin{pmatrix} \sigma_1^2 & \sigma_{12} \\ \sigma_{21} & \sigma_2^2 \end{pmatrix} = B^{-1} \begin{bmatrix} \mathrm{var}(\varepsilon_1) & 0 \\ 0 & \mathrm{var}(\varepsilon_2) \end{bmatrix} (B^{-1})'
$$

or

$$
\begin{pmatrix} \sigma_1^2 & \sigma_{12} \\ \sigma_{21} & \sigma_2^2 \end{pmatrix} = \begin{pmatrix} 1 & b_{12} \\ b_{21} & 1 \end{pmatrix}^{-1} \begin{bmatrix} \mathrm{var}(\varepsilon_1) & 0 \\ 0 & \mathrm{var}(\varepsilon_2) \end{bmatrix} \left[\begin{pmatrix} 1 & b_{12} \\ b_{21} & 1 \end{pmatrix}^{-1} \right]'
$$

Since the four values of Σ are known, it would appear that there are four equations to determine the four unknown values b_{12}, b_{21}, $\mathrm{var}(\varepsilon_1)$, and $\mathrm{var}(\varepsilon_2)$. However, the symmetry of the system is such that $\sigma_{21} = \sigma_{12}$ so that there are only three independent equations to determine the four unknown values. To generalize the argument to an nth-order VAR system, we have

$$\Sigma = B^{-1} \Sigma_\varepsilon (B^{-1})'$$

where Σ, B^{-1}, and Σ_ε are $n \cdot n$ matrices. Using the same logic, it is possible to show that it is necessary to impose $(n^2 - n)/2$ additional restrictions on B^{-1} to completely identify the system. Some specific examples are considered in the next section.

11. EXAMPLES OF STRUCTURAL DECOMPOSITIONS

To illustrate a Sims–Bernanke decomposition, suppose there are five residuals for e_{1t} and e_{2t}. Although a usable sample size of five is unacceptable for estimation purposes, it does allow us to do the necessary calculations in a simple fashion. Thus, suppose that the five error terms are

t	1	2	3	4	5
e_{1t}	1.0	−0.5	0.0	−1.0	0.5
e_{2t}	0.5	−1.0	0.0	−0.5	1.0

Since $\{e_{1t}\}$ and $\{e_{2t}\}$ are regression residuals, their sums are zero. It is simple to verify that $\sigma_1^2 = 0.5$, $\sigma_{12} = \sigma_{21} = 0.4$, and $\sigma_2^2 = 0.5$; hence, the variance/covariance matrix Σ is

$$\Sigma = \begin{bmatrix} 0.5 & 0.4 \\ 0.4 & 0.5 \end{bmatrix}$$

Although the covariance between ε_{1t} and ε_{2t} is zero, the variances of ε_{1t} and ε_{2t} are presumably unknown. As in the previous section, let the variance/covariance matrix of these structural shocks be denoted by Σ_ε so that

$$\Sigma_\varepsilon = \begin{bmatrix} \mathrm{var}(\varepsilon_1) & 0 \\ 0 & \mathrm{var}(\varepsilon_2) \end{bmatrix}$$

The reason that the covariance terms are equal to zero is that ε_{1t} and ε_{2t} are deemed to be pure structural shocks. Moreover, the variance of each shock is time-invariant. For notational convenience, the time subscript can be dropped; for example, $\mathrm{var}(\varepsilon_{1t}) = \mathrm{var}(\varepsilon_{1t-1}) = \dots = \mathrm{var}(\varepsilon_1)$. The relationship between the variance/covariance matrix of the forecast errors (i.e., Σ) and the variance/covariance matrix of the pure shocks (i.e., Σ_ε) is such that $\Sigma_\varepsilon = B\Sigma B'$. Recall that e_t and ε_t are the column vectors $(e_{1t}, e_{2t})'$ and $(\varepsilon_{1t}, \varepsilon_{2t})'$, respectively. Hence,

$$e_t e_t' = \begin{bmatrix} e_{1t}^2 & e_{1t}e_{2t} \\ e_{1t}e_{2t} & e_{2t}^2 \end{bmatrix}$$

so that

$$\Sigma = \frac{1}{T} \sum_{t=1}^{T} e_t e_t' \qquad (5.53)$$

Similarly, Σ_ε is

$$\Sigma_\varepsilon = \frac{1}{T}\sum_{t=1}^{T}\varepsilon_t\varepsilon_t' \qquad (5.54)$$

To link the two variance/covariance matrices, note that the relationship between ε_t and e_t is such that $\varepsilon_t = Be_t$. Substitute this relationship into (5.54) and recall that the transpose of a product is the product of the transposes [i.e., $(Be_t)' = e' + B_t'$], so that

$$\Sigma_\varepsilon = \frac{1}{T}\sum_{t=1}^{T}Be_te_t'B'$$

Using (5.53), we get

$$\Sigma_\varepsilon = B\Sigma B'$$

Using the specific numbers in the example, it follows that

$$\begin{bmatrix} \text{var}(\varepsilon_1) & 0 \\ 0 & \text{var}(\varepsilon_2) \end{bmatrix} = \begin{bmatrix} 1 & b_{12} \\ b_{21} & 1 \end{bmatrix}\begin{bmatrix} 0.5 & 0.4 \\ 0.4 & 0.5 \end{bmatrix}\begin{bmatrix} 1 & b_{21} \\ b_{12} & 1 \end{bmatrix}$$

Since both sides of this equation are equivalent, they must be the same element by element. Carry out the indicated multiplication of $B\Sigma B'$ to obtain

$$\text{Var}(\varepsilon_1) = 0.5 + 0.8b_{12} + 0.5b_{12}^2 \qquad (5.55)$$

$$0 = 0.5b_{21} + 0.4b_{21}b_{12} + 0.4 + 0.5b_{12} \qquad (5.56)$$

$$0 = 0.5b_{21} + 0.4b_{12}b_{21} + 0.4 + 0.5b_{12} \qquad (5.57)$$

$$\text{Var}(\varepsilon_2) = 0.5b_{21}^2 + 0.8b_{21} + 0.5 \qquad (5.58)$$

As you can see, equations (5.56) and (5.57) are identical. There are three independent equations to solve for the four unknowns b_{12}, b_{21}, $\text{var}(\varepsilon_1)$, and $\text{var}(\varepsilon_2)$. As we saw in the last section, in a two-variable system, one restriction needs to be imposed if the structural model is to be identified. Now consider the Choleski decomposition one more time. If $b_{12} = 0$, we find

$\text{var}(\varepsilon_1) = 0.5$
$\qquad 0 = 0.5b_{21} + 0.4$ so that $b_{21} = -0.8$
$\qquad 0 = 0.5b_{21} + 0.4$ so that again we find $b_{21} = -0.8$
$\text{var}(\varepsilon_2) = 0.5(b_{21})^2 + 0.8b_{21} + 0.5$ so that $\text{var}(\varepsilon_2) = 0.5(0.64) - 0.64 + 0.5 = 0.18$

Using this decomposition, we can recover each $\{\varepsilon_{1t}\}$ and $\{\varepsilon_{2t}\}$ as $\varepsilon_t = Be_t$:

$$\varepsilon_{1t} = e_{1t}$$

and

$$\varepsilon_{2t} = -0.8e_{1t} + e_{2t}$$

Thus, the identified structural shocks are

t	1	2	3	4	5
ε_{1t}	1.0	−0.5	0.0	−1.0	0.5
ε_{2t}	−0.3	−0.6	0.0	0.3	0.6

If you want to take the time, you can verify that $\text{var}(\varepsilon_1) = \Sigma(\varepsilon_{1t})^2/5 = 0.5$, $\text{var}(\varepsilon_{2t})$ $= \Sigma(\varepsilon_{2t})^2/5 = 0.18$, and $\text{cov}(\varepsilon_{1t}, \varepsilon_{2t}) = \Sigma\varepsilon_{1t}\varepsilon_{2t}/5 = 0$. Instead, if we impose the alternative restriction of a Choleski decomposition and set $b_{21} = 0$, from (5.55) through (5.58) we obtain

$$\text{var}(\varepsilon_1) = 0.5 + 0.8b_{12} + 0.5b_{12}{}^2$$
$$0 = 0.4 + 0.5b_{12} \qquad\qquad \text{so that } b_{12} = -0.8$$
$$0 = 0.4 + 0.5b_{12} \qquad\qquad \text{so again } b_{12} = -0.8$$
$$\text{var}(\varepsilon_2) = 0.5$$

Since $b_{12} = -0.8$, $\text{var}(\varepsilon_1) = 0.5 + 0.8(-0.8) + 0.5(0.64) = 0.18$. Now B is identified as

$$B = \begin{bmatrix} 1 & -0.8 \\ 0 & 1 \end{bmatrix}$$

If we use the identified values of B, the structural innovations are such that $\varepsilon_{1t} = e_{1t} - 0.8e_{2t}$ and $\varepsilon_{2t} = e_{2t}$. Hence, we have the structural innovations

t	1	2	3	4	5
ε_{1t}	0.6	0.3	0.0	−0.6	−0.3
ε_{2t}	0.5	−1.0	0.0	−0.5	1.0

In this example, the ordering used in the Choleski decomposition is very important. This should not be too surprising since the correlation coefficient between e_{1t} and e_{2t} is 0.8. The point is that the ordering will have important implications for the resulting variance decompositions and impulse response functions. Selecting the first ordering (i.e., setting $b_{12} = 0$) gives more importance to innovations in ε_{1t}. The assumed timing is such that ε_{1t} can have a contemporaneous effect on x_{1t} and x_{2t} while ε_{2t} shocks can affect x_{1t} only with a one-period lag. Moreover, the amplitude of the impulse responses attributable to ε_{1t} shocks will be increased since the ordering affects the magnitude of a "typical" (i.e., one-standard deviation) shock in ε_{1t} and decreases the magnitude of a "typical" ε_{2t} shock.

The important point to note is that *the Choleski decomposition is only one type of identification restriction*. With three independent equations among the four unknowns b_{12}, b_{21}, $\text{var}(\varepsilon_{1t})$, and $\text{var}(\varepsilon_{2t})$, any other linearly independent restriction will allow for the identification of the structural model. Consider some of the other alternatives:

1. *A coefficient restriction.* Suppose that we know that a one-unit innovation ε_{2t} has a one-unit effect on x_{1t}; hence, suppose we know that $b_{12} = 1$. By using the other three independent equations, it follows that $\text{var}(\varepsilon_{1t}) = 1.8$, $b_{21} = -1$ and $\text{var}(\varepsilon_{2t}) = 0.2$.

Given that $\varepsilon_t = Be_t$, we obtain

$$\begin{bmatrix} \varepsilon_{1t} \\ \varepsilon_{2t} \end{bmatrix} = \begin{bmatrix} 1 & 1 \\ -1 & 1 \end{bmatrix}\begin{bmatrix} e_{1t} \\ e_{2t} \end{bmatrix}$$

so that $\varepsilon_{1t} = e_{1t} + e_{2t}$ and $\varepsilon_{2t} = -e_{1t} + e_{2t}$. If we use the five hypothetical regression residuals, the decomposed innovations become

t	1	2	3	4	5
ε_{1t}	1.5	−1.5	0.0	−1.5	1.5
ε_{2t}	−0.5	−0.5	0.0	0.5	0.5

2. *A variance restriction.* Given the relationship between Σ_ε and Σ (i.e., $\Sigma_\varepsilon = B\Sigma B'$), a restriction on the variances contained within Σ_ε will always imply multiple solutions for the coefficients of B. To keep the arithmetic simple, suppose that we know $\mathrm{var}(\varepsilon_{1t}) = 1.8$. The first equation yields two possible solutions for $b_{12} = 1$ and $b_{12} = -2.6$; unless we have a theoretical reason to discard one of these magnitudes, there are two solutions to the model. If $b_{12} = 1$, the remaining solutions are $b_{21} = -1$, and $\mathrm{var}(\varepsilon_{2t}) = 0.2$. If $b_{12} = -2.6$, the solutions are $b_{21} = -5/3$ and $\mathrm{var}(\varepsilon_{2t}) = 5/9$.

   The two solutions can be used to identify two different $\{\varepsilon_{1t}\}$ and $\{\varepsilon_{2t}\}$ sequences, and innovation accounting can be performed using both solutions. Even though there are two solutions, both satisfy the theoretical restriction concerning $\mathrm{var}(\varepsilon_{1t})$.

3. *Symmetry restrictions.* A linear combination of the coefficients and variances can be used for identification purposes. For example, the symmetry restriction $b_{12} = b_{21}$ can be used for identification. If we use equation (5.56), there are two solutions: $b_{12} = b_{21} = -0.5$ or $b_{12} = b_{21} = -2.0$. For the first solution, we find $\mathrm{var}(\varepsilon_{1t}) = 0.225$ and for the second solution $\mathrm{var}(\varepsilon_{1t}) = 0.9$.[11]

   Nevertheless, for the first solution,

$$\begin{bmatrix} \varepsilon_{1t} \\ \varepsilon_{2t} \end{bmatrix} = \begin{bmatrix} 1 & -0.5 \\ -0.5 & 1 \end{bmatrix}\begin{bmatrix} e_{1t} \\ e_{2t} \end{bmatrix}$$

so that

t	1	2	3	4	5
ε_{1t}	0.75	0.0	0.0	−0.75	0.0
ε_{2t}	0.0	−0.75	0.0	0.0	0.75

Overidentified Systems

It may be that economic theory suggests more than $(n^2 - n)/2$ restrictions. If so, it is necessary to modify the method above. The procedure for identifying an overidentified system entails the following steps:

STEP 1: The restrictions on B or $\text{var}(\varepsilon_{it})$ do not affect the estimation of VAR coefficients. Hence, estimate the unrestricted VAR, $x_t = A_0 + A_1 x_{t-1} + \ldots + A_p x_{t-p} + e_t$. Use the standard lag length and block causality tests to help determine the form of the VAR.

STEP 2: Obtain the unrestricted variance/covariance matrix Σ. The determinant of this matrix is an indicator of the overall fit of the model.

STEP 3: Restricting B and/or Σ_ε will affect the estimate of Σ. Select the appropriate restrictions and maximize the likelihood function with respect to the free parameters of B and Σ_ε. This will lead to an estimate of the restricted variance/covariance matrix. Denote this second estimate by Σ_R.

For those wanting a more technical explanation, note that the log likelihood function is

$$-\frac{T}{2}\ln|\Sigma| - \frac{1}{2}\sum_{t=1}^{T}(e_t'\Sigma^{-1}e_t)$$

Fix each element of e_t (and e_t') at the level obtained using OLS; call these estimated OLS residuals $\hat{e}_t$. Now use the relationship $\Sigma_\varepsilon = B\Sigma B'$ so that the log likelihood function can be written as

$$-\frac{T}{2}\ln|B^{-1}\Sigma_\varepsilon(B')^{-1}| - \frac{1}{2}\sum_{t=1}^{T}(\hat{e}_t'B'\Sigma_\varepsilon^{-1}B\hat{e}_t)$$

Now select the restrictions on B and Σ_ε and maximize with respect to the remaining free elements of these two matrices. The resulting estimates of B and Σ_ε imply a value of Σ that we have dubbed Σ_R. A number of popular software packages can perform this type of estimation using the Generalized Method of Moments.

STEP 4: If the restrictions are not binding, Σ and Σ_R will be equivalent. Let $R =$ the number of overidentifying restrictions; i.e., $R =$ number of restrictions exceeding $(n^2 - n)/2$. Then the χ^2 test statistic

$$\chi^2 = |\Sigma_R| - |\Sigma|$$

with R degrees of freedom can be used to test the restricted system.[12] If the calculated value of χ^2 exceeds that in a χ^2 table, the restrictions can be rejected. Now allow for two sets of overidentifying restrictions such that the number of restrictions in R_2 exceeds that in R_1. In fact, if $R_2 > R_1 \geq (n^2 - n)/2$, the significance of the extra $R_2 - R_1$ restrictions can be tested as

$$\chi^2 = |\Sigma_{R2}| - |\Sigma_{R1}| \text{ with } R_2 - R_1 \text{ degrees of freedom}$$

Similarly, in an overidentified system, the t-statistic for the individual coefficients can be obtained. Sims warns that the calculated standard errors may not be very accurate.

Sims' Structural VAR

Sims (1986) uses a six-variable VAR of quarterly data over the period 1948:1 to 1979:3. The variables included in the study are real GNP (y), real business fixed investment (i), the GNP deflator (p), the money supply as measured by M1 (m), unemployment (u), and the treasury bill rate (r). An unrestricted VAR was estimated with four lags of each variable and a constant term. Sims obtained the 36 impulse response functions using a Choleski decomposition with the ordering $y \rightarrow i \rightarrow p \rightarrow m \rightarrow u \rightarrow r$. Some of the impulse response functions had reasonable interpretations. However, the response of real variables to a money supply shock seemed unreasonable. The impulse responses suggested that a money supply shock had little effect on prices, output, or the interest rate. Given a standard money demand function, it is hard to explain why the public would be willing to hold the expanded money supply. Sims proposes an alternative to the Choleski decomposition that is consistent with money market equilibrium. Sims restricts the B matrix such that

$$
\begin{bmatrix}
1 & b_{11} & 0 & 0 & 0 & 0 \\
b_{21} & 1 & b_{23} & b_{24} & 0 & 0 \\
b_{31} & 0 & 1 & 0 & 0 & b_{36} \\
b_{41} & 0 & b_{43} & 1 & 0 & b_{46} \\
b_{51} & 0 & b_{53} & b_{54} & 1 & b_{56} \\
0 & 0 & 0 & 0 & 0 & 1
\end{bmatrix}
\begin{bmatrix}
r_t \\
m_t \\
y_t \\
p_t \\
u_t \\
i_t
\end{bmatrix}
=
\begin{bmatrix}
\varepsilon_{rt} \\
\varepsilon_{mt} \\
\varepsilon_{yt} \\
\varepsilon_{pt} \\
\varepsilon_{ut} \\
\varepsilon_{it}
\end{bmatrix}
$$

Notice there are 17 zero restrictions on the b_{ij}—the system is overidentified; with six variables, exact identification requires only $(6^2 - 6)/2 = 15$ restrictions. Imposing these restrictions, Sims identifies the following six relationships among the contemporaneous innovations:

$$r_t = 71.20m_t + \varepsilon_{rt} \tag{5.59}$$

$$m_t = 0.283y_t + 0.224p_t - 0.0081r_t + \varepsilon_{mt} \tag{5.60}$$

$$y_t = -0.00135r_t + 0.132i_t + \varepsilon_{yt} \tag{5.61}$$

$$p_t = -0.0010r_t + 0.045y_t - 0.00364i_t + \varepsilon_{pt} \tag{5.62}$$

$$u_t = -0.116r_t - 20.1y_t - 1.48i_t - 8.98p_t + \varepsilon_{ut} \tag{5.63}$$

$$i_t = \varepsilon_{it} \tag{5.64}$$

Sims views (5.59) and (5.60) as money supply and demand functions, respectively. In (5.59), the money supply rises as the interest rate increases. The demand for money in (5.60) is positively related to income and the price level and negatively related to the interest rate. Investment innovations in (5.64) are completely autonomous. Otherwise,

Sims sees no reason to restrict the other equations in any particular fashion. For simplicity, he chooses a Choleski-type block structure for GNP, the price level, and the unemployment rate. The impulse response functions appear to be consistent with the notion that money supply shocks affect prices, income, and the interest rate.

One limitation of the technique is that the restrictions on the signs of the $c_{ij}(0)$ can have important effects on statistical inference in an overidentified system. The essence of the argument developed in Waggoner and Zha (1997) relies on the fact that the contemporaneous impulse responses are obtained as the solutions to

$$\begin{bmatrix} e_{1t} \\ e_{2t} \end{bmatrix} = \begin{bmatrix} c_{11}(0) & c_{12}(0) \\ c_{21}(0) & c_{22}(0) \end{bmatrix} \begin{bmatrix} \varepsilon_{1t} \\ \varepsilon_{2t} \end{bmatrix}$$

Suppose that $c_{11}(0)$ is small and is estimated with a large standard error. Restricting $c_{11}(0)$ to be positive (so that ε_{1t} shocks are estimated to increase output with probability one) can artificially inflate the standard errors of the remaining $c_{ij}(0)$.

12. THE BLANCHARD–QUAH DECOMPOSITION

Blanchard and Quah (1989) provide an alternative way to obtain a structural VAR. Their aim is to reconsider the Beveridge and Nelson (1981) decomposition of real GNP into its temporary and permanent components. Toward this end, they develop a macroeconomic model such that real GNP is affected by demand-side and supply-side disturbances. In accord with the natural rate hypothesis, demand-side disturbances have no long-run effect on real GNP. On the supply side, productivity shocks are assumed to have permanent effects on output. In a univariate model, there is no unique way to decompose a variable into its temporary and permanent components. However, using a bivariate VAR, Blanchard and Quah show how to decompose real GNP and recover the two pure shocks.

To take a general example, suppose we are interested in decomposing an $I(1)$ sequence, say $\{y_t\}$, into its temporary and permanent components. Let there be a second variable $\{z_t\}$ that is affected by the same two shocks. For the time being, suppose that $\{z_t\}$ is stationary. If we ignore the intercept terms, the bivariate moving average (BMA) representation of the $\{y_t\}$ and $\{z_t\}$ sequences will have the form

$$\Delta y_t = \sum_{k=0}^{\infty} c_{11}(k)\varepsilon_{1t-k} + \sum_{k=0}^{\infty} c_{12}(k)\varepsilon_{2t-k} \tag{5.65}$$

$$z_t = \sum_{k=0}^{\infty} c_{21}(k)\varepsilon_{1t-k} + \sum_{k=0}^{\infty} c_{22}(k)\varepsilon_{2t-k} \tag{5.66}$$

or in a more compact form,

$$\begin{bmatrix} \Delta y_t \\ z_t \end{bmatrix} = \begin{bmatrix} C_{11}(L) & C_{12}(L) \\ C_{21}(L) & C_{22}(L) \end{bmatrix} \begin{bmatrix} e_{1t} \\ e_{2t} \end{bmatrix}$$

where ε_{1t} and ε_{2t} = independent white-noise disturbances, each having a constant variance and the $C_{ij}(L)$ are polynomials in the lag operator L such that the individual coefficients of $C_{ij}(L)$ are denoted by $c_{ij}(k)$. For example, the third coefficient of $C_{21}(L)$ is $c_{21}(3)$. For convenience, the time subscripts on the variances and the covariance terms are dropped and the shocks are normalized so that var$(\varepsilon_1) = 1$ and var$(\varepsilon_2) = 1$. If we call Σ_ε the variance/covariance matrix of the innovations, it follows that

$$\Sigma_\varepsilon = \begin{bmatrix} \text{var}(\varepsilon_1) & \text{cov}(\varepsilon_1, \varepsilon_2) \\ \text{cov}(\varepsilon_1, \varepsilon_2) & \text{var}(\varepsilon_2) \end{bmatrix}$$

$$= \begin{bmatrix} 1 & 0 \\ 0 & 1 \end{bmatrix}$$

In order to use the Blanchard and Quah technique, at least one of the variables must be nonstationary since $I(0)$ variables do not have a permanent component. However, to use the method, both variables must be in a stationary form. Since $\{y_t\}$ is $I(1)$, (5.65) uses the first difference of the series. Note that (5.66) implies that the $\{z_t\}$ sequence is $I(0)$; if in your own work you find $\{z_t\}$ is also $I(1)$, use its first difference.

In contrast to the Sims–Bernanke procedure, Blanchard and Quah do not directly associate the $\{\varepsilon_{1t}\}$ and $\{\varepsilon_{2t}\}$ shocks with the $\{y_t\}$ and $\{z_t\}$ sequences. Instead, the $\{y_t\}$ and $\{z_t\}$ sequences are the endogenous variables, and the $\{\varepsilon_{1t}\}$ and $\{\varepsilon_{2t}\}$ sequences represent what an economic theorist would call the exogenous variables. In their example, y_t is the logarithm of real GNP, z_t is unemployment, ε_{1t} is an aggregate demand shock, and ε_{2t} is an aggregate supply shock. The coefficients of $C_{11}(L)$, for example, represent the impulse responses of an aggregate demand shock on the time path of change in the log of real GNP.[13]

The key to decomposing the $\{y_t\}$ sequence into its permanent and stationary components is to assume that one of the shocks has a temporary effect on the $\{y_t\}$ sequence. It is this dichotomy between temporary and permanent effects that allows for the complete identification of the structural innovations from an estimated VAR. For example, Blanchard and Quah assume that an aggregate demand shock has no long-run effect on real GNP. In the long run, if real GNP is to be unaffected by the demand shock, it must be the case that the cumulated effect of an ε_{1t} shock on the Δy_t sequence must be equal to zero. Hence, the coefficients $c_{11}(k)$ in (5.65) must be such that

$$\sum_{k=0}^{\infty} c_{11}(k) \, \varepsilon_{1t-k} = 0$$

Since this must hold for any possible realization of the $\{\varepsilon_{1t}\}$ sequence, it must be the case that

$$\sum_{k=0}^{\infty} c_{11}(k) = 0 \tag{5.67}$$

Since the demand-side and supply-side shocks are not observed, the problem is to recover them from a VAR estimation. Given that the variables are stationary, we know there exists a VAR representation of the form

$$\begin{bmatrix} \Delta y_t \\ z_t \end{bmatrix} = \begin{bmatrix} A_{11}(L) & A_{12}(L) \\ A_{21}(L) & A_{22}(L) \end{bmatrix} \begin{bmatrix} \Delta y_{t-1} \\ z_{t-1} \end{bmatrix} + \begin{bmatrix} e_{1t} \\ e_{2t} \end{bmatrix} \tag{5.68}$$

or to use a more compact notation

$$x_t = A(L)x_{t-1} + e_t$$

where: x_t = the column vector $(\Delta y_t, z_t)'$
   e_t = the column vector $(e_{1t}, e_{2t})'$
   $A(L)$ = the $2 \cdot 2$ matrix with elements equal to the polynomials $A_{ij}(L)$
and the coefficients of $A_{ij}(L)$ are denoted by $a_{ij}(k)$.[14]

The critical insight is that the VAR residuals are composites of the pure innovations ε_{1t} and ε_{2t}. For example, e_{1t} is the one-step-ahead forecast error of y_t; i.e., $e_{1t} = \Delta y_t - E_{t-1} \Delta y_t$. From the BMA, the one-step-ahead forecast error is $c_{11}(0)\varepsilon_{1t} + c_{12}(0)\varepsilon_{2t}$. Since the two representations are equivalent, it must be the case that

$$e_{1t} = c_{11}(0)\varepsilon_{1t} + c_{12}(0)\varepsilon_{2t} \tag{5.69}$$

Similarly, since e_{2t} is the one-step-ahead forecast error of z_t,

$$e_{2t} = c_{21}(0)\varepsilon_{1t} + c_{22}(0)\varepsilon_{2t} \tag{5.70}$$

or, combining (5.69) and (5.70), we get

$$\begin{bmatrix} e_{1t} \\ e_{2t} \end{bmatrix} = \begin{bmatrix} c_{11}(0) & c_{12}(0) \\ c_{21}(0) & c_{22}(0) \end{bmatrix} \begin{bmatrix} \varepsilon_{1t} \\ \varepsilon_{2t} \end{bmatrix}$$

If $c_{11}(0)$, $c_{12}(0)$, $c_{21}(0)$, and $c_{22}(0)$ were known, it would be possible to recover ε_{1t} and ε_{2t} from the regression residuals e_{1t} and e_{2t}. Blanchard and Quah show that the relationship between (5.68) and the BMA model plus the long-run restriction of (5.67) provide exactly four restrictions that can be used to identify these four coefficients. The VAR residuals can be used to construct estimates of var(e_1), var(e_2), and cov(e_1, e_2).[15] Hence, there are the following four restrictions:

RESTRICTION 1

Given (5.69) and noting that $E\varepsilon_{1t}\varepsilon_{2t} = 0$, the normalization var($\varepsilon_1$) = var($\varepsilon_2$) = 1 means that the variance of e_{1t} is

$$\text{var}(e_1) = c_{11}(0)^2 + c_{12}(0)^2 \tag{5.71}$$

RESTRICTION 2

Similarly, using (5.70), the variance of e_{2t} is related to $c_{21}(0)$ and $c_{22}(0)$ as
$$\text{var}(e_2) = c_{21}(0)^2 + c_{22}(0)^2 \tag{5.72}$$

RESTRICTION 3

The product of e_{1t} and e_{2t} is

$$e_{1t}e_{2t} = [c_{11}(0)\varepsilon_{1t} + c_{12}(0)\varepsilon_{2t}][c_{21}(0)\varepsilon_{1t} + c_{22}(0)\varepsilon_{2t}]$$

If we take the expectation, the covariance of the VAR residuals is

$$Ee_{1t}e_{2t} = c_{11}(0)c_{21}(0) + c_{12}(0)c_{22}(0) \tag{5.73}$$

Thus, equations (5.71), (5.72), and (5.73) can be viewed as three equations in the four unknowns $c_{11}(0)$, $c_{12}(0)$, $c_{21}(0)$, and $c_{22}(0)$. The fourth restriction is embedded in the assumption that the $\{\varepsilon_{1t}\}$ has no long-run effect on the $\{y_t\}$ sequence. The problem is to transform the restriction (5.67) into its VAR representation. Since the algebra is a bit messy, it is helpful to rewrite (5.68) as

$$x_t = A(L)Lx_t + e_t$$

so that

$$[I - A(L)L]x_t = e_t$$

and, by premultiplying by $[I - A(L)L]^{-1}$, we obtain

$$x_t = [I - A(L)L]^{-1} e_t \qquad (5.74)$$

Denote the determinant of $[I - A(L)L]$ by the expression D. It should not take too long to convince yourself that (5.74) can be written as

$$\begin{bmatrix} \Delta y_t \\ z_t \end{bmatrix} = \frac{1}{D} \begin{bmatrix} 1 - A_{22}(L)L & A_{12}(L)L \\ A_{21}(L)L & 1 - A_{11}(L)L \end{bmatrix} \begin{bmatrix} e_{1t} \\ e_{2t} \end{bmatrix}$$

or, using the definitions of the $A_{ij}(L)$, we get

$$\begin{bmatrix} \Delta y_t \\ z_t \end{bmatrix} = \frac{1}{D} \begin{bmatrix} 1 - \sum a_{22}(k)L^{k+1} & \sum a_{12}(k)L^{k+1} \\ \sum a_{21}(k)L^{k+1} & 1 - \sum a_{11}(k)L^{k+1} \end{bmatrix} \begin{bmatrix} e_{1t} \\ e_{2t} \end{bmatrix}$$

where the summations run from $k = 0$ to infinity.

Thus, the solution for Δy_t in terms of the current and lagged values of $\{e_{1t}\}$ and $\{e_{2t}\}$ is

$$\Delta y_t = \frac{1}{D} \left\{ \left[1 - \sum_{k=0}^{\infty} a_{22}(k)L^{k+1} \right] e_{1t} + \sum_{k=0}^{\infty} a_{12}(k)L^{k+1}e_{2t} \right\} \qquad (5.75)$$

Now e_{1t} and e_{2t} can be replaced by (5.69) and (5.70). Making these substitutions, the restriction that the $\{\varepsilon_{1t}\}$ sequence has no long-run effect on y_t is

$$\left[1 - \sum_{k=0}^{\infty} a_{22}(k)L^{k+1} \right] c_{11}(0)\varepsilon_{1t} + \sum_{k=0}^{\infty} a_{12}(k)L^{k+1}c_{21}(0)\varepsilon_{1t} = 0$$

RESTRICTION 4

For all possible realizations of the $\{\varepsilon_{1t}\}$ sequence, ε_{1t} shocks will have only temporary effects on the Δy_t sequence (and on y_t itself) if

$$\left[1 - \sum_{k=0}^{\infty} a_{22}(k) \right] c_{11}(0) + \sum_{k=0}^{\infty} a_{12}(k)c_{21}(0) = 0$$

With this fourth restriction, there are four equations that can be used to identify the unknown values $c_{11}(0)$, $c_{12}(0)$, $c_{21}(0)$, and $c_{22}(0)$. To summarize, the steps in the procedure are as follows:

STEP 1: Begin by pretesting the two variables for time trends and for unit roots. If $\{y_t\}$ does not have a unit root, there is no reason to proceed with the decomposition. Appropriately transform the two variables so that the resulting sequences are both $I(0)$. Perform lag-length tests to find a reasonable specification for the VAR. The residuals of the estimated VAR should pass the standard diagnostic checks for white-noise processes (of course, e_{1t} and e_{2t} can be correlated with each other).

STEP 2: Using the residuals of the estimated VAR, calculate the variance/covariance matrix; i.e., calculate $\mathrm{var}(e_1)$, $\mathrm{var}(e_2)$, $\mathrm{cov}(e_1, e_2)$. Also calculate the sums:

$$1 - \sum_{k=0}^{p} a_{22}(k) \text{ and } \sum_{k=0}^{p} a_{12}(k)$$

where p = lag length used to estimate the VAR.

Use these values to solve the following four equations for $c_{11}(0)$, $c_{12}(0)$, $c_{21}(0)$, and $c_{22}(0)$:

$$\mathrm{Var}(e_1) = c_{11}(0)^2 + c_{12}(0)^2$$
$$\mathrm{Var}(e_2) = c_{21}(0)^2 + c_{22}(0)^2$$
$$\mathrm{Cov}(e_1, e_2) = c_{11}(0)c_{21}(0) + c_{12}(0)c_{22}(0)$$
$$0 = c_{11}(0)[1 - \Sigma a_{22}(k)] + c_{21}(0)\Sigma a_{12}(k)$$

Given these four values $c_{ij}(0)$ and the residuals of the VAR, the entire $\{\varepsilon_{1t}\}$ and $\{\varepsilon_{2t}\}$ sequences can be identified using the formulas[16]

$$e_{1t-i} = c_{11}(0)\varepsilon_{1t-i} + c_{12}(0)\varepsilon_{2t-i}$$

and

$$e_{2t-i} = c_{21}(0)\varepsilon_{1t-i} + c_{22}(0)\varepsilon_{2t-i}$$

STEP 3: As in a traditional VAR, the identified $\{\varepsilon_{1t}\}$ and $\{\varepsilon_{2t}\}$ sequences can be used to obtain impulse response functions and variance decompositions. The difference is that the interpretation of the impulses is straightforward. For example, Blanchard and Quah are able to obtain the impulse responses of the change in the log of real GNP to a typical supply-side shock. Moreover, it is possible to obtain the historical decomposition of each series. For example, set all $\{\varepsilon_{1t}\}$ shocks equal to zero and use the actual $\{\varepsilon_{2t}\}$ series (i.e., use the identified values of ε_{2t}) to obtain the permanent changes in $\{y_t\}$ as[17]

$$\Delta y_t = \sum_{k=0}^{\infty} c_{12}(k)\, \varepsilon_{2t-k}$$

The Blanchard and Quah Results

In their study, Blanchard and Quah (1989) use the first difference of the logarithm of real GNP and the level of unemployment. They note that unemployment exhibits an apparent time trend and that there is a slowdown in real growth beginning in the mid-1970s. Since there is no obvious way to address these difficult issues, they estimate four different VARs. Two include a dummy allowing for the change in the rate of growth in output, and two include a deterministic time trend in unemployment. Using quarterly GNP and unemployment data over the period 1950:2 through 1987:4, they estimated a VAR with eight lags.

Imposing the restriction that demand-side shocks have no long-run effect on real GNP, Blanchard and Quah identify the two types of shocks. The impulse response functions for the four VARs are quite similar:

- The time paths of demand-side disturbances on output and unemployment are hump-shaped. The impulse responses are mirror images of each other; initially output increases while unemployment decreases. The effects peak after four quarters; afterwards they converge to their original levels.

- Supply-side disturbances have a cumulative effect on output. A supply disturbance having a positive effect on output has a small positive initial effect on unemployment. After this initial increase, unemployment steadily decreases and the cumulated change becomes negative after four quarters. Unemployment remains below its long-run level for nearly five years.

Blanchard and Quah find that the alternative methods of treating the slowdown in output growth and the trend in unemployment affect the variance decompositions. Since the goal here is to illustrate the technique, consider only the variance decomposition using a dummy variable for the decline in output growth and detrended unemployment.

Percent of Forecast Error Variance Due to Demand-Side Shocks

Forecasting Horizon (Quarters)	Output	Unemployment
1	99.0	51.9
4	97.9	80.2
12	67.6	86.2
40	39.3	85.6

At short-run horizons, the huge preponderance of the variation in output is due to demand-side innovations. Demand shocks account for almost all of the movement in GNP at short horizons. Since demand shock effects are necessarily temporary, the findings contradict those of Beveridge and Nelson. The proportion of the forecast error variance falls steadily as the forecast horizon increases; the proportion converges to zero since these effects are temporary. Consequently, the contribution of supply-side innovations to real GNP movements increases at longer forecasting horizons. On the other hand, demand-side shocks generally account for increasing proportions of the variation in unemployment at longer forecasting horizons.

13. DECOMPOSING REAL AND NOMINAL EXCHANGE RATES: AN EXAMPLE

In Enders and Lee (1997), we decompose real and nominal exchange rate movements into the components induced by real and nominal factors. This section presents a small portion of the paper in order to further illustrate the methodology of the Blanchard and Quah technique. One aim of the study is to explain the deviations from purchasing power parity. As in Chapter 4, the real exchange rate (r_t) can be defined as[18]

$$r_t = e_t + p_{ft} - p_t$$

where p_{ft} and p_t refer to the logarithms of U.S. and Canadian wholesale price indices and e_t is the logarithm of the Canadian dollar/U.S. dollar nominal exchange rate.

To explain the deviations from PPP, we suppose that there are two types of shocks: a real shock and a nominal shock. The theory suggests that real shocks can cause permanent changes in the real exchange rate but that nominal shocks can cause only temporary movements in the real rate. For example, in the long run, if Canada doubles its nominal money supply, the Canadian price level and the exchange rate will both double (i.e., p_t and e_t will double). Hence, in the long run, the real exchange rate remains invariant to a money supply shock.

For Step 1, we perform various unit root tests on the monthly Canadian/U.S. dollar real and nominal exchange rates over the 1973:1 to 1989:12 period. Consistent with other studies focusing on the post–Bretton Woods period, it is clear that real and nominal rates can be characterized by nonstationary processes. We use the first difference of the logarithm of each in the decomposition. Our BMA model has the form:

$$\begin{bmatrix} \Delta r_t \\ \Delta e_t \end{bmatrix} = \begin{bmatrix} C_{11}(L) & C_{12}(L) \\ C_{21}(L) & C_{22}(L) \end{bmatrix} \begin{bmatrix} \varepsilon_{rt} \\ \varepsilon_{nt} \end{bmatrix}$$

where ε_{rt} and ε_{nt} represent the zero-mean mutually uncorrelated real and nominal shocks, respectively.

The restriction that the nominal shocks have no long-run effect on the real exchange rate is represented by the restriction that the sum of the coefficients in $C_{12}(L)$ sum to zero; thus, if $c_{ij}(k)$ is the kth coefficient in $C_{ij}(L)$, as in (5.67), the restriction is

$$\sum_{k=0}^{\infty} c_{12}(k) = 0 \qquad (5.76)$$

The restriction in (5.76) implies that the cumulative effect of ε_{nt} on Δr_t is zero, and consequently, that the long-run effect of ε_{nt} on the level of r_t itself is zero. Put another way, the nominal shock ε_{tn} has only short-run effects on real exchange rate. Note that there is no restriction on the effects of a real shock on the real rate or on the effects of either real or nominal shocks on the nominal exchange rate.

For Step 2, we estimate a bivariate VAR model for several lag lengths. At conventional significance levels, formal tests indicate that one lag is sufficient. However, to avoid the possibility of omitting important effects at longer lags, we performed the entire analysis using lag lengths of 1 month, 6 months, and 12 months.

The variance decomposition using the actual $\{\varepsilon_{nt}\}$ and $\{\varepsilon_{rt}\}$ sequences allows us to assess the relative contributions of the real and nominal shocks to forecast error variance of the real and nominal exchange rate series.

Percent of Forecast Error Variance Accounted for by Real Shocks

Horizon	Δr_t	Δe_t
1 month	100.0%	81.5%
3 months	99.9	79.2
12 months	98.5	78.1
36 months	98.5	78.1

As is immediately evident, real shocks explain almost all of the forecast error variance of the real exchange rate at any forecast horizon. Nominal shocks accounted for approximately 20 percent of the forecast error variance of the nominal exchange rate. Our interpretation is that real shocks are responsible for movements in real *and* nominal exchange rates. Hence, we should expect them to display sizable comovements.

Figure 5.9 shows the impulse response functions of the real and nominal exchange rates to both types of shocks. For clarity, the results are shown for the levels of exchange rates (as opposed to first differences) measured in terms of standard deviations. For real shocks:

1. The effect of a "real" shock is to cause an immediate increase in the real and nominal exchange rate. It is interesting to note that the jump in the real value of the dollar is nearly the same as that of the nominal dollar. Moreover, these changes are all of a permanent nature. Real and nominal rates converge to their new long-run levels in about nine months.

2. The movement in the real rate to its long-run level is almost immediate while the nominal value of the U.S. dollar generally rises over time (i.e., the U.S. dollar price of the Canadian dollar falls). There is little evidence of exchange rate overshooting.

3. Long-run changes in the two rates are almost identical, but surprisingly, the long-run real rate jumps more rapidly than does the nominal rate.

As required by our identification restriction, the effect of a nominal shock on the real exchange rate is necessarily temporary. Notice that the effects of typical "nominal" shocks of one standard deviation are all significantly smaller than the effects of typical "real" shocks. A typical nominal shock causes a rise in the nominal value of the U.S. dollar with no evidence of overshooting. Finally, the real U.S. dollar initially moves in the same direction as does the U.S. nominal dollar.

It is instructive to examine the hypothetical time paths of the nominal rate that result from the decomposition. Normalize both rates such that January 1973 = 1.0. Figure 5.10 shows that if all shocks had been nominal shocks, the Canadian dollar would have declined (i.e., the U.S. dollar would have appreciated) rather steadily throughout the entire period; it appears that the rate of depreciation would have accelerated beginning in the early 1980s and continuing throughout 1989. The role of the "real" shock was generally reinforcing that of the nominal shock. It is particularly

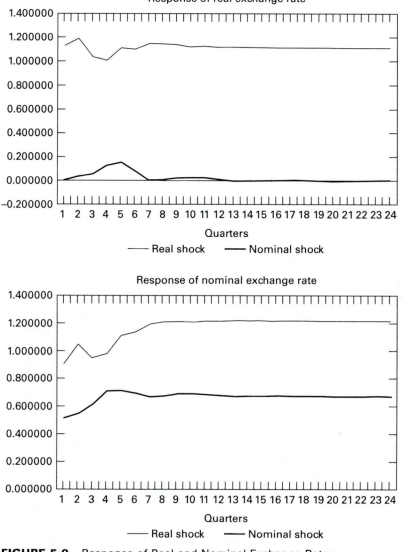

FIGURE 5.9 Response of Real and Nominal Exchange Rates

interesting to note that the real shock captures the major turning points of actual rates. The sharp depreciation beginning in 1978 and the sharp appreciation beginning around 1986 are the result of real, as opposed to nominal, factors.

Limitations of the Technique

A problem with this type of decomposition is that there are many types of shocks. As recognized by Blanchard and Quah (1989), the approach is limited by its ability to

——— Actual   ---- Real   ——— Nominal

FIGURE 5.10 Decomposed Real Canadian Dollar

identify *at most* only as many types of distinct shocks as there are variables. Blanchard and Quah prove several propositions that are somewhat helpful when the presence of three or more structural shocks is suspected. Suppose there are several disturbances having permanent effects but only one having a temporary effect on $\{y_t\}$. If the variance of one type of permanent disturbance grows "arbitrarily" small relative to the other, then the decomposition scheme approaches the correct decomposition. The second proposition they prove is if there are multiple permanent disturbances (temporary disturbances), the correct decomposition is possible if and only if the individual distributed lag responses in the real and nominal exchange rate are sufficiently similar across equations. By "sufficiently similar," Blanchard and Quah mean that the coefficients may differ up to a scalar lag distribution. Yet both propositions essentially imply that there are only two types of disturbances. For the first proposition, the third disturbance must be arbitrarily small. For the second proposition, the third disturbance must have a sufficiently similar path to one of the others. It is wise to avoid such a decomposition when the presence of three or more important disturbances is suspected. Alternatively, as in Clarida and Gali (1994), you might be able to develop a model implying three long-run restrictions among three variables.

Waggoner and Zha (1997) show that the normalizations used to identify the shocks are not innocuous. The Blanchard–Quah restrictions produce a system of quadratic equations so that the signs of the $c_{ij}(0)$ are not identified. In these circumstances, Taylor (2003) recommends the use of overidentifying restrictions or those normalizations that are consistent with an underlying economic model.

14. SUMMARY AND CONCLUSIONS

Intervention analysis was used to determine the effects of installing metal detectors in airports. More generally, intervention analysis can be used to ascertain how any *deterministic* function affects an economic time series. Usually the shape of the intervention function is clear, as in the metal detector example. However, there is a wide variety of possible intervention functions. If there is an ambiguity, the shape of the intervention function can be determined using the standard Box–Jenkins criteria for model selection. The crucial assumption in intervention analysis is that the intervention function has only deterministic components.

Transfer function analysis is appropriate if the "intervention" sequence is stochastic. If $\{y_t\}$ is endogenous and $\{z_t\}$ is exogenous, a transfer function can be fit using a five-step procedure discussed in Section 2. The procedure is a straightforward modification of the standard Box–Jenkins methodology. The resulting impulse response function traces out the time path of $\{z_t\}$ realizations on the $\{y_t\}$ sequence. This technique was illustrated by a study showing that terrorist attacks caused Italy's tourism revenues to decline by a total 600 million SDR.

With economic data, it is not always clear that one variable is dependent and the others are independent. In the presence of feedback, intervention and transfer function analysis are inappropriate. Instead, use a vector autoregression, which treats all variables as jointly endogenous. Each variable is allowed to depend on its past realizations and on the past realizations of all other variables in the system. There is no special attention paid to parsimony since the imposition of the "incredible identification restrictions" may be inconsistent with economic theory. Granger causality tests, block exogeneity, and lag-length tests can help select a more parsimonious model.

Ordinary least squares yield efficient estimates of the VAR coefficients. One difficulty with VAR analysis is that the underlying structural model cannot be recovered from estimated VAR. An arbitrary Choleski decomposition provides an extra equation necessary for identification of the structural model. For each variable in the system, innovation accounting techniques can be used to ascertain: (i) the percentage of the forecast error variance attributable to each of the other variables and (ii) the impulse responses to the various innovations. This technique was illustrated by examining the relationship between terrorism and tourism in Spain.

Another difficulty of VAR analysis is that the system of equations is overparameterized. The Bayesian approach combines a set of prior beliefs with the traditional VAR methods presented in this text. West and Harrison (1989) provide an approachable introduction to the Bayesian approach. Litterman (1980) proposes a sensible set of Bayesian priors that have become the standard in Bayesian VAR models. Todd (1984) and Leamer (1986) provide very accessible applications of the Bayesian approach.

An important development is the convergence of traditional economic theory and the VAR framework. Structural VARs impose an economic model on the contemporaneous movements of the variables. As such, they allow for the identification of the parameters of the economic model and the structural shocks. The Bernanke–Sims procedure can be used to identify (or overidentify) the structural innovations. The Blanchard and Quah methodology imposes long-run restrictions on the impulse response functions to exactly identify the structural innovations. An especially useful feature of the technique is that it provides a unique decomposition of an economic time series into its temporary and permanent components.

QUESTIONS AND EXERCISES

1. Consider three forms of the intervention variable:

   pulse: $z_i = 1$ and all other $z_i = 0$
   pure jump: $z_1 = z_2 = \ldots = 1$ and all other $z_i = 0$
   prolonged impulse: $z_1 = 1$; $z_2 = 0.75$; $z_3 = 0.5$; $z_4 = 0.25$; and all other values of $z_i = 0$

   a. Show how each of the following $\{y_t\}$ sequences responds to the three types of interventions:

   i. $y_t = 0.5y_{t-1} + z_t + \varepsilon_t$

    ii. $y_t = -0.5y_{t-1} + z_t + \varepsilon_t$

    iii. $y_t = 1.25y_{t-1} - 0.5y_{t-2} + z_t + \varepsilon_t$

    iv. $y_t = y_{t-1} + z_t + \varepsilon_t$

    v. $y_t = 0.75y_{t-1} + 0.25y_{t-2} + z_t + \varepsilon_t$

  b. Notice that the intervention models in iv and v have unit roots. Show that the intervention variable $z_1 = 1$; $z_2 = -1$; and all other values of $z_i = 0$ has only a temporary effect on these two sequences.

  c. Show that an intervention variable will not have a permanent effect on a unit root process if all values of z_i sum to zero.

  d. Discuss the plausible models you might choose if the $\{y_t\}$ sequence is:

    i. stationary and you suspect that the intervention has a permanent effect on Ey_t.

    ii. stationary and you suspect that the intervention has a growing and then a diminishing effect.

    iii. nonstationary and you suspect that the intervention has a permanent effect on the level of $\{y_t\}$.

    iv. nonstationary and you suspect that the intervention has a temporary effect on the level of the $\{y_t\}$.

    v. nonstationary and you suspect that the intervention increases the trend growth of $\{y_t\}$.

2. Let the realized value of the $\{z_t\}$ sequence be such that $z_1 = 1$ and all other values of $z_i = 0$.

  a. Use equation (5.11) to trace out the effects of the $\{z_t\}$ sequence on the time path of y_t.

  b. Use equation (5.12) to trace out the effects of the $\{z_t\}$ sequence on the time paths of y_t and Δy_t.

  c. Use equation (5.13) to trace out the effects of the $\{z_t\}$ sequence on the time paths of y_t and Δy_t.

  d. Would your answers to parts (a) through (c) change if $\{z_t\}$ was assumed to be a white-noise process and you were asked to trace out the effects if a z_t shock of the various $\{y_t\}$ sequences?

  e. Assume that $\{z_t\}$ is a white-noise process with a variance equal to unity.

    i. Use (5.11) to derive the cross-correlogram between $\{z_t\}$ and $\{y_t\}$.

    ii. Use (5.12) to derive the cross-correlogram between $\{z_t\}$ and $\{\Delta y_t\}$.

    iii. Use (5.13) to derive the cross-correlogram between $\{z_t\}$ and $\{\Delta y_t\}$.

    iv. Now suppose that z_t is the random walk process $z_t = z_{t-1} + \varepsilon_{zt}$. Trace out the effects of an ε_{zt} shock on the Δy_t sequence.

3. Consider the transfer function model: $y_t = 0.5y_{t-1} + z_t + \varepsilon_t$

where z_t is the autoregressive process: $z_t = 0.5z_{t-1} + \varepsilon_{zt}$.

  a. Derive the cross-correlations between the filtered $\{y_t\}$ sequence and the $\{\varepsilon_{zt}\}$ sequence.

  b. Now suppose $y_t = 0.5y_{t-1} + z_t + 0.5z_{t-1} + \varepsilon_t$ and $z_t = 0.5z_{t-1} + \varepsilon_{zt}$. Derive the standardized cross-covariances between the filtered $\{y_t\}$ sequence and ε_{zt}. Show that the first and second cross-covariances are proportional to the cross-correlations. Show that the cross-covariances decay at the rate 0.5.

4.   Use (5.28) to find the appropriate second-order stochastic difference equation for y_t.

$$\begin{bmatrix} y_t \\ z_t \end{bmatrix} = \begin{bmatrix} 0.8 & 0.2 \\ 0.2 & 0.8 \end{bmatrix} \begin{bmatrix} y_{t-1} \\ z_{t-1} \end{bmatrix} + \begin{bmatrix} e_{1t} \\ e_{2t} \end{bmatrix}$$

    a.   Determine whether the $\{y_t\}$ sequence is stationary.

    b.   Discuss the shape of the impulse response function of y_t to a one-unit shock in e_{1t} and to a one-unit shock in e_{2t}.

    c.   Suppose $e_{1t} = \varepsilon_{yt} + 0.5\varepsilon_{zt}$ and that $e_{2t} = \varepsilon_{zy}$. Discuss the shape of the impulse response function of y_t to a one-unit shock in ε_{yt}. Repeat for a one-unit shock in ε_{zt}.

    d.   Suppose $e_{1t} = \varepsilon_{yt}$ and that $e_{2t} = 0.5\varepsilon_{zy} + \varepsilon_{zt}$. Discuss the shape of the impulse response function of y_t to a one-unit shock in ε_{yt}. Repeat for a one-unit shock in ε_{zt}.

    e.   Use your answers to c and d to explain why the ordering in a Choleski decomposition is important.

    f.   Using the notation in (5.27), find A_1^2 and A_1^3. Does A_1^n appear to approach zero (i.e., the null matrix)?

5.   Using the notation of (5.20) and (5.21) suppose: $a_{10} = 0$, $a_{20} = 0$, $a_{11} = 0.8$, $a_{12} = 0.2$, $a_{21} = 0.4$, and $a_{22} = 0.1$.

    a.   Find the appropriate second-order stochastic difference equation for y_t. Determine whether the $\{y_t\}$ sequence is stationary.

    b.   Answer parts b through f of Question 4 using these new values of the a_{ij}.

    c.   How would the solution for y_t change if $a_{10} = 0.2$?

6.   Suppose the residuals of a VAR are such that $\text{var}(e_1) = 0.75$, $\text{var}(e_2) = 0.5$ and $\text{cov}(e_{1t}, e_{2t}) = 0.25$.

    a.   Using (5.55) – (5.58) as guides, show that it is not possible to identify the structural VAR.

    b.   Using Choleski decomposition such that $b_{12} = 0$, find the identified values of b_{21}, $\text{var}(\varepsilon_1)$, and $\text{var}(\varepsilon_2)$.

    c.   Using Choleski decomposition such that $b_{21} = 0$, find the identified values of b_{12}, $\text{var}(\varepsilon_1)$, and $\text{var}(\varepsilon_2)$.

    d.   Using a Sims–Bernanke decomposition such that $b_{12} = 0.5$, find the identified values of b_{21}, $\text{var}(\varepsilon_1)$, and $\text{var}(\varepsilon_2)$.

    e.   Using a Sims–Bernanke decomposition such that $b_{21} = 0.5$, find the identified values of b_{21}, $\text{Var}(\varepsilon_1)$, and $\text{Var}(\varepsilon_2)$.

    f.   Suppose that the first three values of e_{1t} are estimated to be 1, 0, –1 and that the first three values of e_{2t} are estimated to be –1, 0, 1. Find the first three values of ε_{1t} and ε_{2t} using each of the decompositions in parts b–e.

7.   This set of exercises uses data from the file entitled QUARTERLY.XLS. In Chapter 2, the logarithmic changes in the U.S. Producer Price Index (PPI) and M1 (not seasonally adjusted) were both estimated using the Box–Jenkins method. Here, the goal is to model both simultaneously using a VAR.

    a.   Construct the rate of growth of the money supply (m_t) and the inflation rate as measured by the PPI (π_t) as

$$m_t = \log(\text{M1NSA}_t) - \log(\text{M1NSA}_{t-1})$$
$$\pi_t = \log(\text{PPI}_t) - \log(\text{PPI}_{t-1})$$

Recall that both variables seemed to have some seasonality. In VAR analysis, it is common practice to include seasonal dummy variables to capture the seasonality. Construct the dummy variables D_1, D_2, and D_3, where $D_i = 1$ in the i-th quarter of each year and zero otherwise. Interpret the effects of the seasonal dummies in the following bivariate VAR:

$$m_t = A_{10} + A_{10}(1)D_1 + A_{10}(2)D_2 + A_{10}(3)D_3 + A_{11}(L)m_{t-1} + A_{12}(L)\pi_{t-1} + e_{1t}$$
$$\pi_t = A_{20} + A_{20}(1)D_1 + A_{20}(2)D_2 + A_{20}(3)D_3 + A_{21}(L)m_{t-1} + A_{22}(L)\pi_{t-1} + e_{2t}$$

b. Estimate the VAR above using 12 lags of each variable and save the residuals.

  i. Explain why the estimation cannot begin earlier than 1963:Q2.

  ii. Estimate the model (with the seasonal dummies) using 12 lags of each variable and save the residuals. You should find that $\log(|\Sigma_{12}|) = -18.72418$. Estimate same model *over the same sample period* now using only using 8 lags of each variable. You should find $\log(|\Sigma_8|) = -18.59680$.

  iii. Construct the likelihood ratio test for the null hypothesis of 8 lags. How many restrictions are there in the system? How many regressors are there in each of the unrestricted equations? If you answer correctly, you should find that the calculated value χ^2 with 16 degrees of freedom is 20.149669 with a significance level 0.214. Hence, the restriction 8 lags is not binding.

  iv. Repeat the procedure in order to determine if it is possible to further restrict the system to 4 lags of each variable. Now estimate models with 8 and 4 lags over the sample period 1962:Q2 – 2002:Q1. (Note that the number of regressors in the unrestricted model is now 20.) You should find:

$$\log(|\Sigma_8|) = -18.596804$$
$$\log(|\Sigma_4|) = -18.404343$$
$$\chi^2_{16} = 26.94462 \text{ with significance level 0.04}$$

  Hence, we reject the null hypothesis of only 4 lags.

  v. Now estimate the model with 8 lags. Perform the chi-square test to determine whether the seasonal dummy variables belong in the model. You should find that the sample value of $\chi^2_6 = 26.212510$. With six degrees of freedom, the *prob*-value is 0.0002.

c. Do you find the same lag lengths and the presence of the seasonal factors if you estimate the VAR in levels [i.e., if you estimate the VAR using $\log(M1NSA_t)$ and $\log(PPI_t)$ as variables]?

8. Question 7 indicated that an 8-lag VAR with the seasonal dummy variables is appropriate for the bivariate VAR containing the logarithmic changes of the U.S. Producer Price Index and M1 (not seasonally adjusted).

a. Determine whether m_t Granger causes π_t. You should find that F-statistic is 1.5226 with a *prob*-value of 0.154. How do you interpret this result?

b. Verify that the inflation rate Granger causes the money supply. You should find that the F-statistic is 2.7 with a *prob*-value of 0.008.

c. Verify that each variable Granger causes itself. Hence, inflation Granger causes money growth and Granger causes itself. Money growth, however, does not Granger cause inflation. Explain why it is important to know the correlation coefficient before concluding that money growth has no effect on inflation.

d. It turns out that the correlation coefficient between e_{1t} and e_{2t} is 0.05. Explain why the ordering in a Choleski decomposition is not likely to be important for obtaining the impulse responses. Let the ordering be such that m_t shocks have a contemporaneous effect on π_t. Verify:

Percent of Forecast Error Variance

	due to money shock	
Steps ahead	m_t	π_t
1	100.00	0.000
4	89.728	10.272
12	85.666	14.334

e.   What are the major weaknesses of this bivariate VAR study? Comment on the following issues:

   i.   The treatment of seasonality

   ii.   Other variables that may affect the relationship between money growth and inflation

   iii.   Changes in the conduct of monetary policy

f.   Some would argue that it would be better to estimate the VAR using the log-levels of the variables instead of the logarithmic first differences. Show that an eight-lag model (with seasonals) is appropriate using the log-levels of the variables.

   i.   Why might it be inappropriate to use Granger causality tests for this model?

   ii.   Do the causality tests using undifferenced data differ from those using the differenced data?

   iii.   Obtain the variance decompositions using the levels of the variables. Compare your results to those obtained in part d.

9.   The data set MONEY_DEM.XLS contains real U.S. GDP (RGDP), nominal GDP, the money supply as measured by M2 and the three-month rate on U.S. Treasury bills. As described in Chapter 2 of the Programming Manual, construct the following four variables

$$dlrgdp_t = \log(RGDP_t) - \log(RGDP_{t-1})$$
$$price_t = GDP_t / RGDP_t$$
$$dlrm2_t = \log(M2_t / price_t) - \log(M2_{t-1} / price_{t-1})$$
$$drs = tb3mo_t - tb3mo_{t-1}$$

Hence, $dlrgdp$ is the logarithmic change in real GDP, price is the GDP deflator, $dlrm2$ is the logarithmic change in the real money supply and drs is the change in the short-term interest rate.

a.   Estimate a three-variable VAR with twelve lags of $dlrgdp_t$, $dlrm2_t$ and drs_t. Include a constant but do not use any seasonal dummy variables.

b.   Calculate the multivariate AIC and SBC. Note that there are 37 coefficients (12 lags of three variables plus a constant) in each equation for a total of 111 estimated coefficients in the system.

c.   Reestimate the model using eight lags of each variable. Be sure to estimate the system over the same period used in part A. Note that the multivariate AIC selects the 12-lag model and the SBC selects the 8-lag model. Test for the appropriate lag length using the likelihood ratio test. Given the calculated value of $\chi^2 = 55.33$, the restriction is binding at the 5 percent (but not the 1 percent) significance level.

d.   Using the 12-lag model, show that drs_t is not block exogenous for the other two variables in the system.

e. Perform the Granger causality tests.

f. Jane obtained the impulse response functions (for 12-steps) with two standard deviation confidence intervals surrounding each. The results are shown in Figure 5.11.

    i. What was the ordering Jane used for the Choleski decomposition?

    ii. The vertical axis contains the magnitude of the effects. Why do you suppose that many econometricians prefer to scale the responses to a variable by the standard deviation of its own shock? What is the standard deviation of the $dlrgdp_t$ shock?

    iii. What variables have significant short-term responses for the other variables in the system?

g. Set up a near-VAR such that the lags of $dlrgdp_t$ are excluded from the equation for $dlrgdp_t$ and $dlrm2_t$. How does the near-VAR perform relative to the unrestricted VAR?

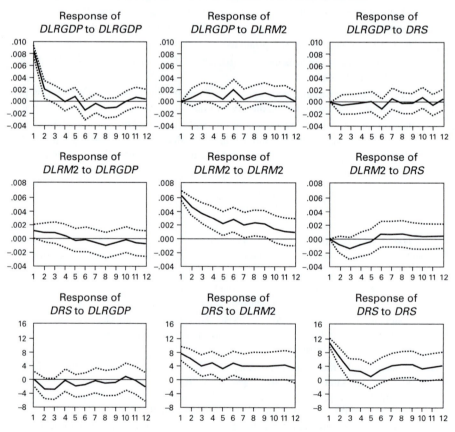

Response to Cholesky One S.D. Innovations ±2 S.E.

FIGURE 5.11 Impulse Responses for the Three-Variable VAR

10. Question 9 suggests that it is appropriate to estimate three-variable twelve-lag VAR for $dlrdgp_t$, $dlrm2_t$, and drs_t. Now suppose we want the contemporaneous relationships among the variables to be

$$\begin{bmatrix} e_{yt} \\ e_{mt} \\ e_{rt} \end{bmatrix} = \begin{bmatrix} 1 & 0 & 0 \\ g_{21} & 1 & g_{23} \\ 0 & 0 & 1 \end{bmatrix} \begin{bmatrix} \varepsilon_{yt} \\ \varepsilon_{mt} \\ \varepsilon_{rt} \end{bmatrix}$$

where e_{yt}, e_{mt}, and e_{rt} are the regression residual from the $dlrgdp_t$, $dlrm2_t$, and drs_t equations, and ε_{yt}, ε_{mt}, and ε_{rt} are the pure shocks (i.e., the structural innovations) to $dlrgdp_t$, $dlrm2_t$, and drs_t, respectively.

a. Provide a plausible economic interpretation of this set of restrictions.
b. Is the system identified?
c. Verify that the impulse responses of an interest rate shock are those provided in the Programming Manual. Compare these results to Jane's results shown in Figure 5.11.

ENDNOTES

1. In terms of the notation of Chapter 4, z_t is equivalent to the level dummy variable D_L.
2. In other words, if $c_0 \neq 0$, predicting y_{t+1} necessitates predicting the value of z_{t+1}.
3. In the identification process, we are primarily interested in the shape, not the height, of the cross-correlation function. It is useful to standardize the covariance by dividing through by σ_z^2; the shape of the correlogram is proportional to the standardized covariance. The text follows the procedure used by most software packages by plotting the standardized cross-covariances.
4. In such circumstances, Box and Jenkins (1976) recommend differencing y_t and/or z_t so that the resulting series are both stationary. The modern view cautions against this approach; as shown in the next chapter, a linear combination of nonstationary variables may be stationary. In such circumstances, the Box–Jenkins recommendation leads to overdifferencing. For the time being, it is assumed that $\{y_t\}$ and $\{z_t\}$ are both stationary processes.
5. We were able to obtain quarterly data from 1970:I to 1988:IV for Austria, Canada, Denmark, Finland, France, West Germany, Greece, Italy, the Netherlands, Norway, the United Kingdom, and the United States. The International Monetary Fund's *Balance of Payments Statistics* reports all data in Special Drawing Rights (SDR). Our dependent variable is the logarithm of nation's revenues divided by the sum of the revenues for all twelve countries.
6. Tourism is highly seasonal; we tried several alternative deseasonalization techniques. The results reported here were obtained using seasonal dummy variables. Hence, y_t represents the deseasonalized logarithmic share of tourism receipts. The published paper reports results using quarterly differencing. Using either type of deseasonalization, the final results were similar.
7. Expectations of the future can also be included in this framework. If the temperature $\{y_t\}$ is an autoregressive process, the expected value of next period's temperature (i.e., y_{t+1}) will depend on the current and past values. In (5.18), the presence of the terms y_t and y_{t-1} can represent how predictions of next period's temperature affect the current thermostat setting.
8. It is easily verified that this representation implies that $\rho_{12} = 0.8$. By definition, the correlation coefficient ρ_{12} is defined to be $\sigma_{12}/(\sigma_1\sigma_2)$ and the covariance is $Ee_{1t}e_{2t} = \sigma_{12}$. If we use the numbers in the example, $Ee_{1t}e_{2t} = E[\varepsilon_{zt}(\varepsilon_{yt} + 0.8\varepsilon_{zt})] = 0.8\sigma_z^2$. Since the decomposition equates var(e_{2t}) with σ_z^2, it follows that $\rho_{12} = 0.8$ if $\sigma_1^2 = \sigma_2^2$.
9. Other types of identification restrictions are included in Sections 10 through 13.
10. Note that γ_1 cannot equal zero if $\{y_t\}$ is $I(1)$. If $\gamma_1 = 0$, $y_t = a_{12}\Delta y_{t-1} + b_{12}\Delta z_{t-1} + \varepsilon_t$, the equation is unbalanced. The left-hand side contains the $I(1)$ variable y_t while the right-hand side contains only the three stationary variables Δy_t, Δz_t, and ε_t.

11. In the example under consideration, the symmetry restriction on the coefficients means that $\text{var}(\varepsilon_{1t})$ is equal to $\text{var}(\varepsilon_{2t})$. This result does not generalize; it holds in the example because of the assumed equality $\text{var}(e_{1t}) = \text{var}(e_{2t})$.

12. The value $|\Sigma_R| - |\Sigma|$ is asymptotically distributed as a χ^2 distribution with R degrees of freedom.

13. Since a key assumption of the model of the technique is that $E(\varepsilon_{1t}, \varepsilon_{2t}) = 0$, you might wonder how it is possible to assume that aggregate demand and supply shocks are independent. After all, if the stabilization authorities follow a feedback rule, aggregate demand will change in response to aggregate supply shocks. The key to understanding this apparent contradiction is that ε_{1t} is intended to be the orthogonalized portion of the demand shock, i.e., the portion of the demand shock that does not change in response to aggregate supply.

14. For example, $A_{11}(L) = a_{11}(0) + a_{11}(1)L + a_{11}(2)L^2 + \ldots$.

15. The VAR residuals also have a constant variance/covariance matrix. Hence, the time subscripts can be dropped.

16. Since two of the restrictions contain squared terms, there will be a positive value and an equal but opposite negative value for some of the coefficients. In Blanchard and Quah's example, if $c_{11}(0)$ is positive, positive demand shocks have a positive effect on output, and if $c_{11}(0)$ is negative, the positive shock has a negative effect on output. Taylor (2003) considers the problem of selecting among the alternative sets of solutions. Waggoner and Zha (1997) argue that the normalization can have important effects on statistical inference. In particular, the choice of the $c_{ij}(0)$ can have profound effects on the shape of the likelihood and, thus, confidence intervals for the impulse responses.

17. In doing so, it will be necessary to treat all $\varepsilon_{2t-i} = 0$ for $t - i < 1$.

18. Here, Canada is treated as the home country so that e_t is the Canadian dollar price of U.S. dollars and p_{ft} refers to the U.S. price level.

CHAPTER 6

COINTEGRATION AND ERROR-CORRECTION MODELS

This chapter explores an exciting new development in econometrics: the estimation of a structural equation or a VAR containing nonstationary variables. In univariate models, we have seen that a stochastic trend can be removed by differencing. The resulting stationary series can be estimated using univariate Box–Jenkins techniques. At one time, the conventional wisdom was to generalize this idea and difference all nonstationary variables used in a regression analysis. However, the appropriate way to treat nonstationary variables is not so straightforward in a multivariate context. It is quite possible for there to be a linear combination of integrated variables that is stationary; such variables are said to be **cointegrated.** Many economic models entail such cointegrating relationships. This chapter has three aims:

1. Introduce the basic concept of cointegration and show that it applies in a variety of economic models. Any equilibrium relationship among a set of nonstationary variables implies that their stochastic trends must be linked. After all, the equilibrium relationship means that the variables cannot move independently of each other. This linkage among the stochastic trends necessitates that the variables be cointegrated.

2. Consider the dynamic paths of cointegrated variables. Since the trends of cointegrated variables are linked, the dynamic paths of such variables must bear some relation to the current deviation from the equilibrium relationship. This connection between the change in a variable and the deviation from equilibrium is examined in detail. It is shown that the dynamics of a cointegrated system are such that the conventional wisdom was incorrect. After all, if the linear relationship is already stationary, differencing the relationship entails a misspecification error.

3. Study the alternative ways to test for cointegration. The econometric methods underlying the test procedures stem from the theory of simultaneous difference equations. The theory is explained and used to develop the two most popular cointegration tests. The proper way to estimate a system of cointegrated variables is examined. Several illustrations of each testing methodology are provided. Moreover, the two methods are compared by applying each to the same data set.

1. LINEAR COMBINATIONS OF INTEGRATED VARIABLES

Since money demand studies stimulated much of the cointegration literature, we begin by considering a simple model of money demand. Theory suggests that individuals want to hold a real quantity of money balances, so that the demand for nominal money holdings should be proportional to the price level. Moreover, as real income and the associated number of transactions increase, individuals will want to hold increased money balances. Finally, since the interest rate is the opportunity cost of holding money, money demand should be negatively related to the interest rate. In logarithms, an econometric specification for such an equation can be written as

$$m_t = \beta_0 + \beta_1 p_t + \beta_2 y_t + \beta_3 r_t + e_t \tag{6.1}$$

where: m_t = demand for money
  p_t = price level
  y_t = real income
  r_t = interest rate
  e_t = *stationary* disturbance term
  β_i = parameters to be estimated
and all variables but the interest rate are expressed in logarithms.

The hypothesis that the money market is in equilibrium allows the researcher to collect time-series data of the money supply (= money demand if the money market always clears), the price level, real income (possibly measured using real GDP), and an appropriate short-term interest rate. The behavioral assumptions require that $\beta_1 = 1$, $\beta_2 > 0$, and $\beta_3 < 0$; a researcher conducting such a study would certainly want to test these parameter restrictions. Be aware that the properties of the unexplained portion of the demand for money (i.e., the $\{e_t\}$ sequence) are an integral part of the theory. If the theory is to make any sense at all, any deviation in the demand for money must necessarily be temporary in nature. Clearly, if e_t has a stochastic trend, the errors in the model will be cumulative so that deviations from money market equilibrium will not be eliminated. Hence, a key assumption of the theory is that the $\{e_t\}$ sequence is stationary.

The problem confronting the researcher is that real GDP, the money supply, price level, and interest rate can all be characterized as nonstationary $I(1)$ variables. As such, each variable can meander without any tendency to return to a long-run level. However, the theory expressed in (6.1) asserts that there exists a linear combination of these nonstationary variables that is stationary! Solving for the error term, we can rewrite (6.1) as

$$e_t = m_t - \beta_0 - \beta_1 p_t - \beta_2 y_t - \beta_3 r_t \tag{6.2}$$

Since $\{e_t\}$ must be stationary, it follows that the linear combination of integrated variables given by the right-hand side of (6.2) must also be stationary. Thus, the theory necessitates that the time paths of the four nonstationary variables $\{m_t\}$, $\{p_t\}$, $\{y_t\}$, and $\{r_t\}$ be linked. This example illustrates the crucial insight that has dominated much of the macroeconometric literature in recent years: *Equilibrium theories involving nonstationary variables require the existence of a combination of the variables that is stationary.*

The money demand function is just one example of a stationary combination of nonstationary variables. Within any equilibrium framework, the deviations from equilibrium must be temporary. Other important economic examples involving stationary combinations of nonstationary variables include:

1. *Consumption function theory.* A simple version of the permanent income hypothesis maintains that total consumption (c_t) is the sum of permanent consumption (c_t^p) and transitory consumption (c_t^t). Since permanent consumption is proportional to permanent income (y_t^p), we can let β be the constant of proportionality and write $c_t = \beta y_t^p + c_t^t$. Transitory consumption is necessarily a stationary variable, and both consumption and permanent income are reasonably characterized as $I(1)$ variables. As such, the permanent income hypothesis requires that the linear combination of two $I(1)$ variables given by $c_t - \beta y_t^p$ be stationary.

2. *Unbiased forward rate hypothesis.* One form of the efficient market hypothesis asserts that the forward (or futures) price of an asset should equal the expected value of that asset's spot price in the future. The argument that the foreign exchange market is efficient requires that the one-period forward exchange rate equal the expectation of the spot rate in the next period. Letting f_t denote the log of the one-period price of forward exchange in t and s_t the log of the spot price of foreign exchange in t, the theory asserts that $E_t s_{t+1} = f_t$. If this relationship fails, speculators can expect to make a pure profit on their trades in the foreign exchange market. If agents' expectations are rational, the forecast error for the spot rate in $t + 1$ will have a conditional mean equal to zero, so that $s_{t+1} - E_t s_{t+1} = \varepsilon_{t+1}$ where $E_t \varepsilon_{t+1} = 0$. Combining the two equations yields $s_{t+1} = f_t + \varepsilon_{t+1}$. Since $\{s_t\}$ and $\{f_t\}$ are $I(1)$ variables, the **unbiased forward rate hypothesis** necessitates that there be a linear combination of nonstationary spot and forward exchange rates that is stationary.

3. *Commodity market arbitrage and purchasing power parity.* Theories of spatial competition suggest that in the short run, prices of similar products in varied markets might differ. However, arbiters will prevent the various prices from moving too far apart even if the prices are nonstationary. Similarly, the prices of Apple computers and PCs have exhibited sustained declines. Economic theory suggests that these simultaneous declines are related to each other since a price discrepancy between these similar products cannot continually widen. Also, as we saw in Chapter 4, purchasing power parity places restrictions on the movements of nonstationary price levels and exchange rates. If e_t denotes the log of the price of foreign exchange and p_t and p_{ft} denote, respectively, the logs of domestic and foreign price levels, long-run PPP requires that the linear combination $e_t + p_{ft} - p_t$ be stationary.

All of these examples illustrate the concept of **cointegration** as introduced by Engle and Granger (1987). Their formal analysis begins by considering a set of economic variables in long-run equilibrium when

$$\beta_1 x_{1t} + \beta_2 x_{2t} + \ldots + \beta_n x_{nt} = 0$$

Letting β and x_t denote the vectors $(\beta_1, \beta_2, ..., \beta_n)$ and $(x_{1t}, x_{2t}, ..., x_{nt})'$, the system is in long-run equilibrium when $\beta x_t = 0$. The deviation from long-run equilibrium—called the **equilibrium error**—is e_t, so that

$$e_t = \beta x_t$$

If the equilibrium is meaningful, it must be the case that the equilibrium error process is stationary. In a sense, the use of the term *equilibrium* is unfortunate because economic theorists and econometricians use the term in different ways. Economic theorists usually use the term to refer to an equality between desired and actual transactions. The econometric use of the term makes reference to any long-run relationship among nonstationary variables. Cointegration does not require that the long-run relationship be generated by market forces or by the behavioral rules of individuals. In Engle and Granger's use of the term, the equilibrium relationship may be causal, behavioral, or simply a reduced-form relationship among similarly trending variables. Engle and Granger (1987) provide the following definition of cointegration:

The components of the vector $x_t = (x_{1t}, x_{2t}, ..., x_{nt})'$ are said to be *cointegrated of order d, b*, denoted by $x_t \sim CI(d, b)$ if

1. All components of x_t are integrated of order d
2. There exists a vector $\beta = (\beta_1, \beta_2, ..., \beta_n)$ such that the linear combination $\beta x_t = \beta_1 x_{1t} + \beta_2 x_{2t} + ... + \beta_n x_{nt}$ is integrated of order $(d - b)$ where $b > 0$.

The vector β is called the **cointegrating vector.**[1]

In terms of equation (6.1), if the money supply, price level, real income, and interest rate are all $I(1)$ and the linear combination $m_t - \beta_0 - \beta_1 p_t - \beta_2 y_t - \beta_3 r_t = e_t$ is stationary, then the variables are cointegrated of order $(1, 1)$. The vector x_t is $(m_t, 1, p_t, y_t, r_t)'$ and the cointegrating vector β is $(1, -\beta_0, -\beta_1, -\beta_2, -\beta_3)$. The deviation from long-run money market equilibrium is e_t; since $\{e_t\}$ is stationary, this deviation is temporary in nature.

There are four important points to note about the definition:

1. Cointegration refers to a *linear* combination of nonstationary variables. Theoretically, it is quite possible that nonlinear long-run relationships exist among a set of integrated variables. However, the current state of econometric practice is just beginning to allow for tests of nonlinear cointegrating relationships. Also note that the cointegrating vector is not unique. If $(\beta_1, \beta_2, ..., \beta_n)$ is a cointegrating vector, then for any nonzero value of λ, $(\lambda\beta_1, \lambda\beta_2, ..., \lambda\beta_n)$ is also a cointegrating vector. Typically, one of the variables is used to *normalize* the cointegrating vector by fixing its coefficient at unity. To normalize the cointegrating vector with respect to x_{1t}, simply select $\lambda = 1/\beta_1$.

2. From Engle and Granger's original definition, cointegration refers to variables that are integrated of the same order. Of course, this does not imply that all integrated variables are cointegrated; usually, a set of $I(d)$ variables is *not* cointegrated. Such a lack of cointegration implies no long-run equilibrium among the variables, so that they can wander arbitrarily far from each other. If two variables are integrated of different orders, they cannot

be cointegrated. Suppose x_{1t} is $I(d_1)$ and x_{2t} is $I(d_2)$ where $d_2 > d_1$. Question 6 at the end of this chapter asks you to prove that any linear combination of x_{1t} and x_{2t} is $I(d_2)$.

Nevertheless, it is possible to find equilibrium relationships among groups of variables that are integrated of different orders. Suppose that x_{1t} and x_{2t} are $I(2)$ and that the other variables under consideration are $I(1)$. As such, there cannot be a cointegrating relationship between x_{1t} (or x_{2t}) and x_{3t}. However, if x_{1t} and x_{2t} are $CI(2,1)$, there exists a linear combination of the form $\beta_1 x_{1t} + \beta_2 x_{2t}$ which is $I(1)$. It is possible that *this* combination of x_{1t} and x_{2t} is cointegrated with the $I(1)$ variables. Lee and Granger (1990) use the term **multicointegration** to refer to this type of circumstance.

3. If x_t has n nonstationary components, there may be as many as $n - 1$ linearly independent cointegrating vectors. Clearly, if x_t contains only two variables, there can be *at most* one independent cointegrating vector. The number of cointegrating vectors is called the **cointegrating rank** of x_t. For example, suppose that the monetary authorities followed a feedback rule such that they decreased the money supply when nominal GDP was high and increased the nominal money supply when nominal GDP was low. This feedback rule might be represented by

$$m_t = \gamma_0 - \gamma_1(y_t + p_t) + e_{1t}$$
$$= \gamma_0 - \gamma_1 y_t - \gamma_1 p_t + e_{1t} \tag{6.3}$$

where $\{e_{1t}\}$ = a stationary error in the money supply feedback rule.

Given the money demand function in (6.1), there are two cointegrating vectors for the money supply, price level, real income, and the interest rate. Let β be the $(5 \cdot 2)$ matrix:

$$\beta = \begin{bmatrix} 1 & -\beta_0 & -\beta_1 & -\beta_2 & -\beta_3 \\ 1 & -\gamma_0 & \gamma_1 & \gamma_1 & 0 \end{bmatrix}$$

The two linear combinations given by βx_t are stationary. As such, the cointegrating rank of x_t is 2. As a practical matter, if multiple cointegrating vectors are found, it may not be possible to identify the behavioral relationships from what may be reduced-form relationships.

4. Most of the cointegration literature focuses on the case in which each variable contains a single unit root. The reason is that traditional regression or time-series analysis applies when variables are $I(0)$ and few economic variables are integrated of an order higher than unity.[2] When it is unambiguous, many authors use the term *cointegration* to refer to the case in which variables are $CI(1, 1)$. The remainder of the text follows this convention. Of course, many other possibilities arise. For example, a set of $I(2)$ variables may be cointegrated of order $CI(2, 1)$ so that there exists a linear combination which is $I(1)$.

Worksheet 6.1 illustrates some of the important properties of cointegration relationships. In Case 1, both the $\{y_t\}$ and $\{z_t\}$ sequences were constructed so as to be random walk plus noise processes. Although the 20 realizations shown generally

WORKSHEET 6.1

ILLUSTRATING COINTEGRATED SYSTEMS

CASE 1: The series $\{\mu_t\}$ is a random walk process and $\{\varepsilon_{yt}\}$ and $\{\varepsilon_{zt}\}$ are white noise. Hence, the $\{y_t\}$ and $\{z_t\}$ sequences are both random walk plus noise processes. Although each is nonstationary, the two sequences have the same stochastic trend; hence they are cointegrated such that the linear combination $(y_t - z_t)$ is stationary. The equilibrium error term $(\varepsilon_{yt} - \varepsilon_{zt})$ is an $I(0)$ process.

CASE 2: All three sequences are random walk plus noise processes. As constructed, no two are cointegrated. However, the linear combination $(y_t + z_t - w_t)$ is stationary; hence, the three variables are cointegrated. The equilibrium error is an $I(0)$ process.

decline, extending the sample would eliminate this tendency. In any event, neither series shows any tendency to return to a long-run level, and formal Dickey–Fuller tests are not able to reject the null hypothesis of a unit root in either series. Although each series is nonstationary, you can see that they do move together. In fact, the difference between the series $(y_t - z_t)$—shown in the second graph—is stationary; the *equilibrium error* term $e_t = (y_t - z_t)$ has a zero mean and a constant variance.

Case 2 illustrates cointegration among three random walk plus noise processes. As in Case 1, no series exhibits a tendency to return to a long-run level, and formal Dickey–Fuller tests are not able to reject the null hypothesis of a unit root in any of the three. In contrast to the previous case, no two of the series appear to be cointegrated; each series seems to "meander" away from the other two. However, as shown in the second graph, there exists a stationary linear combination of the three such that $e_t = y_t + z_t - w_t$. Thus, it follows that the dynamic behavior of *at least* one variable must be restricted by the values of the other variables in the system.

Figure 6.1 displays the information of Case 1 in a scatter plot of $\{y_t\}$ against the associated value of $\{z_t\}$; each of the 20 points represents the ordered pairs (y_1, z_1), (y_2, z_2), ..., (y_{20}, z_{20}). Comparing Worksheet 6.1 and Figure 6.1, you can see that low values in the $\{y_t\}$ sequence are associated with low values in the $\{z_t\}$ sequence and that values near zero in one series are associated with values near zero in the other. Since both series move together over time, there is a positive relationship between the two. The least-squares line in the scatter plot reveals this to be a strong positive association. In fact, this line is the "long-run" equilibrium relationship between the series, and the deviations from the line are the stationary deviations from long-run equilibrium.

For comparison purposes, Panel (a) in Worksheet 6.2 shows the time paths of two random walk plus noise processes that are not cointegrated. Each seems to meander without any tendency to approach the other. The scatter plot shown in Panel (b) confirms the impression of no long-run relationship between the variables. The deviations from the straight line showing the regression of z_t on y_t are substantial. Plotting the regression residuals against time, [see Panel (c)] suggests that the regression residuals are not stationary.

2. COINTEGRATION AND COMMON TRENDS

Stock and Watson's (1988) observation that cointegrated variables share common stochastic trends provides a very useful way to understand cointegration relationships.[3]

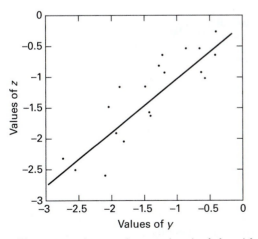

The scatter plot was drawn using the $\{y_t\}$ and $\{z_t\}$ sequences from Case 1 of Worksheet 6.1. Since both series decline over time, there appears to be a positive relationship between the two. The equilibrium regression line is shown.

FIGURE 6.1   Scatter Plot of Cointegrated Variables

WORKSHEET *6.2*

NONCOINTERATED VARIABLES

The $\{y_t\}$ and $\{z_t\}$ sequences are constructed as independent random walk plus noise processes. There is **no** cointegrating relationship between the two variables. As shown in Panel (*a*), both seem to meander without any tendency to come together. Panel (*b*) shows the scatter plot of the two sequences and the regression line $z_t = \beta_0 + \beta_1 y_t$. However, this regression line is spurious. As shown in Panel (*c*), the regression residuals are nonstationary.

Panel (*a*)

Panel (*b*)

Panel (*c*)

For ease of exposition, return to the case in which the vector x_t contains only two variables so that $x_t = (y_t, z_t)'$. Ignoring cyclical and seasonal terms, we can write each variable as a random walk plus an irregular (but not necessarily a white noise) component:

$$y_t = \mu_{yt} + e_{yt} \tag{6.4}$$

$$z_t = \mu_{zt} + e_{zt} \tag{6.5}$$

where: μ_{it} = a random walk process representing the trend in variable i

e_{it} = the stationary (irregular) component of variable i

If $\{y_t\}$ and $\{z_t\}$ are cointegrated of order $(1, 1)$, there must be nonzero values of β_1 and β_2 for which the linear combination $\beta_1 y_t + \beta_2 z_t$ is stationary. Consider the sum

$$\beta_1 y_t + \beta_2 z_t = \beta_1(\mu_{yt} + e_{yt}) + \beta_2(\mu_{zt} + e_{zt})$$
$$= (\beta_1 \mu_{yt} + \beta_2 \mu_{zt}) + (\beta_1 e_{yt} + \beta_2 e_{zt}) \qquad (6.6)$$

For $\beta_1 y_t + \beta_2 z_t$ to be stationary, the term $(\beta_1 \mu_{yt} + \beta_2 \mu_{zt})$ must vanish. After all, if either of the two trends appears in (6.6), the linear combination $\beta_1 y_t + \beta_2 z_t$ will also have a trend. Since the second term in parentheses is stationary, the necessary and sufficient condition for $\{y_t\}$ and $\{z_t\}$ to be $CI(1, 1)$ is

$$\beta_1 \mu_{yt} + \beta_2 \mu_{zt} = 0 \qquad (6.7)$$

Clearly, μ_{yt} and μ_{zt} are variables whose realized values will be continually changing over time. Since we preclude both β_1 and β_2 from being equal to zero, it follows that (6.7) holds for all t if and only if

$$\mu_{yt} = -\beta_2 \mu_{zt} / \beta_1$$

For nonzero values of β_1 and β_2, the only way to ensure the equality is for the stochastic trends to be *identical* up to a scalar. Thus, up to the scalar $-\beta_2/\beta_1$, *two $I(1)$ stochastic processes $\{y_t\}$ and $\{z_t\}$ must have the same stochastic trend if they are cointegrated of order $(1, 1)$.*

Return your attention to Worksheet 6.1. In Case 1, the $\{y_t\}$ and $\{z_t\}$ sequences were constructed so as to satisfy

$$y_t = \mu_t + \varepsilon_{yt}$$
$$z_t = \mu_t + \varepsilon_{zt}$$
and $$\mu_t = \mu_{t-1} + \varepsilon_t$$

where ε_{yt}, ε_{zt}, and ε_t are independently distributed white-noise disturbances.

By construction, μ_t is a pure random walk process representing the same stochastic trend for both the $\{y_t\}$ and $\{z_t\}$ sequences. The value of μ_0 was initialized to zero, and three sets of 20 random numbers were drawn to represent the $\{\varepsilon_{yt}\}$, $\{\varepsilon_{zt}\}$, and $\{\varepsilon_t\}$ sequences. Using these realizations and the initial value of μ_0, the $\{y_t\}$, $\{z_t\}$, and $\{\mu_t\}$ sequences were constructed. As you can clearly determine, subtracting the realized value of z_t from y_t results in a stationary sequence:

$$y_t - z_t = (\mu_t + \varepsilon_{yt}) - (\mu_t + \varepsilon_{zt}) = \varepsilon_{yt} - \varepsilon_{zt}$$

To state the point using Engle and Granger's terminology, multiplying the cointegrating vector $\beta = (1, -1)$ by the vector $x_t = (y_t, z_t)'$ yields the stationary sequence $\varepsilon_t = \varepsilon_{yt} - \varepsilon_{zt}$. Indeed, the equilibrium error term shown in the second graph of Worksheet 6.1 has all the hallmarks of a stationary process. The essential insight of Stock and Watson (1988) is that the parameters of the cointegrating vector must be such that they purge the trend from the linear combination. Any other linear combination of the two variables contains a trend so that the cointegrating vector is unique up to a normalizing scalar. Hence, $\beta_3 y_t + \beta_4 z_t$ cannot be stationary unless $\beta_3/\beta_4 = \beta_1/\beta_2$.

Recall that Case 2 illustrates cointegration between three random walk plus noise processes. Each process is $I(1)$, and Dickey–Fuller unit root tests would not be able to reject the null hypothesis that each contains a unit root. As you can see in the lower portion of Worksheet 6.1, no pairwise combination of the series appears to be cointegrated. Each series seems to meander, but, as opposed to Case 1, no one single series appears to remain close to any other series. However, by construction, the trend in w_t is the simple summation of the trends in y_t and z_t:

$$\mu_{wt} = \mu_{yt} + \mu_{zt}$$

Here, the vector $x_t = (y_t, z_t, w_t)'$ has the cointegrating vector $(1, 1, -1)$, so that the linear combination $y_t + z_t - w_t$ is stationary. Consider:

$$y_t + z_t - w_t = (\mu_{yt} + \varepsilon_{yt}) + (\mu_{zt} + \varepsilon_{zt}) - (\mu_{wt} + \varepsilon_{wt})$$
$$= \varepsilon_{yt} + \varepsilon_{zt} - \varepsilon_{wt}$$

This example illustrates the general point that cointegration will occur whenever the trend in one variable can be expressed as a linear combination of the trends in the other variable(s). In such circumstances it is always possible to find a vector β such that the linear combination $\beta_1 y_t + \beta_2 z_t + \beta_3 w_t$ does not contain a trend. The result easily generalizes to the case of n variables. Consider the vector representation:

$$x_t = \mu_t + e_t \tag{6.8}$$

where: $x_t =$ the vector $(x_{1t}, x_{2t}, \ldots, x_{nt})'$
$\mu_t =$ the vector of stochastic trends $(\mu_{1t}, \mu_{2t}, \ldots, \mu_{nt})'$
$e_t =$ an $n \cdot 1$ vector of stationary components

If one trend can be expressed as a linear combination of the other trends in the system, it means that there exists a vector β such that

$$\beta_1 \mu_{1t} + \beta_2 \mu_{2t} + \ldots + \beta_n \mu_{nt} = 0$$

Premultiply (6.8) by this set of β_i's to obtain

$$\beta x_t = \beta \mu_t + \beta e_t$$

Since $\beta \mu_t = 0$, it follows that $\beta x_t = \beta e_t$. Hence, the linear combination βx_t is stationary. As shown in Section 8, this argument easily generalizes to the case of multiple cointegrating vectors.

3. COINTEGRATION AND ERROR CORRECTION

A principal feature of cointegrated variables is that their time paths are influenced by the extent of any deviation from long-run equilibrium. After all, if the system is to return to long-run equilibrium, the movements of at least some of the variables must respond to the magnitude of the disequilibrium. For example, theories of the term structure of interest rates imply a long-run relationship between long- and short-term rates. If the gap between the long- and short-term rates is "large" relative to the long-run relationship, the short-term rate must ultimately rise relative to the long-term rate. Of course, the gap can be closed by (1) an increase in the short-term rate and/or a decrease in the long-term rate, (2) an increase in the long-term rate but a commensurately larger rise in the short-term rate, or (3) a fall in the long-term rate but a smaller fall in the short-term rate. Without a full dynamic specification of the model, it is not possible to determine which of the possibilities will occur. Nevertheless, the short-run dynamics must be influenced by the deviation from the long-run relationship.

The dynamic model implied by this discussion is one of **error correction.** In an error-correction model, the short-term dynamics of the variables in the system are influenced by the deviation from equilibrium. If we assume that both interest rates are $I(1)$, a simple error-correction model that could apply to the term structure of interest rates is[4]

$$\Delta r_{St} = \alpha_S(r_{Lt-1} - \beta r_{St-1}) + \varepsilon_{St} \qquad \alpha_S > 0 \qquad (6.9)$$

$$\Delta r_{Lt} = -\alpha_L(r_{Lt-1} - \beta r_{St-1}) + \varepsilon_{Lt} \qquad \alpha_L > 0 \qquad (6.10)$$

where ε_{St} and ε_{Lt} are white-noise disturbance terms which may be correlated, r_{Lt} and r_{St} are the long- and short-term interest rates, and α_S, α_L, and β are parameters.

As specified, the short- and long-term interest rates change in response to stochastic shocks (represented by ε_{St} and ε_{Lt}) *and* in response to the previous period's deviation from long-run equilibrium. Everything else being equal, if this deviation happened to be positive (so that $r_{Lt-1} - \beta r_{St-1} > 0$), the short-term interest rate would rise and the long-term rate would fall. Long-run equilibrium is attained when $r_{Lt} = \beta r_{St}$.

Here you can see the relationship between error-correcting models and cointegrated variables. By assumption, Δr_{St} is stationary so that the left-hand side of (6.9) is $I(0)$. For (6.9) to be sensible, the right-hand side must be $I(0)$ as well. Given that ε_{St} is stationary, it follows that the linear combination $r_{Lt-1} - \beta r_{St-1}$ must also be stationary; hence, the two interest rates must be cointegrated with the cointegrating vector $(1, -\beta)$. Of course, the identical argument applies to (6.10). The essential point to note is that the error-correction representation necessitates that the two variables be cointegrated of order $CI(1,1)$. This result is unaltered if we formulate a more general model by introducing the lagged changes of each rate into both equations:[6]

$$\Delta r_{St} = a_{10} + \alpha_S(r_{Lt-1} - \beta r_{St-1}) + \Sigma a_{11}(i) \Delta r_{St-i} + \Sigma a_{12}(i) \Delta r_{Lt-i} + \varepsilon_{St} \quad (6.11)$$

$$\Delta r_{Lt} = a_{20} - \alpha_L(r_{Lt-1} - \beta r_{St-1}) + \Sigma a_{21}(i) \Delta r_{St-i} + \Sigma a_{22}(i) \Delta r_{Lt-i} + \varepsilon_{Lt} \quad (6.12)$$

Again, ε_{St}, ε_{Lt}, and all terms involving Δr_{St-i} and Δr_{Lt-i} are stationary. Thus, the linear combination of interest rates $r_{Lt-1} - \beta r_{St-1}$ must also be stationary.

Inspection of (6.11) and (6.12) reveals a striking similarity to the VAR models of the previous chapter. This two-variable error-correction model is a bivariate VAR in first differences augmented by the error-correction terms $\alpha_S(r_{Lt-1} - \beta r_{St-1})$ and $-\alpha_L(r_{Lt-1} - \beta r_{St-1})$. Notice that α_S and α_L have the interpretation of *speed of adjustment* parameters. The larger α_S is, the greater the response of to the previous period's deviation from long-run equilibrium. At the opposite extreme, very small values of α_S imply that the short-term interest rate is unresponsive to last period's equilibrium error. For the $\{\Delta r_{St}\}$ sequence to be unaffected by the long-term interest rate sequence, α_S *and* all the $a_{12}(i)$ coefficients must be equal to zero. Of course, at least one of the speed of adjustment terms in (6.11) and (6.12) must be nonzero. If both α_S and α_L are equal to zero, the long-run equilibrium relationship does not appear and the model is not one of error correction or cointegration.

The result can easily be generalized to the n-variable model. Formally, the $(n \cdot 1)$ vector $x_t = (x_{1t}, x_{2t}, \ldots, x_{nt})'$ has an error-correction representation if it can be expressed in the form

$$\Delta x_t = \pi_0 + \pi x_{t-1} + \pi_1 \Delta x_{t-1} + \pi_2 \Delta x_{t-2} + \ldots + \pi_p \Delta x_{t-p} + \varepsilon_t \qquad (6.13)$$

where: $\pi_0 =$ an $(n \cdot 1)$ vector of intercept terms with elements π_{i0}
$\pi_i = (n \cdot n)$ coefficient matrices with elements $\pi_{jk}(i)$
$\pi =$ a matrix with elements π_{jk} such that one or more of the $\pi_{jk} \neq 0$
$\varepsilon_t =$ an $(n \cdot 1)$ vector with elements ε_{it}

Note that the disturbance terms are such that ε_{it} may be correlated with ε_{jt}.

Let all variables in x_t be $I(1)$. Now, if there is an error-correction representation of these variables as in (6.13), there is necessarily a linear combination of the $I(1)$ variables that is stationary. Solving (6.13) for πx_{t-1} yields

$$\pi x_{t-1} = \Delta x_t - \pi_0 - \Sigma \pi_i \Delta x_{t-i} - \varepsilon_t$$

Since each expression on the right-hand side is stationary, πx_{t-1} must also be stationary. Since π contains only constants, each row of π is a cointegrating vector of x_t. For example, the first row can be written as $(\pi_{11} x_{1t-1} + \pi_{12} x_{2t-1} + \ldots + \pi_{1n} x_{nt-1})$. Since each series is $I(1)$, $(\pi_{11}, \pi_{12}, \ldots, \pi_{1n})$ must be a cointegrating vector for x_t.

The key feature in (6.13) is the presence of the matrix π. There are two important points to note:

1.   If all elements of π equal zero, (6.13) is a traditional VAR in first differences. In such circumstances there is no error-correction representation since Δx_t does not respond to the previous period's deviation from long-run equilibrium.

2.   If one or more of the π_{jk} differs from zero, Δx_t responds to the previous period's deviation from long-run equilibrium. Hence, *estimating x_t as a VAR in first differences is inappropriate if x_t has an error-correction representation.* The omission of the expression πx_{t-1} entails a misspecification error if x_t has an error-correction representation as in (6.13).

A good way to examine the relationship between cointegration and error correction is to study the properties of the simple VAR model:

$$y_t = a_{11} y_{t-1} + a_{12} z_{t-1} + \varepsilon_{yt} \qquad (6.14)$$

$$z_t = a_{21} y_{t-1} + a_{22} z_{t-1} + \varepsilon_{zt} \qquad (6.15)$$

where ε_{yt} and ε_{zt} are white-noise disturbances that may be correlated with each other and, for simplicity, intercept terms have been ignored. Using lag operators, we can write (6.14) and (6.15) as

$$(1 - a_{11}L)y_t - a_{12}Lz_t = \varepsilon_{yt}$$
$$-a_{21}Ly_t + (1 - a_{22}L)z_t = \varepsilon_{zt}$$

The next step is to solve for y_t and z_t. Writing the system in matrix form, we obtain

$$\begin{bmatrix} (1 - a_{11}L) & -a_{12}L \\ -a_{21}L & (1 - a_{22}L) \end{bmatrix} \begin{bmatrix} y_t \\ z_t \end{bmatrix} = \begin{bmatrix} \varepsilon_{yt} \\ \varepsilon_{zt} \end{bmatrix}$$

Using Cramer's Rule or matrix inversion, we can obtain the solutions for y_t and z_t as

$$y_t = \frac{(1-a_{22}L)\varepsilon_{yt} + a_{12}L\varepsilon_{zt}}{(1-a_{11}L)(1-a_{22}L) - a_{12}a_{21}L^2} \tag{6.16}$$

$$z_t = \frac{a_{21}L\varepsilon_{yt} + (1-a_{11}L)\varepsilon_{zt}}{(1-a_{11}L)(1-a_{22}L) - a_{12}a_{21}L^2} \tag{6.17}$$

We have converted the two-variable first-order system represented by (6.14) and (6.15) into two univariate second-order difference equations of the type examined in Chapter 2. Note that both variables have the same inverse characteristic equation: $(1 - a_{11}L)(1 - a_{22}L) - a_{12}a_{21}L^2$. Setting $(1 - a_{11}L)(1 - a_{22}L) - a_{12}a_{21}L^2 = 0$ and solving for L yields the two roots of the inverse characteristic equation. In order to work with the characteristic roots (as opposed to the inverse characteristic roots), define $\lambda = 1/L$ and write the characteristic equation as

$$\lambda^2 - (a_{11} + a_{22})\lambda + (a_{11}a_{22} - a_{12}a_{21}) = 0 \tag{6.18}$$

Since the two variables have the same characteristic equation, the characteristic roots of (6.18) determine the time paths of both variables. The following remarks summarize the time paths of $\{y_t\}$ and $\{z_t\}$:

1. If both characteristic roots (λ_1, λ_2) lie inside the unit circle, (6.16) and (6.17) yield stable solutions for $\{y_t\}$ and $\{z_t\}$. If t is sufficiently large or if the initial conditions are such that the homogenous solution is zero, the stability condition guarantees that the variables are stationary. The variables cannot be cointegrated of order (1, 1) since each is stationary.

2. If either root lies outside the unit circle, the solutions are explosive. Neither variable is difference stationary, so they cannot be $CI(1, 1)$. In the same way, if both characteristic roots are unity, the second difference of each variable will be stationary. Since each is $I(2)$, the variables cannot be $CI(1, 1)$.

3. As you can see from (6.14) and (6.15), if $a_{12} = a_{21} = 0$, the solution is trivial. For $\{y_t\}$ and $\{z_t\}$ to be unit root processes, it is necessary for $a_{11} = a_{22} = 1$. It follows that $\lambda_1 = \lambda_2 = 1$ and that the two variables evolve without any long-run equilibrium relationship; hence, the variables cannot be cointegrated.

4. For $\{y_t\}$ and $\{z_t\}$ to be $CI(1, 1)$, it is necessary for one characteristic root to be unity and the other to be less than unity in absolute value. In this instance, each variable will have the same stochastic trend and the first difference of each variable will be stationary. For example, if $\lambda_1 = 1$, (6.16) will have the form:

$$y_t = [(1 - a_{22}L)\varepsilon_{yt} + a_{12}L\varepsilon_{zt}]/[(1 - L)(1 - \lambda_2 L)]$$

or, multiplying by $(1 - L)$, we get

$$(1 - L)y_t = \Delta y_t = [(1 - a_{22}L)\varepsilon_{yt} + a_{12}L\varepsilon_{zt}]/(1 - \lambda_2 L)$$

which is stationary if $|\lambda_2| < 1$.

Thus, to ensure that the variables are $CI(1, 1)$, we must set one of the characteristic roots equal to unity and the other to a value that is less than unity in absolute value. For the larger of the two roots to equal unity, it must be the case that

$$0.5(a_{11} + a_{22}) + 0.5\sqrt{(a_{11}^2 + a_{22}^2) - 2a_{11}a_{22} + 4a_{12}a_{21}} = 1$$

so that after some simplification, the coefficients are seen to satisfy[5]

$$a_{11} = [(1 - a_{22}) - a_{12}\, a_{21}]/(1 - a_{22}) \tag{6.19}$$

Now consider the second characteristic root. Since a_{12} and/or a_{21} must differ from zero if the variables are cointegrated, the condition $|\lambda_2| < 1$ requires

$$a_{22} > -1 \tag{6.20}$$

and

$$a_{12}a_{21} + (a_{22})^2 < 1 \tag{6.21}$$

Equations (6.19), (6.20), and (6.21) are restrictions we must place on the coefficients of (6.14) and (6.15) if we want to ensure that the variables are cointegrated of order $(1, 1)$. To see how these coefficient restrictions bear on the nature of the solution, write (6.14) and (6.15) as

$$\begin{bmatrix} \Delta y_t \\ \Delta z_t \end{bmatrix} = \begin{bmatrix} a_{11} - 1 & a_{12} \\ a_{21} & a_{22} - 1 \end{bmatrix} \begin{bmatrix} y_{t-1} \\ z_{t-1} \end{bmatrix} + \begin{bmatrix} \varepsilon_{yt} \\ \varepsilon_{zt} \end{bmatrix} \tag{6.22}$$

Now, (6.19) implies that $a_{11} - 1 = -a_{12}a_{21}/(1 - a_{22})$ so that after a bit of manipulation, (6.22) can be written in the form

$$\Delta y_t = -[a_{12}a_{21}/(1 - a_{22})]y_{t-1} + a_{12}z_{t-1} + \varepsilon_{yt} \tag{6.23}$$

$$\Delta z_t = a_{21}y_{t-1} - (1 - a_{22})z_{t-1} + \varepsilon_{zt} \tag{6.24}$$

Equations (6.23) and (6.24) form an error-correction model. If both a_{12} and a_{21} differ from zero, we can normalize the cointegrating vector with respect to either variable. Normalizing with respect to y_t, we get

$$\Delta y_t = \alpha_y(y_{t-1} - \beta z_{t-1}) + \varepsilon_{yt}$$

$$\Delta z_t = \alpha_z(y_{t-1} - \beta z_{t-1}) + \varepsilon_{zt}$$

where: $\alpha_y = -a_{12}a_{21}/(1 - a_{22})$
$\beta = (1 - a_{22})/a_{21}$
$\alpha_z = a_{21}$

You can see that y_t and z_t change in response to the previous period's deviation from the long-run equilibrium $y_{t-1} - \beta z_{t-1}$. If $y_{t-1} = \beta z_{t-1}$, y_t and z_t change only in response to ε_{yt} and ε_{zt} shocks. Moreover, if $\alpha_y < 0$ and $\alpha_z > 0$, y_t decreases and z_t increases in response to a positive deviation from long-run equilibrium.

You can easily convince yourself that conditions (6.20) and (6.21) ensure that $\beta \neq 0$ and that at least one of the speed of adjustment parameters (i.e., α_y and α_z) is not equal to zero. Now, refer to (6.9) and (6.10); you can see this model is in exactly the same form as the interest rate example presented in the beginning of this section.

Although a_{12} and a_{21} cannot both equal zero, an interesting special case arises if one of these coefficients is zero. For example, if we set $a_{12} = 0$, the speed of adjustment coefficient $\alpha_y = 0$. In this case, y_t changes only in response to ε_{yt} as $\Delta y_t = \varepsilon_{yt}$.[7] The $\{z_t\}$ sequence does all of the correction to eliminate any deviation from long-run equilibrium.

To highlight some of the important implications of this simple model, we have shown:

1. *The restrictions necessary to ensure that the variables are CI(1, 1) guarantee that an error-correction model exists.* In our example, both $\{y_t\}$ and $\{z_t\}$ are unit root processes but the linear combination $y_t - \beta z_t$ is stationary; the normalized cointegrating vector is $[1, -(1 - a_{22})/a_{21}]$. The variables have an error-correction representation with speed of adjustment coefficients $\alpha_y = -a_{12}a_{21}/(1 - a_{22})$ and $\alpha_z = a_{21}$. It was also shown that an error-correction model for $I(1)$ variables necessarily implies cointegration. This finding illustrates the **Granger representation theorem** stating that for any set of $I(1)$ variables, error correction and cointegration are equivalent representations.

2. *A cointegration necessitates coefficient restrictions in a VAR model.* It is important to realize that a cointegrated system can be viewed as a restricted form of a general VAR model. Let $x_t = (y_t, z_t)'$ and $\varepsilon_t = (\varepsilon_{yt}, \varepsilon_{zt})'$ so that we can write (6.22) in the form

$$\Delta x_t = \pi x_{t-1} + \varepsilon_t \qquad (6.25)$$

Clearly, it is inappropriate to estimate a VAR of cointegrated variables using only first differences. Estimating (6.25) without the expression πx_{t-1} would eliminate the error-correction portion of the model. It is also important to note that the rows of π are *not* linearly independent if the variables are cointegrated. Multiplying each element in row 1 by $-(1 - a_{22})/a_{12}$ yields the corresponding element in row 2. Thus, the determinant of π is equal to zero, and y_t and z_t have the error-correction representation given by (6.23) and (6.24).

This two-variable example illustrates the very important insights of Johansen (1988) and Stock and Watson (1988) that *we can use the rank of π to determine whether or not two variables $\{y_t\}$ and $\{z_t\}$ are cointegrated.* Compare the determinant of π to the characteristic equation given by (6.18). If the largest characteristic root equals unity, ($\lambda_1 = 1$), it follows that the determinant of π is zero and that π has a rank equal to unity. If π were to have a rank of zero, it would be necessary for $a_{11} = 1$, $a_{22} = 1$, and $a_{12} = a_{21} = 0$. The VAR represented by (6.14) and (6.15) would be nothing more than $\Delta y_t = \varepsilon_{yt}$ and $\Delta z_t = \varepsilon_{zt}$. In this case, both the $\{y_t\}$ and $\{z_t\}$ sequences are unit root processes without any cointegrating vector. Finally, if the rank of π is full, then neither characteristic root can be unity, so the $\{y_t\}$ and $\{z_t\}$ sequences are jointly stationary.

3. In general, both variables in a cointegrated system will respond to a deviation from long-run equilibrium. However, it is possible that one (but not both) of the speed of adjustment parameters is zero. For example, if $\alpha_y = 0$, $\{y_t\}$ does not respond to the discrepancy from long-run equilibrium and

$\{z_t\}$ does all of the adjustment. In this circumstance, $\{y_t\}$ is said to be **weakly exogenous.** As such, an econometric model for $\{z_t\}$ can be estimated and hypothesis testing can be conducted without reference to a specific model for $\{y_t\}$. Section 10 and Appendix 6.1 consider modeling in a cointegrated system when a variable is weakly exogenous.

Also, *it is necessary to reinterpret Granger causality in a cointegrated system.* In a cointegrated system, $\{y_t\}$ does not Granger cause $\{z_t\}$ if lagged values Δy_{t-i} do not enter the Δz_t equation *and if* z_t does not respond to the deviation from long-run equilibrium. Hence, $\{z_t\}$ must be weakly exogenous. If $a_{21} = 0$ in (6.24), $\{z_t\}$ is weakly exogenous and is not Granger caused by $\{y_t\}$. Similarly, in the cointegrated system of (6.11) and (6.12), $\{r_{Lt}\}$ does not Granger cause $\{r_{St}\}$ if all $a_{12}(i) = 0$ and if $\alpha_S = 0$.

The *n*-Variable Case

Little is altered in the *n*-variable case. The relationship between cointegration, error correction and the rank of the matrix π is invariant to adding additional variables to the system. The interesting feature introduced in the *n*-variable case is the possibility of multiple cointegrating vectors. Now consider a more general version of (6.25):

$$x_t = A_1 x_{t-1} + \varepsilon_t \tag{6.26}$$

where: x_t = the $(n \cdot 1)$ vector $(x_{1t}, x_{2t}, ..., x_{nt})'$
ε_t = the $(n \cdot 1)$ vector $(\varepsilon_{1t}, \varepsilon_{2t}, ..., \varepsilon_{nt})'$
A_1 = an $(n \cdot n)$ matrix of parameters

Subtracting x_{t-1} from each side of (6.26) and letting I be an $(n \cdot n)$ identity matrix, we get

$$\Delta x_t = -(I - A_1)x_{t-1} + \varepsilon_t$$
$$= \pi x_{t-1} + \varepsilon_t \tag{6.27}$$

where π is the $(n \cdot n)$ matrix $-(I - A_1)$ and π_{ij} denotes the element in row i and column j of π. As you can see, (6.27) is a special case of (6.13) such that all $\pi_i = 0$.

Again, the crucial issue for cointegration concerns the rank of the $(n \cdot n)$ matrix π. If the rank of this matrix is zero, each element of π must equal zero. In this instance, (6.27) is equivalent to an *n*-variable VAR in first differences:

$$\Delta x_t = \varepsilon_t$$

Here, each $\Delta x_{it} = \varepsilon_{it}$ so that the first difference of each variable in the vector x_t is $I(0)$. Since each $x_{it} = x_{it-1} + \varepsilon_{it}$, all the $\{x_{it}\}$ sequences are unit root processes and there is no linear combination of the variables that is stationary.

At the other extreme, suppose that π is of full rank. The long-run solution to (6.27) is given by the n independent equations

$$\pi_{11}x_{1t} + \pi_{12}x_{2t} + \pi_{13}x_{3t} + ... + \pi_{1n}x_{nt} = 0$$
$$\pi_{21}x_{1t} + \pi_{22}x_{2t} + \pi_{23}x_{3t} + ... + \pi_{2n}x_{nt} = 0$$
$$\cdot$$
$$\cdot$$
$$\cdot$$
$$\pi_{n1}x_{1t} + \pi_{n2}x_{2t} + \pi_{n3}x_{3t} + ... + \pi_{nn}x_{nt} = 0 \tag{6.28}$$

Each of these n equations is an independent restriction on the long-run solution of the variables; the n variables in the system face n long-run constraints. In this case, each of the n variables contained in the vector x_t must be stationary with the long-run values given by (6.28). The variables cannot be $CI(1, 1)$ since all are stationary.

In intermediate cases, in which the rank of π is equal to $r < n$, there are r cointegrating vectors. With r independent equations and n variables, there are $n - r$ stochastic trends in the system. If $r = 1$, there is a single cointegrating vector given by any row of the matrix π. Each $\{\Delta x_{it}\}$ sequence can be written in error-correction form. For example, we can write Δx_{1t} as

$$\Delta x_{1t} = \pi_{11} x_{1t-1} + \pi_{12} x_{2t-1} + \dots + \pi_{1n} x_{nt-1} + \varepsilon_{1t}$$

or, normalizing with respect to x_{1t-1}, we can set $\alpha_1 = \pi_{11}$ and $\beta_{1j} = \pi_{1j} / \pi_{11}$ to obtain

$$\Delta x_{1t} = \alpha_1 (x_{1t-1} + \beta_{12} x_{2t-1} + \dots + \beta_{1n} x_{nt-1}) + \varepsilon_{1t} \tag{6.29}$$

In the long run, the $\{x_{it}\}$ will satisfy the relationship

$$x_{1t} + \beta_{12} x_{2t} + \dots + \beta_{1n} x_{nt} = 0$$

Hence, the normalized cointegrating vector is $(1, \beta_{12}, \beta_{13}, \dots, \beta_{1n})$ and the speed of adjustment parameter is α_1. In the same way, with two cointegration vectors the long-run values of the variables will satisfy the two relationships

$$\pi_{11} x_{1t} + \pi_{12} x_{2t} + \dots + \pi_{1n} x_{nt} = 0$$
$$\pi_{21} x_{1t} + \pi_{22} x_{2t} + \dots + \pi_{2n} x_{nt} = 0$$

which can be appropriately normalized.

The main point here is that there are two important ways to test for cointegration. The Engle–Granger methodology seeks to determine whether the residuals of the equilibrium relationship are stationary. The Johansen (1988) and Stock–Watson (1988) methodologies determine the rank of π. The Engle–Granger approach is the subject of the next three sections. Sections 7 through 10 examine the Johansen (1988) and Stock–Watson (1988) methodologies.

4. TESTING FOR COINTEGRATION: THE ENGLE–GRANGER METHODOLOGY

To explain the Engle–Granger testing procedure, let's begin with the type of problem likely to be encountered in applied studies. Suppose that two variables—say y_t and z_t—are believed to be integrated of order 1 and we want to determine whether there exists an equilibrium relationship between the two. Engle and Granger (1987) propose a four-step procedure to determine if two $I(1)$ variables are cointegrated of order $CI(1, 1)$.

STEP 1: Pretest the variables for their order of integration. By definition, cointegration necessitates that two variables be integrated of the same order. Thus, the first step in the analysis is to pretest each variable to determine its order of integration. The augmented Dickey–Fuller test discussed in Chapter 4 can be used to infer the number of unit roots (if any) in each of the variables. If both variables are stationary, it is not necessary to proceed since standard time-series methods apply to stationary variables. If the variables are integrated of different orders, it is possible to conclude they are *not* cointegrated in the usual sense of the term. However, as detailed in Section 5, if some variables are $I(1)$ and some are $I(2)$, you may want to determine whether the variables are multicointegrated.

STEP 2: Estimate the long-run equilibrium relationship. If the results of Step 1 indicate that both $\{y_t\}$ and $\{z_t\}$ are $I(1)$, the next step is to estimate the long-run equilibrium relationship in the form

$$y_t = \beta_0 + \beta_1 z_t + e_t \tag{6.30}$$

If the variables are cointegrated, an OLS regression yields a "super-consistent" estimator of the cointegrating parameters β_0 and β_1. Stock (1987) proves that the OLS estimates of β_0 and β_1 converge faster than in OLS models using stationary variables. To explain, reexamine the scatter plot shown in Figure 6.1. You can see that the effect of the common trend dominates the effect of the stationary component; both variables seem to rise and fall in tandem. Hence, there is a strong linear relationship as shown by the regression line drawn in the figure.

In order to determine if the variables are actually cointegrated, denote the residual sequence from this equation by $\{\hat{e}_t\}$. Thus, the $\{\hat{e}_t\}$ series are the estimated values of the deviations from the long-run relationship. If these deviations are found to be stationary, the $\{y_t\}$ and $\{z_t\}$ sequences are cointegrated of order $(1, 1)$. It would be convenient if we could perform a Dickey–Fuller test on these residuals to determine their order of integration. Consider the autoregression of the residuals:

$$\Delta\hat{e}_t = a_1\hat{e}_{t-1} + \varepsilon_t \tag{6.31}$$

Since the $\{\hat{e}_t\}$ sequence is a residual from a regression equation, there is no need to include an intercept term; the parameter of interest in (6.31) is a_1. If we cannot reject the null hypothesis $a_1 = 0$, we can conclude that the residual series contains a unit root. Hence, we conclude that the $\{y_t\}$ and $\{z_t\}$ sequences are *not* cointegrated. The more precise wording is awkward because of a triple negative, but to be technically correct, *if it is not possible to reject the null hypothesis $|a_1| = 0$, we cannot reject the hypothesis that the variables are not cointegrated.* Instead, the rejection of the null hypothesis implies that the residual sequence is stationary.[8] Given that $\{y_t\}$ and $\{z_t\}$ were both found to be $I(1)$ and that the residuals are stationary, we can conclude that the series are cointegrated of order $(1, 1)$.

In most applied studies it is not possible to use the Dickey–Fuller tables themselves. The problem is that the $\{\hat{e}_t\}$ sequence is generated from a regression equation; the researcher does not know the actual error e_t, only the estimate of the error $\hat{e}_t$. The methodology of fitting the regression in (6.30) selects values of β_0 and β_1 that minimize the sum of squared residuals. Since the residual variance is made as small as possible, the procedure is prejudiced toward finding a stationary error process in (6.31). Hence, the test statistic used to test the magnitude of a_1 must reflect this fact. Only if β_0 and β_1 were known in advance and used to construct the true $\{e_t\}$ sequence would an ordinary Dickey–Fuller table be appropriate. When you estimate the cointegrating vector, use the critical values provided in Table C at the end of the text. These critical values depend on sample size and the number of variables used in the analysis. For example, to test for cointegration between two variables using a sample size of 100, the critical value at the 5 percent significance level is –3.398.

If the residuals of (6.31) do not appear to be white noise, an augmented form of the test can be used instead of (6.31). Suppose that diagnostic checks indicate that the $\{\varepsilon_t\}$ sequence of (6.31) exhibits serial correlation. Instead of using the results from (6.31), estimate the autoregression:

$$\Delta\hat{e}_t = a_1\hat{e}_{t-1} + \sum_{i=1}^{n}a_{i+1}\,\Delta\hat{e}_{t-i} + \varepsilon_t \tag{6.32}$$

Again, if we reject the null hypothesis $a_1 = 0$, we can conclude that the residual sequence is stationary and that the variables are cointegrated.

STEP 3: Estimate the error-correction model. If the variables are cointegrated (i.e., if the null hypothesis of no cointegration is rejected), the residuals from the equilibrium regression can be used to estimate the error-correction model. If $\{y_t\}$ and $\{z_t\}$ are $CI(1, 1)$, the variables have the error-correction form

$$\Delta y_t = \alpha_1 + \alpha_y\,[y_{t-1} - \beta_1 z_{t-1}] + \sum_{i=1}\alpha_{11}(i)\Delta y_{t-i} + \sum_{i=1}\alpha_{12}(i)\Delta z_{t-i} + \varepsilon_{yt} \tag{6.33}$$

$$\Delta z_t = \alpha_2 + \alpha_z\,[y_{t-1} - \beta_1 z_{t-1}] + \sum_{i=1}\alpha_{21}(i)\Delta y_{t-i} + \sum_{i=1}\alpha_{22}(i)\Delta z_{t-i} + \varepsilon_{zt} \tag{6.34}$$

where β_i = the parameters of the cointegrating vector given by (6.30), ε_{yt} and ε_{zt} = white-noise disturbances (which may be correlated with each other), and α_1, α_2, α_y, α_z, $\alpha_{11}(i)$, $\alpha_{12}(i)$, $\alpha_{21}(i)$, and $\alpha_{22}(i)$ are all parameters.

Engle and Granger (1987) propose a clever way to circumvent the cross-equation restrictions involved in the direct estimation of (6.33) and (6.34). The magnitude of the residual $\hat{e}_{t-1}$ is the deviation from long-run equilibrium in period $(t-1)$. Hence, it is possible to use the saved residuals $\{\hat{e}_{t-1}\}$ obtained in Step 2 as an instrument for the expression $y_{t-1} - \beta_1 z_{t-1}$ in (6.33) and (6.34). Thus, using the saved residuals from the estimation of the long-run equilibrium relationship, estimate the error-correcting model as

$$\Delta y_t = \alpha_1 + \alpha_y\,\hat{e}_{t-1} + \sum_{i=1}\alpha_{11}(i)\Delta y_{t-i} + \sum_{i=1}\alpha_{12}(i)\Delta z_{t-i} + \varepsilon_{yt} \tag{6.35}$$

$$\Delta z_t = \alpha_2 + \alpha_z\,\hat{e}_{t-1} + \sum_{i=1}\alpha_{21}(i)\Delta y_{t-i} + \sum_{i=1}a_{22}(i)\Delta z_{t-i} + \varepsilon_{zt} \tag{6.36}$$

Other than the error-correction term $\hat{e}_{t-1}$, (6.35) and (6.36) constitute VAR in first differences. This VAR can be estimated using the same methodology developed in Chapter 5. All of the procedures developed for a VAR apply to the system represented by the error-correction equations. Notably:

1. OLS is an efficient estimation strategy since each equation contains the same set of regressors.

2. Since all terms in (6.35) and (6.36) are stationary [i.e., Δy_t and its lags, Δz_t and its lags, and $\hat{e}_{t-1}$ are $I(0)$], the test statistics used in traditional VAR analysis are appropriate for (6.35) and (6.36). For example, lag lengths can be determined using a χ^2-test, and the restriction that all $\alpha_{jk}(i) = 0$ can be checked using an F-test. If there is a single cointegrating vector, restrictions concerning α_y or α_z can be conducted using a t-test.

STEP 4: Assess model adequacy. There are several procedures that can help determine whether the error-correction estimated model is appropriate.

1. You should be careful to assess the adequacy of the model by performing diagnostic checks to determine whether the residuals of the error-correction equations approximate white noise. If the residuals are serially correlated, lag lengths may be too short. Reestimate the model using lag lengths that yield serially uncorrelated errors. It may be that you need to allow longer lags of some variables than of others. If so, you can gain efficiency by estimating the near-VAR using the seemingly unrelated regressions (SUR) method.

2. The *speed of adjustment* coefficients α_y and α_z are of particular interest in that they have important implications for the dynamics of the system.[9] If we focus on (6.36) it is clear that for any given value of $\hat{e}_{t-1}$, a large value of α_z is associated with a large value of Δz_t. If α_z is zero, the change in z_t does not at all respond to the deviation from long-run equilibrium in $(t-1)$. If α_z is zero and if all $\alpha_{21}(i) = 0$, then it can be said that $\{\Delta y_t\}$ does not Granger cause $\{\Delta z_t\}$. We know that α_y and/or α_z should be significantly different from zero if the variables are cointegrated. After all, if both α_y and α_z are zero, there is no error correction and (6.35) and (6.36) comprise nothing more than a VAR in first differences. Moreover, the absolute values of these speed of adjustment coefficients must not be too large. The point estimates should imply that Δy_t and Δz_t converge to the long-run equilibrium relationship.[10]

    If all but one variable is weakly exogenous, you may want to estimate that variable using the general-to-specific technique described in Section 10.

3. As in a traditional VAR analysis, Lutkepohl and Reimers (1992) show that innovation accounting (i.e., impulse responses and variance decomposition analysis) can be used to obtain information concerning the interactions among the variables. As a practical matter, the two innovations ε_{yt} and ε_{zt} may be contemporaneously correlated if y_t has a contemporaneous effect on z_t and/or if z_t has a contemporaneous effect on y_t. In obtaining impulse response functions and variance decompositions, some method—such as a Choleski Decomposition—must be used to orthogonalize the innovations.

The shape of the impulse response functions and the results of the variance decompositions can indicate whether the dynamic responses of the variables conform to theory. Since all variables in (6.35) and (6.36) are $I(0)$, the impulse responses of Δy_t and Δz_t should converge to zero. You should reexamine your results from each step if you obtain a nondecaying or explosive impulse response function.

Before closing this section, a word of warning is in order. It is very tempting to use t-statistics to perform significance tests on the cointegrating vector. However, you must avoid this temptation since the coefficients have an asymptotic t-distribution only in one special circumstance. Suppose that the cointegration relationship between $\{y_t\}$ and $\{z_t\}$ is such that

$$y_t = \beta_0 + \beta_1 z_t + \varepsilon_{1t}$$
$$\Delta z_t = \varepsilon_{2t}$$

where $E\varepsilon_{1t}\varepsilon_{2t} = 0$.

The notation is designed to illustrate the point that the residuals from both equations are uncorrelated white-noise disturbances. The set of assumptions is fairly restrictive in that the residuals from both equations must be serially uncorrelated and the cross-correlations must be zero. If these conditions hold, the OLS estimates of β_0 and β_1 can be tested using t-tests and F-tests. If the disturbances are not normally distributed, the asymptotic results are such that t-tests and F-tests are appropriate. Be aware that both conditions are necessary to perform such tests. If $E\varepsilon_{1t}\varepsilon_{2t} \neq 0$, $\{z_t\}$ is not exogenous since shocks to ε_{1t} affect z_t. Moreover, as in a standard regression, if the residuals of the cointegrating vector are serially correlated, inference of the coefficients is inappropriate. Phillips and Hansen (1990) develop a procedure you can use in such circumstances. The details are outlined in Appendix 1 of this chapter.

5. ILLUSTRATING THE ENGLE–GRANGER METHODOLOGY

Figure 6.2 shows three simulated variables that can be used to illustrate the Engle–Granger procedure. Inspection of the figure suggests that each is nonstationary, and there is no visual evidence that any pair is cointegrated. As detailed in Table 6.1, each series is constructed as the sum of a stochastic trend component plus an autoregressive irregular component.

The first column of the table contains the formulas used to construct the $\{y_t\}$ sequence. First, 150 realizations of a white-noise process were drawn to represent the $\{\varepsilon_{yt}\}$ sequence. Initializing $\mu_{y0} = 0$, we constructed 150 values of the random walk process $\{\mu_{yt}\}$ using the formula $\mu_{yt} = \mu_{yt-1} + \varepsilon_{yt}$ (see the first cell of the table). Another 150 realizations of a white-noise process were drawn to represent the $\{\eta_{yt}\}$ sequence; given the initial condition $\delta_{y0} = 0$, these realizations were used to construct $\{\delta_{yt}\}$ as $\delta_{yt} = 0.5\delta_{yt-1} + \eta_{yt}$ (see the next lower cell). Adding the two constructed series yields 150 realizations for $\{y_t\}$. To help ensure randomness, only the last 100 observations are used in the simulated study. Hence, $\{y_t\}$ is the sum of a stochastic trend and a stationary (i.e., irregular) component.

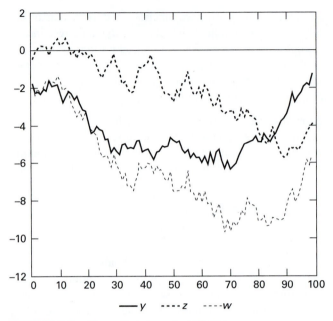

FIGURE 6.2   Three Cointegrated Series

Table 6.1   The Simulated Series

	(y_t)	(z_t)	(w_t)
Trend	$\mu_{yt} = \mu_{yt-1} + \varepsilon_{yt}$	$\mu_{zt} = \mu_{zt-1} + \varepsilon_{zt}$	$\mu_{wt} = \mu_{yt} + \mu_{zt}$
Pure irregular	$\delta_{yt} = 0.5\delta_{yt-1} + \eta_{yt}$	$\delta_{zt} = 0.5\delta_{zt-1} + \eta_{zt}$	$\delta_{wt} = 0.5\delta_{wt-1} + \eta_{wt}$
Series	$y_t = \mu_{yt} + \delta_{yt}$	$z_t = \mu_{zt} + \delta_{zt} + 0.5\delta_{yt}$	$w_t = \mu_{wt} + \delta_{wt} + 0.5\delta_{yt} + 0.5\delta_{zt}$

The $\{z_t\}$ sequence was constructed in a similar fashion; the $\{\varepsilon_{zt}\}$ and $\{\eta_{zt}\}$ sequences are each represented by two different sets of 150 random numbers. The trend $\{\mu_{zt}\}$ and the autoregressive irregular term $\{\delta_{zt}\}$ were constructed as shown in the second column of the table. The $\{\delta_{zt}\}$ sequence can be thought of as a pure irregular component in the $\{z_t\}$ sequence. In order to introduce correlation between the $\{y_t\}$ and $\{z_t\}$ sequences, the irregular component in $\{z_t\}$ was constructed as the sum: $\delta_{zt} + 0.5\delta_{yt}$. In the third column you can see that the trend in $\{w_t\}$ is the simple summation of the trends in the other two series. As such, the three series have the cointegrating vector $(1, 1, -1)$. The irregular component in $\{w_t\}$ is the sum of pure innovation δ_{wt} and 50 percent of the innovations δ_{yt} and δ_{zt}.

Now pretend that we do not know the data-generating process. The issue is whether the Engle–Granger methodology can uncover the essential details of the process. The first step is to pretest the variables in order to determine their order of integration. Consider the augmented Dickey–Fuller regression equation for $\{y_t\}$:

$$\Delta y_t = \alpha_0 + \alpha_1 y_{t-1} + \sum_{i=1}^{n} \alpha_{i+1}\Delta y_{t-i} + \varepsilon_t$$

If the data happened to be quarterly, it would be natural to perform the augmented Dickey–Fuller tests using lag lengths that are multiples of 4 (i.e., $n = 4, 8, \ldots$). For each series, the results of the Dickey–Fuller test and the augmented test using 4 lags are reported in Table 6.2.

With 100 observations and a constant, the 5 percent critical value of the Dickey–Fuller test is –2.89. Since the absolute values of all t-statistics are well below this critical value, we cannot reject the null hypothesis of a unit root in any of the series. Of course, if there were any serious doubt about the presence of a unit root, we could use the procedures in Chapter 4 to test for the presence of a trend or drift. If various lag lengths yield different results, we would want to test for the most appropriate lag length.

The luxury of using simulated data is that we can avoid these potentially sticky problems and move on to Step 2. Since all three variables are presumed to be jointly determined, the long-run equilibrium regression can be estimated using either y_t, z_t, or w_t as the "left-hand-side" variable. The three estimates of the long-run relationship (with t-values in parentheses) are

$$y_t = -0.4843 \quad - 0.9273z_t \quad + 0.97687w_t + e_{yt}$$
$$(-0.5751)(-38.095) \quad (53.462)$$

$$z_t = 0.0589 \quad - 1.0108y_t \quad + 1.02549w_t + e_{zt}$$
$$(0.6709) \; (-38.095) \quad (65.323)$$

$$w_t = 0.0852 \quad + 0.9901y_t \quad + 0.95347z_t + e_{wt}$$
$$(-1.0089) \; (52.462) \quad (65.462)$$

where e_{yt}, e_{zt}, and e_{wt} = the residuals from the three equilibrium regressions.

The essence of the test is to determine whether the residuals from the equilibrium regression are stationary. Again, in performing the test, there is no presumption that any one of the three residual series is preferable to any of the others. If we use each of the three series to estimate an equation in the form of (6.31) [or (6.32)], the estimated values of a_1 are given in Table 6.3.

From Table C, you can see that the critical values of the t-statistic as –3.398. Hence, using any one of the three equilibrium regressions, we can conclude that the series are cointegrated of order (1, 1). Fortunately, all three equilibrium regressions yield this same conclusion. We should be very wary of a result indicating that the variables are

Table 6.2 Estimated α_1 and the Associated t-statistic

	No Lags	4 Lags
Δy_t	-0.01995	-0.02691
	(-0.74157)	(-1.0465)
Δz_t	-0.02069	-0.25841
	(-0.99213)	(-1.1437)
Δw_t	-0.03501	-0.03747
	(-1.9078)	(-1.9335)

Table 6.3 Estimated a_1 and the Associated t-statistic

	No Lags	4 Lags
Δe_{yt}	-0.44301	-0.59525
	(-5.17489)	(-4.0741)
Δe_{zt}	-0.45195	-0.59344
	(-5.37882)	(-4.2263)
Δe_{wt}	-0.45525	-0.60711
	(-5.3896)	(-4.2247)

cointegrated using one variable for the normalization but are not cointegrated using another variable for the normalization. In such circumstances, it is possible that only a subset of the variables are cointegrated. Suppose that x_{1t}, x_{2t}, and x_{3t} are three $I(1)$ variables and that x_{1t} are x_{2t} are cointegrated such that $x_{1t} - \beta_2 x_{2t}$ is stationary. A regression of x_{1t} on the other two variables should yield the stationary relationship $x_{1t} = \beta_2 x_{2t} + 0x_{3t}$. Similarly, a regression of x_{2t} on the other variables should yield the stationary relationship $x_{2t} = (1/\beta_2)x_{1t} + 0x_{3t}$. However, a regression of x_{3t} on x_{1t} and x_{2t} cannot reveal the cointegrating relationship. Nevertheless, the possibility of a contradictory result is a weakness of the test; other methods can be tried if mixed results are found.

You must be careful in conducting significance tests on the estimated equilibrium regressions. The coefficients *do not* have an asymptotic *t*-distribution unless the right-hand-side variables are actually independent and the error terms are serially uncorrelated.

Step 3 entails estimating the error-correction model. Consider the first-order system shown with *t*-statistics in parentheses:

$$\Delta y_t = 0.009 + 0.441 e_{wt-1} + 0.190 \Delta y_{t-1} + 0.332 \Delta z_{t-1} - 0.380 \Delta w_{t-1} + \varepsilon_{yt} \quad (6.37)$$
$$ (0.291) \ (2.94) \quad\quad (1.15) \quad\quad\quad (2.05) \quad\quad (-2.35)$$

$$\Delta z_t = -0.042 + 0.054 e_{wt-1} + 0.139 \Delta y_{t-1} + 0.253 \Delta z_{t-1} - 0.304 \Delta w_{t-1} + \varepsilon_{zt} \quad (6.38)$$
$$ (-1.11) \ (0.304) \quad\quad (0.711) \quad\quad\quad (1.32) \quad\quad (-1.59)$$

$$\Delta w_t = -0.041 - 0.065 e_{wt-1} + 0.157 \Delta y_{t-1} + 0.302 \Delta z_{t-1} - 0.421 \Delta w_{t-1} + \varepsilon_{wt} \quad (6.39)$$
$$ (-0.31) \ (-0.907) \quad\quad (0.688) \quad\quad\quad (1.35) \quad\quad (-1.88)$$

where $e_{wt-1} = w_{t-1} + 0.0852 - 0.9901 y_{t-1} - 0.95347 z_{t-1}$ so that e_{wt-1} is the lagged value of the residual from the equilibrium relationship using w_t as the dependent variable.

Equations (6.37) through (6.39) comprise a first-order VAR augmented with the single error-correction term e_{wt-1}. Again, there is an area of ambiguity since the residuals from any of the "equilibrium" relationships could have been used in the estimation. The signs of the speed of adjustment coefficients are in accord with convergence toward the long-run equilibrium. In response to a positive discrepancy in e_{wt-1}, both y_t and z_t tend to increase while w_t tends to decrease. The error-correction term, however, is significant only in (6.37).

Finally, the diagnostic methods discussed in the last section should be applied to (6.37) through (6.39) in order to assess the model's adequacy. Using actual data, lag-length tests and the properties of the residuals need to be considered. Moreover, innovation accounting could help determine whether the model is adequate. These tests are not performed here since there is no economic theory associated with the simulated data.

The Engle–Granger Procedure with I(2) Variables

Multicointegration refers to a situation in which a linear combination of $I(2)$ and $I(1)$ variables is integrated of order zero. For example, suppose that x_{1t} and x_{2t} are $I(2)$ and that z_t is $I(1)$. It is possible that a linear combination of x_{1t} and x_{2t} is $I(1)$ and that this combination is cointegrated with z_t. Hence, it is possible to have a long-run equilibrium relationship of the form[11]

$$x_{1t} = \beta_2 x_{2t} + \gamma_1 z_t$$

However, a richer set of possibilities is given by the stationary relationship:

$$x_{1t} = \beta_2 x_{2t} + \gamma_1 \Delta x_{2t} + \alpha_1 z_t$$

This specification allows for the possibility that the linear combination $x_{1t} - \beta_2 x_{2t}$ is $I(1)$ and cointegrated with the other $I(1)$ independent variables in the system: Δx_{2t} and z_t. To make sure you understand the issue, ask yourself if it is possible for β_2 to be zero. The answer is a resounding no. If $\beta_2 = 0$, the $I(2)$ variable x_{1t} cannot, by itself, be cointegrated with the $I(1)$ variables.

In principle, it is possible to check for multicointegration using a two-step procedure. First, search for a cointegrating relationship among the $I(2)$ variables and then use this relationship to check for a possible cointegrating relationship with the remaining $I(1)$ variables. Engsted, Gonzalo and Haldrup (1997) show that this procedure is effective only if the cointegrating vector for the first step is known. Otherwise, the second step is contaminated with the errors generated in the first step. In the most general form of the one-step procedure, you estimate an equation in the form

$$x_{1t} = a_0 + a_1 t + a_2 t^2 + \beta_2 x_{2t} + \beta_3 x_{3t} + \gamma_1 \Delta x_{2t} + \gamma_2 \Delta x_{3t} + \alpha_1 z_t + e_t \quad (6.40)$$

where x_{1t}, x_{2t}, and x_{3t} are $I(2)$ variables, z_t is a vector of $I(1)$ variables, and the deterministic regressors can include a quadratic time trend.

Hence, the test allows you to include up to two $I(2)$ variables and an unrestricted number of $I(1)$ variables as regressors. You might want to include the quadratic time trend if $\Delta^2 x_{1t}$ contains a drift. Since the key issue is the stationarity of the $\{e_t\}$ series, estimate a regression of the form

$$\Delta \hat{e}_t = \rho \hat{e}_{t-1} + \sum_{i=1}^{p} \rho_i \Delta \hat{e}_{t-i} + v_t$$

where $\{\hat{e}_t\}$ are the regression residuals from (6.40).

If it is possible to reject the null hypothesis $\rho = 0$, it is possible to conclude that there is multicointegration. In addition to sample size, the critical values of the t-statistic for the null hypothesis $\rho = 0$ depend on the number of $I(2)$ regressors ($m_2 = 1$ or 2), the number of $I(1)$ regressors ($m_1 = 0$ to 4), and the form of the deterministic regressors. The critical values are shown in Table D at the end of the text. Consider the U.K. money demand equations for the sample period 1963:Q1 to 1989:Q2 estimated by Haldrup (1994):

$$m_t = a_0 + 0.68 p_t + 1.57 y_t - 2.67 r_t - 2.55 \Delta p_t \quad (6.41)$$

and

$$m_t = a_0 + a_1 t + 0.89 p_t + 2.39 y_t - 2.69 r_t - 3.25 \Delta p_t \quad (6.42)$$

Pretesting the variables indicated that m_t (as measured by $M1$) and p_t (the implicit price deflator) were $I(2)$ and that y_t (total final expenditure) and r_t (a measure of the interest rate differential) were $I(1)$. The only variable needing explanation is the presence of Δp_t in the money demand function. The idea is to allow for the demand for money to depend on the inflation rate (i.e., change in the log of the price level) since high inflation should reduce the desire to hold money balances. Since there is a total of 105 observations, one $I(2)$ regressor (so that $m_2 = 1$), and three $I(1)$ regressors, the

5 percent critical values for models without and with the linear trend are –4.56 and –4.91, respectively. Using the residuals from the money demand equations given by (6.41) and (6.42), Haldrup found that the t-statistics for the null hypothesis $\rho = 0$ were –2.35 and –2.66, respectively. Hence, it is possible to conclude that the two regressions are spurious (i.e., it is not possible to reject the null hypothesis of no multicointegration).

Even though multicointegration fails, Haldrup goes on to experiment with various estimates of the error-correction mechanism. One interesting model (with standard errors in parentheses) is

$$\Delta^2 m_t = -0.04 \hat{e}_{t-1} + \text{stationary regressors}$$
$$(0.02)$$

where the stationary regressors can include lagged values of $\Delta^2 m_t$ as well as current and lagged values of $\Delta^2 p_t$, Δy_t, Δp_t, and Δr_t. The point estimate is such that $\Delta^2 m_t$ is expected to decline in response to a positive discrepancy from the long-run relationship. The t-statistic of $-0.04/0.02 = 2$ suggests that the effect is just significant at the 5 percent level.

6. COINTEGRATION AND PURCHASING POWER PARITY

To illustrate the Engle–Granger methodology using "real world" data, reconsider the theory of *purchasing power parity (PPP)*. Respectively, if e_t, p_{ft}, and p_t denote the logarithms of the price of foreign exchange, the foreign price level, and the domestic price level, long-run PPP requires that $e_t + p_{ft} - p_t$ be stationary. The unit root tests reported in Chapter 4 indicate that real exchange rates—defined as $r_t = e_t + p_{ft} - p_t$—appear to be nonstationary. Cointegration offers an alternative method to check the theory; if PPP holds, the sequence formed by the sum $\{e_t + p_{ft}\}$ should be cointegrated with the $\{p_t\}$ sequence. Call the constructed dollar value of the foreign price level f_t; that is, $f_t = e_t + p_{ft}$. Long-run PPP asserts that there exists a linear combination of the form $f_t = \beta_0 + \beta_1 p_t + \mu_t$ such that $\{\mu_t\}$ is stationary *and* the cointegrating vector is such that $\beta_1 = 1$.

As reported in Chapter 4, in Enders (1988), I used price and exchange rate data for Germany, Japan, Canada, and the United States for both the Bretton Woods (1960–1971) and post–Bretton Woods (1973–1988) periods.[12] Pretesting the data indicated that for each period, the U.S. price level $\{p_t\}$ and the dollar values of the foreign price levels $\{e_t + p_{ft}\}$ both contained a single unit root. With differing orders of integration, it would have been possible to immediately conclude that long-run PPP had failed.

The next step was to estimate the long-run equilibrium relation by regressing each $f_t = e_t + p_{ft}$ on p_t:

$$f_t = \beta_0 + \beta_1 p_t + \mu_t \tag{6.43}$$

Absolute PPP asserts $f_t = p_t$, so this version of the theory requires $\beta_0 = 0$ and $\beta_1 = 1$. The intercept β_0 is consistent with the relative version of PPP, requiring only that domestic and foreign price levels are proportional to each other. Unless there are compelling reasons to omit the constant, the recommended practice is to include an intercept term in the equilibrium regression. In fact, Engle and Granger's (1987) Monte Carlo simulations all include intercept terms.

The estimated values of β_1 and their associated standard errors are reported in Table 6.4. Note that five of the six values are estimated to be quite a bit below unity. Be especially careful not to make too much of these findings. It is *not* appropriate to conclude that each value of β_1 is significantly different from unity simply because the values of $(1 - \beta_1)$ exceed two or three standard deviations. It is hard to overstate the point that the assumptions underlying this type of t-test are not applicable because there is no presumption that p_t is the exogenous variable while f_t is the dependent variable, or that $\{\mu_t\}$ is white noise.[13]

The residuals from each regression equation, called $\{\hat{\mu}_t\}$, were checked for unit roots. The unit root tests are straightforward because the residuals from a regression equation have a zero mean and do not have a time trend. The following two equations were estimated using the residuals from each long-run equilibrium relationship:

$$\Delta\hat{\mu}_t = a_1\hat{\mu}_{t-1} + \varepsilon_t \tag{6.44}$$

and

$$\Delta\hat{\mu}_t = a_1\hat{\mu}_{t-1} + \Sigma a_{i+1}\Delta\hat{\mu}_{t-i} + \varepsilon_t \tag{6.45}$$

Table 6.5 reports the estimated values of a_1 from (6.44) and from (6.45) using a lag length of four. It bears repeating that failure to reject the null hypothesis $a_1 = 0$ means we cannot reject the null of no cointegration. Alternatively, if $-2 < a_1 < 0$, it is possible to conclude that the $\{\hat{\mu}_t\}$ sequence does not have a unit root and that the $\{f_t\}$ and $\{p_t\}$ sequences are cointegrated. Also note that it is not appropriate to use the confidence intervals reported in Dickey and Fuller. The Dickey–Fuller statistics are inappropriate because the residuals used in (6.44) and (6.45) are not the actual error terms. Rather, these residuals are estimated error terms that are obtained from the estimate of the equilibrium regression. If we knew the magnitudes of the actual errors in each period, we could use the Dickey–Fuller tables.

Under the null hypothesis $a_1 = 0$, the critical values for the t-statistic depend on sample size. Comparing the results reported in Table 6.5 with the critical values provided by Table C indicates that only for Japan during the fixed exchange rate period is it possible to reject the null hypothesis of no cointegration. With four lags,

Table 6.4 The Equilibrium Regressions

	Germany	Japan	Canada
1973–1986			
Estimated β_1	0.5374	0.8938	0.7749
Standard error	(0.0415)	(0.0316)	(0.0077)
1960–1971			
Estimated β_1	0.6660	0.7361	1.0809
Standard error	(0.0262)	(0.0154)	(0.0200)

Table 6.5 Dickey–Fuller Tests of the Residuals

	Germany	Japan	Canada
1973–1986			
No lags			
Estimated a_1	–0.0225	–0.0151	–0.1001
Standard error	(0.0169)	(0.0236)	(0.0360)
t-statistic for $a_1 = 0$	–1.331	–0.640	–2.781
4 lags			
Estimated a_1	–0.0316	–0.0522	–0.0983
Standard error	(0.0170)	(0.0236)	(0.0388)
t-statistic for $a_1 = 0$	–1.859	–2.212	–2.533
1960–1971			
No lags			
Estimated a_1	–0.0189	–0.1137	–0.0528
Standard error	(0.0196)	(0.0449)	(0.0286)
t-statistic for $a_1 = 0$	–0.966	–2.535	–1.846
4 lags			
Estimated a_1	–0.0294	–0.1821	–0.0509
Standard error	(0.0198)	(0.0530)	(0.0306)
t-statistic for $a_1 = 0$	–1.468	–3.437	–1.663

the *t*-statistic for the null hypothesis $a_1 = 0$ is calculated to be –3.437. At the 5 per-cent significance level, the critical value of t is –3.398 for two variables and 100 observations. Hence, at the 5 percent significance level we can reject the null of no cointegration (i.e., we accept the alternative that the variables are cointegrated) and find in favor of PPP. For the other countries in each time period, we cannot reject the null hypothesis of no cointegration and must conclude that PPP generally failed.

The third step in the methodology entails estimation of the error-correction model. Only the Japan/U.S. model needs estimation since it is the sole case for which cointegration holds. The final error-correction models for Japanese and U.S. price levels during the 1960 to 1971 period were estimated to be

$$\Delta f_t = 0.00119 - 0.10548\hat{\mu}_{t-1} \tag{6.46}$$
$$(0.00044)\ (0.04184)$$

$$\Delta p_t = 0.00156 + 0.01114\hat{\mu}_{t-1} \tag{6.47}$$
$$(0.00033)\ (0.03175)$$

where $\hat{\mu}_{t-1}$ is the lagged residual from the long-run equilibrium regression. Note that $\hat{\mu}_{t-1}$ is the estimated value of $f_{t-1} - \beta_0 - \beta_1 p_{t-1}$ and that standard errors are in parentheses.

Lag length tests (see the discussion of χ^2 and F-tests for lag length in Chapter 5) indicated that lagged values of Δf_{t-i} or Δp_{t-i} did not need to be included in the error-correction equations. Note that the point estimates in (6.46) and (6.47) indicate a direct convergence to long-run equilibrium. For example, in the presence of a one-unit deviation from long-run PPP in period $t - 1$, the Japanese price level falls by 0.10548 units and the U.S. price level rises by 0.01114 units. Both of these price changes in period t act to eliminate the positive discrepancy from long-run PPP present in period $t - 1$.

Notice the discrepancy between the magnitudes of the two speed of adjustment coefficients; in absolute value, the Japanese coefficient is approximately ten times that of the U.S. coefficient. As compared to the Japanese price level, the U.S. price level responded only slightly to a deviation from PPP. Moreover, the error-correction term is about $\frac{1}{3}$ of a standard deviation from zero for the U.S. ($0.01114/0.03175 =$ 0.3509) and approximately 2.5 standard deviations from zero for Japan ($0.10548/0.04184 = 2.5210$). Hence, at the 5 percent significance level, we can conclude that the speed of adjustment term is insignificantly different from zero for the United States but not for Japan. This result is consistent with the idea that the United States was a large country relative to Japan—movements in U.S. prices evolved independently of events in Japan, but movements in exchange rate adjusted Japanese prices responded to events in the United States.

You can update the study using the data contained on the file COINT_PPP.XLS. The file contains quarterly values of German, Japanese, and Canadian wholesale prices and bilateral exchange rates with the United States. The file also contains the U.S. wholesale price level. Question 3 at the end of the chapter guides you through the process.

7. CHARACTERISTIC ROOTS, RANK, AND COINTEGRATION

Although the Engle and Granger (1987) procedure is easily implemented, it does have several important defects. The estimation of the long-run equilibrium regression requires that the researcher place one variable on the left-hand side and use the others as regressors. For example, in the case of two variables, it is possible to run the Engle–Granger test for cointegration by using the residuals from either of the following two "equilibrium" regressions:

$$y_t = \beta_{10} + \beta_{11}z_t + e_{1t} \tag{6.48}$$

or

$$z_t = \beta_{20} + \beta_{21}y_t + e_{2t} \tag{6.49}$$

As the sample size grows infinitely large, asymptotic theory indicates that the test for a unit root in the $\{e_{1t}\}$ sequence becomes equivalent to the test for a unit root in the $\{e_{2t}\}$ sequence. Unfortunately, the large sample properties on which this result is derived may not be applicable to the sample sizes usually available to economists. In practice, it is possible to find that one regression indicates that the variables are cointegrated, whereas reversing the order indicates no cointegration. This is a very undesirable feature of the procedure because the test for cointegration should be invariant to the choice of the variable selected for normalization. The problem is obviously compounded using three or more variables since any of the variables can be selected as the left-hand-side variable. Moreover, in tests using three or more variables, we know that there may be more than one cointegrating vector. The method has no systematic procedure for the separate estimation of the multiple cointegrating vectors.

Another defect of the Engle–Granger procedure is that it relies on a *two-step* estimator. The first step is to generate the residual series $\{\hat{e}_t\}$, and the second step uses these generated errors to estimate a regression of the form $\Delta\hat{e}_t = a_1\hat{e}_{t-1} + \dots$. Thus, the coefficient a_1 is obtained by estimating a regression using the residuals from another regression. Hence, any error introduced by the researcher in Step 1 is carried into Step 2. Fortunately, several methods have been developed that avoid these problems. The Johansen (1988) and the Stock and Watson (1988) maximum likelihood estimators circumvent the use of two-step estimators *and* can estimate and test for the presence of multiple cointegrating vectors. Moreover, these tests allow the researcher to test restricted versions of the cointegrating vector(s) and the speed of adjustment parameters. Often, we want to determine whether it is possible to verify a theory by testing restrictions on the magnitudes of the estimated coefficients.

Both the Johansen (1988) and the Stock and Watson (1988) procedures rely heavily on the relationship between the rank of a matrix and its characteristic roots. Appendix 6.2 to this chapter reviews the essentials of these concepts; those of you wanting more details should review this appendix. For those wanting an intuitive explanation, notice that the Johansen procedure is nothing more than a multivariate generalization of the Dickey–Fuller test. In the univariate case, it is possible to view the stationarity of $\{y_t\}$ as being dependent on the magnitude $(a_1 - 1)$; that is,

$$y_t = a_1 y_{t-1} + \varepsilon_t$$

or

$$\Delta y_t = (a_1 - 1)y_{t-1} + \varepsilon_t$$

If $(a_1 - 1) = 0$, the $\{y_t\}$ process has a unit root. Ruling out the case in which $\{y_t\}$ is explosive, if $(a_1 - 1) \neq 0$ we can conclude that the $\{y_t\}$ sequence is stationary. The Dickey–Fuller tables provide the appropriate statistics to formally test the null hypothesis $(a_1 - 1) = 0$. Now consider the simple generalization to n variables; as in (6.26), let

$$x_t = A_1 x_{t-1} + \varepsilon_t$$

so that

$$
\begin{aligned}
\Delta x_t &= A_1 x_{t-1} - x_{t-1} + \varepsilon_t \\
&= (A_1 - I)x_{t-1} + \varepsilon_t \\
&= \pi x_{t-1} + \varepsilon_t
\end{aligned}
\tag{6.50}
$$

where: x_t and ε_t are $(n \cdot 1)$ vectors
$A_1 =$ an $(n \cdot n)$ matrix of parameters
$I =$ an $(n \cdot n)$ identity matrix
π is defined to be $(A_1 - I)$

As indicated in the discussion surrounding (6.27), the rank of $(A_1 - I)$ equals the number of cointegrating vectors. By analogy to the univariate case, if $(A_1 - I)$ consists of all zeroes—so that rank(π) $= 0$—all of the $\{x_{it}\}$ sequences are unit root processes. Since there is no linear combination of the $\{x_{it}\}$ processes that is stationary, the variables are not cointegrated. If we rule out characteristic roots that are greater than unity and if rank(π) $= n$, (6.50) represents a convergent system of difference equations, so that all variables are stationary.

There are several ways to generalize (6.50). The equation is easily modified to allow for the presence of a drift term; simply let

$$\Delta x_t = A_0 + \pi x_{t-1} + \varepsilon_t \qquad (6.51)$$

where A_0 = the $(n \cdot 1)$ vector of constants $(a_{01}, a_{02}, \ldots, a_{0n})'$.

The effect of including the various a_{0i} is to allow for the possibility of a linear time trend in the data-generating process. You would want to include the drift term if the variables exhibited a decided tendency to increase or decrease. Here, the rank of π can be viewed as the number of cointegrating relationships existing in the "detrended" data. In the long run, $\pi x_{t-1} = 0$ so that each $\{\Delta x_{it}\}$ sequence has an expected value of a_{i0}. Aggregating all such changes over t yields the deterministic expression $a_{i0}t$.

Figure 6.3 illustrates the effects of including a drift in the data-generating process. Two random sequences with 100 observations each were generated; denote these sequences as $\{\varepsilon_{yt}\}$ and $\{\varepsilon_{zt}\}$. Initializing $y_0 = z_0 = 0$, we constructed the next 100 values of the $\{y_t\}$ and $\{z_t\}$ sequences as

$$\begin{bmatrix} \Delta y_t \\ \Delta z_t \end{bmatrix} = \begin{bmatrix} -0.2 & 0.2 \\ 0.2 & -0.2 \end{bmatrix} \begin{bmatrix} y_{t-1} \\ z_{t-1} \end{bmatrix} + \begin{bmatrix} \varepsilon_{yt} \\ \varepsilon_{zt} \end{bmatrix}$$

so that the cointegrating relationship is

$$-0.2y_{t-1} + 0.2z_{t-1} = 0$$

or

$$y_t = z_t$$

In Panel (a) of Figure 6.3, you can see that each sequence resembles a random walk process and that neither wanders too far from the other. Panel (b) adds drift coefficients such that $a_{10} = a_{20} = 0.1$; now each series tends to increase by 0.1 units in each period. In addition to the fact that each sequence shares the same stochastic trend, note that each also has the same deterministic time trend. The fact that each has the same deterministic trend is *not* a result of the equivalence between a_{10} and a_{20}; the general solution to (6.51) necessitates that each have the same linear trend. For verification, Panel (c) sets $a_{10} = 0.1$ and $a_{20} = 0.4$. Again, the sequences have the same stochastic and deterministic trends. As an aside, note that increasing a_{20} and decreasing a_{10} would have an ambiguous effect on the slope of the deterministic trend. This point will be important in a moment; by appropriately manipulating the elements of A_0 it is possible to include a constant in the cointegrating vector(s) without imparting a deterministic time trend to the system.

One way to include a constant in the cointegrating relationships is to restrict the values of the various a_{i0}. For example, if rank(π) = 1, the rows of π can differ by only a scalar, so that it is possible to write each $\{\Delta x_{it}\}$ sequence in (6.51) as

$$\Delta x_{1t} = \pi_{11}x_{1t-1} + \pi_{12}x_{2t-1} + \ldots + \pi_{1n}x_{nt-1} + a_{10} + \varepsilon_{1t}$$
$$\Delta x_{2t} = s_2(\pi_{11}x_{1t-1} + \pi_{12}x_{2t-1} + \ldots + \pi_{1n}x_{nt-1}) + a_{20} + \varepsilon_{2t}$$
$$\ldots$$
$$\Delta x_{nt} = s_n(\pi_{11}x_{1t-1} + \pi_{12}x_{2t-1} + \ldots + \pi_{1n}x_{nt-1}) + a_{n0} + \varepsilon_{nt}$$

where s_i = scalars such that $s_i \pi_{1j} = \pi_{ij}$.

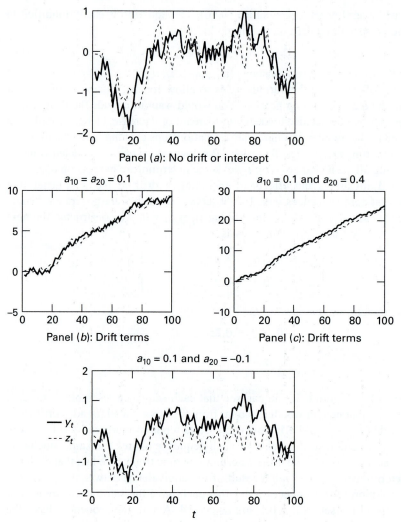

Panel (a): No drift or intercept

Panel (b): Drift terms

Panel (c): Drift terms

Panel (d): Constant in the cointegrating vector

FIGURE 6.3 Drifts and Intercepts in Cointegrating Relationships

If the a_{i0} can be restricted such that $a_{i0} = s_i a_{10}$, it follows that the all of the $\{\Delta x_{it}\}$ sequences can be written with the constant included in the cointegrating vector:

$$\Delta x_{1t} = (\pi_{11}x_{1t-1} + \pi_{12}x_{2t-1} + \ldots + \pi_{1n}x_{nt-1} + a_{10}) + \varepsilon_{1t}$$
$$\Delta x_{2t} = s_2(\pi_{11}x_{1t-1} + \pi_{12}x_{2t-1} + \ldots + \pi_{1n}x_{nt-1} + a_{10}) + \varepsilon_{2t}$$
$$\ldots$$
$$\Delta x_{nt} = s_n(\pi_{11}x_{1t-1} + \pi_{12}x_{2t-1} + \ldots + \pi_{1n}x_{nt-1} + a_{10}) + \varepsilon_{nt}$$

or in compact form,

$$\Delta x_t = \pi^* x^*_{t-1} + \varepsilon_t \qquad (6.52)$$

where: $x_t = (x_t, x_{2t}, \ldots, x_{nt})'$
$x^*_{t-1} = (x_{1t-1}, x_{2t-1}, \ldots, x_{nt-1}, 1)'$

$$\pi^* = \begin{bmatrix} \pi_{11} & \pi_{12} & \cdots & \pi_{1n} & a_{10} \\ \pi_{21} & \pi_{22} & \cdots & \pi_{2n} & a_{20} \\ \cdot & \cdot & \cdots & \cdot & \cdot \\ \pi_{n1} & \pi_{n2} & \cdots & \pi_{nn} & a_{n0} \end{bmatrix}$$

The interesting feature of (6.52) is that the linear trend is purged from the system. In essence, the various a_{i0} have been altered in such a way that the general solution for each $\{x_{it}\}$ does not contain a time trend. The solution to the set of difference equations represented by (6.52) is such that all Δx_{it} are expected to equal zero when $\pi_{11}x_{1t-1} + \pi_{12}x_{2t-1} + \ldots + \pi_{1n}x_{nt-1} + a_{10} = 0$.

To highlight the difference between (6.51) and (6.52), Panel (*d*) of Figure 6.3 illustrates the consequences of setting $a_{10} = 0.1$ and $a_{20} = -0.1$. You can see that neither sequence contains a deterministic trend. In fact, for the data shown in the figure, the trend will vanish so long as we select values of the drift terms maintaining the relationship $a_{10} = -a_{20}$. (You are asked to demonstrate this result in the Questions and Exercises section at the end of this chapter.)

Some econometricians prefer to include an intercept term in the cointegrating vector along with a drift term. This makes sense if the variables contain a drift and if economic theory suggests that the cointegrating vector contains an intercept. However, it should be clear that the intercept in the cointegrating vector is not identified in the presence of a drift term. After all, some portion of the unrestricted drift can always be included in the cointegration vector. In terms of the example above, the system can always be written as

$$\Delta x_{1t} = (\pi_{11}x_{1t-1} + \pi_{12}x_{2t-1} + \ldots + \pi_{1n}x_{nt-1} + b_{10}) + b_{11} + \varepsilon_{1t}$$
$$\ldots$$
$$\Delta x_{nt} = s_n(\pi_{11}x_{1t-1} + \pi_{12}x_{2t-1} + \ldots + \pi_{1n}x_{nt-1} + b_{10}) + b_{n1} + \varepsilon_{nt}$$

where b_{i1} is defined to the value that satisfies $s_i b_{10} + b_{i1} = a_{10}$.

All that was done is to divide a_{10} into two parts and to place one part inside the cointegrating relationship. As such, some identification strategy is necessary since the proportion of the drift to include in the cointegrating vector is arbitrary. The popular software package E-Views, for example, identifies the portion belonging in the cointegrating vector as the amount necessary to force the error-correction term to have a sample mean of zero. Nevertheless, as you can see from Figure 6.3, a drift term outside of the cointegrating relationship is necessary to capture the effects of a sustained tendency for the variables to increase (or decrease). Most researchers include drift terms if the data match Panels (*b*) or (*c*) of Figure 6.3. Otherwise, they include intercepts in the cointegrating vector or exclude the deterministic regressors altogether. If you are unsure, you can use the methods described in the next section to test whether the drifts can be appropriately restricted. Some software packages allow you to include a deterministic time trend in the model. However, it is best to avoid the use of a trend as an explanatory variable unless you have a good reason to include it in the model. Johansen (1994) discusses the role of the deterministic regressors in a cointegrating relationship.

As with the augmented Dickey–Fuller test, the multivariate model can also be generalized to allow for a higher-order autoregressive process. Consider:

$$x_t = A_1 x_{t-1} + A_2 x_{t-2} + \ldots + A_p x_{t-p} + \varepsilon_t \tag{6.53}$$

where: $x_t =$ the $(n \cdot 1)$ vector $(x_{1t}, x_{2t}, \ldots, x_{nt})'$

$\varepsilon_t =$ an independently and identically distributed n-dimensional vector with zero mean and variance matrix Σ_ε.

Equation (6.53) can be put in a more usable form by adding and subtracting $A_p x_{t-p+1}$ to the right-hand side to obtain

$$x_t = A_1 x_{t-1} + A_2 x_{t-2} + A_3 x_{t-3} + \ldots + A_{p-2} x_{t-p+2} + (A_{p-1} + A_p) x_{t-p+1} - A_p \Delta x_{t-p+1} + \varepsilon_t$$

Next, add and subtract $(A_{p-1} + A_p) x_{t-p+2}$ to obtain

$$x_t = A_1 x_{t-1} + A_2 x_{t-2} + A_3 x_{t-3} + \ldots - (A_{p-1} + A_p) \Delta x_{t-p+2} - A_p \Delta x_{t-p+1} + \varepsilon_t$$

Just as in the augmented Dickey–Fuller test developed in Chapter 4, we can continue in this fashion to obtain

$$\Delta x_t = \pi x_{t-1} + \sum_{i=1}^{p-1} \pi_i \Delta x_{t-i} + \varepsilon_t \tag{6.54}$$

where $\pi = -(I - \sum_{i=1}^{p} A_i)$ and $\pi_i = - \sum_{j=i+1}^{p} A_j$.

Again, the key feature to note in (6.54) is rank of the matrix π; the rank of π is equal to the number of independent cointegrating vectors. Clearly, if rank$(\pi) = 0$, the matrix is null and (6.54) is the usual VAR model in first differences. Instead, if π is of rank n, the vector process is stationary. In intermediate cases, if rank$(\pi) = 1$, there is a single cointegrating vector and the expression πx_{t-1} is the error-correction term. For other cases in which $1 < \text{rank}(\pi) < n$, there are multiple cointegrating vectors.

As detailed in Appendix 6.2, the number of distinct cointegrating vectors can be obtained by checking the significance of the characteristic roots of π. We know that the rank of a matrix is equal to the number of its characteristic roots that differ from zero. Suppose we obtained the matrix π and ordered the n characteristic roots such that $\lambda_1 > \lambda_2 > \ldots > \lambda_n$. If the variables in x_t are *not* cointegrated, the rank of π is zero and all of these characteristic roots will equal zero. Since $\ln(1) = 0$, each of the expressions $\ln(1 - \lambda_i)$ will equal zero if the variables are not cointegrated. Similarly, if the rank of π is unity, $0 < \lambda_1 < 1$ so the first expression $\ln(1 - \lambda_1)$ will be negative and all the other $\lambda_i = 0$ so that $\ln(1 - \lambda_2) = \ln(1 - \lambda_3) = \ldots = \ln(1 - \lambda_n) = 0$.

In practice, we can obtain only estimates of π and its characteristic roots. The test for the number of characteristic roots that are insignificantly different from unity can be conducted using the following two test statistics:

$$\lambda_{\text{trace}}(r) = -T \sum_{i=r+1}^{n} \ln(1 - \hat{\lambda}_i) \tag{6.55}$$

$$\lambda_{max}(r, r+1) = -T \ln(1 - \hat{\lambda}_{r+1}) \qquad (6.56)$$

where: $\hat{\lambda}_i$ = the estimated values of the characteristic roots (also called eigenvalues) obtained from the estimated π matrix

T = the number of usable observations

When the appropriate values of r are clear, these statistics are simply referred to as λ_{trace} and λ_{max}.

The first statistic tests the null hypothesis that the number of distinct cointegrating vectors is less than or equal to r against a general alternative. From the previous discussion, it should be clear that λ_{trace} equals zero when all $\lambda_i = 0$. The further the estimated characteristic roots are from zero, the more negative is $\ln(1 - \hat{\lambda}_i)$ and the larger is the λ_{trace} statistic. The second statistic tests the null that the number of cointegrating vectors is r against the alternative of $r + 1$ cointegrating vectors. Again, if the estimated value of the characteristic root is close to zero, λ_{max} will be small.

Critical values of the λ_{trace} and the λ_{max} statistics are obtained using the Monte Carlo approach. The critical values are reproduced in Table E at the end of this text. The distribution of these statistics depends on two things:

1. The number of nonstationary components under the null hypothesis (i.e., $n - r$).

2. The form of the vector A_0. Use the top portion of Table E if you do not include either a constant in the cointegrating vector or a drift term. Use the middle portion of the table if you include a drift term A_0. Use the bottom portion of the table if you include a constant in the cointegrating vector.

Using quarterly data for Denmark over the sample period 1974:1 to 1987:3, Johansen and Juselius (1990) let the x_t vector be represented by

$$x_t = (m2_t, y_t, i_t^d, i_t^b)'$$

where: $m2$ = log of the real money supply as measured by $M2$ deflated by a price index

y = log of real income

i^d = deposit rate on money representing a direct return on money holding

i^b = bond rate representing the opportunity cost of holding money

Including a constant in the cointegrating relationship (i.e., augmenting x_{t-1} with a constant), they report that the residuals from (6.54) appear to be serially uncorrelated. The four characteristic roots of the estimated π matrix are given in the first column of the following table:[14]

	λ_{max} $-T \ln(1 - \hat{\lambda}_{r+1})$	λ_{trace} $-T \sum \ln(1 - \hat{\lambda}_i)$
$\hat{\lambda}_1 = 0.4332$	30.09	49.14
$\hat{\lambda}_2 = 0.1776$	10.36	19.05
$\hat{\lambda}_3 = 0.1128$	6.34	8.69
$\hat{\lambda}_4 = 0.0434$	2.35	2.35

The second column reports the various λ_{max} statistics as the number of usable observations ($T = 53$) multiplied by $\ln(1 - \hat{\lambda}_{r+1})$. For example, $-53 \ln(1 - 0.0434) = 2.35$ and $-53 \ln(1 - 0.1128) = 6.34$. The last column reports the λ_{trace} statistics as the summation of the λ_{max} statistics. Simple arithmetic reveals that $8.69 = 2.35 + 6.34$ and $19.05 = 2.35 + 6.34 + 10.36$.

To test the null hypothesis $r = 0$ against the general alternative $r = 1, 2, 3,$ or 4, use the λ_{trace} statistic. Since the null hypothesis is $r = 0$ and there are four variables (i.e., $n = 4$), the summation in (6.55) runs from 1 to 4. If we sum over the four values, the calculated value of λ_{trace} is 49.14. Since Johansen and Juselius (1990) include the constant in the cointegrating vector, this calculated value of 49.14 is compared to the critical values reported in the bottom portion of Table E. For $n - r = 4$, the critical values of λ_{trace} are 49.65, 53.12, and 60.16 at the 10, 5, and 1 percent significance levels, respectively. Thus, at the 10 percent level, the restriction is *not* binding, so that the variables are *not* cointegrated using this test.

To make a point and to give you practice in using the table, suppose you want to test the null hypothesis $r \leq 1$ against the alternative $r = 2, 3,$ or 4. Under this null hypothesis, the summation in (6.55) runs from 2 to 4 so that the calculated value of λ_{trace} is 19.05. For $n - r = 3$, the critical values of λ_{trace} are 32.00, 34.91, and 41.07 at the 10, 5, and 1 percent significance levels, respectively. The restriction $r = 0$ or $r = 1$ is not binding.

In contrast to the λ_{trace} statistic, the λ_{max} statistic has a specific alternative hypothesis. To test the null hypothesis $r = 0$ against the specific alternative $r = 1$, use equation (6.56). The calculated value of the $\lambda_{max}(0, 1)$ statistic is $-53 \ln (1 - 0.4332) = 30.09$. For $n - r = 4$, the critical values of λ_{max} are 25.56, 28.14, 30.32, and 33.24 at the 10, 5, 2.5, and 1 percent significance levels, respectively. Hence, it is possible to reject the null hypothesis $r = 0$ at the 5 percent significance level (but not the 2.5 percent level) and conclude that there is only one cointegrating vector (i.e., $r = 1$). Before reading on, you should take a moment to examine the data and convince yourself that the null hypothesis $r = 1$ against the alternative $r = 2$ cannot be rejected at conventional levels. You should find that the calculated value of the λ_{max} statistic for $r = 1$ is 10.36 and that the critical value at the 10 percent level is 19.77. Hence, there is no significant evidence of more than one cointegrating vector.

The example illustrates the important point that the results of the λ_{trace} and λ_{max} tests can conflict. The λ_{max} test has the sharper alternative hypothesis. It is usually preferred for trying to pin down the number of cointegrating vectors.

8. HYPOTHESIS TESTING

In the Dickey–Fuller tests discussed in Chapter 4, it was important to correctly ascertain the form of the deterministic regressors. A similar situation applies in the Johansen procedure. As you can see in Table E, the critical values of the λ_{trace} and λ_{max} statistics tend to be smallest without any deterministic regressors and largest with an intercept term included in the cointegrating vector. Instead of cavalierly positing the form of A_0, it is possible to test restricted forms of the vector.

One of the most interesting aspects of the Johansen procedure is that it allows for testing restricted forms of the cointegrating vector(s). In a money demand study, you might want to test restrictions concerning the long-run proportionality between money and prices, or the sizes of the income and interest rate elasticities of demand for money. In terms of equation (6.1) (i.e., $m_t = \beta_0 + \beta_1 p_t + \beta_2 y_t + \beta_3 r_t + e_t$), the restrictions of interest are $\beta_1 = 1$, $\beta_2 > 0$, and $\beta_3 < 0$.

The key insight to all such hypothesis tests is that *if there are r cointegrating vectors, only these r linear combinations of the variables are stationary*. All other linear combinations are nonstationary. Thus, suppose you reestimate the model restricting the parameters of π. If the restrictions are not binding, you should find that the number of cointegrating vectors has *not* diminished.

To test for the presence of an intercept in the cointegrating vector as opposed to the unrestricted drift A_0, estimate the two forms of the model. Denote the ordered characteristic roots of the unrestricted π matrix by $\hat{\lambda}_1, \hat{\lambda}_2, \ldots, \hat{\lambda}_n$ and the characteristic roots of the model with the intercept(s) in the cointegrating vector(s) by $\hat{\lambda}_1^*, \hat{\lambda}_2^*, \ldots, \hat{\lambda}_n^*$. Suppose that the unrestricted form of the model has r nonzero characteristic roots. Asymptotically, the statistic

$$-T \sum_{i=r+1}^{n} [\ln(1-\hat{\lambda}_i^*) - \ln(1-\hat{\lambda}_i)] \qquad (6.57)$$

has a χ^2 distribution with $(n-r)$ degrees of freedom.

The intuition behind the test is that all values of $\ln(1-\hat{\lambda}_i^*)$ and $\ln(1-\hat{\lambda}_i)$ should be equivalent if the restriction is not binding. Hence, small values for the test statistic imply that it is permissible to include the intercept in the cointegrating vector. However, the likelihood of finding a stationary linear combination of the n variables is greater with the intercept in the cointegrating vector than if the intercept is absent from the cointegrating vector. Thus, a large value of $\hat{\lambda}_{r+1}^*$ [and a corresponding large value of $-T\ln(1-\hat{\lambda}_{r+1}^*)$] implies that the restriction artificially inflates the number of cointegrating vectors. Thus, as proven by Johansen (1991), if the test statistic is sufficiently large, it is possible to reject the null hypothesis of an intercept in the cointegrating vector(s) and conclude that there is a linear trend in the variables. This is precisely the case represented by the middle portion of Figure 6.3.

Johansen and Juselius (1990) test the restriction that their estimated Danish money demand function does not have a drift. Since they found only one cointegrating vector among $m2$, y, i^d, and i^b, set $n = 4$ and $r = 1$. The calculated value of the χ^2 statistic in (6.57) is 1.99. With three degrees of freedom, this is insignificant at conventional levels; they conclude that the variables do not have a linear time trend and find it appropriate to include the constant in the cointegrating vector.

In order to test other restrictions on the cointegrating vector, Johansen defines the two matrices α and β, both of dimension $(n \cdot r)$ where r is the rank of π. The properties of α and β are such that

$$\pi = \alpha\beta'$$

Note that β is the matrix of cointegrating parameters and α is the matrix of weights with which each cointegrating vector enters the n equations of the VAR. In a sense, α can be viewed as the matrix of the speed of adjustment parameters. Due to the cross-equation restrictions, it is not possible to estimate α and β using OLS.[15] However, using maximum likelihood estimation, it is possible to (1) estimate (6.54) as an error-correction model; (2) determine the rank of π; (3) use the r most significant cointegrating vectors to form β'; and (4) select α such that $\pi = \alpha\beta'$. Question 5 at the end of this chapter asks you to find several such α and β' matrices.

It is easy to understand the process in the case of a single cointegrating vector. Given that rank(π) = 1, the rows of π are all linear multiples of each other. Hence, the equations in (6.54) have the form

$$\Delta x_{1t} = \pi_{11}x_{1t-1} + \pi_{12}x_{2t-1} + \ldots + \pi_{1n}x_{nt-1} + \ldots + \varepsilon_{1t}$$
$$\Delta x_{2t} = s_2\,(\pi_{11}x_{1t-1} + \pi_{12}x_{2t-1} + \ldots + \pi_{1n}x_{nt-1}) + \ldots + \varepsilon_{2t}$$
$$\ldots$$
$$\Delta x_{nt} = s_n\,(\pi_{11}x_{1t-1} + \pi_{12}x_{2t-1} + \ldots + \pi_{1n}x_{nt-1}) + \ldots + \varepsilon_{nt}$$

where the s_i are scalars and, for notational simplicity, the matrices $\pi_i \Delta x_{t-i}$ have not been written out.

Now define $\alpha_i = s_i \pi_{1j}$ and $\beta_i = \pi_{1i}/\pi_{11}$, so that each equation can be written as

$$\Delta x_{it} = \alpha_i\,(x_{1t-1} + \beta_2 x_{2t-1} + \ldots + \beta_n x_{nt-1}) + \ldots + \varepsilon_{it} \quad (i = 1, \ldots, n)$$

or in matrix form,

$$\Delta x_t = \sum_{i=1}^{p-1} \pi_i \Delta x_{t-i} + \alpha\beta' x_{t-1} + \varepsilon_t \tag{6.58}$$

where the single cointegrating vector is $\beta = (1, \beta_2, \beta_3, \ldots, \beta_n)'$ and the speed of adjustment parameters are given by $\alpha = (\alpha_1, \alpha_2, \ldots, \alpha_n)'$.

Once α and β are determined, testing various restrictions on α and β is straightforward if you remember the fundamental point that if there are r cointegrating vectors, only these r linear combinations of the variables are stationary. Thus, the test statistics involve comparing the number of cointegrating vectors under the null and alternative hypotheses. Again, let $\hat{\lambda}_1, \hat{\lambda}_2, \ldots, \hat{\lambda}_n$ and $\hat{\lambda}_1^*, \hat{\lambda}_2^*, \ldots, \hat{\lambda}_n^*$ denote the ordered characteristic roots of the unrestricted and restricted models, respectively. To test restrictions on β, form the test statistic:

$$T \sum_{i=1}^{r} [\ln\,(1 - \hat{\lambda}_i^*) - \ln\,(1 - \hat{\lambda}_i)] \tag{6.59}$$

Asymptotically, this statistic has a χ^2 distribution with degrees of freedom equal to the number of restrictions placed on β. Small values of $\hat{\lambda}_i^*$ relative to $\hat{\lambda}_i$ (for $i \leq r$) imply a reduced number of cointegrating vectors. Hence, the restriction embedded in the null hypothesis is binding if the calculated value of the test statistic exceeds that in a χ^2 table. For example, Johansen and Juselius test the restriction that money and income move proportionally. Their estimated long-run equilibrium relationship is

$$m2_t = 1.03y_t - 5.21i_t^b + 4.22i_t^d + 6.06$$

They restrict the coefficient of income to be unity and find the restricted values of the $\hat{\lambda}_i^*$ to be such that

	$\hat{\lambda}_i^*$	$T \ln(1 - \hat{\lambda}_i^*)$
$i = 1$	0.433	−30.04
$i = 2$	0.172	−10.01
$i = 3$	0.044	−2.36
$i = 4$	0.006	−0.32

Given that the unrestricted model has $r = 1$ and $-T \ln(1 - \hat{\lambda}_1) = 30.09$, (6.59) becomes $-30.04 + 30.09 = 0.05$. Since there is only 1 restriction imposed on β, the test statistic has a χ^2 distribution with 1 degree of freedom. A χ^2 table indicates that 0.05 is not significant; hence, they conclude that the restriction is not binding.

Restrictions on α can be tested in the same way. The procedure is to restrict α and compare the r most significant characteristic roots for the restricted and unrestricted models using (6.59). If the calculated value of (6.59) exceeds that from a χ^2 table, with degrees of freedom equal to the number of restrictions placed on α, the restrictions can be rejected. For example, Johansen and Juselius (1990) test the restriction that only money demand (i.e., $m2_t$) responds to the deviation from long-run equilibrium. Formally, they test the restriction that $\alpha_2 = \alpha_3 = \alpha_4 = 0$. Restricting the three values of α_i to equal zero, they find the largest characteristic root in the restricted model is such that $T \ln(1 - \hat{\lambda}_1^*) = -23.42$. Since the unrestricted model is such that $T \ln(1 - \hat{\lambda}_1) = -30.09$, equation (6.59) becomes $-23.42 - (-30.09) = 7.67$. The χ^2 statistic with three degrees of freedom is 7.81 at the 5 percent significance level. Hence, they find mild support for the hypothesis that the restriction is not binding.

If there is a single cointegrating vector, the Engle–Granger and Johansen methods have the same asymptotic distribution. If it can be determined that only one cointegrating vector exists, it is common to rely on the estimated error-correction model to test restrictions on α. If $r = 1$, and a single value of α is being tested, the usual t-statistic is asymptotically equivalent to the Johansen test.

Lag Length and Causality Tests

The simplest way to understand lag length tests is to consider the system in the form of (6.54)

$$\Delta x_t = \pi x_{t-1} + \sum_{i=1}^{p-1} \pi_i \Delta x_{t-i} + \varepsilon_t$$

Regardless of the rank of π, all of the Δx_{t-i} are stationary variables. Hence, we can use Rule 1 of Sims, Stock, and Watson (1990). Recall that the rule implies that the coefficients of interest on zero-mean stationary variables can be tested using a normal distribution. Since lag length depends solely on the values of the π_i, a χ^2 distribution is appropriate to test any restriction concerning lag length. As in the case of any VAR, let Σ_u and Σ_r be the variance/covariance matrices of the unrestricted and restricted systems, respectively. As in Chapter 5, let c denote the maximum number of regressors contained in the longest equation. The test statistic

$$(T-c)(\log|\Sigma_r| - \log|\Sigma_u|)$$

can be compared to a χ^2 distribution with degrees of freedom equal to the number of restrictions in the system. Alternatively, you can use the multivariate AIC or SBC to determine the lag length. If you want to test the lag lengths for a single equation, an F-test is appropriate.

The rule also means that you cannot perform Granger causality tests in a cointegrated system using a standard F-test. First, suppose that rank $(\pi) = 0$ so that

$$\Delta x_t = \sum_{i=1}^{p-1} \pi_i \Delta x_{t-i} + \varepsilon_t$$

As such, Granger causality involves only stationary variables. Yet, this was precisely the case discussed in Chapter 5 when the variables in a VAR are not cointegrated. Hence, Granger causality tests can be conducted using a standard F distribution. However, if the variables are cointegrated, a Granger causality test involves the coefficients of π. Since these coefficients multiply nonstationary variables, it is not appropriate to use a F-statistic to test for Granger causality. Block exogeneity tests are also ruled out. If w_t is cointegrated with y_t or z_t, you cannot use a standard χ^2 test to determine whether w_t belongs in the equations for y_t and z_t.

To Difference or Not to Difference

We have reached a point where it is possible to address the issue of differencing the nonstationary variables in an unrestricted VAR. There is no question that differencing leads to a misspecification error if the variables are cointegrated. Suppose that the actual data-generating process is given by the cointegrated system of (6.54) but you estimate the following VAR in first differences:

$$\Delta x_t = \sum_{i=1}^{p-1} \pi_i \Delta x_{t-i} + \varepsilon_t$$

The system is misspecified since it excludes the long-run equilibrium relationships among the variables that are contained in πx_{t-1}. Given the misspecification error, all of the coefficient estimates, t-tests, F-tests, tests of cross-equation restrictions, impulse responses and variance decompositions are not representative of the true process. Hence, there is a substantial penalty to pay if you estimate a VAR in first differences when the data are actually cointegrated; differencing "throws away" information contained in the cointegrating relationship(s).

Why not simply estimate all VARs in levels? The answer is that it is preferable to use the first differences if the $I(1)$ variables are not cointegrated. There are three consequences if the $I(1)$ variables are not cointegrated and you estimate the VAR in levels:

1. Tests lose power because you estimate n^2 more parameters (one extra lag of each variable in each equation).

2. For a VAR in levels, tests for Granger causality conducted on the $I(1)$ variables do not have a standard F distribution. If you use first differences, you can use the standard F distribution to test for Granger causality.

3. When the VAR has $I(1)$ variables, the impulse responses at long forecast horizons are inconsistent estimates of the true responses. Since the impulse responses need not decay, any imprecision in the coefficient estimates will have a permanent effect on the impulse responses. If the VAR is estimated in first differences, the impulse responses decay to zero and so the estimated responses are consistent.

The suggestion is that it is important to properly determine whether the $I(1)$ variables are cointegrated. You can perform lag length tests regardless of whether the variables are cointegrated. As such, the suggested methodology is to estimate an unrestricted VAR. Most researchers would begin with a lag length of approximately $T^{1/3}$. You may want to extend the number of lags if you suspect a substantial amount of seasonality. For example, with 100 observations of two variables using quarterly data, you might want to begin with 12 lags even though $T^{1/3}$ is approximately five. Select the most appropriate lag length and then perform a cointegration test. If the variables are not cointegrated, estimate the system in first differences. If the variables are cointegrated, you can work with the error-correction model. Since the error-correction term and all values of Δx_{t-i} are stationary, you can inference on any variable (except those appearing within the cointegrating vectors) using the usual test statistics. Impulse responses and variance decompositions will yield consistent estimates of the actual values.

The Test in the Presence of *I*(2) Variables

It is also possible to test for multicointegration using Johansen's methodology. Consider the VAR system:

$$\Delta^2 x_t = \pi x_{t-1} + \Gamma \Delta x_{t-1} + \sum_{i=1}^{p-2} \pi_i \Delta^2 x_{t-i} + \varepsilon_t \tag{6.60}$$

The issue of multicointegration concerns the ranks of both π and Γ. In principle, it is possible to consider all possible orders of cointegration for the variables in the system. However, to illustrate the procedure, it is useful to begin with a three-variable system consisting of the three *I*(2) variables x_{1t}, x_{2t}, and x_{3t} that are multicointegrated such that

$$\pi_{11}x_{1t} + \pi_{12}x_{2t} + \pi_{13}x_{3t} + \Gamma_{11}\Delta x_{1t} + \Gamma_{12}\Delta x_{2t} + \Gamma_{13}\Delta x_{3t} = 0$$

Let r denote the rank of π and r_1 denote the rank of Γ so that (6.60) is such that $r = r_1 = 1$. Clearly, if $r = 0$, multicointegration fails since there is no linear combination of the three *I*(2) variables that forms an equilibrium relationship. If $r = 1$ and $r_1 = 0$, the equilibrium relationship has the form $\pi_{11}x_{1t} + \pi_{12}x_{2t} + \pi_{13}x_{3t} = 0$. As such, $\Delta^2 x_t = \pi x_{t-1} + I(0)$ variables so that $\pi_{11}x_{1t} + \pi_{12}x_{2t} + \pi_{13}x_{3t}$ is necessarily a stationary relationship—the variables are *CI*(2, 2). All of this may seem straightforward, but there is a complicating factor when the ranks of π and Γ have to be estimated. To illustrate the point, suppose that the *I*(2) variables are cointegrated such that

$$\pi_{11}x_{1t} + \pi_{12}x_{2t} + \pi_{13}x_{3t} \sim I(1)$$

where $\sim I(d)$ indicates the order of integration.

If you take the first difference, it follows that $\pi_{11}\Delta x_{1t} + \pi_{12}\Delta x_{2t} + \pi_{13}\Delta x_{3t} \sim I(0)$. You should be able to figure out the problem. For any cointegrating vector in π, it is possible to estimate an identical cointegration vector for the first differences of the variables. Yet a linear combination of the two relationships is not stationary. Consider the result obtained by subtracting the *I*(0) relationship from the *I*(1) relationship:

$$\pi_{11}x_{1t} + \pi_{12}x_{2t} + \pi_{13}x_{3t} - \pi_{11}\Delta x_{1t} - \pi_{12}\Delta x_{2t} - \pi_{13}\Delta x_{3t} = \pi_{11}x_{1t-1} + \pi_{12}x_{2t-1} + \pi_{13}x_{3t-1}$$

Since $\pi_{11}x_{1t-1} + \pi_{12}x_{2t-1} + \pi_{13}x_{3t-1}$ is *I*(1), all that has been done is to change the time subscript for the variables in the cointegrating relationship. The point is that it is necessary to find cointegrating vectors in Γ that are not linear combinations of those in π.[17]

If we take the more general case considered by Johansen (1995), let rank(π) = r and let s denote the number of cointegrating vectors in Γ that are orthogonal to those in π. In an n-variable system such that some of the variables are $I(2)$, you should be able to verify that:

1. If $r = 0$, there is no relationship among the variables that is stationary.

2. In a n variable system, if $r + s = n - 1$, there is a unique multicointegrating vector. The number of $I(2)$ stochastic trends in a n-variable system is given by $n - r - s$.

3. The value of s must be such that $s < n - r$. For the analysis of $I(2)$ variables to be appropriate, the values of r and s must be such that $s + r < n$. If $s = n - r$, then x_t contains no $I(2)$ variables.

Johansen's cointegration test with $I(2)$ variables is actually a two-step procedure. In the first step, you estimate a model as in (6.60) to determine the rank of π. Determine the value of r using the λ_{trace} and λ_{max} statistics in the usual way. In the second step, you determine the value of s conditional on the value of r.[18] Let the null hypothesis be $s = s_0$ and consider:

$$Q_{r,s}^* = -T \sum_{i=s_0+1}^{n} \ln(1 - \hat{\lambda}_i) \qquad (6.61)$$

Hence, $Q_{r,s}^*$ is constructed in the same fashion as a λ_{trace} statistic. The principal differences are that you test the rank of Γ conditional on the value of r and that you obtain the number of cointegrating vectors orthogonal to those in π.[19] As such, the critical values needed to determine the value of s have to be modified. Given the value of r, if the sample value of $Q_{r,s}^*$ exceeds the critical value calculated by Johansen, reject the null hypothesis $s = s_0$ in favor of the alternative $s > s_0$. For $r = 1$, the critical values at the 10 percent, 5 percent, and 1 percent significance levels are

Critical Values for $Q_{1,s}^*$

	$s = 0$	$s = 1$
10%	31.88	17.79
5%	34.80	19.99
1%	40.84	24.74

For example, let $r = 1$ and suppose that the sample value of $Q_{1,s}^*$ is found to be 35.00. As such, the null hypothesis $s = 0$ can be rejected at the 5 percent significance level.

Tests on Multiple Cointegrating Vectors

If the rank of π exceeds one, it is not straightforward to interpret the cointegrating vectors. When there are multiple cointegrating vectors, any linear combination of these vectors is also a cointegrating vector. Fortunately, it is often possible to identify separate behavioral relationships by appropriately restricting the individual cointegrating vectors. The only complication is that you need to be clear about the number of restrictions you impose on the system. It is important to note that *if there are r cointegration relationships in an n-variable system, there exists a cointegrating vector for each subset of (n − r + 1) variables.* For example, if there are two cointegrating vectors in a three-variable system, there is a cointegrating vector for each bilateral pair of the variables ($2 = n - r + 1$). To demonstrate the point, let $x_t = (x_{1t}, x_{2t}, x_{3t}, x_{4t})'$ and suppose there are two cointegrating vectors for these four variables. If we normalize each vector with respect to x_{1t}, we can write that condition $\beta'x_t = 0$ as

$$\begin{bmatrix} 1 & -\beta_{12} & -\beta_{13} & -\beta_{14} \\ 1 & -\beta_{22} & -\beta_{23} & -\beta_{24} \end{bmatrix} \begin{bmatrix} x_{1t} \\ x_{2t} \\ x_{3t} \\ x_{4t} \end{bmatrix} = \begin{bmatrix} 0 \\ 0 \end{bmatrix}$$

Consider the $2 \cdot n$ matrix β' consisting of the cointegrating parameters. Subtract row 1 from row 2 to obtain

$$\begin{bmatrix} 1 & -\beta_{12} & -\beta_{13} & -\beta_{14} \\ 0 & -\beta_{22} + \beta_{12} & -\beta_{23} + \beta_{13} & -\beta_{24} + \beta_{14} \end{bmatrix}$$

Now, renormalize row 2 by dividing each of its elements by $(\beta_{12} - \beta_{22})$ to obtain

$$\begin{bmatrix} 1 & -\beta_{12} & -\beta_{13} & -\beta_{14} \\ 0 & 1 & -\beta_{23}^* & -\beta_{24}^* \end{bmatrix}$$

where $-\beta_{23}^* = (\beta_{13} - \beta_{23})/(\beta_{12} - \beta_{22})$ and $-\beta_{24}^* = (\beta_{14} - \beta_{24})/(\beta_{12} - \beta_{22})$. Hence, x_{2t}, x_{3t}, and x_{4t} are cointegrated such that $x_{2t} = \beta_{23}^* x_{3t} + \beta_{24}^* x_{4t}$. Similarly, add β_{12} times row 2 to row 1 to obtain

$$\begin{bmatrix} 1 & 0 & -\beta_{13}^* & -\beta_{14}^* \\ 0 & 1 & -\beta_{23}^* & -\beta_{24}^* \end{bmatrix}$$

where $\beta_{1j}^* = \beta_{1j} + \beta_{12}\beta_{2j}^*$.

Thus, x_1, x_3, and x_4 are cointegrated such that $x_{1t} = \beta_{13}^* x_{3t} + \beta_{14}^* x_{4t}$. Since the labeling of the variables is irrelevant, it follows that there exists a cointegrating vector for each subset of three variables. More generally, β' will be a $r \cdot n$ matrix of cointegrating parameters, and each subset of $n - r + 1$ variables will be cointegrated. From the preceding discussion, it should be clear that standard row and column operations on β' *do not* entail restrictions on the cointegrating vectors. Such operations merely result in additional cointegrating vectors that are linear combinations of the original vectors.

EXAMPLE 1: VARIABLE EXCLUSION WITHIN AN EQUATION   With multiple cointegrating vectors, you cannot test whether any one particular $\beta_{ij} = 0$ since this assumption does not restrict the cointegrating space. In the general case where β' is an $r \cdot n$ matrix, a testable exclusion restriction entails the exclusion of r or more variables from a cointegrating vector. Hence, excluding r variables from a cointegrating vector entails only one restriction. If the sample value of the χ^2 statistic with one degree of freedom (since there is only one restriction involved) exceeds a critical value, reject the null hypothesis that this set of variables contains a cointegrating relationship.

EXAMPLE 2: VARIABLE EXCLUSION ACROSS EQUATIONS Next, suppose that you want to test whether x_{4t} can be excluded from the set of cointegrating relationships. The restriction $\beta_{14} = \beta_{24} = 0$ entails only one restriction on the cointegrating space. In the general case where β' is an $r \cdot n$ matrix, the test $\beta_{1j} = \beta_{2j} = \ldots = \beta_{rj} = 0$ still involves only one restriction. This follows since x_{it} can be eliminated from $r - 1$ equations using simple row and column operations.

EXAMPLE 3: CONDITIONAL RESTRICTIONS It is also possible to restrict one cointegrating vector conditional on the values of all other cointegrating vectors. For example, you might want to determine if $(1, \beta_{22}, 0, \beta_{24})'$ is a cointegrating vector for the fixed normalized values of β_{12}, β_{13}, and β_{14}. Thus, you fix the values of β_{12}, β_{13}, and β_{14} and determine whether you can exclude x_{3t} from the second vector. Cutler, Davis, and Smith (1999) consider the identification issue in considerable detail. They examine the following four behavioral relationships in a seven variable system:

$$m_t = d_0 + d_1 y_t + d_2 r_t + d_3 p_t + e_{1t}$$
$$c_t = a_0 + a_1 y_t + a_2 r_t + e_{2t}$$
$$i_t = b_0 + b_1 y_t + b_2 r_t + e_{3t}$$
$$im_t = g_0 + g_1 y_t + g_2 r_t + e_{4t}$$

where: m_t = log of nominal money holdings
y_t = log of real income
r_t = real interest rate
c_t = log of real consumption
i_t = log of real investment
p_t = log of the price level
im_t = log of real imports
e_{1t}, e_{2t}, e_{3t}, and e_{4t} are stationary error terms.

The first equation is the money demand equation. The next three equations are a simple consumption function, an investment function, and an import demand function, respectively. Consumption, investment, and imports are each assumed to be functions of only income and the interest rate. The issue is to determine whether it is possible to identify these four equations from a seven-variable system. Toward this end, they obtained estimates of a (7×7) π matrix over a number of sample periods. There were at least four cointegrating vectors in every case considered. Over the entire sample, 1960:2 to 1990:4, Cutler, Davis, and Smith (1999) found that they could not reject the restrictions at conventional significance levels (the *prob*-value was 16 percent).

9. ILLUSTRATING THE JOHANSEN METHODOLOGY

An interesting way to illustrate the Johansen methodology is to use exactly the same data shown in Figure 6.2. Although the Engle–Granger technique did find that the simulated data were cointegrated, a comparison of the two procedures is useful. Use the following four steps when implementing the Johansen procedure.

STEP 1: It is good practice to pretest all variables to assess their order of integration. Plot the data to see if a linear time trend is likely to be present in the data-generating process. In most instances you will have variables that are integrated of the same order. In other cases, you can check for multicointegration.

The results of the test can be quite sensitive to the lag length, so it is important to be careful. The most common procedure is to estimate a vector autoregression using the *undifferenced* data. Then use the same lag-length tests as in a traditional VAR. Begin with the longest lag length deemed reasonable and test whether it can be shortened. For example, if we want to test whether lags 2 through 4 are important, we can estimate the following two VARs:

$$x_t = A_0 + A_1 x_{t-1} + A_2 x_{t-2} + A_3 x_{t-3} + A_4 x_{t-4} + e_{1t}$$
$$x_t = A_0 + A_1 x_{t-1} + e_{2t}$$

where: x_t = the $(n \cdot 1)$ vector of variables
$A_0 = (n \cdot 1)$ matrix of intercept terms
$A_i = (n \cdot n)$ matrices of coefficients
e_{1t} and e_{2t} = $(n \cdot 1)$ vector of error terms

Estimate the first system with four lags of each variable in each equation and call the variance/covariance matrix of residuals Σ_4. Now estimate the second equation using only one lag of each variable in each equation and call the variance/covariance matrix of residuals Σ_1. Even though we are working with nonstationary variables, we can perform lag length tests using the likelihood ratio test statistic recommended by Sims (1980):

$$(T-c)(\log|\Sigma_1| - \log|\Sigma_4|)$$

where: T = number of observations

c = number of parameters in the unrestricted system

$\log|\Sigma_i|$ = natural logarithm of the determinant of Σ_i

Following Sims, use the χ^2 distribution with degrees of freedom equal to the number of coefficient restrictions. Since each A_i has n^2 coefficients, constraining $A_2 = A_3 = A_4 = 0$ entails $3n^2$ restrictions. Alternatively, you can select lag length p using the multivariate generalizations of the AIC or SBC.

STEP 2: Estimate the model and determine the rank of π. Many time-series statistical software packages contain a routine to estimate the model. Here, it suffices to say that OLS is not appropriate because it is necessary to impose cross-equation restrictions on the π matrix. In most circumstances, you may choose to estimate the model in three forms: (1) with all elements of A_0 set equal to zero, (2) with a drift, or (3) with a constant term in the cointegrating vector.

For example, we can use the simulated data shown in Figure 6.2 so that $x_t = (y_t, z_t, w_t)'$. If we pretend that we do not know the form of the data-generating process, we might want to include an intercept term in the cointegrating vector(s). As we saw in the last section, it is possible to test for the presence of the intercept. Lag-length tests indicate setting $p = 2$ so that the estimated form of the model is

$$\Delta x_t = A_0 + \pi x_{t-1} + \pi_1 \Delta x_{t-1} + \varepsilon_t \tag{6.62}$$

where A_0 was constrained so as to force the intercept to appear in the cointegrating vector.

As always, carefully analyze the properties of the residuals of the estimated model. Any evidence that the errors are not white noise usually means that lag lengths are too short. Figure 6.4 shows deviations of y_t from the long-run relationship ($\mu_t = -0.01331 - y_t - 1.0350z_t + 1.0162w_t$) and one of the error sequences (i.e., the $\{\varepsilon_{yt}\}$ sequence that equals the residuals from the y_t equation in (6.62)). Both sequences conform to their theoretical properties in that the residuals from the long-run equilibrium appear to be stationary and the estimated values of the $\{\varepsilon_{yt}\}$ series approximate a white-noise process.

The estimated values of the characteristic roots of the π matrix in (6.62) are

$$\lambda_1 = 0.32600; \ \lambda_2 = 0.14032; \text{ and } \lambda_3 = 0.033168$$

Since $T = 98$ (100 observations less the two lost as a result of using 2 lags), the calculated values of λ_{max} and λ_{trace} for the various possible values of r are reported in the center column of Table 6.6.

Consider the hypothesis that the variables are not cointegrated (so that the rank $\pi = 0$). Depending on the alternative hypothesis, we have a choice of two possible test statistics. If we are interested in the hypothesis that the variables are not cointegrated ($r = 0$) against the alternative of one or more cointegrating vectors ($r > 0$), we can calculate the $\lambda_{trace}(0)$ statistic:

$$\begin{aligned}\lambda_{trace}(0) &= -T\left[\ln(1 - \lambda_1) + \ln(1 - \lambda_2) + \ln(1 - \lambda_3)\right] \\ &= -98\left[\ln(1 - 0.326) + \ln(1 - 0.14032) + \ln(1 - 0.033168)\right] \\ &= 56.786\end{aligned}$$

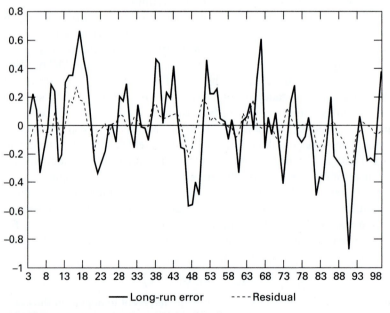

FIGURE 6.4   Long-Run and Short-Run Errors

Table 6.6 The λ_{max} and λ_{trace} Tests

Null Hypothesis	Alternative Hypothesis	5% Critical Value	10% Critical Value
λ_{trace} tests	λ_{trace} value		
r = 0	r > 0	56.786	34.91	32.00
r ≤ 1	r > 1	18.123	19.96	17.85
r ≤ 2	r > 2	3.306	9.24	7.52
λ_{max} tests	λ_{max} value		
r = 0	r = 1	38.663	22.00	19.77
r = 1	r = 2	14.817	15.67	13.75
r = 2	r = 3	3.306	9.24	7.52

Since 56.786 exceeds the 5 percent critical value of the λ_{trace} statistic (in the bottom panel of Table E, the critical value is 34.91), it is possible to reject the null hypothesis of no cointegrating vectors and accept the alternative of one or more cointegrating vectors. Next, we can use the $\lambda_{trace}(1)$ statistic to test the null of $r \leq 1$ against the alternative of two or three cointegrating vectors. In this case, the $\lambda_{trace}(1)$ statistic is

$$\lambda_{trace}(1) = -T\,[\ln(1 - \lambda_2) + \ln(1 - \lambda_3)]$$
$$= -98\,[\ln\,(1 - 0.14032) + \ln(1 - 0.033168)]$$
$$= 18.123$$

Since 18.123 is less than the 5 percent critical value of 19.96, we cannot reject the null hypothesis at this significance level. However, 18.123 does exceed the 10 percent critical value of 17.85; some researchers might reject the null and accept the alternative of two or three cointegrating vectors. The $\lambda_{trace}(2)$ statistic indicates no more than two cointegrating vectors at the 10 percent significance level.

The λ_{max} statistic does not help to clarify the issue. The null hypothesis of no cointegrating vectors ($r = 0$) against the specific alternative $r = 1$ is clearly rejected. The calculated value $\lambda_{max}(0, 1) = -98\,\ln(1 - 0.326) = 38.663$ exceeds the 5 percent critical value of 22.00. Note that the test of the null hypothesis $r = 1$ against the specific alternative $r = 2$ cannot be rejected at the 5 percent, but can be rejected the 10 percent, significance level. The calculated value of $\lambda_{max}(1, 2)$ is $-98\,\ln(1 - 0.14032) = 14.817$, whereas the critical values at the 5 and 10 percent significance levels are 15.67 and 13.75, respectively. Even though the actual data-generating process contains only one cointegrating vector, the realizations are such that researchers willing to use the 10 percent significance level would incorrectly conclude that there are two cointegrating vectors. Failing to reject an incorrect null hypothesis is always an inherent danger of using wide confidence intervals.

STEP 3: Analyze the normalized cointegrating vector(s) and speed of adjustment coefficients. If we select $r = 1$, the estimated cointegrating vector ($\beta_0\ \beta_1\ \beta_2\ \beta_3$) is

$$\beta = (0.00553\ 0.41532\ 0.42988\ -0.42207)$$

If we normalize with respect to β_1, the normalized cointegrating vector and the speed of adjustment parameters are

$$\beta = (-0.01331 \ {-1.0000} \ {-1.0350} \ 1.0162)$$
$$\alpha_y = 0.54627$$
$$\alpha_z = 0.16578$$
$$\alpha_w = 0.21895$$

Recall that the data were constructed imposing the long-run relationship $w_t = y_t + z_t$; hence, the estimated coefficients of the normalized β vector are close to their theoretical values of $(0 \ {-1} \ {-1} \ 1)$.[16] Consider the following tests:

1. The test that $\beta_0 = 0$ entails one restriction on one cointegrating vector; hence, the likelihood ratio test has a χ^2 distribution with one degree of freedom. The calculated value of $\chi^2 = 0.011234$ is not significant at conventional levels. Hence, we cannot reject the null hypothesis that $\beta_0 = 0$. Thus, it is possible to use the form of the model in which there is neither a drift nor an intercept in the cointegrating vector. Thus, to clarify the issue concerning the number of cointegrating vectors, it would be wise to reestimate the model excluding the constant from the cointegrating vector.

2. To restrict the normalized cointegrating vector such that $\beta_2 = -1$ and $\beta_3 = 1$ entails two restrictions on one cointegrating vector; hence, the likelihood ratio test has a χ^2 distribution with two degrees of freedom. The calculated value of $\chi^2 = 0.55350$ is not significant at conventional levels. Hence, we cannot reject the null hypothesis that $\beta_2 = -1$ and $\beta_3 = 1$.

3. To test the joint restriction $\beta = (0, -1, -1, 1)$ entails the three restrictions $\beta_0 = 0$, $\beta_2 = -1$, and $\beta_3 = 1$. The calculated value of χ^2 with three degrees of freedom is 1.8128 so that the significance level is 0.612. Hence, we cannot reject the null hypothesis that the cointegrating vector is $(0, -1, -1, 1)$.

STEP 4: Finally, innovation accounting and causality tests on the error-correction model of (6.62) could help to identify a structural model and determine whether the estimated model appears to be reasonable. Since the simulated data have no economic meaning, innovation accounting is not performed here.

10. GENERAL-TO-SPECIFIC MODELING

In some sense, the general-to-specific approach is a compromise between a pure error-correction model and a traditional regression-based approach. An error-correction model can be overparameterized while a pure regression can seem *ad hoc* unless you are sure of the correct specification. The general-to-specific modeling approach is more of a philosophy than a specific statistical test. As the name suggests, you begin with an extremely general model and pare it down by testing various coefficient restrictions. In this way, the final model is always nested within the initial model.

The theoretical framework underling the approach begins with an autoregressive distributed lag (ADL) model. In the two-variable first-order case, the ADL model is

$$y_t = a_{11}y_{t-1} + a_{12}z_t + a_{13}z_{t-1} + \varepsilon_t$$

As will be demonstrated shortly, it is useful to write the ADL model in the equivalent form

$$\Delta y_t = \alpha(y_{t-1} - \beta z_{t-1}) + \rho\Delta z_t + \varepsilon_t \tag{6.63}$$

where $\alpha = (a_{11} - 1)$, $\rho = a_{12}$, and $\beta = (a_{12} + a_{13})/(1 - a_{11})$.

In a more general setting, with n variables, the ADL model has the form

$$x_{1t} = A_1(L)x_{1t-1} + A_2(L)x_{2t} + \ldots + A_n(L)x_{nt} + \varepsilon_t$$

The point is that the ADL is extremely general; as such, it is a useful way to begin modeling the variable x_{1t}. For our purposes, the essential point is that an error-correction model is embedded within the ADL; as such, appropriately restricting the ADL yields an error-correction model. To return to the two-variable case, suppose that y_t and z_t are cointegrated of order $(1, 1)$ and that the error-correcting model is represented by

$$\Delta y_t = \alpha_1(y_{t-1} - \beta z_{t-1}) + e_{1t} \tag{6.64}$$

$$\Delta z_t = \alpha_2(y_{t-1} - \beta z_{t-1}) + e_{2t} \tag{6.65}$$

Notice that (6.64) and (6.65) are in reduced form and not in structural form. As in Chapter 5, there is no reason to suppose that the error terms are uncorrelated with each other. Given that we do not want to impose that restriction $Ee_{1t}e_{2t} = 0$ we can we can let the variance/covariance matrix of the errors be given by

$$\Sigma = \begin{bmatrix} \sigma_{11} & \sigma_{12} \\ \sigma_{12} & \sigma_{22} \end{bmatrix}$$

where $\sigma_{ij} = Ee_ie_j$.

As long as $\sigma_{12} \neq 0$, e_{1t} and e_{2t} are correlated. It is possible to write the contemporaneous relationship between the two errors as

$$e_{1t} = \rho e_{2t} + \varepsilon_t \tag{6.66}$$

where ρ is σ_{12}/σ_{22} and ε_t is a white-noise error term.

If we substitute (6.65) and (6.66) into (6.64), we obtain

$$\begin{aligned} \Delta y_t &= \alpha_1(y_{t-1} - \beta z_{t-1}) + \rho e_{2t} + \varepsilon_t \\ &= \alpha_1(y_{t-1} - \beta z_{t-1}) + \rho[\Delta z_t - \alpha_2(y_{t-1} - \beta z_{t-1})] + \varepsilon_t \\ &= (\alpha_1 - \rho\alpha_2)(y_{t-1} - \beta z_{t-1}) + \rho\Delta z_t + \varepsilon_t \end{aligned}$$

Now, if we let $\alpha = \alpha_1 - \rho\alpha_2$, we can write

$$\Delta y_t = \alpha(y_{t-1} - \beta z_{t-1}) + \rho\Delta z_t + \varepsilon_t \tag{6.67}$$

Hence, we can write the error-correction equation for y_t given by (6.64) and (6.65) in the exact form as the reparameterized ADL given by (6.63). Of course, if we start from a higher-order process, additional lags of Δy_{t-i} and Δz_{t-i} should be added to the equation.

Weak Exogeneity

In a cointegrated system, if a variable does not respond to the discrepancy from the long-run equilibrium relationship, it is **weakly exogenous.**[20] Hence, if the speed of adjustment parameter α_i is zero, the variable in question is weakly exogenous. The practical importance is that a weakly exogeneous variable does not experience the type of feedback that necessitates the use of a VAR.

To explain (see Appendix 6.1 for more details), suppose that you estimate an ADL using OLS. You know that this equivalent to estimating the equation in the form of (6.67). Hence, when z_t is *not* weakly exogenous (i.e., when $\alpha_2 \neq 0$), you estimate the unrestricted equation

$$\Delta y_t = \beta_1 y_{t-1} + \beta_2 z_{t-1} + \beta_3 \Delta z_t + \varepsilon_t \qquad (6.68)$$

where from (6.67) the estimated coefficients are such that $\beta_1 = \alpha_1 - \rho\alpha_2$, $\beta_2 = (\alpha_1 - \rho\alpha_2)\beta$ and $\beta_3 = \rho$.

Notice that the contemporaneous correlation coefficient between e_{1t} and e_{2t} (i.e., ρ) appears in the estimate for each coefficient of (6.68). However, if z_t is weakly exogenous (i.e., when $\alpha_2 = 0$), your coefficient estimates are such that $\beta_1 = \alpha_1$, $\beta_2 = \alpha_1\beta$, and $\beta_3 = \rho$. Hence, you can identify α_1, β, and ρ from β_1, β_2, and β_3. More importantly, the fact that $\alpha_2 = 0$ means that the contemporaneous correlation between e_{1t} and e_{2t} does not affect the estimate of the cointegrating parameter $\beta = \beta_2/\alpha_1$. The fact that z_t is correlated with the innovations in e_{1t} is not important for the estimates of α_1 and β when $\alpha_2 = 0$. Hence, if $\alpha_2 = 0$, it is appropriate to estimate (6.68) by OLS and to construct confidence intervals for β and/or α_1 using the normal distribution.[21]

Inflation in Australia

In a very instructive paper, de Brouwer and Ericsson (1998) show the proper way to model a single variable in a cointegrated system using the general-to-specific approach. Two other excellent examples of the approach include Hendry and Ericsson (1991) and Davidson, Hendry, Srba, and Yeo (1987).

The goal is to develop a model of the Australian inflation rate as measured by the "underlying" CPI. This measure of inflation excludes certain volatile items such as fruit and vegetables, automotive fuel, and mortgage interest rates. Without investigating the underlying theoretical model, for our purposes, it is sufficient to posit that the price index may be represented by

$$p_t = \beta_0 + \beta_1 ulc_t + \beta_2 ip_t + \beta_3 pet_t + e_t \qquad (6.69)$$

where: p_t = the underlying CPI
  ulc_t = an index of unit labor costs
  ip_t = index of tariff–adjusted import prices converted to Australian dollars
  pet_t = index of gasoline prices measured in Australian dollars
  e_t = the deviation from the long-run equilibrium
All variables are expressed in natural logs.

In a cost–push model of inflation, increases in unit labor costs, import prices, and gasoline prices should all increase the Australian CPI. Hence, β_1, β_2, and β_3 should all be positive. Moreover, proportional increases in each of the subcomponent prices should have a proportional effect on the CPI. As such, a testable hypothesis is $\beta_1 + \beta_2 + \beta_3 = 1$. Of course, the theory also requires that the $\{e_t\}$ sequence be stationary.

The paper used quarterly data for each of the four variables over the 1976:3 to 1993:3 period for a total of 69 observations. The time paths of the CPI, unit labor costs, and import prices are shown in Figure 6.5.[22] All three series have a decidedly upward movement and seem to track each other reasonably well. The first step is to analyze each for possible unit roots versus deterministic time trends. Since the orders of integration are unclear, tests are also conducted for multiple unit roots. The augmented Dickey–Fuller tests (using four lags of each variable) have the following form:

$$\Delta y_t = a_0 + \gamma y_{t-1} + a_2 t + \sum_{i=1}^{4} \beta_i \Delta y_{t-i} + \sum_{i=1}^{3} \phi_i D_{it} + \varepsilon_t \qquad (6.70)$$

The only variables needing explanation are the centered seasonal dummy variables $\{D_{1t}\}$, $\{D_{2t}\}$, and $\{D_{3t}\}$. Each seasonal dummy D_{it} has a value of 3/4 in quarter i and $-1/4$ in the other three quarters. In this way, each dummy has a mean value of zero (i.e., it is centered around zero) and so cannot contribute to the magnitude of the drift. The estimated values of γ and the associated t-statistics for the null hypothesis $\gamma = 0$ are

	p_t	ulc_t	ip_t	pet_t
γ	0.02	−0.05	−0.06	−0.12
t-statistic	(0.91)	(−0.93)	(−1.25)	(−2.20)

At the 5 percent significance level, the Dickey–Fuller critical value is −3.50; hence, the null hypothesis of a unit root cannot be rejected. Moreover, there is support for the claim that $\{p_t\}$ and $\{ip_t\}$ are both $I(2)$ variables since the null of a unit root cannot be rejected for the $\{\Delta p_t\}$ and $\{\Delta ip_t\}$ series. At this point, there is a critical choice to make. One is to allow for the possibility of multicointegration.

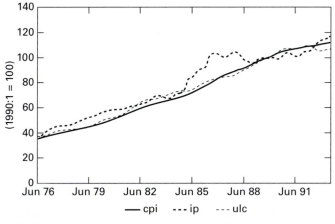

FIGURE 6.5   Prices and Costs in Australia

However, with only 69 total observations, the Dickey–Fuller tests have very low power to detect a truly stationary process. Moreover, if an equation in the form of (6.70) is estimated using the second differences of these two variables (i.e., $\Delta^2 p_t$ and $\Delta^2 ip_t$), the values of γ are found to be -0.44 ($t = -3.01$) and -0.68 ($t = -2.55$), respectively. Given that the point estimates of the characteristic roots are far from unity, the authors decided to treat all four variables as $I(1)$ processes.

The next step was to obtain the appropriate lag length for the VAR. Given that the data set is quarterly and that the sample size is small, they estimated an equation in the form of (6.54) using four lags of $\{\Delta x_t\}$, a constant, and three centered seasonal dummy variables. The multivariate SBC for the models with four through one lags are -29.05, -29.99, -30.49, and -31.15, respectively.[23] Since the SBC continually decreases as the lag length is reduced, the authors chose to use the first-order VAR to test for cointegration.

The values of the λ_{trace} and λ_{max} statistics are such that the null hypothesis of no cointegration (i.e., $r = 0$) is soundly rejected. Also notice that the λ_{trace} statistic is such that the null hypothesis of $r \leq 1$ cannot be rejected and the λ_{max} statistic is such that the null of $r = 1$ against the alternative of $r = 2$ cannot be rejected. As such, it is evident that there is only one cointegrating vector among the four variables.

	$r = 0$	$r \leq 1$	$r \leq 2$	$r \leq 3$
λ_{trace}	101.7	22.2	12.6	3.9
λ_{max}	79.4	9.7	8.7	3.9

Given that there exists a single cointegrating vector, the issue is to see if it is possible to impose the homogeneity restriction $\beta_1 + \beta_2 + \beta_3 = 1$. The sample value of χ^2 is 0.61, and the critical value at the 5 percent significance level is 3.8. Hence, the restriction is not binding; the normalized cointegrating vector with the restriction imposed is

$$p_t = \beta_0 + 0.426 ulc_t + 0.481 ip_t + 0.093 pet_t \qquad (6.71)$$

Equation (6.71) indicates that the long-run elasticity of gasoline prices for the CPI is approximately 9 percent. The elasticities of unit labor costs and import prices are about 42 and 48 percent, respectively. Next, a χ^2 test is used to determine whether each of the coefficients is statistically different from zero. The sample values of χ^2 for the exclusion of ulc_t, ip_t, and pet_t are 7.3, 29.2, and 2.8, respectively. If you compare these values to 3.8 (i.e., the critical value at the 5 percent significance level), you can see that only the coefficient for pet_t can be set equal to zero.

Weak Exogeneity Again

If we ignore the deterministic regressors and the stationary dynamics, each variable has the error-correction form

$$\Delta x_{it} = \alpha_i (p_{t-1} - \beta_0 - 0.426 ulc_{t-1} - 0.481 ip_{t-1} - 0.093 pet_{t-1}) + \dots$$

where the notation x_{it} ($i = 1$ to 4) refers to the variables p_t, ulc_t, ip_t, and pet_t, respectively.

Each speed of adjustment coefficient (i.e., each value of α_i) measures the degree to which the variable in question responds to the deviation from the long-run equilibrium relationship. It is interesting to note that the speed of adjustment coefficient of the Δp_t equation is -1.0. As such, the Australian CPI experiences sharp increases with increases in unit labor costs, import prices and gasoline prices. On the other hand, the values of the α_i for the unit labor cost, import price and gasoline price equations are only -0.061, -0.075, and -0.096, respectively. Not only are these coefficients small in absolute value (implying a slow adjustment), they are of the "wrong" sign. As already noted, this is not especially troublesome since the Johansen test indicates that the characteristic root of the system implies convergence to the long-run equilibrium.

Next, de Brouwer and Ericsson (1998) go on to formally test whether the four values of α_i are equal to zero. The sample values of χ^2 for the restrictions $\alpha_1 = 0$, $\alpha_2 = 0$, $\alpha_3 = 0$, and $\alpha_4 = 0$ are 25.4, 1.89, 1.34, and 0.43, respectively. Only the speed of adjustment coefficient for the p_t equation has a χ^2 value exceeding 3.8. Hence, ulc_t, ip_t, and pet_t are all weakly exogenous. As such, the CPI equation can be estimated and tested in a single-equation framework.

Now consider an equation in the form of (6.69) that is estimated using OLS. As discussed in Appendix 6.1, it is appropriate to conduct inference on the cointegrating vector if the errors in the equations that determine ulc_t, ip_t, and pet_t are uncorrelated with e_t and if $\{e_t\}$ is not serially correlated. The weak exogeneity tests suggest that the errors in the equations that determine ulc_t, ip_t, and pet_t are not correlated with e_t. One way to eliminate any serial correlation in $\{e_t\}$ is to include lagged changes of the endogenous variable and the regressors. Thus, a reasonable specification is

$$p_t = \beta_0 + \beta_1 ulc_t + \beta_2 ip_t + \beta_3 pet_t + A_1(L)\Delta p_{t-1} \\ + A_2(L)\Delta ulc_{t-1} + A_3(L)\Delta ip_{t-1} + A_4(L)\Delta pet_{t-1} + \varepsilon_t$$

or the more general autoregressive distributed lag model

$$p_t = A_1(L)p_{t-1} + A_2(L)ulc_t + A_3(L)ip_t + A_4(L)pet_t \\ + \text{deterministic regressors} + \varepsilon_t \tag{6.72}$$

where variables up to lag four are included in the estimation and the deterministic regressors consist of a dummy variable to account for changes in tax rates, an intercept, and three centered seasonal dummy variables.

Note that the ADL represented be (6.72) can be estimated by OLS. The individual coefficients of (6.72) are not especially important. However, the long-run solution of the estimated equation is such that

$$p_t = -0.094 + 0.516 ulc_t + 0.463 ip_t + 0.55 pet_t \tag{6.73}$$

where the coefficient i is obtained as $A_i(1)/[1 - A_1(1)]$.

There are two interesting features of the long-run solution. First, (6.73) looks remarkably like the long-run equilibrium relationship (6.71) obtained from the Johansen methodology. Second, (6.72) is quite general in its structure. In particular, the error-correction model is clearly a special case of (6.72). Towards this end, the authors used standard t-tests and F-tests to determine whether it is possible to pare down the ADL model to an error-correcting form. Not only did they test exclusion restrictions on the various lags, but they were not able to reject these hypotheses:

1. The coefficients of lags two through four on all variables can be set equal to zero.

2. The sum of the coefficients on ulc_{t-1}, ip_{t-1}, and pet_{t-1} minus the coefficient on p_{t-1} equals zero.

3. The coefficients on the contemporaneous values of Δy_t, Δulc_t, and Δip_t equal zero.

The final model (with standard errors in parenthesis) is

$$\Delta p_t = 0.0141\Delta pet_t + 0.0763gap_{t-1} - 0.0891(p_{t-1} - 0.465ulc_{t-1}$$
$$\quad (0.006) \qquad\qquad (0.011) \qquad\qquad (0.007) \qquad\qquad (0.056)$$

$$- 0.443ip_{t-1} - 0.092pet_{t-1}) + \text{deterministic regressors} + \varepsilon_t \qquad (6.74)$$
$$\quad (0.050) \qquad (0.026)$$

where gap_t was added a measure of the Australian output gap obtained as the residual from a regression of output on a linear time trend.

As it stands, (6.74) is extremely parsimonious as compared with an equation in an unrestricted VAR or error-correction model. As such, it is important to put the regression equation through a battery of diagnostic tests. Obviously, the residuals of the final model should appear to be white noise. Moreover, goodness-of-fit measures and the out-of-sample forecasts should be superior to those of rival models. There is little point in reporting the details of such tests here. Instead, there is a general point to be made about cointegrated variables. Suppose that x_{1t} through x_{nt} are cointegrated of order $CI(1, 1)$ and that the following regression has been estimated by OLS:

$$x_{1t} = \beta_0 + \beta_2 x_{2t} + \ldots + \beta_n x_{nt} + e_t$$

If x_{2t} through x_{nt} are all weakly exogenous, and $\{e_t\}$ is not serially correlated, it is possible to perform inference on the β_i using standard t-tests or F-tests. If e_t is serially correlated, the regression can be augmented by lagged changes (or levels) of the endogenous and exogenous variables. The general specification of a distributed-lag model allows for single-equation estimation and testing. As in any OLS equation using $I(1)$ variables, you perform lag length (but not Granger causality or exogeneity) tests.

11. SUMMARY AND CONCLUSIONS

Many economic theories imply that a linear combination of certain nonstationary variables must be stationary. For example, if the variables $\{x_{1t}\}$, $\{x_{2t}\}$, and $\{x_{3t}\}$ are $I(1)$ and the linear combination $e_t = \beta_0 + \beta_1 x_{1t} + \beta_2 x_{2t} + \beta_3 x_{3t}$ is stationary, the variables are said to be cointegrated of order $(1, 1)$. The vector $(\beta_0, \beta_1, \beta_2, \beta_3)$ is called the cointegrating vector. Cointegrated variables share the same stochastic trends and so cannot drift too far apart. Cointegrated variables have an error-correction representation such that each responds to the deviation from "long-run equilibrium."

One way to check for cointegration is to examine the residuals from the long-run equilibrium relationship. If these residuals have a unit root, the variables cannot be cointegrated of order $(1, 1)$. Another way to check for cointegration among $I(1)$ variables is to estimate a VAR in first differences and include the lagged level of the variables. If we use a multivariate generalization of the Dickey–Fuller test, the vector can be checked for the presence of unit roots. In an n equation system, n minus the number of unit roots equals the number of cointegrating vectors.

The λ_{trace} and λ_{max} test statistics can be used to help determine the number of cointegrating vectors. These tests are sensitive to the presence of the deterministic regressors included in the cointegrating vector(s). Restrictions on the cointegrating vector(s) and/or the speed of adjustment parameters can be tested using χ^2 statistics. You should be aware of the role of the deterministic regressors in a cointegration framework. Johansen (1994) shows how to test to determine whether there is a deterministic trend, drift terms outside of the cointegrating vector or constants appearing in the cointegrating vector.

The Johansen and Juselius tables are extended to allow for more than five variables in Osterwald–Lenum (1992). Also, there is a growing body of work that examines hypothesis testing in a cointegrated system. Park (1992) develops a nonparametric method for the estimation and testing of cointegrating vectors. Johansen and Juselius (1992) and Horvath and Watson (1993) discuss the testing of structural hypotheses within a cointegration framework. A useful review of the hypothesis tests are found in Johansen (1991). Appendix 6.1 and Section 10 discuss the Phillips-Hansen (1990) method.

If all but one variable is weakly exogenous, that variable can be modeled in a single equation framework. In an example of the Australian inflation rate, it was shown how to use a general-to-specific modeling strategy to obtain a parsimonious model.

The literature is proceeding in several interesting directions. Friedman and Kuttner (1992) use cointegration tests to show that significant relationships between money, income, and interest rates break down in the 1980s. The paper makes an excellent companion piece with this chapter since it also uses innovation accounting techniques. Another interesting money demand study using the techniques in this chapter is Baba, Hendry, and Starr (1992). Gregory and Hansen (1992) consider the possibility of a structural break in a cointegrated system. The intercept and/or slope coefficients of the cointegrating vector are allowed to experience a regime shift at an unknown date. Baltagi (2000) contains a collection of papers that try to extend the results of panel unit toot tests to cointegrated systems. King, et al. (1991) combine cointegration tests with the type of structural decompositions considered in Chapter 5.

QUESTIONS AND EXERCISES

1. Let equations (6.14) and (6.15) contain intercept terms such that

$$y_t = a_{10} + a_{11}y_{t-1} + a_{12}z_{t-1} + \varepsilon_{yt} \quad \text{and} \quad z_t = a_{20} + a_{21}y_{t-1} + a_{22}z_{t-1} + \varepsilon_{zt}$$

   a. Show that the solution for y_t can be written as

$$y_t = [(1 - a_{22}L)\varepsilon_{yt} + (1 - a_{22})a_{10} + a_{12}L\varepsilon_{zt} + a_{12}a_{20}] / [(1 - a_{11}L)(1 - a_{22}L) - a_{12}a_{21}L^2]$$

   b. Find the solution for z_t.

   c. Suppose that y_t and z_t are $CI(1, 1)$. Use the conditions in (6.19), (6.20), and (6.21) to write the error-correcting model. Compare your answer to (6.22) and (6.23). Show that the error-correction model contains an intercept term.

   d. Show that $\{y_t\}$ and $\{z_t\}$ have the same deterministic time trend (i.e., show that the slope coefficients of the time trends are identical).

   e. What is the condition such that the slope of the trend is zero? Show that this condition is such that the constant can be included in the cointegrating vector.

2. The data file COINT6.PRN contains the three simulated series used in Sections 5 and 9. You should find the properties of the data are such that

Series	Obs	Mean	Std Error	Minimum	Maximum
Y	100	-4.2810736793	1.4148612773	-6.3307043375	-1.2512548288
Z	100	-2.1437335637	1.7951179043	-5.7040632238	0.6257029853
W	100	-6.3677952867	2.3914380011	-9.6848404427	-1.4460513399

   a. Use the data to reproduce the results in Section 5

   b. Use the data to reproduce the results in Section 9.

3. The file COINT_PPP.XLS contains quarterly values of German, Japanese, and Canadian wholesale prices and bilateral exchange rates with the United States. The file also contains

the U.S. wholesale price level. The names on the individual series should be self-evident. For example, p_us is the U.S. price level and ex_g is the German exchange rate with the United States. All variables except the mark/dollar exchange rates run from 1973:Q4 to 2001:Q4 and all have been normalized to equal 100 in 1973:Q4.

a.   Form the log of each variable. Estimate the long-run relationship between Canada and the United States as

$$log(ex\_ca) = 4.12 + 0.937log(p\_ca) - 0.830log(p\_us)$$

Do the point estimates of the slope coefficients seem to be consistent with long-run PPP?

b.   Let μ_t denote the residuals from the long-run relationship. Use these residuals to perform the Engle–Granger test for cointegration. If you use three lagged changes, you should find

$$\Delta\mu_t = -0.089\mu_{t-1} - 0.063\Delta\mu_{t-1} + 0.048\Delta\mu_{t-2} + 0.236\Delta\mu_{t-3} + v_t$$

The t-statistic on the coefficient for μ_{t-1} is -2.17. Explain why the test indicates that long-run PPP fails.

c.   Repeat parts i and ii using Germany and Japan.

4. The second, fourth, and fifth columns of the file labeled INT_RATES.XLS contain the interest rates paid on U.S. 3-month, 3-year, and 10-year U.S. government securities. The data run from 1954:7 to 2002:12. These columns are labeled TBILL, R3, and R10, respectively.

a.   Pretest the variables to show that the rates all act as unit root processes. Specifically, perform augmented Dickey–Fuller tests using the lag length selected by the AIC. If you include an intercept (but no time trend) you should obtain

Series	Lags	Estimated a_1	t-statistic	prob-value
TBILL	12	−0.0140	−2.08	0.259
R3	12	−0.0106	−1.95	0.308
R10	12	−0.0078	−1.85	0.355

b.   Estimate the cointegrating relationships using the Engle–Granger procedure. Perform augmented Dickey–Fuller tests on the residuals. Using TBILL as the "dependent" variable, you should find

$$TBILL_t = -0.101 + 1.899R3_t - 0.997\,R10_t$$
$$(-0.147)(41.762)\ (-21.183)$$

where t-statistics are in parentheses.

Perform the Engle–Granger test on the residuals from the equation above. Why is it appropriate to use nine lags in the augmented form of the test? If you use nine lags, you should find that the coefficient on the lagged residual (i.e., e_{t-1}) is -0.1347 with a t-statistic of -5.18.

The 5 percent critical value is about -3.76. Based on this data, do you conclude that the variables are cointegrated?

c.   Repeat part b using R10 as the dependent variable. If you use 4 and 12 lags in the augmented form of the Engle–Granger test, (i.e., estimate $\Delta e_t = \alpha_1 e_{t-1} + \ldots$) you should find

lags	estimated α_1	t–statistic
4	−0.074	−4.01
12	−0.072	−3.35

Using R10 as the dependent variable, are the three interest rates cointegrated?

d. Estimate an error-correcting model using 12 lags of each variable. Use the residuals from part b as the error-correction term and do not include a separate intercept. You should find that the error-corrections are such that

$$\Delta \text{TBILL}_t = -0.040e_{t-1} + \dots \qquad t\text{-statistic for the error-correction term: } -0.983$$
$$\Delta R3_t = 0.088e_{t-1} + \dots \qquad t\text{-statistic for the error-correction term: } 2.638$$
$$\Delta R10_t = 0.096e_{t-1} + \dots \qquad t\text{-statistic for the error-correction term: } 3.741$$

where e_{t-1} is the lagged residual from your estimate in part b.

i. Perform the appropriate diagnostic tests on the system. In particular, determine whether the three residual series appear to be white noise. Are the lags lengths unnecessarily long?

ii. Discuss the nature of the adjustment. Are any of the rates weakly exogenous? In response to a deviation from the long-run relationship, how are the three rates predicted to change?

e. Estimate the model using the Johansen procedure. Use 12 lags and include an intercept in the cointegrating vector. You should find the following:

List of characteristic roots (i.e., eigenvalues) in descending order:
0.055   0.025   0.007

Trace Tests				Maximum Eigenvalue Tests			
Null	Alternative	λ_{trace}	5% Value	Null	Alternative	λ_{max}	5% Value
$r = 0$	$r \geq 1$	50.78	34.91	$r = 0$	$r = 1$	32.41	22.00
$r \leq 1$	$r \geq 2$	18.38	19.96	$r = 1$	$r = 2$	14.45	15.67
$r \leq 2$	$r = 3$	3.93	9.24	$r = 2$	$r = 3$	3.93	9.24

i. Explain why the λ_{trace} test strongly suggests there is exactly one cointegrating vector.

ii. To what extent is this result reinforced by the λ_{max} test?

f. Verify that the normalized cointegrating vector is

$$\text{TBILL}_t = -0.379 + 1.603R3_t - 0.665R10_t$$

i. Compare this result to your answer in part b.

ii. Verify that the three speeds of adjustment parameters (with t-statistics in parentheses) are

TBILL: -0.037	R3: 0.082	R10: 0.101
(-0.930)	(2.45)	(3.98)

5. Suppose you estimate π to be

$$\pi = \begin{bmatrix} 0.6 & -0.5 & 0.2 \\ 0.3 & -0.25 & 0.1 \\ 1.2 & -1.0 & 0.4 \end{bmatrix}$$

a. Show that the determinant of π is zero.

b. Show that two of the characteristic roots are zero and that the third is 0.75.

c. Let $\beta' = (3, -2.5, 1)$ be the single cointegrating vector normalized with respect to x_{3t}. Find the $(3 \cdot 1)$ vector α such that $\pi = \alpha\beta'$. How would α change if you normalized β with respect to x_{1t}?

d. Describe how you could test the restriction $\beta_1 + \beta_2 = 0$.

Now suppose you estimate π to be:

$$\pi = \begin{bmatrix} 0.8 & 0.4 & 0.0 \\ 0.1 & 0.1 & 0.0 \\ 0.75 & 0.25 & 0.5 \end{bmatrix}$$

e. Show that the three characteristic roots are 0.0, 0.5, and 0.9.

f. Select β such that:

$$\beta = \begin{bmatrix} 0.8 & 0.75 \\ 0.4 & 0.25 \\ 0.0 & 0.5 \end{bmatrix}$$

Find the $(3 \cdot 2)$ matrix α such that $\pi = \alpha\beta'$.

6. Suppose that x_{1t} and x_{2t} are integrated of orders 1 and 2, respectively. You are to sketch the proof that any linear combination of x_{1t} and x_{2t} is integrated of order 2. Toward this end:

a. Allow x_{1t} and x_{2t} to be the random walk processes

$$x_{1t} = x_{1t-1} + \varepsilon_{1t} \qquad \text{and} \qquad x_{2t} = x_{2t-1} + \varepsilon_{2t}$$

   i. Given the initial conditions x_{10} and x_{20}, show that the solutions for x_{1t} and x_{2t} have the form $x_{1t} = x_{10} + \Sigma\varepsilon_{1t-i}$ and $x_{2t} = x_{20} + \Sigma\varepsilon_{2t-i}$.

   ii. Show that the linear combination $\beta_1 x_{1t} + \beta_2 x_{2t}$ will generally contain a stochastic trend.

   iii. What assumption is necessary to ensure that x_{1t} and x_{2t} are $CI(1, 1)$?

b. Now let x_{2t} be integrated of order 2. Specifically, let $\Delta x_{2t} = \Delta x_{2t-1} + \varepsilon_{2t}$. Given initial condition for x_{20} and x_{21}, find the solution for x_{2t}. (You may allow ε_{1t} and ε_{2t} to be perfectly correlated.)

   i. Is there any linear combination of x_{1t} and x_{2t} that contains only a stochastic trend?

   ii. Is there any linear combination of x_{1t} and x_{2t} that does not contain a stochastic trend?

c. Provide an intuitive explanation for the statement: If x_{1t} and x_{2t} are integrated of orders d_1 and d_2 where $d_2 > d_1$, any linear combination of x_{1t} and x_{2t} is integrated of order d_2.

7. The Programming Manual that accompanies this text contains a discussion of nonlinear least squares and maximum likelihood estimation. If you have not already done so, download the manual and programs from the Wiley Web site.

a. Section 5.5 in Chapter 4 contains discussion of the problem of conducting inference on the parameters of a cointegrating vector. Execute Program 4.10. Why is it a problem that only 16.8 percent of the true values of β_1 lie within a 95 percent confidence interval?

b. How would you modify the program so as to generate the Engle–Granger critical values?

8. Section 3 of Chapter 2 of the Programming Manual that comes with this text estimates the relationship between the long-term and short-term interest rate as

$$tb1yr_t = 0.698 + 0.916tb3mo_t$$

a. Use the data set MONEYDEM.XLS to estimate the error-correction model. Use five lags of each variable.

b. As shown in the manual, you can use the error-correction model to obtain the impulse response functions with a Choleski decomposition. Your responses should look like:

Impulse Response Functions

c. In the equation for $\Delta tb1yr_t$, the coefficient on the error-correction term is –0.098 with a t-statistic equal to –0.427. Why is it possible to argue that $tb1yr_t$ is weakly exogenous? How can you model the long-term rate using the general-to-specific approach?

ENDNOTES

1. To include an intercept term, simply set all realizations of one $\{x_{it}\}$ sequence equal to unity. In the text, the long-run relationship with an intercept will be denoted by $\beta_0 + \beta_1 x_{1t} + \ldots + \beta_n x_{nt} = 0$. Also note that the definition rules out the trivial case in which all elements of β equal zero. Obviously if all the $\beta_i = 0$, $\beta x_t' = 0$.

2. As a technical point, note that if all elements of x_t are $I(0)$, it is possible for e_t to be integrated of order –1. However, this case is of little interest for economic analysis. Also note that if $\{x_t\}$ is stationary, $\Delta^d x_t$ is stationary for all $d > 0$.

3. The issue is trivial if both trends are deterministic. Simply detrend each of the variables using a deterministic polynomial time trend of the form $\alpha_0 + \alpha_1 t + \alpha_2 t^2 + \ldots$.

4. The error-correction term could have been written in the form $\alpha_S'(\beta_1 r_{Lt-1} - \beta_2 r_{St-1})$. Normalization with respect to the long-term rate yields (6.9), where $\alpha_S = \alpha_S' \beta_1$ and $\beta = \beta_2/\beta_1$. Here, the cointegrating vector is $(1, -\beta)$.

5. Note that (6.11) and (6.12) represent a system of first-order difference equations. The stability conditions place restrictions on the magnitudes of α_S, α_L, and the various values of $a_{ij}(k)$.

6. Equation (6.18) can be written as $\lambda^2 = a_1 \lambda + a_2$ where $a_1 = (a_{11} + a_{22})$ and $a_2 = (a_{12}a_{21} - a_{11}a_{22})$. Now refer all the way back to Figure 1.5 in Chapter 1. For $\lambda_1 = 1$, the coefficients of (6.18) must lie along line segment BC. Hence, $a_1 + a_2 = 1$, or $a_{11} + a_{22} + a_{12}a_{21} - a_{11}a_{22} = 1$. Solving for a_{11} yields (6.19). For $|\lambda_2| < 1$, the coefficients must lie inside region A0BC. Given (6.19), the condition $a_2 - a_1 = 1$ is equivalent to that in (6.21).

7. Another interesting way to obtain this result is to refer back to (6.14). If $a_{12} = 0$, $y_t = a_{11}y_{t-1} + \varepsilon_{yt}$. Imposing the condition that $\{y_t\}$ is a unit root process is equivalent to setting $a_{11} = 1$ so that $\Delta y_t = \varepsilon_{yt}$.

8. The stability condition is that $-2 < a_1 < 0$. Hence, if a_1 is found to be sufficiently negative, we need to be able to reject the null hypothesis: $a_1 = -2$.

9. As shown in Section 3, the values of α_y and α_z are directly related to the characteristic roots of the difference equation system. Direct convergence necessitates that α_y be negative and α_z be positive.

10. Engle and Granger (1987) do provide a statistic to test the joint hypothesis $\alpha_y = \alpha_z = 0$. However, their simulations suggest this statistic is not very powerful, and they recommend against its use.

11. Of course, x_{1t} and x_{2t} can be $CI(2, 2)$ so that the linear combination $x_{1t} - \beta_2 x_{2t}$ is stationary. In this circumstance, $\gamma_1 = 0$ since z_t cannot be cointegrated with $x_{1t} - \beta_2 x_{2t}$. However, this is a rather unusual circumstance, so that the literature focuses on the case in which x_{1t} and x_{2t} are $CI(2, 1)$.

12. Wholesale prices and period average exchange rates were used in the study. Each series was converted into an index number such that each series was equal to unity at the beginning of its respective period (either 1960 or 1973). In the fixed exchange rate period, all values of $\{e_t\}$ were set equal to unity.

13. A second set of regressions of the form $p_t = \beta_0 + \beta_1 f_t + \mu_t$ was also estimated. The results using this alternative normalization are very similar to those reported here.

14. The numbers are slightly different from those reported by Johansen and Juselius (1990) due to rounding.

15. As discussed in Appendix 6.2, the Johansen procedure consists of the matrix of vectors of the squared canonical correlations between the residuals of x_t and Δx_{t-1} regressed on lagged values of Δx_t. The cointegrating vectors are the rows of the normalized eigenvectors.

16. You can normalize with respect to any variable with only one caveat. If the true value of $\beta_i = 0$ (so that x_{it} does not enter the cointegrating relationship), normalizing with respect to x_{it} will wildly inflate the other coefficients and their significance levels. In essence, you will have divided all other magnitudes by a coefficient that is estimated to be near zero.

17. In the general case of an n–variable system, let rank(π) = r and define the $n \cdot r$ matrices α and β such that $\alpha\beta' = \pi$. Also, let $a_\perp$ and $\beta_\perp$ denote the orthogonal complements of α and β. Johansen (1995) obtains the value of s from $a_\perp'\Gamma\beta_\perp$ once the value of r has been chosen.

18. Johansen shows that this two-step procedure has the following properties: (i) if the rank of π is r and there are no $I(2)$ components, the procedure picks out the true value of r with a high probability, (ii) a value of r that is too low is selected with a limiting probability of zero, and (iii) if there are $I(2)$ components, the procedure will accept no $I(2)$ components with a small probability. Jorgensen, Kongsted, and Rahbek (1996) show how to simultaneously select the values of r and s.

19. Hence, the characteristic roots are those of $a_\perp'\Gamma\beta_\perp$

20. Engle, Hendry, and Richard (1983) provide a comprehensive analysis of various types of exogeneity. In general, a variable x_{it} is weakly exogenous for the parameter set P if the marginal distribution of x_{it} contains no useful information for conducting inference on P. Hence, x_{it} can be exogenous in one econometric model but not another.

21. However, since $\{y_t\}$ and $\{z_t\}$ are $I(1)$, the test statistics of the null hypothesis $\beta_1 = 0$ and $\beta_2 = 0$ are nonstandard.

22. The data shown in Figure 6.5 were provided by David Gruen.

23. The paper also reports the results of the likelihood ratio statistics for testing the reduced lag lengths. These tests reinforce the results of the SBC.

APPENDIX 6.1: INFERENCE ON A COINTEGRATING VECTOR

The Johansen procedure allows you to test restrictions on one or more cointegrating vectors. However, it is very tempting to use the t-statistics on a coefficient of a cointegrating vector estimated by OLS in the Engle–Granger methodology. Nevertheless, you must avoid this temptation since the coefficients *do not* have asymptotic t-distributions except in one special circumstance. The problem is that the coefficients are super-consistent but the standard errors are not. Nevertheless, it is typical for a published study to report the coefficients of the cointegrating vector and the associated t-statistics or standard errors. For example, the cointegrating relationship between y_t, z_t, and w_t in Section 5 was reported as (with t-statistics in parentheses)

$$y_t = -0.4843 \quad - 0.9273z_t + 0.97687w_t + e_{yt}$$
$$(-0.5751)(-38.095) \quad (53.462)$$

However, $\{e_{yt}\}$ may be serially correlated and z_t and w_t may not be exogenous variables. As in a traditional regression with stationary variables, you need to correct for serial correlation and the problem of endogenous regressors. To illustrate the *fully modified least squares* procedure developed by Phillips and Hansen (1990), consider the simple two-variable example

$$y_t = \beta_0 + \beta_1 z_t + e_{1t}$$
$$\Delta z_t = e_{2t}$$

The first equation is the cointegrating relationship and the second indicates that $\{z_t\}$ is the stochastic trend. The notation e_{1t} and e_{2t} is designed to illustrate the point that the residuals from both equations are stationary. However, they may be serially correlated and may be correlated with each other. As such, the second equation is actually quite general since Δz_t can be correlated with its own lags and with values of y_t.

Clearly, the relationship between the two errors is crucial. We begin with the simple case wherein:

$$\begin{bmatrix} e_{1t} \\ e_{2t} \end{bmatrix} = N \; i.d.d. \left(\begin{bmatrix} 0 \\ 0 \end{bmatrix}, \begin{bmatrix} \sigma_1^2 & 0 \\ 0 & \sigma_2^2 \end{bmatrix} \right)$$

Case 1: In this circumstance, the errors are serially uncorrelated and the cross-correlations are zero. Hence, the OLS regression of y_t on z_t and a constant is such that the explanatory variable (i.e., z_t) is independent of the error term e_{1t}. As indicated in the text, the OLS estimates of β_0 and β_1 can be tested using the normal distribution. Hence, t-tests and F-tests are appropriate. If the disturbances are not normally distributed, the asymptotic results are such that t-tests and F-tests are appropriate.

Case 2: In general, e_{1t} and e_{2t} will be correlated with each other so that $Ee_{1t}e_{2t} \neq 0$. In order to conduct inference on the parameters of the cointegrating vector, it is necessary to correct for the endogeneity of z_t. You do this by including leads and lags of $\{\Delta z_t\}$ in the cointegrating relationship. Hence, you estimate the equation

$$y_t = \beta_0 + \beta_1 z_t + \ldots + \gamma_{-1}\Delta z_{t+1} + \gamma_0 \Delta z_t + \gamma_1 \Delta z_{t-1} + \ldots + e_{1t}$$

In essence, you are controlling for innovations in z_t since the equation is equivalent to

$$y_t = \beta_0 + \beta_1 z_t + \ldots + \gamma_{-1} e_{2t+1} + \gamma_0 e_{2t} + \gamma_1 e_{2t-1} + \ldots + e_{1t}$$

Let var(e_{1t}) be denoted by σ_e^2. If $\{e_{1t}\}$ is serially uncorrelated, you can form a t-statistic to determine whether the estimated value of β_1 (i.e., $\hat{\beta}_1$) equals the hypothesized value β_1 using the t-statistic

$$t = (\hat{\beta}_1 - \beta_1)/\sigma_e$$

Case 3: In the most general case, $Ee_{1t}e_{2t} \neq 0$ and the residuals from the cointegrating vector (i.e., the estimated values of e_{1t}) are likely to be serially correlated. Hence, you also need to modify the t-statistic so that you use the appropriate estimate of the variance of e_{1t}. If the $\{e_{1t}\}$ series is serially correlated, you adjust the t-statistic using the following procedure:

STEP 1: Estimate the equation for y_t and obtain the estimated $\{e_{1t}\}$ series. Denote the t-statistic for the null hypothesis $\hat{\beta}_1 = \beta_1$ as t_0.

STEP 2: Estimate the $\{e_{1t}\}$ series as an AR(p) process to correct for autocorrelation. In particular, use the residuals from Step 1 to estimate the equation

$$e_{1t} = \alpha_1 e_{1t-1} + \ldots + \alpha_p e_{1t-p} + \varepsilon_t$$

Let σ^2 denote the estimated variance of ε_t so that σ is the standard deviation. Construct the value λ as

$$\lambda = \sigma/(1 - \alpha_1 - \ldots - \alpha_p)$$

STEP 3: Multiply t_0 by σ_e/λ. The resulting value is the appropriate t-statistic for the null hypothesis $\hat{\beta}_1 = \beta_1$. Compare the corrected t-statistic to that in a t-table. As you can see, the corrected t-statistic uses a more appropriate estimator for var(e_{1t}).

Little is altered if we allow z_t to be a vector of variables. However, a word of caution is in order. There are many possible sources of error in the three-step methodology outlined above. You could use too few or too many lags in Step 1. A similar problem arises in Step 2 because p is unknown. The Johansen procedure circumvents many of these problems in that all variables are treated as jointly endogenous and the VAR residuals are not serially correlated. Hence, you can conduct inference on the cointegrating vector(s) directly.

The procedure is not always as difficult as it sounds. As a practical matter, many researchers correct for serial correlation by adding lagged changes of Δy_t to the estimated equation. If the augmented equation eliminated the serial correlation, Steps 2 and 3 are unnecessary. The estimated equation has the form

$$y_t = \beta_0 + \beta_1 z_t + A_1(L)\Delta y_{t-1} + \ldots + \gamma_{-1}\Delta z_{t+1} + \gamma_0 \Delta z_t + \gamma_1 \Delta z_{t-1} + \ldots + \varepsilon_t$$

where $A_1(L)$ is a polynomial in the lag operator L and $\{\varepsilon_t\}$ is serially uncorrelated.

Section 10 contains an interesting example applied to the Australian price level. The key feature of the example is that the regressors are shown to be weakly exogenous.

APPENDIX 6.2: CHARACTERISTIC ROOTS, STABILITY, AND RANK

Characteristic Roots Defined

Let A be an $(n \cdot n)$ square matrix with elements a_{ij} and let x be an $(n \cdot 1)$ vector. The scalar λ is called a characteristic root of A if

$$Ax = \lambda x \tag{A6.1}$$

Let I be an $(n \cdot n)$ identity matrix so that we can rewrite (A6.1) as

$$(A - \lambda I)x = 0 \tag{A6.2}$$

Since x is a vector containing values not identically equal to zero, (A6.2) requires that the rows of $(A - \lambda I)$ be linearly dependent. Equivalently, (A6.2) requires that the determinant $|A - \lambda I| = 0$. Thus, we can find the characteristic root(s) of (A6.1) by finding the values of λ that satisfy

$$|A - \lambda I| = 0 \tag{A6.3}$$

Example 1

Let A be the matrix:

$$A = \begin{bmatrix} 0.5 & -0.2 \\ -0.2 & 0.5 \end{bmatrix}$$

so that

$$|A - \lambda I| = \begin{vmatrix} 0.5 - \lambda & -0.2 \\ -0.2 & 0.5 - \lambda \end{vmatrix}$$

Solving for the value of λ such that $|A - \lambda I| = 0$ yields the quadratic equation:

$$\lambda^2 - \lambda + 0.21 = 0$$

The two values of λ which solve the equation are $\lambda = 0.7$ and $\lambda = 0.3$. Hence, 0.7 and 0.3 are the two characteristic roots.

Example 2

Now change A such that each element in column 2 is twice the corresponding value in column 1. Specifically,

$$A = \begin{bmatrix} 0.5 & 1 \\ -0.2 & -0.4 \end{bmatrix}$$

Now,

$$|A - \lambda I| = \begin{vmatrix} 0.5 - \lambda & 1 \\ -0.2 & -0.4 - \lambda \end{vmatrix}$$

Again, there are two values of λ which solve $|A - \lambda I| = 0$. Solving the quadratic equation $\lambda^2 - 0.1\lambda = 0$ yields the two characteristic roots $\lambda_1 = 0$ and $\lambda_2 = 0.1$.

Characteristic Equations

Equation (A6.3) is called the characteristic equation of the square matrix A. Notice that the characteristic equation will be an nth-order polynomial in λ. The reason is that the determinant $|A - \lambda I| = 0$ contains the nth degree term λ^n resulting from the expression:

$$(a_{11} - \lambda)(a_{22} - \lambda)(a_{33} - \lambda) \dots (a_{nn} - \lambda)$$

As such, the characteristic equation will be an nth-order polynomial of the form

$$\lambda^n + b_1 \lambda^{n-1} + b_2 \lambda^{n-2} + b_3 \lambda^{n-3} + \dots + b_{n-1}\lambda + b_n = 0 \qquad (A6.4)$$

From (A6.4) it immediately follows that an $(n \cdot n)$ square matrix will necessarily have n characteristic roots. As we saw in Chapter 1, some of the roots may be repeating and some may be complex. In practice, it is not necessary to actually calculate the values of the roots solving (A6.4). The necessary and sufficient conditions for all characteristic roots to lie within the unit circle are given in the appendix to Chapter 1.

Notice that the term b_n is of particular relevance because $b_n = (-1)^n |A|$. After all, b_n is the only expression resulting from $|A - \lambda I|$ that is not multiplied by λ. In terms of (A6.4), the expressions λ^n and b_n will have the same sign if n is even and opposite signs if n is odd. In Example 1, the characteristic equation is $\lambda^2 - \lambda + 0.21 = 0$ so that $b_2 = 0.21$. Since $|A| = 0.21$, it follows that $b_2 = (-1)^2(0.21)$. Similarly, in Example 2, the characteristic equation is $\lambda^2 - 0.1\lambda = 0$, so that $b_2 = 0$. Since it is also the case that $|A| = 0$, it also follows that $b_2 = (-1)^2 |A|$. In Example 3 below, we consider the case in which $n = 3$.

Example 3
Let A be such that

$$|A - \lambda I| = \begin{bmatrix} 0.5 - \lambda & 0.2 & 0.2 \\ 0.2 & 0.5 - \lambda & 0.2 \\ 0.2 & 0.2 & 0.5 - \lambda \end{bmatrix}$$

The characteristic equation is

$$\lambda^3 - 1.5\lambda^2 + 0.63\lambda - 0.081 = 0$$

and the characteristic roots are

$$\lambda_1 = 0.9, \ \lambda_2 = 0.3, \text{ and } \lambda_3 = 0.3$$

The determinant of A is 0.081 so that $b_3 = -0.081 = (-1)^3 |A|$.

Determinants and Characteristic Roots

The determinant of an $(n \cdot n)$ matrix is equal to the product of its characteristic roots, that is

$$|A| = \prod_{i=1}^{n} \lambda_i \qquad (A6.5)$$

where $\lambda_1, \lambda_2, \dots, \lambda_n$ are the n characteristic roots of the $(n \cdot n)$ matrix A.

The proof of this important proposition is straightforward since the values λ_1, λ_2, ..., λ_n solve (A6.4). Yet, from the algebra of polynomials, the product of the factors of (A6.4) is equal to $(-1)^n b_n$:

$$\prod_{i=1}^{n} \lambda_i = (-1)^n b_n$$

From the discussion, we also know that $(-1)^n b_n = |A|$. Hence (A6.5) must hold in that the product $(\lambda_1)(\lambda_2) \ldots (\lambda_n) = (-1)^n b_n = |A|$.

Examples 1 to 3 Continued

In Examples 1 and 2, the characteristic equation is quadratic of the form $\lambda^2 + b_1\lambda + b_2 = 0$. To find the roots of this quadratic equation, we seek the factors λ_1 and λ_2 such that

$$(\lambda - \lambda_1)(\lambda - \lambda_2) = 0$$

or

$$\lambda^2 - (\lambda\lambda_1 + \lambda\lambda_2) + \lambda_1\lambda_2 = 0$$

or

$$\lambda^2 - (\lambda_1 + \lambda_2)\lambda + \lambda_1\lambda_2 = 0$$

Clearly, the value of $\lambda_1\lambda_2$ must equal b_2. To check the formulas in Example 1, recall that the characteristic equation is $\lambda^2 - \lambda + 0.21 = 0$. In this problem, the value of b_2 is 0.21, the product of the characteristic roots is $\lambda_1\lambda_2 = (0.7)(0.3) = 0.21$, and the determinant of A is $(0.5)^2 - (0.2)^2 = 0.21$. In Example 2, the characteristic equation is $\lambda^2 - 0.1\lambda = 0$ so that $b_2 = 0$. The product of the characteristic roots is $\lambda_1\lambda_2 = (0.0)(0.1) = 0.0$, and the determinant of A is $(0.5)(0.4) - (0.2) = 0$.

In Example 3, the characteristic equation is cubic: $\lambda^3 - 1.5\lambda^2 + 0.63\lambda - 0.081 = 0$. The value of b_3 is -0.081, product of the characteristic roots is $(0.9)(0.3)(0.3) = 0.081$, and the determinant of A is 0.081.

Characteristic Roots and Rank

The rank of a square $(n \cdot n)$ matrix A is the number of linearly independent rows (columns) in the matrix. The notation rank$(A) = r$ means that the rank of A is equal to r. The matrix A is said to be of full rank if rank$(A) = n$.

From the discussion above, it follows that *the rank of A is equal to the number of its nonzero characteristic roots.* Certainly, if all rows of A are linearly independent, the determinant of A is not equal to zero. From (A6.5) it follows that none of the characteristic roots can equal zero if $|A| \neq 0$. At the other extreme, if rank$(A) = 0$, each element of A must equal zero. When rank$(A) = 0$, the characteristic equation degenerates into $\lambda^n = 0$ with the solutions $\lambda_1 = \lambda_2 = \ldots = \lambda_n = 0$. Consider the intermediate cases wherein $0 < \text{rank}(A) = r < n$. Since interchanging the various rows of a matrix does not alter the absolute value of its determinant, we can always rewrite $|A - \lambda I| = 0$ such that the first r rows comprise the r linearly independent rows of A. The determinant of these first r rows will contain r characteristic roots. The other $(n-r)$ roots will be zeroes.

In Example 2, rank(A) = 1 since each element in row 1 equals –2.5 times the corresponding element in row 2. For this case, $|A| = 0$ and exactly one characteristic root is equal to zero. In the other two examples, A is of full rank and all characteristic roots differ from zero.

Example 4

Now consider a (3 · 3) matrix A such that rank(A) = 1. Let

$$|A - \lambda I| = \begin{bmatrix} 0.5 - \lambda & 0.2 & 0.2 \\ 1 & 0.4 - \lambda & 0.4 \\ -0.25 & -0.1 & -0.1 - \lambda \end{bmatrix}$$

The rank of A is unity since row 2 is twice row 1 and row 3 is –0.5 times row 1. The determinant of A equals zero and the characteristic equation is given by

$$\lambda^3 - 0.8\lambda^2 = 0$$

The three characteristic roots are $\lambda_1 = 0.8$, $\lambda_2 = 0$, and $\lambda_3 = 0$.

Stability of a First-order VAR

Let x_t be the (n · 1) vector $(x_{1t}, x_{2t}, ..., x_{nt})'$ and consider the first-order VAR

$$x_t = A_0 + A_1 x_{t-1} + \varepsilon_t \tag{A6.6}$$

where: $A_0 = (n \cdot 1)$ vector with elements a_{i0}
   $A_1 = (n \cdot n)$ square matrix with elements a_{ij}
   $\varepsilon_t = (n \cdot 1)$ vector of white-noise disturbances $(\varepsilon_{1t}, \varepsilon_{2t}, ..., \varepsilon_{nt})'$

To check the stability of the system, we need only examine the homogeneous equation:

$$x_t = A_1 x_{t-1} \tag{A6.7}$$

We can use the method of undetermined coefficients and for each x_{it} posit a solution of the form

$$x_{it} = c_i \lambda^t \tag{A6.8}$$

where c_i is an arbitrary constant.

If (A6.8) is to be a solution, it must satisfy each of the n equations represented by (A6.7). Substituting $x_{it} = c_i \lambda^t$ and $x_{it-1} = c_i \lambda^{t-1}$ for each of the x_{it} in (A6.7), we get

$$c_1 \lambda^t = a_{11} c_1 \lambda^{t-1} + a_{12} c_2 \lambda^{t-1} + ... + a_{1n} c_n \lambda^{t-1}$$
$$c_2 \lambda^t = a_{21} c_1 \lambda^{t-1} + a_{22} c_2 \lambda^{t-1} + ... + a_{2n} c_n \lambda^{t-1}$$
$$c_3 \lambda^t = a_{31} c_1 \lambda^{t-1} + a_{32} c_2 \lambda^{t-1} + ... + a_{3n} c_n \lambda^{t-1}$$
$$...$$
$$c_n \lambda^t = a_{n1} c_1 \lambda^{t-1} + a_{n2} c_2 \lambda^{t-1} + ... + a_{nn} c_n \lambda^{t-1}$$

Now, divide each equation by λ^{t-1} and collect terms to form

$$c_1(a_{11} - \lambda) + c_2 a_{12} + c_3 a_{13} ... + c_n a_{1n} = 0$$
$$c_1 a_{21} + c_2(a_{22} - \lambda) + c_3 a_{23} ... + c_n a_{2n} = 0$$
$$...\qquad...\qquad...\qquad...\qquad...$$
$$c_1 a_{n1} + c_2 a_{n2} + c_3 a_{n3} ... + c_n(a_{nn} - \lambda) = 0$$

so that the following system of equations must be satisfied:

$$\begin{bmatrix} a_{11} - \lambda & a_{12} & a_{13} & \cdots & a_{1n} \\ a_{21} & a_{22} - \lambda & a_{23} & \cdots & a_{2n} \\ \cdots & \cdots & \cdots & \cdots & \cdots \\ a_{n1} & a_{n2} & a_{n3} & \cdots & a_{nn} - \lambda \end{bmatrix} \begin{bmatrix} c_1 \\ c_2 \\ \cdots \\ c_n \end{bmatrix} = \begin{bmatrix} 0 \\ 0 \\ \cdots \\ 0 \end{bmatrix}$$

For a nontrivial solution to the system of equations, the following determinant must equal zero:

$$\begin{vmatrix} (a_{11} - \lambda) & a_{12} & a_{13} & \cdots & a_{1n} \\ a_{21} & (a_{22} - \lambda) & a_{23} & \cdots & a_{2n} \\ \cdots & \cdots & \cdots & \cdots & \cdots \\ a_{n1} & a_{n2} & a_{n3} & \cdots & (a_{nn} - \lambda) \end{vmatrix} = 0$$

The determinant will be an nth-order polynomial that is satisfied by n values of λ. Denote these n characteristics roots by $\lambda_1, \lambda_2, \ldots \lambda_n$. Since each is a solution to the homogeneous equation, we know that the following linear combination of the homogeneous solutions is also a homogeneous solution:

$$x_{it} = d_1 \lambda_1{}^t + d_2 \lambda_2{}^t + \ldots + d_n \lambda_n{}^t$$

Note that each $\{x_{it}\}$ sequence will have the same roots. The necessary and sufficient condition for stability is that all characteristic roots lie within the unit circle.

Cointegration and Rank

The relationship between the rank of a matrix and its characteristic roots is critical in the Johansen procedure. Using the notation from Section 7, let

$$x_t = A_1 x_{t-1} + \varepsilon_t$$

so that

$$\Delta x_t = (A_1 - I)x_{t-1} + \varepsilon_t$$
$$= \pi x_{t-1} + \varepsilon_t$$

If the rank of π is unity, all rows of π can be written as a scalar multiple of the first. Thus, each of the $\{\Delta x_{it}\}$ sequences can be written as

$$\Delta x_{it} = s_i (\pi_{11} x_{1t-1} + \pi_{12} x_{2t-1} + \ldots + \pi_{1n} x_{nt-1}) + \varepsilon_{it}$$

where $s_1 = 1$ and $s_i = \pi_{ij} / \pi_{1j}$.

Hence, the linear combination: $\pi_{11} x_{1t-1} + \pi_{12} x_{2t-1} + \ldots + \pi_{1n} x_{nt-1} = (\Delta x_{it} - \varepsilon_{it})/s_i$ is stationary since Δx_{it} and ε_{it} are both stationary.

The rank of π equals the number of cointegrating vectors. If rank(π) = r, there are r linearly independent combinations of the $\{x_{it}\}$ sequences that are stationary. If rank(π) = n, all variables are stationary.

The rank of π is equal to the number of its characteristic roots that differ from zero. Order the roots such that $\lambda_1 > \lambda_2 > \ldots > \lambda_n$. The Johansen methodology allows you to determine the number of roots that are statistically different from zero. The relationship between A_1 and π is such that if all characteristic roots of A_1 are in the unit circle, π is of full rank.

Calculating the Characteristic Roots in Johansen's Method

Although commercially available software packages can obtain the characteristic roots of π, you might be interested in programming the method yourself (or at least understanding the method). First select the most appropriate lag length p in for the VAR

$$x_t = A_1 x_{t-1} + \ldots + A_p x_{t-p} + \varepsilon_t$$

STEP 1: Estimate the VAR in first differences, that is, estimate

$$\Delta x_t = B_1 \Delta x_{t-1} + \ldots + B_{p-1} \Delta x_{t-p+1} + e_{1t}$$

STEP 2: Regress x_{t-1} on the lagged changes; that is, estimate a VAR of the form

$$x_{t-1} = C_1 \Delta x_{t-1} + \ldots + C_{p-1} \Delta x_{t-p+1} + e_{2t}$$

STEP 3: Compute the squares of the canonical correlations between e_{1t} and e_{2t}. In an n-equation VAR, the n canonical correlations are the n values of λ_i. The λ_i are obtained as the solutions to

$$\left| \lambda_i S_{22} - S_{12} S_{11}^{-1} S_{12}' \right| = 0$$

where $S_{ii} = T^{-1} \sum_{i=1}^{T} e_{it}(e_{it})'$, $S_{12} = T^{-1} \sum_{i=1}^{T} (e_{2t} e_{1t})'$

and e_{1t} and e_{2t} are the column vectors of residuals obtained in Steps 1 and 2.

STEP 4: The maximum likelihood estimates of the cointegrating vectors are the n columns that are nontrivial solutions for

$$\lambda_i S_{22} \pi_i = S_{12} S_{11}^{-1} S_{12}' \pi_i$$

CHAPTER 7

NONLINEAR TIME-SERIES MODELS

Economic theory suggests that a number of important time-series variables should exhibit nonlinear behavior. The observation that wages display downward rigidity is a key feature of many macroeconomic models. Moreover, it has been established that downturns in the business cycle are sharper than recoveries in that key macroeconomic variables, such as output and employment, fall more sharply than they rise. Since the standard ARMA model relies on linear difference equations, new dynamic specifications are necessary to capture nonlinear behavior. In fact, research in this new area of time-series econometrics seems to be growing exponentially (itself, a nonlinear process). This chapter has three aims:

1. Compare the ARMA model to various types of nonlinear models. Once the assumption of linearity is abandoned, it is possible to estimate any number of potential nonlinear processes. Several nonlinear forms have proved themselves to be especially useful. The text will focus on those nonlinear models that can be estimated by OLS methods, nonlinear least squares or maximum likelihood techniques.

2. Develop a number of tests that can detect the presence of nonlinear adjustment. The time-series literature contains a number of tests that are useful in determining whether or not a series is nonlinear. It will be shown that detecting nonlinearity is far simpler than trying to establish the precise nature of the nonlinearity.

3. Illustrate the process of estimating a nonlinear model. To a large extent, estimating a nonlinear process entails learning by doing. Toward this end, a number of series will be estimated using nonlinear techniques. Moreover, several studies that have appeared in the time-series literature will be reviewed. The issue of unit roots and cointegration in a nonlinear setting will also be examined.

1. LINEAR VERSUS NONLINEAR ADJUSTMENT

On a long automobile trip to a new location, you might take along a road atlas. Since the earth is not flat, the maps contained in the atlas are a linear approximation to the actual path of your journey. Nevertheless, for most trips, such a linear approximation is extremely useful. Try to envision the nuisance of a nonlinear road atlas. For other types of trips, the linearity assumption is clearly inappropriate. It would be disastrous for NASA to use a flat map of the earth to plan the trajectory of a rocket launch. Similarly, the assumption that economic processes are linear can provide useful approximations to the actual time-paths of economic variables. Nevertheless, policy makers could make a serious error if they ignore the empirical evidence that unemployment increases more sharply than it decreases.

One example of a nonlinear model that has been used in the literature is the threshold autoregressive (TAR) model. To explain how it might be useful, let r_{Lt} and r_{St} be the long-term and short-term interest rates on two similar financial instruments. Suppose that the spread, defined as $s_t = r_{Lt} - r_{St}$, adjusts to the long-run value $\overline{s}$. A simple AR(1) representation of the dynamic adjustment mechanism might be

$$s_t = a_0 + a_1 s_{t-1} + \varepsilon_t \qquad \text{where } 0 < a_1 < 1$$

For our purposes, it convenient to define $\overline{s}$ as the long-run value $a_0/(1 - a_1)$ and write the adjustment process as

$$s_t = \overline{s} + a_1(s_{t-1} - \overline{s}) + \varepsilon_t$$

If $s_t = \overline{s}$, the system is said to be in long-run equilibrium. In other circumstances, a_1 percent of the current period's deviation from the long-run value tends to persist into the next period. In fact, there is evidence that interest rate spreads display a nonlinear adjustment pattern. Periods in which the spread is low relative to its long-run value (so that $s_{t-1} - \overline{s} < 0$) are far more persistent than periods in which $s_{t-1} - \overline{s} > 0$. It is possible model these differing degrees of persistence using

$$s_t = \begin{cases} \overline{s} + a_1(s_{t-1} - \overline{s}) + \varepsilon_{1t} & \text{when } s_{t-1} > \overline{s} \\ \overline{s} + a_2(s_{t-1} - \overline{s}) + \varepsilon_{2t} & \text{when } s_{t-1} \leq \overline{s} \end{cases} \qquad (7.1)$$

where ε_{1t} and ε_{2t} are white-noise processes.

In (7.1), when s_{t-1} is above the threshold value $\overline{s}$, the spread follows the AR(1) process $s_t = \overline{s} + a_1(s_{t-1} - \overline{s}) + \varepsilon_{1t}$ and when s_{t-1} is below the threshold, the spread follows the AR(1) process $s_t = \overline{s} + a_2(s_{t-1} - \overline{s}) + \varepsilon_{2t}$. As long as $|a_2| > |a_1|$, periods when $s_{t-1} < \overline{s}$ will tend to be more persistent than other periods.

To better illustrate the difference between linear and nonlinear adjustment, consider the homogeneous part of the first-order AR(1) model:

$$y_t = a_1 y_{t-1}$$

Given that $-1 < a_1 < 1$, we know that the long-run mean is such that $Ey_t = 0$. The nature of the adjustment process is such that a_1 percent of any current deviation from the long-run equilibrium persists into the next period. For example, if $a_1 = 0.5$ and the initial condition is such that $y_{t-1} = 1.0$, it immediately follows that $E_{t-1}y_t = 0.5$ and $E_{t-1}y_{t+1} = 0.25$. Let $\{y_{t-1}^*\}$ denote the specific sequence $\{1, 0.50, 0.25, 0.125, \ldots\}$ generated by assuming the initial condition $y_{t-1} = 1$. The linearity of the adjustment process can be demonstrated by considering alternative values for y_{t-1}. If the initial condition is such that $y_{t-1} = 2$, the subsequent values of the new sequence are exactly twice that of the previous case. In fact, multiplying the initial value of y_{t-1} by any scalar λ results in the sequence $\{\lambda y_{t-1}^*\}$. The **phase diagram** shown in Panel (a) of Figure 7.1 represents

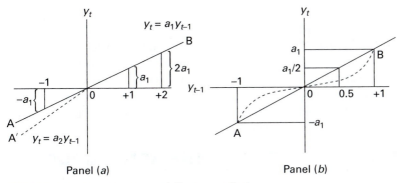

Panel (a)   Panel (b)

FIGURE 7.1 Two Nonlinear Adjustment Paths

the linear nature of this adjustment process. The solid straight line labeled AB is constructed to have a slope equal to a_1. Hence, for any value of y_{t-1}, you can obtain the next value in the sequence by using line AB to project y_{t-1} onto the y_t axis. Since the slope is constant, any scalar multiple of y_{t-1} will result in the proportional value of y_t. As shown in the figure, if $y_{t-1} = 1$, the expected value of $y_t = a_1$ and if $y_{t-1} = 2$, the expected value of $y_t = 2a_1$.

Also note that adjustment is symmetric around zero. If $y_{t-1} = -1$, $E_{t-1}y_t = -0.5$ and $E_{t-1}y_{t+1} = -0.25$ and so on. Hence, for the linear model, multiplying the initial condition y_{t-1} by -1 results in the sequence $\{-y^*_{t-1}\}$.

Now suppose that the phase diagram is such that adjustment occurs along the kinked line passing through A'0B. Thus $y_t = a_1 y_{t-1}$ when $y_{t-1} > 0$ and $y_t = a_2 y_{t-1}$ when $y_{t-1} \leq 0$. Again, if $y_{t-1} = 1$, the next value in the sequence equals a_1. However, if $y_{t-1} = -1$, the next value in the sequence equals $-a_2$. Since $a_2 > a_1$, it should be clear that the $\{y_t\}$ sequence will approach zero more slowly when beginning from a negative value of y_{t-1} than a positive value. Hence, the adjustment process is not linear since the choice λy_{t-1} does not necessarily result in the sequence $\{\lambda y^*_{t-1}\}$. This is precisely the type of adjustment represented by (7.1); if $a_2 > a_1$ and $\bar{s} = 0$, the $\{s_t\}$ sequence has precisely the phase diagram shown by A'0B in Panel (a) of Figure 7.1.

A different type of nonlinear model is needed to represent the process of gravitational attraction. From elementary physics, we know that the speed of an object in space will increase as it falls toward the earth. We can represent the earth as being located at point 0 and suppose that the object in space is attracted to point 0. If y_t denotes the distance of the object from 0 at time t, gravitational attraction can be represented by the curve passing through A0B in Panel (b) of Figure 7.1. As shown in the figure, if we let $y_{t-1} = 1$, the value of y_t will be a_1. Instead, if y_{t-1} is 0.5, the value of y_t must be less than $a_1/2$. Hence, the adjustment process is not linear because the choice λy_{t-1} does not result in the sequence $\{\lambda y^*_{t-1}\}$. The straight line $y_t = a_1 y_{t-1}$ passing through A0B does not capture this feature of the adjustment process.

Take a moment to imagine other types of nonlinear processes. For example, transport costs might deter arbitrage of a slight discrepancy between cotton prices in Alabama and Mississippi. In contrast, large price discrepancies might be eliminated almost immediately. You should be able to think of several other examples. The point is that once we decide to leave the realm of linearity, there are many potential types of nonlinearity. It can be especially important to determine the most appropriate form of the nonlinearity. After all, adopting an incorrect nonlinear specification may be more problematic than simply ignoring the nonlinearity altogether. Since selecting the proper nonlinear model can be difficult, it is not surprising that this remains an important area of current research. However, some special forms of nonlinearity have proven to be particularly useful in applied time-series research. We begin by presenting an overview of the most important nonlinear models.

2. SIMPLE EXTENSIONS OF THE ARMA MODEL

The simplest form of the nonlinear autoregressive (NLAR) model is

$$y_t = f(y_{t-1}) + \varepsilon_t$$

This is a first-order nonlinear autoregressive model, denoted by NLAR(1), in that the longest lag length is one. It is possible to reparameterize the model in a more interesting way:

$$y_t = a_1(y_{t-1}) \cdot y_{t-1} + \varepsilon_t \tag{7.2}$$

where $a_1(y_{t-1}) \cdot y_{t-1} \equiv f(y_{t-1})$.

Equation (7.2) looks exactly like an AR(1) model except for the fact that the autoregressive coefficient a_1 is allowed to be a function of the value of y_{t-1}. If we do not know the functional form of $f(\ )$, the usual dichotomy between nonlinearity in variables and time-varying parameters is not really clear-cut. It can be very difficult for a statistical test to detect the difference between a model in which some of the regressors are not raised to the power one and a model in which the parameters are varying over time. More generally, the p-th order nonlinear autoregressive model is

$$y_t = f(y_{t-1}, y_{t-2}, \ldots, y_{t-p}) + \varepsilon_t \tag{7.3}$$

and is denoted by NLAR(p).

The difficulty in estimating (7.3) is that the functional form of $f(\ )$ is unknown. One way to proceed is to use a Taylor series approximation of the unknown functional form. For the NLAR(2) model $y_t = f(y_{t-1}, y_{t-2}) + \varepsilon_t$, the Taylor series approximation using terms no higher than order-three is

$$y_t = a_0 + a_1 y_{t-1} + a_2 y_{t-2} + a_{12} y_{t-1} y_{t-2} + a_{11} y_{t-1}^2$$
$$+ a_{22} y_{t-2}^2 + a_{112} y_{t-1}^2 y_{t-2} + a_{122} y_{t-1} y_{t-2}^2 + a_{111} y_{t-1}^3 + a_{222} y_{t-2}^3 + \varepsilon_t$$

For the more general NLAR(p) we need a more compact notation. A simple way of writing such a Taylor series approximation is

$$y_t = a_0 + \sum_{i=1}^{p} a_i y_{t-i} + \sum_{i=1}^{p} \sum_{j=1}^{p} \sum_{k=1}^{r} \sum_{l=1}^{s} a_{ijkl} y_{t-i}^k y_{t-j}^l + \varepsilon_t \tag{7.4}$$

where p is the order of the process and r and s are integers that are greater than or equal to 1. In order to avoid a very large number of parameters, the sum of r and s is usually restricted to be less than or equal to 4.

The GAR Model

Equation (7.4) is called the generalized autoregressive (GAR) model. GAR models extend the standard AR model by including various powers of the lagged values of y_{t-i} and cross-products of the powers of y_{t-i} and y_{t-j}. As a Taylor series approximation, the GAR model is capable of mimicking a wide variety of functional forms—all that is required is that the function be differentiable. Moreover, the model is easy to estimate; simply form the variables y_{t-i}^j and their cross-products and estimate the model using OLS. A test for nonlinearity can be carried out directly since the linear model is nested with the GAR model. If it is not possible to reject the null hypothesis that all values of $a_{ijkl} = 0$, it can be concluded that the process is linear. On the downside, the resulting model is likely to be overparameterized. This is especially true if the number of lags in the model is more than two. You can use traditional t-tests and F-tests to pare down the number of parameters estimated. Alternatively, you can use model selection criteria such as the AIC or SBC.

The Bilinear Model

Just as a parsimonious ARMA model can well-approximate a high-order AR(p) process, it is possible to use moving average terms in a nonlinear model. Consider the simple bilinear (BL) model:

$$y_t = \alpha_0 + \alpha_1 y_{t-1} + \beta_1 \varepsilon_{t-1} + c_1 \varepsilon_{t-1} y_{t-1} + \varepsilon_t$$

The intent is to use moving average terms and the interactions of autoregressive and MA terms to approximate a high-order GAR model. As such, bilinear models are a natural extension of ARMA models in that they add the cross products of y_{t-i} and ε_{t-j} to account for nonlinearity. The general form of the bilinear model BL (p, q, r, s) is

$$y_t = \alpha_0 + \sum_{i=1}^{p} \alpha_i y_{t-i} + \varepsilon_t + \sum_{i=1}^{q} \beta_i \varepsilon_{t-i} + \sum_{i=1}^{r}\sum_{j=1}^{s} c_{ij} y_{t-i}\varepsilon_{t-j} \qquad (7.5)$$

Notice that the linear ARMA(p, q) model is nested within (7.5); if all values of $c_{ij} = 0$, (7.5) is identical to an ARMA(p, q) model. As with the GAR model, the bilinear model can be viewed as having stochastic parameter variation. To understand the point, consider the BL model:

$$y_t = \alpha_0 + \alpha_1 y_{t-1} + c_1 y_{t-1}\varepsilon_{t-1} + \varepsilon_t$$

so that

$$y_t = \alpha_0 + (\alpha_1 + c_1 \varepsilon_{t-1}) y_{t-1} + \varepsilon_t \qquad (7.6)$$

Equation (7.6) looks like an autoregressive model except for the fact that the autoregressive coefficient is $\alpha_1 + c_1\varepsilon_{t-1}$. In a sense, the autoregressive coefficient is a random variable with a mean equal to α_1. If c_1 is positive, the autoregressive coefficient will increase with ε_{t-1}. In this way positive ε_{t-1} shocks will be more persistent than negative shocks.

Now for a little quiz. You cannot use OLS to estimate (7.5) since you cannot directly form the variables $y_{t-i}\varepsilon_{t-j}$. The question is: If you have the single time series

$\{y_t\}$, how can you estimate the series as a bilinear process? The standard procedure is to use maximum likelihood estimation. Many of the standard econometric software packages allow you to perform the estimation using a straightforward generalization of the method developed in Appendix 1 of Chapter 2 for the estimation of an MA process.

An Example

Rothman (1998) compared the in-sample fit and out-of-sample forecasting performance of a number of nonlinear models of the U.S. unemployment rate. Toward this end, he detrended the log of the unemployment rate and estimated the following three models over the 1948:Q1 to 1979:Q4 period:

AR $\quad u_t = 1.563u_{t-1} - 0.670u_{t-2} + \varepsilon_t$
$\qquad\quad$ (22.46) $\quad$ (−10.06)

GAR $\quad u_t = 1.500u_{t-1} - 0.553u_{t-2} - 0.745u_{t-2}^3 + \varepsilon_t \qquad$ variance ratio = 0.965
$\qquad\quad$ (23.60) $\qquad$ (−6.72) $\qquad$ (−2.33)

BL $\quad u_t = 1.910u_{t-1} - 0.690u_{t-2} - 0.585u_{t-1}\varepsilon_{t-3} + \varepsilon_t \qquad$ variance ratio = 0.936
$\qquad\quad$ (24.11) $\qquad$ (−10.55) $\qquad$ (−2.08)

where: $\qquad\qquad u_t$ = the detrended log of the unemployment rate
$\qquad$ *variance ratio* = the ratio of the residual variance of the estimated model to the residual variance of the AR model

The AIC was used to select the most appropriate values of p and q from the general class of ARMA(p, q) models. The AR(2) specification yielded the best fit from the class of linear ARMA models. A general specification search within the class of GAR models was undertaken and the AIC was used to select the one with the best fit. Simply, for the given lag length of two, all models of the form given by (7.4) were estimated and the one with the lowest AIC was retained. Notice that only the cubic term on the second lag of the unemployment rate was deemed to be important. Since the GAR model incorporates the AR(2) models as a special case, it is not surprising that it has a smaller residual variance. As Rothman indicates, it is instructive to write the estimated GAR model as

$$u_t = 1.500u_{t-1} - [0.553 + 0.745u_{t-2}^2]u_{t-2} + \varepsilon_t$$

In this form, the GAR model can be viewed as an AR(2) process such that the coefficient on the second lag is $-[0.553 + 0.745u_{t-2}^2]$. As such, large deviations from trend unemployment (so that u_{t-2}^2 is large) are associated with lower autoregressive persistence then small deviations from trend. As such, the speed of adjustment is faster when unemployment is far from its trend value than when it is close to the trend. Hence, the speed of adjustment is opposite to that of gravitational attraction. As an exercise, you should sketch the phase diagram for this adjustment process and compare your answer to Panel (*b*) of Figure 7.1.

Of the three models, the BL model has the smallest residual variance. The general BL model in the form of (7.5) was estimated for various values of r and s. Again the AIC was used to select the best fitting model from this class. Notice that the estimated bilinear model uses the cross-product $u_{t-1}\varepsilon_{t-3}$ even though the linear model contains only two lags (i.e., r and s were allowed to exceed the order of the linear portion of the equation). Rothman indicates that u_{t-1} and ε_{t-3} are positively correlated. Since the coefficient on $u_{t-1}\varepsilon_{t-3}$ is negative, large shocks to the unemployment rate imply a faster speed of adjustment than small shocks. As u_{t-1} and ε_{t-3} tend to move together, the larger $u_{t-1}\varepsilon_{t-3}$, the smaller is the degree of persistence.

3. THRESHOLD AUTOREGRESSIVE MODELS

A **regime switching model** allows the behavior of $\{y_t\}$ to depend on the state of the system. In a recession, the unemployment rate is likely to rise sharply and then slowly decline to its long-run value. However, the unemployment rate does not fall sharply in an economic expansion. As such, the dynamic adjustment equation for the unemployment rate depends on whether the economy is in an expansionary state (or regime) or in a recession. When the economy changes from an expansionary regime to a contractionary regime, the dynamic adjustment of the unemployment rate is likely to change. In other circumstances, regime switches might be due to the magnitude of the variable of interest, the result of an election that changes the behavior of policymakers, or may be completely unobservable. As you might expect, a number of regime switching models have been developed to analyze these types of regime changes.

Before proceeding, you need to know that most regime switching models can be quite difficult to estimate. Although many software packages allow you to estimate a linear model by appropriately clicking on a menu, this is not true for nonlinear models. In general, you need to use a statistical package that has its own programming language if you want to estimate a regime-switching model. A simple threshold autoregressive (TAR) model can be estimated using OLS. Other models with thresholds need to be estimated using nonlinear least squares or maximum likelihood methods. The artificial neural network and Markov switching models require methods that are more sophisticated. As such, discussion in the text emphasizes the threshold models. The programming manual that accompanies this text has a number of examples.

Models with Thresholds

Panel (a) of Figure 7.1 illustrates a simple TAR process. Recall that the degree of autoregressive persistence is a_1 when $y_{t-1} > 0$ and a_2 when $y_{t-1} \le 0$. As in equation (7.1), if we include a disturbance term, the behavior of the $\{y_t\}$ sequence can be represented by

$$y_t = \begin{cases} a_1 y_{t-1} + \varepsilon_{1t} & \text{if } y_{t-1} > 0 \\ a_2 y_{t-1} + \varepsilon_{2t} & \text{if } y_{t-1} \le 0 \end{cases} \tag{7.7}$$

You can think of the equation $y_{t-1} = 0$ as being a threshold. On one side of the threshold, the $\{y_t\}$ sequence is governed by one autoregressive process and on the other side of the threshold, there is a different autoregressive process. Although $\{y_t\}$ is linear in each regime, the possibility of regime switching means that the entire $\{y_t\}$ sequence is nonlinear. Shocks to $\{\varepsilon_{1t}\}$ or $\{\varepsilon_{2t}\}$ are responsible for regime switching. If, for example, $y_{t-1} > 0$, the subsequent values of the sequence will tend to decay toward zero at the rate a_1. However, a negative realization of ε_{1t} can cause y_t to fall by such an extent that it lies below the threshold. In the negative regime, the behavior of the process is governed by $y_t = a_2 y_{t-1} + \varepsilon_{2t}$. As you can infer, the larger the variance of $\{\varepsilon_{1t}\}$, the more likely is a switch from the positive regime to the negative regime.

Another common variant of the TAR model is to assume that the variances of the two error terms are equal [i.e., $\text{var}(\varepsilon_{1t}) = \text{var}(\varepsilon_{2t})$]. In this circumstance, (7.7) can be written as

$$y_t = a_1 I_t y_{t-1} + a_2 (1 - I_t) y_{t-1} + \varepsilon_t \tag{7.8}$$

where $I_t = 1$ if $y_{t-1} > 0$ and $I_t = 0$ if $y_{t-1} \leq 0$.

In equation (7.8), I_t is an indicator function, or dummy variable, that takes on the value of 1 if y_{t-1} is above the threshold and a value of 0 otherwise. When $y_{t-1} > 0$, $I_t = 1$ and $(1 - I_t) = 0$, so that (7.8) is equivalent to $a_1 y_{t-1} + \varepsilon_t$. When $y_{t-1} \leq 0$, $I_t = 0$, and $(1 - I_t) = 1$, so that (7.8) is equivalent to $a_2 y_{t-1} + \varepsilon_t$. Figure 7.2 provides a visual comparison of the AR, GAR, BL, and TAR models. A series of 200 random numbers were drawn from a standardized normal distribution so as to simulate the $\{\varepsilon_t\}$ sequence. The initial value y_1 was set equal to ε_1 and the next 199 values of $\{y_t\}$ were created according to the formula

$$y_t = 0.7 y_{t-1} + \varepsilon_t$$

Panel (a) of Figure 7.2 shows the time path of this simulated AR(1) process. Notice that the series fluctuates around a mean of zero. Although it may not be possible to

FIGURE 7.2   Comparison of Linear and Nonlinear Processes

discern with visual inspection alone, the degree of autoregressive decay is always the same; on average, 70 percent of the current value of y_t persists into the next period. Next, the same random numbers were used to generate the GAR process:

$$y_t = 0.7y_{t-1} - 0.06y_{t-1}^2 + \varepsilon_t$$

or

$$y_t = [0.7 - 0.06y_{t-1}]\,y_{t-1} + \varepsilon_t$$

The nature of this particular GAR process is that it behaves as an AR(1) process with a random coefficient. The greater is the value of y_{t-1}, the smaller is the autoregressive coefficient. For values of $y_{t-1} = -2$, 0, and 2, the degrees of autoregressive persistence are 0.82, 0.7, and 0.58, respectively. This pattern can be seen in Panel (b) of Figure 7.2 because negative values of the simulated GAR process are far more persistent than positive values. Compare Panels (a) and (b) and note the values of the two series surrounding period 55. You can clearly see that the GAR series returns to its mean far more slowly than the AR series.

The identical random numbers were used to construct the BL sequence shown in Panel (c). After initializing $y_1 = \varepsilon_1$, the remaining values of the sequence were generated from

$$y_t = 0.7y_{t-1} - 0.3y_{t-1}\varepsilon_{t-1} + \varepsilon_t$$

or

$$y_t = [0.7 - 0.3\varepsilon_{t-1}]\,y_{t-1} + \varepsilon_t$$

In the BL model, the degree of persistence depends on the value of ε_{t-1}; the larger is ε_{t-1}, the smaller the degree of persistence. In fact, for those periods in which $\varepsilon_{t-1} < -1.0$, the sequence behaves like an explosive process (since the value of $0.7 - 0.3\varepsilon_{t-1}$ exceeds unity). In Panel (c), you can see the extreme movements in the BL process if you examine the time interval that surrounds period 55. Nevertheless, the successive values of ε_t are more likely to exceed -1, so the BL process does not continue its decline.

Panel (d) of Figure 7.2 illustrates the time path of the TAR process

$$y_t = 0.3I_t y_{t-1} + 0.7(1 - I_t)y_{t-1} + \varepsilon_t$$

where $I_t = 1$ if $y_{t-1} > 0$ and $I_t = 0$ otherwise.

When $y_{t-1} \leq 0$, this TAR process behaves exactly like the AR(1) process shown in Panel (a). Thus, the lower portions of Panels (a) and (d) are nearly identical. However, for the TAR process, only 30 percent of the current value of y_t tends to persist into the subsequent period when $y_{t-1} > 0$. Hence, in contrast to the AR(1) process of Panel (a), the TAR process displays a substantial degree of mean reversion whenever $y_{t-1} > 0$.

In actuality, the TAR models developed by Tong (1983, 1990) allow for a number of different regimes with separate higher-order AR(p) processes in each regime. A more general version of equation (7.7) is the two-regime TAR model:

$$y_t = \begin{cases} \alpha_{10} + \alpha_{11}y_{t-1} + \dots + \alpha_{1p}y_{t-p} + \varepsilon_{1t} & \text{if } y_{t-1} > \tau \\ \alpha_{20} + \alpha_{21}y_{t-1} + \dots + \alpha_{2r}y_{t-r} + \varepsilon_{2t} & \text{if } y_{t-1} \leq \tau \end{cases} \tag{7.9}$$

In (7.9), there are two separate regimes defined by the value of y_{t-1}. Unlike the TAR models depicted in Figures 7.1 and 7.2, the value of the threshold τ can differ from zero. Moreover, the particular phase diagram shown in the figure was a special type of TAR model in that it is continuous. The specification in equation (7.9) allows the two segments of the phase diagram to be discontinuous at the threshold.

If τ is known, the estimation of a TAR model is straightforward. Separate the observations according to whether y_{t-1} is above or below the threshold. Each segment of (7.9) can then be estimated using OLS. The lag lengths p and r can be determined as in an AR model. Hence, you can determine the lag lengths using t-tests on the individual coefficients, F-tests on groups of coefficients, or the AIC and/or SBC. A simple numerical example might be helpful. Suppose that the first seven observations of a time series are as follows:

t	1	2	3	4	5	6	7
y_t	0.5	0.3	−0.2	0.0	−0.5	0.4	0.6
y_{t-1}	NA	0.5	0.3	−0.2	0.0	−0.5	0.4

If you know that the threshold is zero, sort the observations into two groups according to whether y_{t-1} is greater than or less than zero. Since values when $y_{t-1} = 0$ are included with those when $y_{t-1} < 0$, the two regimes would look like this:

Positive		Negative	
y_t	y_{t-1}	y_t	y_{t-1}
0.3	0.5	0.0	−0.2
−0.2	0.3	−0.5	0.0
0.6	0.4	0.4	−0.5

The two separate AR(1) processes can be estimated for each regime. For each (y_t, y_{t-1}) pair, the first regression would use (0.3, 0.5), (−0.2, 0.3), and (0.6, 0.4) and the second regression would use (0.0, −0.2), (−0.5, 0.0), and (0.4, −0.5). It is only a bit more complicated to estimate an AR(2) model for each regime. For an AR(2), the first regression would use the (y_t, y_{t-1}, y_{t-2}) values (−0.2, 0.3, 0.5) and (0.6, 0.4, −0.5) and the second regression would use (0.0, −0.2, 0.3), (−0.5, 0.0, −0.2), and (0.4, −0.5, 0.0).

If we restrict $\text{var}(\varepsilon_{1t}) = \text{var}(\varepsilon_{2t})$, we can rewrite (7.9) as

$$y_t = I_t \left[\alpha_{10} + \sum_{i=1}^{p} \alpha_{1i} y_{t-i} \right] + (1 - I_t) \left[\alpha_{20} + \sum_{i=1}^{r} \alpha_{2i} y_{t-i} \right] + \varepsilon_t \tag{7.10}$$

where $I_t = 1$ if $y_{t-1} > \tau$ and $I_t = 0$ if $y_{t-1} \leq \tau$.

When $y_{t-1} > 0$, $I_t = 1$ and $(1 - I_t) = 0$, so that (7.10) is equivalent to $\alpha_{10} + \alpha_{11} y_{t-1} + \ldots + \alpha_{1p} y_{t-p} + \varepsilon_t$. When $y_{t-1} \leq 0$, $I_t = 0$ and $(1 - I_t) = 1$, so that (7.10) is equivalent to $\alpha_{20} + \alpha_{21} y_{t-1} + \ldots + \alpha_{2r} y_{t-r} + \varepsilon_t$. Thus, to estimate a TAR model in the form of (7.10), create the indicator function and form the variables $I_t y_{t-i}$ and $(1 - I_t) y_{t-i}$. You can then estimate the equation using OLS. In terms of the seven observations from the numerical example, suppose that you want to estimate (7.7) using a value of $\tau = 0$. You should be able to verify that the time path of the indicator function I_t and the values of $I_t y_{t-1}$, $I_t y_{t-2}$, $(1 - I_t)y_{t-1}$, and $(1 - I_t)y_{t-2}$ are those shown in the table.

t	1	2	3	4	5	6	7
y_t	0.5	0.3	-0.2	0.0	-0.5	0.4	0.6
y_{t-1}	NA	0.5	0.3	-0.2	0.0	-0.5	0.4
y_{t-2}	NA	NA	0.5	0.3	-0.2	0.0	-0.5
I_t	NA	1	1	0.0	0.0	0.0	1
$I_t y_{t-1}$	NA	0.5	0.3	0.0	0.0	0.0	1
$(1 - I_t)y_{t-1}$	NA	0.0	0.0	-0.2	0.0	-0.5	0
$I_t y_{t-2}$	NA	NA	0.5	0.0	0.0	0.0	-0.5
$(1 - I_t)y_{t-2}$	NA	NA	0.0	0.3	-0.3	0.0	0.0

To estimate a model using one lag in each regime, you estimate a model using the four variables I_t, $(1 - I_t)$, $I_t y_{t-1}$ and $(1 - I_t)y_{t-1}$. To estimate a model with two lags in each regime, you estimate the six values of α_{ij} from the regression equation

$$y_t = \alpha_{10}I_t + \alpha_{11}I_t y_{t-1} + \alpha_{12}I_t y_{t-2} + \alpha_{20}(1 - I_t) + \alpha_{21}(1 - I_t)y_{t-1} + \alpha_{22}(1 - I_t)y_{t-2} + \varepsilon_t$$

Hence, when $y_{t-1} > 0$, $I_t = 1$ and $(1 - I_t) = 0$, so that

$$y_t = \alpha_{10} + \alpha_{11}y_{t-1} + \alpha_{12}y_{t-2} + \varepsilon_t$$

Similarly, when $y_{t-1} \leq 0$, $I_t = 0$ and $(1 - I_t) = 1$, so that

$$y_t = \alpha_{20} + \alpha_{21}y_{t-1} + \alpha_{22}y_{t-2} + \varepsilon_t$$

Regardless of whether you restrict the residual variances to be equal, OLS gives consistent estimates of the intercept and slope coefficients conditional on the threshold being correct.

Unknown Threshold

In most instances, the value of the threshold is unknown and must be estimated along with the other parameters of the TAR model. Fortunately, Chan (1993) shows how to obtain a super-consistent estimate of the threshold τ. To best explain the logic of the procedure, the TAR series shown in Panel (*d*) of Figure 7.2 is reproduced in Figure 7.3. If the threshold is to be meaningful, the series must actually cross the threshold. It would be nonsense to use a threshold of four to estimate the TAR model since the series never crosses that threshold. Thus, τ must lie between the maximum and minimum values of the series. In practice, the highest and lowest 15 percent of the values are excluded from the search to ensure an adequate number of observations on each side of the threshold. Your estimates will be very imprecise if, for example, one regime has only twenty observations. If you have a very large number of observations, you may want to exclude only the highest and lowest 10 percent of the observations as potential thresholds.

In the example at hand, τ should lie within the band containing the middle 70 percent of the observations. Each data point within the band has the potential to be the threshold. Thus, try a value of $\tau = y_1$ (i.e., the first observation in the band) and estimate

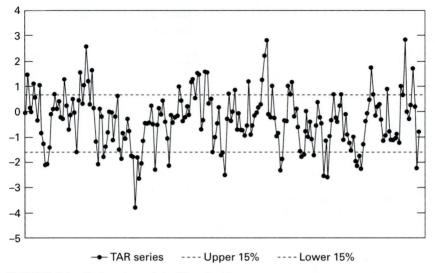

FIGURE 7.3   Estimation of the Threshold

an equation in the form of (7.9) or (7.10). As you can see in the figure, y_2 lies outside the band. Hence, there is no need to estimate a regression using $\tau = y_2$. Next, estimate TAR models using $\tau = y_3$ and $\tau = y_4$ since these two values lie within the band. Continue in this fashion for each observation within the band. With 200 observations, there should be 141 estimates of the TAR model. The regression containing the smallest residual sum of squares contains the consistent estimate of the threshold.

Now you can see why you need to use a software package that contains a programming language. Instead of estimating the 141 equations one at a time, as illustrated in the Programming Manual, you could embed the estimations within a Do-End loop or a For-Next loop.

Rothman's (1998) TAR estimate of the U.S. unemployment rate tells an interesting story. His two-regime model in the form of (7.9) is

$$u_t = 0.0529 + 1.349u_{t-1} - 0.665u_{t-2} + \varepsilon_{1t} \quad \text{if } u_{t-1} \geq 0.062$$
$$\quad (3.46) \quad (16.03) \quad \quad (-9.37)$$

$$u_t = 1.646u_{t-1} - 0.733u_{t-2} + \varepsilon_{2t} \quad \quad \quad \text{if } u_{t-1} < 0.062$$
$$\quad (14.27) \quad \quad (-6.37)$$

There is a high-unemployment and a low-unemployment regime separated by the value $u_{t-1} = 0.062$. Rothman notes that unemployment is more persistent in the high-unemployment regime than the low-unemployment regime in that shocks that increase unemployment do not readily decay to zero. The variance ratio for the TAR model is 0.942. As measured by the residual sum of squares, the TAR model fits the data better than the AR(2) and GAR models, but not as well as the BL model. Notice that the estimated AR(2), GAR, BL, and TAR models contain 2, 3, 3, and 6 parameters (remember that τ is an estimated parameter in the TAR model). As such, a different pattern emerges if AIC is used to select the most appropriate model. The BL model has the lowest value of the AIC followed by the AR, GAR, and TAR models. Based on the AIC, most applied econometricians would discard the TAR model.

4. EXTENSIONS AND OTHER NONLINEAR MODELS

Note that there is something very different about the TAR model versus the GAR and BL models. The latter two are designed to be useful when the functional form of the nonlinear process is unknown. Usually, there is no particular reason why a squared or cubed term should be included in the analysis for any reason other than the fit. In contrast, the TAR model posits a type of adjustment mechanism that corresponds to the state of the economic system. This has lead to a growing popularity of TAR models and a number of interesting extensions.

Selecting the Delay Parameter

In the TAR models considered thus far, the regime is determined by the value of y_{t-1}. However, it might be that the timing of the adjustment process is such that it takes more than one period for the regime switch to occur. In such circumstances, we could allow the regime switch to occur according to the value of y_{t-d} where $d = 1, 2, 3, \ldots$. Thus, the system would be in regime 1 if $y_{t-d} > \tau$ and in regime 2 if $y_{t-d} \leq \tau$. There are several procedures available to select the value of the **delay parameter** d. The standard procedure is to estimate a TAR model for each potential value of d. The one with the smallest value of the residual sum of squares contains the most appropriate value of the delay parameter. Alternatively, you can choose the delay parameter that leads to the smallest value of the AIC or the SBC. This second approach is most useful when the optimal values for p and r (i.e., the lag lengths in the various regimes) depend on the choice of d.

Multiple Regimes

In some instances, it may be reasonable to assume that there are more than two regimes. The introductory section to this section discussed the following TAR model of the interest rate spread:

$$s_t = \begin{cases} \bar{s} + a_1(s_{t-1} - \bar{s}) + \varepsilon_t & \text{when } s_{t-1} > \bar{s} \\ \bar{s} + a_2(s_{t-1} - \bar{s}) + \varepsilon_t & \text{when } s_{t-1} \leq \bar{s} \end{cases}$$

Now suppose that there is a transaction cost c that prevents complete adjustment of the spread to $\bar{s}$. If the gap between s_{t-1} and $\bar{s}$ is less than the cost of undertaking the transaction, it would not be profitable to switch funds between the securities. As such, there may be a neutral band within which the spread may fluctuate. Within this band, there are no economic incentives to act in a way that equates the spread with $\bar{s}$. Outside of the band, however, there may be strong incentives for individuals to act in a way that drives the spread toward $\bar{s}$. A simple way to model this behavior is with the **band-TAR** model:

$$s_t = \bar{s} + a_1(s_{t-1} - \bar{s}) + \varepsilon_t \quad \text{when } s_{t-1} > \bar{s} + c$$
$$s_t = s_{t-1} + \varepsilon_t \quad\quad\quad\quad\quad \text{when } \bar{s} - c < s_{t-1} \leq \bar{s} + c$$
$$s_t = \bar{s} + a_2(s_{t-1} - \bar{s}) + \varepsilon_t \quad \text{when } s_{t-1} \leq \bar{s} - c$$

For this specification, there tends to be no tendency for mean reversion unless s_{t-1} lies outside of the neutral band formed by adding and subtracting the transaction cost from the long-run value of the spread. Hence, inside the band, the behavior of the spread is a random walk. Balke and Fomby (1997) use this type of band threshold process to estimate a model of the term structure of interest rates.

In a more general multiple regime model, each regime can be represented by a distinct autoregressive process. As shown in Section 5, a number of graphical techniques can be used to detect the presence of multiple thresholds.

Regression Models

It has also become popular to use a threshold in the context of a traditional regression model. Consider the following specification:

$$y_t = a_0 + (a_1 + b_1 I_t) x_t + \varepsilon_t$$

where $I_t = 1$ if $y_{t-1} > \tau$ and $I_t = 0$ otherwise.

Here, $a_1 + b_1$ measures the effect of x_t on y_t when $y_{t-1} > \tau$. When $y_{t-1} \leq \tau$, the effect of x_t on y_t is a_1. You can estimate the value of the threshold using Chan's method described above. For example, Shen and Hakes (1995) estimate a nonlinear reaction function for the central band of Taiwan. The idea is that the central bank will respond differently to changes in economic variables in a high inflationary environment than in a low inflationary environment. Similarly, Galbraith (1996) shows that for Canada and the United States, the effect of money on output depends on whether credit conditions are already tight or loose.

Smooth Transition Models

For some processes, it may not seem reasonable to assume that the threshold is sharp. Instead the speed of adjustment may be the type of nonlinear process shown in Panel (*b*) of Figure 7.1. Smooth transition autoregressive (STAR) models allow the autoregressive parameters to change slowly. Consider the special NLAR model given by

$$y_t = \alpha_0 + \alpha_1 y_{t-1} + \beta_1 y_{t-1} f(y_{t-1}) + \varepsilon_t$$

If $f(\ )$ is a smooth continuous function, the autoregressive coefficient $(\alpha_1 + \beta_1)$ will change smoothly along with the value of y_{t-1}. There are two particularly useful forms of the STAR model that allow for a varying degree of autoregressive decay. The logistic–STAR (LSTAR) model generalizes the standard autoregressive model such that the autoregressive coefficient is a logistic function:

$$y_t = \alpha_0 + \alpha_1 y_{t-1} + \dots + \alpha_p y_{t-p} + \theta [\beta_0 + \beta_1 y_{t-1} + \dots + \beta_p y_{t-p}] + \varepsilon_t \quad (7.11)$$

where $\theta = [1 + \exp(-\gamma(y_{t-1} - c))]^{-1}$.

Note that γ is called the *smoothness* parameter. In the limit, as $\gamma \to 0$ or ∞, the LSTAR model becomes an $AR(p)$ model since the value of θ is constant. For intermediate values of γ, the degree of autoregressive decay depends on the value of y_{t-1}. As $y_{t-1} \to -\infty$, $\theta \to 0$ so that the behavior of y_t is given by $\alpha_0 + \alpha_1 y_{t-1} + \dots + \alpha_p y_{t-p} + \varepsilon_t$. Similarly, as $y_{t-1} \to +\infty$, $\theta \to 1$ so that the behavior of y_t is given by $(\alpha_0 + \beta_0) +$

$(\alpha_1 + \beta_1)y_{t-1} + \ldots + \varepsilon_t$. Thus, the intercept and the autoregressive coefficients smoothly change between these two extremes as the value of y_{t-1} changes.

The exponential form of the model (ESTAR) replaces (7.11) with

$$\theta = 1 - \exp\left[-\gamma(y_{t-1} - c)^2\right] \quad \gamma > 0$$

For the ESTAR model, as γ approaches zero or infinity, the model becomes an AR(p) model since θ is constant. Otherwise, the model displays nonlinear behavior. Notice that the coefficients for the ESTAR model are symmetric around $y_{t-1} = c$. As y_{t-1} approaches c, θ approaches 0 so that the behavior of y_t is given by $\alpha_0 + \alpha_1 y_{t-1} + \ldots + \alpha_p y_{t-p} + \varepsilon_t$. As y_{t-1} moves further from c, θ approaches 1 so that the behavior of y_t is given by $(\alpha_0 + \beta_0) + (\alpha_1 + \beta_1)y_{t-1} + \ldots + \varepsilon_t$. The ESTAR model has proven to be useful for periods surrounding the turning points of a series (i.e., periods in which y_{t-1}^2 will be extreme) in that such periods have different degrees of autoregressive decay than others. Notice that the ESTAR model is symmetric around $y_{t-1} = c$ so that it can approximate gravitational attraction as in Figure 7.1.

Michael, Nobay, and Peel (1997) make the point that transactions costs are an important feature of international trade. Such costs may include the purchase of foreign exchange or forward cover, the payment of tariffs and import licensing fees, and transportation costs. As in the band–TAR model, small deviations from PPP will not be corrected through the process of commodity arbitrage. Larger discrepancies are expected to be mean-reverting such that speed of adjustment is an increasing function of the size of the discrepancy. The idea is that very large discrepancies are quickly eliminated but mid-size discrepancies are eliminated more slowly.

This type of behavior can be captured by an ESTAR process. The particular form of the ESTAR model they consider is

$$\Delta y_t = \alpha_0 + a_1 y_{t-1} + \sum_{i=1}^{p-1} \alpha_i \Delta y_{t-i}$$

$$+ \left[1 - \exp(-\gamma(y_{t-d} - c)^2)\right]\left(\beta_0 + b_1 y_{t-1} + \sum_{i=1}^{p-1} \beta_i \Delta y_{t-i}\right) + \varepsilon_t$$

where y_t is the real exchange rate.

When $y_{t-d} = c$, the adjustment process is given by

$$\Delta y_t = \alpha_0 + a_1 y_{t-1} + \sum_{i=1}^{p-1} \alpha_i \Delta y_{t-i} + \varepsilon_t$$

and as $y_{t-d} \to \pm\infty$, the adjustment process is given by

$$\Delta y_t = (\alpha_0 + \beta_0) + (a_1 + b_1)y_{t-1} + \sum_{i=1}^{p-1} (\alpha_i + \beta_i)\Delta y_{t-i} + \varepsilon_t$$

The nature of transactions costs implies that a_1 may be very small (or zero). After all, when $y_{t-d} \approx c$, there is little incentive to arbitrage the market. However, since large deviations are mean reverting, b_1 should be negative. The specific testing strategy is discussed in Section 6. For now, it is sufficient to report their model for the United States–United Kingdom real exchange rate over the 201-year period 1791 to 1992 (with t-statistics in parentheses) is

$$\Delta y_t = 0.40 \Delta y_{t-1} + [1 - \exp(-532.4(y_{t-1} - 0.038)^2](-y_{t-1} + 0.59 \Delta y_{t-2} + 0.57 \Delta y_{t-4} - 0.017)$$
$$\quad\; (3.37) \qquad\qquad\qquad\quad (2.44) \quad\;\; (7.21) \qquad\qquad (3.90) \qquad (2.89) \qquad (5.17)$$

The point estimates imply that when the real rate is near 0.038, there is no tendency for mean reversion since $a_1 = 0$. However, when $(y_{t-1} - 0.038)^2$ is very large, the speed of adjustment coefficient is quite rapid. Hence, the adjustment of the real exchange rate is consistent with the presence of transaction costs.

The Artificial Neural Network

The artificial neural network (ANN) can be useful for nonlinear processes that have an unknown functional form. The simple form of the ANN model is

$$y_t = a_0 + a_1 y_{t-1} + \sum_{i=1}^{n} \alpha_i f_i(y_{t-1}) + \varepsilon_t \qquad (7.12)$$

where the function $f_i(y_{t-1})$ is a cumulative distribution or a logistic function such as that in (7.11). For the case of the logistic function, we can write

$$y_t = a_0 + a_1 y_{t-1} + \sum_{i=1}^{n} \alpha_i [1 + \exp(-\gamma_i(y_{t-1} - c_i))]^{-1} + \varepsilon_t$$

Although the ANN is very similar to the LSTAR model, there are some important differences. First, the ANN allows only the intercept to be time-varying; the autoregressive coefficient a_1 is constant. As such, the level of the series is changing over time. Second, the ANN uses n different logistic functions (called **nodes**). Kuan and White (1994) prove that, for sufficiently large n, this type of model can approximate any first-order nonlinear model arbitrarily closely. As such, the ANN is particularly useful for estimating nonlinear relationships that are difficult to fit.

Although the model can fit the data extraordinarily well, there is an obvious difficulty in that the model does not have a clear economic interpretation. Since the ANN can be extended to high-order autoregressive processes, it can have an extremely large number of parameters. As such, there is a danger of overfitting the data. If you let n become too large (i.e., if you use too many nodes) you will wind up fitting the noise component of the data. The fact that $R^2 \to 1$ as n grows increasingly large should not be especially comforting if the goal is to forecast subsequent values of the series. Many researchers would select the value of n using the parsimonious SBC.

Notice that the parameters are not globally identified for $n > 1$. Numerical optimization routines have difficulty finding the parameter values that minimize the sum of squared residuals since many local minima often exist. To circumvent the problem, a number of different routines are used to estimate the parameter values. Although the details are not necessary for our purposes, it is instructive to consider the "recursive learning" method discussed in White (1989). Suppose you use the first t observations of your data set to obtain the nonlinear least squares estimates of the parameters. Let $\hat{\theta}_t$ denote the vector of estimated parameters using these t observations and let $\hat{y}_{t+1}$ denote the predicted value y_{t+1}. The value of $\hat{\theta}_t$ acts as an initial condition in the difference equation:

$$\hat{\theta}_{t+1} = \hat{\theta}_t + \eta_t (y_{t+1} - \hat{y}_{t+1})$$

where η_t is generally taken to be a multiple of vector of partial derivatives of (7.12) with respect to the parameters evaluated at the point estimates of θ_t. The successive values of $\hat{\theta}_{t+1}$ are obtained until all the parameter estimates converge.

We can follow White (1989) and explore the ability of the ANN to mimic **chaos**. A sequence $\{y_t\}$ is said to be chaotic if it is generated from a deterministic difference equation such that it does not explode or converge to a constant or to a repetitive cycle. Thus, the sequence may appear to be random even though it is completely deterministic. In particular, let $y_1 = y_2 = 0.5$ and suppose that the next 98 values of the $\{y_t\}$ sequence are generated according to

$$y_t = 1 - 1.4 y_{t-1}^2 + 0.3 y_{t-2}$$

The actual and fitted values of the series are shown in Figure 7.4. Although just two nodes were used to estimate the series, the fit of the ANN is quite reasonable. The example illustrates the point that the ANN is capable of capturing a highly nonlinear process when the functional form is completely unknown.

The Markov Switching Model

The basic threshold model allows the regime switch to depend on the magnitude of an observable variable. If y_{t-d} exceeds some threshold value, the system is in regime

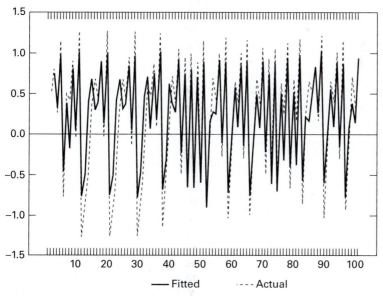

FIGURE 7.4 The ANN Fitted to Chaos

one; otherwise, the system is in regime two. Although regime switching is more gradual in the STAR and ANN models, the adjustment process depends on the current
state of the system. In contrast, the Markov switching model developed by Hamilton
(1989) posits that regime switches are exogenous. To take a simple example, suppose
there are two regimes (or states of the world) and that the autoregressive process for
y_t is regime-dependent. In particular, let

$$y_t = a_{10} + a_1 y_{t-1} + \varepsilon_{1t} \qquad \text{if the system is in regime 1}$$
$$y_t = a_{20} + a_2 y_{t-1} + \varepsilon_{2t} \qquad \text{if the system is in regime 2}$$

At this point, the model looks very much like a TAR model of (7.7) in that the
autoregressive coefficient is a_1 in regime 1 and a_2 in regime 2. However, in contrast
to the TAR model, there are fixed probabilities of a regime change. If p_{11} denotes the
probability that the system remains in regime one, $(1 - p_{11})$ denotes the probability
that the system switches from regime one to regime two. Similarly, if p_{22} denotes the
probability that the system remains in regime two, $(1 - p_{22})$ is the probability that the
system switches from regime two to regime one. Thus, the switching process is actually a first-order Markov process. No attempt is made to explain the reason that
regime changes occur and no attempt is made to explain the timing of such changes.
There are several important features of the Markov switching model:

1. Since the transition probabilities (i.e., p_{11} and p_{22}) are unknown, they need
    to be estimated along with the coefficients of the two autoregressive
    processes. As in the TAR model, if one of the regimes rarely occurs, the
    coefficients for that regime will be poorly estimated.

2. The overall degree of persistence depends on the autoregressive parame-
    ters *and* the transition probabilities. For example, if $a_1 > a_2$ and p_{11} is
    large, the process will tend to remain in the regime with substantial autore-
    gressive persistence. Moreover if p_{22} is small, the system will have a ten-
    dency to switch into regime one from regime two.

3. The probabilities p_{11}, $(1 - p_{11})$, p_{22}, and $(1 - p_{22})$ are all *conditional* prob-
    abilities. For example, if the system is in regime two, $(1 - p_{22})$ is the con-
    ditional probability that the system switches into regime one. It is also of
    interest to calculate the *unconditional* probability that the system is in
    regime one (p_1) and in regime two (p_2). In Exercise 3 at the end of this
    chapter, you are asked to show that

$$p_1 = (1 - p_{22})/(2 - p_{11} - p_{22})$$
$$p_2 = (1 - p_{11})/(2 - p_{11} - p_{22})$$

Thus, if $p_{11} = 0.75$ and $p_{22} = 0.5$, $p_1 = 2/3$ and $p_2 = 1/3$.

Usually, Markov switching models are used to estimate the model for the mean
of a series. However, in an interesting study, Edwards and Susmel (2000) use a
regime-switching model to examine the interest rate volatility in emerging markets.
It is argued that the standard GARCH model is not applicable to emerging markets
because of the occurrence of large shocks. Although a GARCH model estimated
using a t-distribution could account for fat-tailed returns, such models will typically

predict too much volatility persistence. As illustrated in Chapter 3, the sum of the coefficients in a GARCH model is often close to unity. As an alternative, consider a three-state model containing a low-volatility regime, a moderate-volatility regime and a high-volatility regime. If the probability of switching out of a high-volatility state is large, high volatility does not need to be extremely persistent.

Edwards and Susmel use weekly interest rate data for Argentina, Brazil, Chile, Hong Kong, and Mexico. They begin by estimating an AR(1) equation for the model of the mean and a GARCH(1, 1) model for the variance. Consider the estimated set of equations for Brazil (with standard errors in parentheses) over the April 18, 1994, through April 16, 1999, period:

$$\Delta r_t = -0.0133 - 0.217\Delta r_{t-1} + \varepsilon_t$$
$$(0.04) \quad (0.10)$$

$$h_t = 0.058 + 1.321\varepsilon_{t-1}^2 + 0.395h_{t-1}$$
$$(0.03) \quad (0.25) \quad (0.05)$$

where r_t is the Brazilian short-term interest rate and h_t is the conditional variance. The model of the mean is in first differences since r_t is a unit root process.

Although the coefficients are significant at the 5 percent level, there is a disturbing feature of the model. Notice that the sum of the coefficients in the equation for h_t exceeds unity. As such, the model predicts that volatility is explosive. As an alternative, Edward and Susmel consider the volatility switching ARCH (SWARCH) model. The basic form of the model is

$$h_t / \gamma_s = \alpha_0 + \sum_{i=1}^{q} \alpha_i (\varepsilon_{t-i}^2 / \gamma_s)$$

where $s = 1$, 2 or 3 refers to the current state (i.e., low, moderate, or high).

Note that one of the values of γ_s must be normalized to equal unity. Moreover, if $\gamma_1 = 1$, the other values of γ_s measures the ratio of the conditional variance in state s relative to that in state 1. The estimated SWARCH model for Brazil is

$$\Delta r_t = -0.087 + 0.016\Delta r_{t-1} + \varepsilon_t$$
$$(0.03) \quad (0.05)$$

$$h_t / \gamma_s = 0.131 + 0.068\varepsilon_{t-1}^2 / \gamma_s$$
$$(0.03) \quad (0.10)$$

and

$$\gamma_1 = 1, \ \gamma_2 = 4.851, \text{ and } \gamma_3 = 128.51$$

It is striking that the high-volatility state is more than 128 times more volatile than the low-volatility state. Nevertheless, the probability of a switch from the high-volatility state to the other states was found to be high. Hence, the high-volatility state was found to be short-lived.

5. TESTING FOR NONLINEARITY

Before you begin a general specification search to find a model that fits your particular data set, it is important to test for the presence of nonlinearity. This section will present a number of procedures that have been developed to determine if the data seem to be nonlinear and to help to determine the form of the nonlinearity. Be forewarned that no set of tests can actually pin down the proper form of nonlinearity. Rather, the tests can only suggest the form of the nonlinearity.

The ACF and the McLeod–Li Test

In estimating an ARMA model, the autocorrelation function can help you select the proper values of p and q, and the ACF of the residuals is an important diagnostic tool. Unfortunately, the ACF as used in linear models may be misleading for nonlinear models. The reason is that the autocorrelation coefficients measure the degree of *linear* association between y_t and y_{t-i}. As such, the ACF may fail to detect important nonlinear relationships present in the data. Consider the following example:

$$y_t = \varepsilon_{t-1}^2 + \varepsilon_t \qquad (7.13)$$

where $\{\varepsilon_t\}$ is a normally distributed white-noise process.

Since y_{t-1} is a function of ε_{t-1}, the value of y_t is dependent on the value of y_{t-1}. Nevertheless, with a little bit of algebra, it is possible to show that all of the autocorrelations are equal to zero. To derive this result, call $\text{var}(\varepsilon_t) = \text{var}(\varepsilon_{t-i}) = \sigma^2$. If you take the conditional expectation of (7.13), it follows that $Ey_t = Ey_{t-1} = \sigma^2$. Thus, the autocorrelations are

$$\rho_i = E(y_t - \sigma^2)(y_{t-i} - \sigma^2)$$
$$= E(\varepsilon_{t-1}^2 + \varepsilon_t - \sigma^2)(\varepsilon_{t-1-i}^2 + \varepsilon_{t-i} - \sigma^2)$$
$$= E(\varepsilon_{t-1}^2 \varepsilon_{t-1-i}^2 + \varepsilon_{t-1}^2 \varepsilon_{t-i} - \varepsilon_{t-1}^2 \sigma^2 + \varepsilon_t \varepsilon_{t-1-i}^2$$
$$+ \varepsilon_t \varepsilon_{t-i} - \varepsilon_t \sigma^2 - \sigma^2 \varepsilon_{t-1-i}^2 - \sigma^2 \varepsilon_{t-i} + \sigma^2 \sigma^2)$$

Note that $E(\varepsilon_{t-i}^2 \varepsilon_{t-j}^2) = \sigma^2 \sigma^2$, $E(\varepsilon_t \varepsilon_{t-i}^2) = 0$ and $E(\varepsilon_t \sigma^2) = 0$. As such:

$$\rho_i = \sigma^2 \sigma^2 + E\varepsilon_{t-1}^2 \varepsilon_{t-i} - \sigma^2 \sigma^2 - \sigma^2 \sigma^2 + \sigma^2 \sigma^2 = E\varepsilon_{t-1}^2 \varepsilon_{t-i}$$

Clearly, all values of $E_{t-1}^2 \varepsilon_{t-i} = 0$ if $i \neq 1$. Moreover, if ε_t is normally distributed, the third moment $E\varepsilon_t^3 = E\varepsilon_{t-1}^3 = 0$. Hence, all values of ρ_i ($i \neq 0$) are equal to zero. Now suppose that you observe the sample ACF for $\{y_t\}$ but are unaware that the data were generated by (7.13). Based on the observation that the sample autocorrelations are small, you might mistakenly conclude that the series is white noise. You would not be the first person to fall into the trap of confusing a lack of correlation with statistical independence. Although the autocorrelations are zero, the value of y_t is clearly dependent on the value of y_{t-1}.

Since we are interested in nonlinear relationships in the data, a useful diagnostic tool is to examine the ACF of the squares or cubed values of a series. For example, the ACF of y_t^2 (or the squares of the residuals from an estimated equation) can reveal a nonlinear pattern. To illustrate the point, Granger and Teräsvirta (1993) show that the ACF from **chaos** may be indicative of white noise but that the ACF of squared values of the sequence may be large. Recall that a nonexplosive sequence is chaotic if it is generated from a deterministic difference equation such that it does not converge to a constant or to a repetitive cycle. Consider the following chaotic process:

$$y_t = 4y_{t-1}(1 - y_{t-1}) \text{ for } 0 < y_1 < 1 \tag{7.14}$$

In (7.14), y_t is related to the level and the squared value of y_{t-1}. However, the autocorrelations of $\{y_t\}$ will all be small but the ACF of $\{y_t^2\}$ will be large. To follow along using your software package, set $y_1 = 0.7$ and generate the next 99 values of $\{y_t\}$ using (7.14). Even though the sequence is perfectly predictable, you should find that the first six autocorrelations are

ρ_1	ρ_2	ρ_3	ρ_4	ρ_5	ρ_6
−0.074	−0.072	0.008	0.032	−0.016	−0.030

All of the correlations are less than one standard deviation from zero. However, the correlation coefficient between y_t^2 and y_{t-1}^2 is −0.281 and the autocorrelation coefficient between y_t^3 and y_{t-1}^3 is −0.386. With 100 observations, these two correlations are highly significant. The point of the example is to show that any neglected nonlinearity in your data can be checked using the ACF of the squared (or cubed) values of the series. To be a bit more formal, the McLeod–Li (1983) test seeks to determine if there are significant autocorrelations in the squared residuals from a linear equation. To perform the test, estimate your series using the best-fitting linear model and call the residuals $\hat{e}_t$. As in a formal test for ARCH errors (see Section 2 of Chapter 3), form the autocorrelations of the squared residuals. Let ρ_i denote the sample correlation coefficient between squared residuals $\hat{e}_t^2$ and $\hat{e}_{t-i}^2$ and use the Ljung–Box statistic to determine whether the squared residuals exhibit serial correlation. Hence, form

$$Q = T(T+2)\sum_{i=1}^{n}\rho_i/(T-i)$$

The value Q has an asymptotic χ^2 distribution with n degrees of freedom if the $\{\hat{e}_t^2\}$ sequence is uncorrelated. Rejecting the null hypothesis is equivalent to accepting that the model is nonlinear. Alternatively, you can estimate the regression

$$\hat{e}_t^2 = \alpha_0 + \alpha_1\hat{e}_{t-1}^2 + \ldots + \alpha_n\hat{e}_{t-n}^2 + v_t$$

If there are no nonlinearities, α_1 through α_n should be zero. With a sample of T residuals, if there are no nonlinearities, the test statistic TR^2 will converge to a χ^2 distribution with n degrees of freedom. In small samples you can use an F-test for the null hypothesis $\alpha_1 = \alpha_2 = \ldots = \alpha_n = 0$. If you are astute, you will remember that this test was used to detect ARCH-type errors. It turns out that the McLeod–Li (1983) test is the exact Lagrange multiplier test for ARCH errors. However, the test has substantial power to detect various forms of nonlinearity. Notice that the actual form of the nonlinearity is not specified by the test. Rejecting the null hypothesis of linearity does not tell you the nature of the nonlinearity present in the data.

The RESET

The Regression Error Specification Test (RESET) also posits the null hypothesis of linearity against a general alternative hypothesis of nonlinearity. If the residuals from a linear model are independent, they should not be correlated with the regressors used in the estimating equation or with the fitted values. Hence, a regression of the residuals on these values should not be statistically significant. To perform the RESET:

STEP 1: Estimate the best-fitting linear model. Let $\{e_t\}$ be the residuals from the model and denote the fitted values by $\hat{y}_t$.

STEP 2: Select a value of H (usually 3 or 4) and estimate the regression equation:

$$e_t = \delta z_t + \sum_{h=2}^{H} \alpha_i \hat{y}_t^h \text{ for } H \geq 2$$

where z_t is the vector that contains the variables included in the model estimated in Step 1. For example, if you estimate an ARMA(p, q) model, z_t will include a constant, y_{t-1} through y_{t-p}, and ε_{t-1} through ε_{t-q}. Note that the test can also be applied to a regression model. As such, z_t may also include exogenous explanatory variables.

This regression should have little explanatory power if the model is truly linear. As such, the sample value of F should be small. Hence, you can reject linearity if the sample value of the F-statistic for the null hypothesis $\alpha_1 = \alpha_2 = \ldots = \alpha_H$ exceeds the critical value from a standard F-table. The RESET is easy to implement, does not require the estimation of a large number of parameters, and has reasonable power to detect nonlinearities.

Other Portmanteau Tests

Portmanteau tests (translated as "a little brown suitcase") are residual-based tests that do not have a specific alternative hypothesis. The Ljung–Box Q-statistics are a good example of this type of catch-all test. Similarly, the popular Brock, Dechert, Scheinkman, and LeBaron (1996) test, called the BDS test, is a portmanteau test for independence. In essence, the test examines the distance between different pairs of residuals. Let d represent a given distance and let ε_t and ε_{t-1} be two realizations of the $\{\varepsilon_t\}$ sequence. If all values of $\{\varepsilon_t\}$ are independent, then the probability that the distance between any pair of residuals (ε_i, ε_j) is less than d should be the same for all i and j. Although very popular, the BDS test is able to detect serial correlation, parameter instability, neglected nonlinearity, structural breaks and other misspecification problems. Hence, rejecting the null hypothesis of independence does little to help identify the nature of the problem. Also be aware that the BDS test does not have especially good small-sample performance unless you bootstrap the critical values.

The point is that the McLeod–Li Test, the RESET, and other portmanteau tests all have a very general alternative hypothesis. As such, the tests are helpful in determining whether a nonlinear model is appropriate but not in determining the nature of the nonlinearity. As noted by Clements and Hendry (1998, pp. 168–69), "parameter change appears in many guises and can cause significant forecast error when models are used in practice." They also establish that it can be difficult to distinguish model misspecification from the problem of nonconstant parameters. As such, it is worthwhile to examine Lagrange multiplier tests for nonlinearity since they have a specific null hypothesis and a specific alternative hypothesis.

Lagrange Multiplier Tests

Lagrange multiplier (LM) tests can be used to test for a specific type of nonlinearity. Thus, an LM test can help you to select the proper functional form to use in your nonlinear estimation. To keep the analysis simple, we will assume that var$(\varepsilon_t) = \sigma^2$ is constant. Let $f(\ )$ be the nonlinear functional form and let α denote the parameters of $f(\ )$. In these circumstances, the LM test can be conducted as follows:[1]

STEP 1: Estimate the linear portion of the model to get the residuals $\{e_t\}$.

STEP 2: Obtain all of the partial derivatives $\partial f(\ )/\partial \alpha$ evaluated under the null hypothesis of linearity. Typically, these partial derivatives will be nonlinear functions of the regressors used in Step 1. Estimate the **auxiliary regression** by regressing e_t on these partial derivatives.

STEP 3: The value of TR^2 has a χ^2 distribution with degrees of freedom equal to the number of regressors used in Step 2. If the calculated value of TR^2 exceeds the critical value from a χ^2 table, reject the null hypothesis of linearity and accept the alternative. With a small sample, it is standard to use an F-test.

One benefit of the method is that you need not estimate the nonlinear model itself. More importantly, the use of a number of LM tests can help you select the form of the nonlinearity. It could be the case, for example, that an LM test rejects the GAR model but accepts the BL model. Unfortunately, this is not the typical case. Instead, the two LM tests are likely to accept the GAR model and the BL model. Nevertheless, comparing the *prob*-values of the two can be helpful. Another problem of the LM test is that the parameters of $f(\ )$ must be identified under the null hypothesis of linearity. These issues are explained in the three examples below.

THREE EXAMPLES

Example 1 Suppose you want to determine whether $\{y_t\}$ has the specific GAR form:

$$y_t = \alpha_0 + \alpha_1 y_{t-1} + \alpha_2 y_{t-2} + \alpha_3 y_{t-1} y_{t-2} + \varepsilon_t \qquad (7.15)$$

Of course, it would be straightforward to estimate (7.15) directly and obtain the t-statistic for the null hypothesis $\alpha_3 = 0$. However, the point of this section is to illustrate the appropriate use of the LM test. Toward this end, estimate the sequence an AR(2) process and obtain the residuals $\{e_t\}$. Now, you need to find the partial derivatives of the nonlinear functional form. It should be clear that

$$\partial y_t/\partial \alpha_0 = 1; \ \partial y_t/\partial \alpha_1 = y_{t-1}; \ \partial y_t/\partial \alpha_2 = y_{t-2} \text{ and } \partial y_t/\partial \alpha_3 = y_{t-1} y_{t-2}$$

Hence, Step 2 indicates that you regress e_t on a constant (i.e., a vector of 1's), y_{t-1}, y_{t-2}, and $y_{t-1}y_{t-2}$. Thus, the auxiliary regression is

$$e_t = a_0 + a_1 y_{t-1} + a_2 y_{t-2} + a_3 y_{t-1} y_{t-2} + v_t \qquad (7.16)$$

Obtain the sample value of TR^2. If this value exceeds the critical value of χ^2 with four degrees of freedom, reject the null hypothesis of linearity and accept the alternative of the GAR model. Alternatively, you can perform an F-test for the joint hypothesis $a_0 = a_1 = a_2 = a_3 = 0$.

Example 2   A similar procedure can be used to determine whether $\{y_t\}$ has the BL form:

$$y_t = \alpha_0 + \alpha_1 y_{t-1} + \alpha_2 y_{t-2} + \alpha_3 \varepsilon_{t-1} y_{t-2} + \varepsilon_t$$

Again, estimate the sequence an AR(2) process and obtain the residuals $\{e_t\}$. The desired partial derivatives are

$$\partial y_t / \partial \alpha_0 = 1; \; \partial y_t / \partial \alpha_1 = y_{t-1}; \; \partial y_t / \partial \alpha_2 = y_{t-2} \text{ and } \partial y_t / \partial \alpha_3 = \varepsilon_{t-1} y_{t-2}$$

so that auxiliary regression is

$$e_t = a_0 + a_1 y_{t-1} + a_2 y_{t-2} + a_3 \varepsilon_{t-1} y_{t-2} + v_t \tag{7.17}$$

Since the actual values of $\{\varepsilon_{t-1}\}$ are unobserved, use the estimated residuals to form $\varepsilon_{t-1} y_{t-2}$ in (7.17). If the sample value of TR^2 exceeds the critical value of χ^2 with four degrees of freedom, reject the null hypothesis of linearity and accept the alternative of the BL model. Alternatively, you can use an F-test for the null hypothesis $a_0 = a_1 = a_2 = a_3 = 0$.

Notice that (7.16) and (7.17) are very similar. Since ε_{t-1} will be highly correlated with y_{t-1}, the values of TR^2 from the two equations will be quite similar. Hence, the results of both tests should be quite similar; if (7.16) indicates that a GAR model is appropriate, (7.17) should indicate that a BL model is appropriate. Nevertheless, the two tests can be useful. If both accept the null hypothesis of linearity, you can be reasonably confident that the AR(2) model is adequate. If both reject the null hypothesis, you can be somewhat confident that a nonlinear model is appropriate. However, unless the *prob*-values of the two tests are quite different, the tests will not provide much guidance as to which nonlinear form is the most appropriate.

Example 3   Now suppose that you want to test for the specific LSTAR form:

$$y_t = \alpha_0 + \alpha_1 y_{t-1} + (\beta_0 + \beta_1 y_{t-1})\{[1 + \exp(-\gamma(y_{t-1} - c))]\}^{-1} + \varepsilon_t$$

For the LSTAR model, the null hypothesis that the model is linear is identical to setting $\gamma = 0$. You should be able to see the problem with using the LM test. If $\gamma = 0$, the magnitudes of β_0, β_1, and c are completely irrelevant! Clearly, if $\gamma = 0$, it makes no difference whether β_1 is -0.5 or $+1$. The point is that the values of β_0, β_1, and c are unidentified under the null hypothesis that the model is linear.[2] As such, it is not possible to perform an LM test. It is worth a few minutes of your time to try the following exercise. Find the partial derivatives of the LSTAR model and evaluate each under the null hypothesis $\gamma = 0$. Indicate the functional form of the resulting auxiliary regression (*Hint:* $\partial y_t / \partial c$ evaluated at $\gamma = 0$ is zero).

Tests for STAR Models

Since the LM test fails for LSTAR (and ESTAR) adjustment, other means are necessary to detect the presence of a smooth transition model. Teräsvirta (1994) develops a framework that can often detect the presence of nonlinear behavior. Moreover, the method can be used to determine whether a series is best modeled as an LSTAR or an ESTAR process. The test is based on a Taylor series expansion of the general STAR model. For the LSTAR model, we can write θ as

$$\theta = [1 + \exp(-\gamma(y_{t-d} - c))]^{-1} \equiv [1 + \exp(-h_{t-d})]^{-1}$$

so that $h_{t-d} = \gamma(y_{t-d} - c)$.

Now, the trick is to take a third-order Taylor series approximation of θ with respect to h_{t-d} evaluated $h_{t-d} = 0$. Of course, this is identical to evaluating the expansion at $\gamma = 0$. Although taking the partial derivatives is a bit tedious, after a bit of manipulations it is possible to obtain.[3]

	Equals	**Evaluated at $h_{t-d} = 0$**
$\partial\theta/\partial h_{t-d}$	$\exp(-h_{t-d})/[1 + \exp(-h_{t-d})]^2$	$1/4$
$\partial^2\theta/\partial h_{t-d}^2$	$-\exp(-h_{t-d})[1 - \exp(-h_{t-d})]/[1 + \exp(-h_{t-d})]^3$	0
$\partial^3\theta/\partial h_{t-d}^3$	$\exp(-h_{t-d})[1 + \exp(-2h_{t-d}) - 4\exp(-h_{t-d})]/[1 + \exp(-h_{t-d})]^4$	$-1/8$

Thus, since the second derivative is zero, the desired expansion has the form: $\theta = h_{t-d}/4 - h_{t-d}^3/48 = \gamma(y_{t-d} - c)/4 - \gamma^3(y_{t-d} - c)^3/48$. Hence, we can write the approximation of the LSTAR model in the form

$$y_t = \alpha_0 + \alpha_1 y_{t-1} + \ldots + a_p y_{t-p} + (\beta_0 + \beta_1 y_{t-1}) + \ldots + \beta_p y_{t-p} \ (\pi_1 h_{t-d} + \pi_3 h_{t-d}^3) + \varepsilon_t$$

Because h_{t-d} depends only on the value of y_{t-d}, we can write the model in the more compact form

$$y_t = z_t + z_t y_{t-d} + z_t y_{t-d}^2 + z_t y_{t-d}^3 + \varepsilon_t$$

where $z_t = (\alpha_0, y_{t-1}, y_{t-2}, \ldots, y_{t-p})$.

Thus, you form the products of the regressors with the powers of y_{t-d}. Then, you test for the presence of LSTAR behavior by estimating an auxiliary regression:

$$e_t = a_0 + a_1 y_{t-1} + \ldots + a_p y_{t-p} + a_{11} y_{t-1} y_{t-d} + \ldots$$
$$+ a_{1p} y_{t-p} y_{t-d} + a_{21} y_{t-1} y_{t-d}^2 + \ldots + a_{2p} y_{t-1} y_{t-d}^2$$
$$+ a_{31} y_{t-1} y_{t-d}^3 + \ldots + a_{3p} y_{t-p} y_{t-d}^3 + \varepsilon_t \quad (7.18)$$

The test for linearity is identical to testing the joint restriction that all nonlinear terms are zero (i.e., $a_{11} = \ldots = a_{1p} = a_{21} = \ldots = a_{2p} = a_{31} = \ldots = a_{3p} = 0$). You can perform the test using a standard F-test with $3p$ degrees of freedom in the numerator. If you are not sure of the delay factor, the recommendation is to run the test using all plausible values of d. The value of d that results in the smallest *prob*-value (i.e., the value of d providing the best fit) is the best estimate of d.

With all of the background work completed, it is straightforward to rework the details for an ESTAR model. Let θ be

$$\theta = 1 - \exp(-h_{t-d}^2)$$

so that $h_{t-d} \equiv \gamma^{1/2}(y_{t-d} - c)$. Now, the partial derivatives are:

	Equals	**Evaluated at $h_{t-d} = 0$**
$\partial\theta / \partial h_{t-d}$	$2h_{t-d}\exp(-h_{t-d}^2)$	0
$\partial^2\theta / \partial h_{t-d}^2$	$2\exp(-h_{t-d}^2) - 4h_{t-d}^2 \exp(-h_{t-d}^2)$	2
$\partial^3\theta / \partial h_{t-d}^3$	$-12h_{t-d}\exp(-h_{t-d}^2) + 8h_{t-d}^3 \exp(-h_{t-d}^2)$	0

Unlike the LSTAR model, the expansion for the ESTAR model has the quadratic form: $\theta = \pi_2 h_{t-d}^2$. Thus, we can write the expansion of the ESTAR model without h_{t-d} and h_{t-d}^3. Hence, the Taylor series approximation has the form

$$y_t = \alpha_0 + \alpha_1 y_{t-1} + \ldots + \alpha_p y_{t-p} + (\beta_0 + \beta_1 y_{t-1} + \ldots + \beta_p y_{t-p})(\pi_2 h_{t-d}^2) + \varepsilon_t$$

$$= z_t + z_t y_{t-d} + z_t y_{t-d}^2 + \varepsilon_t$$

The key insight in Teräsvirta (1994) is that the auxiliary equation for the ESTAR model is nested within that for an LSTAR model. If the ESTAR is appropriate, it should be possible to exclude all of the terms in the cubic expression $z_t y_{t-d}^3$ from (7.18). Hence, the testing procedure follows these steps:

STEP 1: Estimate the linear portion of the AR(p) model to determine the order p and to obtain the residuals $\{e_t\}$.

STEP 2: Estimate the auxiliary equation (7.18). Test the significance of the entire regression by comparing TR^2 to the critical value of χ^2. If the calculated value of TR^2 exceeds the critical value from a χ^2 table, reject the null hypothesis of linearity and accept the alternative hypothesis of a smooth transition model. (Alternatively, you can perform an F-test.)

STEP 3: If you accept the alternative hypothesis (i.e., if the model is nonlinear), test the restriction $a_{31} = a_{32} = \ldots = a_{3n} = 0$ using an F-test. If you reject the $a_{31} = a_{32} = \ldots = a_{3n} = 0$, the model has the LSTAR form. If you accept the restriction, conclude that the model has the ESTAR form.

Testing for a TAR Model

The TAR model is not differentiable at the threshold so that it does not have a Taylor series representation. Nevertheless, the test for LSTAR and ESTAR models has been shown to work for the TAR model as well. However, there is not a specific test to determine whether a TAR or an STAR model is best. Unless there is a theoretical reason for selecting a particular specification, most would use the AIC or SBC to select between the alternatives. The delay parameter is chosen as in the LSTAR test—use the value of d providing the best fit. The key remaining issue is how to determine whether there are multiple thresholds. Tsay (1998) develops a formal test for multiple thresholds. However, one commonly used technique is based on Chan's (1993) method of finding the consistent estimate of the threshold. We can think of the sum of squared residuals from any TAR model as being a function of the threshold value used in the estimation, i.e., $ssr = ssr(\tau)$. The closer we come to the true threshold the smaller should be the sum of squared residuals. Hence, ssr should be minimized at the true value of the threshold. The basic idea is that the sum of squared residuals will have several local minima if there are several thresholds. To use this method, follow these steps:

STEP 1: Sort the threshold variable (i.e., sort y_{t-d}) from the lowest to the highest value. Let s_i denoted the i-th value of the sorted series. Hence, in a sample with T observations, s_1 is the smallest value of y_{t-d} and s_T is largest value.

STEP 2: Estimate a TAR model in the form of (7.9) or (7.10) using the successive values of $\{s_i\}$ as thresholds. Save the sum of squared residuals associated with each model. Since you want to maintain 15 percent of the observations on each side of the threshold, use only the middle 70 percent of the values of s_i. For example, if you have 200 observations, estimate 141 TAR models beginning with $\tau = s_{30}$ and ending with $\tau = s_{170}$. When you are done, you will have 141 values of the sum of squared residuals.

STEP 3: Create a graph of the successive values of the sum of squared residuals. If ssr_{30} is the sum of squared residuals using $\tau = s_{30}$ and ssr_{170} is the sum of squared residuals using $\tau = s_{170}$, plot the values of ssr_{30} through ssr_{170}.

If there is a single threshold, there should be a single trough in the graph you create in Step 3. For example, if there is a trough at ssr_{132}, the consistent estimate of the threshold is s_{132}. After all, $\tau = s_{132}$ results in the TAR model with the best fit. If there are two troughs, there are two potential thresholds. To explain in a bit more detail, suppose that the correct model is the one used to generate the 200 values shown in Figure 7.3:

$$y_t = 0.3I_t y_{t-1} + 0.7(1 - I_t)y_{t-1} + \varepsilon_t$$

where $I_t = 1$ if $y_{t-1} > 0$ and $I_t = 0$ otherwise.

Figure 7.5 reproduces the same numerical values sorted from low to high. As shown in both figures, the first value lying within the 70 percent band (i.e., s_{30}) is

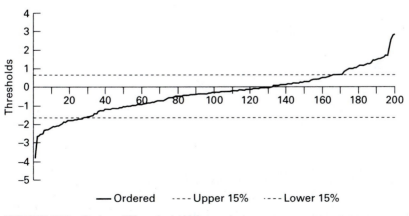

—— Ordered   ---- Upper 15%   ---- Lower 15%

FIGURE 7.5 Ordered Threshold Values

–1.623. Hence, the first estimate of the TAR model uses $\tau = -1.623$. The second estimation uses the next sorted observation as the threshold. This second value happens to be –1.601; thus, the second estimation uses $\tau = -1.601$. Continuing in this fashion brings us closer to the true threshold value of zero. As such, the fit of the TAR model should continue to improve as we move from threshold values of –1.623 towards $\tau = 0$. However, once we cross the true threshold and use values of τ that are greater than zero, the sum of squared residuals should begin to increase. As such, the plot of the residual sum of squares should reach a minimum at $\tau = 0$. If you examine Figure 7.5, you can see that $\tau = 0$ corresponds to s_{132}.

What would happen if the true model contained two thresholds? In particular, suppose one threshold is –1 and the other is zero. As you can see from Figure 7.5, the value of $s_{55} = -1$ and $s_{132} = 0$. Now consider the idealized plot of the residual sum of squares shown in Figure 7.6. As we estimate TAR models beginning with s_{30} and proceed toward s_{55}, the sum of squared residuals declines. Also depicted is the fact that the sum of squared residuals should begin to increase as we use threshold values in excess of –1. This increase continues until you approach the second threshold. In the example at hand, at ordered observation 95 (i.e., at s_{95}), the sum of squared residuals begins another decline as we approach the second threshold of 0. The second trough at ordered observation 132 indicates the second threshold $\tau = 0$.

6. ESTIMATES OF REGIME SWITCHING MODELS

This section illustrates a number of techniques used in the estimation of regime switching models. The goal is to demonstrate a number of practical issues that arise in applied work.

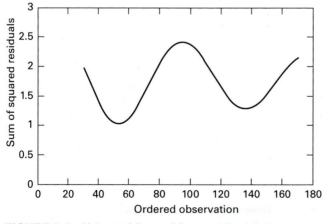

FIGURE 7.6   Values of Sum of Squared Residuals

An LSTAR Model

To illustrate the process of estimating an LSTAR model, 250 realizations of the following sequence were generated:

$$y_t = 1 + 0.9y_{t-1} + (3 - 1.7y_{t-1})/(1 + \exp(-10(y_{t-1} - 5))) + \varepsilon_t \qquad (7.19)$$

If you compare (7.19) to (7.11) you will see that the smoothness parameter $\gamma = 10$ and that $\theta = 1/[1 + \exp(-10(y_{t-1} - 5))]$. As $y_{t-1} \rightarrow -\infty$, the behavior of y_t is governed by the autoregressive process $1 + 0.9y_{t-1} + \varepsilon_t$ and as $y_{t-1} \rightarrow +\infty$, the behavior of y_t is governed by $4 - 0.8y_{t-1} + \varepsilon_t$. Note that in the neighborhood of $y_{t-1} = 0$, the value of θ is approximately equal to zero. The 250 realizations are shown in Figure 7.7. The simulated sequence has a sample mean of 0.62 and a standard deviation of 3.43. The first six autocorrelations are

ρ_1	ρ_2	ρ_3	ρ_4	ρ_5	ρ_6
0.552	0.270	0.067	−0.039	−0.136	−0.161

The first few autocorrelations seem to exhibit geometric decay and those for lags 5 and 6 have *prob*-values near 5 percent ($2 \cdot 250^{1/2} = 0.1265$). If we did not know the actual data-generating process, we might be tempted to estimate the series as a linear AR(1) process. In fact, the estimated linear model looks to be quite plausible; consider

$$y_t = 0.278 + 0.552y_{t-1} + e_t \qquad (7.20)$$
$$(1.50) \ (10.42)$$

and AIC = 1901.18885   SBC = 1908.22375.

The residual autocorrelations are such that there is no *linear* relationship in the residuals. The first 12 autocorrelations of the residuals are

ρ_1	ρ_2	ρ_3	ρ_4	ρ_5	ρ_6	ρ_7	ρ_8	ρ_9	ρ_{10}	ρ_{11}	ρ_{12}
0.03	0.01	−0.06	−0.02	−0.1	−0.04	−0.11	−0.09	0.07	−0.00	−0.05	−0.06

FIGURE 7.7   The Simulated LSTAR Process

The Ljung–Box Q-statistics are such that the *prob*-values for the first 4, 8, and 12 lags are 0.900, 0.347, and 0.471, respectively. Since the autocorrelations of the residuals are not significant at conventional levels, you might be tempted to conclude that the true data-generating process was an AR(1). However, a battery of nonlinear diagnostic testing reveals a very different picture. Note first that the autocorrelations of the squared residuals also suggest that the linear model is adequate. The autocorrelations of the squared residuals are

ρ_1	ρ_2	ρ_3	ρ_4	ρ_5	ρ_6	ρ_7	ρ_8	ρ_9	ρ_{10}	ρ_{11}	ρ_{12}
0.032	−0.039	−0.068	−0.101	−0.091	−0.099	−0.076	−0.069	0.136	0.004	−0.016	−0.046

In contrast, the RESET test indicates a nonlinear relationship. Call e_t and $\hat{y}_t$ the residuals and the fitted values from the linear model, respectively. Given that the best-fitting model is an AR(1), to perform the RESET test, estimate a regression of the form

$$e_t = a_0 + a_1 y_{t-1} + \alpha_1 \hat{y}_t^2 + \alpha_2 \hat{y}_t^3 + \alpha_3 \hat{y}_t^4 + v_t$$

If we use the data from (7.20), we obtain

$$e_t = 0.932 + 0.710 y_{t-1} + 0.058 \hat{y}_t^2 - 0.157 \hat{y}_t^3 - 0.034 \hat{y}_t^4$$
$$(4.24) \quad (9.04) \qquad (0.64) \qquad (-9.39) \quad (-4.84)$$

Notice that a number of the individual coefficients appear to be statistically significant. However, you should not rely on the individual t-statistics because the regressors are highly correlated; for example, large values of $\hat{y}_t^2$ will be associated with large values of $\hat{y}_t^4$. The issue is whether the values of $\hat{y}_t^i$ have any explanatory power as a group. The F-statistic for the null hypothesis $\alpha_1 = \alpha_2 = \alpha_3 = 0$ equals 95.60. Since there are three degrees of freedom in the numerator (we impose three restrictions) and 244 in the denominator (250 observations minus 5 estimated coefficients and 1 lost observation resulting from the lagged value y_{t-1}), we can reject the null hypothesis at any conventional significant level (the 1 percent critical value is 3.86). Hence, we conclude that the series exhibits some form of nonlinear behavior.

It is quite a bit more difficult to pin down the form of the nonlinearity. Since the data are simulated, there is no possibility of using economic theory to suggest the most probable form of nonlinearity. Hence, one way to proceed is to estimate a number of nonlinear models and select the one that fits the best. However, the danger of this procedure is that you are likely to overfit the data. A more prudent way to proceed is to perform a number of Lagrange multiplier tests to determine which models are likely to be the most plausible.

One test that can be useful to select the functional form is Teräsvirta's test for LSTAR versus ESTAR behavior. Pretend that we do not know the value of the delay parameter d. It seems natural to begin with $d = 1$. From the Taylor series expansion for a first-order LSTAR model, we need to regress the residuals from the linear model on the regressors (i.e., a constant and y_{t-1}) and on y_{t-1}, y_{t-1}^2, and y_{t-1}^3 multiplied by the regressors. The estimated auxiliary regression is

$$e_t = 0.933 + 0.076 y_{t-1} - 0.027 y_{t-1}^2 - 0.039 y_{t-1}^3 - 0.003 y_{t-1}^4$$
$$(4.35) \quad (9.21) \qquad (-0.987) \quad (-11.52) \quad (-4.84)$$

The F-statistic for the entire regression is 71.70; with four numerator and 244 denominator degrees of freedom, the regression is highly significant. Moreover, the F-statistic for the presence of the nonlinear terms y_{t-1}^2, y_{t-1}^3, and y_{t-1}^4 is 95.60; with three numerator and 244 denominator degrees of freedom, we can conclude that there is threshold behavior. Next, we can determine if LSTAR or ESTAR behavior is the most appropriate. Given the t-statistic on the coefficient for y_{t-1}^4, we cannot exclude this expression from the auxiliary equation. Hence, we can rule out ESTAR behavior in favor of LSTAR behavior. It is possible that the delay parameter is two even though y_{t-2} does not directly appear in the model. To determine whether the y_{t-1} or y_{t-2} is the most appropriate threshold variable, you can estimate the following auxiliary equation

$$e_t = 0.738 + 0.047 y_{t-1} - 0.158 y_{t-1} y_{t-2} - 0.005 y_{t-1} y_{t-2}^2 + 0.003 y_{t-1} y_{t-2}^3$$

The F-value for this regression was only 5.73. Since the $d = 1$ yields a substantially better fit than the $d = 2$, we can conclude that the y_{t-1} is the most appropriate threshold variable. Thus, it seems reasonable to estimate a nonlinear model of the form

$$y_t = \alpha_0 + \alpha_1 y_{t-1} + (\beta_0 + \beta_1 y_{t-1})/(1 + \exp(-\gamma(y_{t-1} - c))) + \varepsilon_t$$

Since the coefficients are multiplicative, OLS cannot be used to obtain the least squares estimates of the coefficients. Instead, it is standard to use nonlinear least squares (NLLS) to obtain the estimates of the parameter values. Unfortunately, many of the numerical methods used to estimate the parameter values have difficulty in simultaneously finding γ and c. It is crucial to provide the numerical routine with very good initial guesses. One common technique is to posit a plausible initial guess and simultaneously estimate the coefficients using NLLS. At this point you have the preliminary estimates of γ and c. Reestimate the model fixing c at the preliminary estimate in order to obtain a second estimate of γ. Next, fix γ at the estimated value and obtain an updated estimate of c. Continue to iterate until the values of successive values of c and γ stabilize. Once the parameter values seem to be steady from one iteration to the next, you should be able to estimate all parameter values simultaneously. An example of this iterative method is shown next.

For the given value of $c = 4.4$, the estimates of α_0, α_1, β_0, β_1, and γ are reported in the first row of Table 7.1. You can see that the estimates of α_0, α_1, and β_0 (but not

Table 7.1   Successive Iterations of the LSTAR Model

Iteration	Given	$\hat{\alpha}_0$	$\hat{\alpha}_1$	$\hat{\beta}_0$	$\hat{\beta}_1$	$\hat{\gamma}$	$\hat{c}$
1	$c = 4.40$	1.011	0.954	25.15	−6.38	3.83	
2	$\gamma = 3.83$	1.050	0.970	−20.66	0.787		5.15
3	$c = 5.15$	0.950	0.925	−21.85	1.17	5.81	
4	$\gamma = 5.81$	0.993	0.946	−13.31	−0.141		8.72
5	$c = 8.72$	0.938	0.921	−11.50	−0.323	5.01	
6	$\gamma = 5.01$	0.956	0.930	−8.26	−0.833		5.02
...							
9	$c = 5.02$	0.942	0.923	−5.87	−1.179	11.21	

β_1) are reasonably close to the actual values used in the data-generating process. The key point to note is that this first iteration yields a value of $\hat{\gamma} = 3.83$. Next, fix the value of $\gamma = 3.83$ to estimate α_0, α_1, β_0, β_1, and c. The new estimate of c is 5.15. At this point we have completed the first round of the iterations. Now, if we fix $c = 5.15$, the estimated value of γ is 5.81. The results of nine such iterations are shown in the table. If we use the ninth iteration values of $\gamma = 11.21$ and $c = 5.02$ as initial guesses for a simultaneous NLLS estimation, we obtain the final estimate:

$$y_t = 0.941 + 0.923y_{t-1} + (-5.86 - 1.18y_{t-1})/(1 + \exp(-11.206(y_{t-1} - 5.01))) + \varepsilon_t$$
$$\quad (14.43)\ (45.15) \qquad (-2.07)(-2.45) \qquad\qquad\qquad (6.77) \qquad (312.33)$$

AIC = 1365.22154   SBC = 1386.32626

The point estimates that all the parameters except β_0 and β_1 are very close to their true values. The estimated value of β_1, but not β_0, is contained within a confidence interval of ± 2 standard deviations of its actual value. Moreover, the AIC and the SBC both select the LSTAR model over the linear model. Note that you need to be wary of the t-statistics for two reasons. First, the nonlinear least squares estimates do not make the assumptions that the estimated coefficients have normal distributions. Second, the estimates are all performed using numerical methods. Given these caveats, the estimated model captures the essential features of (7.19).

The Real Exchange Rate as an ESTAR Process

As indicated earlier, Michael, Nobay, and Peel (1997) argue that transactions costs should make real exchange rates behave as ESTAR processes. For our purposes, the series of interest is the annual observations of the U.K.–U.S. real rate over the 1791 to 1992 period. The first issue is to determine whether or not the rates are stationary; after all, if the rates are unit root processes, the theory of PPP fails. As such, they use augmented Dickey–Fuller tests to determine whether the series contains a unit root. The use of annual data results in very short lags. If we ignore the intercept, the estimated equation for the U.K.–U.S. rate is

$$\Delta y_t = -0.12y_{t-1} + 0.12\Delta y_{t-1} + \varepsilon_t \qquad\qquad (7.21)$$
$$\quad (-3.62) \qquad (1.75)$$

In absolute value, the t-statistic of -3.62 exceeds critical value reported in the Dickey–Fuller table; as such, it is possible to reject the null hypothesis of a unit root in the real exchange rate. The point estimate of -0.12 implies a fairly slow speed of adjustment; approximately 88 percent of the current period's discrepancy from PPP is expected to persist into the next year. Nevertheless, this linear model forces the speed of adjustment to be constant. The next issue is to determine whether Teräsvirta's four-step methodology indicates the presence of ESTAR adjustment.

Given the lag lengths, the most plausible value of the delay parameter d is unity. Nevertheless, the authors follow the standard procedure and select the value of d that results in the best fit of the auxiliary equation. As suspected, the value $d = 1$ fits the data better than the alternatives $d = 2$ or $d = 3$. The auxiliary regression has the same form as (7.18). The *prob*-value of the F-statistic for the null hypothesis that all values of $a_{ij} = 0$ in the U.K.–U.S. auxiliary equation is 0.076. Hence, there is weak evidence of nonlinear behavior in the U.K.–U.S. rate.

Given the presence of threshold adjustment, the next issue is to test for LSTAR versus ESTAR adjustment. The F-test for the null hypothesis that all values of $a_{3i} = 0$ has a *prob*-value 0.522; as such, it is not possible to reject the null hypothesis of ESTAR adjustment. Notice that the test for nonlinearity has less power than the test for ESTAR versus linear adjustment. The auxiliary equation for nonlinear adjustment has coefficients for both the LSTAR and ESTAR models. If there is ESTAR adjustment, a number of the coefficients are unnecessary. Hence, the authors constrain all values of $a_{3i} = 0$, and test whether the remaining coefficients are zero. The F-statistic for this test has a *prob*-value of 0.028. Hence, this test with enhanced power suggests ESTAR versus linear adjustment.

Estimating a TAR Model

A number of papers have indicated that U.S. industrial production displays nonlinear behavior. You can follow along the estimation process using the data set INDPROD_60.XLS. Figure 7.8 shows the percentage change in the monthly values of the index over the period January 1960 through June 2002. In December 1974 the index fell by as much as 4.25 percent and in April 1978, the index rose by 3.35 percent. The average percentage change of the 510 values was 0.26 percent with a standard deviation of 0.80 percent. After some experimentation, it was found that the best-fitting AR(p) model is

$$y_t = 0.127 + 0.282y_{t-1} + 0.145y_{t-2} + 0.102y_{t-3} + \varepsilon_t \qquad (7.22)$$
$$\quad (3.60) \quad (6.37) \qquad (3.19) \qquad (2.34)$$

and AIC = 2836.49104   SBC = 2853.40508.

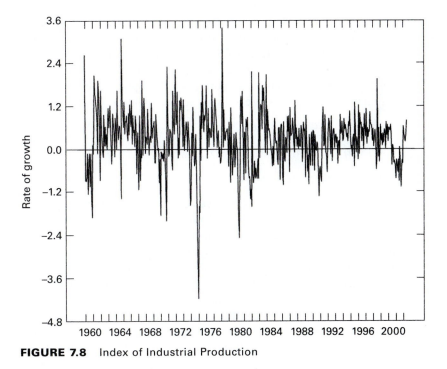

FIGURE 7.8   Index of Industrial Production

The residual autocorrelations are small and the Q-statistics indicate no remaining linear relationships in the data. Consider:

ρ_1	ρ_2	ρ_3	ρ_4	ρ_5	ρ_6
−0.009	0.006	0.000	0.054	−0.046	−0.045

$Q(4) = 1.535$, significance level $= 0.820$
$Q(8) = 3.881$, significance level $= 0.868$
$Q(12) = 9.480$, significance level $= 0.661$

Diagnostic checking indicates a potential problem with the linear specification. The autocorrelations of the squared residuals are

ρ_1	ρ_2	ρ_3	ρ_4	ρ_5	ρ_6	ρ_7	ρ_8	ρ_9	ρ_{10}	ρ_{11}	ρ_{12}
0.222	0.008	−0.003	0.059	0.004	0.010	−0.005	−0.023	0.054	−0.012	0.119	0.060

With 510 observations, the value of 0.22 is highly significant. However, the RESET is not supportive of nonlinearity. If we regress the residuals on the regressors and the powers of the fitted values, we obtain

$$e_t = 0.003 + 0.025y_{t-1} - 0.025y_{t-2} + 0.006y_{t-3} + 0.179\hat{y}_t - 0.229\hat{y}_t^2 - 0.336\hat{y}_t^3$$
$$(0.072)\ (0.425)\quad (-0.003)\quad\quad (0.0123)\quad\quad (0.496)\ (-1.036)\ (-1.304)$$

The F-statistic for the joint restriction that the coefficients on $\hat{y}_t$, $\hat{y}_t^2$, and $\hat{y}_t^3$ jointly equal zero is 0.649. With three degrees of freedom in the numerator and 500 in the denominator, the *prob*-value is 0.22. Hence, the RESET does not detect the presence of nonlinear behavior. Notice that the RESET has a very general alternative hypothesis; as such, it does not have power against all types of nonlinearity. Suppose we believed that the process exhibited some type of LSTAR adjustment and wanted to apply the Teräsvirta's test for LSTAR and ESTAR behavior. In this case, the test entails regressing the residuals from the linear model on a constant, the three lags of y_{t-i}, and products of these regressors on three powers of y_{t-d}. Specifically, for a given value of d, we estimate the auxiliary regression:

$$e_t = a_0 + a_1 y_{t-1} + a_2 y_{t-2} + a_3 y_{t-3} + a_{d1} y_{t-d} y_{t-1} + a_{d2} y_{t-d} y_{t-2}$$
$$+ a_{d3} y_{t-d} y_{t-3} + a_{d21} y_{t-d}^2 y_{t-1} + a_{d22} y_{t-d}^2 y_{t-2} + a_{d23} y_{t-d}^2 y_{t-3}$$
$$+ a_{d31} y_{t-d}^3 y_{t-1} + a_{d32} y_{t-d}^3 y_{t-2} + a_{d33} y_{t-d}^3 y_{t-3} + v_t$$

If $d = 1$, we obtain an F-value of 10.24; this value is highly significant so we can conclude that there is some type of threshold behavior. It might be the case that $d = 2$ or 3. If we estimate the auxiliary equation using y_{t-2} as the threshold variable, the F-statistic for the entire regression is 8.941. If we let y_{t-3} be the threshold variable, the F-statistic for the entire regression is 9.681. All of the F-values are very significant. Nevertheless, since $d = 1$ yields the best fit, we conclude that y_{t-1} is the transition variable. Ordinarily, the next issue would be to test for LSTAR or ESTAR behavior. As it turns out, the F-statistic for the exclusion restriction for all nonlinear terms in the auxiliary equation is 2.115; with nine degrees of freedom in the numerator and 494 in the denominator, the test has a *prob*-value of 0.027. Hence, at the

5 percent (but not the 1 percent) significance level, we would conclude that the series exhibits LSTAR behavior.

However, there is no specific test for TAR versus linear adjustment or TAR versus LSTAR adjustment. The problem is that the TAR model is not differentiable at τ so that a Taylor series expansion (or an LM test) is not possible. Nevertheless, suppose that the goal is to estimate a TAR model. For example, it seems quite plausible that positive growth rates exhibit different autoregressive behavior than negative growth rates. If the threshold is known to be zero it is straightforward to set the indicator function—create the variable $I_t \geq 0$ if y_{t-1} is positive and zero otherwise. After multiplying each variable by the indicator, the estimate of the best-fitting TAR regression in the form of (7.10) is

$$y_t = (0.171 + 0.205y_{t-1} + 0.088y_{t-2} + 0.152y_{t-3}) \, I_t + (0.222 + 0.475y_{t-1}$$
$$\quad (2.39) \quad (2.64) \qquad (1.49) \qquad (2.66) \qquad \qquad (3.16) \quad (4.29)$$
$$+ \, 0.184y_{t-2} + 0.021y_{t-3}) \, (1 - I_t) + \varepsilon_t$$
$$\quad (2.38) \qquad (0.309)$$

AIC = 2836.42158 SBC = 2870.24967

As measured by the SBC, the fit of the linear model is clearly superior. The restriction that all values of $\alpha_i = \beta_i$ is such that $F(4,499) = 2.001$ with significance level 0.093. Hence, at the 5 percent significance level, the TAR model with $\tau = 0$ does not display a significant degree of asymmetry. One possible explanation is that the threshold might not be zero. As such, it is possible to use Chan's method to obtain a consistent estimate of the threshold. The sorted values of the potential thresholds were such to ensure that no less than 15 percent of the observations occur in each regime. When the values of y_{t-1} were sorted from low to high, the 77th value (510 · 0.15 = 76.6) was –0.44859 and the 434th observation was 0.95953. Hence, we looked for potential thresholds within this interval. The residual sum of squares was minimized using a threshold value of $\tau = -0.3488$.

Figure 7.9 shows the value of the sum of squared residuals for each threshold value considered. You can clearly see that the smallest residual sum of squares occurs around –0.35; hence, this is the consistent estimate of τ. Notice that there appears to be a second trough in the residual sum of squares in the neighborhood of –0.12. However, the decline is small so that we proceed under the assumption that there is a single threshold at –0.3488. When the TAR model was estimated using this value, it was found

$$y_t = (0.139 + 0.209y_{t-1} + 0.170y_{t-2} + 0.136y_{t-3}) \, I_t$$
$$\quad (2.66) \quad (3.28) \qquad (3.28) \qquad (2.70)$$
$$+ \, (0.517 + 0.774y_{t-1} - 0.065y_{t-2} + 0.058y_{t-3}) \, (1 - I_t) + \varepsilon_t$$
$$\quad (3.76) \quad (5.41) \qquad (-0.560) \qquad (0.658)$$

where $\tau = -0.3488$, AIC = 2831.87602 and SBC = 2869.93262.

The point estimates suggests that there is far more persistence when y_{t-1} is below the threshold than when y_{t-1} is above the threshold. The F-value of the test of symmetry is 3.648; with 4 numerator and 499 denominator degrees of freedom, this has a *prob*-value of 0.006. Hence, there is strong evidence of threshold adjustment. Notice that the AIC, but not the SBC, selects the model with the consistent estimate of the threshold over the linear model. Even if the two insignificant coefficients are eliminated, the values of the AIC and SBC are 2828.41382 and

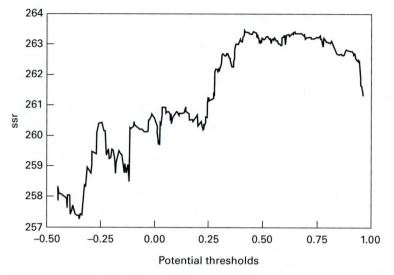

FIGURE 7.9 Residual Sum of Squares and the Potential Thresholds

2858.01340, respectively. Since the SBC continues to select the linear specification, we should maintain a healthy skepticism of this TAR model.

Inference in a TAR Model

Suppose you estimate the TAR model in the form

$$y_t = \alpha_{11} I_t y_{t-1} + \alpha_{21}(1 - I_t)y_{t-1} + \varepsilon_{1t}$$

where $I_t = 1$ of $y_{t-1} > \tau$ and $I_t = 0$ if $y_{t-1} \le \tau$.

Under the null hypothesis of linearity, the model is the AR(1) process

$$y_t = \alpha y_{t-1} + \varepsilon_{2t}$$

If the threshold τ is known, it is possible to use a standard F-test to determine whether $\alpha_{11} = \alpha_{21}$. However, if the threshold is unknown, another method must be used since you have searched over all values of τ to estimate the values of α_{11} and α_{21}. Hansen (1997) shows how to appropriately perform the test using a bootstrapping procedure. Search over all values of τ to find the best-fitting TAR model. Let σ_1^2 denote the estimated variance of ε_{1t}. Next, estimate the linear model to obtain an estimate of the variance of ε_{2t} called σ_2^2. If you have T observations, a traditional F-statistic could be constructed as

$$F = T\left(\sigma_2^2 - \sigma_1^2\right)/\sigma_1^2$$

However, this sample value cannot be compared to the critical value found in a table for F. Instead, you need to draw T normally distributed random numbers with a mean of zero and a variance of unity; let μ_t denote this set of random numbers. You treat μ_t as the dependent variable. Regress u_t on the actual values of y_{t-1} to obtain an estimate of σ_2^2 called σ_2^{*2}. Similarly, for each potential value of τ regress μ_t on $I_t y_{t-1}$ and $(1 - I_t)y_{t-1}$ [i.e., estimate a regression in the form $\mu_t = \alpha I_t y_{t-1} + \beta(1 - I_t)y_{t-1}$] and use the regression providing the best fit. Call the variance of the residuals from this regression σ_1^{*2}. Use these two variances to form

$$F^* = T\left(\sigma_2^{*2} - \sigma_1^{*2}\right)/\sigma_1^{*2}$$

Repeat this process several thousand times to obtain the distribution of F^*. If the value of F from your sample exceeds the 95th percentile for F^*, you can reject the null hypothesis of linearity at the 5 percent significance level. The method generalizes to testing the null hypothesis a linear model against the alternative of (7.10). Create σ_1^2 and σ_2^2 by estimating (7.10) and the linear model that constrains all values of $\alpha_{1i} = \alpha_{2i}$. Create σ_2^{*2} by regressing μ_t on all of the regressors the linear model and create σ_1^{*2} by regressing μ_t on all of the regressors in (7.10). After several thousand replications, you have the distribution of F^*.

7. GENERALIZED IMPULSE RESPONSES AND FORECASTING

This section presents two different estimated threshold models. Each was selected to emphasize a different aspect of the general methodology. First, Potter's (1995) TAR model of U.S. GNP is presented. The interesting feature of Potter's study is the calculation of impulse responses from a TAR model. Second, Enders and Sandler's (2002) forecast function for the number of casualties caused by transnational terrorists is examined.

Nonlinear Estimates of GNP Growth

Potter (1995) argues that a nonlinear model of U.S. GNP growth performs much better than a linear one. To begin, Potter estimates the following AR(5) model of the logarithmic change in the quarterly values of real U.S. gross national product (*GNP*) growth over the 1947:1 to 1990:4 period:

$$y_t = 0.540 + 0.330y_{t-1} + 0.193y_{t-2} - 0.105y_{t-3} - 0.092y_{t-4} - 0.024y_{t-5} + \varepsilon_t \quad \text{AIC} = 8.00$$
$$\quad\ (4.42)\quad (4.23)\qquad (2.35)\qquad\ (-1.27)\qquad (-1.12)\qquad (-0.308)$$

where $y_t = 100*[\log(GNP_t) - \log(GNP_{t-1})]$.

Potter also estimates a two-regime TAR model allowing the variances to differ across regimes. He states that pre-testing yields a delay factor of 2 (i.e., $d = 2$) and a threshold of zero. After purging the threshold regression of insignificant coefficients, Potter reports the following TAR model:

$$y_t = 0.517 + 0.299y_{t-1} + 0.189y_{t-2} - 1.143y_{t-5} + \varepsilon_{1t} \qquad y_{t-2} > 0$$
$$\quad\ (3.21)\quad (3.74)\qquad (1.77)\quad (-16.57)$$

$$y_t = -0.808 + 0.516y_{t-1} - 0.946y_{t-2} - 0.352y_{t-5} + \varepsilon_{2t} \qquad y_{t-2} \leq 0$$
$$\quad\ (-1.91)\quad (2.79)\qquad (-2.68)\qquad (-1.63)$$

The presence of the AR(5) terms is unusual because the data are seasonally adjusted and there is no particular reason to suppose that the fifth lag (but not lags 3 and 4) affect the contemporaneous value of GNP. However, Potter reports that the AR(3) and AR(4) coefficients are not statistically different from zero at the 5 percent significance level. There are 37 observations in the contractionary regime ($y_{t-2} \leq 0$) and 133 observations in the expansionary regime ($y_{t-2} > 0$). The estimated variance of $\varepsilon_{1t} = 0.763$ and the estimated variance of $\varepsilon_{2t} = 1.50$. Thus, the magnitudes of shocks while in the contractionary regime tend to be quite large. The large negative coefficient in the AR(2) term in the contractionary regime has an interesting economic implication. When $y_{t-2} < 0$, there tends to be a sharp reversal in the contraction of output since the product of -0.946 and y_{t-2} is positive.

RECURSIVE FORECASTS The AIC was constructed by combining the residual sums of squares from the two segments of the TAR model. This value of the AIC ($= -4.89$) clearly selects the TAR model over the linear model. In order to compare the out-of-sample forecasts, the following procedure was used. Beginning with the sample period 1947:1 through 1960:1, linear and TAR models were estimated. For each model, the one-step-ahead forecast was obtained. Then, the sample period was updated by one quarter and new linear and TAR models were estimated. These updated models were used to obtain one-step-ahead forecasts. Repeating this procedure though the end of the sample yielded two sets of one-step-ahead forecasts. The correlation of the forecasts with the actual values of output growth was 0.23 for the linear model and 0.35 for the TAR model. As such, the forecasting performing performance of the TAR model exceeds that of the linear model.

Impulse Responses

In a linear model, the impulse responses are not history dependent and the magnitude of the shock does not alter the time-profile of the responses. For example, in the linear AR(1) model $y_t = \rho y_{t-1} + \varepsilon_t$, the impulse responses are given by

$$y_t = \sum_{i=0}^{\infty} \rho^i \varepsilon_{t-i}$$

Hence, the effect of a one-unit shock on y_t is 1, the effect of the shock on y_{t+1} is predicted to be ρ (i.e., $\partial y_{t+1}/\partial \varepsilon_t = \partial y_t/\partial \varepsilon_{t-1} = \rho$), the effect the shock on y_{t+2} is predicted to be ρ^2, and so forth. Moreover, the effects of a two-unit shock are simply twice those for the one-unit shock and the effects of a negative shock are simply the negative of those for positive shocks. However, the interpretation of impulse response functions for a nonlinear model is not straightforward. The reason is that the impulse responses are history dependent. The effect of an ε_t shock on the time path of the system depends on the magnitudes of the current and subsequent shocks. Clearly, the sign of the shocks can matter. To take a simple example, in a TAR model with $\tau = 0$, the impulse responses for a one-unit positive shock will have a different time path than a one-unit negative shock. Moreover, the size of the shocks matter; if you are in the contractionary regime, a small positive shock can imply a different time profile than a very large shock since the small shock is less likely to induce a regime change. Thus, to calculate impulse responses, it is necessary to specify the history of the system and the magnitude of the shock. Moreover, the effects of a shock to ε_t on y_{t+10} will depend on the magnitudes of the shocks that take place in periods $(t + 1)$ through $(t + 9)$. There are several ways to attack the problem. Potter considers shocks of four different magnitudes: –2 percent, –1 percent, 1 percent, and 2 percent. Moreover, he considers several different histories. Consider:

- In the three quarters of 1983:3, 1983:1 and 1984:1, real GNP growth at an annual rate was a remarkable 7.1 percent, 8.2 percent, and 8.2 percent, respectively. As such, even a –2 percent shock would cause GDP growth to remain in the positive regime. Hence, the responses are very similar to those that would be obtained from a linear model. Since there is no regime switching, the 1 percent and 2 percent shocks are multiples of each other. The four impulse responses for this particular history are shown in Panel (*a*) of Figure 7.10.

- The situation was very different in 1970:2 in that the economy experienced a mild downturn. For 1969:4, 1970:1 and 1970:2, GNP growth measured at an annual rate was –1.9 percent, –0.46 percent, and 0.91 percent, respectively.

FIGURE 7.10   Impulse Responses for Two Histories

Hence, the negative, but not the positive, shocks push GNP growth across the threshold of zero. Panel (*b*) of Figure 7.10 shows the asymmetric responses. Given that the contractionary regime has a AR(2) coefficient that is nearly –1.0, negative shocks are less persistent then positive shocks. As such, you can see the rather quick turnaround in GNP growth predicted to begin in 1970:3. Also notice that the effects of the –1 percent and –2 percent shocks are not proportional to each other.

Notice that these impulse response functions trace out the effects of different sized ε_t shocks (t = 1984:$Q$1 and 1970:$Q$2) assuming subsequent shocks are all zero. Using the methods discussed below, it is possible to generalize the impulse response functions to allow for the effects of any ensuing shocks. To preview the method, consider Potter's –1 percent shock used as value for $\varepsilon_{1972:Q2}$. It is possible to draw eight random values to simulate a possible sequence for $\varepsilon_{1972:Q3}$ through $\varepsilon_{1974:Q3}$. This set of shocks can then be used to obtain the impulse responses through 1974:$Q$3. If this procedure is repeated several thousand times, it is possible to obtain the mean values of the impulse responses along with the various percentiles. Hence, it is possible to obtain a 5 percent or 10 percent confidence band around the calculated mean values of the impulses.

Terrorist Incidents with Casualties

A realistic way to capture the nature of terrorist campaigns is to use a two-regime TAR model. In relatively tranquil regimes, terrorists can replenish and stockpile resources, recruit new members, raise funds, and plan for future attacks. Terrorism can remain low until an event occurs that switches the system into the high-terrorism regime. Because each terrorist attack utilizes scarce resources, high-terrorism states are not anticipated to exhibit a high degree of persistence when a shock raises the level of terrorism. On the other hand, periods with little terrorism can be highly persistent to shocks. In order to measure the differing persistence across the two states, Enders and Sandler (2002) acquired quarterly data on the number of incidents containing one or more casualties over the 1968:1 to 2000:4 period. We first estimated the number of incidents with casualties (*cas*) as the linear AR(3) autoregressive process:

$$cas_t = 5.91 + 0.261cas_{t-1} + 0.310cas_{t-2} + 0.209cas_{t-3} + \varepsilon_t \quad \text{AIC} = 1205.72$$
$$(2.83)\ (2.98) \qquad (3.59) \qquad (2.40)$$

where cas_t represents the number of incidents with casualties.

The model appears adequate in that it satisfies the standard diagnostic tests. All *t*-statistics are significant at conventional levels and the point estimates of the autoregressive coefficients imply stationarity. The results of a Dickey–Fuller test allow us to reject the null hypothesis of a unit root at the 5 percent significance level. Moreover, the Ljung–Box Q-statistics indicate that the residuals are serially uncorrelated. For example, Q-statistics using the first 4, 8, and 12 lags of the residual autocorrelations have *prob*-values of 0.98, 0.52, and 0.72, respectively.

Correlation coefficients are measures of linear association and may not detect nonlinearities in the data. We begin a search for the most appropriate TAR representation by estimating a model in the form of (7.10) using a value of $p = 3$. By applying Chan's method to search over all potential thresholds, we obtained

$$cas_t = (17.05 + 0.173cas_{t-1} + 0.236cas_{t-2} + 0.053cas_{t-3})\, I_t$$
$$\quad (2.89)\ (1.59) \qquad (1.72) \qquad\ (0.458)$$
$$+ (2.57 + 0.361cas_{t-1} + 0.207cas_{t-2} + 0.362cas_{t-3})\,(1 - I_t) + \varepsilon_t \quad (7.23)$$
$$\quad (0.08)\ (2.28) \qquad (0.91) \qquad\ (2.71)$$

where the estimates of the threshold and the delay are $\tau = 25$ and $d = 2$.

Equation (7.23) is clearly overparameterized, since there are a number of coefficients with t-statistics less than 1.96 in absolute value. To purge the model of the "unimportant" coefficients, we use the following strategy. If the t-statistics indicate that one or more of the coefficients have a *prob*-value below 5 percent, we reestimate the model excluding the "least significant" term. Thus, (7.23) is re-estimated without $I_t cas_{t-3}$. If the AIC of the resulting model is smaller than that of the original model, the term is purged. The exceptions to this procedure are the two intercept terms, because the absence of an intercept implies a zero mean. This procedure yields the final TAR estimate:

$$cas_t = (17.87 + 0.189cas_{t-1} + 0.237cas_{t-2})\, I_t$$
$$\quad (3.19)\ (1.83) \qquad (1.83)$$
$$+ (3.92 + 0.423cas_{t-1} + 0.398cas_{t-3})\,(1 - I_t) + \varepsilon_t \quad (7.24)$$
$$\quad (1.48)\ (2.97) \qquad (3.12)$$

where AIC $= 1205.07$, $\tau = 25$, and $d = 2$.

Diagnostic checking indicates that the model is appropriate. For example, the first twelve autocorrelations of the residuals are less than 0.14 in absolute value and the *prob*-values for the Ljung–Box $Q(4)$, $Q(8)$, and $Q(12)$ statistics are 0.98, 0.57, and 0.81, respectively. Even though the TAR model contains seven parameters (i.e., six coefficients plus τ), the AIC selects it over the linear model.

The threshold model yields very different implications about the behavior of the cas_t series than the linear model. The latter indicates that the cas_t sequence convergences to the long-run mean of approximately 26.9 incidents per quarter [5.91 / (1.0 $- 0.261 - 0.301 - 0.209)$]. Since the linear specification makes no distinction between high- and low-terrorism states, the degree of autoregressive decay is always constant. Regardless of whether the number of incidents is above or below the mean, the degree of persistence is quite large; the largest characteristic root of the linear model is 0.88.

A useful way to conceptualize the time path of the TAR model is to refer to the **skeleton.** The skeleton is the model excluding the error term; hence, it captures the properties of the underlying nonlinear difference equation. For example, the skeleton of (7.24) is

$$cas_t = [17.87 + 0.189cas_{t-1} + 0.237cas_{t-2}]I_t + [3.92 + 0.423cas_{t-1} + 0.398cas_{t-3}](1 - I_t)$$

In the high-terrorism regime (i.e., when the number of incidents is 25 or more), $I_t = 1$, so that $cas_t = 17.87 + 0.189cas_{t-1} + 0.237cas_{t-2}$. Thus, the number of incidents gravitates toward the attractor 31.1 [$= 17.87 \div (1 - 0.189 - 0.237)$]. As measured by the largest characteristic root, the speed of adjustment is 0.59; when terrorism is high, approximately 60 percent of each incident is expected to persist into the next period.

In the low-terrorism state, $I_t = 0$, so that $cas_t = 3.92 + 0.423cas_{t-1} + 0.398cas_{t-3}$. The attractor is 21.9 and the largest characteristic root is 0.88. When the number of incidents is below the threshold value of 25, there is little tendency to return to a long-run mean value. Perhaps a better way to understand the nature of the system is to consider the forecast function. As analyzed in Koop, Pesaran, and Potter (1996), the forecasts and impulse responses from a nonlinear model are state-dependent. In terms of (7.24), a positive shock when $y_{t-2} > 25$ will be less persistent than the same shock when y_{t-2} is far below the threshold. Since we are interested in comparing short-run and long-run forecasts in the two states (rather than a generalized impulse response function), we use a modified version of Koop, Pesaran, and Potter's methodology.

For a model with three lags, we select a particular history for y_t, y_{t-1}, and y_{t-2}. For example, in the last three quarters of 1985—a high-terrorism regime—the number of casualty incidents were 33, 50, and 40, respectively. Hence, to forecast the subsequent number of incidents from the perspective of 1985:4, we let $y_{t-2} = y_{1985:2} = 33$, $y_{t-1} = y_{1985:3} = 50$, and $y_t = y_{1985:4} = 40$. We then select 25 randomly drawn realizations of the residuals of (7.24). Since the residuals may not have a normal distribution, the residuals are selected using standard bootstrapping procedures. In particular, the residuals are drawn with replacement using a uniform distribution. Call these residuals ε_{t+1}^*, ε_{t+2}^*, ..., ε_{t+25}^*. We then generate y_{t+1}^* through y_{t+25}^* by substituting these bootstrapped residuals into (7.24) and setting I_t appropriately for high- or low-terrorism states. In essence, y_{t+1}^* is one possible realization of the cas_t series for 1986:1, y_{t+2}^* is one possible realization of the cas_t series for 1986:2, and so on. For this particular history, we repeat the process 1,000 times. Under very weak conditions, the Law of Large Numbers guarantees that the sample average of the 1,000 values of y_{t+i}^* converges to the conditional mean of y_{t+1} denoted by $E_t y_{t+1}$. Similarly, the Law of Large Numbers guarantees that the sample means of the various y_{t+i}^* (called $y_{t+i}^*(k)$) converge to the true conditional i-step-ahead forecasts, that is

$$\lim_{N \to \infty} \left[\sum_{k=1}^{N} y_{t+i}^*(k) / N \right] = E_t y_{t+i}$$

The essential point is that the sample averages of y_{t+1}^* through y_{t+25}^* yield the 1-step- through 25-step-ahead conditional forecasts of the cas_t series from the perspective of 1985:4. Intuitively, because the number of casualty incidents exceeds the threshold, the value of cas_t should quickly decline from 40 toward the attractor of 31.1. Nevertheless, the long-run forecast need not equal the attractor, which can be seen by examining the conditional forecasts (indicated by the solid line) shown in Panel (a) of Figure 7.11. Although the expected number of cas_t incidents does decline toward 31.1, there are two reasons why the long-term forecasts continue to decline. Since incidents below the threshold are (on average) more persistent than those above, the system's mean will be below the attractor. Moreover, the forecasts allow for the possibility of a regime-switch into the low-terrorism state. As shown in Panel (a) of the figure, the long-run expected value is about 28.5 casualty incidents per quarter. When the number of incidents is high, there is a rapid decline to the threshold, as terrorist networks cannot maintain high-level, resource-using offensives. A

FIGURE 7.11   Nonlinear Forecasts of Casualty Incidents

comparison of the forecasts with the actual number of casualty incidents (the dashed line in the figure) is instructive. The close fit is remarkable given that the forecasts are not the successive one-step-ahead forecasts. Instead, the figure traces out the 1-step- through 25-step-ahead forecasts from the perspective of 1985:4.

In contrast, the number of terrorist incidents in the last three quarters of 1998 were quite low; $y_{1998:2} = 5$, $y_{1998:3} = 15$, and $y_{1998:4} = 6$. As shown in Panel (b) of Figure 7.11, reversion back toward the attractor of 21.9 is quite slow in the low-terrorism state. In fact, conditional on the history of 1998:4, the forecasts remain below 21.9 until the third quarter of 2001. The forecasts seem to track the actual number of incidents occurring through the end of our data set reasonably well and ultimately converge to those for Panel (a). In either case, these long-run forecasts are relatively close to the attractor for the high-terrorism state (31.1).

8. UNIT ROOTS AND NONLINEARITY

Suppose you were convinced that the interest rate spread displays the type of nonlinear adjustment given by (7.1). Before estimating the TAR model directly, you might want to determine whether the series does revert to a long-run equilibrium value (called an **attractor**). However, the established tests for the presence of an attractor assume a linear adjustment process. For example, the Dickey–Fuller (1979) test for a unit root uses a linear adjustment process of the form

$$y_t = a_1 y_{t-1} + \varepsilon_t \quad [\text{or } \Delta y_t = \rho y_{t-1} + \varepsilon_t] \tag{7.25}$$

If the null hypothesis $a_1 = 1$ can be rejected in favor of the alternative $-1 < a_1 < 1$, it can be concluded that the $\{y_t\}$ sequence decays to the attractor $y^* = 0$. However, if the $\{y_t\}$ sequence is generated from a nonlinear model, the Dickey–Fuller test might fail to detect an attractor since it is misspecified. Although (7.25) can be augmented with deterministic regressors and lagged changes of $\{y_t\}$, the crucial point to note is that the dynamic adjustment process is assumed to be linear. The issue is important since Pippenger and Goering (1993) and Balke and Fomby (1997) show that tests for unit roots have low power in the presence of asymmetric adjustment. After all, (7.25) does not appropriately capture the dynamic adjustment process of a nonlinear model.

Notice that the discussion above is directly applicable to the findings of Michael, Nobay, and Peel (1997). Recall that their aim was to determine whether real exchange rates should be modeled as an ESTAR process. Nevertheless, the dynamic equation used to determine whether the U.K.–U.S. real exchange rate was stationary [i.e., equation (7.21)] assumes a linear adjustment process. As it turned out, they were able to reject the null hypothesis of a unit root. However, in other circumstances, a linear test may not be able to detect the presence of an attractor for a nonlinear process.

To circumvent this problem, there is a large and growing literature designed to test for the presence of an attractor in the presence of nonlinear adjustment. For example, in Enders and Granger (1998), we generalized the Dickey–Fuller methodology to consider the null hypothesis of a unit root against the alternative hypothesis of a threshold autoregressive (TAR) model. The simple version TAR model is

$$\Delta y_t = I_t \rho_1 (y_{t-1} - \tau) + (1 - I_t)\rho_2 (y_{t-1} - \tau) + \varepsilon_t \tag{7.26}$$

$$I_t = \begin{cases} 1 & if \ y_{t-1} \geq \tau \\ 0 & if \ y_{t-1} < \tau \end{cases} \tag{7.27}$$

As shown by the phase diagram illustrated in Figure 7.12, when $y_{t-1} = \tau$, $\Delta y_t = 0$. However, Δy_t equals $\rho_1 (y_{t-1} - \tau)$ if the lagged value of the series is above τ and equals $\rho_2 (y_{t-1} - \tau)$ if the lagged value of the series is below τ. The attractor is τ since Δy_t has an expected value of zero when $y_{t-1} = \tau$. Hence, if $y_{t-1} = a$, Δy_t equals the distance ab.

If we use the specification given by (7.26) and (7.27), it is possible to test for an attractor even though the adjustment process is nonlinear. Notice that if $\rho_1 = \rho_2 = 0$, the process is a random walk. A sufficient condition for the $\{y_t\}$ sequence to be stationary is $-2 < (\rho_1, \rho_2) < 0$.[4] Also notice that the Dickey–Fuller test emerges as the special case in which $\rho_1 = \rho_2$. If it is possible to reject the null hypothesis $\rho_1 = \rho_2 = 0$, it can be concluded that there is an attractor. However, as in the Dickey–Fuller test, it is not possible to use a classical F-statistic to test the null hypothesis $\rho_1 = \rho_2 = 0$. Instead, the F-statistics for the null hypothesis $\rho_1 = \rho_2 = 0$ are reported in Table F at the end of the text.

If the null hypothesis of nonstationarity is rejected, it is possible to test for symmetric versus asymmetric adjustment. In particular, if the null is rejected (so that the

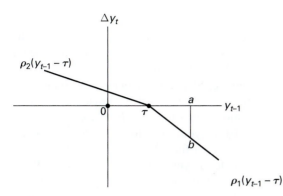

FIGURE 7.12   Phase Diagram for the TAR Model in Equation 7.26

sequence has an attractor), then you can perform the test for symmetric adjustment (i.e., $\rho_1 = \rho_2$) using a standard F-distribution. If the threshold is unknown (but estimated consistently using Chan's method), the conjecture is that you can also use a standard F-test. However, Hansen shows that small sample properties of the OLS estimates of the individual ρ_1 and ρ_2 values have inflated standard errors and the convergence properties of the OLS estimates can be poor. To avoid this problem, you can use Hansen's (1997) method that was described at the end of Section 6.

An alternative to the basic TAR model is the momentum threshold autoregressive (M-TAR) model. Since the exact nature of the nonlinearity may be unknown, it is possible to allow the adjustment to depend on the change in y_{t-1} (i.e., Δy_{t-1}) instead of the level of y_{t-1}. In this case, the model becomes (7.26) along with the indicator function

$$I_t = \begin{cases} 1 & \text{if } \Delta y_{t-1} > 0 \\ 0 & \text{if } \Delta y_{t-1} \leq 0 \end{cases} \tag{7.28}$$

This variant of the basic model, used by Enders and Granger (1998) and Caner and Hansen (1998), allows a variable to display differing amounts of autoregressive decay depending on whether it is increasing or decreasing. This specification is especially relevant when the adjustment is such that the series exhibits more momentum in one direction than the other; the resulting model is called momentum-threshold autoregressive (M-TAR) model. The F-statistics for the null hypothesis $\rho_1 = \rho_2 = 0$ using the M-TAR specification is called ϕ_M. As there is generally no presumption as to whether to use the TAR or the M-TAR model, the recommendation is to select the adjustment mechanism (7.27) or (7.28) by a model selection criterion such as the AIC or SBC.

To perform the test, follow these steps:

STEP 1: If you know the value of τ (for example $\tau = 0$), estimate (7.26). Otherwise, use Chan's method; for each potential threshold τ, set the indicator function using (7.27). Estimate (7.26) for each potential threshold value and select the value of τ from the regression containing the smallest value for the sum of squared residuals.

STEP 2: If you are unsure as to the nature of the adjustment process, repeat Step 1 using the M-TAR model. For each potential threshold τ set the indicator function using (7.28). Select the value of τ resulting in the best fit. Use the AIC or SBC to select the TAR or M-TAR specification.

STEP 3: Use the model selected from Step 1 or Step 2 to calculate the F-statistic for the null hypothesis $\rho_1 = \rho_2 = 0$. For the TAR model, compare this sample statistic with the appropriate critical value in Table F. The critical values depend on sample size (T) and whether you augment the model with lagged changes. Use Panel (a) if you estimate τ for a TAR model and Panel (b) if you estimate τ for an M-TAR model. If you know the threshold and estimate an M-TAR model, use Panel (c). In the case of a TAR model with a known threshold, the test seems to have low power relative to the Dickey–Fuller test. As such, the critical values for this case are not reported.

STEP 4: If the alternative hypothesis is accepted (i.e., if there is an attractor), it is possible to test for symmetric versus asymmetric adjustment since the asymptotic joint distribution of ρ_1 and ρ_2 converges to a multivariate normal. As such, the restriction that adjustment is symmetric (i.e., the null hypothesis $\rho_1 = \rho_2$) can be tested using a standard F-test or using Hansen's (1997) method.

STEP 5: Diagnostic checking of the residuals should be undertaken to ascertain whether the estimated $\{\varepsilon_t\}$ series could reasonably be characterized by a white-noise process. If the residuals are correlated, return to Step 1 and re-estimate the model in the form:

$$\Delta y_t = I_t \rho_1 (y_{t-1} - \tau) + (1 - I_t) \rho_2 (y_{t-1} - \tau) + \sum_{i=1}^{p} \alpha_i \Delta y_{t-i} + \varepsilon_t \qquad (7.29)$$

In working with this specification, it is possible to use diagnostic checks of the residuals and/or the various model selection criteria to determine the lag length. In principle, it is possible to allow the lagged changes to appear asymmetrically. However, this particular extension has not been explored in the literature.

An Example

Enders and Granger use quarterly values of the 10-year government securities (r_{Lt}) and the Federal Funds rate (r_{St}) over the period 1958:1 through 1994:1. You can find the data used in the study on the file labeled GRANGER.XLS. The issue is to determine how to model the relationship between the two interest rates. First form the interest rate spread as $s_t = r_{Lt} - r_{St}$. After a bit of experimentation, the most appropriate equation for the Dickey–Fuller test is

$$\Delta s_t = 0.120 - 0.156 s_{t-1} + 0.162 \Delta s_{t-1} + \varepsilon_t$$
$$\quad\;\; (1.52)\,(-3.56) \qquad\;\; (1.94)$$

AIC = 669.79   SBC = 678.68

These are the identical results found by Engle and Granger. The coefficient on s_{t-1} has a t-statistic of -3.56; hence, the null hypothesis of a unit root can be soundly rejected. Since the point of this section is to illustrate the test for threshold adjustment, we can pretend that the results of the Dickey–Fuller test are ambiguous. Nevertheless, diagnostic checking reveals that the equation is inadequate. For example, the RESET with $H = 3$ and $H = 4$ have *prob*-values of 0.0016 and 0.00009, respectively. Hence, there is substantial evidence of neglected nonlinearity.

Next, estimate a TAR model in the form of (7.27) and (7.29). The value of τ yielding the best fit is -0.27 so that the resulting TAR model of the spread is

$$\Delta s_t = -0.066 I_t(s_{t-1} + 0.27) - 0.286(1 - I_t)(s_{t-1} + 0.27) + 0.172\Delta s_{t-1} + \varepsilon_t$$
$$\quad (-1.59) \qquad\qquad (-3.67) \qquad\qquad\qquad (2.07)$$

AIC = 669.12   SBC = 680.97

For Step 2, we can estimate an M-TAR model by replacing (7.27) with (7.28). The value of τ yielding the best fit is 1.64 so that the resulting M-TAR model of the spread is

$$\Delta s_t = -0.299 I_t(s_{t-1} - 1.64) - 0.007(1 - I_t)(s_{t-1} - 1.64) + 0.016\Delta s_{t-1} + \varepsilon_t$$
$$\quad (-4.75) \qquad\qquad (-0.145) \qquad\qquad\qquad (1.183)$$

AIC = 662.55   SBC = 674.40

Notice that the AIC and the SBC both select the M-TAR model even though it has two coefficients that are statistically insignificant. You might want to experiment and estimate the model without these two extraneous coefficients. The F-statistic for the null hypothesis that $\rho_1 = \rho_2 = 0$ is 11.44. If we compare this to the critical values for Φ_M, we can reject the null hypothesis of no attractor. As such, we can test whether adjustment is symmetric or asymmetric. The F-statistic for the null hypothesis $\rho_1 = \rho_2$ is 12.24 with a *prob*-value of 0.0006. Hence, we can conclude that the M-TAR best captures the adjustment process of the interest rate spread. The point estimates suggest that the equilibrium value of the spread is 1.64. When the spread is increasing (i.e., when $\Delta s_{t-1} > 0$), the speed of adjustment is fairly rapid. However, when the spread is decreasing (so that the long-term rate is falling relative to the referral funds rate), the adjustment of -0.007 is almost nonexistent. This is in contrast to the linear model; the linear model suggests that the speed of adjustment is -0.158 regardless of whether the spread is increasing or decreasing. Moreover, the linear specification suggests that the long-run equilibrium value of the spread is zero since the intercept has a t-statistic of 1.52.

NONLINEAR ERROR-CORRECTION   If you experiment with the data set, you will find that both r_{Lt} and r_{St} act as $I(1)$ processes. Since there is a linear combination of these two $I(1)$ variables that is stationary, the Granger representation theorem indicates that there is an error-correction model. However, there is nothing requiring that the dynamic adjustment mechanism must be linear. Instead, it seems plausible that the error-correction model has the M-TAR form

$$\Delta r_{Lt} = -0.03 I_t(s_{t-1} - 1.64) - 0.07(1 - I_t)(s_{t-1} - 1.64) + A_{11}(L)\Delta r_{Lt-1} + A_{12}(L)\Delta r_{St-1} + \varepsilon_{1t}$$
$$\quad (-0.766) \qquad\qquad (-2.11) \qquad\qquad\qquad F_{11} = 0.087 \quad F_{12} = 0.521$$

$$\Delta r_{St} = 0.21 I_t(s_{t-1} - 1.64) - 0.04(1 - I_t)(s_{t-1} - 1.64) + A_{21}(L)\Delta r_{Lt-1} + A_{22}(L)\Delta r_{St-1} + \varepsilon_{2t}$$
$$\quad (2.67) \qquad\qquad (-0.67) \qquad\qquad\qquad F_{21} = 0.001 \quad F_{22} = 0.844$$

where t-statistics are in parentheses, two lags of each variable are used in each equation, $F_{ij} =$ is the *prob*-value that all coefficients in the polynomial $A_{ij}(L) = 0$, and I_t is the M-TAR indicator given by (7.28).

The t-statistics suggest an interesting adjustment process towards the long-run equilibrium. Increases in the spread tend to be accompanied by changes in the federal funds rate while decreases are accompanied by changes in the 10-year rate. When the spread is increasing (i.e., if $\Delta s_{t-1} > 0$), we would expect the Fed-funds rate to increase by 21 percent of the discrepancy between s_{t-1} and the long-run value of 1.64. When the spread is decreasing, the long-term rate declines by 7 percent of the discrepancy. Nevertheless, since the threshold was estimated, some might want to use bootstrap t-statistics to perform inference on the coefficients.

The linear error-correction model tells a very different story. If we use the type of linear error-correction model used in Chapter 6, we obtain

$$\Delta r_{Lt} = -0.114\hat{e}_{t-1} + A_{11}(L)\Delta r_{Lt-1} + A_{12}(L)\Delta r_{St-1} + \varepsilon_{1t}$$
$$(-3.30) \qquad F_{11} = 0.062 \qquad F_{12} = 0.288$$

$$\Delta rs_t = -0.002\hat{e}_{t-1} + A_{21}(L)\Delta rl_{t-1} + A_{22}(L)\Delta rs_{t-1} + \varepsilon_{2t}$$
$$(-0.04) \qquad F_{21} = 0.000 \qquad F_{22} = 0.333$$

where $\hat{e}_{t-1}$ is the residual from the regression of r_{Lt} on a constant and r_{St}. Hence, $\hat{e}_{t-1}$ is the estimated deviation from the long-run relationship obtained by using the Engle–Granger technique.

Hence, the linear model implies that only the 10-year interest rate responds to the discrepancy from the long-run equilibrium.

9. SUMMARY AND CONCLUSIONS

There are many important economic variables that exhibit nonlinear behavior. The difficulty is to properly capture the form of the nonlinearity. Once you abandon the linear framework, you must address the specification problem. As surveyed in this chapter, there are many nonlinear models and there is no clear way to decide which nonlinear specification is the best. The issue is important since the use of an incorrect nonlinear specification may be worse than ignoring the nonlinearity. Moreover, a linear model can always be viewed as a local approximation of a nonlinear process.

There are some standard recommendations for estimating a nonlinear process. The most important is to use a specific to general modeling strategy. In particular:

1. Always start by plotting your data. Visual inspection of the data can help you detect the nature of the nonlinearity. Moreover, an outlier or a structural break will appear as a departure from the standard linear model with constant coefficients. You can save yourself substantial modeling time if you inspect the data for these features.

2. Fit the series of interest using the best linear model possible. For example, you might fit $\{y_t\}$ as an ARMA process using the Box–Jenkins methodology. The coefficients should be well estimated and the residuals should show no evidence of any serial correlation.

3. There are a number of tests designed to detect nonlinear behavior. The McLeod–Li, RESET and various Lagrange multiplier tests can be used to detect nonlinear behavior. A Lagrange multiplier test has a specific nonlinear model as its alternative hypothesis. Nevertheless, even a battery of such tests is not able to reveal the precise nature of the nonlinearity.

4. If nonlinearity is detected, you have to decide on the appropriate form of the nonlinear specification. There is no substitute for an underlying theoretical model of the adjustment process. For example, if your model suggests that prices increase more readily than they decrease, some form of threshold model is likely to be the most appropriate.

5. The fitted nonlinear model(s) should fit the data better than the linear specification and all coefficients should be statistically significant. In most instances, you will search over a number of plausible specifications. As such, the individual t-statistics and F-statistics are likely to be misleading. After all, you are examining the t-statistic on the best-fitting specification. If you examine 10 different specifications, on average, you should find one that is significant at the 10 percent level. Because overfitting is a distinct possibility, many researchers would use the parsimonious SBC as a measure of fit. Moreover, traditional t-tests and F-tests may not be appropriate in some nonlinear settings. Hansen (1997) considers the issue of inference in TAR models.

6. The generalized impulse response function can help you detect whether the nonlinear model is plausible. A useful diagnostic check is to use a Granger–Newbold or Diebold–Mariano test (see Section 9 of Chapter 2) to check the out-of-sample forecasting performance of the various models.

The nonlinear models discussed in this chapter were used to estimate a series $\{y_t\}$. However, it is possible to apply nonlinear models to the equation for the conditional variance. For example, the TARCH model discussed in Chapter 3 is an example of a nonlinearity applied to the equation for the conditional variance. Hamilton and Susmel (1994) show how to apply the Markov switching model to the conditional variance of a time series. Higgens and Bera (1992) develop a nonlinear ARCH (NARCH) model that posits a "constant elasticity of substitution" functional form for the model of the conditional variance.

In addition, a large literature is growing concerning the presence of unit roots and cointegration in the presence of nonlinearities. For example, Granger, Inoue, and Morin (1997) develop some of the issues in terms of a nonlinear error correction model. Enders and Siklos (2001) extend the TAR unit root test discussed in Section 8 to allow for a cointegrated system. Tsay (1998) develops a test that can be used to detect threshold cointegration. The appropriate use of the test is illustrated using spot and futures prices. Caner and Hansen (2001) develop a maximum likelihood method to test for a threshold unit root and Hansen and Seo (2002) extend the analysis to a cointegrated system. Kapetanios, Shin, and Snell (2003) develop a simple way to test for a unit root against the alternative of an ESTAR model. Another way to think about nonlinear models is in the frequency domain. Granger and Joyeux (1980) provide an introduction to the notion that a series may be integrated of some order other than an integer. Such nonlinear processes may be mean-reverting yet can behave similarly to unit root processes.

QUESTIONS AND EXERCISES

1. Let p_A and p_M denote the price of cotton in Alabama and Mississippi, respectively. The price gap, or discrepancy, is $p_A - p_M$. For each part, present a nonlinear model that captures the dynamic adjustment mechanism given in the brief narrative.

   a. A large price gap (in absolute value) tends to be eliminated quickly as compared to a small gap.

   b. The price gap is closed more quickly if it is positive than if it is negative.

   c. It costs 10 cents to transport cotton between Alabama and Mississippi. Hence, a price discrepancy of less than 10 cents will not be eliminated by arbitrage. However, 50 percent of any price gap exceeding 10 cents will be eliminated within a period.

   d. The value of p_A, but not the value of p_M, responds to a price gap.

2. Draw the phase diagram for each of the following processes:

   a. The GAR model: $y_t = 1.5y_{t-1} - 0.5y_{t-1}^3 + \varepsilon_t$

   b. The TAR model: $y_t = 1 + 0.5y_{t-1} + \varepsilon_t$ if $y_{t-1} > 2$ and $y_t = 0.5 + 0.75y_{t-1} + \varepsilon_t$ if $y_{t-1} \le 2$

   c. The TAR model: $y_t = 1 + 0.5y_{t-1} + \varepsilon_t$ if $y_{t-1} > 0$ and $y_t = -1 + 0.5y_{t-1} + \varepsilon_t$ if $y_{t-1} \le 0$

      Notice that this model is discontinuous at the threshold. Show that $y_{t-1} = +2$ and $y_{t-1} = -2$ are both stable equilibrium values for the skeleton.

   d. The TAR model: $y_t = -1 + 0.5y_{t-1} + \varepsilon_t$ if $y_{t-1} > 0$ and $y_t = +1 + 0.5y_{t-1} + \varepsilon_t$ if $y_{t-1} \le 0$

      Show that there is no stable equilibrium for the skeleton.

   e. The LSTAR model: $y_t = 0.75y_{t-1} + 0.25y_{t-1}/[1 + \exp(-y_{t-1})] + \varepsilon_t$

   f. The ESTAR model: $y_t = 0.75y_{t-1} + 0.25y_{t-1}[1 - \exp(-y_{t-1}^2)] + \varepsilon_t$

3. In the Markov switching model, let p_1 denote the *unconditional* probability that the system is in regime one and let p_2 denote the *unconditional* probability that the system is in regime two. As in the text, let p_{ii} denote the probability that the system remains in regime i. Prove the assertion

$$p_1 = (1 - p_{22})/(2 - p_{11} - p_{22})$$
$$p_2 = (1 - p_{11})/(2 - p_{11} - p_{22})$$

4. The file labeled LSTAR.XLS contains the 250 realizations of the series used in Section 6.

   a. Verify that (7.20) represents the best-fitting linear model for this process.

   b. Perform the RESET using $H = 3$. How does this compare to the result using $H = 4$?

   c. If your software package can perform the BDS test, determine whether the residuals from (7.20) pass the BDS test for white noise.

   d. Perform the LM tests for LSTAR adjustment and for ESTAR adjustment.

   e. If you estimate the process as a GAR process, you should find

$$y_t = 2.03 + 0.389y_{t-1} + 0.201y_{t-2} - 0.147y_{t-1}^2 + \varepsilon_t$$
$$(8.97) \quad (6.97) \qquad (3.48) \qquad (-10.57)$$

      All of the t-statistics imply that the coefficients are well estimated. Show that all of the residual autocorrelations are less than 0.1 in absolute value.

      How would you determine whether the GAR model or the LSTAR model is preferable?

5. The file INDPROD_60.XLS contains the industrial production series used to estimate the TAR model in Section 6. Use the data to replicate the results reported in the text.

6. The file GRANGER.XLS contains the interest rate series used to estimate the TAR and M-TAR models in Section 8.

   a. Estimate the TAR and M-TAR models reported in Section 8.

   b. Estimate the M-TAR model without the two insignificant coefficients.

   c. Calculate the AIC and the SBC for the TAR model and the M-TAR model without the insignificant coefficients. In your calculations, be sure to adjust the two model selection criteria to allow for the fact that you estimated the threshold.

   d. Calculate the multivariate AIC for the linear error correction model. How does this value compare to the multivariate AIC for the nonlinear error correction model?

7. Consider the linear process $y_t = 0.75y_{t-1} + \varepsilon_t$. Given $y_t = 1$, find $E_t y_{t+1}$, $E_t y_{t+2}$ and $E_t y_{t+3}$.

   a. Now consider the GAR process $y_t = 0.75y_{t-1} - 0.25y_{t-1}^2 + \varepsilon_t$. Given $y_t = 1$, find $E_t y_{t+1}$. Can you find $E_t y_{t+2}$ and $E_t y_{t+3}$? [Hint: $(E_t y_{t+1})^2 \neq E_t(y_{t+1}^2)$].

b. Use your answer to Part a to explain why it is difficult to perform multi-step-ahead forecasting with a nonlinear model.

8. Chapters 1.4 and 1.5 of the Programming Manual that accompanies this text contain a discussion of nonlinear least squares and maximum likelihood estimation. If you have not already done so, download the manual from the Wiley Web site. Also download the data set MONEYDEM.XLS and the programs.

   a. Consider the LSTAR model

$$y_t = \alpha_0 + \sum_{i=1}^{p} \alpha_i y_{t-i} + \theta(\beta_0 + \sum_{i=1}^{p} \beta_i y_{t-i}) + \varepsilon_t$$

   where $\theta = [1 + \exp(-\gamma y_{t-1})]^{-1}$ and $\gamma > 0$ is a scale parameter.

   Program 1.3 of the Programming Manual shows the relationship between γ, θ, and y_{t-1}. Specifically, the program produces the graph shown below. Values of y_{t-1} ranging from −5 to +5 are shown on the horizontal axis. As y_{t-1} increases from −5 to +5, the value of θ is shown to increase as well. However, this functional relationship is a function of γ. As γ increases from 0.5 to 5.0, the curve becomes steeper. Explain the relationships depicted in the figure.

Effects of Gamma on Theta

b. Program 1.4 uses nonlinear least squares to estimate the logarithmic change in M3 (*dlm3₁*) as an LSTAR model. Use the program to reproduce the results shown in the Programming Manual.

c. Program 1.4 also estimates the same LSTAR model using maximum likelihood methods. Compare the results of the two estimations. Why are there slight discrepancies between the two estimation methods?

d. Use your software package to estimate the logarithmic change in M3 as a bilinear process. You should find that the best-fitting model is

$$dlm3_t = 0.977 dlm3_{t-1} + \varepsilon_t - 0.273\varepsilon_{t-1} + 9.12 dlm3_{t-1}\varepsilon_{t-1}$$

9. Section 4.3 of the Programming Manual contains a discussion of the appropriate way to program a TAR model. If you have not already done so, download the manual from the

Wiley Web site. As shown in Program 4.3, use the data in MONEYDEM.XLS to construct the logarithmic change in real GDP ($dlrgdp_t$).

a. Estimate $dlrgdp_t$ as an AR(2) process.

b. Estimate the series as a TAR process such that $d = 1$, and $\tau = 0$. Your answer should be consistent with that reported in the manual.

c. Use Chan's method to find the consistent estimate of the threshold. You should find that $\tau = 0.01724$. Create the variables I_t, $I_t y_{t-1}$, $I_t y_{t-2}$, $(1 - I_t)$, $(1 - I_t)y_{t-1}$ and $(1 - I_t)y_{t-2}$. You should find

$$y_t = (0.022 - 0.444y_{t-1} - 0.037y_{t-2})I_t + (1 - I_t)(0.005 + 0.0238y_{t-1} + 0.0142y_{t-3}) + \varepsilon_t$$

Eliminate all insignificant coefficients and use the AIC to compare your answer to the model found in part a.

d. As shown in the programming manual, there might be a second threshold at 0.0025. Use the two thresholds to estimate a three-regime TAR model.

10. Section 5.4 of Chapter 4 in the Programming Manual shows you how to generate the critical values used in Enders and Granger (1998).

a. Reproduce the results for a sample size of 100 but use only 2000 Monte Carlo replications. How do your answers compare to those reported in the programming manual?

b. How would you obtain critical values for other sample sizes?

ENDNOTES

1. In these circumstances, the log likelihood for observation t is: $-(1/2)\ln(2\pi) - (1/2)\ln\sigma^2 - (1/2\sigma^2)\varepsilon_t^2$. Hence, the partial derivatives of the log likelihood with respect to α do not depend on the variance.

2 If a parameter is not identified under the null hypothesis, its partial derivative has no effect on the log likelihood function evaluated under the null hypothesis. Hence, in this circumstance, any type of likelihood test fails.

3 Recall that the third-order Taylor series expansion of $y = f(x)$ around the point $x = x_0$ is $y = f(x_0) + f'(x_0)(x - x_0) + (1/2)f''(x_0)(x - x_0)^2 + (1/6)f'''(x_0)(x - x_0)^3$ where ' denotes differentiation.

4 Petrucelli and Woolford (1984) show that a weaker set of sufficient conditions for the stationarity of $\{y_t\}$ is $\rho_1 < 0$, $\rho_2 < 0$ and $(1 + \rho_1)(1 + \rho_2) < 1$. It is also possible for one value of ρ_i to equal zero. Although there is no mean-reversion in this regime, if the variance of ε_t is sufficiently large, the system will switch into the convergent regime.

STATISTICAL TABLES

Table A   **Empirical Cumulative Distribution of τ**

Sample Size T	Significance level			
	0.01	0.025	0.05	0.10

The τ statistic: No Constant or Time Trend ($a_0 = a_2 = 0$)

Sample Size T	0.01	0.025	0.05	0.10
25	−2.66	−2.26	−1.95	−1.60
50	−2.62	−2.25	−1.95	−1.61
100	−2.60	−2.24	−1.95	−1.61
250	−2.58	−2.23	−1.95	−1.62
300	−2.58	−2.23	−1.95	−1.62
∞	−2.58	−2.23	−1.95	−1.62

The τ_μ statistic: Constant but No Time Trend ($a_2 = 0$)

Sample Size T	0.01	0.025	0.05	0.10
25	−3.75	−3.33	−3.00	−2.62
50	−3.58	−3.22	−2.93	−2.60
100	−3.51	−3.17	−2.89	−2.58
250	−3.46	−3.14	−2.88	−2.57
500	−3.44	−3.13	−2.87	−2.57
∞	−3.43	−3.12	−2.86	−2.57

The τ_τ statistic: Constant + Time Trend

Sample Size T	0.01	0.025	0.05	0.10
25	−4.38	−3.95	−3.60	−3.24
50	−4.15	−3.80	−3.50	−3.18
100	−4.04	−3.73	−3.45	−3.15
250	−3.99	−3.69	−3.43	−3.13
500	−3.98	−3.68	−3.42	−3.13
∞	−3.96	−3.66	−3.41	−3.12

Source: The table is reproduced from Fuller (1976). It is used by permission of John Wiley & Sons, Inc.

Table B   **Empirical Distribution of ϕ**

Sample size T	Significance level			
	0.10	0.05	0.025	0.01
ϕ_1				
25	4.12	5.18	6.30	7.88
50	3.94	4.86	5.80	7.06
100	3.86	4.71	5.57	6.70
250	3.81	4.63	5.45	6.52
500	3.79	4.61	5.41	6.47
∞	3.78	4.59	5.38	6.43
ϕ_2				
25	4.67	5.68	6.75	8.21
50	4.31	5.13	5.94	7.02
100	4.16	4.88	5.59	6.50
250	4.07	4.75	5.40	6.22
500	4.05	4.71	5.35	6.15
∞	4.03	4.68	5.31	6.09
ϕ_3				
25	5.91	7.24	8.65	10.61
50	5.61	6.73	7.81	9.31
100	5.47	6.49	7.44	8.73
250	5.39	6.34	7.25	8.43
500	5.36	6.30	7.20	8.34
∞	5.34	6.25	7.16	8.27

Source: Dickey, David, and Wayne A. Fuller (1981). Used by permission of the Econometric Society.

Table C   **Critical Values for the Engle–Granger
Cointegration Test**

T	1%	5%	10%	1%	5%	10%
	Two Variables			**Three Variables**		
50	−4.123	−3.461	−3.130	−4.592	−3.915	−3.578
100	−4.008	−3.398	−3.087	−4.441	−3.828	−3.514
200	−3.954	−3.368	−3.067	−4.368	−3.785	−3.483
500	−3.921	−3.350	−3.054	−4.326	−3.760	−3.464
	Four Variables			**Five Variables**		
50	−5.017	−4.324	−3.979	−5.416	−4.700	−4.348
100	−4.827	−4.210	−3.895	−5.184	−4.557	−4.240
200	−4.737	−4.154	−3.853	−5.070	−4.487	−4.186
500	−4.684	−4.122	−3.828	−5.003	−4.446	−4.154

The critical values are for cointegrating relations (with a constant in the
cointegrating vector) estimated using the Engle-Granger methodology.

Source: Critical values are interpolated using the response surface in
MacKinnon (1991).

Table D   **Residual Based Cointegration Test with *I*(1) and *I*(2) Variables**

m_1	T	Intercept Only				Linear Trend			
		$m_2 = 1$		$m_2 = 2$		$m_2 = 1$		$m_2 = 2$	
		prob-value		*prob*-value		*prob*-value		*prob*-value	
		0.01	0.05	0.01	0.05	0.01	0.05	0.01	0.05
0	50	−4.18	−3.51	−4.70	−4.02	−4.66	−4.01	−5.14	−4.45
	100	−4.09	−3.42	−4.51	−3.86	−4.55	−3.90	−4.93	−4.31
	250	−4.02	−3.38	−4.35	−3.80	−4.41	−3.83	−4.81	−4.20
1	50	−4.65	−3.93	−5.15	−4.40	−5.11	−4.42	−5.62	−4.89
	100	−4.51	−3.89	−4.85	−4.26	−4.85	−4.26	−5.23	-4.62
	250	−4.39	−3.80	−4.71	−4.18	−4.73	−4.19	−5.11	-4.50
2	50	−4.93	−4.30	−5.54	−4.77	−5.47	−4.74	−5.98	−5.17
	100	−4.81	−4.25	−5.29	−4.59	−5.21	−4.58	−5.59	−4.93
	250	−4.77	−4.16	−5.06	−4.49	−5.07	−4.51	−5.35	−4.80
3	50	−5.38	−4.71	−5.76	−5.08	−5.89	−5.13	−6.23	−5.48
	100	−5.20	−4.56	−5.58	−4.92	−5.52	−4.91	−5.97	−5.25
	250	−5.05	−4.48	−5.44	−4.83	−5.38	−4.78	−5.69	−5.07
4	50	−5.81	−5.09	−6.24	−5.48	−6.35	−5.47	−6.64	−5.82
	100	−5.58	−4.93	−5.88	−5.20	−5.86	−5.20	−6.09	−5.50
	250	−5.39	−4.28	−5.64	−5.07	−5.66	−5.08	−5.95	−5.34

Note: m_1 is the number of $I(1)$ variables and m_2 is the number of $I(2)$ variables on the right-hand side of the multicointegrating relationship.

Source: The critical values for the intercept only case are from Haldrup (1994) and critical values for the linear trend are from Engsted, Gonzalo, and Haldrup (1997).

Table E   **Empirical Distributions of the λ_{max} and λ_{trace} Statistics**

Significance level

	10%	5%	2.5%	1%	10%	5%	2.5%	1%

λ_{max} and λ_{trace} **statistics without any deterministic regressors**

$n-r$		λ_{max}				λ_{trace}		
1	2.86	3.84	4.93	6.51	2.86	3.84	4.93	6.51
2	9.52	11.44	13.27	15.69	10.47	12.53	14.43	16.31
3	15.59	17.89	20.02	22.99	21.63	24.31	26.64	29.75
4	21.56	23.80	26.14	28.82	36.58	39.89	42.30	45.58
5	27.62	30.04	32.51	35.17	54.44	59.46	62.91	66.52

λ_{max} and λ_{trace} **statistics with drift**

$n-r$		λ_{max}				λ_{trace}		
1	2.69	3.76	4.95	6.65	2.69	3.76	4.95	6.65
2	12.07	14.07	16.05	18.63	13.33	15.41	17.52	20.04
3	18.60	20.97	23.09	25.52	26.79	29.68	32.56	35.65
4	24.73	27.07	28.98	32.24	43.95	47.21	50.35	54.46
5	30.90	33.46	35.71	38.77	64.84	68.52	71.80	76.07

λ_{max} and λ_{trace} **statistics with a constant in the cointegrating vector**

		λ_{max}				λ_{trace}		
1	7.52	9.24	10.80	12.97	7.52	9.24	10.80	12.95
2	13.75	15.67	17.63	20.20	17.85	19.96	22.05	24.60
3	19.77	22.00	24.07	26.81	32.00	34.91	37.61	41.07
4	25.56	28.14	30.32	33.24	49.65	53.12	56.06	60.16
5	31.66	34.40	36.90	39.79	71.86	76.07	80.06	84.45

Source: Osterwald–Lenum (1992). The tables reported here are reproduced with permission from Blackwell Publishers.

Table F   **Critical Values for Threshold Unit Roots**

Panel (*a*): Consistent Estimate of the Threshold Using the TAR Model

T	No Lagged Changes				One Lagged Change				Four Lagged Changes			
	90%	95%	97.5%	99%	90%	95%	97.5%	99%	90%	95%	97.5%	99%
50	5.15	6.19	7.25	8.64	5.55	6.62	7.66	9.10	5.49	6.55	7.59	9.00
100	5.08	6.06	6.93	8.19	5.39	6.34	7.30	8.54	5.38	6.32	7.29	8.56
250	5.11	6.03	6.88	8.04	5.26	6.12	6.99	8.14	5.36	6.29	7.15	8.35

Panel (*b*): Consistent Estimates of the Threshold Using the M-TAR Model

T	No Lagged Changes				One Lagged Change				Four Lagged Changes			
	90%	95%	97.5%	99%	90%	95%	97.5%	99%	90%	95%	97.5%	99%
50	5.02	6.05	7.09	8.59	4.98	6.07	7.15	8.56	4.93	5.96	7.01	8.48
100	4.81	5.77	6.73	7.99	4.77	5.71	6.56	7.90	4.74	5.70	6.67	7.97
250	4.70	5.64	6.51	7.64	4.64	5.54	6.40	7.56	4.64	5.54	6.39	7.61

Panel (*c*): Known Threshold Value in the M-TAR Model

T	No Lagged Changes				One Lagged Change				Four Lagged Changes			
	90%	95%	97.5%	99%	90%	95%	97.5%	99%	90%	95%	97.5%	99%
50	4.21	5.19	6.15	7.55	4.12	5.11	6.05	7.25	3.82	4.73	5.65	6.84
100	4.11	5.04	5.96	7.10	4.08	4.97	5.87	7.06	3.81	4.72	5.63	6.83
250	4.08	4.97	5.83	6.91	4.05	4.93	5.78	6.83	3.69	4.71	5.63	6.78

REFERENCES

Anderson, L. and J. Jordan. "Monetary and Fiscal Actions: A Test of their Relative Importance in Economic Stabilization." *Federal Reserve Bank of St. Louis Review* (Nov. 1968), 11–24.

Baba, Yoshihisa, David F. Hendry, and Ross M. Starr. "The Demand for M1 in the U.S.A., 1960–1988." *Review of Economic Studies* 59 (Jan. 1992), 25–61.

Balke, Nathan. S., and Thomas B. Fomby. "Threshold Cointegration." *International Economic Review* 38, (1997), 627–43.

Baltagi, Badi. "Nonstationary Panels, "Panel Cointegration, and Dynamic Panels." *Advances in Econometrics*, 15. Amsterdam: Elsevier Science, 2000.

Bell, W., and S. Hilmer. "Issues Involved with the Seasonal Adjustment of Economic Time Series." *Journal of Business and Economic Statistics* 2 (1984), 291–320.

Ben-David, Dan. and Papell, David. "The Great Wars, the Great Crash, and Steady State Growth: Some New Evidence About an Old Stylized Fact." *Journal of Monetary Economics* 36 (1995), 453–75.

Bernanke, Ben. "Alternative Explanations of Money-Income Correlation." *Carnegie-Rochester Conference Series on Public Policy* 25 (1986), 49–100.

Beveridge, Stephen, and Charles Nelson. "A New Approach to Decomposition of Economic Time Series into Permanent and Transitory Components with Particular Attention to Measurement of the Business Cycle." *Journal of Monetary Economics* 7 (March 1981), 151–74.

Blanchard, Oliver, and Danny Quah. "The Dynamic Effects of Aggregate Demand and Supply Disturbances." *American Economic Review* 79 (Sept. 1989), 655–673.

Bollerslev, Tim. "Generalized Autoregressive Conditional Heteroscedasticity." *Journal of Econometrics* 31 (1986), 307–27.

Box, George, and D. Cox. "An Analysis of Transformations." *Journal of the Royal Statistical Society*, Series B.26 (1964), 211–52.

Box, George, and D. Pierce. "Distribution of Autocorrelations in Autoregressive Moving Average Time Series Models." *Journal of the American Statistical Association* 65 (1970), 1509–26.

Box, George, and Gwilym Jenkins. *Time Series Analysis, Forecasting, and Control*. San Francisco: Holden Day, 1976.

Brock, William, Davis Dechert, Jose Scheinkman, and Blake LeBaron. "A Test for Independence Based Upon the Correlation Dimension." *Econometric Reviews* 15, (1997), 197–235.

de Brouwer, Gordon and Neil Ericsson. "Modeling Inflation in Australia." *Journal of Business and Economic Statistics* 16, (1998), 433–49.

Bureau of the Census. X-11 Information for the User, U.S. Department of Commerce. Washington D.C.: U.S. Government Printing Office, 1969.

445

Cagan, Phillip. "The Monetary Dynamics of Hyperinflation." Milton Friedman, ed., *Studies in the Quantity Theory of Money*. Chicago, Ill.: University of Chicago Press, 1956, pp. 25–120.

Campbell, John Y., and Pierre Perron. "Pitfalls and Opportunities: What Macroeconomists Should Know About Unit Roots." Technical Working Paper 100, NBER Working Paper Series. April 1991.

Caner, Mehmet, and Bruce Hansen. "Threshold Autoregression with a Unit Root." *Econometrica* 69, (2001), 1555—96.

Chan, K. S. "Consistency and Limiting Distribution of the Least Squares Estimator of a Threshold Autoregressive Model." *The Annals of Statistics* 21, (1993) 520–33.

Clarida, Richard H., and Jordi Gali, "Sources of Real Exchange Rate Fluctuations: How Important Are Nominal Shocks?" Carnegie-Rochester Conference Series on Public Policy 41, (1994), 1–56.

Clements, Michael P., and David Hendry. *Forecasting Economic Time Series*. MIT Press: Cambridge, 1998.

Davisdon, J., D. Hendry, F. Srba, and S. Yeo. "Econometric Modeling of the Aggregate Time-Series Relationship Between Consumers' Expenditure and Income in the United Kingdom." *The Economic Journal* 88 (1978), 661–92.

Dickey, David, and Wayne A. Fuller. "Distribution of the Estimates for Autoregressive Time Series with a Unit Root." *Journal of the American Statistical Association* 74 (June 1979), 427–31.

____."Likelihood Ratio Statistics for Autoregressive Time Series with a Unit Root." *Econometrica* 49 (July 1981), 1057–72.

Dickey, David, W. Bell, and R. Miller. "Unit Roots in Time Series Models: Tests and Implications." *American Statistician* 40 (1986), 12–26.

Dickey, David, and S. Pantula. "Determining the Order of Differencing in Autoregressive Processes." *Journal of Business and Economic Statistics* 15 (1987), 455–61.

Diebold, Francis, and Roberto Mariano. "Comparing Predictive Accuracy." *Journal of Business and Economic Statistics* 13, (1995), 253–63.

Doan, Thomas. *RATS User's Manual*. Evanston, Ill.: Estima, 1992.

Doldado, Juan, Tim Jenkinson, and Simon Sosvilla-Rivero. "Cointegration and Unit Roots." *Journal of Economic Surveys* 4 (1990), 249–73.

Dornbusch, Rudiger. "Expectations and Exchange Rate Dynamics." *Journal of Political Economy* 84 (1976), 1161–76.

Edwards, Sebastian, and Raul Susmel. "Interest Rate Volatility and Contagion in Emerging Markets: Evidence from the 1990s." National Bureau of Economic Research Working Paper 7813. (2000).

Efron, Bradley. "Bootstrap Methods: Another Look at the Jackknife." *Annals of Statistics* 7, (1979),1–26.

Efron, Bradley, and Robert Tibshirani. *An Introduction to the Bootstrap*. Chapman and Hall: New York. 1993.

Elliott, Graham, Thomas Rothenberg, and James Stock. "Efficient Tests for an Autoregressive Unit Root." *Econometrica* 64 (1996), 813–36.

Enders, Walter. "ARIMA and Cointegration Tests of Purchasing Power Parity." *Review of Economics and Statistics* 70 (Aug. 1988), 504–08.

Enders, Walter, and C.W.J. Granger. Unit-root Tests and Asymmetric Adjustment with an Example Using the Term Structure of Interest Rates. *Journal of Business and Economic Statistics* 16, (1998), 304–11.

Enders, Walter, and Bong-Soo Lee. "Accounting for Real and Nominal Exchange Rate Movements in the Post-Bretton Woods Period." *Journal of International Money and Finance* 16 (1997), 233–54.

Enders, Walter, and Todd Sandler. "Causality Between Transnational Terrorism and Tourism: The Case of Spain." *Terrorism* 14 (Jan. 1991), 49–58.

Enders, Walter, Todd Sandler, and Jon Cauley. "Assessing the Impact of Terrorist-Thwarting Policies: An Intervention Time Series Approach." *Defense Economics* 2 (Dec. 1990), 1–18.

Enders, Walter, Todd Sandler, and Gerald F. Parise. "An Econometric Analysis of the Impact of Terrorism on Tourism." *Kyklos* 45 (1992), 531–554.

Enders, Walter, and Pierre Siklos. "Cointegration and Threshold Adjustment." *Journal of Business and Economic Statistics* 19, (2001), 166–76.

Engle, Robert F. "Autoregressive Conditional Heteroscedasticity with Estimates of the Variance of United Kingdom Inflation." *Econometrica* 50 (July 1982), 987–1007.

Engle, Robert E., and Tim Bollerslev. "Modeling the Persistence of Conditional Variances." *Econometric Reviews* 5 (1986), 1–50.

Engle, Robert E., and Clive W. J. Granger. "Cointegration and Error-Correction: Representation, Estimation, and Testing. *Econometrica* 55 (March 1987), 251–76.

Engle, Robert F., and David Kraft. "Multiperiod Forecast Error Variances of Inflation Based on the ARCH Model." A. Zellner, ed., *Applied Time Series Analysis of Economic Data*. Washington, D.C.: Bureau of the Census, 1983, pp. 293–302.

Engle, Robert F., David Lilien, and Russell Robins. "Estimating Time Varying Risk Premia in the Term Structure: The ARCH-M Model." *Econometrica* 55 (March 1987), 391–407.

Evans, G. and N. Savin. "Testing for Unit Roots: 1." *Econometrica* 49 (1981), 753–79.

Engsted, Tom, Jesus Gonzalo, and Neils Haldrup. "Testing for Multicointegration." *Economics Letters* 56 (1997), 259–66.

Farmer, Roger E. *The Macroeconomics of Self-Fulfilling Prophecies*. Cambridge, Mass.: MIT Press, 1993.

Friedman, Benjamin, and Kenneth Kuttner. "Money, Income, Prices, and Interest Rates." *American Economic Review* 82 (June 1992), 472–92.

Galbraith, John W. "Credit Rationing and Threshold Effects in the Relation Between Money and Output." *Journal of Applied Econometrics* 11, (1996), 419–29.

Granger, Clive, T. Inoue, and N. Morin. "Nonlinear Stochastic Trends." *Journal of Econometrics* 81 (1997), 65–92.

Granger, Clive, and R. Joyeux. "An Introduction to Long Memory Time Series Models and Fractional Differencing." *Journal of Time Series Analysis* 1 (1980), 15–29.

Granger, Clive, and Tae-Hwy Lee. "Multicointegration." *Advances in Econometrics* 8, (1990), 77–84.

Granger, Clive, and Paul Newbold. "Spurious Regressions in Econometrics." *Journal of Econometrics* 2 (1974), 111–20.

_____ . "Forecasting Transformed Series." *Journal of the Royal Statistical Society* B 38, (1976), 189–203.

Granger, Clive and Timo Teräsvirta. *Modeling Nonlinear Economic Relationships*. Oxford University Press: Oxford. 1993.

Gregory, Allen, and Bruce Hansen. *Residual Based Tests for Cointegration in Models with Regime Shifts*. Kingston: Queens University, 1992.

Haldrup, Neils. "The Asymptotics of Single-Equation Cointegration Regressions with I(1) and I(2) Variables." *The Journal of Econometrics* 63 (1994), 153–81.

Hamilton, James. "A New Approach to the Economic Analysis of Nonstationary Time Series and the Business Cycle." *Econometrica* 57. (1989), 357–84.

Hamilton, James, and Raul Susmel. "Autoregressive Conditional Heteroskedasticity and Changes in Regime." *Journal of Econometrics* 64 (1994), 307–33.

Hansen, Bruce. "Inference in TAR Models." *Studies in Nonlinear Dynamics and Econometrics* 2 (1997), 1–14.

_____ . "Inference When a Nuisance Parameter Is Not Identified Under the Null Hypothesis." *Econometrics* 64 (1996), 413–30.

Hansen, Bruce, and Byeongseon Seo. "Testing for Two-Regime Threshold Cointegration in Vector Error-Correction Models." *Journal of Econometrics* 110, (2002), 293–318.

Harvey, Andrew. *Forecasting, Structural Time Series Models, and the Kalman Filter*. Cambridge: Cambridge University Press, 1989.

Hendry, David, A. Neale, and N. Ericsson. *PC-NAIVE: An Interactive Program for Monte Carlo Experimentation in Econometrics*. Institute for Economics and Statistics: Oxford University, 1990.

Hendry, David F., and Neil Ericsson. "An Economic Analysis of U.K. Money Demand in 'Monetrary Trends in the United States and the United Kingdom by Milton Friedman and Anna J. Schwartz.'" *American Economic Review* 81 (1991), 8–39.

Higgens, M. and Anil Bera. "A Class of Nonlinear ARCH Models." *International Economic Review* 33 (1992) 137–58.

Hodrick, Robert, and Edward Prescott. "Postwar Business Cycles." *Journal of Money, Credit and Banking* 29 (1997), 1–16.

Holt, Matthew, and Satheesh Aradhyula. "Price Risk in Supply Equations: An Application of GARCH Time-Series Models to the U.S. Broiler Market." *Southern Economic Journal* 57 (July 1990), 230–42.

Horvath, Michael, and Mark Watson. *Testing for Cointegration When Some of the Cointegrating Vectors Are Known*. Chicago, Ill.: Federal Reserve Bank of Chicago, 1993.

Hylleberg, S., R. Engle, C. Granger, and B. Yoo. "Seasonal Integration and Cointegration." *Journal of Econometrics* 44 (1990), 215–38.

Johansen, Soren. "Statistical Analysis of Cointegration Vectors." *Journal of Economic Dynamics and Control* 12 (June–Sept. 1988), 231–54.

_____. "Estimation and Hypothesis Testing of Cointegrating Vectors in Gaussian Vector Autoregressive Models." *Econometrica* 59 (Nov. 1991), 1551–80.

_____ . "The Role of the Constant and Linear Terms in Cointegration Analysis of Non-Stationary Variables." *Econometric Reviews* 13, (1994), 205–30.

Johansen, Soren, and Katerina Juselius. "Maximum Likelihood Estimation and Inference on Cointegration with Application to the Demand for Money." *Oxford Bulletin of Economics and Statistics* 52 (1990), 169–209.

___. "Testing Structural Hypotheses in a Multivariate Cointegration Analysis of PPP and the UIP for UK." *Journal of Econometrics* 53 (1992), 211–44.

Kapetanios, George, Yongcheol Shin, and Andy Snell. "Testing for a Unit Root in the Nonlinear STAR Framework." *Journal of Econometrics* 112 (2003), 359–79.

King, Robert, Charles Plosser, James Stock, and Mark Watson. "Stochastic Trends and Economic Fluctuations." *American Economic Review* 81 (Sept. 1991), 819–40.

Koop, Gary, M. Hashem Pesaran, and Simon Potter. "Impulse Response Analysis in Nonlinear Multivariate Models." *Journal of Econometrics* 74 (1996), 119–47.

Kuan, Chung-Ming, and Halbert White. "Artificial Neural Networks: An Econometric Perspective." *Econometric Reviews* 13, (1994), 1–91.

Kwiatkowski, D., Peter Phillips, Peter Schmidt, and Y. Shin. "Testing the Null Hypothesis of Stationarity Against the Alternative of a Unit Root: How Sure Are WE That Economic Tine Series Have a Unit Root?" *Journal of Econometrics* 54 (1992), 159–78.

Leamer, Edward. "A Bayesian Analysis of the Determinants of Inflation." P. A. Belsey and E. Kuh, eds., *Model Reliability*. Cambridge, Mass.: MIT Press, 1986, pp. 62–89.

Levin, Andrew, Chien-Fu Lin, and Chia-Shang Chu. "Unit Root Tests in Panel Data: Asymptotic and Finite-Sample Properties." *Journal of Econometrics* 108 (2002), 1–24.

Litterman, Robert. "A Bayesian Procedure for Forecasting with Vector Autoregressions." Federal Reserve Bank of Minneapolis, Minneapolis, 1981.

Ljung, G., and George Box. "On a Measure of Lack of Fit in Time Series Models." *Biometrica* 65 (1978), 297–303.

Lutkepohl, Helmut, and Hans-Eggert Reimers. "Impulse Response Analysis of Cointegrated Systems." *Journal of Economic Dynamics and Control* 16 (Jan. 1992), 53–78.

Maddla, G. S. and S. Wu. "Comparative Study of Unit Root Tests with Panel Data and a New Simple Test." *Oxford Bulletin of Economics and Statistics* 61 (1999), 631–52.

McLeod, A., and W. Li. "Diagnostic Checking ARMA Time Series Models Using Squared Residual Correlations." *Journal of Time Series Analysis* 4, (1983), 269–73.

Meese, R., and Ken Singleton. "On Unit Roots and Empirical Modeling of Exchange Rates." *Journal of Finance* 37 (1982), 1029–35.

Michael, Panos, A. Robert Nobay, and David Peel. "Transactions Costs and Nonlinear Adjustment in Real Exchange Rates: An Empirical Investigation." *Journal of Political Economy* 105 (1997), 862–79.

Nelson, Charles, and Charles Plosser. "Trends and Random Walks in Macroeconomic Time Series: Some Evidence and Implications." *Journal of Monetary Economics* 10 (1982), 130–62.

Osterwald-Lenum, Michael. "A Note with Quantiles of the Asymptotic Distribution of the Maximum Likelihood Cointegration Rank Test Statistics." *Oxford Bulletin of Economics and Statistics* 54 (1992), 461–71.

Park, Joon. "Canonical Cointegrating Regressions." *Econometrica* 60 (Jan. 1992), 119–43.

Perron, Pierre. "The Great Crash, the Oil Price Shock, and the Unit Root Hypothesis." *Econometrica* 57 (Nov. 1989), 1361–1401.

_____. "Further Evidence on Breaking Trend Functions in Macroeconomic Variables." *Journal of Econometrics* 80 (1997), 355–85.

Perron, Pierre, and Timothy Vogelsang. "Nonstationary and Level Shifts with an Application to Purchasing Power Parity." *Journal of Business and Economic Statistics* 10 (1992), pp. 301–20.

Petrucelli, J., and S. Woolford. "A Threshold AR(1) Model." *Journal of Applied Probability* 21 (1984), 270–86.

Phillips, Peter. "Understanding Spurious Regressions in Econometrics." *Journal of Econometrics* 33 (1986), 311–40.

Phillips, Peter and Bruce Hansen. "Statistical Inference in Instrumental Variables Regression with I(1) Processes." *Review of Economic Studies* 57 (1990), 99–125.

Phillips, Peter, and Pierre Perron. "Testing for a Unit Root in Time Series Regression." *Biometrica* 75 (June 1988), 335–46.

Pippenger, Michael K., and Gregory E. Goering . 'A Note on the Empirical Power of Unit Root Tests under Threshold Processes.' *Oxford Bulletin of Economics and Statistics* 55 (1993), 473–81.

Potter, Simon. "A Nonlinear Approach to US GNP." *Journal of Applied Econometrics* 10 (1995), 109–25.

Quah, Danny. "The Relative Importance of Permanent and Transitory Components: Identification and Some Theoretical Bounds." *Econometrica* 60 (Jan. 1992), 107–18.

Rothman, Philip. "Forecasting Asymmetric Unemployment Rates." *Review of Economics and Statistics* 80 (1998), 164–68.

Said, S., and David Dickey. "Testing for Unit Roots in Autoregressive-Moving Average Models with Unknown Order." *Biometrica* 71 (1984), 599–607.

Samuelson, Paul. "Interactions Between the Multiplier Analysis and Principle of Acceleration." *Review of Economics and Statistics* 21 (May 1939), 75–78.

___. "Conditions That the Roots of a Polynomial Be Less than Unity in Absolute Value." *Annals of Mathematics Statistics* 12 (1941), 360–64.

Schmidt, Peter. "Dickey–Fuller Tests with Drift." *Advances in Econometrics* 8 (1990), 161–200.

Shen, Chung Hua, and David Hakes. "Monetary Policy as a Decision-Making Hierarchy: The Case of Taiwan." *Journal of Macroeconomics* 17 (1995), 357–68.

Sims, Christopher. "Macroeconomics and Reality." *Econometrica* 48 (Jan. 1980), 1–49.

___. "Are Forecasting Models Usable for Policy Analysis?" *Federal Reserve Bank of Minneapolis Quarterly Review* (Winter 1986), 3–16.

___. "Bayesian Skepticism on Unit Root Econometrics." *Journal of Economic Dynamics and Control* 12 (1988), 463–74.

Sims, Christopher, James Stock and Mark W. Watson. "Inference in Linear Time Series Models with some Unit Roots." *Econometrica* 58 (1990), 113–44.

Stock, James. "Asymptotic Properties of Least-Squares Estimators of Cointegrating Vectors." *Econometrica* 55 (1987), 1035–56.

Stock, James and Mark Watson. "Testing for Common Trends." *Journal of the American Statistical Association* 83 (Dec. 1988), 1097–1107.

Suits, Daniel, and Gorden Sparks. "Consumption Regressions with Quarterly Data." T. S. Duesenberry, G. Fromm, L. R. Klein, and E. Kuh, eds., *The Brookings Quarterly Econometric Model of the United States*. Chicago, Ill.: Rand McNally, 1965, pp. 203–23.

Taylor, Mark. "Estimating Structural Macroeconomic Shocks Through Long-Run Recursive Restrictions on Vector Autoregressive Models: The Problem of Identification." Department of Economics Working Paper: University of Warwick. (2003).

Teräsvirta, Timo. "Specification, Estimation and Evaluation of Smooth Transition Autoregressive Models." *Journal of the American Statistical Association* 89, (1994), 208–18.

Todd, Richard M. "Improving Economic Forecasting with Bayesian Autoregression." *Federal Reserve Bank of Minnesota Quarterly Review* (Fall 1984), 18–29.

Tong, H. *Threshold Models in Nonlinear Time Series Analysis*. SpringerVerlag: New York. 1983.

Tsay, Ruey. "Testing and Modeling Multivariate Threshold Models." *Journal of the American Statistical Association* 93 (1998), 1188–1202.

Vogelsang, Timothy, and Pierre Perron. "Additional Tests for a Unit Root Allowing for a Break in the Trend Function at an Unknown Time." *International Economic Review* 39 (1998), 1073–1100.

Watson, Mark. "Univariate Detrending Methods with Stochastic Trends." *Journal of Monetary Economics* 18 (1986), 49–75.

West, Mike, and Jeff Harrison. *Bayesian Forecasting and Dynamic Models*. New York: Springer-Verlag, 1989.

White, Halbert. "Some Asymptotic Results for Learning in Single Hidden-Layer Feedforward Network Models." *Journal of the American Statistical Association* 84 (1989), 1003–13.

Zellner, Arnold. "Bayesian Analysis in Econometrics." *Journal of Econometrics* 37 (1988), 27–50.

Zivot, Eric, and Donald Andrews. "Further Evidence on the Great Crash, the Oil-Price Shock, and the Unit-Root Hypothesis." *Journal of Business and Economic Statistics* 20, (2002), 25–44.

INDEX

WILEY SERIES IN PROBABILITY AND STATISTICS

Established by WALTER A. SHEWHART and SAMUEL S. WILKS

Editors: *David J. Balding, Peter Bloomfield, Noel A. C. Cressie, Nicholas I. Fisher, Iain M. Johnstone, J. B. Kadane, Louise M. Ryan, David W. Scott, Adrian F. M. Smith, Jozef L. Teugels*

Editors Emeriti: *Vic Barnett, J. Stuart Hunter, David G. Kendall*

The *Wiley Series in Probability and Statistics* is well established and authoritative. It covers many topics of current research interest in both pure and applied statistics and probability theory. Written by leading statisticians and institutions, the titles span both state-of-the-art developments in the field and classical methods.

Reflecting the wide range of current research in statistics, the series encompasses applied, methodological and theoretical statistics, ranging from applications and new techniques made possible by advances in computerized practice to rigorous treatment of theoretical approaches.

This series provides essential and invaluable reading for all statisticians, whether in academia, industry, government, or research.

ABRAHAM and LEDOLTER · Statistical Methods for Forecasting
AGRESTI · Analysis of Ordinal Categorical Data
AGRESTI · An Introduction to Categorical Data Analysis
AGRESTI · Categorical Data Analysis, *Second Edition*
ANDEL · Mathematics of Chance
ANDERSON · An Introduction to Multivariate Statistical Analysis, *Second Edition*
*ANDERSON · The Statistical Analysis of Time Series
ANDERSON, AUQUIER, HAUCK, OAKES, VANDAELE, and WEISBERG Statistical Methods for
    Comparative Studies
ANDERSON and LOYNES · The Teaching of Practical Statistics
ARMITAGE and DAVID (editors) · Advances in Biometry
ARNOLD, BALAKRISHNAN, and NAGARAJA · Records
*ARTHANARI and DODGE · Mathematical Programming in Statistics
*BAILEY · The Elements of Stochastic Processes with Applications to the Natural Sciences
BALAKRISHNAN and KOUTRAS · Runs and Scans with Applications
BARNETT · Comparative Statistical Inference, *Third Edition*
BARNETT and LEWIS · Outliers in Statistical Data, *Third Edition*
BARTOSZYNSKI and NIEWIADOMSKA-BUGAJ · Probability and Statistical Inference
BASILEVSKY · Statistical Factor Analysis and Related Methods: Theory and Applications
BASU and RIGDON · Statistical Methods for the Reliability of Repairable Systems
BATES and WATTS · Nonlinear Regression Analysis and Its Applications
BECHHOFER, SANTNER, and GOLDSMAN · Design and Analysis of Experiments for Statistical
    Selection, Screening, and Multiple Comparisons
BELSLEY · Conditioning Diagnostics: Collinearity and Weak Data in Regression
BELSLEY, KUH, and WELSCH · Regression Diagnostics: Identifying Influential Data and Sources
    of Collinearity
BENDAT and PIERSOL · Random Data: Analysis and Measurement Procedures, *Third Edition*
BERRY, CHALONER, and GEWEKE · Bayesian Analysis in Statistics and Econometrics: Essays in
    Honor of Arnold Zellner
BERNARDO and SMITH · Bayesian Theory
BHAT and MILLER · Elements of Applied Stochastic Processes, *Third Edition*
BHATTACHARYA and JOHNSON · Statistical Concepts and Methods
BHATTACHARYA and WAYMIRE · Stochastic Processes with Applications
BILLINGSLEY · Convergence of Probability Measures, *Second Edition*
BILLINGSLEY · Probability and Measure, *Third Edition*
BIRKES and DODGE · Alternative Methods of Regression
BLISCHKE AND MURTHY (editors) · Case Studies in Reliability and Maintenance
BLISCHKE AND MURTHY · Reliability: Modeling, Prediction, and Optimization
BLOOMFIELD · Fourier Analysis of Time Series: An Introduction, *Second Edition*

*Now available in a lower-priced paperback edition in the Wiley Classics Library.

BOLLEN · Structural Equations with Latent Variables

BOROVKOV · Ergodicity and Stability of Stochastic Processes

BOULEAU · Numerical Methods for Stochastic Processes

BOX · Bayesian Inference in Statistical Analysis

BOX · R. A. Fisher, the Life of a Scientist

BOX and DRAPER · Empirical Model-Building and Response Surfaces

*BOX and DRAPER · Evolutionary Operation: A Statistical Method for Process Improvement

BOX, HUNTER, and HUNTER · Statistics for Experimenters: An Introduction to Design, Data Analysis, and Model Building

BOX and LUCEÑO · Statistical Control by Monitoring and Feedback Adjustment

BRANDIMARTE · Numerical Methods in Finance: A MATLAB-Based Introduction

BROWN and HOLLANDER · Statistics: A Biomedical Introduction

BRUNNER, DOMHOF, and LANGER · Nonparametric Analysis of Longitudinal Data in Factorial Experiments

BUCKLEW · Large Deviation Techniques in Decision, Simulation, and Estimation

CAIROLI and DALANG · Sequential Stochastic Optimization

CHAN · Time Series: Applications to Finance

CHATTERJEE and HADI · Sensitivity Analysis in Linear Regression

CHATTERJEE and PRICE · Regression Analysis by Example, *Third Edition*

CHERNICK · Bootstrap Methods: A Practitioner's Guide

CHERNICK and FRIIS · Introductory Biostatistics for the Health Sciences

CHILÈS and DELFINER · Geostatistics: Modeling Spatial Uncertainty

CHOW and LIU · Design and Analysis of Clinical Trials: Concepts and Methodologies

CLARKE and DISNEY · Probability and Random Processes: A First Course with Applications, *Second Edition*

*COCHRAN and COX · Experimental Designs, *Second Edition*

CONGDON · Bayesian Statistical Modelling

CONOVER · Practical Nonparametric Statistics, *Second Edition*

COOK · Regression Graphics

COOK and WEISBERG · Applied Regression Including Computing and Graphics

COOK and WEISBERG · An Introduction to Regression Graphics

CORNELL · Experiments with Mixtures, Designs, Models, and the Analysis of Mixture Data, *Third Edition*

COVER and THOMAS · Elements of Information Theory

COX · A Handbook of Introductory Statistical Methods

*COX · Planning of Experiments

CRESSIE · Statistics for Spatial Data, *Revised Edition*

CSÖRGÖ and HORVÁTH · Limit Theorems in Change Point Analysis

DANIEL · Applications of Statistics to Industrial Experimentation

DANIEL · Biostatistics: A Foundation for Analysis in the Health Sciences, *Sixth Edition*

*DANIEL · Fitting Equations to Data: Computer Analysis of Multifactor Data, *Second Edition*

DASU and JOHNSON · Exploratory Data Mining and Data Cleaning

DAVID · Order Statistics, *Second Edition*

*DEGROOT, FIENBERG, and KADANE · Statistics and the Law

DEL CASTILLO · Statistical Process Adjustment for Quality Control

DETTE and STUDDEN · The Theory of Canonical Moments with Applications in Statistics, Probability, and Analysis

DEY and MUKERJEE · Fractional Factorial Plans

DILLON and GOLDSTEIN · Multivariate Analysis: Methods and Applications

DODGE · Alternative Methods of Regression

*DODGE and ROMIG · Sampling Inspection Tables, *Second Edition*

*DOOB · Stochastic Processes

DOWDY and WEARDEN · Statistics for Research, *Second Edition*

DRAPER and SMITH · Applied Regression Analysis, *Third Edition*

DRYDEN and MARDIA · Statistical Shape Analysis

DUDEWICZ and MISHRA · Modern Mathematical Statistics

*Now available in a lower-priced paperback edition in the Wiley Classics Library.

DUNN and CLARK · Applied Statistics: Analysis of Variance and Regression, *Second Edition*
DUNN and CLARK · Basic Statistics: A Primer for the Biomedical Sciences, *Third Edition*
DUPUIS and ELLIS · A Weak Convergence Approach to the Theory of Large Deviations
*ELANDT-JOHNSON and JOHNSON · Survival Models and Data Analysis
ENDERS · Applied Econometric Time Series
ETHIER and KURTZ · Markov Processes: Characterization and Convergence
EVANS, HASTINGS, and PEACOCK · Statistical Distributions, *Third Edition*
FELLER · An Introduction to Probability Theory and Its Applications, Volume I, *Third Edition*, Revised; Volume II, *Second Edition*
FISHER and VAN BELLE · Biostatistics: A Methodology for the Health Sciences
*FLEISS · The Design and Analysis of Clinical Experiments
FLEISS · Statistical Methods for Rates and Proportions, *Second Edition*
FLEMING and HARRINGTON · Counting Processes and Survival Analysis
FULLER · Introduction to Statistical Time Series, *Second Edition*
FULLER · Measurement Error Models
GALLANT · Nonlinear Statistical Models
GHOSH, MUKHOPADHYAY, and SEN · Sequential Estimation
GIFI · Nonlinear Multivariate Analysis
GLASSERMAN and YAO · Monotone Structure in Discrete-Event Systems
GNANADESIKAN · Methods for Statistical Data Analysis of Multivariate Observations, *Second Edition*
GOLDSTEIN and LEWIS · Assessment: Problems, Development, and Statistical Issues
GREENWOOD and NIKULIN · A Guide to Chi-Squared Testing
GROSS and HARRIS · Fundamentals of Queueing Theory, *Third Edition*
*HAHN and SHAPIRO · Statistical Models in Engineering
HAHN and MEEKER · Statistical Intervals: A Guide for Practitioners
HALD · A History of Probability and Statistics and their Applications Before 1750
HALD · A History of Mathematical Statistics from 1750 to 1930
HAMPEL · Robust Statistics: The Approach Based on Influence Functions
HANNAN and DEISTLER · The Statistical Theory of Linear Systems
HEIBERGER · Computation for the Analysis of Designed Experiments
HEDAYAT and SINHA · Design and Inference in Finite Population Sampling
HELLER · MACSYMA for Statisticians
HINKELMAN and KEMPTHORNE: · Design and Analysis of Experiments, Volume 1: Introduction to Experimental Design
HOAGLIN, MOSTELLER, and TUKEY · Exploratory Approach to Analysis of Variance
HOAGLIN, MOSTELLER, and TUKEY · Exploring Data Tables, Trends and Shapes
*HOAGLIN, MOSTELLER, and TUKEY · Understanding Robust and Exploratory Data Analysis
HOCHBERG and TAMHANE · Multiple Comparison Procedures
HOCKING · Methods and Applications of Linear Models: Regression and the Analysis of Variance, *Second Edition*
HOEL · Introduction to Mathematical Statistics, *Fifth Edition*
HOGG and KLUGMAN · Loss Distributions
HOLLANDER and WOLFE · Nonparametric Statistical Methods, *Second Edition*
HOSMER and LEMESHOW · Applied Logistic Regression, *Second Edition*
HOSMER and LEMESHOW · Applied Survival Analysis: Regression Modeling of Time to Event Data
HØYLAND and RAUSAND · System Reliability Theory: Models and Statistical Methods
HUBER · Robust Statistics
HUBERTY · Applied Discriminant Analysis
HUNT and KENNEDY · Financial Derivatives in Theory and Practice
HUSKOVA, BERAN, and DUPAC · Collected Works of Jaroslav Hajek—with Commentary
IMAN and CONOVER · A Modern Approach to Statistics
JACKSON · A User's Guide to Principle Components
JOHN · Statistical Methods in Engineering and Quality Assurance
JOHNSON · Multivariate Statistical Simulation
JOHNSON and BALAKRISHNAN · Advances in the Theory and Practice of Statistics: A Volume in Honor of Samuel Kotz

*Now available in a lower-priced paperback edition in the Wiley Classics Library.

JUDGE, GRIFFITHS, HILL, LÜTKEPOHL, and LEE · The Theory and Practice of Econometrics, *Second Edition*

JOHNSON and KOTZ · Distributions in Statistics

JOHNSON and KOTZ (editors) · Leading Personalities in Statistical Sciences: From the Seventeenth Century to the Present

JOHNSON, KOTZ, and BALAKRISHNAN · Continuous Univariate Distributions, Volume 1, *Second Edition*

JOHNSON, KOTZ, and BALAKRISHNAN · Continuous Univariate Distributions, Volume 2, *Second Edition*

JOHNSON, KOTZ, and BALAKRISHNAN · Discrete Multivariate Distributions

JOHNSON, KOTZ, and KEMP · Univariate Discrete Distributions, *Second Edition*

JURECKOVÁ and SEN · Robust Statistical Procedures: Aymptotics and Interrelations

JUREK and MASON · Operator-Limit Distributions in Probability Theory

KADANE · Bayesian Methods and Ethics in a Clinical Trial Design

KADANE AND SCHUM · A Probabilistic Analysis of the Sacco and Vanzetti Evidence

KALBFLEISCH and PRENTICE · The Statistical Analysis of Failure Time Data, *Second Edition*

KASS and VOS · Geometrical Foundations of Asymptotic Inference

KAUFMAN and ROUSSEEUW · Finding Groups in Data: An Introduction to Cluster Analysis

KEDEM and FOKIANOS · Regression Models for Time Series Analysis

KENDALL, BARDEN, CARNE, and LE · Shape and Shape Theory

KHURI · Advanced Calculus with Applications in Statistics, *Second Edition*

KHURI, MATHEW, and SINHA · Statistical Tests for Mixed Linear Models

KLUGMAN, PANJER, and WILLMOT · Loss Models: From Data to Decisions

KLUGMAN, PANJER, and WILLMOT · Solutions Manual to Accompany Loss Models: From Data to Decisions

KOTZ, BALAKRISHNAN, and JOHNSON · Continuous Multivariate Distributions, Volume 1, *Second Edition* with Index

KOTZ and JOHNSON (editors) · Encyclopedia of Statistical Sciences: Supplement Volume

KOTZ, READ, and BANKS (editors) · Encyclopedia of Statistical Sciences: Update Volume 1

KOTZ, READ, and BANKS (editors) · Encyclopedia of Statistical Sciences: Update Volume 2

KOVALENKO, KUZNETZOV, and PEGG · Mathematical Theory of Reliability of Time-Dependent Systems with Practical Applications

LACHIN · Biostatistical Methods: The Assessment of Relative Risks

LAD · Operational Subjective Statistical Methods: A Mathematical, Philosophical, and Historical Introduction

LAMPERTI · Probability: A Survey of the Mathematical Theory, *Second Edition*

LANGE, RYAN, BILLARD, BRILLINGER, CONQUEST, and GREENHOUSE · Case Studies in Biometry

LARSON · Introduction to Probability Theory and Statistical Inference, *Third Edition*

LAWLESS · Statistical Models and Methods for Lifetime Data, *Second Edition*

LAWSON · Statistical Methods in Spatial Epidemiology

LE · Applied Categorical Data Analysis

LE · Applied Survival Analysis

LEE and WANG · Statistical Methods for Survival Data Analysis, *Third Edition*

LEPAGE and BILLARD · Exploring the Limits of Bootstrap

LEYLAND and GOLDSTEIN (editors) · Multilevel Modelling of Health Statistics

LIAO · Statistical Group Comparison

LINDVALL · Lectures on the Coupling Method

LINHART and ZUCCHINI · Model Selection

LITTLE and RUBIN · Statistical Analysis with Missing Data, *Second Edition*

LLOYD · The Statistical Analysis of Categorical Data

MAGNUS and NEUDECKER · Matrix Differential Calculus with Applications in Statistics and Econometrics, *Revised Edition*

MALLER and ZHOU · Survival Analysis with Long Term Survivors

MALLOWS · Design, Data, and Analysis by Some Friends of Cuthbert Daniel

MANN, SCHAFER, and SINGPURWALLA · Methods for Statistical Analysis of Reliability and Life Data

*Now available in a lower-priced paperback edition in the Wiley Classics Library.

MANTON, WOODBURY, and TOLLEY · Statistical Applications Using Fuzzy Sets

MARDIA and JUPP · Directional Statistics

MASON, GUNST, and HESS · Statistical Design and Analysis of Experiments with Applications to Engineering and Science, *Second Edition*

McCULLOCH and SEARLE · Generalized, Linear, and Mixed Models

McFADDEN · Management of Data in Clinical Trials

McLACHLAN · Discriminant Analysis and Statistical Pattern Recognition

McLACHLAN and KRISHNAN · The EM Algorithm and Extensions

McLACHLAN and PEEL · Finite Mixture Models

McNEIL · Epidemiological Research Methods

MEEKER and ESCOBAR · Statistical Methods for Reliability Data

MEERSCHAERT and SCHEFFLER · Limit Distributions for Sums of Independent Random Vectors: Heavy Tails in Theory and Practice

*MILLER · Survival Analysis, *Second Edition*

MONTGOMERY, PECK, and VINING · Introduction to Linear Regression Analysis, *Third Edition*

MORGENTHALER and TUKEY · Configural Polysampling: A Route to Practical Robustness

MUIRHEAD · Aspects of Multivariate Statistical Theory

MURRAY · X-STAT 2.0 Statistical Experimentation, Design Data Analysis, and Nonlinear Optimization

MYERS and MONTGOMERY · Response Surface Methodology: Process and Product Optimization Using Designed Experiments, *Second Edition*

MYERS, MONTGOMERY, and VINING · Generalized Linear Models. With Applications in Engineering and the Sciences

NELSON · Accelerated Testing, Statistical Models, Test Plans, and Data Analyses

NELSON · Applied Life Data Analysis

NEWMAN · Biostatistical Methods in Epidemiology

OCHI · Applied Probability and Stochastic Processes in Engineering and Physical Sciences

OKABE, BOOTS, SUGIHARA, and CHIU · Spatial Tesselations: Concepts and Applications of Voronoi Diagrams, *Second Edition*

OLIVER and SMITH · Influence Diagrams, Belief Nets and Decision Analysis

PANKRATZ · Forecasting with Dynamic Regression Models

PANKRATZ · Forecasting with Univariate Box-Jenkins Models: Concepts and Cases

*PARZEN · Modern Probability Theory and Its Applications

PEÑA, TIAO, and TSAY · A Course in Time Series Analysis

PIANTADOSI · Clinical Trials: A Methodologic Perspective

PORT · Theoretical Probability for Applications

POURAHMADI · Foundations of Time Series Analysis and Prediction Theory

PRESS · Bayesian Statistics: Principles, Models, and Applications

PRESS · Subjective and Objective Bayesian Statistics, *Second Edition*

PRESS and TANUR · The Subjectivity of Scientists and the Bayesian Approach

PUKELSHEIM · Optimal Experimental Design

PURI, VILAPLANA, and WERTZ · New Perspectives in Theoretical and Applied Statistics

PUTERMAN · Markov Decision Processes: Discrete Stochastic Dynamic Programming

*RAO · Linear Statistical Inference and Its Applications, *Second Edition*

RENCHER · Linear Models in Statistics

RENCHER · Methods of Multivariate Analysis, *Second Edition*

RENCHER · Multivariate Statistical Inference with Applications

RIPLEY · Spatial Statistics

RIPLEY · Stochastic Simulation

ROBINSON · Practical Strategies for Experimenting

ROHATGI and SALEH · An Introduction to Probability and Statistics, *Second Edition*

ROLSKI, SCHMIDLI, SCHMIDT, and TEUGELS · Stochastic Processes for Insurance and Finance

ROSENBERGER and LACHIN · Randomization in Clinical Trials: Theory and Practice

ROSS · Introduction to Probability and Statistics for Engineers and Scientists

ROUSSEEUW and LEROY · Robust Regression and Outlier Detection

RUBIN · Multiple Imputation for Nonresponse in Surveys

RUBINSTEIN · Simulation and the Monte Carlo Method

*Now available in a lower-priced paperback edition in the Wiley Classics Library.

RUBINSTEIN and MELAMED · Modern Simulation and Modeling

RYAN · Modern Regression Methods

RYAN · Statistical Methods for Quality Improvement, *Second Edition*

SALTELLI, CHAN, and SCOTT (editors) · Sensitivity Analysis

*SCHEFFE · The Analysis of Variance

SCHIMEK · Smoothing and Regression: Approaches, Computation, and Application

SCHOTT · Matrix Analysis for Statistics

SCHUSS · Theory and Applications of Stochastic Differential Equations

SCOTT · Multivariate Density Estimation: Theory, Practice, and Visualization

*SEARLE · Linear Models

SEARLE · Linear Models for Unbalanced Data

SEARLE · Matrix Algebra Useful for Statistics

SEARLE, CASELLA, and McCULLOCH · Variance Components

SEARLE and WILLETT · Matrix Algebra for Applied Economics

SEBER and LEE · Linear Regression Analysis, *Second Edition*

SEBER · Multivariate Observations

SEBER and WILD · Nonlinear Regression

SENNOTT · Stochastic Dynamic Programming and the Control of Queueing Systems

*SERFLING · Approximation Theorems of Mathematical Statistics

SHAFER and VOVK · Probability and Finance: It's Only a Game!

SMALL and MCLEISH · Hilbert Space Methods in Probability and Statistical Inference

SRIVASTAVA · Methods of Multivariate Statistics

STAPLETON · Linear Statistical Models

STAUDTE and SHEATHER · Robust Estimation and Testing

STOYAN, KENDALL, and MECKE · Stochastic Geometry and Its Applications, *Second Edition*

STOYAN and STOYAN · Fractals, Random Shapes and Point Fields: Methods of Geometrical Statistics

STYAN · The Collected Papers of T. W. Anderson: 1943–1985

SUTTON, ABRAMS, JONES, SHELDON, and SONG · Methods for Meta-Analysis in Medical Research

TANAKA · Time Series Analysis: Nonstationary and Noninvertible Distribution Theory

THOMPSON · Empirical Model Building

THOMPSON · Sampling, *Second Edition*

THOMPSON · Simulation: A Modeler's Approach

THOMPSON and SEBER · Adaptive Sampling

THOMPSON, WILLIAMS, and FINDLAY · Models for Investors in Real World Markets

TIAO, BISGAARD, HILL, PEÑA, and STIGLER (editors) · Box on Quality and Discovery: with Design, Control, and Robustness

TIERNEY · LISP-STAT: An Object-Oriented Environment for Statistical Computing and Dynamic Graphics

TSAY · Analysis of Financial Time Series

UPTON and FINGLETON · Spatial Data Analysis by Example, Volume II: Categorical and Directional Data

VAN BELLE · Statistical Rules of Thumb

VIDAKOVIC · Statistical Modeling by Wavelets

WEISBERG · Applied Linear Regression, *Second Edition*

WELSH · Aspects of Statistical Inference

WESTFALL and YOUNG · Resampling-Based Multiple Testing: Examples and Methods for p-Value Adjustment

WHITTAKER · Graphical Models in Applied Multivariate Statistics

WINKER · Optimization Heuristics in Economics: Applications of Threshold Accepting

WONNACOTT and WONNACOTT · Econometrics, *Second Edition*

WOODING · Planning Pharmaceutical Clinical Trials: Basic Statistical Principles

WOOLSON and CLARKE · Statistical Methods for the Analysis of Biomedical Data, *Second Edition*

WU and HAMADA · Experiments: Planning, Analysis, and Parameter Design Optimization

YANG · The Construction Theory of Denumerable Markov Processes

*ZELLNER · An Introduction to Bayesian Inference in Econometrics

ZHOU, OBUCHOWSKI, and MCCLISH · Statistical Methods in Diagnostic Medicine

---

*Now available in a lower-priced paperback edition in the Wiley Classics Library.